Contents

Plates and figures

Contributors

J. M. Berg, M.Sc., M.B., B.Ch., M.R.C.Psych., Director of Research, Mental Retardation Centre; Staff Geneticist and Psychiatrist, Hospital for Sick Children, Toronto; and Associate Professor, University of Toronto. Formerly Clinical Research Consultant, Kennedy-Galton Centre, Harperbury Hospital, Hertfordshire.

A. D. B. Clarke, Ph.D., F.B.Ps.S., Professor of Psychology, University of Hull. Formerly Consultant Psychologist, The Manor Hospital, Epsom.

Ann M. Clarke, Ph.D., F.B.Ps.S., Reader in Educational Psychology, Department of Educational Studies, University of Hull, Formerly Principal Psychologist, The Manor Hospital, Epsom.

M. Fawcus, M.Sc., L.C.S.T., Senior Tutor, School for the Study of Disorders of Communication, London.

R. Fawcus, B.Sc., L.C.S.T., Lecturer in Human Communication Studies, Guy's Hospital Medical School, London.

H. C. Gunzburg, M.A., Ph.D., F.B.Ps.S., Consultant Psychologist, Director of Psychological Services, Hospitals for the Subnormal, Birmingham Area.

B. M. E. Hermelin, Ph.D., Research Psychologist, M.R.C. Developmental Psychology Research Unit, London.

C. C. Kiernan, B.A., Ph.D., Senior Lecturer in Child Development, Child Development Research Unit, University of London Institute of Education.

P. J. Mittler, M.A., Ph.D., F.B.Ps.S., Director, Hester Adrian Research Centre for the Study of Learning Processes in the Mentally Handicapped and Professor of the Education of the Mentally Handicapped, University of Manchester.

N. O'Connor, M.A., Ph.D., F.B.Ps.S., Director, M.R.C. Developmental Psychology Research Unit, London.

J. Tizard, M.A., B.Litt., Ph.D., F.B.Ps.S., Research Professor of Child Development in the University of London Institute of Education. Formerly Professor of Child Development in the University of London Institute of Education.

Acknowledgements*

The contributors and editors have drawn heavily upon the publications of many workers in this field, to all of whom they wish to express their gratitude. They would like in particular to thank the following:

Dr J. M. Berg. The late Professor L. S. Penrose F.R.S. for providing Plate 5. The late Dr D. H. H. Thomas for permission to photograph the children who were in his care, shown in Plates 3, 6 and 7. Mr M. A. C. Ridler for his photography of all the patients shown in the plates.

Professor A. D. B. Clarke and *Dr Ann M. Clarke.* The late Dr H. M. Skeels for permission to quote much data from his studies. The Editor, *American Journal of Mental Deficiency,* and the American Association on Mental Deficiency, for allowing the reprinting, as Chapter 1, of a substantial proportion of a guest editorial by the authors. Dr Sheila C. B. Duncan, Dr F. Peter Woodford and Mr R. G. B. Clarke for advice in connection with Chapter 1.

Mrs M. Fawcus and *Mr R. Fawcus.* Shulamith Kastein for permission to quote material on p. 329. Mr James Paterson for data quoted on p. 341. Mr B. Schneider and Mr J. Vallon for permission to quote their writings on p. 328.

Dr H. C. Gunzburg. The late Dr C. J. C. Earl and Dr R. J. Stanley for their stimulating discussions which helped in the formulation of much of the material presented.

Dr C. C. Kiernan. The Department of Health and Social Security for support by means of Research Grants. J. F. Budde, F. J. Menolascino and the editor of the journal for fig. 7, from *Mental Retardation,* vol. 9 (1971). J. F. Budde for fig. 8, from *The Lattice Systems Approach: A Development Tool for Behavioral Research and Program Models* (Parsons Research Center, 1971). Dr H. F. Boozer for fig. 9.

Professor P. J. Mittler. Dr W. A. Bricker and Churchill Livingstone for fig. 4,

---

* Some other acknowledgements will be found in the text.

from *Assessment for Learning in the Mentally Handicapped*, edited by P. J. Mittler (1973). Dr V. R. Hall and the American Speech and Hearing Association for fig. 6, from *A Functional Approach to Speech and Language*, edited by F. L. Girardeau and J. E. Spradlin (ASHA Monograph 14, 1970). Dr H. N. Sloane, Dr M. K. Johnston, Dr F. R. Harris and the Houghton Mifflin Company for fig. 5, from *Operant Procedures in Remedial Speech and Language Training*, edited by H. N. Sloane and B. D. Macaulay (1968).

Professor J. Tizard. Dr Henry V. Cobb for permission to quote from *The Prediction of Fulfilment* (Teachers' College Press, 1972). Dr Mervyn Susser for permission to quote from *Community Psychiatry* (Random House, 1968).

Preface to the paperback edition

The first edition of *Mental Deficiency: The Changing Outlook*, published in 1958, was designed to provide a reasonably comprehensive overview of new material, both for practitioners and research workers, and a relatively short and inexpensive volume was produced. By 1974, however, the third edition needed to be a much larger and more costly project, to do justice to the wealth of material arising from many expanding research areas. The outlook had changed beyond the pockets of many who wanted to own the book.

It was then suggested that we should publish a selection of representative articles to convey, as economically as possible, the conceptual changes which have catalysed recent research and those which resulted from it. Inevitably the selection has been very difficult; we have been guided largely by reviewers' comments, together with a need to ensure adequate balance and perspective.

Of the twenty-five original chapters, twelve are reproduced here, and we have added an entirely new first chapter which offers an integration of the whole research field in relation to prevention and amelioration of mental subnormality. Our conclusions point to the very real prospects of substantially reducing the incidence of handicapping conditions. There remains, however, a substantial gap between these optimistic 'prospects' indicated by research, and the changes which our societies are prepared to support. If all research were to stop today, it would still take many years to implement our knowledge. The changing outlook for subnormality is perhaps now most dependent upon social implementation and its careful scientific evaluation.

We are once again glad to express our gratitude to Mrs Moira Phillips for work on author and subject indexes; also to Mr M. Norman of Hull University Computer Centre who kindly provided a conversion of page numbers for these. Miss Jane Hunter, Miss Jane Armstrong and Miss Sandra Fox of Methuen and Company Ltd have been most helpful during the production of this book.
April 1977   A. M. C.
                                                                            A. D. B. C.

I

A. D. B. Clarke and A. M. Clarke

Prospects for prevention and amelioration of mental subnormality: an overview

Introduction

The field of mental subnormality is a meeting point for all the biological and behavioural sciences, with implications both for our understanding of human development in general and retarded development in particular. In the first edition of this book (1958) we noted that 'traditionally mental deficiency has been a neglected field of study, with the exception of some aspects of neuropathology and genetics'. In the second edition (1965) we commented on this earlier statement, indicating that 'between 1958 and 1964, however, many developments have occurred, and the pace of change has been greatly accelerated'. In this, the third edition, even greater changes are recorded, and prospects for prevention and amelioration of subnormality are better than ever before.

In the past, as at present, different countries have employed different practices for, and concepts of, mental subnormality. Definitions, however, tend to use similar phrases, such as 'incomplete or insufficient general mental development', 'sub-average general intellectual functioning' or 'arrested or incomplete development of mind . . . which includes subnormality of intelligence'. Such descriptions are necessarily vague when upper borderlines between the milder conditions and dullness are arbitrary, and depend upon an interaction between social attitudes, the complexity of society, and the provision of services. These problems are considered in detail later in this book. In the meanwhile it may be helpful to show how British and international terminology relate to IQ level and to aetiology (see Fig. 1).

As implied above, the milder levels of subnormality cannot be regarded as a scientific category but rather comprise a theoretical, administrative group of well below average individuals some of whom, usually temporarily, are 'at risk' of needing special educational or social assistance. The natural history of the majority of such persons is vastly different from those below about IQ 50, and, as indicated in Chapter 2, only a minority is in receipt of any specialized services for any length of time.

The endeavours of biological and behavioural scientists can be subsumed under three headings. First, the description of the many conditions which comprise subnormality, whether at chromosomal, biochemical or behavioural levels. Second, much work – again biological and behavioural – is related to the task of primary prevention of handicapping conditions. Third, the two approaches include in their aims the amelioration of existing mental subnormality. This classification of research work is over-simple, but will serve its purpose for subsequent discussion. In particular, there is an overlap between prevention and amelioration, for really successful treatment becomes preventive of further retardation.

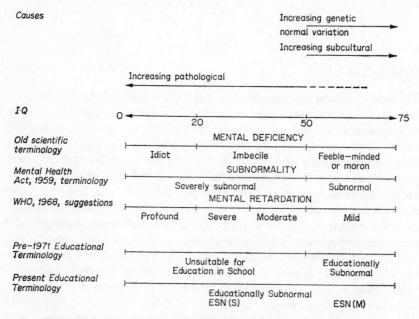

Fig. 1 Relation of IQ to aetiology and terminology, old and new.

Belmont (1971), in an important paper, draws attention to the contents of symposia held on the occasion of the Joseph P. Kennedy Jr Foundation international awards for research, leadership and service in retardation. The vast majority of these papers were related to chromosomal aberrations and inborn errors of metabolism. These contributions which are very important nevertheless only apply to the aetiology of a minority of the subnormal. Belmont points out that retardation is a behavioural deficiency and the majority of these research workers have nothing to say about behaviour, other than that it is retarded. He calls for an increase in bio-behavioural research, a view which we would endorse.

A World Health Organization (1968) document also stresses that no single profession has the key to the problems posed by mental subnormality, and calls for multi-disciplinary research. The primary aim of this shortened book, however, is to offer and discuss the results of investigations into retarded behaviour, the main presenting feature of mental subnormality. In attempting this, however, we do not subscribe to a narrow professional viewpoint, and sufficient will be offered of the biological level of analysis to indicate its achievements, problems and limitations.

The largest society in the world dedicated to the study of mental subnormality, the American Association of Mental Deficiency, recently (1976) celebrated its centenary. This has proved to be an appropriate period for taking stock, for evaluating the progress of the past and for attempting to predict the future. In this overview, however, we will not aim to assess the history of the last hundred years, for that has been undertaken admirably by Sloan and Stevens (1976). As in all fields of human endeavour, we stand on the shoulders of others. In paying tribute to our predecessors, however, we must also be aware that they were people of their time, constrained by contemporary philosophical, social and political ideologies. In the light of the 1970s, some of the earlier history of the AAMD makes astonishing reading. Of course we too are creatures of our time, but we have the advantage of well-developed scientific methodologies which allow the distinction to be made between value judgements and facts. We do not, for example, confuse correlates with causes, we are aware of the vital importance of controls, replication and validation. To be humane, as were many of those who went before, is not enough if the problems of prevention and amelioration are to be tackled effectively.

This chapter, then, will offer an assessment of our present knowledge and its applications to prevention and amelioration. The argument will hinge upon two statements: 'Using present knowledge and techniques from the biomedical and behavioural sciences it is possible to reduce the occurrence of mental retardation by 50 per cent before the end of the century' (President's Committee, 1972). This became a Major National Goal. Notice the phrase 'present knowledge and techniques', and 'it is possible'. Whether the possible becomes probable may be a different matter, dependent on the resources which become available. But explicit in this passage is the argument that if research had stopped dead some four years ago, we would still have the potential for halving the incidence of mental retardation. Is there any real sign that this is beginning to happen? The second statement complements the first: 'Using present knowledge and techniques it is possible substantially to improve the levels of functioning of most of the retarded' (Clarke, 1976). Again, is this really happening?

It will be appropriate, in trying to answer these questions, to dichotomize the field of subnormality into those conditions below about IQ 50, and those which constitute the milder grades. While it is clear that there are overlapping problems, these are on the whole separate populations, differing considerably in aetiology, incidence, prevalence, in present capabilities and in prognosis. It is therefore proposed to over-simplify a little by first discussing our knowledge of research upon the causes, prevention and amelioration of the severer grades of retardation, and then assessing the same factors in relation to milder conditions.

Severe subnormality

It cannot be urged too strongly that careful epidemiological work must be available for the evaluation of trends of decrease, increase or stability of various conditions. An important study in England compared results of surveys in the 1920s and 1960s. There is an unfortunate dearth of such comparative research, since little epidemiological work was carried out in the earlier part of this century. The results suggested that the *incidence* of below IQ 50 conditions had decreased by about a third, a decrease masked in overall *prevalence* rates by the increased lifespan of the two-thirds, particularly Down's syndrome (Tizard, 1964). Thus, social and health advances, most of them not specifically aimed at reducing mental subnormality, may have already had a considerable impact. These are likely to include the widespread use of immunization techniques against common childhood illnesses that can have neurological *sequelae*; early diagnosis of the rare cases where inborn errors of metabolism can be corrected; better ante-natal and natal care, in particular the increasing percentage of deliveries in hospitals rather than home, and the more careful monitoring, therefore, of the course of labour; genetic counselling and family planning; better public health; and the reducing age at which mothers complete their families. But a word of warning here: if the social changes which reduce the age of primiparous women continue, we may well run into an increase in handicapping conditions associated with low maternal age.

Probably the single most important biomedical advance came in 1959 with the discovery of chromosomal aberrations. Since then new findings have been frequent and more than 100 chromosome disorders have been identified. Down's syndrome is, of course, the most common, accounting for between a quarter and a third of all below IQ 50 cases. Much rarer conditions such as maple syrup urine disease and homocystinuria have been discovered, and illustrate the progress being made in the differentiation of various forms of retardation by mainly biochemical techniques (see Chapter 3).

Amniocentesis for mothers at risk, and the termination of pregnancies where positive results are found, are likely to make an impact, and this should clearly become a routine service for all older mothers. This, together with the reducing maternal age for family completion, should reduce the incidence of Down's syndrome. As yet, except perhaps in New York City (Stein, Susser and Guterman, 1973), there appear to be no firm figures available reflecting such a drop, which should already have started (Alberman, 1976). Two additional points should be made. First, there may well be some small risk of abortion from amniocentesis, although a recent NIH study of over 2,000 women suggests that this is not so (President's Committee, 1976). Second, for Down's syndrome results are seldom clear before the eighteenth week of pregnancy, some weeks after the optimal period for termination of pregnancy (Wynne Griffiths, 1973).

As Brock (1976) indicates, recent discoveries that chemical components leak into the amniotic fluid from foetuses with neural tube defects has opened a new chapter in prenatal diagnosis. In particular, the importance of alpha-fetoprotein

(AFP) measurements in the early prenatal diagnosis of spina bifida and anencephaly has been established. This protein occurs as early as the sixth week of gestation in foetal serum. While amniotic fluid assessment can be used to protect the mother with a history of previous abnormal pregnancies involving neural tube defects, it will not normally be applied to the vast majority of mothers for whom this is a first-time event. But AFP may be detected in very low concentrations in normal serum by radio-immunoassay, and its concentration increases in maternal blood during pregnancy. In 1974 studies established that a proportion of cases both of anencephaly and spina bifida were associated with serum AFP values at the extreme of, or outside, the normal range. Two conclusions have already emerged from a collaborative study organized by the Institute for Research into Mental Retardation, London. First, that attempts to detect neural tube defects before the end of the first trimester are unlikely to be successful; second, that anencephaly is easier to detect than spina bifida and that in both the efficiency is well short of 100 per cent (Brock, 1976). Clearly we may expect advances in these techniques, with amniocentesis following the serum screening as confirmation or otherwise of abnormal findings. Milunsky and Alpert (1976) warn, however, that 'in view of the significant true false-positive rate, the greatest caution is advised in interpreting raised AFP concentrations, especially in patients not specifically at risk for having offspring with NTD'.

Another major advance in the last decade, has been the discovery of a method for immunizing rhesus negative mothers against Rh sensitization by rhesus positive foetuses (Clarke, 1967); another is the production of a rubella vaccine. The increasing use of surgical treatment of some forms of infantile hydrocephalus is a further example, although here evaluation is complicated by the fact that spontaneous arrest may occur in some cases, and by possible selective factors determining treatment/non-treatment: those with the better prognosis are more likely to be chosen for surgery (Guthkelch, 1970). One is bound to add, however, that the efforts of some physicians and some surgeons, using heroic methods, to keep alive grossly damaged babies for whom survival presents a continuing tragedy, are now giving way to a more sober appreciation of prognostic factors.

There is no shortage of potentially fertile hypotheses in the biomedical field. We offer just two examples. The first is the well-known suggestion by Stoller and Collmann (1965) that a hepatitis virus, interacting with maternal age, plays a part in the aetiology of Down's syndrome. Currently there is evidence both for and against this hypothesis (e.g. Kucera, 1970; Baird and Miller, 1968). The second example, in a different area, is provided by C. A. Clarke *et al.*'s (1975) suggestion that spina bifida and anencephaly may result from the presence of residual trophoblastic material arising from a recent miscarriage. The cases for and against this view, and the possible mechanism of interaction with the new foetus are carefully discussed and some potentially crucial research suggested in this paper.

Work in the field of prevention must take account of man-made agents;

mercury poisoning, for example, was the cause of the dramatic Minamata Disease. The dangers of ionizing radiations are well known, and the more extreme forms of lead poisoning are well appreciated. As a matter of fact, they were understood in the eighteenth century when lead miners in Yorkshire found it necessary to erect one mile long stone chimneys, built on the surface of the hillsides to the very tops where the toxic fumes were dispersed. We also know of the dangers to young children from the internal use in buildings of lead paint. In some countries professional decorators are forbidden by law to use lead-based paint inside houses, but tenement dwellers, if they paint at all, are likely to do it themselves, and are not subject to such restrictions. In how many countries is it legally obligatory to define the dangers on tins of lead paint? There seems to be a lack of public health education on these matters. Again, lead fumes are ceaselessly belched into the air from cars, and legislation to reduce this emission is being implemented in too few countries. Old lead water pipes are also suspect, according to Beattie *et al.* (1975), although there is controversy about this paper (see subsequent correspondence in the *Lancet*) and Elwood *et al.* (1976) conclude that, if a hazard does exist, it is likely to be confined to homes in which lead water levels of over 0·8 p.p.m. occur.

Summarizing, it is evident that the potentials for decreasing the incidence of the severer grades of subnormality are present, and have probably been operating for some time as a result of general social changes. Add to these the specific biomedical advances of the type mentioned and the outlook seems promising. Do we really have prospects of halving the incidence of these types of subnormality? So far as conditions where a single cause-effect relationship is concerned the potential is evidently present. In these cases it may not be essential to comprehend the exact mechanisms by which such unitary causes operate (e.g. the extra chromosome in Down's syndrome). But their identification usually suggests the path to preventive measures. For example, the decline in birth-rate in some developed countries may be differentially greater among older women (S.L.B. Duncan, personal communication), and this social trend is likely to have a considerable effect. But so far as preventive services are concerned, we suspect that a considerable gap exists between what is on offer and what is taken up. It is not enough to have preventive or ameliorative services available if they are not used by all those for whom they are intended. In England, for example, there is at least one amniocentesis centre in every hospital region, but it has been suggested (S.L.B. Duncan, personal communication) that probably less than 10 per cent of mothers over 35 years are having this test. We suspect that there is the usual social class gradient in the take-up of available free services. Public health education in its ordinary form will probably fail to touch the lowest social groups, and this problem relates to most other aspects of social disadvantage.

Turning now to the amelioration of severe subnormality, it is of interest that from about 1951 and onwards two independent streams of work in England and Holland, the one strictly experimental and the other in training centres, produced an identical finding that, under certain circumstances, the moderately and severely retarded could learn well, retain that learning and even transfer their new-found skills to different tasks. Much later, the strategies which such approaches reflected were termed 'normalization'. As Grunewald (1969) has written, 'the term implies . . . a *striving* in various ways towards what is normal . . . normalization does not imply any denial of the retardate's handicap. It involves rather exploiting his other mental and physical capacities so that his handicap becomes less pronounced . . .'

It became increasingly clear in the 1950s that proper programming of learning, proper incentives and knowledge of results could transform the skills of the moderately and sometimes some of the severely retarded. Then behaviour modification as a formalized system developed rapidly in the following decade, again with the same general implications as the earlier work, but this time more often applied to the more profoundly handicapped. As a technology of learning its implications are, of course, far wider than for subnormality alone. Its very considerable efficacy for those whose learning deficits are their main problem accounts for the rapid spread of these techniques. It has also become clear that early and prolonged intervention in the home, using parents as educators, can have significant effects upon the early development of the moderately or severely retarded child. So twenty-five years of research have totally transformed our *expectations* of what can be done.

These are great achievements, but have they been translated into practice? In the main, the more severely retarded persons, except in a few centres, very rarely get the sort of help from which they can benefit. What is needed is lengthy, skilled and hence costly help, not unskilled caretaking. The findings to which we have referred are often either unknown to practitioners, totally misunderstood or thought to be inappropriate. Hence, even among professionals there tends to be a widespread underestimation of what can be done. This is serious, for low expectancies are clearly associated with poor provision and hence poor outcome. A vicious circle is then perpetuated. Moreover, Grant, Moores and Whelan (1973) have shown that those staff in day training centres who are most closely in touch with these handicapped adults consistently underestimate their potential work performance.

Mild subnormality

Assessing trends in the incidence and prevalence of mild subnormality is much more difficult, because these are associated with so many complex and inter-acting factors: changes in the provision of services, the efficacy of schooling, the availability of employment and the degree of public understanding, all in the context of increasingly demanding urban societies. It is easy, in fact, to demonstrate large increases in the numbers designated mildly subnormal as a consequence of better provision. Then again, there are very large differences in prevalence rates at different ages, which complicate the picture.

The role of malnutrition in damaging the young, vulnerable animal brain has received much attention in recent years (Dobbing and Smart, 1974). It is much more difficult to establish its effect on man, however, because malnutrition does not exist in isolation, normally being part of a generally adverse situation. Moreover, the mediating mechanisms could involve either arrest or deceleration of brain growth, or relative non-responsiveness socially of parents and children under conditions of malnourishment, or the reflection of a wider unstimulating social context, or all of these. And even an apparently more ideal investigation, such as the Dutch Famine study (Stein *et al.*, 1975), permits a number of alternative explanations (see correspondence in the *Lancet*: September 1975– January 1976). Moreover, a given degree and duration of human malnutrition cannot be taken in isolation, but must be related to subsequent life history (Richardson, 1976). This important question will continue to be debated (Tizard, 1976). We cannot afford to remain uninvolved in the problem of malnutrition, for it is part and parcel of the tragic conditions under which a large proportion of our 4,000 million fellow human beings continue to live.

Where, in the minority of mild cases, organic factors are implicated, the same general preventive principles apply as with the more severe grades. Of the remainder, a proportion owe their existence to normal genetic variation. It has recently been shown that the whole question of parent-child resemblances in intelligence is very much more complex than most writers have maintained (McAskie and Clarke, 1976). The polygenic model predicts that, without assortative mating, the single parent-child correlation is ·5 and the mid-parent-child correlation ·71. But there commonly is assortative mating which should increase both of these; indeed assortative mating for intelligence is greater than for any characteristic other than race. Genetic and environmental factors are themselves correlated, so that environment should add to genetic parent-child resemblances. Nevertheless, such resemblances are imperfect and a number of mildly retarded are born to normal parents of average or below average intelligence, reared in normal environments and without suspicion of organic involvement. These are the normal variants. There remains the very large group of subcultural retarded, where it is assumed that a combination of genetic and social adversity is responsible. A multiplicity of additive and inter-active factors appear to be relevant.

From the work of Skeels and onwards, it became increasingly obvious that this group can have quite a good social prognosis. But Skeels's intervention was life-long and complete, and the social outcome from average adoptive homes was very much better than that of a contrast group, and from what might have been inferred from the social origin of the children (Skeels, 1966). The classic paper by Skodak and Skeels (1949) following up, at age 13, 100 adopted children, shows much the same thing in terms of IQ rather than social outcome. With an increasing recognition that adverse environment played a part in the aetiology of mild retardation, intervention from then onwards became an 'in' concept. But with it was associated the belief that intervention would only be effective in the early years. Thus, one of the roots of the Head-Start concept was an unquestioning faith in the crucial and disproportionate influence of early experience upon later development. By now there is clear evidence against this still fashionable view (Clarke and Clarke, 1976), and even in the study of animal behaviour such workers as Harlow (Novak and Harlow, 1975) have substantially rescinded their earlier pronouncements about critical periods.

Kirk's (1958) careful work, which exactly predicted the failure of Project Head-Start, was brushed aside in the liberal euphoria of the mid-1960s. Jensen (1969) was correct in concluding from various reviews of Head-Start that 'compensatory education has been tried, and it apparently has failed', although many writers subsequently indicated that these programmes were neither compensatory nor educational, being mainly of short duration, offering free rather than cognitive activity supervised by mostly unskilled 'teachers' and treating the child out of the context of his home. Incidentally, the cost of Head-Start between 1965 and 1970 was more than $2,000 million. Here was a case of the national application of programmes against which research evidence already existed.

Bronfenbrenner's excellent review (1974) of some twenty-one of the better studies, selected from many hundreds of totally inadequate ones, comes near to the heart of the matter. Intervention in the home is likely to be more successful than in the pre-school; but those most likely to respond come from the 'upper crust' of poor families. As has been shown repeatedly, those most in need of help fail to seek it, or to accept it or benefit from it when offered.

The Follow-Through project recognizes the deficiencies of Head-Start on its own, and sponsors four-year compensatory programmes for both Head-Start and non-Head-Start children, from kindergarten to the third grade. The effects of one such programme have been evaluated very carefully and cautiously by Abelson, Zigler and DeBlasi (1974). They conclude that 'the gains accruing from compensatory education programmes are commensurate with the duration and amount of effort which are expended on these programmes'. We would predict with considerable confidence, however, that four years of Follow-Through, even added to Head-Start, will be insufficient to make any great impact on the later lives of these children while they remain in poor homes, both economically and culturally disadvantaged. While it is at last generally conceded that brief early intervention has effects which fade, it is less often appreciated that the effects of much longer early intervention which is not followed by similar stimulation will also fade. Early life is not a 'critical period' psychosocially (Clarke and Clarke, 1976). This suggests that, although early intervention is desirable, since prevention is better than cure, later intervention may also considerably ameliorate or even overcome mild retardation. Feuerstein is one of the few researchers who are clear about this in discussing the theoretical underpinning of his successful treatment of culturally deprived adolescents (Feuerstein and Krasilowsky, 1972).

It is apparent that among the more severely disadvantaged, serious social problems may recur in succeeding generations of the same family. This, indeed, was the basis for the early twentieth-century notion of 'bad stock'. Nevertheless, there appears to be quite a large 'escape rate' by children from multiple-problem families, and, of course, there is also new recruitment into a 'cycle of disadvantage'. Comparatively little is known of the factors promoting such inter-generational continuities or changes (Rutter and Madge, 1976). But there must always be a bottom 2–3 per cent on qualities which society values, in this case arising from a range of pathologies, biological and social, together with genetic factors, the effects of which are enhanced by assortative mating. Here we are considering one extreme of the whole issue of the correlates of occupational class, which apparently operate across vastly different political systems, whether capitalist or socialist. For example, an interesting epidemiological study has been carried out in Warsaw which indicates that, after thirty years of greatly diminished economic, housing and school inequalities, occupational class still relates to backwardness and mild retardation. Thus, using a re-standardization of Raven's Progressive Matrices Test on well over 13,000 10- to 11-year-old children (96 per cent of the population of that age), and a four-category occu-of Raven's Progressive Matrices Test on well over 13,000 10 to 11 year-old children 96 per cent of the population of that age), and a four-category occupational classification for parents, a 15 IQ point difference between Class I and IV children's average IQs emerged. Whereas 2·8 per cent of Class I children had low scores, 16·8 per cent of those from Class IV were similarly placed. The conclusion is thus inescapable that ecological and school variables contribute little to intellectual differences between these children, possibly because these factors are in Warsaw restricted in range. On the other hand, familial correlates (e.g. parental occupation and education) are strong (Czarkowski et al., 1977).

There is no doubt that for attainment, intelligence and a whole gamut of other mental and physical qualities, the correlates of occupational class represent the most universal and firmly established findings in the field of human behaviour. Familial, economic and ecological factors are usually so pervasively inter-correlated that it is normally difficult to disentangle the mechanisms; the Warsaw study has a particular advantage in this respect. It has yet to report school attainment results, but represents an important attempt to separate familial from ecological and school variables.

In discussing the effects of perinatal complications, Sameroff and Chandler (1975) have shown that, except for cases of extreme damage, the social class context in which the child is reared can have a considerable effect in amplifying, modifying or completely overcoming such handicaps. This again emphasizes the incorrectness of regarding damage as setting unalterable limits on human development, since a given degree may have a spectrum of outcomes in different individuals and in different situations.

Society needs to grasp the fact that children, unwanted and unplanned, reared by parents who are *both* intellectually limited *and* emotionally unstable, have a poor prognosis, but a normal one if adopted, and possibly even if adopted late (Kadushin, 1970). There is much reluctance to move children from their parents, but sometimes keeping families together is clearly against the better interests of all concerned. In extreme cases, social worker support is of little avail. There is an urgent need for severely disadvantaged families to have, among other things, the privileges of the advantaged in the form of voluntary family planning. The provision of clinics will have little impact, but the offer of birth control techniques taken into the home, as part of a general habilitation effort, may prevent an intolerable situation for inadequate, disturbed parents and the potential victims of their union. Society needs to look less emotively and more unflinchingly at these problems, particularly in a world where the population has doubled since 1930, and continues to increase by 75 million per year.

The fact that all cross-sectional prevalence and all longitudinal follow-up studies indicate, as age increases, a considerable diminution in mild subnormality, is firmly established. These results are the most hopeful in the whole field. They probably reflect (1) 'camouflage' after the final years of greatest intellectual demands in school or initial 'prop up' by 'benefactors' (Edgerton and Bercovici, 1976); (2) prolonged social learning and delayed responsiveness to society in general; and (3) delayed maturation which appears to be a feature associated with prolonged adversity – a catch-up phenomenon also apparent for growth after mild malnutrition. They may illustrate what Sameroff and Chandler (1975) term a 'self-righting tendency which appears to move children towards normality in the face of pressure towards deviation'.

As Cobb has shown (1972) in an excellent review of all follow-up studies, 'the most consistent and outstanding finding . . . is the high proportion of the adult retarded who achieve satisfactory adjustments, by whatever criteria are employed . . .' Cobb was in the main talking of follow-up studies of those for whom rather little had been done, the least fortunate of this group. But one cannot entirely discount the possible effects of some sort of long-term intervention or care. Of course, there remains a proportion who contribute to problem families and other social deviancies. But it can no longer be said that mild retardation 'underlies all our social problems' (Goddard, 1914), although one might add that this expresses in extreme form some of the major problems of society.

Future prospects

This overview has merely sampled recent researches, but it may be appropriate to summarize, to offer a balance sheet, to answer the questions posed at the beginning and to consider possible implications.

First, the prospects of halving the incidence of mental subnormality in the next twenty-three years. So far as the severer grades in developed countries are concerned, these possibilities are indeed likely to be achieved. Such a reduction will arise from a complex of improvements: for example, the social trend downwards in the maternal ages at which children are born, diminution in family size, and improvements in public health and medical care. If one adds to these the application of methods specifically aimed at reducing the incidence of mental retardation, genetic counselling, prenatal diagnosis, and the correction of metabolic defects, then the prospects seem encouraging. However, this carries with it the implication that increasing reduction in numbers may affect the provision of facilities for those who are born. This would isolate their families even further.

So far as mild subnormality is concerned, prospects of halving the incidence seem to be very slight, even though some follow-up studies, some adoption studies, or even the evidence from later intervention indicate a relatively good adult prognosis. The knowledge gained from some expensive and careful schemes, such as those of Garber and Heber (1977), is of inestimable value. But there seems to be little prospect of applying these nationally, and even immense social change could not at once defeat the problem, for there is a fundamental human tendency to persist in attitudes and parental behaviour which, even when unreinforced by gross social inequalities, play a part in producing the subcultural retarded. And, as noted, there must always exist a bottom 2 or 3 per cent on qualities which societies value. The question is whether we can become sufficiently humane to help develop limited assets so that the individual can function usefully and happily. Will 'the brotherhood of man' remain an empty phrase?

Since the mildly subnormal comprise about 75 per cent of the whole group, and since the subcultural contribute largely to it, the prospects of reducing the overall incidence of designated mental retardation seem nothing like so good as suggested by the President's Committee.[1]

The second question posed at the outset relates to the potentially substantial improvement in the functioning of most of the subnormal, using present knowledge and techniques. Here the position is in general extremely bad. A few centres and a few institutions are doing excellent work, and using to the full our new knowledge. But where substantial new resources have been offered, authorities have more often been bewitched by the need for splendid new buildings than convinced of the need to plan splendid new programmes, which are more important. So here again is an ominous and, we fear, growing gap between our knowledge and our practice. It is usually characterized by an underestimation of what can be achieved. Grant, Moores and Whelan (1973) were right to express surprise (which should perhaps have been indignation)

that this underestimation should still occur nearly two decades after the published findings of Clarke and Hermelin (1955) who demonstrated that although the severely subnormal had exceedingly low initial ability levels in

[1] Since these lines were written, this point appears to have been implicitly conceded by the President's Committee (1976) in *Mental Retardation: Century of Decision*. Washington, DC: Government Printing Office Stock No. 040-000-00343-6.

industrial and other tasks these bore little relationship to the much higher levels that could be achieved with training.

Furthermore, it is still not known why some professionals appear to be very much more successful than others at releasing the social and learning potentials of the retarded.

If this analysis is correct, or even only partly so, what are the implications? The main ones appear to include the following:

1. In this field, as in others, we are competing for limited resources. Hence the growing need for independently monitored cost benefit analyses which clearly distinguish the benefit to the individual, to the family and to society. A recent and exemplary analysis on the use of amniocentesis for preventing the birth of Down's syndrome children has been provided by Hagard and Carter (1976). The National Institute of Health (USA) have also funded a controlled trial involving about 2,000 pregnancies (President's Committee, 1976). Laurence and Gregory (1976) urge the concentration of such services in specialist centres, where experienced staff keep the rate of abortion to a minimum and achieve a high rate of success in culturing amnion cells. We need more of these centres.

2. There is thus an increasing need for pre-natal screening for those at risk and for older mothers. Equally important, the ways in which the take-up of these services may be increased requires urgent investigation. Here there is certainly another large gap between our knowledge and its application.

3. In view of the characteristic underestimation of what can be achieved, there is an urgent need for staff retraining at all levels. Pioneer demonstration projects and staff workshops are much more likely to be effective than the written or spoken word. Resistance to change among some staff in all professions is considerable.

4. No parent of a moderately, severely or profoundly handicapped child should be expected to rear that child without the fullest support, from birth onwards. Where parents are unwilling or unable to provide care, the provision of small units needs to be increased.

5. Mild subnormality poses seemingly intractable problems, exhibiting in extreme form the major social problems with which developed countries are beset. It is exaggerated by the gross inequalities which are obvious in most societies, but even so, desirable social change by itself is unlikely to cancel out these difficulties at once. It is fortunate that many of the mildly subnormal tend to show a shift towards normality as age increases; it seems that life experiences and the passage of time may be compensatory. But can we not do better in diminishing the familial, social and gross economic inequalities which are involved, and at the same time offer better help?

6. Of many necessary omissions from this chapter, the gravest has been our failure to consider the developing countries. The World Health Organization has an important part to play here, and has already (1968) produced a report

on the organization of services, with the needs of developing countries in mind. It is to be regretted that there is no one in the headquarters at Geneva whose sole concern is mental retardation. But the Joint Commission, formed by the International Association for the Scientific Study of Mental Deficiency and the International League of Societies for the Mentally Handicapped, officially recognized by WHO as a Non-Governmental Organization, is expected soon to offer position statements on Prevention and Amelioration. It is hoped that these will alert international agencies to these problems.

7. In the light of limited resources, the expansion of volunteer services is greatly to be encouraged. There is much latent sympathy in our society, and many of its resources remain untapped.

8. Although the distinction between pure and applied research has been over-stressed to some extent, it seems that current opinion is weighted against applied research. For some, the field of subnormality offers a captive population in which rather general theories, which may have little relevance to retardation, may be tested. Others use a *blitzkreig* approach, rejecting the potentially more rewarding toil of longer experiments. Our journals, particularly, but not solely, in the behavioural sciences, are replete with material, the 'real-life' implications of which are never assessed. The practical testing and application of research findings needs much higher priority than at present occurs. We now possess powerful methodologies for evaluating the effects of both contrived and natural changes (e.g. Campbell, 1975). In this whole connection it is good to note the increasing interest in the ethics of human experimentation.

9. Scientists, though often overworked, occupy a privileged position in society. They therefore have a considerable responsibility for ensuring that their discoveries are field tested and applied. As indicated earlier, there is already far too large a gap between current knowledge and its application. Thus we urge a greater involvement in the corridors of power, and in the sometimes tedious dialogue with governmental agencies.

Man is becoming increasingly aware that he can be a predatory, cruel and callous creature, and that the environment, like the the bank, imposes limited credit and high rates of interest for repayment. He is belatedly coming to realize that environmental exploitation must be radically reduced. The world-wide wastage of human capabilities is no less obvious than that of material resources. In extreme form it is reflected in our approach to mental retardation. It is the task of science to reveal the ways in which our biological and social pathologies can be alleviated, and it is our task as scientists to see that these findings are widely disseminated and used with profit.

References

ABELSON, W. D., ZIGLER, E. and DeBLASI, C. L. (1974) Effects of a four-year follow through program on economically disadvantaged children. *J. educ. Psychol.*, **66**, 756–71.

ALBERMAN, E. (1976) The prevention of Down's syndrome. *Developm. Med. Child Neurol.*, **17**, 793–801.

BAIRD, P. A. and MILLER, J. R. (1968) Some epidemiological aspects of Down's syndrome in British Columbia. *Brit. J. prev. soc. Med.*, **22**, 81–5.

BEATTIE, A. D., MOORE, M. R., GOLDBERG, A., FINLAYSON, M. J. W., GRAHAM, J. F., MACKIE, E. M., MAIN, J. C., MCLAREN, D. A., MURDOCH, R. M. and STEWART, G. T. (1975) Role of chronic low-level lead exposure in the aetiology of mental retardation. *Lancet*, **i**, 589–92.

BELMONT, J. M. (1971) Medical-behavioural research in retardation. *Internat. Rev. Res. ment. Retard.*, **5**, 1–81.

BROCK, D. J. H. (1976) Prenatal diagnosis – chemical methods. In *Human Malformations*. *Brit. med. Bull.*, **32**, no. 1, 16–20.

BRONFENBRENNER, U. (1974) *A Report on Longitudinal Evaluations of Pre-School Programs*, Vol. 2. *Is early Intervention Effective?* Washington, DC: DHEW Publication No. (OHD) 74–25.

CAMPBELL, D. T. (1975) Reforms as experiments. In STRUENING, E. L. and GUTTENTAG, M. (eds.) *Handbook of Evaluation Research*, Vol. 1, 71–100. Beverley Hills: Sage.

CLARKE, A. D. B. (1977) Presidential address: from research to practice. In MITTLER, P. (ed.) *Research to Practice in Mental Retardation*, Vol. I, 7–19. Baltimore: Univ. Park Press.

CLARKE, A. D. B. and HERMELIN, B. F. (1955) Adult imbeciles: their abilities and trainability. *Lancet*, **ii**, 337–9.

CLARKE, A. M. and CLARKE, A. D. B. (eds.) (1976) *Early Experience: Myth and Evidence*. London. Open Books; New York: Free Press.

CLARKE, C. A. (1967) Prevention of Rh-haemolytic disease. *Brit. med. J.*, **4**, 484–5.

CLARKE, C. A., HOBSON, D., MCKENDRICK, O. M., ROGERS, S. G. and SHEPHARD, P. M. (1975) Spina bifida and anencephaly: miscarriage as a possible cause. *Brit. med. J.*, **2**, 743–6.

COBB, H. V. (1972) *The Forecast of Fulfilment*. New York: Teachers' College Press, Columbia Univ.

CZARKOWSKI, M., FIRKOWSKA-MANKIEWICZ, A., OSTROWSKA, A., SOKOLOWSKA, M., STEIN, Z., SUSSER, M. and WALD, I. (1977) Some ecological, school and family factors in the intellectual performance of children: the Warsaw study. In MITTLER, P. (ed.) *Research to Practice in Mental Retardation*, Vol. I, 89–95. Baltimore: Univ. Park Press.

DOBBING, J. and SMART, J. L. (1974) Undernutrition in the developing brain. In GAZE, R. M. and KEATING, M. J. (eds.) *Development and Regeneration in the Nervous System,* **30**: 2, 164–8. London: British Council.

EDGERTON, R. B. and BERCOVICI, S. M. (1976) The cloak of competence: years later. *Amer. J. ment. Defic.,* **80**, 485–97.

ELWOOD, P. C., MORTON, M., ST LEGER, A. S. (1976) Lead in water and mental retardation. *Lancet,* **i**, 590–1.

FEUERSTEIN, R. and KRASILOWSKY, D. (1972) International strategies for the significant modification of congitive functioning in the disadvantaged adolescent. *J. Amer. Acad. Child Psychiat.,* **11**, 572–82.

GARBER, H. and HEBER, R. (1977) The Milwaukee Project: indications of the effectiveness of early intervention in preventing mental retardation. In MITTLER, P. (ed.) *Research to Practice in Mental Retardation,* Vol. I, 119–27. Baltimore: Univ. Park Press.

GODDARD, H. (1914) *Feeble-mindedness: its Causes and Consequences.* New York: Macmillan.

GRANT, G. W. B., MOORES, B. and WHELAN, E. (1973) Assessing the work needs and work performance of mentallyhandicapped adults. *Brit. J. ment. Subnorm.,* **19**, 71–9.

GRUNEWALD, K. (1969) *The Mentally Retarded in Sweden.* Stockholm: The Swedish Institute.

GUTHKELCH, A. N. (1970) Hydrocephalus and its treatment. *Proc. Roy. Soc. Med.,* **60**, 1263–5.

HAGARD, S. and CARTER, F. A. (1976) Preventing the birth of infants with Down's syndrome: a cost-benefit analysis. *Brit. Med. J.,* **1**, 753–6.

JENSEN, A. R. (1969) How much can we boost IQ and scholastic achievement? *Harvard Educ. Rev.,* **39**, 1–123.

KADUSHIN, A. (1970) *Adopting Older Children.* New York: Columbia Univ. Press.

KIRK, S. A. (1958) *Early Education of the Mentally Retarded.* Urbana, Ill.: Univ. of Illinois Press.

KUCERA, T. (1970) Down's syndrome and infectious hepatitis. *Lancet,* **i**, 569–70.

LAURENCE, K. M. and GREGORY, P. (1976) Prenatal diagnosis of chromosome disorders. In *Human Malformations. Brit. Med. Bull.,* **32**, no. 1, 9–15.

MCASKIE, M. and CLARKE, A. M. (1976) Parent-offspring resemblances in intelligence: theories and evidence. *Brit. J. Psychol.,* **67**, 243–73.

MILUNSKY, A. and ALPERT, E. (1976) Routine testing for Alpha-fetoprotein in amniotic fluid. *Lancet,* **i**, 1015.

NOVAK, M. A. and HARLOW, H. F. (1975) Social recovery of monkeys isolated for the first year of life: I. Rehabilitation and therapy. *Developm. Psychol.,* **11**, 453–65.

PRESIDENT'S COMMITTEE ON MENTAL RETARDATION (1972) *Entering the*

Era of Human Ecology. Washington, DC: DHEW Publication No. (OS) 72–7.

PRESIDENT'S COMMITTEE ON MENTAL RETARDATION (1976) PCMR Message No. 42 Amniocentesis safe. Washington, DC: DHEW.

RICHARDSON, S. A. (1976) The relation of severe malnutrition in infancy to the intelligence of school children with differing life histories. *Pediat. Res.*, **10**, 57–61.

RUTTER, M. and MADGE, N. (1976) *Cycles of Disadvantage*. London: Heinemann.

SAMEROFF, A. J. and CHANDLER, M. J. (1975) Reproductive risk and the continum of caretaking casualty. In HOROWITZ, F. D., HETHERINGTON, M., SCARR-SALAPATEK, S. and SIEGEL, G. (eds.) *Rev. Child Developm. Res.*, **4**, 187–224. Chicago: Univ. of Chicago Press.

SKEELS, H. M. (1966) Adult status of children with contrasting early life histories: a follow-up study. *Monogr. Soc. Res. Child Developm.*, **31**, no. 3. Serial no. 105.

SKODAK, M. and SKEELS, H. M. (1949) A final follow-up study of 100 adopted children. *J. genet. Psychol.*, **75**, 85–125.

SLOAN, W. and STEVENS, H. A. (1976) *A Century of Concern*. Washington, DC: Amer. Assoc. Ment. Defic., Inc.

STEIN, Z. A., SUSSER, M. and GUTERMAN, A. G. (1973) Screening programme for prevention of Down's syndrome. *Lancet*, **i**, 305–10.

STEIN, Z. A., SUSSER, M. W., SAENGER, G. and MAROLLA, F. (1975) A historical cohort of the Dutch famine, 1944–45. In PRIMROSE, D. A. A. (ed.) *Proc. 3rd Cong. internat. Assoc. scient. Stud. ment. Defic.*, 44–53. Warsaw: Polish Medical Publishers.

STOLLER, A. and COLLMANN, R. D. (1965) Virus aetiology for Down's syndrome (mongolism). *Nature*, **208**, 903–4.

TIZARD, J. (1964) *Community Services for the Mentally Handicapped*. London: Oxford Univ. Press.

TIZARD, J. (1976) Nutrition, growth and development. *Psychol. Med.*, **6**, 1–5.

WORLD HEALTH ORGANIZATION (1968) *Organization of Services for the Mentally Retarded*. Wld. Hlth. Org. techn. Rep. Ser., 392. Generva: WHO.

WYNNE GRIFFITHS, G. (1973) The prevention" of Down's syndrome (mongolism). *Hlth Trends*, **5**, 59–60.

2

A. M. Clarke and A. D. B. Clarke

Criteria and classification
of subnormality

Some historical aspects of classification

The need to classify is deeply embedded in human beings, indeed it appears to be a fundamental basis of cognitive activities. As Bruner puts it, categorization allows the complexity of stimuli to be reduced by treating phenomena as equivalent when indeed they can be differentiated from each other in a variety of ways. It is thus important to recognize that the tendency to classify, either implicitly or explicitly, is part of the biological basis of man.

The categories which man will create are intimately related to the overall society in which he finds himself, and to his role in that society. For example, the 'man-in-the-street' and the architect will 'see' a given building in terms of very different selective categories. Moreover, the degree of selective categorization itself tends to change during individual development, as more and more knowledge is gained. Thus the young child's concept of a kangaroo will differ markedly from that of a zoologist, even though both have a clear and overlapping concept of this animal.

There is a close parallel between the use of classifications by the individual and those used by society. Different classifications of the same phenomenon serve different purposes and themselves change as the purposes change. This in turn is intimately related to prevailing social orientations at a given point in time. For example, the word 'crétin' is derived from the French '*chrétien*' (Christian) and is testimony to the fact that in early times the severely handicapped were cared for by monastic communities.

Classification involves 'labelling' and there is a constant act of changing labels as new knowledge is acquired or as society's view of the concept changes. Langdon Down first described in 1866 the condition of mongolism, a label based upon the physical appearance of a particular clinical type, together with the aetiological notion of 'atavistic regression' which itself really implied that the 'Mongolian race' was inferior. In the mid-twentieth century, as world biological science expanded, it became necessary to reject this archaic label in the interest both of scientific precision, and to oppose the perpetuation of an offensive racist label. The 'Langdon Down syndrome' or 'Down's syndrome' was thus invented, and the word 'Syndrome' of course rightly underlines the constellation of possible symptoms in this condition. With even more recent genetic discoveries, sub-classifications of Down's syndrome such as 'Trisomy 21' or 'mosaicism' became necessary.

Labels for a given concept may also change in response to popular feeling. Thus in this country the terms 'mental deficiency', 'feeble-mindedness', 'imbecility' and 'idiocy' were dropped, in favour of 'subnormality' and 'severe subnormality', in the 1959 Mental Health Act, as being less pejorative. Similarly, the words 'mental retardation' are seen as less offensive than 'mental deficiency' in the United States. And now, 'mental handicap' shows every sign of being a more favoured label. Finally, it should be pointed out that a given label carries with it different connotations for different people, and may lead to great confusion in discussion if the number or quality of assumptions underlying the same label differs between two communicators (e.g. between a geneticist and a teacher, or a paediatrician and a relatively naïve parent).

Historical documents provide an insight into the varying social reasons why certain members of society have been classified as mentally subnormal. Early in history, the reasons for classification were clearly linked with administrative matters. In England, statutory mention of the mentally subnormal dates as far back as the reign of Edward I (1272–1307), when the distinction was made for the first time on record between the born fool and the lunatic. In the Statute of Prerogatives in the reign of Edward II, a similar division is recorded, between 'born fool' (*fatuus naturalis*) and the person of unsound mind who may yet have certain lucid intervals (*non compos mentis, sicut quidam sunt per lucida intervalla*). The purpose of this distinction in feudal times was to facilitate the disposal of property: thus, if a man were found by questioning to be a lunatic, the Crown took possession of his belongings only during the period of his illness; whereas, if a man were found to be an idiot, his property reverted permanently to the Crown, subject only to an obligation to provide for his person and estate.

Scientific views, however, began from the beginning of this century to make a larger impact upon administrative and social concepts. Thus over-simple and confused genetic theories, in the context of a type of social Darwinism, began to emerge with the work of Goddard (1912) and others. From then on one can perceive an interplay between social and scientific concepts.

Sarasen and Doris (1969) have given extended consideration to this interplay between the development of biological science and social attitudes towards mental subnormality. They trace the origin and consequences of the degeneration theory, the confusion between insanity and mental subnormality, the impact of social Darwinism, the development of the eugenics movement and the role of the intelligence testing movement, among other topics. Their book is essential reading for all those interested in the origins of different forms of provision and changing social attitudes. Here, however, space forbids little more than the briefest excursion into this area.

We propose to trace very briefly the changing use of the word 'idiot', a word derived from the Greek, and meaning 'a private person'. It has also been used to denote 'layman' (1660), and professional fool or jester, as in Shakespeare ('a tale told by an idiot'), or an ignorant, uneducated man. For a considerable period of time the word idiot appeared to denote anyone who was mentally subnormal, and it is of course impossible to know what level of impairment was then defined. John Locke (1623–1704) was fully aware of the distinction between insanity and subnormality: 'Madmen put wrong ideas together, and so make wrong propositions, but argue and reason right from them; but idiots make very few or no propositions, and reasons scarce at all'. In the late eighteenth century, Blackstone mentions that the 'idiot or natural fool is one that hath had no understanding from his nativity; and therefore is by law never likely to attain any'. At the beginning of the nineteenth century Pinel considered idiocy as being a variant of the general class of psychosis, involving a partial or total abolition of the intellectual powers. The idiots' natural indolence and stupidity might, however, be obviated by engaging them in manual occupations, suitable to their respective 'capacities'.

Esquirol (1772–1840) wrote that 'idiocy is not a disease, but a condition in which the intellectual faculties are never manifested; or have never been developed sufficiently to enable the idiot to acquire such an amount of knowledge, as persons of his own age, and placed in similar circumstances as himself, are capable of receiving'. In the United States, Howe in 1848 refers to the difficulty of distinguishing dementia from idiocy. He contrasts those whose understanding is undeveloped, or developed to a very feeble degree, with those who have lost their understanding, the demented: '. . . by far the greater part of the idiots are children of parents, one or both of whom were of scrofulous temperaments, and poor flabby organization'. Alcoholism was seen as a major aetiological factor; however, Howe began to distinguish between idiots, fools and simpletons.

The classic book by Séguin (1866) *Idiocy: its Treatment by the Physiological Method* perpetuated for a while the use of idiocy as a generic term. But increasing awareness of differences within the broad group, as well as differing prognosis, was fully recognized terminologically by the Idiots Act of 1886. Here lunacy, on the one hand, and idiocy and imbecility, on the other, are distinguished. Idiots and imbeciles from birth or from an early age would be placed in any registered hospital or institution for the care and training of such persons. In using the term imbecile, it indicated that a class of subnormals existed, less defective than the idiot. It also recognized that the idiot might be trained. Before long the Education Act of 1870 showed that there existed yet other groups, the 'educable imbecile and the feeble-minded'. In 1897 a Departmental Committee was set up, among other things, to 'report particularly upon the best practicable means for distinguishing on the one hand between the educable and non-educable children . . .' In turn this led to the Elementary Education (Defective and Epileptic Children) Act of 1899 with its distinction between those who could, and those who could not, be sufficiently educated to become at least partially self-supporting in later life. Within a few years, Binet was to be faced with objectifying this same distinction .

The Royal Commission of 1904 reported in 1908, and as a result the Mental Deficiency Act of 1913 was passed. In this, idiots, imbeciles, feeble-minded persons and moral imbeciles were for the first time clearly defined: 'Idiots; that is to say, persons so deeply defective in mind from birth or from an early age as to be unable to guard themselves against common physical dangers . . .'

We need take this survey of 'idiocy' no further, for the 1913 definition, perpetuated in the amending Act of 1927, to all intents and purposes is synonymous with 'profound retardation' of the World Health Organization today. It has been clear that a specific meaning in Greek gave way to a number of alternatives in 'plain English'. It took on a pathological connotation in the seventeenth century, was seen in the nineteenth century variously as a form of psychosis, or the result of alcoholism and degeneration, or as the most severe degree of defect, as well as being used as a generic term for all grades of defect. Only at the end of the century was the more recent diagnostic synonym foreshadowed, while latterly the term has been omitted from the new vocabulary of scientists and administrators.

Society's changing outlook

What is subnormality? It is difficult to discuss this question without first examining the historical models of classification, and the assumptions made by those creating them.

Even in the simplest of societies from the beginning of history there have probably been those who perceived that some of their fellow men were socially incompetent and very stupid, and reasoned that these factors were causally connected. During the nineteenth century the 'disease model' became basic to a consideration of this population, for society placed those in need of care in the hands of the medical profession. At first, such persons seem to have been predominantly fairly severely retarded but by the end of the century, as legislation developed, a wider range of persons became designated as mentally deficient. As our brief considerations of the development of attitudes will show, the subnormal were regarded as a race apart in the early years of the present century. The social problems which some of them posed in a developing, complex, urban society, were 'explained' by reference to an over-simple genetic model, in the context of social Darwinism. This is well exemplified by Goddard's (1912) work on the Kallikak family which had very wide social and legislative repercussions both in the United States and this country. Both Goddard and Walter E. Fernald found themselves members of the same committee of the American Breeders' Association, and it is probably no accident therefore that through this connection Fernald (quoted by Sarason and Doris, 1969) was able to express such views in an alarming and succinct form to the Massachusetts Medical Society in 1912:

The social and economic burdens of uncomplicated feeble-mindedness are only too well known. The feeble-minded are a parasitic, predatory class, never capable of self-support or of managing their own affairs. The great majority ultimately become public charges in some form. They cause unutterable sorrow at home and are a menace and danger to the community. Feeble-minded women are almost invariably immoral, and if at large usually become carriers of venereal disease or give birth to children who are as defective as themselves. The feeble-minded woman who marries is twice as prolific as the normal woman.

We have only begun to understand the importance of feeble-mindedness as a factor in the causation of pauperism, crime and other social problems. Hereditary pauperism, or pauperism of two or more generations of the same family, generally means hereditary feeble-mindedness. In Massachusetts there are families who have been paupers for many generations. Some of the members were born or even conceived in the poor house.

Every feeble-minded person, especially the high-grade imbecile, is a potential criminal, needing only the proper environment and opportunity for the development and expression of his criminal tendencies. The unrecognized imbecile is a most dangerous element in the community.

Until fairly recently (the 1950s) such an analysis as that of Fernald, albeit in an attenuated form, underlay much thinking about subnormality. No doubt humane attitudes also played a part in legal provision, but basically legislation was conceived as protecting society. In this country, until 1959, the procedure was thus of 'certification as mentally deficient' provided the individual could be proved as 'subject to be dealt with'. Periodic reassessment or alleged reassessment took place, with visits of Justices of the Peace, followed in some cases by trial in daily employment, trial in residential employment and ultimately, if the 'patient' was fortunate, 'discharge from care'.

In any consideration of the classification of the mentally subnormal, two elementary but, none the less, important general points must be made. Classification always has a purpose. Its function has often been to allow some administrative action to be taken, sometimes investing it with a precision and scientific flavour it does not possess. Secondly, while no doubt boundaries do exist in nature, these are seldom as sharply defined or as rigid as we seek to make them. It is generally agreed that intellectual abilities, and also social competence, form graded continua, so that any dividing line must, in effect, be arbitrary.

Within the subnormal group, sub-classification equally has a purpose; sometimes the bias may be educational, sometimes aetiological or prognostic, and here again boundaries are often arbitrary, although those conditions in which the biological basis is fairly well understood (e.g. Down's syndrome) may be more precisely delineated than those in which it is not (e.g. autism).

During the latter half of the present century several factors have combined to alter considerably society's view of the mentally subnormal and therefore of appropriate provisions for them. These include (1) an awareness that genetic variation is a much more complex matter than was formerly realized; (2) evidence that the national degeneracy earlier predicted by certain prophets of doom was not taking place; (3) indications that nutritional and social factors may be implicated in some forms of subnormality; (4) the success of programmes of remediation undertaken in a few institutions which yielded hopeful results; and (5) a more humane and tolerant attitude towards at least mild forms of social deviation. It followed that the subnormal person should not be shut away in remote hospitals, but community care and integration became the watchwords, with plans for ultimately a very large number of hostel places. Moreover, in the 1970s the belief that half the present inmates of mental subnormality hospitals could and should find a place in the community is generally accepted. At the same time, voluntary admission as opposed to 'certification' caters for the vast majority, and legislation has shifted from primarily protecting society to primarily protecting the rights of handicapped individuals.

Purposes of classification

The different purposes of modern classification will now be briefly described.

(1) ADMINISTRATIVE

Some specific action may be needed on behalf of an individual, a group or for the sake of the home. The act of labelling a person as mentally subnormal enables the administrative machinery to take steps which, because of regulations or law, it otherwise could not do. They may be educational, institutional or protective. Nowadays a legally arranged deprivation of liberty, so common in the past, is unusual. The emphasis is upon voluntary admission to, for example, hospital or training centre.

(2) SCIENTIFIC

(a) *Diagnostic*. The social deviant (of whatever form) stands out as different from his peers. Natural curiosity suggests that the nature of this difference should be described – 'What is wrong with this person?' is the usual question in response to a grossly deviant appearance or grossly deviant behaviour. Then comes the question 'What is the cause or what are the causes of the condition?' and a diagnostic assessment may in itself suggest the approach to remediation, whether biochemical, educational or psychological (e.g. behaviour modification).

(b) *Prognostic*. Close on the heels of the question 'What is wrong?', comes the query 'What are his prospects?' Prognostic evaluation may often be linked with diagnosis, and can include an assessment of the likely contribution, and interaction, of biological and social factors in determining the handicap. It is appreciated, for example, that some children, drawn from very adverse social conditions, whose behaviour is indistinguishable from others in terms of their present personal characteristics, mature later, and during adolescence or early adult life show marked improvement in behavioural characteristics. Or again, some pathological conditions carry with them a prognosis of deterioration and early death. The complex question of prediction has recently been considered by Clarke and Clarke (1972 and 1973).

(c) *Research.* Classification, using well-defined criteria, allows scientists at different periods or from different areas to compare findings and communicate with each other. Is the survival rate for mongols increasing? Is the incidence of severe subnormality decreasing? Is encephalitis an equally grave cause of subnormality in Africa as in India? Do adults originally suffering from mild subnormality continue to improve after the age of 20, or indeed 40? These are but a few of the innumerable questions which can only be asked validly if the classification method and the constituent population are clearly defined.

Criteria of subnormality

Once the potential conceptual confusion of mental subnormality and mental illness has been clarified, three interlinked aspects of the behaviour of certain social deviants have been commonly considered: poor intelligence, lack of social skills, and poor academic achievements. The latter has never been advocated as a major or sole criterion, presumably since it has long been apparent to the most casual observer that many socially competent people are deficient in the skills of literacy or numeracy. Various authorities have, however, advocated intellectual or social incompetence, either separately or in combination, as being definitive of mental subnormality. These will, therefore, be examined for their validity and their adequacy.

(I) SOCIAL INCOMPETENCE AS A CRITERION

This concept is self-evidently so vague as nowadays rarely to be discussed seriously as a sufficient sole criterion of subnormality. Standards of what constitutes competence must be arbitrary, must differ not only between societies, but also within a society in different areas or social classes, as well as differing at various points in time. Social difficulties are clearly not confined to the subnormal but are symptomatic of a very wide range of causes, acting singly or in combination. Those who fail to conform to society's norms will include all criminals and *some* members of the following: the mentally ill, the mentally subnormal, the exceptionally brilliant, and the social or political innovator. In the latter case some countries appear to regard non-conformers as by definition socially incompetent and mentally ill.

Nevertheless, social incompetence as the major criterion of mental deficiency has been advocated by influential experts, with profound implications for legislation and the nature of the group thus classified. The 1913 British Mental Deficiency Act (amended in 1927) nowhere mentioned intelligence explicitly, but rather 'arrested or incomplete development of mind' was the central feature of the definition. The concept of mind was perceived as being wider than intelligence and included 'moral deficiency'. In discussing the then legal definition, Tredgold (1952) stated that although the Act made no reference to the permanency of the condition, there is no doubt that mental arrest, sufficient to cause the social incapacity envisaged by the Act, would be permanent and incurable. He further pointed out that when the Act referred to 'arrested development of mind', there was no legal justification for assuming that the only really important aspect of mind is the intellectual one: 'an arrested development of any process or department of mind, provided it resulted in social incapacity, constitutes mental deficiency'.

This latter interpretation has been advocated by several authorities and is typified by the British Medical Association and Magistrates' Association's memorandum of 1947 ('Interpretation of Definitions in the Mental Deficiency Act, 1927'), which states that 'the purpose of this memorandum is to point out that the concept of mind is wider than that of intellect, and that mental defect (i.e. deficiency of mind) is not the same thing as intellectual deficiency, though it includes it'. A similar point of view was later expressed by the Board of Control (1954) and the Royal Medico-Psychological Association (1954) in their memoranda to the Royal Commission on the Law relating to Mental Illness and Mental Deficiency. Thus, the Board of Control say: 'We regard the present definitions as enabling medical practitioners to certify mentally defective patients on the ground that they have characteristics from early youth which make them anti-social, although their intelligence might be quite normal.' The RMPA, in its discussion of the nature of mental deficiency, stated:

This 'condition of arrested or incomplete development of mind' may, however, be manifested in very varied ways. A usual manifestation is failure to develop what is commonly known as intelligence-functions which can be measured by psychometric methods and assessed under such terms as 'mental age' or 'intelligence quotient'; but this is by no means invariable, and in other cases the undeveloped mind may be manifested chiefly by failure to attain normal control of the emotions or to achieve the qualities needed for normal social behaviour.

The practical outcome of this point of view was that in England a large number of individuals of dull-normal and normal intellect were certified as mentally defective and compulsorily detained. O'Connor and Tizard (1954) showed that in their 5 per cent sample of nearly 12,000 patients, over half were classified as 'feeble-minded'; they found, in conformity with their previous researches, and that of other psychologists working in institutions, that the *average* IQ of *young* adult feeble-minded defectives was a little above 70 points. Various tests have been used by different examiners with substantially similar results. Commenting on this state of affairs, the British Psychological Society (1955) wrote that 'During this century, the British concept of mental deficiency has widened until it is no longer closely related to biological, psychological, or genetic definitions of the condition'. It seems that something like one-quarter of all institutionalized mentally deficient patients had IQs of 70 or above at the time these reports were made, a fact never envisaged by Tredgold. As already implied, this position did not appear to have altered substantially during the mid-1960s (apart from a welcome and dramatic drop in the numbers compulsorily detained) after the passing of the 1959 Mental Health Act (Castell and Mittler, 1965). Since then, however, there has been a considerable reduction in numbers of mildly subnormal admitted to hospital.

(2) EDUCATIONAL RETARDATION AS A CRITERION

The MD Act of 1927 in its definition of those to be classed as feeble-minded says '... in the case of children, that they appear to be permanently incapable by reason of such defectiveness (already defined) of receiving proper benefit from the instruction in ordinary schools'. This definition was in effect amended by the 1944 Education Act, which makes provision for the teaching of educationally subnormal children of all sorts, including the cognitively defective (above IQ 50), without certification as mentally deficient. Persistent educational failure has never been regarded as a sole criterion of mental defect and, as Wallin (1949) pointed out, such a procedure would classify as subnormal, millions of children of backward and borderline levels of intelligence who could not be regarded as feeble-minded, socially considered. Nevertheless, it is commonly used as one of the facts supporting a diagnosis of mental subnormality, and deserves, therefore, a passing reference.

(3) THE IQ AS A CRITERION

The advantages and disadvantages of IQ measurements have been discussed by many writers. It is thus intended here to offer the briefest account of the problems, as follows: (1) the IQ is liable to some degree of measurement error, either because of imperfect standardization or because of individual cognitive or motivational fluctuations possessing no long-term significance; (2) the same IQ on different tests may not, for reasons of standardization, mean the same thing. In practice this may be overcome with the use of standard scores but this is seldom undertaken by clinicians or administrators; (3) intellectual growth over long periods of time (and particularly among some of the mildly subnormal) does not necessarily proceed in a constant fashion with reference to age peers. Like physical growth, intellectual growth may change, sometimes markedly, in its rate of increase. This does not lead to error in the sense defined in (1) above;

rather it indicates that IQ changes may reflect real growth changes.

The difficulty is expressed by Kushlick (1968) in his attempt to assess the prevalence and prognosis of mild subnormality. The IQ range 50 to 70, he writes, has not proved useful either clinically or administratively. Among the many examples he offers, the classification of children as educationally subnormal may be cited. The total number of children in ESN schools seldom exceeds half of the 2 per cent to be expected if all children of IQ 50–70 were to attend, but anyway a report indicates that almost 40 per cent of the ESN have IQs above 70. One cannot, therefore, escape the conclusion that a minority of the 50–70 IQ group actually find their way into ESN schools.

From the foregoing it seems obvious that an upper borderline for subnormality is impossible to define with any degree of precision in IQ terms. Two considerations may, however, prove to be useful. First, to think of a proportion of the population as 'at risk' of needing special services at some time during their lives, while acknowledging that opinions will vary about what proportion this might represent (e.g. 2 per cent in England versus 3 per cent, as proposed by Heber, 1959). Second, an arbitrary upper limit should be imposed, if only to ensure that services designed as appropriate for an intellectually homogeneous section of the population are not misapplied by being extended to include a much wider range of the population, probably manifesting different needs. This appears in England to be occurring with an influx of ex-ESN children into some Adult Training Centres originally designed for the severely subnormal.

There does, however, appear to remain considerable agreement for the view expressed by Burt (1922) that for adults a mental age of 8 or IQ 50 is helpful in distinguishing between those who are almost invariably 'social parasites' and those who can, albeit at a low level, fend for themselves in the community. Despite the problems outlined above, some kind of classification system is necessary, (a) for administrative and (b) for scientific purposes. The major use here seems to be for research and for communication between scientists. We have suggested that mild mental subnormality is not a scientific category in itself. This does, of course, imply that scientific work on those so classified may not prove very useful.

In practice, behavioural criteria of subnormality are hard to define with precision. An extreme expression of this problem is given by Garfunkel (1964) and Brabner (1967) quoted by Sarason and Doris (1969). They argue that diagnostic categories or definitions confuse rather than clarify issues and that the concept of subnormality, like that of mental illness, is a useless one for understanding and modifying non-adaptive behaviour, primarily because the so-called 'condition' of subnormality is not an identifiable behavioural entity. Brabner goes on to state that medical men have initially lumped together in single categories several diseases of unknown aetiology. Later knowledge allows them to subdivide or re-classify these once vague categories.

The present writers have considerable sympathy with this view, and offer as an illustrative example the results of an attempt to account for those who might be presumed to be in need of assistance in a country offering well-established and extensive free services for the mentally subnormal. As already noted, it is generally estimated that about 2 per cent of the population may be regarded as intellectually subnormal and severely subnormal, in the porportion of three to one, respectively. With a population in England and Wales of about 48 million, therefore, one would expect to identify something like 960,000 subnormal persons of all grades. What do we know of the status of this large group? It is possible, in a rough-and-ready way, to account for a proportion by examining statistics for a given year, in this case 1966 (see Table 1).

TABLE 1. *Total identified subnormal population (subnormal and severely subnormal) in England and Wales, 1966*

Population of England and Wales	approx.	48,000,000
2% of total population		960,000
In schools for the ESN	approx.	45,000
On ESN waiting lists	''	10,000
In mental subnormality hospitals	''	65,000
On mental subnormality hospital waiting lists	''	5,000
Under care of local health authorities	''	93,000
In Junior Training Centres	''	17,000
In Adult Training Centres	''	18,000
Total	''	253,000

Note: The total of 253,000 is considerably inflated because the Training Centre numbers are almost certainly also included in those under care of local health authorities. Moreover, in mental subnormality hospitals and training centres, the majority will be of severely subnormal grade.

It should be added that in 1966 there were a little over 4 million children under five; 2 per cent of this figure is 80,000. Of these, perhaps 60,000 are potentially ESN, but these will not have been identified until the school years. The balance, about 20,000, is severely subnormal and some of these pre-school children will be under the care of local health authorities or in special care units or in subnormality hospitals. All these considerations justify the conclusion that a relatively small percentage of the *mildly* subnormal (unlike the severely subnormal) are in receipt of special facilities at any one time. (Part of this information is taken from Table 7 in Worters, 1968.)

The table accounts for all those specifically designated subnormal (whether of mild or severe grade) and dealt with as such by various social agencies. It is certain that the table includes the vast majority of those who are severely subnormal. There remains the possibility, however, that other types of community provision include significant numbers of the mildly subnormal, of which the criminal population is the only one worth serious consideration. In an as yet unpublished recent study, Dr C. Banks (personal communication) gave individual Stanford-Binet tests to 900 randomly sampled men, aged 17–20, in detention, prison or borstal. She found that 2 per cent (i.e. roughly the expected representation from the total population) had IQs of 70 and below. Unfortunately, there is no study available of the intelligence of a randomly selected prison population, but according to Dr R. V. G. Clarke (personal communication) studies of selected samples of the prison population, while showing an over-representation of the dull normal, do not suggest any marked over-representation of the subnormal.

If one were to add, say, a further 25,000 (probably a considerable overestimate) to cover the mildly subnormal receiving care in prisons, borstals, approved schools, or charitable hostels, one would account only for less than a third of the estimated total subnormal and severely subnormal population. The conclusion seems inescapable that at any one point in time the majority of the *mildly subnormal* (who comprise three-quarters of the whole) function within the limits of community tolerance in a welfare state, receiving no special official provision. For these very reasons, little is known of the 'ordinary' mildly subnormal in the community, and precise data relate in the main to the most disadvantaged members of the group.

The rather crude analysis offered above is supported by the results of long-term social follow-up of mildly retarded persons (Charles, 1953; Miller, 1965). A large group identified as retarded and attending 'opportunity classes' was originally studied in the 1930s. Detailed analysis of the ways in which its members differed from the general population has been provided and the successively improving outcome carefully documented. A final monograph by Baller, Charles and Miller (1967) indicated that the majority were functioning adequately as low-average members of the population, working in unskilled or semi-skilled employment. Of average age 53 years, this group has 'continued to fare much better than could have been predicted or even hoped for'. See also Chapter 5.

If we perceive the mentally subnormal as a group of people 'at risk' of requiring special facilities provided by a welfare state (and this operational definition is at least as reasonable as any other), then it appears that *at any one point in time* only a third of those who may be presumed to represent the bottom 2 per cent of the distribution of intelligence are in fact using those facilities. The proportion *who at some period in their lives* require the special help of welfare agencies, will, of course, be greater. The above analysis is offered, not as evidence of some undisclosed qualities among the subnormal, nor as evidence of a necessarily perfect state of affairs. It does, however, imply (1) that a large proportion of the group at risk are not classified as subnormal for specific administrative purposes; and (2) where special help is required, it may be only temporarily.

In these terms, therefore, the mildly and severely subnormal are both 'at risk' of needing some form of community provision. The 'risk' is absolute so far as the lower group is concerned, and much less so in the higher group. In the former, the cause is primarily intellectual, and in the latter very often a compound of social, intellectual and environmental factors.

Decisions concerning the upper limit for the mildly subnormal will reflect an interaction of social provision, the threshold for social tolerance of deviant behaviour, the employment situation and, commonly, the existence of areas of social degradation, as well as the belief that it is wise in education or training not to deal with a group which is very heterogeneous in character.

It is concluded, therefore, that mild subnormality is primarily a social concept which may alter from time to time and which has some convenience so far as treatment is concerned. The label does not in practice constitute a scientific entity, which is not to say, of course, that the group so delineated may not be scientifically of very great interest, providing a very rewarding field of work.

THE AAMD COMMITTEE

In an endeavour to bring order into the chaotic status of terminology and classification in the field of mental retardation, the American Association on Mental Deficiency set up a broadly based committee of experts to inquire into the problem and make proposals. The recommended new system of classification was published (Heber, 1959), and represents an important advance in the field. Since the definitions and concepts proposed differ substantially from, for example, those embodied in the new British Mental Health Act, passed in the same year, it remains to be seen how effective the American Association on Mental Deficiency classification will be in producing a more uniform system of statistical reporting on an international basis.

The Manual starts with a section on definition, presenting a general concept of mental retardation which is interdisciplinary in character and which serves to distinguish mental retardation from other disorders of behaviour.

Definition: 'Mental retardation refers to subaverage general intellectual functioning which originates during the development period and is associated with impairment in one or more of the following: (1) maturation, (2) learning, and (3) social adjustment.'

'Subaverage' refers to performance more than one standard deviation below the population mean; 'general intellectual functioning' may be assessed by one or more of the various objective tests developed for the purpose; the upper age limit of the 'developmental period', although it cannot be precisely defined, is regarded as approximately 16 years; rate of 'maturation' refers to the rate of sequential development of self-help skills of infancy and early childhood and is regarded as of prime importance as a criterion during the pre-school years; 'learning ability' refers to the facility with which knowledge is acquired as a function of experience, and is particularly important as a qualifying condition during the school years. Social adjustment is particularly important as a qualifying condition of mental retardation at the adult level where it is assessed in terms of the degree to which the individual is able to maintain himself independently in the community and in gainful employment, as well as his ability to meet and conform to other personal and social responsibilities and standards set by the community. Since adequate population norms and highly objective measures of the various aspects of adaptive behaviour are not yet available, it is not possible to establish precise criteria of functioning in these areas.

The report stresses finally that within the framework of the present definition, mental retardation is a term descriptive of the *current* status of the individual.

The Manual outlines excellent classificatory schemes under medical and behavioural headings, and also includes a section on statistical reporting (Heber, 1959; see also footnote on p. 116 of this volume).

The reader is referred to an interesting polemic on some of the concepts used in the AAMD Manual between Garfield and Wittson (1960a, b) and Cantor (1960, 1961). In the last paper the author discusses at length the concept of 'incurability', and stresses the dangers inherent in the persistent tendency of clinicians to 'entitize' mental retardation.

WHO EXPERT COMMITTEE ON MENTAL HEALTH, 1968

The WHO Expert Committee (1968) takes account of most of the foregoing discussion of problems concerning criteria and classification. The report suggests IQ borderlines for the different grades of defect, assuming a population mean of 100 and a standard deviation of 15 points. Taken in conjunction with social factors, it is argued that the sub-classification of the mentally retarded should be associated with the following approximate IQ ranges: mild, −2·0 to −3·3 standard deviations from the mean (i.e. IQs 50–70); moderate, −3·3 to −4·3 standard deviations from the mean (i.e. IQs 35–50); severe, −4·3 to −5·3 standard deviations from the mean (i.e. IQs 20–35); and profound, more than −5·3 standard deviations from the mean. As the report indicates, 'It should again be stressed that these are not exact measurements, nor should they be considered the sole criteria; in practice, the categories will tend to overlap, but the IQ has some value within the range of mental retardation, both as a diagnostic and as a prognostic guide.' It might be added that the lower the IQ, the more profound are its implications both diagnostically and prognostically.

The Expert Committee's discussion on these points was related to the text of the eighth revision of the ICD (World Health Organization, 1967). The Committee thus accepted the sub-classification but made it more precise. It strongly opposed, however, the classification of those with an IQ in the range 68–85 as 'borderline mentally retarded' as shown in category 310. On this basis at least 16 per cent of the population would be labelled mentally retarded or borderline mentally retarded. The widening of the concept implied by this definition would greatly damage the quality of available services, which are geared to lower abilities, and would make mental retardation a repository for other deviant conditions. A similar viewpoint was advanced during a 1969 WHO Seminar held in Washington DC, where the following main recommendations were made for the ninth revision of the ICD: (1) A scheme of classification should be instituted requiring the recording of four types of information: (a) degree of mental handicap, (b) aetiological or associated biological or organic factors, (c) associated psychiatric disorder, and (d) psychosocial factors.

(2) The grades of mental retardation recommended in the 1968 report should be used, and the category 'borderline mental retardation' should be replaced by a category 'normal variations in intelligence'. Rather than being included in the ICD Manual, IQ ranges should be specified in an accompanying glossary which should draw attention to the limitations as well as to the usefulness of IQ data, and the need to take into account social and cultural background when evaluating grade of intellectual retardation (Moser, 1971, and personal communication).

The pathological / subcultural dichotomy

A most important classification, on the basis of aetiology, was proposed by E. O. Lewis (1933). Although subsequently modified, it remains fundamental, has influenced later classificatory systems and thus finds a penultimate place in this chapter.

Lewis stated that the term mental deficiency is an abstraction used to cover a heterogeneous and complex group of clinical conditions due to a variety of biological factors, and preferred, therefore, to speak of 'mental deficiencies'. On the basis of clinical studies in the field, he suggested that there are two forms of variation: (1) the *pathological* type, and (2) the *subcultural* type. Adopting Tredgold's classification of clinical varieties of secondary amentia, Lewis included in the pathological group all cases of mental deficiency attributable to trauma, inflammatory conditions, hydrocephalus, syphilis, epilepsy, cretinism, and nutritional and sensory defects. He also included several other conditions, such as mongolism, amaurotic family idiocy, hyperteliorism, naevoid amentiae, progressive degeneration, and many cases of sclerotic amentiae. In the causation of all these varieties of defect, one finds the intervention of some new or alien factors of a pathological character not found in the normal constitution. In Lewis's classification, such conditions as phenylketonuria and amaurotic idiocy, which are known to be due to recessive genes, were included in the pathological type.

On the other hand, the subcultural group included those cases of defect in which no alien factor was found, and where the deficiency was only an extreme variety of the normal variation of mental endowments. Thus, the higher grades of subcultural deficiency merged imperceptibly into the lower grades of dullness or temperamental instability in the normal population. Although Lewis inclined to the view that subcultural deficiency is inherited, he believed that unfavourable environmental factors may in some cases account for the condition.

As Penrose (1962) has indicated, an interesting change has occurred in our understanding of aetiological mechanisms. Whereas, in Lewis's day, most cases of pathological, mainly low-grade subnormality were thought to result from trauma, infection or toxicity, it is now increasingly recognized that rare (often recessive) genetic mechanisms are sometimes responsible for the damage (e.g. phenylketonuria). And whereas subnormals of about IQ 50 upward were at one time thought to owe their condition largely to unfavourable genetic mechanisms, evidence now suggests that early and prolonged social adversity is an important, though not the sole, feature. The pathological/subcultural dichotomy remains useful although there has been some reinterpretation of its aetiological mechanisms.

Clarke (1966, 1969) has suggested a tripartite system of aetiological classification, effectively splitting the Lewis subcultural category into subcultural versus normal genetic variation. Recognizing that parental-child intelligence correlations rarely exceed 0·5, he indicates that a proportion of the mildly subnormal groups must owe their status, not primarily to social factors, but to normal genetic variation. Fig. 1 in Chapter 1 indicated the relationship of these three aetiological headlines to terminology and to IQ.

Conclusions

Criteria and classification of subnormality possess a long history of development and change. At the root of all systems is the need of societies to take action of some kind. The nature of the procedures adopted is profoundly influenced by current perceptions of deviance on the one hand, and the type of responsibilities owed to their members on the other. From the thirteenth century consideration of problems concerning disposal of property, these concepts have changed to include, implicitly, biological and social theories of man. These ranged from the need for Christian brotherhood and charity for the oppressed, to post-Darwinian theories concerning the supposed evolutionary threat of 'feeble-mindedness' to civilized society. Currently, these have moved away from segregation to the notion of integration of the handicapped in the community and their maximal 'normalization'.

We have stressed throughout that subnormality is primarily an administrative concept, used for the purposes of social action. Our brief overview of the major criteria of subnormality, namely IQ below 70, social incompetence and educational retardation, has made clear that each is overinclusive of other conditions. It has been argued that (1) the IQ criterion includes many socially competent members at the above IQ 50 level; (2) that social incompetence is to be found in many other conditions than subnormality and is thus not specifically pathognomonic; and (3) that educationally, as Burt once put it, 'the dull are usually backward, but the backward are not necessarily dull'.

In combination, these criteria are highly intercorrelated in that small section of the population below about IQ 50. Above this level, in the individual case, an intercorrelation of all three will suggest the need for special help, which may be of a temporary or a longer-term nature. This combination provides the purest measure of administrative prevalence, that is, of society's need to take action.

References

BALLER, W. R., CHARLES, D. C. and MILLER, E. L. (1967) Mid-life attainment of the mentally retarded: a longitudinal study. *Genet. Psychol. Monogr.*, **75,** 235–329.

Board of Control (1954) *Memorandum of Evidence before the Royal Commission on the Law relating to Mental Illness and Mental Deficiency.* Day 1. London: HMSO.

BRABNER, G. (1967) The myth of mental retardation. *Training School Bull.*, **63,** 149–52.

British Medical Association and Magistrates' Association (1947) *Interpretations of Definitions in the Mental Deficiency Act, 1927.* London: BMA.

British Psychological Society (1955) *Memorandum of Evidence before the Royal Commission on the Law relating to Mental Illness and Mental Deficiency.* Day 17. London: HMSO.

BURT, C. (1922) *Mental and Scholastic Tests* (2nd edn, 1924). London: P. S. King.

CANTOR, G. N. (1960) A critique of Garfield and Wittson's reaction to the revised Manual on Terminology and Classification. *Amer. J. ment. Defic.*, **64,** 954–6.

CANTOR, G. N. (1961) Some issues involved in category VIII of the A.A.M.D. 'Terminology and Classification Manual'. *Amer. J. ment. Defic.*, **65,** 561–6.

CASTELL, J. H. F. and MITTLER, P. J. (1965) Intelligence of patients in subnormality hospitals: a survey of admissions in 1961. *Brit. J. Psychiat.*, **111,** 219–25.

CHARLES, D. C. (1953) Ability and accomplishment of persons earlier judged mentally deficient. *Genet. Psychol. Monogr.*, **47,** 3–71.

CLARKE, A. D. B. (1966) *Recent Advances in the Study of Subnormality.* London: National Association for Mental Health.

CLARKE, A. D. B. (1969) *Recent Advances in the Study of Subnormality.* (2nd edn). London: National Association for Mental Health.

CLARKE, A. D. B. and CLARKE, A. M. (1972) Consistency and variability in the growth of human characteristics. In WALL, W. D. and VARMA, V. (eds.) *Advances in Educational Psychology*, I. London: Univ. of London Press.

CLARKE, A. M. and CLARKE, A. D. B. (1973) Assessment and prediction in the severely subnormal. In MITTLER, P. J. (ed.) *Psychological Assessment of the Mentally Handicapped.* London: Churchill.

GARFIELD, S. L. and WITTSON, C. (1960a) Some reactions to the revised Manual on Terminology and Classification in Mental Retardation. *Amer. J. ment. Defic.*, **64,** 951–3.

GARFIELD, S. L. and WITTSON, C. (1960b) Comments on Dr Cantor's remarks. *Amer. J. ment. Defic.*, **64,** 957–9.

GARFUNKEL, F. (1964). Probabilities and possibilities for modifying behaviour of mentally retarded children: tactics for research. *Boston Univ. J. Educ.*, **147**, 45–52.

GODDARD, H. H. (1912) *TheKallikak Family*. New York: Macmillan.

HEBER, R. (1959) A manual on terminology and classification in mental retardation. *Amer. J. ment. Defic. Monogr. Suppl.*, **64.**

KUSHLICK, A. (1968) Social problems in mental subnormality. In MILLER, E. (ed.) *Foundations of Child Psychiatry*. Oxford: Pergamon.

LEWIS, E. O. (1933) Types of mental deficiency and their social significance. *J. ment. Sci.*, **79**, 298–304.

MILLER, E. L. (1965) Ability and social adjustment at midlife of persons earlier judged mentally deficient. *Genet. Psychol. Monogr.*, **72**, 139–98.

MOSER, J. (1971) World Health Organization activities concerning mental retardation. In PRIMROSE, D. A. (ed.) *Proc. 2nd Congr. Internat. Assoc. Scient. Stud. Ment. Defic.*, 546–7. Warsaw: Ars Polona; Amsterdam: Swets & Zeitlinger.

O'CONNOR, N. and TIZARD, J. (1954) A survey of patients in twelve mental deficiency institutions. *Brit. med. J.*, **i**, 16–18.

PENROSE, L. S. (1962) Biological aspects. *Proc. Lond. Conf. Scient. Stud. Ment Defic.*, **1**, 11–18.

Royal Medico-Psychological Association (1954) *Memorandum of Evidence before the Royal Commission on the Law relating to Mental Illness and Mental Deficiency*. Day 8. London: HMSO.

SARASON, S. B. and DORIS, J. (1969) *Psychological Problems in Mental Deficiency* (4th edn). New York: Harper & Row.

TREDGOLD, A. F. (1949) *A Text-book of Mental Deficiency* (7th edn reprinted; 8th edn 1952). London: Baillière, Tindall & Cox.

WALLIN, J. E. W. (1949) *Children with Mental and Physical Handicaps*. New York and London: Staples.

World Health Organization (1967) *Manual of the International Statistical Classification of Diseases, Injuries and Causes of Death, 1965 Revision*. Geneva.

World Health Organization (1968) *Organization of Services for the Mentally Retarded*. Fifteenth Report of the WHO Expert Committee on Mental Health. WHO Tech. Rep. Ser. 392. Geneva.

WORTERS, A. R. (1968) Subnormality – terminology and prevalence. In O'GORMAN, G. (ed.) *Modern Trends in Mental Health and Subnormality*. London: Butterworth.

3

J. M. Berg

Aetiological aspects of mental subnormality: pathological factors

Introduction

A wide variety of individuals with different clinical characteristics and different degrees of intellectual retardation are considered to be mentally defective or subnormal. Criteria of social competence and educational capability enter into such considerations, as well as the intellectual level *per se* as measured by tests of intelligence. Persons who can be classified as mentally subnormal on the basis of these criteria range from the helpless idiot to the dullard whose behaviour is regarded as disturbed or otherwise inappropriate. From the aetiological point of view, the term mental subnormality has no more meaning than, for example, a term such as diminished head size. Like smallness of the head, mental subnormality is not a disease entity but a symptom which can be determined by a large number of different causal agencies. These agencies operate, in given circumstances, to produce the symptom, in varying degrees of severity, together with other clinical manifestations. This chapter considers complementary aspects of these basic issues. (See also Chapter 2.)

General approach to the problem

Some subnormal persons, in particular those with severe mental defect, suffer from demonstrable organic disease or pathology which, however determined, can reasonably be regarded as being responsible for the subnormality. Aided by knowledge of the personal and family history, these pathological conditions may be detected, even pre-natally in certain particular circumstances,[1] by means of various diagnostic techniques including clinical, radiological, biochemical, cytological and neuropathological ones. In other cases of subnormality, no physical abnormality can be found which could account for the mental defect. A considerable clinical problem which arises in these cases is that of trying to decide whether the inability to demonstrate organic pathology is due to inadequacy of available methods of diagnosis or due to the absence of such pathology. Important diagnostic aids have been developed in recent years, notably in the fields of biochemistry and cytogenetics, which have led to the detection of

[1] Since this chapter was written, the scope of prenatal diagnosis has extended substantially. This trend will undoubtedly continue, with significant preventive implications in regard to some varieties of mental subnormality. Milunsky (1973) has published a comprehensive survey of developments in these spheres.

previously undifferentiated pathological types of mental subnormality. There is little doubt that more such types will be recognized in the future, though very many persons are likely to remain who function at a low intellectual level for reasons other than the operation of specific disease processes. Lewis (1933) called such cases 'subcultural', as opposed to 'pathological', and regarded them as representing the lower end of the normal variations in intelligence which occur in the general population. Most of these cases have relatively mild intellectual deficit and many are not obviously distinct from the normal population as a whole.

Lewis's (1933) subdivision of the mentally retarded into those who are organically diseased variants of the general population and those who are normal variants provides a helpful approach to the aetiology of mental subnormality. Two groups of causal agencies emerge for consideration:

1. Specific organic pathological processes directly responsible for, or closely associated with, mental defect. In the main, these lead to severe subnormality. However, a few (for example, the triple-X condition in females) are more usually associated with mild defect and many (for example, phenylketonuria) can result in intellectual states varying from gross idiocy to levels within the range of normality.
2. An interaction of genetical and environmental influences, of the same kind as those operating in the normal population, not responsible for specific physical disease but sufficient to produce some (usually mild) impairment of intellectual function. This will lead to a diagnosis of subnormality if the individual is considered also to be socially incompetent.

The influences mentioned in the second group are considered in Chapter 4 and will not be discussed further here. In this chapter an account is given of specific pathological causes of, and some distinct physical syndromes closely associated with, mental subnormality. The subject cannot be dealt with extensively within the confines of one chapter, so that the data are presented with emphasis on principles rather than details.

Heredity and environment in the causation of pathological types of mental subnormality

The pathological types of mental subnormality can be divided conveniently into those which are genetically and those which are environmentally determined. It should be borne in mind, however, that the two sets of causal factors are not mutually exclusive. The effects on the individual of abnormal events and diseases having their origin in the environment will be influenced by the inherited constitution of that individual; for example, the occurrence of an obviously environmental event, such as injury at birth, will be dependent to some extent on characteristics of the newborn infant, like his birth weight, which are partly genetically determined. Conversely, inherited defects can be determined by

earlier environmental events as, for instance, when irradiation produces mutations in germ cells (ova and sperms) which are harmful to offspring derived from
these cells. Further, even when mental subnormality is due to inherited disease,
environmental influences, such as a stable and stimulating home, appropriate
educational facilities, and specific medical treatments, can have a substantial
effect on the actual level and quality of mental function achieved. Haemolytic
disease of the newborn, due to *Rhesus* incompatibility between mother and
foetus, provides a notable example of the interaction between hereditary and
environmental factors in the production of mental effects. In this condition, an
inherited antigenic difference between the mother and her foetus can result in
the formation of maternal antibodies which constitute an environmental hazard
to the foetus; its red cells may be haemolysed with consequent serious damage to
foetal tissues, including those of the brain. Mental subnormality of variable
degree can thus occur in survivors. Both mortality and morbidity rates have been
reduced by the environmental alteration achieved by exchange transfusions
undertaken soon after birth. This technique involves the removal of the infant's
blood, containing harmful ingredients, and its replacement by normal donor
blood. Even more important current developments, involving the use of prophylactic Rh immunoglobulin, could result in a decline of Rhesus haemolytic
disease by as much as 95 per cent (Finn, 1970).

Without prejudice to the reservations made above, the conditions to be discussed in this chapter are subdivided into those of genetical and those of environmental origin. As Penrose (1963a) pointed out, the distinction between hereditary
and environmental causes must be based upon temporal sequence; the former
are determined prior to conception (in parental, or more remote ancestral, germ
cells) and the latter subsequent to it (before, during or after birth). It is perhaps
as well to add a reminder here that the terms hereditary and congenital are not
synonymous. The latter term is more comprehensive in that it is applicable both
to conditions which are inherited and to those which arise from events occurring
during intra-uterine life. Thus, all hereditary conditions may be considered as
congenital in origin, though some congenital ones are not hereditary. The point
can be illustrated by reference to congenital cataract. One variety of this, described by Garland and Moorhouse (1953), occurs in association with subnormality and ataxia and is due to a recessively transmitted gene. Another variety is a
well-known consequence, together with other abnormalities including mental
defect, of foetal infection with the rubella virus during the early stages of pregnancy. A further point which emerges from this reference to congenital cataract
is that genetical and environmental events can give rise to similar defects.
Goitrous cretinism, discussed on page 44, provides another example of this.

I. MENTAL SUBNORMALITY OF SPECIFIC GENETICAL ORIGIN

Genetically determined conditions closely associated with pathological types of
mental subnormality may be due to:

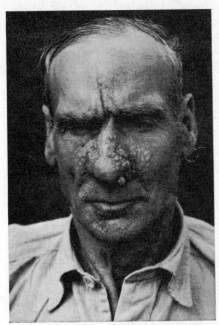

1. *Epiloia:* severely subnormal man aged 64 years. Note adenoma sebaceum

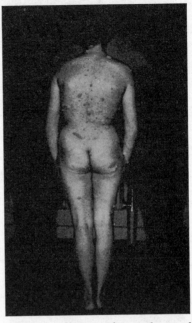

2. *Neurofibromatosis:* subnormal woman aged 32 years. Note multiple tumours and pigmentation of skin

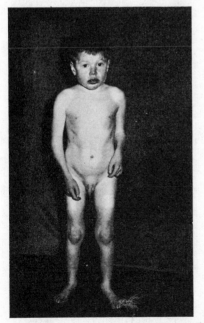

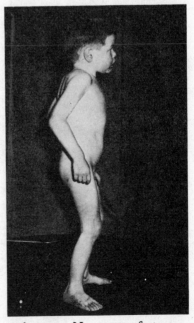

3. *Gargoylism:* severely subnormal boy aged 9 years. Note coarse features and limitation of extension of joints

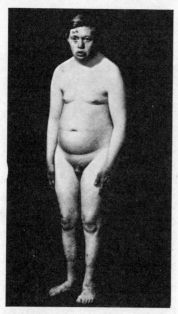

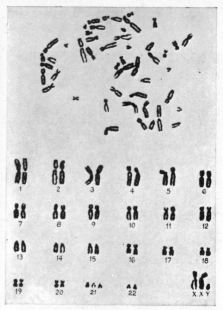

4. *Association of Down's syndrome and Klinefelter syndrome:* severely subnormal man aged 49 years. Note slanting eyes and breast enlargement

5. *Chromosomes from dividing cell* of patient on left with analysis (Denver classification). Note extra No. 21 and extra X chromosome

(Published by permission of the Council of the Hunterian Society)

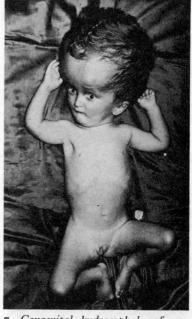

6. *Tuberculous meningitis resulting in severe subnormality:* boy aged 15 years. He also has enlarged head and spastic diplegia

7. *Congenital hydrocephaly* of uncertain aetiology associated with severe subnormality: boy aged $3\frac{1}{2}$ years. Head circumference = 79 cm (norm = 51 cm)

1. Harmful genes. Autosomal dominant, autosomal recessive and X-linked abnormalities are the main ones in this category. The genes resulting in pathological types of subnormality are rare specific ones, in contrast to commoner non-specific genes which may be supposed to be operating to produce what Lewis (1933) called 'subcultural' variation.
2. Aberrant chromosomes. These aberrations may involve the autosomes or the sex chromosomes and, sometimes, both.

Each of these will be considered in turn. An understanding of the mechanisms involved in the production of these abnormalities presupposes some knowledge of the characteristics of chromosomes and of the genetical units, or genes, which are regarded as an essential part of their nature. Some aspects of this subject are referred to in the context of the data presented below, though a comprehensive account of it is beyond the scope of the main theme of this chapter. Stimulating general introductions to the science of human genetics include those of Carter (1962) and of Penrose (1963b). Among valuable recent editions of more formal introductory textbooks, those of Roberts (1970) and Thompson and Thompson (1973) may be mentioned as examples.

(1) *Conditions due to harmful genes*

(a) *Autosomal dominant abnormalities.* Several conditions, in which mental subnormality is not uncommon, fulfil the criteria of dominant inheritance. Such conditions are due to a single gene transmitted by a parent (of either sex) to half the offspring, though actually, because human sibships are relatively small, frequently more or less than half the children are affected. The parent, say the father, is capable of transmitting the gene either because it has arisen by fresh mutation in his germ cells or because he himself inherited it. In the former case, the parent will not himself suffer from the disease and, in the latter, he must be sufficiently mildly afflicted to be capable of reproduction even though his affected offspring may be so grossly diseased as to be infertile. Fresh gene mutations and variability in the manifestations of disease therefore play an important role in dominant conditions associated with severe abnormalities. These considerations can make the demonstration of dominant inheritance of such abnormalities very difficult in practice.

Epiloia illustrates these points. Bourneville (1880) was the first to recognize the pathological features of the condition which he called *sclérose tubéreuse* (tuberous or tuberose sclerosis) in view of the tuber-like nodules which are found in the brain. Feeling the need for a name based on clinical rather than neuro-pathological considerations, Sherlock (1911) coined the term epiloia for the disease. Three of its main features are mental subnormality, epilepsy, and various skin anomalies of which the most important is adenoma sebaceum, consisting of multiple papules in a mainly butterfly-shaped distribution on both cheeks (see Plate 1). Mental subnormality is usually severe but can be absent. Though often noted in infancy, subnormality may not be apparent for a number, or even many, years, particularly when it is of a mild degree. Epilepsy commonly begins in the first year of life and may be the first sign of abnormality noted. There is wide variability in the frequency of fits, and remissions can occur, lasting for months or years, even without the use of anticonvulsants. Adenoma sebaceum, which is a most valuable diagnostic sign, does not usually appear till the child is a few years old, though it may possibly be present at birth (Walsh et al., 1938) and has been observed also, for the first time, at the age of 26 years (Finlayson, 1955). In addition to these variable manifestations, many internal tissues, apart from those of the brain, can be involved (for example, the kidneys, heart and lungs) with the production of a wide range of clinical signs. Various combinations of pathological and clinical findings occur in individual cases, even in the same family, making it difficult to obtain accurate data concerning the familial and overall incidence of the disease. Incomplete forms, with some of the more obvious features absent, add to the difficulty. Nevertheless, many pedigrees show a dominant mode of inheritance. A considerable number of cases, perhaps about half, seem to occur sporadically and many of these are thought to be due to new gene mutations. Penrose (1963a) estimated the frequency of epiloia due to a dominant gene to be one in 30,000 in the general population of England. The condition is not unusual in populations of severely subnormal persons; there were 10 instances of it among 800 consecutive admissions of idiot and imbecile children to the Fountain Hospital, London (Berg, 1963).

Among other conditions which can reasonably be regarded as dominant, and which are not infrequently associated with mental subnormality, are neurofibromatosis, acrocephalosyndactyly and craniofacial dysostosis. As in epiloia, new gene mutations are thought to determine many instances of these conditions and they display considerable variation in symptomatology.

Neurofibromatosis (von Recklinghausen's disease), with an estimated incidence, in all its forms, of the order of 1 in 2,000 in the general population (Neel, 1954), is partially characterized by nerve tumour formation which may involve many parts of the body (see Plate 2). If there is cerebral involvement, mental subnormality can be one of the sequelae. Preiser and Davenport (1918) noted that 7.8 per cent of 243 reported cases of neurofibromatosis were feeble-minded, and, more recently, Canale et al. (1964) reported a 10 per cent incidence of retardation among 92 affected patients seen in a Detroit hospital. However, the disease is rare among the severely subnormal. In the Fountain Hospital series of 800 children referred to above, there were only 2 examples of it. Penrose (1963a) pointed out that many pedigrees are consistent with the hypothesis that an irregularly dominant gene is responsible for the disease.

Acrocephalosyndactyly (Apert's syndrome) is a condition in which, as the name indicates, a high, wide and short cranium is associated with malformation of the fingers and/or toes. A characteristic facial appearance, including widely set bulging eyes, underdeveloped maxillae, crowded teeth and a prominent lower jaw, facilitates correct diagnosis. According to Sirkin (1944), the intelligence of most reported cases is normal. However, Penrose (1963a) noted that mental defect, though not usually severe, is a common accompaniment. Blank (1960) distinguished two main clinical categories of acrocephalosyndactyly, 'typical' and 'atypical', interdigital osseous union being a conspicuous feature of the former and absent in the latter. He described the former as being commoner and estimated its incidence at birth to be about 1 in 160,000. Most cases are thought to be due to fresh gene mutations. Among additional varieties of acrocephalosyndactyly which have been recorded are two rare types in which there are extra, as well as fused, digits. One of these types (Noack's syndrome) is considered to be dominant, and the other (Carpenter's syndrome) recessive (McKusick, 1968).

Craniofacial dysostosis (Crouzon's disease) is another condition in which cranial deformity can be associated with mental subnormality. The physical characteristics of the condition include a thin, acrocephalic skull, prognathism, exophthalmos and optic atrophy. These characteristics are variable, and a considerable range of associated anomalies also are sometimes reported under the heading of Crouzon's disease. They may not all be instances of the same disease. The incidence of the condition in some families suggests a dominant mode of inheritance. In a well-illustrated example of such a family, recorded by Vulliamy and Normandale (1966), the authors were able to trace fourteen affected members over four generations. According to Dodge *et al.* (1959), about one-quarter of reported cases have no history of other relatives being affected.

(b) *Autosomal recessive abnormalities.* A larger number of recessive conditions are known to be closely associated with severe subnormality than is the case with dominant conditions. This is not surprising as the heterozygous carriers of genes responsible for recessive abnormalities are not themselves affected, in the sense of being diseased, and so are fertile despite the fact that the genes they transmit can produce, in the homozygous state, major defects resulting in infertility. It should be added that important advances have been made in recent years in the detection of heterozygous carriers of genes for recessive abnormalities by means of special examinations. Examples of such examinations are chemical loading or tolerance tests, in which the response to a standard oral dose of phenylalanine or galactose is measured, for purposes of detection of carriers of the gene for phenylketonuria and that for galactosaemia, respectively. Heterozygotes for each of these conditions usually show a higher rise and slower decline in the blood level of the relevant ingested chemical than do non-carrier controls. Another valuable method of carrier detection, with applications to some recessively determined biochemical types of subnormality, involves direct assays of body tissues for specific enzyme deficiencies.

Both parents must be carriers of the gene determining a recessive abnormality for that abnormality to occur in offspring. As this is more likely to happen if the parents are blood relations, there is a higher incidence of consanguinity among the parents of children with rare recessive defects than would be expected on the basis of chance alone. Parental consanguinity is thus a useful pointer to the presence of rare recessively inherited defects though, of course, many non-consanguineous parents have children with recessive abnormalities and many consanguineous parents have normal children only. The increased incidence of parental consanguinity in series of cases of severe subnormality indicates that rare recessive conditions are likely to be found in such series. Among 800 consecutive admissions of severely subnormal children to the Fountain Hospital, London, 10 (1·25 per cent) had parents who were first cousins (Berg, 1963, unpublished observations), compared with a figure of 0·4 per cent for children admitted to general hospitals in England (Bell, 1940).

When both parents are the carriers of a gene for any particular recessive abnormality, there is a one in four risk of any one child inheriting the gene in duplicate, one from each parent, and thus being affected. As with dominant conditions, however, small individual human sibships do not provide a statistically adequate sample for the precise Mendelian ratio of affected to unaffected children to occur often in practice, quite apart from the difficulty created by early death of some cases.

A brief account follows of some conditions, considered to be recessive, which are connected with mental subnormality. Each of these conditions is rare in the general population with frequencies usually less than 1 in 10,000.

Phenylketonuria, a metabolic disease discovered by Fölling (1934), is characterized chemically by an inability to convert phenylalanine to tyrosine, due to deficiency of a specific enzyme, phenylalanine 4-hydroxylase, in the liver. This leads to an accumulation of phenylalanine in blood serum and other tissues. One result is that phenylpyruvic acid is excreted in the urine from a few weeks after birth onwards, and this substance can be conveniently identified by the green colour reaction produced on the addition of ferric chloride solution to urine containing it. Mental subnormality, usually of a severe degree, is present in most cases though a number of persons with the disease have near normal, and even normal, intelligence. There may be substantial differences in intelligence between phenylketonurics even in the same sibship (Coutts and Fyfe, 1971). These considerations must be borne in mind in assessing the effect on mental level of a phenylalanine-low diet given as treatment. Though some controversy persists about the precise efficacy of such treatment, there is widespread agreement that an important prerequisite for its success is commencement in early infancy (before 3 months); less certain is the age at which dietary restrictions can be appropriately abandoned. A possible future therapeutic prospect, mentioned by Rosenberg and Scriver (1969), is that of liver transplants from normal donors as a source of missing enzyme.

The basic reason for mental subnormality in phenylketonuria is obscure, but post-mortem examinations of brains of affected cases show definite abnormalities including reduction in size and fibrous gliosis (Crome and Pare, 1960). In addition to intellectual deficit, behavioural peculiarities are fairly frequent (Pitt, 1971). Other clinical features include dilution of hair and eye colour in comparison with unaffected sibs, a tendency to dermatitis, broad, widely spaced incisors, brisk reflexes and, as in many other types of severe subnormality, reduced stature and head size and a liability to have fits. Gross physical deformities are relatively uncommon.

It has become apparent, in recent years, that the condition discussed above, now sometimes referred to as classical phenylketonuria, is not the only variety of disordered phenylalanine metabolism. Mild and transient variants have been described, as well as a benign persistent type, each with its own biochemical and clinical characteristics (Rosenberg and Scriver, 1969). An issue of particular relevance to mental subnormality is that concerned with hyperphenylalaninaemia in fertile women. High phenylalanine levels in such women have grave implications for foetal development. The seriousness of the problem is indicated in Yu and O'Halloran's (1970) review of sixty-eight offspring of phenylketonuric mothers. Sixty-five of these children were retarded, and some had such additional abnormalities as small heads, convulsions and heart defects. The authors emphasize the importance of careful dietary control prior to and during pregnancy in these circumstances.

Over the past two decades, a number of new diseases have been discovered which, like phenylketonuria, appear to be recessively inherited, are characterized by the excretion of specific amino-acids in the urine and are associated with mental subnormality. They include *maple syrup urine disease* (Menkes *et al.*, 1954), *argininosuccinicaciduria* (Allan *et al.*, 1958), *cystathioninuria* (Harris *et al.*, 1959), *homocystinuria* (Carson *et al.*, 1963), and *lysinuria* (Oyanagi *et al.*, 1970). Relatively few examples of these rare conditions are known as yet and available information about them is considerably more scanty than in the case of phenylketonuria. They illustrate, however, the progress being made in the differentiation of specific types of mental subnormality by the application of new techniques of investigation, in these instances mainly biochemical ones.

Galactosaemia is a disorder of carbohydrate metabolism in which the absence of a particular enzyme, known as galactose-1-phosphate uridyl transferase, prevents the normal transformation of galactose to certain glucose products. As galactose is an ingredient in milk, ordinary feeding of an affected baby exposes it to serious clinical consequences. These include failure to thrive, jaundice and liver enlargement in the early stages of the disease; subsequently, mental subnormality and cataract formation may be noted. The symptomatology can be attributed to undue concentrations of chemical substances both intracellularly and in body fluids (Harris, 1970). Many reports testify to the value of early treatment with a galactose-free diet in preventing or ameliorating these abnormalities. An instance has been recorded (Roe *et al.*, 1971) of an apparently healthy child born to a galactosaemic woman who had been maintained on a galactose-restricted diet since infancy.

Amaurotic idiocy is the term often used for conditions in which there are complex disturbances of lipid metabolism resulting in intracellular deposits of abnormal substances, mainly in the brain and retina. These disease states are associated clinically, as the name implies, with visual defects and mental subnormality. Manifestations appear at different ages, the two most documented varieties being the infantile type (Tay-Sachs disease) and the juvenile type (Batten's or Vogt-Spielmeyer disease). In the former, neurological and ophthalmological abnormalities develop within several months of birth and are distinctly progressive with gross mental defect, paralysis, epilepsy, a so-called 'cherry-red spot' in the macula, optic atrophy and blindness as common features, followed by death by the age of about 2 to 4 years (Frederickson and Trams, 1966). In the latter, symptoms are similar in some respects, but onset is usually delayed till the child is several years old and the disease advances more slowly until death occurs about five to ten years later (Sjögren, 1931). The two diseases appear to be separate entities in various regards.

Gargoylism (see Plate 3), like amaurotic idiocy, concerns disease in which abnormal substances accumulate within cells. Mucopolysaccharide metabolism is disordered, complex biochemical disturbances occur and many tissues are involved. The grotesque facies and deformed appearance, which produce a close resemblance between affected persons, led Ellis *et al.* (1936) to name the condition gargoylism, a term which has become widely accepted. Abnormalities can be observed in early infancy. The typical facies include coarse features, well-developed bony prominences, bushy eyebrows, corneal clouding, a broad nose and large mouth, lips and tongue. Among other clinical findings are hirsutes, a protuberant abdomen due to enlargement of the liver and spleen, dorso-lumbar kyphosis and limitation of extension of joints. Mental subnormality is usually of severe degree. An X-linked form of the disease, referred to by many as Hunter's syndrome, occurs. This differs clinically from the commoner autosomal recessive variety (frequently also called Hurler's syndrome), described above, in generally showing milder manifestations of later onset, including the absence of corneal involvement. Other, to some extent similar, conditions involving abnormal mucopolysaccharide metabolism also have been documented, often with eponymous designations (McKusick, 1969). These include the syndromes of Sanfilippo, Morquio, Scheie and Maroteaux-Lamy.

Cretinism can be conveniently discussed here as there is considerable evidence that some cases, in which various chemical defects in the synthesis and utilization of thyroid hormone occur, are recessively determined (Stanbury, 1966). Cretinism in these cases is associated with enlargement of the thyroid gland, a circumstance which also can be environmentally determined by insufficient iodine intake in the diet or by the ingestion of goitrogenic agents like thiouracil. Imperfect embryonic development of the thyroid gland, for whatever reason, can result in cretinism as well, in this instance without goitre. Recent data indicate that cretinism is less common than is often assumed. No more than 2 examples were noted among 800 (0·3 per cent) consecutive admissions of severely subnormal children to the Fountain Hospital, London (Berg, 1963). At the larger children's hospitals in Scandinavia, only one or two cases of congenital cretinism are diagnosed annually (Åkerren, 1955). The clinical features can include mental subnormality, general sluggishness, anaemia, small stature, coarse skin, large tongue, low temperature, slow pulse and chronic constipation. If treatment with thyroid extract is started early, the prognosis as regards physical development is generally considered to be good but the effect on mental development is more variable (Hubble, 1953; Lawson, 1955).

Microcephaly literally means smallness of the head and, as such, can be used as a descriptive term for a physical sign that is noted in various different types of mental subnormality. Among these are, for instance, many cases of phenyl-ketonuria and mongolism, and children born to mothers who were exposed to irradiation or to the rubella virus early in pregnancy. When used in this way the term is often restricted, rather arbitrarily, to persons with a head circumference below a certain size, for example less than 17 inches in adults or at least three standard deviations below the mean for age and sex in children. Microcephaly is considered in this section because there is convincing evidence that some mentally subnormal persons with small heads of a particular shape have recessively inherited their condition (Böök *et al.*, 1953; Komai *et al.*, 1955; van den Bosch, 1959). Penrose (1963a) pointed out that such individuals, sometimes referred to as 'true' microcephalics, have heads in which the height and width show relatively greater reduction than the length, and they tend to have a receding forehead and a face approaching the normal in size. Penrose regarded these features, combined with a well-developed, though dwarfed, body and a tendency to a stooping posture and quick, furtive movements, as highly characteristic; some observers (for example, Kirman, 1957), however, dispute this. Another type of microcephaly which appears to be recessively inherited, but is different from the condition discussed above in various respects, is known as Seckel's syndrome or bird-headed dwarfism. Affected persons have small heads with a 'bird-like' facies and show multiple congenital malformations. They are dwarfed in stature and retarded in intellect. McKusick *et al.* (1967) have described a sibship in which two sisters and a brother probably had the disorder.

(c) *X-linked abnormalities*. The abnormalities considered thus far are determined by genes located on the autosomes, consisting, in man, of twenty-two pairs of chromosomes. In addition to these abnormalities, there are a number, closely associated with mental subnormality, which are thought to be due to genes on the X chromosome. These abnormalities are referred to as X-linked. As there are two X chromosomes in females and only one in males (the other sex chromosome in males being a Y), a gene for recessive defects on the X chromosome has different effects in the two sexes. Males with one such harmful gene on the X chromosome would be affected whereas females with the one gene on an X chromosome would be heterozygous carriers of the abnormality; females would be affected if they were homozygous for the gene in question (i.e. if it were located on each of their X chromosomes).

In general, males are affected by X-linked recessive abnormalities and females are carriers, though it is possible for females to be affected also. An affected father, even if fertile, cannot transmit the abnormality to his sons though such a father's daughters would all be carriers despite the mother being normal. If the father is normal and the mother is a carrier, there is a one in two risk that a son will be affected and the same risk that a daughter will be a carrier. In the less likely circumstance of the father being affected and the mother being a carrier, sons will be normal or affected and daughters will be carriers or affected. If both parents were affected, and could have children, all of them would have the abnormality.

Because of its occurrence in royalty, one type of rare X-linked condition, the bleeding disease haemophilia, has become especially well known. The disease has no particular association with mental subnormality. An X-linked form of gargoylism, referred to on page 44, does have such an association and the following abnormalities are further examples.

Oculocerebrorenal syndrome is the name now most usually applied to a condition discovered by Lowe *et al.* (1952). Up to 1968, some seventy characteristic examples had been reported (Abbassi *et al.*, 1968). The disease is so called because of the association of eye abnormalities (such as cataract and glaucoma) with mental subnormality and kidney defects (manifested by excess amino-acids in the urine and other changes). The disease affects boys and is transmitted by females. Abnormalities, particularly cataracts, may be noted at birth or soon after. Life expectancy is substantially reduced, renal disturbances and secondary infections being common causes of death.

Lesch–Nyhan syndrome is the eponymous designation now often applied to a condition described by Lesch and Nyhan (1964) in two brothers, aged 5 and 8 years, in whom hyperuricaemia was associated with mental subnormality, choreoathetosis and an inclination to bite their lips and hands. Other reports of affected boys contributed to the further delineation of this syndrome of severe mental and physical handicaps. Among additional neurological features which may be noted are spasticity, convulsions, dysarthria and dysphagia. Also, increased levels of urinary uric acid can be connected with such manifestations as the passage of blood or calculi in the urine. Hoefnagel *et al.* (1965) raised the question of a possible X-linked recessive mode of inheritance, and subsequently-published pedigrees of afflicted families, for example by Shapiro *et al.* (1966), provided supportive evidence for this view.

Nephrogenic diabetes insipidus is a disease in which excessive excretion of dilute urine is associated with undue thirst. Manifestations appear in early infancy. Unlike other varieties of diabetes insipidus, the condition does not respond to treatment with antidiuretic hormone. Mental subnormality, of variable degree, occurs in some cases. In a study of eight children, aged from 5 to 11 years, with the disease, Ruess and Rosenthal (1963) reported IQ scores ranging from about 20 to 114. Unless adequate fluid intake is maintained, dehydration occurs and this can have an adverse effect on the mental level (Kirman *et al.*, 1956). The disease usually occurs in males, but females are sometimes affected (West and Kramer, 1955; Glaser, 1958). Heterozygous female carriers may be detected by a reduced ability to concentrate urine when fluids are withheld (Carter and Simpkiss, 1956).

Hydrocephaly (see Plate 7), like microcephaly (see p. 45), can be looked upon as a physical sign which may be due to a variety of causes, both genetical and environmental ones. Among the latter causes are, for instance, tuberculous meningitis which is discussed on page 58. Genetical types of hydrocephaly include a variety which is characterized by narrowing of the aqueduct of Sylvius and demonstrates an X-linked pattern of inheritance. Edwards *et al.* (1961) reported a family with a defect of this kind in which there were fifteen affected males and no affected females in three generations. Shannon and Nadler (1968) recently described another such family and briefly reviewed earlier reports. Whatever the cause of a particular case of hydrocephaly, cerebral pathology is present so that subnormality and neurological abnormalities, like spasticity and epilepsy, are common clinical consequences in survivors.

(2) *Conditions due to aberrant chromosomes*

(a) *Autosomal aberrations.* The nuclei of somatic cells in normal humans contain forty-six chromosomes, largely consisting of desoxyribonucleic acid (DNA), of which forty-four are known as autosomes and two as sex chromosomes. Twenty-two autosomes and one sex chromosome are derived from each of the two germ cells (ovum and sperm) which unite to begin the formation of the new individual. The relatively recent development of cytological techniques which enable each of the chromosomes to be clearly seen under the microscope, in suitable preparations of dividing human cells (see Plate 5), has led to the discovery of a substantial number of chromosomal aberrations which are closely connected with various abnormal clinical conditions. Standardization in identification and designation of each chromosome has been greatly facilitated as a result of international conferences held in Denver, London, Chicago and Paris in 1960, 1963, 1966 and 1971 respectively. Based on the proposals of these meetings (Chicago Conference, 1966; Paris Conference, 1971), individual chromosomes are distinguished by such criteria as their length, the position of a constriction called the centromere and characteristic banding patterns produced by certain special stains. They can thus be matched in pairs, numbered or lettered in a uniform manner, and abnormalities can be indicated by recommended notations or symbols. These abnormalities can occur both in the number and in the morphology of the chromosomes. It is possible also for the same person to have some cells in his body showing a chromosomal anomaly and other cells which are normal, or he may have more than one type of chromosomal aberration in different cells. This phenomenon is known as mosaicism.

The first reports of human chromosomal aberrations began to appear in 1959 and it was evident, from the outset, that the aberrations were often associated with mental subnormality. New discoveries have been comparatively frequent in this rapidly advancing field, and more than 100 different types of human chromosome disorders have now been described (Carr, 1969). It can be reasonably expected, in relation to these developments, that a good deal of additional data will be forthcoming on hitherto obscure forms of subnormality and other defects. The following are examples of types of mental subnormality now known to be connected with autosomal aberrations. Much still remains uncertain as to the aetiological factors which determine these aberrations and as to how the latter operate to produce abnormal clinical states.

Mongolism (Down's syndrome) is by far the commonest disease entity detected in subnormal populations. Among 800 consecutive admissions of severely subnormal children to the Fountain Hospital, London, there were 175 (21·9 per cent) cases of the syndrome (Berg, 1963). By contrast, the next most common entity was mental defect due to meningitis with an incidence of 2·8 per cent. The incidence of Down's syndrome in hospital populations of subnormal persons of all ages and grades of defect is often about 10 per cent. Despite the possible implications in the name 'mongolism', the disease is not especially characteristic of, and is not limited to, any particular race. For readers interested in a detailed comprehensive account of the condition, the textbook by Penrose and Smith (1966) is particularly valuable.

The frequency of Down's syndrome at birth was found by Carter and MacCarthy (1951) to be 1 in 666 in London and the Home Counties and this figure agrees closely with other European surveys as well as with a large Australian one (Collmann and Stoller, 1962a). The well-known and striking variation in incidence that occurs at different maternal ages is shown in a table by Penrose (1963a); at birth, the incidence is less than 0·1 per cent up to a maternal age of 34 years and then rises steeply to as much as 2·75 per cent in the maternal age-group of 45 years and over. Respiratory infections, heart defects and other causes result in a higher early mortality in cases of Down's syndrome than in the general population, so that the incidence of the condition falls in older age-groups. In 1958, the incidence was about 1 in 1,000, at the age of 10 years, in and around London (Carter, 1958). The mortality rate of cases of Down's syndrome has decreased markedly in the past few decades as it has also in children in general.

The clinical features of the syndrome have been recorded many times since Langdon Down's original description in 1866 and they will not be considered in detail here. Many, though by no means all (Zappella and Cowie, 1962), cases are recognized at birth; the diagnosis is usually made in the first year of life, and should, in general, be conveyed promptly to the parents (Berg *et al.*, 1969). A wide range of abnormalities occur though manifestations vary and many are found individually in persons not suffering from the disease. Stature is reduced and the limbs are hypotonic. The head tends to be small with greater reduction in length than in breadth. The characteristic facies includes slanting eyes, epicanthic folds, squint, Brushfield's spots (white specks) in the iris, and small nose and ears. The teeth often erupt late and some may be congenitally absent (Barkla, 1966a, b). There is a tendency for the little finger to be curved inwards and for a wide gap to occur between the first and second toes. A single transverse palmar crease is often present, and characteristic dermatoglyphic patterns occur on the hands and feet as they do also in some other conditions in which there are chromosomal aberrations (Penrose, 1963c). The incidence of leukaemia is increased in young children with Down's syndrome (Krivit and Good, 1957). Biochemical studies of the blood and urine have not revealed pathognomonic abnormalities.

Marked neurological handicaps, like epilepsy and cerebral palsy, are unusual and nearly all cases learn to walk. They are often cooperative and friendly. These aspects of their personalities, as well as the traditional views that they are especially fond of music and better mimics than other children, deserve further study. Many cases have IQs between 20 and 40; some, however, are gross idiots and others have IQs above 45 and can benefit from attendance in schools for the educationally subnormal (Dunsdon *et al.*, 1960).

Abnormalities in the pelvic bones (Caffey and Ross, 1956) and absence of a rib (Beber, 1965) have been reported, and many internal organs can be malformed. Heart malformations, of many kinds, are particularly frequent. Contrary to views expressed by some authors, Berg *et al.* (1960) have found no heart defect specific to Down's syndrome though some defects are particularly common. Malformation of the duodenum is also relatively frequent (Bodian *et al.*, 1952). The brain is reduced in weight and tends to be rounded with small frontal lobes, brain-stem and cerebellum, but it does not appear to show constant abnormalities on histological examination (Crome, 1957).

There is no known cure for Down's syndrome and claims for the efficacy of pituitary and thyroid preparations should be viewed with caution (Berg *et al.*, 1961). Advocacy of the value of siccacell treatment is also unconvincing (Bardon, 1964).

An outstanding advance in knowledge about Down's syndrome was made with the discovery that persons with the disease have forty-seven chromosomes in somatic cells instead of the normal forty-six (Lejeune *et al.*, 1959). In these cases there is an extra chromosome No. 21 and this circumstance is often referred to as trisomy 21. It is considered to arise as a result of non-disjunction whereby both, instead of one, members of the relevant pair of chromosomes enter the germ cell during the formation of the latter. The association in these cases of Down's syndrome with advancing maternal age implicates the ovum rather than the sperm. Propositions have been made that maternal exposure to various external agencies before or at about the time of conception, for example ionizing radiation (Sigler *et al.*, 1965) or the virus of infective hepatitis (Stoller and Collmann, 1965), could be aetiologically related to the syndrome. Opinions differ on these questions.

A number of variations in the chromosomal findings can occur in Down's syndrome. In a small minority of cases, forty-six chromosomes are found in somatic cells. The karyotype, however, is still unbalanced because, by a process known as translocation, a considerable portion of a No. 21 chromosome is fused with another autosome, which may be a No. 15 or a No. 22. These cases of the syndrome are not obviously different clinically from those with forty-seven chromosomes. However, in the 15:21 translocation type both maternal and paternal age is close to that in the general population, whereas in the 21:22 type advancing paternal (and not maternal) age may be aetiologically significant (Penrose, 1963d). Balanced translocations may be transmitted through several generations without producing clinical effects unless an extra amount of chromosome material is present. Another chromosomal variation in Down's syndrome is the occurrence of mosaicism, in which circumstance some cells can have a normal chromosome complement whereas others show trisomy 21. Such cases may have only limited signs of the disease. Down's syndrome can be associated also with the Klinefelter syndrome (see Plate 4). This occurs in males with forty-eight chromosomes in their cells, one of which is an extra No. 21 and the other an extra X (see Plate 5). Since the first case with this association was recorded (Ford *et al.*, 1959), a number of further instances have been reported. Down's syndrome with an extra No. 21 has been recorded occasionally also in persons with other additional chromosome abnormalities, such as XXX or XYY sex chromosome constitution and trisomy of a No. 13-15 or a No. 18 autosome (Laxova *et al.*, 1971).

Patau's syndrome occurs in persons who have a characteristic combination of congenital malformations including cerebral and heart defects, microphthalmos, malformed ears, harelip, cleft palate, polydactyly and capillary haemangiomata (Patau *et al.*, 1960; Taylor, 1967, 1968). In addition, diagnostically helpful dermatoglyphic deviations from the normal are often found on the hands and feet (Penrose, 1966). Affected children tend to be born before term, with a low birth weight, and most die soon after. However, even in early infancy, developmental retardation is noted and seizures are common. The condition is often referred to as trisomy 13-15 because there are usually seven chromosomes in this group instead of the normal six, and it has been uncertain to which of the three pairs (13, 14, or 15) the extra chromosome should be designated; it is now generally considered to be an additional No. 13. As with Down's syndrome, this trisomy is commoner among the offspring of older than of younger mothers.

Edwards's syndrome is another trisomic condition in which an extra autosome, either a No. 17 or a No. 18, is associated with multiple congenital abnormalities. These include an abnormally shaped head, peculiar facies, webbing of the neck, syndactyly, chest deformity and heart malformation (Edwards *et al.*, 1960; Taylor, 1967, 1968). Absence of true dermatoglyphic patterns on the finger tips (i.e. the presence of arch formations) is a strikingly frequent finding. Though birth often occurs at term, weight tends to be lower than in Patau's syndrome. In this condition also, delayed mental development is observed in infancy, a period which few survive, and, on the average, maternal age is increased. Taylor (1968) has estimated, from pooled data, that Edwards's and Patau's syndrome each have an incidence of the order of 1 in 7,000 live births. Because of the extremely high infantile mortality, examples of either syndrome are very rarely seen in mental subnormality practice.

The cri du chat syndrome is the name given to a condition, first described by Lejeune and his co-workers (1963, 1964), in which a peculiar cry resembling the mewing of a cat is a characteristic finding. Among other clinical features are gross retardation of mental development, a small head, low-set ears, oblique palpebral fissures and a broad nasal bridge. The initial reports concerned children, but the prospects of survival to adulthood became apparent with the documentation of older examples (Berg *et al.*, 1965; Breg *et al.*, 1970), including one aged 55 years. As the patients get older, the typical cry disappears, the face tends to lose its earlier rounded appearance and premature greying of the hair is quite often noted. The crucial chromosomal error in affected persons is deletion of part of the short arm of one of the No. 5 chromosomes. A like deletion can occur in the morphologically similar No. 4 chromosome, also resulting in mental subnormality, but no cat-like cry and a number of rather different physical consequences (Arias *et al.*, 1970; Miller *et al.*, 1970), such as a flat nose, cleft palate, a preauricular and/or sacral dimple or sinus, and hypospadias.

Partial deletion of No. 18 chromosome, involving either the long or the short arm of that chromosome, has been described in some forty instances and new examples are being documented from time to time. Reported features in persons having a deletion of the long arm (18q— in the Chicago Conference, 1966, notation), in addition to severe mental subnormality, include a small head, anomalies of the ears and eyes, hypotonia and an increased frequency of whorl patterns on the finger tips (de Grouchy *et al.*, 1964; Wertelecki *et al.*, 1966; Insley, 1967). The clinical characteristics of those showing short arm deletion (18p—) appear to have been less uniform, as indicated by Migeon's (1966) summary of twelve recorded cases. However, variable degrees of retardation in mental and physical development have been generally consistent findings in affected individuals surviving beyond infancy.

Other autosomal aberrations of diverse kinds have been found in humans and, particularly with increasing sophistication of techniques, including the important new banding procedures with fluorescent and Giesma dye stains (Hsu, 1973), it is virtually certain that more will be detected. The most frequently documented autosomal aberrations discovered to date include those described above. Trisomy may involve other autosomes also. For instance, Ellis *et al.* (1962) reported trisomy, probably of chromosome No. 22, in a subnormal person with epilepsy. It is also possible for cells to contain 69, 92, and even 184 chromosomes. Apart from abnormalities in the number of chromosomes, morphological aberrations can occur. Several examples of deletions are provided on this page, and translocation has been referred to on page 49. Other rare abnormalities of chromosome structure include duplications, inversions and ring chromosomes. Mental subnormality is commonly associated with many of these aberrations.

(b) *Sex chromosomal aberrations.* Of the two sex chromosomes normally present in humans, an X is derived from the mother and an X or Y from the father. Females have two X chromosomes in their cells and males have an X and a Y. As in the case of the autosomes, aberrations of the sex chromosomes can occur which are closely associated with various abnormal clinical states. Well-documented disorders in this category, particularly relevant to the field of mental subnormality, are the Klinefelter syndrome, the triple-X and double-Y conditions, and some variants of these situations.

The diagnosis of X chromosome anomalies is facilitated by the discovery made by Barr and Bertram (1949) that cell nuclei of normal females contain a sex chromatin structure, known as the Barr body, which is visible under the microscope. Examination of buccal smears shows that some cells contain one Barr body less than the number of X chromosomes in the sex chromosome constitution of that individual. Thus, a normal male (XY sex chromosome constitution), a normal female (XX), a Klinefelter male (XXY), and a triple-X female (XXX) have 0, 1, 1, 2 Barr bodies, respectively, in their cell nuclei. The examination of buccal smears for Barr bodies is a comparatively simple procedure so that a valuable screening test is available for investigations of X chromosome aberrations. Staining techniques, using quinacrine compounds, are currently being developed and refined to enable rapid recognition of the presence of one or more Y chromosomes. Characteristic fluorescent bodies, numerically equal to the number of Y chromosomes in a person's sex chromosome make-up, thus may be observed in appropriate preparations of some interphase nuclei, including those from buccal smears (Pearson et al., 1970). These developments provide prospects for surveying populations for Y chromosome aberrations to complement the well-established X chromosome screening procedure referred to above.

Klinefelter syndrome is the name given to a combination of abnormalities described by Klinefelter et al. (1942). These abnormalities, which become apparent from puberty onwards, occur in males and include gynaecomastia, small testes, azoospermia, poor hair growth and an increased pituitary gonadotropin level. Many cases are mentally subnormal, often mildly so. Manifestations can be variable and not all individuals described as examples of the Klinefelter syndrome have the same features or necessarily suffer from the same disease. Some of these persons have a normal sex chromosome constitution, whereas others have an extra X chromosome and so are of the type XXY. The latter is the usual finding when the chromosome constitution is abnormal but, occasionally, cases with some degree of clinical similarity have 3 or 4 X chromosomes with one Y, or 2 Xs and 2 Ys, or even, though males, 2 Xs and apparently no Ys. Still others (mosaics) have an abnormal sex chromosome complement in only some of their cells. The association of Klinefelter syndrome and Down's syndrome in the same person has been referred to on page 50. Klinefelter syndrome is commoner among patients in hospitals for the mentally subnormal, and among those attending infertility clinics, than in the general population. A number of surveys of males in subnormality hospitals have revealed a frequency of chromatin-positive cases (i.e. those showing Barr bodies) of the order of 1 per cent, compared with, on average, only about one-sixth that frequency in live-born male babies (Court Brown, 1969).

The triple-X condition, which occurs in persons also referred to as 'super-females', is, like the Klinefelter syndrome, a condition in which an extra X chromosome is present. These persons, who are females, thus have an XXX sex chromosome constitution. The clinical features are not strikingly abnormal (Johnston *et al.*, 1961). Subnormality is present in some cases and most of these are mildly retarded. Menstruation can be absent or irregular but some have regular periods, are fertile and can have normal children. The condition is not usually found as frequently as the Klinefelter syndrome in hospitals for the mentally subnormal, and had an incidence of 0·4 per cent in one large series of retarded females studied (Maclean *et al.*, 1962). Chromosomal variants of the condition occur and these include females with 4 or 5 X chromosomes and others who are mosaics of the type XXX/XX or XXX/XO or even the combination XXX/XX/XO.

The double-Y condition, in which an X and two, instead of one, Y chromosomes are present, was first reported in a mentally normal man (Hauschka *et al.*, 1962), but subsequently shown to have an association with mental subnormality, aggressive behaviour and unusual tallness (Jacobs *et al.*, 1965). Later studies of males with these clinical features, in various psychiatric and penal settings, often also revealed an unduly high frequency of XYY sex chromosome complement in comparison with control groups (Court Brown, 1968; Marinello *et al.*, 1969). However, it is important to emphasize that by no means all persons with an extra Y chromosome show a characteristic stereotype of the kind referred to above. In fact, considerable physical differences are found in such persons, as well as a wide mental spectrum ranging from entirely laudable to grossly anti-social behaviour and from superior to severely deficient intellect (Berg and Smith, 1971). Marked deviations from normal intelligence, at either end of the scale, are unusual, most affected cases recorded to date being relatively mildly retarded. These considerations should be borne in mind in making prognostic judgments in a given instance, particularly when the additional Y chromosome is detected in infancy before any clinical peculiarities are apparent. As with other chromosomal disorders described in earlier sections, variants of the double-Y condition may be found, including, on rare occasions, two instead of one extra Y to produce an XYYY sex chromosome constitution, and mosaicism in which only some cells show the chromosome fault. The association of an extra Y with an extra No. 21 chromosome or with an extra X has been mentioned on pages 50 and 52 respectively.

Other sex chromosomal aberrations in humans are also now known and, as with autosomal aberrations, their number is likely to grow. One of these conditions, in which there is a total of forty-five chromosomes in somatic cells (with one X and no Y), is known as Turner's syndrome. Physical abnormalities involving the neck, ovaries, kidneys and heart occur but the condition does not appear to be associated particularly with mental subnormality. Still other rare aberrations consist of abnormalities in the form rather than in the number of X chromosomes. These chromosomes may be shortened, lengthened, or distorted in other ways.

The Y chromosome also may show various structural anomalies, as well as numerical aberrations of the kind already considered.

II. MENTAL SUBNORMALITY OF ENVIRONMENTAL ORIGIN

A large number of agents and events having their origin in the environment have been regarded as causes of pathological types of mental subnormality. Many of these circumstances have been convincingly established as being aetiologically significant whereas others have been postulated on more tenuous grounds. The occurrence of an abnormal environmental event or disease in a person subsequently noted to be subnormal is not, of itself, proof of a causal connection. The likelihood of such a connection is greatly increased if the particular abnormal event produces characteristic features which include signs of cerebral involvement, and if other causes of subnormality can be reasonably excluded.

Environmental events leading to pathological types of mental subnormality can occur before, during, or after birth and they are considered below in each of these categories.

(1) *Pre-natal causes*

The causes of mental subnormality discussed under this heading are those which operate during intra-uterine life. The causes themselves can originate from events occurring before or after conception. Examples in each of these categories are, respectively, maternal infection with the spirochaete producing syphilis and with the virus producing rubella. A brief account follows of these, as well as of some other, pre-natal agencies which can result in mental subnormality.

Congenital syphilis has long been recognized as a cause of mental subnormality in live-born offspring of infected mothers. The spirochaete responsible for syphilis can pass from the mother to the foetus and produce abortion, stillbirth, or mental and physical abnormalities in surviving children. Among the abnormalities which may be noted in childhood are mental defect, blindness, deafness, epilepsy, paralyses, and characteristic anomalies of the skull and teeth. In one variety, juvenile general paresis, manifestations often develop in late childhood or adolescence and include mental disturbance, as well as defect, and characteristic neurological signs. A general decline in the incidence of syphilis in many countries has resulted in a marked reduction of cases of subnormality due to this infection. Compared to a 4 per cent incidence of congenital syphilis found by Penrose (1938) in Colchester, and by Benda (1942) in Massachusetts, a more recent survey in London (Berg and Kirman, 1959) revealed a history of syphilis in only 0·6 per cent of 1,900 defectives.

Rubella in early pregnancy was first shown by Gregg (1941) to be a cause of congenital abnormalities in the offspring of infected mothers, and many reports on the subject have since been published. The most important structures involved are those of the brain, heart, eyes and ears with the production of a characteristic, though variable, symptomatology. Other tissues may be damaged also with, for instance, resultant skeletal and dental defects (Forrest and Menser, 1970). The proportions of affected children reported among those at risk have varied greatly in different studies, but have been of the order of 10 to 20 per cent in some of the more recent prospective surveys. An important fact which emerged from the earlier studies was that the incidence of affected live-born children falls markedly when the mother develops rubella after the first three months of pregnancy. The risk appears to be particularly great if rubella occurs in the first month of pregnancy (Pitt, 1961). Data from the Fountain Hospital, London, indicate that rather less than 1 per cent of cases of severe subnormality were due to maternal rubella (Kirman, 1955). The role of this infection in the production of minor degrees of subnormality is less clear. Developments of prophylactic measures against rubella by the use, in certain circumstances, of gammaglobulin and, more recently and significantly, of an appropriate rubella virus vaccine, though still fraught with unresolved problems (Robbins and Heggie, 1970), hold promise that the disease will become an increasingly rare cause of congenital defects and subnormality.

Irradiation, in the form of *excessive* exposure to x-rays, in the early stages of pregnancy is now well established as a cause of abortion and of mental subnormality, reduced head size, microphthalmia and other defects in surviving children. Early studies on the subject include those of Zappert (1926), Murphy (1928, 1929), and Goldstein (1930). Similar dangers to the foetus of radiation from other sources were demonstrated by Plummer (1952) and by Yamazaki *et al.* (1954) who investigated, respectively, effects of the Hiroshima and Nagasaki atomic explosions. Persisting defects in survivors who were thus exposed in utero were recorded in a twenty-year follow-up study by Wood *et al.* (1967).

Rhesus incompatibility between mother and foetus has been referred to on page 38. In these circumstances, the basal ganglia and other portions of the brain can become stained and damaged by bilirubin pigments, a pathological state to which the term kernicterus is frequently applied (Baar, 1959). Affected liveborn children are jaundiced soon after birth and survivors often suffer from mental subnormality, choreoathetosis, spasticity and deafness. The mental level varies from extreme idiocy to normality. Eleven out of 800 (1·4 per cent) severely subnormal children admitted to the Fountain Hospital, London, were considered to owe their defect to Rhesus incompatibility (Berg, 1963). Maternal-foetal incompatibility involving the ABO blood groups can produce similar effects and they are known to occur also in the absence of evidence of blood group incompatibility.

Other pre-natal causes of subnormality have been implicated or postulated on many occasions. Space does not permit a discussion of each of them in turn so that a brief general account is given in this section of some agencies not specifically considered above.

Many infections, apart from syphilis and rubella, can be transmitted to the foetus, but few of these have been convincingly shown to cause mental subnormality. Interest in maternal virus infections, from this point of view, was stimulated with the discovery of the hazards of rubella. Cytomegalic inclusion-body disease, transmitted through the placenta, can produce microgyria, among other defects in the brain and elsewhere (Crome, 1961), and so result in subnormality. Maternal Asian influenza was noted by Coffey and Jessop (1959, 1963) to be associated with an increased incidence of central nervous system abnormalities in offspring, but Doll et al. (1960) did not find such an association. These and other viral infections, in relation to their possible deleterious effects on the foetus, have been considered in a useful review by Hardy (1965). Bacterial infection in pregnant women has not been proved to cause subnormality in their offspring but maternal toxoplasmosis, a protozoal infection, can do so. Other findings in congenital toxoplasmosis include abnormalities of head size, intra-cranial calcification and ocular defects (Couvreur and Desmonts, 1962). Malaria, another protozoal infection, can be transmitted to the foetus and was found by Archibald (1958) to be associated with a reduction in birth weight; follow-up studies of such children, compared with others, in regard to mental function would be interesting.

Teratogenic effects of various chemical agents have been demonstrated many times in experimental animals (Kalter, 1968). The possibility of grave hazards to the human foetus of particular chemical substances has received increased attention following the thalidomide tragedy which occurred about a decade ago. The commonest malformations resulting from thalidomide, taken during pregnancy, are those involving the limbs (Smithells, 1962; Leck and Millar, 1962) and there appeared to be no specific relationship of this drug with mental subnormality. Other drugs, however, may have such a relationship. Thiouracil (Elphinstone, 1953), for instance, and also large doses of insulin (Wickes, 1954) administered to pregnant women, have been occasionally associated with the birth of subnormal children. Treatment of mothers during pregnancy with radioactive iodine may result in the birth of children with cretinism, though the diagnosis might not be apparent initially (Green et al., 1971). A retrospective survey by Gal et al. (1967) indicated that certain hormonal pregnancy tests might be connected significantly with the birth of some babies with meningomyelocele or hydrocephaly. Apart from the question of therapeutic or diagnostic chemical agents, extensive use of chemicals in agriculture and industry could, in certain circumstances, constitute a danger to the foetus. Reports have been published, for example, of serious neurological abnormalities in infants whose mothers inadvertently ingested, while pregnant, foodstuffs contaminated with mercury (Snyder, 1971). In addition, various deficiencies in the maternal diet may be harmful to the human foetus with the possibility of adverse effects on subsequent mental development (Hepner, 1958).

Deleterious effects on the foetus have been attributed also, from time to time, to various other events occurring during pregnancy. Few of these can be regarded as established causes of mental subnormality. Among ancient explanations of the origin of foetal defects are supernatural intervention, either by gods or devils, intercourse during menstruation, and unpleasant sights and frights during pregnancy (Pitt, 1962). Claims also have been made that acute maternal anxiety and emotional stress can result in foetal malformation, but evidence for this view is unconvincing. Data bearing on this question have been discussed recently by James (1969). Physical trauma sometimes may cause damage to the foetal nervous system (Hinden, 1965). So may anoxia, and Courville (1959) has considered various circumstances where this could occur. Reduction in such variables as birth weight and head circumference has been noted among children of mothers who smoked during pregnancy (Kullander and Källén, 1971). Possibly harmful consequences of the unsuccessful use of chemical contraceptives and abortifacients deserve fuller study, as do a wide range of other factors.

(2) *Natal causes*

The two events at birth which are especially relevant to the question of causation of cerebral damage, and hence of mental subnormality, are mechanical injury and hypoxia or asphyxia. These events are closely associated, and it is often difficult, in clinical practice, to distinguish the role of each. A further difficulty is that of trying to decide whether evidence of birth trauma or hypoxia in a particular case represents the cause or the consequence of abnormality.

Birth injury is a term which is often used to cover the combined effects of mechanical trauma and of hypoxia or anoxia occurring in relation to the birth process. The types of central nervous system damage which can be a consequence of these occurrences have been reviewed by Towbin (1970). Birth injury has been blamed for anything from under 1 per cent to over 50 per cent of cases of subnormality. In general, the higher estimates have been based on retrospective evidence of obstetrical complications or of neonatal distress in subnormal persons, and in many of these cases a causal connection is not convincingly demonstrated. In a detailed study of 1,280 subnormal patients of all types, Penrose (1938) found only 11 cases (0·9 per cent) whose defect could be regarded, with reasonable certainty, as due to birth injury. He added, however, that trauma may have been an unrecognized aetiological factor in a number of other cases. Drillien (1963) concluded, on the evidence from an extensive longitudinal survey of Edinburgh children, that obstetrical hazard is not a major factor in the causation of gross defect.

The risk of birth injury is increased in premature births and this could be a factor in the poorer mental development that has been noted in prematurely born children, as a group, when compared to children in general. A greater liability for twins to be injured at birth may account also for some of the excess of twins found in subnormal populations (Berg and Kirman, 1960). Other circumstances, often interrelated, which have been considered to have a bearing on the problem of birth injury include maternal age, complications of pregnancy such as toxaemia, birth order, and various abnormalities of presentation and delivery.

(3) *Post-natal causes*

A large number of abnormal events and diseases having their origin in the post-natal environment can be responsible for mental subnormality. Though many of these events and diseases are themselves common, they often do not have an obvious effect on mental function. Variations between individuals in suscepti-bility to an illness, its severity, and the efficacy of treatment are among the factors which may influence the outcome. Mental retardation, when it does result, varies widely in degree from case to case.

The aetiological significance of post-natal agencies, particularly when they do not operate till a considerable time after birth, is frequently easier to assess than is the case with either pre-natal or natal events. This is because there is the opportunity of observing the child's development before, as well as after, the post-natal hazard occurs. However, the possibility must be considered that some diseases which are determined earlier, for instance certain types of amaurotic idiocy (see p. 43), may show clinical manifestations only some time after the child is born.

Several examples of post-natal causes of subnormality are described indi-vidually below and others are referred to in a general section.

Tuberculous meningitis, which was nearly always fatal before modern drugs for the treatment of tuberculosis became available, is now periodically seen as a cause of mental subnormality (see Plate 6). Many children with tuberculous meningitis are treated successfully, but some, who would probably otherwise have died during the acute illness, now survive and show mental and physical abnormalities of varying degrees of severity (Todd and Neville, 1964). Among 800 children with IQs below 50 admitted, from 1949 to 1960, to the Fountain Hospital, London, 11 (1·4 per cent) were considered to owe their subnormality to tuberculous meningitis (Berg, 1962a). Other handicaps in these children included, in order of frequency, spastic paralysis of the limbs, blindness, hydrocephaly, epilepsy and deafness.

Whooping cough encephalopathy is a term which may be used to designate the cerebral involvement which sometimes complicates this infectious fever. As a consequence of such involvement, mental subnormality, behaviour disturbances, epilepsy, paralysis, and impairment of vision and hearing can occur (Berg, 1962b). Definite, though variable, abnormalities are found in the brains of children with neurological complications who do not survive the acute illness. These include haemorrhagic, inflammatory and degenerative changes. Levy and Perry (1948) considered that subnormality seemed to be due to whooping cough in 2 per cent of 1,000 children with IQs of 70 or less in a Washington State institution. By contrast, this cause of subnormality has only very occasionally been established among severely subnormal children in the Fountain Hospital, London. Byers and Rizzo (1950), in a follow-up for several years of thirty-five Boston children who had whooping cough before the age of 2 years, found that six (17 per cent) suffered from intellectual or emotional difficulties of sufficient severity to 'compromise their competitive status'.

Lead poisoning in childhood is rarely reported in Great Britain but many cases have been recorded in some countries, notably the United States, Australia and Japan. Pica is a frequent precursor and painted woodwork is a particularly common source of the lead. The average toddler is said to take some three months to nibble away sufficient lead-containing paint to produce symptoms (Shrand, 1961). Apart from paint, other sources of the metal noted in affected children examined in London include red lead in putty, old battery casings and toys (Moncrieff *et al.*, 1964). Cerebral involvement is relatively common in children; clinical manifestations can include changes of temperament, tremors, convulsions, coma and papilloedema. Patchy, widespread lesions are found in the soft, oedematous brains of children who die during the acute illness (Blackman, 1937). Among persisting abnormalities in survivors are subnormality, behaviour disturbances, paralyses of the limbs, and blindness associated with optic atrophy. Intellectual, emotional and sensori-motor handicaps have been found in cases followed up after apparent complete recovery from the original illness (Byers and Lord, 1943). A useful review has been published by Gibb and MacMahon (1955).

Head injury is not infrequently blamed by parents for subnormality in their offspring. In fact, it is rarely established as the cause of gross mental defect in childhood (Berg, 1960). Less severe post-traumatic effects are commoner. Behaviour disturbances and personality changes leading to poor scholastic achievement were noted by Newell (1937) in five out of twenty persons who had had head injuries. A lasting adverse influence on their school careers was thought by Rowbotham *et al.* (1954) to be likely in eight out of eighty-two children with such injuries. A well-documented recent study of the frequency of acute head injuries and their psychiatric consequences in young schoolchildren has been presented by Rune (1970). It is often said that adults tolerate head injuries less well than children (Glaser and Shafer, 1932; Blau, 1936) so that harmful mental effects may be commoner following cerebral trauma in adulthood. In studies of subnormal patients of all grades and ages, post-natal cerebral trauma was thought to be aetiologically significant in 0·9 per cent of 1,280 cases in Colchester (Penrose, 1938) and in 1·5 per cent of 1,000 cases in New York State (Boldt, 1948).

Other post-natal causes also can be implicated, with a fair degree of certainty, in particular cases of pathological types of mental subnormality.

Various organisms can cause meningitis and lead to subnormality and physical defects similar to those due to the tubercle bacillus. Among these organisms are the pneumococcus, meningococcus, staphylococcus, and the influenza bacillus. Between them, they were responsible for the same percentage of cases of severe subnormality (1·4 per cent) as was due to tuberculous meningitis in the Fountain Hospital series referred to above.

Besides whooping cough, other acute infectious fevers (for instance, measles, chickenpox and scarlet fever) can sometimes be followed by mental deterioration. Careful follow-up of cases which appear to recover completely at the time of the acute illness may show a higher incidence of harmful mental effects than is often assumed to occur. Gibbs *et al.* (1956) did electroencephalographic studies on children with whooping cough, measles and mumps who showed no clinical evidence of neurological involvement during, or immediately after, the acute illness. On the basis of these studies, they thought that in some cases a 'state of disorder' is established which might take months or years to run its full course and which might sometimes manifest itself in clinical disorder long after the acute illness. Immunization against whooping cough very occasionally produces neurological complications, including subnormality, similar to those which can occur with whooping cough itself (Berg, 1958). Mental subnormality has also been noted, though rarely, following vaccination against smallpox.

Many other infections and infestations can result in cerebral damage and thus lead to subnormality. Among the various encephalitides, encephalitis lethargica attracted especial attention because of widespread epidemics of the disease in the earlier part of this century. Manifestations of the condition include antisocial behaviour, intellectual retardation, a mask-like expression, and muscular tremors and rigidity. Cerebral involvement also can complicate disease due to certain parasitic worms, protozoa and fungi, so that these are potential, though rarely implicated, causes of subnormality. Subnormality also has been observed as a sequel to gastro-enteritis accompanied by marked dehydration (Crome, 1952), and gross defect can follow sudden catastrophes, associated with anoxia, such as partial drowning or strangulation, carbon monoxide poisoning, and temporary cardiac arrest.

The effect of psychological and social influences on mental function has evoked a great deal of interest in recent years. Adverse influences in this category can play a role in the production of maladjustment and intellectual impairment and thus can be crucial in regard to a diagnosis of mental subnormality in certain cases. This subject falls outside the scope of the present chapter which is concerned with pathological types of subnormality due to organic disease processes. It is dealt with extensively in other sections of this book. (See Chapter 4).

Conclusions

Organic disease or pathology is responsible for nearly all cases of gross mental defect and for some cases in which the defect is relatively mild. The pathological types of mental subnormality determined in this way have been considered in this chapter and shown to be due to the operation of a large number of harmful physical agencies of both genetical and environmental origin.

Clinical evidence of cerebral abnormality, such as paralyses of the limbs and epilepsy, is found in many persons with severe mental subnormality. Cerebral pathology, often widespread and of various kinds, is demonstrable also at post-mortem examination in the great majority of gross defectives (Crome, 1960). Nevertheless, the causes of such pathology, and hence of the subnormality, can be established in the present state of knowledge in only a minority of these cases.

In circumstances relatively favourable for diagnosis because of the availability of a great deal of relevant data, definite causes of, and distinct syndromes closely connected with, subnormality were found in only one-third of 800 children with IQs below 50 (Berg, 1963). If the 175 cases of Down's syndrome in this series of 800 children are excluded, only 100 of the remaining 625 children (16 per cent) are accounted for in terms of aetiology. These data give some impression of the great amount of knowledge that still needs to be accumulated before the causation of pathological types of mental subnormality can be regarded as being satisfactorily understood. It may be added that the causal basis of many clinically distinctive mental retardation syndromes, such as those of de Lange (Berg *et al.*, 1970) and of Rubinstein and Taybi (Rubinstein, 1969), is, thus far, entirely obscure. Even when clear-cut retardation syndromes, known to be closely connected with a specific biological fault, can be recognized, the exact aetiology and pathogenesis of the mental defect in these syndromes is not always altogether clear as yet. The precise reasons why subnormality occurs are still vague in, for instance, conditions associated with chromosomal aberrations and in phenylketonuria.

The problem of the elucidation of the many different causes of pathological types of mental subnormality is deservedly receiving increasing attention from the viewpoint of a variety of scientific disciplines. This problem is, indeed, a fundamental one because understanding of causation is an essential basis for rational preventive and curative measures.

References

ABBASSI, V., LOWE, C. U. and CALCAGNO, P. L. (1968) Oculo-cerebrorenal syndrome: a review. *Amer. J. Dis. Childh.*, **115**, 145–68.

ÅKERRÉN, Y. (1955) Early diagnosis and early therapy in congenital cretinism. *Arch. dis. Childh.*, **30**, 254–6.

ALLAN, J. D., CUSWORTH, D. C., DENT, C. E. and WILSON, V. K. (1958) A disease, probably hereditary, characterized by severe mental deficiency and a constant gross abnormality of amino acid metabolism. *Lancet*, **i**, 182–7.

ARCHIBALD, H. M. (1958) Influence of maternal malaria on newborn infants. *Brit. med. J.*, **2**, 1512–14.

ARIAS, D., PASSARGE, E., ENGLE, M. A. and GERMAN, J. (1970) Human chromosomal deletion: two patients with the 4p-syndrome. *J. Pediat.*, **76**, 82–8.

BAAR, H. S. (1959) Kernicterus. *J. Maine med. Ass.*, **50**, 111–17.

BARDON, L. M. E. (1964) Sicacell treatment of mongolism. *Lancet*, **ii**, 234–5.

BARKLA, D. H. (1966a) Ages of eruption of permanent teeth in mongols. *J. ment. Defic. Res.*, **10**, 190–7.

BARKLA, D. H. (1966b) Congenital absence of permanent teeth in mongols. *J. ment. Defic. Res.*, **10**, 198–203.

BARR, M. L. and BERTRAM, E. G. (1949) A morphological distinction between neurones of the male and female, and the behaviour of the nucleolar satellite during accelerated nucleoprotein synthesis. *Nature* (Lond.), **163**, 676–7.

BEBER, B. A. (1965) Absence of a rib in Down's syndrome. *Lancet*, **ii**, 289.

BELL, J. (1940) A determination of the consanguinity rate in the general hospital population of England and Wales. *Ann. Eugen.*, **10**, 370–91.

BENDA, C. E. (1942) Congenital syphilis in mental deficiency. *Amer. J. ment. Defic.*, **47**, 40–8.

BERG, J. M. (1958) Neurological complications of pertussis immunization. *Brit. med. J.*, **2**, 24–7.

BERG, J. M. (1960) Postnatal head injury as a cause of mental defect. *Arch. Pediat.*, **77**, 207–11.

BERG, J. M. (1962a) Meningitis as a cause of severe mental defect. *Proc. Lond. Conf. Scient. Stud. Ment. Defic.*, *1960*, **1**, 160–4. Dagenham: May & Baker.

BERG, J. M. (1962b) Whooping cough encephalopathy. *Indian Practitioner*, **15**, 559–61.

BERG, J. M. (1963) Causal factors in severe mental retardation. *Proc. 2nd Internat. Congr. Ment. Retard.*, *Vienna*, *1961*, **1**, 170–3.

BERG, J. M. and KIRMAN, B. H. (1959) Syphilis as a cause of mental deficiency. *Brit. med. J.*, **2**, 400–4.

BERG, J. M. and KIRMAN, B. H. (1960) The mentally defective twin. *Brit. med. J.*, **1**, 1911–17.

BERG, J. M. and SMITH, G. F. (1971) Behaviour and intelligence in males with XYY sex chromosomes. In PRIMROSE, D. A. (ed.) *Proc. 2nd Congr. Internat. Assoc. Scient. Study Ment. Defic.* Warsaw: Ars Polona; Amsterdam: Swets & Zeitlinger.

BERG, J. M., CROME, L. and FRANCE, N. E. (1960) Congenital cardiac malformations in mongolism. *Brit. Heart J.*, **22**, 331–46.

BERG, J. M., GILDERDALE, S. and WAY, J. (1969) On telling parents of a diagnosis of mongolism. *Brit. J. Psychiat.*, **115**, 1195–6.

BERG, J. M., DELHANTY, J. D. A., FAUNCH, J. A. and RIDLER, M. A. C. (1965) Partial deletion of short arm of a chromosome of the 4–5 group (Denver) in an adult male. *J. ment. Defic. Res.*, **9**, 219–28.

BERG, J. M., KIRMAN, B. H., STERN, J. and MITTWOCH, U. (1961) Treatment of mongolism with pituitary extract. *J. ment. Sci.*, **107**, 475–80.

BERG, J. M., MCCREARY, B. D., RIDLER, M. A. C. and SMITH, G. F. (1970) *The de Lange Syndrome.* Oxford: Pergamon.

BLACKMAN, S. S. (1937) The lesions of lead encephalitis in children. *Bull. Johns Hopk. Hosp.*, **61**, 1–62.

BLANK, C. E. (1960) Apert's syndrome (a type of acrocephalosyndactyly) – observations on a British series of thirty-nine cases. *Ann. hum. Genet.*, **24**, 151–64.

BLAU, A. (1936) Mental changes following head trauma in children. *Arch. Neurol. Psychiat.* (Chicago), **35**, 723–69.

BODIAN, M., WHITE, L. L. R., CARTER, C. O. and LOUW, J. H. (1952) Congenital duodenal obstruction and mongolism. *Brit. med. J.*, **1**, 77–8.

BOLDT, W. H. (1948) Postnatal cerebral trauma as an etiological factor in mental deficiency. *Amer. J. ment. Defic.*, **53**, 247–67.

BÖÖK, J. A., SCHUT, J. W. and REED, S. C. (1953) A clinical and genetical study of microcephaly. *Amer. J. ment. Defic.*, **57**, 637–60.

BOURNEVILLE, D. M. (1880) Sclérose tubéreuse des circonvolutions cérébrales: idiotie et épilepsie hemiplégique. *Arch. Neurol.*, **1**, 81–9.

BREG, W. R., STEELE, M. W., MILLER, O. J., WARBURTON, D., DE CAPOA, A. and ALLDERDICE, P. W. (1970) The cri du chat syndrome in adolescents and adults: clinical findings in 13 older patients with partial deletion of the short arm of chromosome No. 5 (5p−). *J. Pediat.*, **77**, 782–91.

BYERS, R. K. and LORD, E. E. (1943) Late effects of lead poisoning on mental development. *Amer. J. Dis. Childh.*, **66**, 471–94.

BYERS, R. K. and RIZZO, N. D. (1950) A follow-up of pertussis in infancy. *New Engl. J. Med.*, **242**, 887–91.

CAFFEY, J. and ROSS, S. (1956) Mongolism (mongoloid deficiency) during early infancy. Some newly recognized diagnostic changes in the pelvic bones. *Pediatrics*, **17**, 642–51.

CANALE, D., BEBIN, J. and KNIGHTON, R. S. (1964) Neurologic manifestations of von Recklinghausen's disease of the nervous system. *Confin. neurol.* (*Basel*), **24**, 359–403.

CARR, D. H. (1969) Chromosomal abnormalities in clinical medicine. In STERNBERG, A. G. and BEARN, A. G. (eds.) *Progress in Medical Genetics*, Vol. 6. New York: Grune & Stratton.

CARSON, N. A. J., CUSWORTH, D. C., DENT, C. E., FIELD, C. M. B., NEILL, D. W. and WESTALL, R. G. (1963) Homocystinuria: a new inborn error of metabolism associated with mental deficiency. *Arch. dis. Childh.*, **38**, 425–36.

CARTER, C. O. (1958) A life-table for mongols with the causes of death. *J. ment. Defic. Res.*, **2**, 64–74.

CARTER, C. O. (1962) *Human Heredity*. Harmondsworth: Penguin.

CARTER, C. O. and MACCARTHY, D. (1951) Incidence of mongolism and its diagnosis in the newborn. *Brit. J. prev. soc. Med.*, **5**, 83–90.

CARTER, C. O. and SIMPKISS, M. (1956) The 'carrier' state in nephrogenic diabetes insipidus. *Lancet*, **ii**, 1069–73.

Chicago Conference on Standardization in Human Cytogenetics (1966) *Birth Defects: Original Article Series*, **II** (2). New York: National Foundation.

COFFEY, V. P. and JESSOP, W. J. E. (1959) Maternal influenza and congenital deformities: a prospective study. *Lancet*, **ii**, 935–8.

COFFEY, V. P. and JESSOP, W. J. E. (1963) Maternal influenza and congenital deformities: a follow-up study. *Lancet*, **i**, 748–51.

COLLMANN, R. D. and STOLLER, A. (1962a) Notes on the epidemiology of mongolism in Victoria, Australia, from 1942 to 1957. *Proc. Lond. Conf. Scient. Stud. Ment. Defic.*, *1960*, **2**, 517–26. Dagenham: May & Baker.

COLLMANN, R. D. and STOLLER, A. (1962b) A survey of mongoloid births in Victoria, Australia, 1942–1957. *Amer. J. Publ. Hlth*, **52**, 813–29.

COURT BROWN, W. M. (1968) Males with an XYY sex chromosome complement. *J. med. Genet.*, **5**, 341–59.

COURT BROWN, W. M. (1969) Sex chromosome aneuploidy in man and its frequency, with special reference to mental subnormality and criminal behavior. *Int. Rev. exp. Path.*, **7**, 31–97.

COURVILLE, C. B. (1959) Antenatal and paranatal circulatory disorders as a cause of cerebral damage in early life. *J. Neuropath.*, **18**, 115–40.

COUTTS, N. A. and FYFE, W. M. (1971) Classical and mild phenylketonuria in a family. *Arch. dis. Childh.*, **46**, 550–2.

COUVREUR, J. and DESMONTS, G. (1962) Congenital and maternal toxoplasmosis: a review of 300 congenital cases. *Developm. med. Child. Neurol.*, **4**, 519–30.

CROME, L. (1952) Encephalopathy following infantile gastro-enteritis. *Arch. dis. Childh.*, **27**, 468–72.

CROME, L. (1957) The pathology of certain syndromes. In HILLIARD, L. T. and KIRMAN, B. H. (eds.) *Mental Deficiency*. London: Churchill.

CROME, L. (1960) The brain and mental retardation. *Brit. med. J.*, **1**, 897–904.

CROME, L. (1961) Cytomegalic inclusion-body disease. *Wld Neurol.*, **2**, 447–58.

CROME, L. and PARE, C. M. R. (1960) Phenylketonuria, a review and a report of the pathological findings in four cases. *J. ment. Sci.*, **106**, 862–83.

DE GROUCHY, J., ROYER, P., SALMON, C. and LAMY, M. (1964) Délétion partielle des bras longs du chromosome 18. *Path. Biol.* (Paris), **12**, 579–82.

DODGE, H. W., WOOD, M. W. and KENNEDY, R. L. J. (1959) Craniofacial dysostosis: Crouzon's disease. *Pediatrics*, **23**, 98–106.

DOLL, R., HILL, A. B. and SAKULA, J. (1960) Asian influenza in pregnancy and congenital defects. *Brit. J. prev. soc. Med.*, **14**, 167–72.

DOWN, J. L. H. (1866) Observation on an ethnic classification of idiots. *Lond. Hosp. Rep.*, **3**, 259–62.

DRILLIEN, C. M. (1963) Obstetric hazard, mental retardation and behaviour disturbance in primary school. *Developm. med. Child. Neurol.*, **5**, 3–13.

DUNSDON, M. I., CARTER, C. O. and HUNTLEY, R. M. C. (1960) Upper end of range of intelligence in mongolism. *Lancet*, **i**, 565–8.

EDWARDS, J. H., NORMAN, R. M. and ROBERTS, J. M. (1961) Sex-linked hydrocephalus: report of a family with 15 affected members. *Arch. dis. Childh.*, **36**, 481–5.

EDWARDS, J. H., HARNDEN, D. G., CAMERON, A. H., CROSSE, V. M. and WOLFF, O. H. (1960) A new trisomic syndrome. *Lancet*, **i**, 787–90.

ELLIS, R. W. B., SHELDON, W. and CAPON, N. B. (1936) Gargoylism (chondro-osteo-dystrophy, corneal opacities, hepatosplenomegaly and mental deficiency). *Quart. J. Med.*, **5**, 119–35.

ELLIS, J. R., MARSHALL, R. and PENROSE, L. S. (1962) An aberrant small acrocentric chromosome. *Ann. hum. Genet.*, **26**, 77–83.

ELPHINSTONE, N. (1953) Thiouracil in pregnancy – its effect on the foetus. *Lancet*, **i**, 1281–3.

FINLAYSON, A. (1955) Tuberous sclerosis. *Amer. J. ment. Defic.*, **59**, 617–28.

FINN, R. (1970) The prevention of Rhesus haemolytic disease. In APLEY, J. (ed.) *Modern Trends in Paediatrics*, Vol. 3. London: Butterworth.

FÖLLING, A. (1934) Über Ausscheidung von Phenylbrenztraubensäure in den Harn als Stoffwechselanomalie in Verbindung mit Imbezillität. *Hoppe-Seyler's Z. physiol. Chem.*, **227**, 169–76.

FORD, C. E., JONES, K. W., MILLER, O. J., MITTWOCH, U., PENROSE, L. S., RIDLER, M. and SHAPIRO, A. (1959) The chromosomes in a patient showing both mongolism and the Klinefelter syndrome. *Lancet*, **i**, 709–10.

FORREST, J. M. and MENSER, M. A. (1970) Congenital rubella in school-children and adolescents. *Arch. dis. Childh.*, **45**, 63–9.

FREDERICKSON, D. S. and TRAMS, E. G. (1966) Ganglioside lipidosis: Tay-Sachs disease. In STANBURY, J. B., WYNGAARDEN, J. B. and FREDERICKSON, D. S. (eds.) *The Metabolic Basis of Inherited Disease* (2nd edn). New York: McGraw-Hill.

GAL, I., KIRMAN, B. and STERN, J. (1967) Hormonal pregnancy tests and congenital malformation. *Nature* (Lond.), **216**, 83.

GARLAND, H. and MOORHOUSE, D. (1953) An extremely rare recessive hereditary syndrome including cerebellar ataxia, oligophrenia, cataract and other features. *J. Neurol. Psychiat.*, **16**, 110–16.

GIBB, J. W. G. and MACMAHON, J. F. (1955) Arrested mental development induced by lead poisoning. *Brit. med. J.*, **i**, 320–3.

GIBBS, E. L., GIBBS, F. A. and GROSSMAN, H. (1956) Electroencephalographic evidence of encephalitis in children with supposedly uncomplicated childhood diseases. *Trans. Amer. neurol. Ass.*, 81st Annual Meeting.

GLASER, L. H. (1958) A case of nephrogenic diabetes insipidus. *Brit. med. J.*, **2**, 780–1.

GLASER, M. A. and SHAFER, F. P. (1932) Skull and brain traumas; their sequelae. *J. Amer. med. Ass.*, **98**, 271–6.

GOLDSTEIN, L. (1930) Radiogenic microcephaly. *Arch. Neurol. Psychiat.*, **24**, 102–15.

GREEN, H. G., GAREIS, F. J., SHEPARD, T. H. and KELLEY, V. C. (1971) Cretinism associated with maternal sodium iodide I 131 therapy during pregnancy. *Amer. J. Dis. Childh.*, **122**, 247–9.

GREGG, N. M. (1941) Congenital cataract following German measles in the mother. *Trans. ophthal. Soc. Aust.*, **3**, 35–46.

HARDY, J. B. (1965) Viral infection in pregnancy: a review. *Amer. J. Obstet. Gynec.*, **93**, 1052–65.

HARRIS, H. (1970) *The Principles of Human Biochemical Genetics.* Amsterdam: North-Holland Publishing Co.

HARRIS, H., PENROSE, L. S. and THOMAS, D. H. H. (1959) Cystathioninuria. *Ann. hum. Genet.*, **23**, 442–53.

HAUSCHKA, T. S., HASSON, J. E., GOLDSTEIN, M. N., KOEPF, G. F. and SANDBERG, A. A. (1962) An XYY man with progeny indicating familial tendency to non-disjunction. *Amer. J. hum. Genet.*, **14**, 22–30.

HEPNER, R. (1958) Maternal nutrition and the fetus. *J. Amer. Med. Assoc.*, **168**, 1774–7.

HINDEN, E. (1965) External injury causing foetal deformity. *Arch. dis. Childh.*, **40**, 80–1.

HOEFNAGEL, D., ANDREW, E. D., MIREAULT, N. G. and BERNDT, W. O. (1965) Hereditary choreoathetosis, self-mutilation and hyperuricemia in young males. *New Engl. J. Med.*, **273**, 130–5.

HSU, T. C. (1973) Longitudinal differentiation of chromosomes. In ROMAN, H. L., SANDLER, L. M. and CAMPBELL, A. (eds.) *Ann. Rev. Genet.*, **7**, 153–76.

HUBBLE, D. V. (1953) Endocrine disorders. In MONCRIEFF, A. and EVANS, P. (ed.) *Diseases of Children* (5th edn). London: Edward Arnold.

INSLEY, J. (1967) Syndrome associated with a deficiency of part of the long arm of chromosome No. 18. *Arch. dis. Childh.*, **42**, 140–6.

JACOBS, P. A., BRUNTON, M., MELVILLE, M. M., BRITTAIN, R. P. and MCCLEMONT, W. F. (1965) Aggressive behaviour, mental subnormality and the XYY male. *Nature* (Lond.), **208**, 1351–2.

JAMES, W. H. (1969) The effect of maternal psychological stress on the foetus. *Brit. J. Psychiat.*, **115**, 811–25.

JOHNSTON, A. W., FERGUSON-SMITH, M. A., HANDMAKER, S. D., JONES, H. W. and JONES, G. S. (1961) The triple-X syndrome. Clinical, pathological and chromosomal studies in three mentally retarded cases. *Brit. med. J.*, **2**, 1046–52.

KALTER, H. (1968) *Teratology of the Central Nervous System.* Chicago: Univ. of Chicago Press.

KIRMAN, B. H. (1955) Rubella as a cause of mental deficiency. *Lancet*, **ii**, 1113–15.

KIRMAN, B. H. (1957) In HILLIARD, L. T. and KIRMAN, B. H. (eds.) *Mental Deficiency.* London: Churchill.

KIRMAN, B. H., BLACK, J. A., WILKINSON, R. H. and EVANS, P. R. (1956) Familial pitressin-resistant diabetes insipidus with mental defect. *Arch. dis. Childh.*, **31**, 59–66.

KLINEFELTER, H. F., REIFENSTEIN, E. C. and ALBRIGHT, F. (1942) Syndrome characterized by gynecomastia, aspermatogenesis without a-leydigism, and increased excretion of follicle-stimulating hormone. *J. clin. Endocr.*, **2**, 615–27.

KOMAI, T., KISHIMOTO, K. and OSAKI, Y. (1955) Genetic study of microcephaly based on Japanese material. *Amer. J. hum. Genet.*, **7**, 51–65.

KRIVIT, W. and GOOD, R. A. (1957) Simultaneous occurrence of mongolism and leukemia. *A.M.A.J. dis. Child.*, **94**, 289–93.

KULLANDER, S. and KÄLLÉN, B. (1971) A prospective study of smoking and pregnancy. *Acta obstet. gynec. scand.*, **50**, 83–94.

LAWSON, D. (1955) On the prognosis of cretinism. *Arch. dis. Childh.*, **30**, 75–82.

LAXOVA, R., MCKEOWN, J. A., SALDAÑA, P. and TIMOTHY, J. A. D. (1971) A case of XYY Down's syndrome confirmed by autoradiography. *J. med. Genet.*, **8**, 215–19.

LECK, I. M. and MILLAR, E. L. M. (1962) Incidence of malformations since the introduction of thalidomide. *Brit. med. J.*, **2**, 16–20.

LEJEUNE, J., GAUTIER, M. and TURPIN, R. (1959) Etudes des chromosomes somatiques de neuf enfants mongoliens. *C.R. Acad. Sci.* (Paris), **248**, 1721–2.

LEJEUNE, J., LAFOURCADE, J., BERGER, R., VIALATTE, J., BOESWILLWALD, M., SERINGE, P. and TURPIN, R. (1963) Trois cas de délétion partielle du bras court d'un chromosome 5. *C.R. Acad. Sci. Paris*, **257**, 3098–102.

LEJEUNE, J., LAFOURCADE, J., DE GROUCHY, J., BERGER, R., GAUTIER, M., SALMON, C. and TURPIN, R. (1964) Délétion partielle du bras court du chromosome 5. Individualisation d'un nouvel état morbide. *Sem. Hôp. Paris*, **40**, 1069–79.

LESCH, M. and NYHAN, W. L. (1964) A familial disorder of uric acid metabolism and central nervous system function. *Amer. J. Med.*, **36**, 561–70.

LEVY, S. and PERRY, H. A. (1948) Pertussis as a cause of mental deficiency. *Amer. J. ment. Defic.*, **52**, 217–26.

LEWIS, E. O. (1933) Types of mental deficiency and their social significance. *J. ment. Sci.*, **79**, 298–304.

LOWE, C. U., TERREY, M. and MACLACHLAN, E. A. (1952) Organic-aciduria, decreased renal ammonia production, hydrophthalmos, and mental retardation. *Amer. J. Dis. Childh.*, **83**, 164–84.

MCKUSICK, V. A. (1968) *Mendelian Inheritance in Man: Catalogs of Autosomal Dominant, Autosomal Recessive, and X-linked Phenotypes* (2nd edn). Baltimore: Johns Hopkins Press.

MCKUSICK, V. A. (1969) The nosology of the mucopolysaccharidoses. *Amer. J. Med.*, **47**, 730–47.

MCKUSICK, V. A., MAHLOUDJI, M., ABBOT, M. H., LINDENBERG, R. and KEPAS, D. (1967) Seckel's bird-headed dwarfism. *New Engl. J. Med.*, **277**, 279–86.

MACLEAN, N., MITCHELL, J. M., HARNDEN, D. G., WILLIAMS, J., JACOBS, P. A., BUCKTON, K. A., BAIKIE, A. G., COURT BROWN, W. M., MCBRIDE, J. A., STRONG, J. A., CLOSE, H. G. and JONES, D. C. (1962) A survey of sex-chromosome abnormalities among 4514 mental defectives. *Lancet*, **i**, 293–6.

MARINELLO, M. J., BERKSON, R. A., EDWARDS, J. A. and BANNERMAN, R. M. (1969) A study of the XYY syndrome in tall men and juvenile delinquents. *J. Amer. med. Assoc.*, **208**, 321–5.

MENKES, J. H., HURST, P. L. and CRAIG, J. M. (1954) A new syndrome: progressive familial infantile cerebral dysfunction associated with an unusual urinary substance. *Pediatrics*, **14**, 462–7.

MIGEON, B. R. (1966) Short arm deletions in group E and chromosomal 'deletion' syndromes. *J. Pediat.*, **69**, 432–8.

MILLER, O. J., BREG, W. R., WARBURTON, D., MILLER, D. A., DE CAPOA, A., ALLDERDICE, P. W., DAVIS, J., KLINGER, H. P., MCGILVRAY, E. and ALLEN, F. H. (1970) Partial deletion of the short arm of chromosome No. 4 (4p−): clinical studies in five unrelated patients. *J. Pediat.*, **77**, 792–9.

MONCRIEFF, A. A., KOUMIDES, O. P., CLAYTON, B. E., PATRICK, A. D., RENWICK, A. G. C. and ROBERTS, G. E. (1964) Lead poisoning in children. *Arch. dis. Childh.*, **39**, 1–13.

MILUNSKY, A. (1973) *The Prenatal Diagnosis of Hereditary Disorders.* Springfield, Ill.: Charles C. Thomas.

MURPHY, D. P. (1928) Ovarian irradiation; its effect on the health of subsequent children. *Surg. Gynec. Obstet.*, **47**, 201–15.

MURPHY, D. P. (1929) The outcome of 625 pregnancies in women subjected to pelvic radium or roentgen irradiation. *Amer. J. Obstet. Gynec.*, **18**, 179–87.

NEEL, J. V. (1954) Problems in the estimation of the frequency of uncommon inherited traits. *Amer. J. hum. Genet.*, **6**, 51–60.

NEWELL, H. W. (1937) The effect of head injury on the behavior and personality of children: a study of 20 cases. *Med. Clin. N. Amer.*, **21**, 1335–65.

OYANAGI, K., MIURA, R. and YAMANOUCHI, T. (1970) Congenital lysinuria: a new inherited transport disorder of dibasic amino acids *J. Pediat.*, **77**, 259–66.

Paris Conference on Standardization in Human Cytogenetics (1971) *Birth Defects: Original Article Series*, **viii** (7). New York: National Foundation.

PATAU, K., SMITH, D. W., THERMAN, E., INHORN, S. L. and WAGNER, H. P. (1960) Multiple congenital anomaly caused by an extra autosome. *Lancet*, **i**, 790–3.

PEARSON, P. L., BOBROW, M. and VOSA, C. G. (1970) Technique for identifying Y chromosomes in human interphase nuclei. *Nature* (Lond.), **226**, 78–80.

PENROSE, L. S. (1938) A clinical and genetic study of 1280 cases of mental defect. *Sp. Rep. Ser., Med. Res. Coun.*, No. 229. London: HMSO.

PENROSE, L. S. (1963a) *The Biology of Mental Defect*. London: Sidgwick & Jackson.

PENROSE, L. S. (1963b) *Outline of Human Genetics* (2nd edn). London: Heinemann.

PENROSE, L. S. (1963c) Finger-prints, palms and chromosomes. *Nature*, **197**, 933–8.

PENROSE, L. S. (1963d) Paternal age in mongolism. *Lancet*, **i**, 1101.

PENROSE, L. S. (1966) Dermatoglyphic patterns in large acrocentric trisomy. *J. ment. Defic. Res.*, **10**, 1–18.

PENROSE, L. S. and SMITH, G. F. (1966) *Down's Anomaly*. London: Churchill.

PITT, D. B. (1961) Congenital malformations and maternal rubella: progress report. *Med. J. Aust.*, **1**, 881–90.

PITT, D. B. (1962) Congenital malformations: a review. *Med. J. Aust.*, **1**, 82–7, 121–4.

PITT, D. B. (1971) The natural history of untreated phenylketonuria. *Med. J. Aust.*, **1**, 378–83.

PLUMMER, G. (1952) Anomalies occurring in children exposed *in utero* to the atomic bomb in Hiroshima. *Pediatrics*, **10**, 687–93.

PREISER, S. A. and DAVENPORT, C. B. (1918) Multiple neurofibromatosis (von Recklinghausen's disease) and its inheritance: with description of a case. *Amer. J. med. Sci.*, **156**, 507–40.

ROBBINS, F. C. and HEGGIE, A. D. (1970) The rubella problem. In FRASER, F. C., MCKUSICK, V. A. and ROBINSON, R. (eds.) *Congenital Malformations: Proceedings of Third International Conference, The Hague, Netherlands, September 1969*. Amsterdam: Excerpta Medica.

ROBERTS, J. A. F. (1970) *An Introduction to Medical Genetics* (5th edn). London: Oxford Univ. Press.

ROE, T. F., HALLATT, J. G., DONNELL, G. N. and NG, W. G. (1971) Childbearing by a galactosemic woman. *J. Pediat.*, **78**, 1026–30.

ROSENBERG, L. E. and SCRIVER, C. R. (1969) Disorders of amino acid metabolism. In BONDY, P. K. (ed.) *Duncan's Diseases of Metabolism* (6th edn). Philadelphia: W. B. Saunders.

ROWBOTHAM, G. F., MACIVER, I. V., DICKSON, J. and BOUSFIELD, M. E. (1954) Analysis of 1400 cases of acute injury to the head. *Brit. med. J.*, **1**, 726–30.

RUBINSTEIN, J. H. (1969) The broad thumbs syndrome – progress report 1968. *Birth Defects: Original Article Series*, 5 (2), 25–41.

RUESS, A. L. and ROSENTHAL, I. M. (1963) Intelligence in nephrogenic diabetes insipidus. *Amer. J. Dis. Childh.*, 105, 358–63.

RUNE, V. (1970) Acute head injuries in children: an epidemiologic, child psychiatric and electroencephalographic study of primary school children in Umeå. *Acta Paediat. scand.*, Suppl. 209, 1–122.

SHANNON, M. W. and NADLER, H. L. (1968) X-linked hydrocephalus. *J. med. Genet.*, 5, 326–8.

SHAPIRO, S. L., SHEPPARD, G. L., DREIFUSS, F. E. and NEWCOMBE, D. S. (1966) X-linked recessive inheritance of a syndrome of mental retardation with hyperuricemia. *Proc. Soc. exp. Biol. Med.*, 122, 609–11.

SHERLOCK, E. B. (1911) *The Feeble-Minded.* London: Macmillan.

SHRAND, H. (1961) Treatment of lead poisoning with intramuscular edathamil calcium-disodium. *Lancet*, i, 310–12.

SIGLER, A. T., LILIENFELD, A. M., COHEN, B. H. and WESTLAKE, J. E. (1965) Radiation exposure in parents of children with mongolism (Down's syndrome). *Bull. Johns Hopk. Hosp.*, 117, 374–99.

SIRKIN, J. (1944) Acrocephalosyndactylia: report of a case. *Amer. J. ment. Defic.*, 48, 335–8.

SJÖGREN, T. (1931) Die juvenile amaurotische Idiotie. *Hereditas*, 14, 197–426.

SMITHELLS, R. W. (1962) Thalidomide and malformations in Liverpool. *Lancet*, i, 1270–3.

SNYDER, R. D. (1971) Congenital mercury poisoning. *New Engl. J. Med.*, 284, 1014–16.

STANBURY, J. B. (1966) Familial goiter. In STANBURY, J. B., WYN-GAARDEN, J. B. and FREDERICKSON, D. S. (eds.) *The Metabolic Basis of Inherited Disease* (2nd edn). New York: McGraw-Hill.

STOLLER, A. and COLLMANN, R. D. (1965) Incidence of infective hepatitis followed by Down's syndrome nine months later. *Lancet*, ii, 1221–3.

TAYLOR, A. I. (1967) Patau's, Edwards' and cri du chat syndromes: a tabulated summary of current findings. *Developm. med. Child Neurol.*, 9, 78–86.

TAYLOR, A. I. (1968) Autosomal trisomy syndromes: a detailed study of 27 cases of Edwards' syndrome and 27 cases of Patau's syndrome. *J. med. Genet.*, 5, 227–52.

THOMPSON, J. S. and THOMPSON, M. W. (1973) *Genetics in Medicine* (2nd edn). Philadelphia: W. B. Saunders.

TODD, R. MCL. and NEVILLE, J. G. (1964) The sequelae of tuberculous meningitis. *Arch. dis. Childh.*, 39, 213–25.

TOWBIN, A. (1970) Central nervous system damage in the human fetus and newborn infant: mechanical and hypoxic injury, incurred in the fetal-neonatal period. *Amer. J. Dis. Childh.*, 119, 529–42.

VAN DEN BOSCH, J. (1959) Microcephaly in the Netherlands: a clinical and genetical study. *Ann. hum. Genet.*, **23**, 91–116.

VULLIAMY, D. G. and NORMANDALE, P. A. (1966) Cranio-facial dysostosis in a Dorset family. *Arch. dis. Childh.*, **41**, 375–82.

WALSH, M. N., KOCH, F. L. P. and BRUNSTING, B. A. (1938) The syndrome of tuberous sclerosis, retinal tumors, and adenoma sebaceum: report of case. *Proc. Mayo Clin.*, **13**, 155–60.

WERTELECKI, W., SCHINDLER, A. M. and GERALD, P. S. (1966) Partial deletion of chromosome 18. *Lancet*, **ii**, 641.

WEST, J. R. and KRAMER, J. G. (1955) Nephrogenic diabetes insipidus. *Pediatrics*, **15**, 424–32.

WICKES, I. G. (1954) Foetal defects following insulin coma therapy in early pregnancy. *Brit. med. J.*, **2**, 1029–30.

WOOD, J. W., JOHNSON, K. G. and OMORI, Y. (1967) In utero exposure to the Hiroshima atomic bomb: an evaluation of head size and mental retardation twenty years later. *Pediatrics*, **39**, 385–92.

YAMAZAKI, J. N., WRIGHT, S. W. and WRIGHT, P. M. (1954) Outcome of pregnancy in women exposed to the atomic bomb in Nagasaki. *Amer. J. Dis. Childh.*, **87**, 448–63.

YU, J. S. and O'HALLORAN, M. T. (1970) Children of mothers with phenylketonuria. *Lancet*, **i**, 210–12.

ZAPPELLA, M. and COWIE, V. (1962) A note on time of diagnosis in mongolism. *J. ment. Defic. Res.*, **6**, 82–6.

ZAPPERT, J. (1926) Über rontgenogene fotale mikrozephalie. *Arch. Kinderheilk.*, **80**, 34–50.

4

A. M. Clarke and A. D. B. Clarke

Genetic-environmental interactions in cognitive development

Introduction

The topic implied by the title of this chapter is very complex, and space permits no more than a highly selective review. The nature-nurture issue was the subject of bitter debate in the 1930s, very much on an 'either-or' basis, with the hereditarians and environmentalists each taking an extreme stand. Superficially at least, the present debate is more sophisticated, with most research workers eager to indicate that they are interactionists. This term, however, permits a wide range of interpretations, with Jensen and Eysenck at one extreme (asserting that 80 per cent of the variance for intellectual differences is genetic in origin), and Skeels and Hunt at the other.

The problem of genetic and environmental interaction in the development of human characteristics is central to the behavioural sciences. For the field of mental subnormality, it is of particular relevance to the causation and treatment of mildly handicapped and disadvantaged children. Hence the topic will be treated quite generally in this chapter.

The first point to be considered is the argument by analogy that since important human characteristics like height are known to be strongly influenced by heredity, it is likely that others such as intelligence will also be. Furthermore, it has been shown that animals can, by judicious manipulation of genetic characteristics, be bred for certain behavioural traits. Two points arise in this connection. (1) It is known that various environmental factors affect the development of height, particularly nutrition; to quote an extreme example, a severely rachitic child will not develop to his potential stature. In another connection, a leading geneticist once pointed out that the best dairy cow will cease to give its abundant supply of milk if severely undernourished. (2) The evolutionary development in the highest primates of a complex and sophisticated system of communication, renders them capable of transmitting information from generation to generation, which raises the possibility that some intellectual strategies as well as elaborated verbal codes may be acquired rather than inherited, or, at the least, so modified on the basis of an unobservable hereditary potential as to alter substantially the position of intellectual development by comparison with purely physical characteristics.

We see then that an important conceptual distinction must be made between the operation of the physical environment on the development of elaborated behavioural characteristics and the potential operation of the social environment. In this connection a further distinction needs to be drawn between environmental factors which are likely to have a rapid effect, and those which are likely to operate slowly and cumulatively. In the former category we find certain events may rapidly and permanently damage the genotype, as demonstrated by abnormal mutations following exposure to an atomic bomb explosion; others may damage the developing foetus *in utero*; maternal rubella and placenta collapse being different examples of this. Yet others, such as acute cerebral infections or severe trauma, may render a normally intelligent child severely subnormal in a matter of days or weeks. In the second category, the effect of nutrition on height and other physical characteristics is a slow process, to be measured in years rather than weeks. There is no evidence, nor in our view is there ever likely to be any, that social factors operate rapidly; they must be seen as potentially long-term variables, if they operate at all.

Before considering the data, it may be helpful to outline the research models which are theoretically valid for elucidating the problem. These will include both those which for ethical reasons cannot be used, and those which can and have been used.

(1) EXPERIMENTAL MANIPULATION OF THE ENVIRONMENT

(a) If children born to *two* parents of known high IQ were to be experimentally placed at birth in conditions of poverty and deprivation, reared by foster parents *both* of known low IQ for, say fifteen years, and were found to be very bright, this would be powerful evidence for heredity being of overwhelming importance in determining intelligence.

(b) If children born to two parents of known low IQ were experimentally placed at birth with parents both known to be bright, and brought up in a stimulating and culturally rich environment, and resembled their true parents more than their foster parents, heredity would be presumed to be the powerful factor.

(c) If children born to two parents of known low IQ were experimentally manipulated in such a way that the potentially adverse effects of living with their parents were compensated for, yet developed low intelligence, once again heredity would emerge supreme.

(d) If a cohort of identical twins born to parents of known high (or low) IQ were separated at birth, one twin remaining with the natural parents and the other twin placed with parents varying from very unintelligent to highly intelligent; and if, after fifteen years, those whose environment differed substantially from the natural home resembled each other closely, heredity would be shown predominant.

In practice, of these experimental models (a) and (d) cannot be tried for ethical reasons; there is partial evidence on (b), and (c) is the subject of a recent ongoing experiment in which the results are suggestive, but the children are not as yet old enough for the results to be clearly evaluated.

(2) OBSERVED DATA FROM SITUATIONS WHICH HAVE ARISEN THROUGH NATURAL SOCIAL CAUSES

These form the vast bulk of available evidence on heredity and environment. The following are situations which have been used to elucidate the effects of either heredity or environment on intellectual performance. In all cases the tool used was a standardized intelligence test, usually with a verbal component. The following predictions may be made.

Genetics

1. Correlations between related individuals should show an increasing size according to the closeness of the familial relations.
2. Children separated from their natural mothers and reared in foster homes should resemble their mothers more closely than their foster mothers.
3. Much less certainly, some writers have predicted that there should be regression to the mean across generations. Galton noticed that children of very tall parents tended to be shorter, while children of short parents tended to be taller. It has been suggested that a similar effect will be found with respect to intelligence. One would expect to find studies with IQs of both parents and all their children available for the testing of this hypothesis.
4. Children resident in institutions where the range of environment is limited should show considerable individual differences.
5. Separated identical twins should show a higher intercorrelation of test scores than siblings, and, even if there are wide environmental differences for each member of the twin pair, their scores should be very similar, and the relationship should be much the same as for identical twins reared together.

Environment

1. Converse findings to those above should in general be available, except that correlations between related individuals should show an increasing size according to the closeness of the familial relationships for reasons of environmental similarities. This point is the same as (1) under Genetics.
2. Children whose environments change for a prolonged period should show changing growth rates in the direction predicted by the environmental change.
3. The amount of change noted under (2) above should relate to the degree and duration of environmental alteration.

As will be seen when data are examined, few studies are anywhere near to being crucial, but as Burt (1967) states: 'The logic of the argument should be carefully noted: as in all natural science, the mode of proof is indirect; hence the conclusions can never be "necessary" or "certain", but only probable. The critic ... commonly misses this point and revels in demonstrating that some alternative can be conceived. But one can always think up alternatives; a hypothesis empirically shown to be probable can only be overthrown by proving that the proposed alternative *is still more probable.*'

The predictions mentioned above will now be compared with existing studies and, with one exception, poorer models not so far mentioned will be ignored. The exception relates to the correlates of social class; these variables appear so powerful and pervasive that, whatever the balance of forces that influences their origin, they are clearly of major general importance quite apart from their specific relevance to the problem of mild subnormality. In particular, the models described under Environment (2) and (3) will be closely examined because both natural and contrived experiments are now numerous, and because the methodological problems posed by these approaches are relatively straightforward.

Genetic factors

(1) Correlations between IQs of individuals and their relatives depend upon the closeness of the familial relationships. Erlenmeyer-Kimling and Jarvik (1963) have summarized 52 studies and present median correlations as well as their range. Thus, unrelated children reared together yield median IQ intercorrelations of ·23 (range: ·15 to ·32); foster-parent and child, ·20 (range: ·18 to ·40 – 3 studies); parent-child, ·50 (range: ·22 to ·80 – 12 studies); siblings reared apart, ·40 (range: ·33 to ·47 – 2 studies); siblings reared together, ·49 (range: ·30 to ·77 – 35 studies); dizygotic twins reared together, ·53 (range: ·38 to ·88 – 20 studies); monozygotic twins reared together, ·87 (range: ·76 to ·95 – 14 studies); monozygotic twins reared apart, ·75 (range: ·61 to ·87 – 4 studies). The ranges[1] around these median values are very considerable, and may reflect either (1) differences in design and execution of the studies, or (2) differences in populations studied with respect to genetic and environmental variables; or both.

The work of Erlenmeyer-Kimling and Jarvik is well known and quoted by all those writing upon the inheritance of intelligence (e.g. Jensen, 1969; Eysenck, 1971). It is also well appreciated that the majority of separated monozygotic twins are reared in similar environments (e.g. Shields, 1962). A problem in interpreting kinship data is that environments of relatives are likely themselves to be correlated, and with adequate measures might provide a hierarchy of correlations resembling the IQ correlation matrix. Thus, on an environmental hypothesis one would expect a low relationship between, say, cousins, and a very high correlation between identical twins reared together.

In favour of genetic factors, however, is the fact of very low correlations

[1] These ranges are approximate, having been estimated from a small graph.

between foster parents and children, and on an environmental hypothesis one would surely expect the usual correlation between parent and child IQ (when living together) to be higher than ·50, which is about the same as that for unrelated people who marry.

(2) The correlation between maternal and child IQ has been firmly established as averaging about ·50. Skodak and Skeels (1949) offered a final report on 100 children with inferior social histories adopted in infancy into superior homes. It was shown that these had a normal chance of superiority or inferiority (IQ range at 13 was 70 to 154, with a mean of 117) in spite of the fact that true mothers' IQs averaged well below 100. Nevertheless, by the age of 13 a correlation with true mothers' IQ of ·44 was established, even though there was a mean difference of over 20 points between the mothers and their children. This can only be interpreted as showing the influence of genetic factors on the differences between the children, as well as, of course, an environmental influence, even after allowing for regression to the mean (see below).

(3) Burt (1967) points out that people are apt to think of heredity as a tendency of like to beget like, whereas Mendelian theory is equally applicable to account for differences within families. One of the important areas of debate in this connection is regression to the mean, first noticed by Francis Galton in the context of height. For intelligence this would entail the paradox that if the parents are dull, their children will be brighter, and if the parents are bright, their children will be duller than they are, i.e. in each case the intelligence of the children will tend to be nearer to that of the population average than that of their parents. Of the several studies pertinent to the problem, the best known is one by Burt (1961), while Oden's (1968) report on the follow-up of Terman's gifted group and their children is also often quoted. Burt's evidence appears to provide perfect support for the usual genetic prediction of regression halfway to the mean. Thus with an average paternal IQ of 140, the mean IQ of the children was 121, and with an average paternal IQ of 85, the average of the children was 93.

There are a number of difficulties concerning this study: for example, perfect regression halfway to the mean would only be predicted genetically with random mating, whereas as mentioned above, there is substantial assortative mating for intelligence. The results appear suspiciously perfect, since this amount of regression would not be predicted in an assortatively mated population. The mothers' IQs thus constitute an unknown variable, and Burt's statements that his study 'is intended merely as a pilot enquiry', that 'the data are too crude and limited for a detailed examination by a full analysis of variance' and that 'For obvious reasons the assessments of adult intelligence were less thorough and less reliable' suggest that these findings are by no means as firm as some subsequent authors have interpreted them.

The whole issue of regression to the mean has been subject to misinterpretation and misunderstandings. Firstly, it is incorrectly thought, on the basis of the genetic model, that regression will be predicted *equally* from single parent and mid-parent intelligence. In fact, it only applies in the case of single parent-child correlations, and will, of course, be reduced by the extent to which assortative mating occurs. Secondly, and probably in part due to the first confusion, Burt's study has been treated as though it referred to mid-parent-child regression, whereas in fact the data are on fathers' and sons' intelligence levels only. Thirdly, it has been considered that parent-child regression is not predictable on any environmental hypothesis. In fact, in the case of single-parent-child regression, hypothetically it could be, but the same environmental argument loses plausibility if the fact of sibling differences is considered in conjunction with it. Thus the strength of the genetic explanation of regression does not hinge upon the parent-child relationship alone. However, in the case of mid-parent-child regression, as for example observed by Outhit (1933) and more recently by Reed and Reed (1965), this is not predicted by a simple additive polygenic model; regression here can only be explained on either environmental grounds, or on the basis of a radically different genetic model. In either case, test error would be implicated to some extent. It will thus be obvious that regression to the mean is the weakest and most confused of all the genetic arguments discussed here. The authors are greatly indebted to their colleague, Mr M. McAskie, for much of the section outlined under (3) above.

(4) Institutions usually offer a uniformity of environment, with poor adult-child ratios and relationships. Long residence under such conditions might be expected to produce a uniformity in intellectual functioning in ordinary children. While one or two studies indicate a decreasing IQ variability (e.g. Jones and Carr-Saunders, 1927) the majority show a wide range of individual differences surviving the impact of environmental uniformity (Burt, 1961; 1966).

(5) The universal finding that identical twin IQ correlations are very high, and much higher than sibling correlations, has been accepted as powerful evidence of the role of heredity. Even if one views this from an environmental view (i.e. that identical twins must have a closer environmental similarity than other members of the species, and that identical twins reared apart are commonly brought up in similar environments), there is no environmental reason why identical twins reared apart should correlate *more closely* than siblings reared together, except that in the former case there is identity in ages but not in the latter.

We will now consider twin studies in some detail, since these comprise the most widely quoted area of research in the genetics of intelligence. Various statistical methods have been evolved for estimating the proportion of the variance between individuals that can be ascribed to genetic factors, and Mittler (1971) provides a useful review. McClearn (1970) quotes some surprising results from the work of Vandenberg (1966) in which within-pair variances were calculated for MZ and DZ twins on the six Primary Mental Ability subtests. Significant hereditary determinants for verbal, space, number and fluency were suggested, but no evidence for hereditary determination of memory *or reasoning* was forthcoming.

Burt's (1966) study of identical twins reared apart is widely quoted as meeting the usual objection to such studies, namely that the separated individuals are commonly reared in similar environments. Admittedly there have been exceptions where a few cases, reared in markedly different circumstances, have shown considerable differences (Newman *et al.*, 1937). Apparently Burt had the opportunity over many years to build up a case study of some identical twins separated very early in life and reared in different social classes. His general findings indicated surprisingly high intercorrelations for IQ in spite of social class differences, but a social class effect on school attainments. Yet there are a number of puzzling features about this study which are seldom noticed. First, no raw data are presented, and in particular no indication of the mean IQs for each half of the twin pairs. It could be that the means would indicate social class correlates, yet the intercorrelations of IQ could still remain very high. Second, the class distribution of those remaining with their parents was as follows: social classes I — III = 19; social classes IV — VI = 34. The other twins were distributed in foster homes as follows: social classes I — III = 11; social classes IV — VI = 42. While it is clear that considerable differences in class distribution occurred, they are not overwhelmingly great in most cases. Only about half the sample had twins who experienced a shift of two or more social classes when fostered. Third, the method of assessment of IQ is not entirely clear. Thus Burt (1967), commenting on the views of some of his critics, stated that 'what I was discussing was not acquired knowledge or skill ... but rather the psychologist's attempts to assess the individual's "innate general ability" – a purely "hypothetical factor". My object was to demonstrate that, when these assessments were reached, not by taking scores on some familiar "group test" just as they stand, but *by adopting the more elaborate procedures which my colleagues and I had used*, then the errors of assessment were comparatively slight' (our italics). Reference back to the 'elaborate procedures' in the 1966 paper shows that the tests used were: (1) a group test of non-verbal and verbal items; (2) an individual test, Burt's own revision of the Terman–Burt scale, 'used primarily for standardization, and for doubtful cases'; (3) a set of performance tests. The test results 'were submitted to the teachers for comment or criticism; and, wherever any question arose, the child was re-examined'. It is not stated how often such retests occurred, nor what their effect was. Did they, for example, involve a closer approximation of the IQs of twin pairs ? Table 2 in the 1966 paper includes the mysterious heading 'Final assessment' without indicating there or elsewhere how these were reached, but the effect on correlations was slightly to raise the relationship between IQs of identical twins reared apart.

It will be seen that Burt's paper raises a number of important questions which unfortunately can never be answered now. Knowing what we do about the 'experimenter effect' a much closer enquiry on the mode of assessment would have been desirable in order to exclude this as possessing any possible influence (e.g. knowledge of the hypothesis, knowledge of the other twin test scores). In particular the notion of establishing 'innate general ability', dated though it is, appears to beg the whole question. If those doing the assessments had been able to establish this, then by definition identical twins reared apart in different environments would possess identical innate general ability, which in fact approximates to Burt's reported findings.

Indices of heritability are usually based on the comparison of intra-class correlations between identical and fraternal twins. Using such formulae, whether Holzinger's H or Falconer's h^2, it is usually concluded that about 80 per cent of the variance is genetic in origin. Nevertheless, it is nearly always stated that such estimates are based upon North American or European populations and cannot necessarily be generalized, and that studies of minority populations are also needed.

It must be indicated, however, that there are still a number of problems in this type of approach. As Hunt in his book *Intelligence and Experience* (1961) indicates, the analysis of variance model fits the data too poorly and assumes that genetic and environmental variances are additive and without interaction. A further point, in comparing fraternal twin intercorrelations with identical twin correlations, relates to twin studies in general. These are used because in non-separated twins, whether fraternal or identical, it is assumed that environment is held more or less constant for each member of the twin pair; if this is so, it is scarcely surprising that heredity should emerge as the more powerful variable. But the whole approach to estimating heritability in this fashion is also weakened by the range of findings in twin studies. Thus Erlenmeyer-Kimling and Jarvik (1963) quote the range of ·40 to ·65 for dizygotic twins of opposite sex reared together, ·63 to ·85 for monozygotic twins reared apart, and ·76 to ·95 for mono-zygotics reared together. Indeed, Jarvik and Erlenmeyer-Kimling (1967), who are among those most closely identified with arguments for the importance of genetic factors, protest that 'attempts to assess the relative contribution of genotypic differences to individual differences in psychological characters continue to appear in the literature', and that the 'heritability' estimate 'is usually regarded as an approximation to some true, fixed property of the characteristic under study. The foregoing assumption is incorrect'. They go on to indicate that heritability would receive its highest estimate for a genetically heterogeneous group which had undergone relatively homogeneous environmental circumstances, and would appear low when derived from comparatively homogeneous populations, experiencing a diversity of environmental conditions.

A further source of disagreement has recently been outlined by Jensen (1971). He argues that the established practice of squaring the correlation coefficient in order to obtain the percentage of variance due to genetic factors in kinship correlations is unjustified. Such correlations, unsquared, are themselves the genetic proportion.

McClearn (1970) discusses in some detail these problems and shows that the assumption that comparison of mono- with dizygotic twins will indicate the contribution of heredity is fraught with difficulties.

The straightforward application of twin study results to the population at large is prevented by two features of the twin situation. The magnitude of the genetic effect is assessed by comparing differences between genetically identical individuals to the differences between genetically diverse individuals; the genetic diversity, however, is only that which can exist among progeny of the same parents. This will involve much less variability than exists in the population as a whole. Similarly, the environmental forces whose impact is assessed by MZ pair differences are only those environmental differences that exist within a family. Again this must certainly underestimate the range of environmental forces at work in the population.

Moreover, Penrose (1972) has indicated that on the assumption of an 80 per cent hereditary contribution to intellectual differences, and with the fact of assortative mating, IQ correlations between parents and their children and between siblings should be much higher than they in fact are. He also suggests that psychologists should pay less attention to intra-familial differences in intelligence and more to special abilities.

In summary, in the present state of knowledge one can accept the existence of powerful genetic factors in the development of individual differences in intelligence, scholastic ability and other characteristics, without presuming, on the basis of less than adequate data, to ascribe a particular proportion of the variance to genetics or environment.

This section can be concluded by stating the obvious, that genetic factors exert a strong influence on intellectual development, and may be assumed to account for a large part of observed intellectual differences. Indeed with a genetic theory which is prepared to explain both similarities and differences within families, it is tempting to assume that inheritance accounts for virtually all of the variance in a population with respect to measured intelligence; in fact many serious students of this problem believe that it accounts for by far the major part. We have now to look at evidence on the effect of the environment to account for the fact that some have hesitation in adopting this position as firmly established.

Environmental factors

INTRODUCTION

The word environmental needs definition for the purposes of this section. It is perfectly correct to regard brain damage due to trauma, or resulting from the effects of maternal rubella in early pregnancy, or underdevelopment due to early malnutrition, as environmental in origin, and there is seldom any controversy over these or allied conditions. The present section, however, will be concerned only with the rather less obvious and much more controversial effects of social environments; thus in this section, environmental is used as a synonym for social-psychological.

It may be helpful to start with a logical argument. It does not seem possible, if evolutionary theory is accepted, to conceive of *any* behaviour which does not have a biological foundation – that is, in the final analysis of most cases a hereditary basis. No biological scientist is likely to accept the 'blank slate' hypothesis, and latterly the writings of Chomsky and Lenneberg have added powerfully to the logical argument in showing the biological basis of human language acquisition. Those who work in the field of mental subnormality should have no difficulty in accepting the proposition that there are a few very rare cases of individuals born without a 'language acquisition device', whereas other members of the species appear to have a highly developed and sensitive ability to acquire language. In a beautifully succinct account of his theory, Lenneberg (1964) describes four criteria which may distinguish biologically from culturally determined behaviour, and illustrates these by contrasting walking (biologically determined) with *writing* (culturally determined, although with a biological basis).

Lenneberg does not argue that developed language is a genotypic phenomenon – he asserts that the culturally determined features in language are obvious, and his discussion focuses on the less obvious innate features.

It is self-evident that there is a large environmental component to language as used by any human being. It is an established fact that verbal intelligence tests correlate as well or better with school achievement as do any other behavioural measures. All the data in the previous section on genetic factors in intelligence were based on intelligence tests with a large verbal component. The question is to what extent does the language environment, in which a child develops, determine his efficiency on verbal reasoning tests; are there gross differences in language environment within one culture; are these differences reflected in intelligence tests and scholastic achievement? May some non-verbal strategies of reasoning be shaped by the environment?

THE CORRELATES OF SOCIAL CLASS

An attempt to describe differences within a culture will be mentioned. This is the report of Hess and Shipman (1965), based upon Bernstein's theories. They took a group of 163 Negro mothers of 4-year-old children representing four social classes: college-educated, professional and managerial; skilled, but not college educated; unskilled and semi-skilled, with mostly no high-school education; unskilled or semi-skilled level, but with fathers absent and mothers on public assistance. These mothers were interviewed twice in their homes, and brought to the university for testing and for an interaction session between mother and child in which the mother was taught three simple tasks by the staff member and then asked to teach these tasks to the child.

The results showed (a) a striking difference in verbal output differentiating middle-class mothers from those of the three other groups; (b) a difference in the use of abstract words, scores ranged from an average index of 5·6 for middle-class mothers to 1·8 for the recipient of public assistance; (c) a difference in the use of complex syntactic structures. There were differences in control systems: the middle-class mothers in response to questions concerning how they would deal with such situations as the child breaking school rules, failing to achieve, or having been wronged by someone, showed a marked tendency to offer person-oriented logical and elaborated explanations, while the lowest classes offered status-oriented orders. There were significant differences among the children on cognitive tasks which correlated with observed differences among the mothers in their mode of teaching their own child in an experimental session. On the other hand, the mothers of the four groups differed little in the affective elements of their interaction with their children.

The authors define cultural deprivation in terms of lack of cognitive meaning in the mother-child communication system. The 'meaning of deprivation is a deprivation of meaning, a cognitive environment in which behavior is controlled by status rules rather than by attention to the individual characteristics of a specific situation and one in which behaviour is not mediated by verbal cues or by teaching that relates events to one another and the present to the future.' The end result is the child responsive to authority rather than to rationale, non-reflective and without long-term goals.

Faced with pronounced differences betweeen social classes in their method of communicating with their children, it might be expected that there will be differences among children reflecting the language and cognitive environments in which they are reared. From the foregoing, it could be predicted that:

1. SES differences should be found not only in global IQ measures, but in the qualitative aspects of a child's preferred cognitive strategy. It is to be expected that children reared in circumstances favouring abstract strategies would perform well in tests demanding abstract thinking, and conversely those reared in cultures relatively devoid of cognitive meaning will encourage strategies relying on associative rote learning, at which such children might be expected to excel. (This is borne out by the data; see p. 84.)
2. Since successful achievement at school is increasingly dependent upon abstract cognitive strategies, one would expect a growing disparity between high and low social classes as age increases. (This is confirmed; see p. 85.)
3. One would expect a positive relation between ability to receive and profit from higher education and continued conceptual development. (Again this is confirmed; see p. 85.)

It is of interest that little difference may be found between social groups at around 15 to 18 months (Bayley, 1965; Hindley, 1965). Clear average IQ differences are present by 3 years (Hindley, 1965). Schaefer (1970) suggests that the appearance of differences is probably related to the shift in content from sensori-motor test items to a greater language content, and it is language differences which, as already noted, are obvious features in social class comparison. However, the consequences of a simplistic language, over and above the poor language itself, should not be ignored, nor the improverished surroundings in which such children are reared, nor the potential implications for the development of abstract non-verbal cognitive structures.

Lawton (1968) made a detailed study of language use by middle- and working-class boys, matched for verbal and non-verbal ability, at the ages of 12 and 15 years. Using three different language situations – essay writing, discussion and a structured interview – he obtained data which on the whole confirmed the social class differences postulated by Bernstein. The two major factors which differentiated the groups were, first, a more extensive use of the passive voice in middle-class children, and, second, their facility at switching from a restricted to a more elaborated code in appropriate circumstance.

If language impoverishment is indeed a main way in which low social class effects are mediated, then a remedial language programme for such children might overcome social class differences. There are problems in answering this clearly, because language programmes are seldom applied in isolation. However, Levenstein (1969), quoted by Schaefer (1970), claims to have promoted 17-point average IQ gains by stimulating mother-child verbal interaction over a seven-month period, involving the lending of books and toys (see later section on Head-Start Studies).

Jensen (1970a) has given detailed consideration to the basis of social class differences in intelligence. He believes that these cannot be comprehended without involving the existence of at least two relevant dimensions: (1) the cultural content of the test items; and (2) their complexity, degree of abstraction and problem solving. He cites the classic paper of Eells *et al.* (1951) which indicates that the largest social class differences did not appear in the most culturally loaded items, but rather on those that involved the highest degree of abstraction, conceptual thinking and problem solving ability. Moreover, these items possessed no great cultural content, in the sense of different degrees of exposure in different social classes. In addition, if all the social classes' IQ differences were due to differences in cultural experiences, it should be possible to devise intelligence tests that favour low groups over high. Jensen states that no one has succeeded in doing this, hence culture bias is only a trivial effect compared with intrinsic differences in abstractions and complexity. This seems to be an impressive argument but in reality may be circular if, as already noted in the work of Hess and Shipman (1965), abstractness and complexity may themselves be culturally biased. It is not being argued that Jensen's findings are either unimportant or invalid, but rather that we question the mechanisms by which Level I and Level II types of thinking evolve as the preferred strategies in individual cases.

At this point some discussion of Level I and Level II is necessary. Jensen has elaborated his theory of hierarchical cognitive abilities in various publications (1969), and most recently (1970b) in a chapter entitled 'A theory of primary and secondary familial mental retardation'. He excludes from his argument those mental retardates predominantly below IQ 50 whose condition is due to pathological agents, and goes on to examine the nature and cause of subcultural retardation. Jensen dismisses as unsound the notion that the common correlation between IQ and SES is to a large extent culturally determined, and gives the evidence for regarding genetic factors as the major cause of mild mental sub-normality.

Jensen argues that there is a great deal of evidence that mental abilities stand in some hierarchical relationship to one another. He acknowledges the controversial nature of factor analytic studies alone, but points to the considerable evidence from experimental studies of the training process such as Gagné's and those reviewed by White (1965) as showing that for many abilities there is a natural and invariable order of acquisition or emergence, such that when ability B is found A will always be present, but not conversely. He acknowledges that some basic abilities are learned, but suggests that there are other abilities which are practically impossible to account for except in terms of maturation. These latter abilities can also be seen as hierarchical, in the sense that normal maturation of a lower level of neural structure does not necessarily ensure later maturation of a higher level.

For Jensen the essential characteristic that most generally describes the levels of this hierarchy of mental maturation is the degree of correspondence between 'input' and 'output'. Lower levels in the hierarchy involve relatively little processing or transformation of input (whereas the higher levels do). A continuum is postulated, transcending task difficulty and stimulus complexity, in which tasks requiring little input transformation (e.g. conditioning, reaction-time, discrimination learning) are low in the hierarchy while complex concept learning and problem solving (as in verbal analogies and Raven's Progressive Matrices) are high. The theory states that although all tasks range along a single continuum, the latter is seen as the result of at least two types of ability: Level I or 'associative ability' and Level II or 'cognitive ability'.

Jensen asserts that, in every study performed by his research group, low SES and middle SES groups differ much less on Level I tests than on Level II (Jensen, 1970b).

One could predict Jensen's (1970b) experimental results from those of Hess and Shipman (1965) as well as from the theories of sociologists such as Bernstein. The interpretation of Jensen's findings would, however, be totally different from the one he advances, and consequently the educational implications would also differ. One might predict that the lower-class child would, over a period of many years, cumulatively come to depend upon Level I learning strategies, while the middle-class child would increasingly leave these behind and depend more and more upon Level II.

A series of experiments conducted by the authors on pre-school children of predominantly (but not exclusively) low social class indicated that in sorting tasks demanding, for their correct solution, the use of super-ordinate concepts, the children's initial strategy involved incorrect and often idiosyncratic associations. Training on different material, so organized as to force the child to use a conceptual strategy, resulted in substantially improved performance on transfer back to the initial task (Clarke et al., 1967; Clarke et al., 1969). It is suggested that the biologically normal child has potential for both Level I and II strategies but that his long-term interaction with cultural factors, favouring predominantly one or the other, may be crucial in determining which he employs in a given situation.

It seems, then, that Level II as an available mode of response is superior to, but depends upon, Level I. In suggesting this dichotomy Jensen seems to be doing little more than splitting cognitive processes into simple versus complex, and intelligence into basic, simple versus complex, abstract, symbolic. This may be a useful distinction to make (reminiscent of Bernstein's restricted versus elaborated linguistic codes) but unequivocal evidence on the origins of either is much more difficult to obtain than he suggests. Moreover, Stevenson (1972) indicates that the size of correlations (between ·38 and ·56) between the most extreme representatives of Level I and Level II tasks suggests that these levels are less independent than might be supposed.

It is not possible within the compass of this chapter to present all the evidence on the relationship between home background and intelligence as tested or as revealed in scholastic achievement. Goldberg (1970), in discussing psychosocial issues in the disadvantaged, confirms the second prediction made above (page 82): 'The findings cited throughout this section demonstrate not only a consistently negative relationship between disadvantaged status (economic and ethnic) and academic or intellective attainment; they demonstrate also that the retardation exhibited by such children is cumulative, growing greater and greater as they go up the grades. Whatever the explanation, the fact remains that as they grow older and stay in school longer, disadvantaged children fall further behind their more affluent age mates.'

There is substantial evidence from studies at those ages when educational opportunities are most diverse that higher education improves performance not only on attainment but also on intelligence tests. Vernon (1960) summarizes the position as follows:

... Many studies have shown that high school and college students continue to increase their scores from 15 up to 20 years and over. Indeed, Dearborn and Rothney (1941), on the basis of repeated testing of children in their 'teens, predict that the final maxim is not reached until 30. The only plausible way of reconciling these findings is to allow that growth continues so long as education or other stimulating conditions continue, though probably never beyond 25–30 years, and that when such stimulation ceases decline sets in.

A direct indication of the effects of advanced education is provided by Lorge's (1945) and Husén's (1951) investigations, where the same individuals were tested as children and as adults. Lorge reckoned that, at 34, adults who had received university education were 2 MA years superior to others who possessed the same intelligence at 14 but had had no further schooling. Husén tested 722 men entering the Army at 20 whose IQs at 10 years were known, and found that those who had matriculated had gained 12 IQ points relative to those who had had no secondary education.

That the quality rather than the length of schooling makes a difference is indicated by a research (Vernon, 1957) in which almost all the boys in the 14 secondary schools of an English city were tested at 14 years, and their results compared with their IQs at the time of secondary school selection 3 to 4 years earlier. Allowing for initial differences between boys entering different schools, and for regression effects, there were now differences of up to 12 points between boys in the 'best' and 'worst' schools. The combined grammar and technical school boys had apparently gained 7 points over the combined modern schools. Much of this difference might well be due to the grammar school boys coming from better homes, with more favourable attitudes to education; but this would none the less be an environmental effect.

In addition, Oden (1968), reporting on a follow-up of Terman's gifted group, reports a general increase in CMT score with increased educational level within this highly selective sample. However, she also reports that 146 subjects who did not go beyond high school earned exactly the same CMT score as that of a group of advanced graduate students at a leading university. Lerner (1968) summarizes from what he describes as 'a jungle of literature' the well-known relationship, demonstrated during the first world war in America, between adult intelligence and educational expenditure in the states from which the recruits were drawn.

Finally, in discussing the effects of social class, it must be pointed out that although average differences have long been appreciated, one is dealing with something more than the effects of social class membership. Within each class, there is the same range of ability; it is in their differing proportions of particular levels of ability that these differences reside (Maxwell, 1961). Thus the proportion with superior ability is very low in the children of social class IV and V parents, and very high in social class I. But because of the size of these lower socio-economic groups the absolute number of superior children is greater than for those of the small social group I.

It seems, therefore, that the context of social class influences provides a groundwork for the development of a particular average level of ability and attainment. But this average level for each class is surrounded by wide differences arising from genetic differences and constitutional differences (e.g. the effects of nutrition, the prevalence of illness, the effects of differing birth histories, etc.). Moreover, practices within each social class are far from being uniform and, as pointed out by Burt many years ago, the 'efficiency of the mother' has an enormous influence upon the child's development.

The correlates of social class have been well documented recently by Davie, Butler and Goldstein (1972), and some details of their study are offered later in this chapter. They note that 'One of the most striking features which emerges ... is the very marked differences between children from different circumstances which are already apparent by the age of seven ... the most potent factors were located in the home environment.' There are, of course, large actuarial differences between different classes in material prosperity, child-rearing practices and parental expectations, but in spite of these average differences, the situation within a single social class is obviously far from being uniform. Clearly in this field as in others, multiple genetic and environmental interactions are involved cumulatively and over the whole period of development.

STUDIES OF MAJOR ENVIRONMENTAL CHANGE

One of the most carefully documented studies of environmental change and its effect upon retarded children has been provided by Skeels and Dye (1939), Skeels (1966) and Skodak (1968). The initial observation was accidental. Two children under 18 months old, in residence at a state orphanage, gave unmistakable evidence of marked mental retardation. Kuhlmann–Binet intelligence tests were given to both, the results on one (at 13 months) being IQ 46, and on the second (aged 16 months) IQ 35. Qualitative and behavioural assessments supported these results. There was no indication of organic defects.

These two children were recommended for transfer to a state school for the mentally deficient but the prognosis was at the time regarded as poor. After transfer, they were placed in a ward of older girls whose ages ranged from 18 to 50 years and in mental age from 5 to 9 years. Six months later the psychologist visiting the wards of this institution was surprised to notice the apparently remarkable development of these children. They were accordingly re-examined on the same test as before, this time gaining IQs of 77 and 87 respectively. A year later their IQs had risen to 100 and 88. At the age of about $3\frac{1}{2}$ the two children's scores were 95 and 93.

The hypothesis to explain these results was that the ward attendants had taken a particular fancy to these two babies who were the only pre-school children in their care. They were given outings and special play materials. Similarly, the older and brighter inmates of the ward were particularly attached to the children and would play with them during most of their waking hours; for these two it was clearly a stimulating environment. It was considered that a further change would be desirable if the intellectual alteration was to be maintained, and accordingly they were placed in rather average adoptive homes at the age of $3\frac{1}{2}$. After about fifteen months in these homes re-examination, this time with the Stanford–Binet, resulted in IQs of 94 and 93 respectively. These unexpected findings raised a number of important questions. Observation suggested that similar children left in an orphanage nursery made no such gains in the rate of mental growth. Adult contacts were at a minimum and limited largely to physical care. Adoptive placement was clearly inappropriate, owing to the lack of certainty that progress would occur. The most reasonable solution would seem to lie in a repetition of the 'accidental experiment' but this time in a planned and controlled manner. Thus research was started involving an experimental group of thirteen children whose ages ranged from 7 to 30 months, and Kuhlmann–Binet IQs of 35 to 89. Mean age at the time of transfer to the state school was 19 months and mean IQ was 64. Once again, clinical observation supported the IQ classification; for example, a 7-month-old child in the group could scarcely hold his head up without support, while another at 30 months could not stand alone and required support while sitting in a chair. After the close of the experimental period it was decided to study a contrast group of children remaining in the orphanage. This group consisted of twelve children, whose ages ranged from 11 to 21 months, and IQs from 50 to 103. Mean age at the time of the first test was 16 months, with a mean IQ of 86. No marked differences in the birth histories of the two groups were observed, nor in their medical histories. Family histories indicated that the majority came from homes of low socio-economic levels with parents of low intellect, and there were no important differences between them.

The members of the experimental group in general repeated the experiences of the first two children and also attended the school kindergarten just as soon as they could walk. In the case of almost every child, some adult, either older girl or attendant, would become particularly attached to him or her and would figuratively 'adopt' him. This probably constituted an important aspect of the change. Members of the Contrast Group, however, had environments rather typical of the average orphanage. The outstanding feature was the profound lack of mental stimulation or experiences usually associated with the life of the young child in an ordinary home. Up to the age of 2 years, the children were in the nursery of the hospital. They had good physical care but little beyond this; few play materials were available and they were seldom out of the nursery room except for short walks or periods of exercise. At the age of 2, they graduated to cottages where over-crowding was characteristic. Thirty to thirty-six children of the same sex under 6 years of age were under the care of one matron and three or four untrained and reluctant teenage girls. The matron's duties were so arduous that a necessary regimentation of the children resulted. No child had any personal property. The contrast between these two environments is obvious (cf. Bowlby, 1951).

During the course of the experiment the average increase in IQ of the experimental group was 27·5 points, the final IQs at the conclusion having a mean of 91·8. Gains ranged from 7 to 58 points; three made increments of 45 points or more, and all but two increased by more than 15 points. The length of the experimental period depended in an individual case upon the child's progress, varying from 5·7 months to 52·1, with a mean of 18·9 months.

The development of the children in the contrast group was almost precisely the opposite from those in the experimental group. The average IQ at the beginning was 86·7 and at the end was 60·5, an average loss of 26·2 points. Apart from one child who gained 2 points, all showed losses varying from 8 to 45 points. Ten of the twelve children lost 15 or more points. The average length of the experimental period was 30·7 months.

In commenting upon these data, one notes (a) the initial superiority of the contrast group; (b) the reversal of the status of the two groups; and (c) the differing lengths of the evaluation periods for the groups.

As soon as the experimental group showed intellectual functioning approaching the normal range, with two exceptions they were placed in adoptive homes. The adoptive parents were, with one exception, lower middle class. The selection of relatively modest levels of adoptive homes was made because of the poor social background of the children and the fact that, at one time, they had all been mentally retarded. It was therefore felt advisable to select homes where aspirations for achievement might not be too high.

Contrast children, on the other hand, either remained in unstimulating and in some cases actively adverse orphanages or state schools for the mentally retarded.

Later, Skeels, with the assistance of Marie Skodak, carried out an impressive follow-up of both groups after being completely out of touch with their members for over twenty years (Skeels, 1966; Skodak, 1968). The aims of the follow-up were simple. What happened to the children as adults, how have the early childhood differences been reflected in adult achievement and adjustment, and have the divergent paths been maintained. A major problem was of course to locate the subjects, and the Skeels monograph describes in vivid detail the problems and frustrations in so doing.

Very marked differences between the two groups were found in educational and occupational status and general life style. The experimental group had completed an average of 11·68 grades of school (median 12); their spouses had virtually identical educational attainments. The contrast group, on the other hand, had completed an average of 3·95 grades of school (median 2·75).

In considering occupational levels, it should be noted that the experimental group contained only three males, while the contrast group contained eight.

There were marked differences in the occupational levels of the two groups. The three males in the experimental group were: a vocational counsellor, a sales manager for an estate agent, and a staff sergeant in the Air Force. Eight of the ten girls were married and of those who were employed, one taught elementary school grades, another was a registered nurse, another a licensed practical nurse, another had passed State Board examinations and practised as a beautician. Another girl was a clerk, another after graduating from high school passed the examinations and was accepted as a stewardess in an airline. Two were domestics in private homes.

In the contrast group, four were still residents in institutions, and unable to engage in employment. Seven were employed, one washing dishes in a nursing home, two were dishwashers in small restaurants, another worked in a cafeteria. One of the men had been in and out of institutions for years, and when out lived with his grandmother, doing odd jobs. Another man was a 'floater' travelling from coast to coast, engaging in casual and unskilled labour. Yet another was an employee in the state institution where he was originally a patient. Finally, the deviant of this group, to be referred to later, was a typesetter for a newspaper in a large city. It will be apparent that, of those who were employed, with the exception above (Case 19), all were in unskilled manual occupations. It might also be added that, unlike the experimental group which had shown considerable geographical mobility and whose members were very difficult to trace, there were only minor problems in locating by means of institutional records the members of the contrast group.

Space precludes a detailed consideration of all the evidence presented in the 1966 monograph. Although inevitably in a study of this kind there are some gaps in information available, sufficient data are presented on the status of the children as infants, the socio-economic and educational backgrounds of at least one parent, the status of the adoptive parents and the final outcome for the twenty-five children as adults, for certain conclusions to be drawn with considerable confidence.

Although the majority of the experimental group were adopted, two were not, for reasons which are not stated. The majority of the contrast group remained in poor institutions during their childhood, but there was one exception. What is clear is that the eventual outcome for all these children was closely related to the long-term environmental circumstances surrounding the major part of their later development. It is our belief, based on this and other evidence, that the relatively brief pre-school stimulation programme, which was initially a major focus of interest for Skeels and his colleague Skodak, is probably of little long-term relevance, except as initiating a differentiation between experimental and contrast groups, and thus providing the belief that the experimental children would not grow up to be mentally retarded.

This thesis will be illustrated with reference to the bare outlines of some specific case histories.

Case 10 (experimental group) at 23 months, before transfer to the 'stimulating conditions', had an IQ of 72. On retest at 45 months, his IQ was 79. His natural mother was educated to 8th grade, and had six months of high school education. His natural father was a theatre manager in a small town, and was presumably at least of reasonable intelligence. His adoptive father, educated to 9th grade, was a milkman and his adoptive mother had been educated to 8th grade. The subject himself graduated from high school, and attended college for two and a half years. At the time of follow-up he was sales manager in a real estate firm.

Case 11 (experimental group) at 26 months, before transfer, had an IQ of 75. On retest at 51 months, after the special programme, he had an IQ of 82. His natural mother had an IQ of 66 and was diagnosed as a psychotic mental defective. Nothing is known of his natural father. His adoptive father was a college graduate, the only one of the adoptive sample who occupied a professional post. The adoptive mother was a high school graduate, drawn from a somewhat affluent family. The subject himself was a university graduate, with a BA degree and some postgraduate work at the time of follow-up. His occupation was that of vocational counsellor in a state welfare programme.

By contrast, Case 2 (experimental group) had an IQ of 57 at 13 months. On retest, after the programme, at 37 months her IQ had risen to 77. Her natural mother had completed 8th grade at school and was said to be 'slow mentally'. The natural father, a farm labourer, was also said to be mentally slow; he, too, had completed 8th grade. The subject was never adopted, and completed only five grades at school. On follow-up, about 1942, she was in residence at the institution for the mentally retarded and 'in all probability will continue to show marked mental retardation to a degree necessitating continued institutionalization'. At final follow-up, she was a housewife married to a labourer and had been in domestic service.

Case 24 (contrast group) had an IQ of 50 at 22 months. On retest, at 52 months his IQ was 42. His natural mother went as far as 8th grade at school and then took a short evening class course in business studies. She worked as a telephone operator and did general office work. His natural father graduated from high school but was unemployed at the time of his birth. The subject was brought up in the institution for the mentally retarded where he did rather well. At the age of 20, his Wechsler IQ scores were: Verbal 76; Performance 106; Full Scale, 84. An attempt was made to place him in open employment but this proved unsatisfactory and he asked for return to the institution where, at the time of follow-up, he was assistant to the Head Gardener. He was reported to be an exceedingly good gardener but institutionalized.

Case 19 (contrast group) had an IQ of 87 at 15 months. On retest at 45 months this had decreased to 67. His natural mother graduated from high school and had an IQ of 84; his father was a farmer. Although he was never adopted, he was the only member of the contrast group not brought up in the institution for the mentally retarded. By chance he was included in an intensive stimulation programme as part of a doctoral research which emphasized language training and cognitive development. When he entered regular school he was discovered to have a moderate hearing loss following bilateral mastoidectomy in infancy. At about the time of retest, at the relatively late age of 6, he was accordingly transferred to a residential school for the deaf where the matron of his cottage took a special fancy to him as one of the youngest children, and one who had no family. He was a frequent guest in her home and in that of her daughter and son-in-law. He graduated from high school, had one semester of college and at the time of follow-up was employed as a compositor and typesetter. His marriage was stable, he had four intelligent children, owned his house in a comfortable middle-class district, and was earning as much as the rest of the contrast group put together.

In summary, the diverging early histories of both groups have been maintained in adult life. 'It seems obvious', writes Skeels (1966), 'that under present day conditions there are still countless numbers of infants born with sound biological constitutions and with potentialities for development well within the normal range, who will become mentally retarded and a burden to society unless appropriate intervention occurs ... we have sufficient knowledge to design programs of intervention which can counteract the devastating effects of poverty, sociocultural deprivation and maternal deprivation.'

This study was one of the spiritual fathers of Head-Start Programmes, and some general comments may be in order. As already stated in the previous chapter, infant IQs have virtually no predictive value. The early changing IQ of both Experimental and Contrast subjects are therefore difficult to interpret, and as Jensen (1969) notes, extreme caution must be exercised in evaluating IQ increments. The only university graduate had an IQ of 82 at the age of $4\frac{1}{4}$ years. Yet the long-term changes were congruent with the environmental opportunities the children were initially offered. What seems important is the vast differences among all twenty-five children, in their total histories and in their ultimate status. The intervention programme may be of no more long-term significance than in having inspired confidence in the investigators that the children were potentially adoptable.

The work of Kirk (1958), which was directly inspired by the early Skeels data, showed that although IQ increments can be engineered by careful pre-school programmes, contrast children who had not had such programmes began to catch up with those who had, during their first year in school. Furthermore, Kirk spells out the implications for children living in psycho-socially deprived homes, and writes, 'It should make us reconsider the belief that "a poor home or a poor mother is better than no home or no mother".' Until someone has been able to demonstrate the long-term effects of early intervention without subsequent environmental enrichment, the safest interpretation of Skeels' important data is that adult status is closely related to the whole environmental circumstances between the age of 5 and adulthood.

A few studies of individual children, socially isolated in an extreme and fortunately rare way, also illustrate the retarding effect of grossly adverse environments, as well as the remedial influences (from the age of 6 or 7) of enriched environments. The case described by Mason (1942) and independently by Davis (1947) is a classic but suffers from several omissions. Much more recently, Koluchova (1972) has described quite fully and carefully the rescue from isolation, neglect and cruelty, of twin boys aged 7.

Their mother died shortly after their birth. They were placed 'in care' for a year, after which they went to an aunt for six months. During this time they developed normally, and it is probably very important that their nutrition was normal. When they were 18 months old, their father married again, and their stepmother, an obviously unbalanced woman, took over the care of the twins. They had reached the age of 7 before it was discovered that for most of the intervening period the boys had been kept isolated in a cellar, had been cruelly treated, and were suffering from malnutrition.

Experts who examined them found that they were severely mentally handicapped, their IQs being in the forties. They could barely speak, they could hardly walk, they were terrified of ordinary household objects and were quite unable to recognize the meaning of pictures.

For some time the boys were given very active treatment – partly to repair the physical damage they had suffered and partly to bring their social behaviour and their abilities up to the level that might be expected of more 'normal' retarded children. When they were judged ready for it, they were placed in a school for the mentally handicapped. So good was their progress there that they were moved after a while to an ordinary school. Now they are doing well, though at 11 years of age they are still some years behind average in school attainment. But their IQs – in just four years – have more than doubled, are continuing to increase, and are now in the normal range (one is 94 and the other 95).

The twins have been adopted by dedicated people who are giving them a stable and happy home, and the improvement in their emotional maturity is very obvious. Of course, we do not know what will happen to them eventually, but it is interesting to hear that when they were first discovered a number of experts considered that their terrible condition and the extraordinary way they had been treated must mean that they were damaged beyond hope of recovery. (See also Clarke, 1972.)

On the contrary, it is clear now that the options remained open at the age of 7, even after almost unbelievable adversity. Our own work in the 1950s also illustrated the considerable long-term changes that could take place in adolescent and early adult life following removal from conditions of great adversity (Clarke and Clarke, 1954; Clarke *et al.*, 1958).

The Koluchova study is too recent to have received comment. The studies by Mason, Davis, Skeels and Skodak are, however, well known and the findings generally accepted. Referring to such research, Jensen (1969) offers the argument that environment only acts as a threshold variable. 'There can be no doubt', he writes, 'that moving children from an extremely deprived environment to good average environmental circumstances can boost the IQ some 20 to 30 points and in certain extreme rare cases as much as 60 or 70 points. On the other hand, children reared in rather average circumstances do not show an appreciable IQ gain as a result of being placed in a more culturally enriched environment.' (Here Jensen gives no references.) He goes on to say

> *While there are reports of groups of children going from below average up to average IQs as a result of environmental enrichment, I have found no report of a group of children being given permanently superior IQs by means of environmental manipulations* (our italics).

In brief, it is doubtful that psychologists have found consistent evidence for any social environmental influences short of extreme environmental isolation which have a marked systematic effect on intelligence. This suggests that the influence of the quality of the environment on intellectual development is not a linear function. Below a certain threshold of environmental adequacy, deprivation can have a markedly depressing effect on intelligence. But above this threshold, environmental variations cause relatively small differences in intelligence. . . . When I speak of sub-threshold environmental deprivation, I do not refer to a mere lack of middle-class amenities. I refer to the extreme sensory and motor restrictions in environments such as those described by Skeels and Dye (1939) and Davis (1947) . . . culturally disadvantaged children are not reared in anything like the degree of sensory and motor deprivation that characterizes the children of the Skeels study.

This rather diffuse passage, then, suggests that social environment only possesses a marked effect on intelligence in extreme conditions Moreover, in the sentence which we have italicized it is quite unclear whether Jensen has (a) found no report or (b) has found reports but these had negative results. In either event, it is surprising that he fails to mention Husén's famous (1951) study (see p. 177). Suffice it to say, that having dismissed 'ordinary' environmental differences, Jensen has no need to weigh the evidence from many other studies.

A test of Jensen's threshold theory for the operation of environmental factors would be provided by a prospective and total intervention programme using the disadvantaged population living in their own homes and in their own community. As already noted, these in Jensen's view are above the threshold, since they do not suffer 'anything like the degree of sensory and motor deprivation that characterizes the children of the Skeels study'. The study which will be outlined fulfils these criteria and, although in its early stages, has results which are very suggestive.

Heber and his associates (Heber et al., 1968; Heber and Garber, 1971; Heber, 1971) have been responsible for the most important and best-controlled prospective study designed to test the cultural deprivation hypothesis. It is indicated that over the past thirty years no more intense and bitter controversy has occurred than that concerning the aetiology of cultural-familial retardation, a group comprising perhaps 80 per cent of the total. The study was designed to have a bearing upon this question.

The first step was to institute a survey in an area of Milwaukee with the greatest population density, lowest median family income and the greatest rate of dilapidated housing. The major finding was that maternal intelligence proved to be the best single predictor of low intelligence in the offspring. Mothers with IQs less than 80, comprising less than half the total, accounted for almost four-fifths of children with IQs below 80. Moreover, the lower the maternal IQ, the greater the probability of her child scoring low. Paternal/maternal IQs were found to correspond fairly closely. A major early finding was that child IQs of the below 80 IQ mothers declined with increasing age, from an average of about 84 at age 5 to an average of about 78 at age 10 and considerably lower in adolescence. So far, the data could permit a number of differing explanations. It could be concluded, however, that in the slum, mental retardation was neither randomly distributed nor randomly caused. Thus the view that in a generic way the 'disadvantaged' environment affects cognitive development adversely is questioned. One cannot assume that conditions within a slum are uniform. Large families where maternal intelligence is low provide the context for mild retardation in depressed areas. Hence, whatever the mechanisms, there is a clear need to attempt the prevention of emergent retardation by a comprehensive family approach to rehabilitation.

Trained interviewers visited all mothers in the area with newborn children and used the PPVT as an initial screening device, also collecting extensive data on family history. Scores of 70 or less were checked by a full administration of the WAIS. Forty mothers, on the criterion of a WAIS Full Scale IQ of 75 or less, were randomly assigned to experimental or control conditions and were invited to participate in the study, the experimental part of which comprised (1) an infant stimulation programme, and (2) a maternal rehabilitation programme.

The teachers were paraprofessional, language facile, affectionate people who had had some experience with infants or young children and resided in the same general neighbourhood as the children. At 3 months of age the infant commenced attendance at the Centre. Each was then assigned a teacher who remained with the child until he reached 12 to 15 months of age. At that time he was gradually paired with other teachers and children. He was then grouped with two other children and came into contact with three different teachers. Each teacher was responsible for total care of the infant and had to follow and expand upon a prescribed set of activities. Each teacher of the 18 months and older group was responsible for ten children, seen in groups of two, three or four depending on age. She had to familiarize herself with one of three main academic areas (maths/ problem solving, language and reading). The teacher was expected to evaluate progress and to 'individualize instruction, as well as having a part to play in art, music, field trips and special holiday activities. She also had to establish as a major responsibility, contact and rapport with the child's mother.' The job was clearly a demanding one, and an ongoing training programme for teachers was established.

The philosophy of pre-school education was 'to prevent from occurring those language, problem solving and achievement motivation deficits which are known to be common attributes of mild mental retardation'. Intellectual functioning is regarded as the 'combination of abilities referred to as input, retention, interpretation, integration and utilization of symbols. The specific subject areas of our academic programme are simply vehicles through which we hoped to foster in our children these abilities which underlie normal intellectual development.' The curriculum had a cognitive-language orientation implemented through a structured environment by prescriptive teaching techniques on a daily basis (seven-hour day, five days per week).

Heber takes no particular theoretical stand other than that structured presentation of material is necessary. He considered that there were no ready-made programmes available so the project staff continually adapted existing methods and materials. The area chosen for particular emphasis was language and cognition, and the tasks to which the children were exposed were increased in complexity as they were mastered.

Language is emphasized for it is a tool for recording and processing information as well as for communication. Cognitive development is emphasized for it provides the child with a repertoire or responses enabling him to interpret and refine information. In addition, the child must have the desire to utilize these skills. . . . It is hoped that achievement motivation will be developed by introducing tasks designed to maximize interest, to provide success experiences, to provide supportive and corrective feedback from responsive adults, and to gradually increase the child's responsibility for task completion.

The author goes on to write that by utilizing a structured learning approach, the emphasis is on educating the teacher to plan and present relevant and organized learning situations. The content was presented in small logical steps, in which progress was evaluated and corresponding adjustments made to the programme. Heber's report gives details of the curriculum.

A two-phase programme for the mothers was instituted in parallel with the pre-school project. Attempts were made to give preparation for employment and to improve the home-making and child-rearing skills of the mothers in the experimental group.

Job training was undertaken in two large private nursing homes, both because permanent staff had an understanding of rehabilitation procedures and because employment opportunities existed. Reading, writing and arithmetic were emphasized to increase the mothers' self confidence before the on-the-job training commenced. In addition, they attended classes on home economics, interpersonal relations and child care.

The job training included five weeks on laundry work, three-and-a-half weeks housekeeping, nine weeks food service and nine weeks of simple nursing. During this period there was a remarkable development of group spirit and cohesion. Group counselling sessions on a daily basis were felt to be important. This whole programme was regarded as quite successful, but major problems with respect to adequacy of home-making skills and care and treatment of children remain to be resolved with a number of the families. Hence the maternal programme is now shifting to an increased emphasis on training in general care of family and home, budgeting, instruction and food preparation, family hygiene and the mother's role in child growth and development.

Heber presents the results of repeated measures on the experimental and control children. In the first two years of life these consisted largely of the application of general developmental scales. From then on, in addition, increased emphasis was given to direct measures of learning and performance. Tests are administered by someone not involved in either the maternal or child projects.

At the age of 60 months there was a 26-point difference in the mean IQs for the two groups (Stanford-Binet) and a 20-point difference on the WPPSI. The actual scores are difficult to interpret, due to repeated testing of all the children in both groups; however, the majority of the controls scored below 90. Similar differences were obtained on various measures of language use, including the ITPA.

Thus the data indicate a remarkable acceleration of development in the children of the experimental group. Moreover, their performance is quite homogeneous compared with the range exhibited by the control group, where a quarter function at or above test norms while the remainder show trends towards sub-average performance.

Heber exhibits proper caution in interpreting these data, and raises the question of whether the children in the experimental group have merely benefited from specific training relevant to the tests on which they have been assessed. If this were so, and it seems unlikely to the present writers, then one would expect transfer in a very non-specific manner to occur to other cognitive activities (Clarke *et al.*, 1967). Nevertheless Heber indicates that no comparable group of infants has ever been exposed to the intensive training experienced by the experimental group. But possibly they have merely reached certain developmental stages earlier than usual, asks Heber. Much will depend upon the context of their lives in primary school and later, but just as cumulative deficits can occur, so too a positively reinforcing situation is likely to maintain cumulative assets in the future. We consider that this will necessitate a continuing divergence in the life styles of experimental and control subjects. If this experiment were now to cease, and the experimental children were to revert to control conditions, remaining in these until adulthood, it would be our assumption that there would be little or no difference between these groups at the age of, say, 20. Further work will in fact test this hypothesis, but hopefully, this experiment may have implications for our understanding of human development and the genetic limits upon performance.

If, indeed, the divergence between experimental and control children is maintained or increased as they grow older, the question will ultimately be raised concerning the crucial ingredients of the two-way programme for mothers and their children. This will call for even more ambitious and costly research but it will have to be undertaken if there is to be any hope of general programmes for upgrading the vast section in the population. Experiments already planned with current groups will have some bearing on these problems.

Not only have Heber and his colleagues used standard psychometric procedures but, increasingly, experimental measures of, for example, colour-form matching, sorting, probability, discrimination, and an Ivanov-Smolensky discrimination procedure. These were chosen because they could be made increasingly complex as the child developed. More than half the very lengthy (1971) report is devoted to these experiments, all of which showed superiority of the experimental over the control group. Perhaps the most interesting were inspired by the work of Hess and Shipman (1965) in studying mother-child interaction in both groups.

The experimental techniques and the general plan of Heber's research are impressive. In our view, however, his theoretical position is less than adequately formulated. For example, he appears to accept uncritically the notion of critical periods, which even in the animal field are fast being modified, and the application of which to man is very debatable. This might well lead him to underestimate the need for later enriched experience during the 'critical period' of human development from 5 to 20! Moreover, the published material (as opposed to roneo'd progress reports) is very scanty and one awaits with the greatest interest (and impatience) a detailed and unified account of this work. In addition, the results must not be interpreted as showing equality of biological potential; as

Eysenck (1971) has indicated, Heber's results show the effect of an environment never previously encountered by children of this age. It remains to be seen what might be the effect of similar intervention on children of high IQ parents.

Since the above paragraphs were drafted, further reports by Heber *et al.* (1972) and by Heber and Garber (1974) have become available. As predicted by the present writers, for those members of the experimental group who have reached school age, and for whom the formal programme has ceased, there has been a relative decline, although they are still above average and the gap between them and the controls remains roughly constant. It is our guess that far longer intervention, perhaps 12 to 15 years, is necessary to establish any permanent development change.

SUBTLE ENVIRONMENTAL FACTORS: THE FIRST-BORN PHENOMENON

The most likely explanation of the known facts that children who are first-born in a family tend to be superior in a number of ways is, in the writers' opinion, the operation of subtle, intra-familial psychosocial factors. Jensen (1969), who recognizes that work in this field is a threat to his threshold theory, summarizes in seventeen lines some of the evidence showing that 'first-born children are superior in almost every way, mentally and physically' and goes on to write: 'Since the first-born effect is found throughout all social classes in many countries and has shown up in studies over the past 80 years . . . it is probably a biological rather than a social psychological phenomenon. It is almost certainly not a genetic effect.' If, however, this were a biological, not a genetic outcome, it would imply some uterine superiority for the first-born. There is no evidence for this, and indeed birth hazards, with consequent damage, are greater for first-born than later born children. Furthermore, although no systematic study has been conducted on the superiority of 'first reared' as opposed to first-born, observation suggests that these former also show superiority. Roe (1952) in her classic paper on sixty-four eminent scientists, notes that the majority (thirty-nine) were first-born, of the remainder five were eldest sons and two who were second-born were effectively 'first reared' because of the death of an elder child. For the remainder there was often a considerable difference in age between the subject and his next elder brother (averaging five years).

Without exception all studies of first-born children, as well as others which take this phenomenon into account, show a significant advantage over later born children in terms of achievement, a strong tendency first recognized by Galton in 1874. Schachter (1963) has reviewed earlier studies of relationships between birth order and eminence and birth order and intelligence, concluding that eminent people are far more likely to have been eldest or only children than to have been later born. No clear answer concerning the relationship with intelligence emerged. Bradley (1968), reviewing later evidence of first-born of both sexes in universities and colleges throughout the United States, showed that these and only children are consistently and massively over-represented. Detailed studies of the finalists in National Merit Scholarship competitions showed among the top half per cent of the population in successive large groups there was a 23 per cent over-representation of first-born and only children. The fact that first-born and only children are over-represented in American universities could be established because of the widespread policy of requiring birth order data for university admission. Comparable data for Britain are not available because ordinal birth position is not recorded on UCCA forms. Unpublished studies in the Psychology Departments of Sheffield and Hull Universities, however, confirm these findings. Altus (1966), after considerable research into the pre-eminence of first-born and only children in academic attainment, reported that he was unable to find a single study that showed a divergent trend. More recent writers have added to the picture (Chittenden *et al.*, 1968). Nevertheless, this area has been examined critically by Schooler (1972) who believes that almost no reliable evidence exists for birth order effects in men living in the United States in the mid-1960s. The nub of his argument is that (1) at different periods within a community there are variations in the numbers of families started and, consequently, in the proportion of first-born; and (2) that family size is negatively correlated with social class, that social class is correlated with academic achievement and hence that the chances of an academically achieving individual being first-born are greater than for the general population. It is perfectly correct that many studies have not taken into account the possibly confounding effects of social class, which could certainly be mainly responsible, but there are a number which have controlled for family size and hence probably for social class. For example, Nichols (quoted by Altus, 1966) reported that of the 568 representatives of two-child families who were finalists in the National Merit competition, 66 per cent were first-born (a 16 per cent over-representation); of the 414 from three-child families, 52 per cent were first-born (a 19 per cent over-representation); and of the 244 from four-child families, 59 per cent were first-born (a 34 per cent over-representation). Furthermore as Schooler himself recognizes, there is some evidence that first- and last-born children tend to be more achieving academically than those in an intermediate ordinal position (see also Altus, 1966).

Finally, studies are briefly reviewed which take into account social class effects in assessing first-born achievement.

Thus Douglas (1964) has indicated that first-born children stay at school longer, join more clubs, read better books and push themselves harder than other children. The first-born of two or three children, particularly from working-class families, won far more grammar school places than would be expected from their ability scores alone. Douglas, Ross and Simpson (1968) show that the virtually all-round superiority of elder over younger boys in the same family is established and maintained from about age 8 onwards. Douglas did not, however, find that only children were as a group superior. This leads him to a somewhat different interpretation than is offered in the American reviews, although both have in common the assumption that personality variables relating to need for achievement are involved (see also Sontag *et al.*, 1958). Since the numerous American studies show that the phenomenon includes only children, this interpretation emphasizes adult-child relations while Douglas stresses sibling relationships.

More recently yet another careful study (Davie *et al.*, 1972) shows the effect of birth order on a number of variables in a large random sample of children. Thus at age 7, the difference in reading attainment between first- and fourth- or later-born children was equivalent to 16 months of reading age; for height, first-born were 2·8 cm taller than fourth- or later-born children after allowing for other relevant factors such as social class. Moreover, for a given birth order, those children with no younger siblings were 1·1 cm taller than those with two or more younger siblings. It is also of interest that the number of younger children is associated with adjustment; those with two or more younger siblings are less well adjusted than those with none. The authors assume that findings such as these can best be attributed to the sharing of resources, including parental time and attention. The 'only child' phenomenon has even been observed in a group of young mongols; those reared in families without other children or other young children showed a slight acceleration of mental development over those in families with other young children (Carr, 1971).

Jensen's argument, although not disproved, seems to be a far less likely explanation for the achievements of the first-born.

HEAD-START STUDIES

Following the work of Kirk (1958), Skeels (1966) and many others, and the recognition that deliberate intervention could produce upward shifts in measures of child development, in some cases maintained into adult life, the stage was set in the 1960s for attempts to upgrade the culturally disadvantaged and deprived members of the population in the United States. Thus President Johnson's Anti-Poverty Bill encouraged the initiation of Head-Start Programmes of pre-school education. It was tragic that the wave of enthusiasm, which followed, led in most cases to work which was philosophically, psychologically, educationally and methodologically naïve. Three errors, obvious to any sophisticated observer at the time, were common.

(1) The use of a short duration programme of pre-school stimulation in the summer before school entry. It was hoped that this brief exposure to pre-school education would undo the effects of early deprivation and allow the child to benefit from ordinary schooling. In such studies, few, if any, attempts were made to consider the child in his total context, including the home. No literature on recovery from cultural deprivation (other than from rare and extreme social isolation) gave the slightest hint that developmental paths in childhood could be rapidly shifted in a permanent way, so the philosophy of such intervention was ignorant, even though paying lip-service to research findings.

(2) Coupled with the hope that intervention of short duration could undo the

effects of social deprivation was a failure to realize that early experience involving learning must be subsequently reinforced if there is to be any hope of building up a permanency of such effects (Clarke, 1968).

(3) Many of the pre-school educational programmes were scarcely educational at all, and few attempts were made to analyse the needs of deprived children. Too often they were offered what they already possessed – free activity.

There exist a number of reviews of these attempts, of which those by Bereiter and Engelmann (1966) and Jensen (1969) are perhaps the best known. The former authors begin their book by referring to the sort of evidence already covered in our section on social class. They indicate that in all cognitive measures, disadvantaged children are retarded, or at least below average. In practically every aspect of language development, young children of this type function at the average level of those a year or more younger. Similar findings apply to reasoning ability. Thus for school success, disadvantaged children are retarded in areas that count the most.

Bereiter and Engelmann consider that disadvantaged children lack learning, and not the fundamental capacity to learn. Deficits in the early years are amplified by the school situation and become cumulative; hence it is necessary to remedy this situation in the pre-school years. If they are to catch up, however, they must progress at a faster than normal rate.

The most widely endorsed approach to this problem is the strategy termed 'enrichment'. In the pre-school programme attempts are made to compress the maximum quantity of experiences believed to be associated with the advantaged child's superior performance. Such programmes, write the authors, are often watered down with a humanitarian content which the disadvantaged child is thought to deserve. The most obvious logical error in this 'catch-up' approach is that while the disadvantaged child is being exposed to the programme, the advantaged child is forging ahead. This, then, is a race which cannot be won if its success depends upon well above average rates of absorption of cultural experiences, for a limited period in the day and for a limited overall duration. Such a programme may comprise a mere 500 hours in comparison with the 20,000 hours in which cultural disadvantages have retarded learning. Hence there remain just two ways of approaching the problem: (1) by selecting experiences that produce more learning; and (2) by compressing more experience into the available time. In so doing one cannot replicate the slow, cumulative development of the normal child which builds up under conditions of minor daily increments. 'Normally the young child has a lot of time; but the disadvantaged child who enters a pre-school at the age of four-and-a-half has already used most of his up.'

The basic fallacy in the enrichment strategy is that disadvantaged children must have the same kinds of experience as the privileged. If this were true, there would be no hope of speeding up their learning. More potent experiences are needed if the gap is ever to be reduced. Thus, if a child is one year retarded, and if he is to catch up a further year, he must learn at twice the normal rate.

Hence a narrower than usual spectrum of learning must be offered if this hope is to be realized. Specifically, one must focus upon academic objectives and relegate all others to a secondary position. This logical solution is one that promotes revulsion among many, but as we shall see, is the only possible hope for the full realization of potential in these children. Bereiter and Engelmann go out of their way to answer such criticisms; 'the broad, unfocused educational program', they write, 'recognizes no priorities and tolerates no omissions'. The errors here are (1) that the child's future is not considered; (2) the notion that a well-rounded programme is required reveals an ignorance of the fact that a world exists outside the school, and it may well be that a narrow educational programme amplifies the child's possibilities of benefiting from ordinary non-school experience; (3) the skilful teacher can promote favourable attitudes and emotional adjustment through specific learning activities equally well as through 'broadening' experiences; (4) recent evidence suggests that the child is not just a passive receiver of environmental stimulation. Rather, education hands him the tools needed to pursue his own development actively. The school can offer the specific skills which enable him to develop properly; (5) the teacher who tries to meet all the child's needs is likely to extend herself and dilute herself beyond all effectiveness; (6) the pre-school programme must somehow compromise between the ideals of all-round development and dealing with the severity of the child's deficiencies. The 'whole child' approach amounts to dividing the time, offering a smattering of learning in many areas but leaving him with a lesser degree of all the deficiencies he had before. Bereiter and Engelmann single out language handicaps as the most crucial.

Almost all schools for the disadvantaged are modelled upon upper middle class nursery school methods. These have never been designed with scholastic objectives primarily in mind. Such schools produce small gains in wide behavioural areas. Nevertheless some authors have made much of these gains which are, however, extinguished in comparison with those of controls after some years in the ordinary school. The advantages of such pre-schools thus appear to be slight. Bereiter and Engelmann offer a simple rule that fits the results quite closely. On the average, disadvantaged children going through pre-school will progress half the way to the mean from their initial IQ. No group will ever reach 100 if it starts below this level. On the other hand, the few cases where groups have risen to an average level of 100 relate to programmes which have departed radically from the traditional approach. (But see Heber and Garber, 1970.)

The authors then offer a detailed discussion of the language handicaps which are part and parcel of cultural disadvantage and outline the two possible strategies for overcoming them. The first is to compress a vast amount of miscellaneous verbal material to the limited time available, and the second is to plan activities so as to focus as directly as possible on the objectives. Thus the preferred approach ensures that the child receives an amount of exposure, practice and correction sufficient to teach what is intended. The first has been termed 'verbal bombardment'; the second simply involves direct teaching or instruction. Both imply a radical departure from traditional methods, but the former is less satisfactory because it may miss certain objectives. The latter gives a greater opportunity of planning and control of the syllabus. This approach has been criticized on the grounds of feasibility and whether it is good for young children to be subjected to essentially classroom procedures. The fact that such an approach has long been effective with very young deaf children is quoted as a precedent.

Outlining fifteen educational objectives that a disadvantaged child should attain by the end of a pre-school programme, ranging from being able to distinguish words from pictures to being able to perform certain kinds of 'if-then' deductions, the authors outline their results on a group of severely deprived 4-year-old children. From being retarded in language abilities by one year, these children caught up with the average in language and IQ in nine months of instruction. In summarizing this study, the authors maintain that their approach does not minimize stress but tries to direct it into productive channels; it does not provide the children with 'mothering' but does promote close affectional ties with the teacher. It prepares the child, under the best conditions, for normal schooling. If creativity is equated with freedom, the disadvantaged child usually has too much of it already.

The remainder of Bereiter and Engelmann's book is taken up with a detailed and careful consideration of all aspects of the programme.

In contrast, we now turn to the famous review of Jensen (1969) which opens with the words 'Compensatory education has been tried and it apparently has failed'. He goes on to quote the 1967 evaluation of the US Commission on Civil Rights which concluded that 'none of the programs appear to have raised significantly the achievement of participating pupils, as a group, within the period evaluated by the Commission'. Thus Jensen proposed to examine the presuppositions which underlay this apparent failure, and particularly the social deprivation hypothesis. This suggests that, having lacked certain essential early experiences, the child is thereafter cumulatively handicapped.

Jensen devotes some space to examining the concept of intelligence and IQ, examining the stability of IQ measures, and, incidentally, criticizing the notion popularized by Bloom (1964) that the age at which half the variance in adult intelligence can be predicted (i.e. by a ·7 correlation) implies that half its development has taken place. Jensen concludes that although the IQ is certainly not constant, under normal environmental conditions it is at least as stable as developmental characteristics of a strictly physical nature (see Clarke and Clarke, 1972). He also notes that the question about the normality of distribution of intelligence is meaningless.

Jensen believes that in psychology the importance of heredity has been under-estimated, particularly in individual differences in intelligence. He suggests that this has led to a 'belief in the almost infinite plasticity of intellect, the ostrich-like denial of biological factors in individual differences . . .'. He goes on to consider in detail the results of animal studies and discusses the problems of estimating heritability. He argues that values of H do not represent what the heritability might be under any environmental conditions or in all populations, or even the same populations at different times. These estimates are specific to the population sampled, the point in time, how the measurements were made, and the particular test used to obtain the measurements. He considers evidence from twin studies (particularly Burt, 1966), foster parents versus natural parents and of direct measures of environment. From an examination of correlational studies Jensen concludes that heredity is the major factor in individual IQ differences.

In a section entitled 'How the Environment Works' he advances the notion of environment as a threshold variable, that is, environment only has a marked effect if extremely adverse. The argument here (as pointed out on p. 94) is most unclear, although later (1969, p. 44) Jensen claims that this point is established. Moreover, he refers to the work by Heber in which is demonstrated a declining IQ in children whose mothers (with IQs below 80) resided in a slum, and concludes that this is probably due to genetic factors. Referring to recent work on birth order and achievement, he suggests (without offering any evidence) that this is probably a biological rather than a social-psychological phenomenon (see Clarke and Clarke, 1972). Jensen then discusses social class differences in intelligence and rightly underlines this association as one of the most substantial and least disputed facts in psychology and education. He considers that IQ differences in different classes have hereditary, environmental and interaction components, but environmental factors associated with class status are not a major *independent* source of intelligence variance. After reviewing other areas of research, including race, Jensen tackles the problem of compensatory education in the last twenty pages of his article.

Jensen starts by pointing out that the magnitude of IQ gains arising from enrichment and cognitive stimulation programmes ranges from about 5 to 20 IQ points. Amount of gain is related to the intensity and specificity of the instructional aspects of the programme. Ordinary nursery school attendance – and here there is agreement with Bereiter and Engelmann – generally results in a gain of only 5 or 6 points. With the addition of special cognitive training, particularly in language, the average gain is about 10 points. When an intensive programme is extended into the child's home, with short but demanding daily sessions, about a third of the children have shown gains of as much as 20 points. But, writes Jensen, average gains of 10 or 15 points have not been obtained (1) 'on any sizeable groups' or (2) 'have not been shown to persist or to be replicable'. There have, however, been claims for average 20 point increments, 'achieved by removing certain cultural and attitudinal barriers to learning'.

Jensen states that he had 'found no evidence of comparable gains in non-disadvantaged children'. The exceedingly meagre gains arising from excellent pre-school programmes occurred because the children did not come from sufficiently deprived backgrounds; here Jensen foreshadows his threshold theory for environmental effects, to which attention has already been drawn. He then uses regression to the mean as an explanatory model for some studies. 'The group's mean will increase by an appreciable amount because of the imperfect correlation between test-retest scores over, say, a one-year interval. Since this correlation is known to be considerably lower in younger than older children, there will be considerably greater "gain" due to regression for younger groups of children.' This is a cart-before-horse argument of a type to which we have devoted some discussion in Chapter 6 and in Clarke *et al.* (1960).

Small but significant gains in the Stansford–Binet may also arise from improvement on only one or two items of the test for young children. Moreover, testing under optimal conditions – as opposed to first testing in unfamiliar surroundings – may boost the IQ. Here Jensen foreshadows the views of Labov (1969). Such gains are of the same magnitude as the effects of direct coaching upon the IQ.

Jensen asks 'what is really changed when we boost the IQ?' Is it a gain in 'g', or in something less central to our concept of intelligence? 'I have found no studies that demonstrated gains in relatively non-cultural or non-verbal tests ...' By implication, therefore, the gains seem to represent acquisition of simple information. Moreover, such gains fade after the enrichment programme has ceased (but see Clarke, 1968). Pre-school programmes should, therefore, be evaluated according to long-term results. The present authors agree with Jensen, but would wish to add to this sentence 'and upon the reinforcement or non-reinforcement of the programme subsequently'.

There is little doubt that intellectual development can be stunted by a deprived environment, and that a shift to a good one can undo the damage very largely, writes Jensen. But can enrichment go beyond a mere amelioration of the stunting? Does it act as a hothouse, producing an earlier bloom, or as a fertilizer, producing better yields? As we have seen, the ongoing experiment by Heber and Garber has a bearing on this question.

Jensen concludes that the pay-off from compensatory programmes in terms of IQ gains is small except where methods are sharply focused, as in the Bereiter and Engelmann study where children receive twenty-minute periods of intensive instruction in language, reading and arithmetic. The largest gains were in scholastic performance, and this is the area which can most fruitfully be tackled. It is the present authors' view that Jensen is likely to be proved right in this assessment. We would add that if pre-school learning is regarded as foundational, and followed by a sequence of instruction based upon it (rather than putting the child in a class not geared to his needs) the widening gap in academic achievement characteristic of advantaged and disadvantaged children may well close. In view of the findings of Husén and others (summarized by Vernon, see p. 85) it is altogether possible that at, say, age 12 children progressively accelerated in this way would perform better on intelligence tests as well as in attainment. Some slight evidence for this view is provided by Halsey (1972).

In Volume I of a Report on Educational Priority, Halsey outlines the findings emerging from four English action-research projects. He indicates that, contrary to much American experience, gains induced by pre-school programmes can be maintained into the infant school. He attributes this to 'the high degree of pre-school cover, the continuity of approach from the pre-school groups (mostly attached to the infant schools) through into the schools, the exceptional stability of the area's population, and the considerable interest generated by the fact that the groups were the first to attend any form of pre-school'. We would, however, point out that with the passage of further time the effects could well be extinguished, although the involvement of the child's parents may combat this, depending upon the degree to which their attitudes and abilities have been affected by the programmes. Moreover, in one of the experiments reported, some of the children who had attended pre-school in the previous year were involved during their first school year in an individual instruction programme. Although these children had already made gains on the English Picture Vocabulary Test, they showed a further rise in vocabulary as a result of their further enrichment.

Halsey offers three conclusions from the experience of three years in four districts. First,

> pre-schooling is *par excellence* a point of entry into the development of the community school . . . the point at which the networks of family and formal education can be linked. . . . Second, [it] is the most effective instrument for applying the principle of positive discrimination, and this conviction rests partly on the theory that primary and secondary educational attainment has its social foundations in the child's experience in the pre-school years and partly on the evidence that positive discrimination at the pre-school level can have a multiplier effect on the overwhelmingly important educative influences of the family and peer group to which the child belongs. . . . Third, there is no unique blueprint of either organization or content which could be applied mechanically as national policy.

Halsey goes on to state that 'The home is the most important "educational" influence on the child. Formal pre-schooling is marginal. It cannot in this sense be compensatory. It can, however, define its role as supportive to family influences where support is most needed.' It is necessary to encourage parents to join in the educational process, taking education into the home and bringing parents into the school.

One of the best-controlled minimal intervention studies has been reported by Gray and Klaus (1965, 1970). Two experimental groups started a ten-week per year pre-school programme at ages 3 and 4 respectively; local and distal control groups served for comparison purposes. The experimental programme, which was especially concerned with changing attitudes towards achievement as well as aptitudes relating to achievement, was supplemented by weekly meetings during the remainder of each year by a specially trained home visitor and the parents. Intervention caused a rise in intelligence which was quite sharp at first, then levelled off and finally began to show decline once intervention ceased. It is of interest that those who started the programme at age 4 were fairly consistently superior to those who commenced at age 3. Yet differences between experimentals and controls were still apparent three years after completion of the programme; we would expect these to have been extinguished if there is a later follow-up. Spill-over effects were apparent in the local control group, while the distal control group declined quite sharply. Gray and Klaus conclude that progressive retardation can be offset but such an approach cannot be expected to 'carry the entire burden of off-setting progressive retardation ... without massive changes in the life situation of the child, home circumstances will continue to have their adversive effect upon the child's performance'. These results are entirely consistent with those of Heber, the main variable being totality of intervention, and the authors are completely aware that, as they say, pre-school experience cannot be conceived of as a single-shot inoculation protecting the child for life against the effects of adverse conditions. Human performance is the result of continuous and complex interaction between the individual and his environment.

Conclusions

Throughout this chapter we have attempted to indicate that an 'either-or' discussion of genetics and environment is dated and in many ways ridiculous. Our general thesis, which should by now almost represent a truism but which nevertheless needs stating and restating, is that human development is mediated by slow, unfolding, cumulative and powerful biological and psychosocial interactions. Different processes may well emerge at a particular time by virtue of predominant influences of one or the other, but all testify to these essential interactions.

In spite of the complexity of the field and of the data, we shall try to indicate certain consistencies and their implications.

1. Much has been outlined with respect to intelligence, but this has in the text sometimes been linked with attainment. We offer no apologies, and here we follow Vernon in accepting that an IQ test is just as much an attainment test as is a measure of reading. Unlike the latter, however, it taps a much wider range of cognitive skills. The view is also shared with Vernon that the IQ does not by itself 'cause' scholastic attainments, and indeed we consider there may well be two-way interactions between them. Test results may never be used as direct indications of biological potential. Here there is an open conflict with the views of the late Sir Cyril Burt.

2. Some of the data for genetic influences determining cognitive development regardless of environment are less than satisfactory when examined closely, and some permit alternative explanations. The most compelling evidence, however, resides in the fact that long residence in the relatively uniform conditions of institutions is still associated with wide individual differences; that correlations between foster parents and foster children are normally lower than between parents and their children; and that no environmental reason exists for the higher correlation between separated identical twins reared apart than siblings reared together.

In commenting on some of the correlational data, Penrose (1972) argued that the assumption that intelligence has a real existence, although it can only be measured indirectly, still confuses discussions on social, racial and cultural mental differences. It would be more significant, both for educational and genetical purposes, if psychologists paid more attention to the intra-familial correlations of special abilities.

3. The correlates of social class are well known, and appear quite powerful and pervasive in spite of the crudity of the criteria. While each social class contains within it the whole range of intelligence and scholastic attainments, it is in their proportions in each class that they differ. Membership of Social Class V carries with it, among other factors, a high probability of scholastic backwardness, and in subsections of it (see Heber and Garber, 1971) there is a very strong risk of mild mental retardation. Yet the data do not *of themselves* yield an unequivocal answer to the relative importance of hereditary and environmental influence. It is prudent to interpret them as showing complex and slowly cumulative interactions.

4. Much less equivocal evidence of environmental effects come from studies of children who have undergone a considerable change of circumstances. There are vast differences in long-term outcome for those reared in very poor institutions and those removed from them and adopted (Skeels and Dye, 1939; Skeels, 1966; Skodak, 1968). A similar picture emerges from a study of rare cases of children rescued from social isolation and neglect (Mason, 1942; Davis, 1947; Koluchova, 1972). Such findings are universally accepted and these prompted Jensen's (1969) threshold theory for environmental influences. In this view, only such grossly adverse conditions are likely to influence markedly the course of development, and Jensen specifically draws attention to the much less adverse situation of the culturally disadvantaged child. The threshold theory is thus held to explain why the vast bulk of Head-Start Programmes fail in the long term.

5. It is suggested that Heber and Garber's (1971) important study already provides evidence against the threshold theory for environmental action, although the long-term outcome has yet to be seen. Studies by Husén (1951) and Vernon (1957) have similar indications. We also suggest, contrary to Jensen, that the first-born effect is more likely to be a psychosocial than a biological phenomenon, and thereby has considerable implications for the existence of environmental differences within families.

6. Jensen's view that most Head-Start Programmes have failed is a statement of fact, as well as an indictment of the *naïveté* of those behavioural scientists who played a part in planning such programmes. Before accepting that genetic inferiority is the limiting factor, however, we offer as more plausible the likelihood that the main variables for long-term intervention effects are: (1) the quality of the original environment; (2) the degree to which it was changed; (3) the duration of change; (4) the type of change and the methods of intervention, including its totality or lack of it; (5) the quality and duration of

reinforcement; and (6) the length of follow-up. Unfortunately those organizing the majority of recent intervention studies appear to have believed that a few weeks' intervention would undo several years of under-stimulation, and that this single-shot approach would mark the child for life. A Head-Start Programme as a means of compensating for years of deprivation, followed by further deprivation, is like offering good nutrition to an under-nourished child for a short period before returning him to his original conditions. No Head-Start Programme on its own can ever have long-term effects, and a belief to the contrary testifies to the ubiquity and strength of the mythology surrounding the alleged long-term effects of early experience (Clarke, 1968; Clarke and Clarke, 1972). Early experience in general does not *by itself*, and if unreinforced, have long-term effects, and the notion of critical periods in psychological (as opposed to physical) development receives little if any support from the literature. Indeed, prediction of adult status from the best psychological methods does not become powerful until later childhood, and even then there is considerable intra-individual variability.

Development, whether of cognitive, physical, scholastic or personality processes, involves a slow and very long-term cumulative interaction between biological and psychosocial factors. Hence, if mild mental retardation is to be prevented in those at risk, very long-term programmes are needed. The bold claim of the President's Committee on Mental Retardation (1972) that, *using present techniques from the biomedical and behavioural sciences*, the incidence of mental retardation in general can be reduced by half by the end of this century, depends for its realization quite largely upon acceptance of these simple facts about human development, together with their implications.

References

ALTUS, W. D. (1966) Birth order and its sequelae. *Science*, **151**, 44–9.

BAYLEY, N. (1965) Comparisons of mental and motor test scores for ages 1–15 months by sex, birth order, race, geographical location, and education of parents. *Child Developm.*, **36**, 379–411.

BEREITER, C. and ENGELMANN, S. (1966) *Teaching Disadvantaged Children in the Pre-school*. Englewood Cliffs, NJ: Prentice-Hall.

BLOOM, B. S. (1964) *Stability and Change in Human Characteristics*. London: John Wiley.

BOWLBY, J. (1951) *Maternal Care and Mental Health*. Geneva: World Health Organization.

BRADLEY, R. W. (1968) Birth order and school related behaviour. *Psychol. Bull.*, **70**, 45–51.

BURT, C. (1961) Intelligence and social mobility. *Brit J. statist Psychol.*, **14**, 3–24.

BURT, C. (1966) The genetic determination of differences in intelligence: a study of monozygotic twins reared together and apart. *Brit. J. Psychol.*, **57**, 137–53.

BURT, C. (1967) The genetic determination of intelligence: a reply. *Brit. J. Psychol.*, **58**, 153–62.

BURT, C. (1970) The genetics of intelligence. In DOCKRELL, W. B. (ed.) *On Intelligence*. London: Methuen.

CARR, J. (1971) *A Comparative Study of the Development of Mongol and Normal Children from 0–4 years*. Ph.D. thesis, Univ. of London.

CHITTENDEN, E. A., FOAN, M. W. and ZWEIL, D. M. (1968) School achievement of first and second born children. *Child Developm.*, **39**, 1223–8.

CLARKE, A. D. B. (1968) Learning and human development – the forty-second Maudsley Lecture. *Brit. J. Psychiat.*, **114**, 1061–77.

CLARKE, A. D. B. (1972) A commentary on Koluchova's 'Severe deprivation in twins: a case study'. *J. Child Psychol. Psychiat.*, **13**, 103–6.

CLARKE, A. D. B. and CLARKE, A. M. (1954) Cognitive changes in the feebleminded. *Brit. J. Psychol.*, **45**, 173–9.

CLARKE, A. D. B. and CLARKE, A. M. (1972) Consistency and variability in the growth of human characteristics. In WALL, W. D. and VARMA, V. P. (eds.) *Advances in Educational Psychology: 1*. London: Univ. of London Press.

CLARKE, A. D. B., CLARKE, A. M. and BROWN, R. I. (1960) Regression to the mean: a confused concept. *Brit. J. Psychol.*, **51**, 105–17.

CLARKE, A. D. B., CLARKE, A. M. and REIMAN, S. (1958) Cognitive and social changes in the feebleminded: three further studies. *Brit. J. Psychol.*, **49**, 144–57.

CLARKE, A. M., COOPER, G. M. and CLARKE, A. D. B. (1967) Task complexity and transfer in the development of cognitive structures. *J. exp. Child Psychol.*, **5**, 562–76.

CLARKE, A. M., COOPER, G. M. and LOUDON, E. H. (1969) A set to establish equivalence relations. *J. exp. Child Psychol.*, **8**, 180–9.

DAVIE, R., BUTLER, N. and GOLDSTEIN, H. (1972) *From Birth to Seven*. London: Longmans and The National Children's Bureau.

DAVIS, K. (1947) Final note on a case of extreme isolation. *Amer. J. Sociol.*, **52**, 432–7.

DEARBORN, W. F. and ROTHNEY, J. W. M. (1941) *Predicting the Child's Development*. Cambridge, Mass.: Sci.-Art Publ.

DOUGLAS, J. W. B. (1964) *The Home and the School*. London: MacGibbon & Kee.

DOUGLAS, J. W. B., ROSS, J. M. and SIMPSON, H. R. (1968) *All our Future*. London: Peter Davies.

EELLS, K., DAVIS, A., HAVIGHURST, R. J., HERRICK, V. E. and TYLER, R. (1951) *Intelligence and Cultural Differences*. Chicago: Univ. of Chicago Press.

ERLENMEYER-KIMLING, L. and JARVIK, L. F. (1963) Genetics and intelligence. *Science*, **142**, 1477–9.

EYSENCK, H. J. (1971) *Race, Intelligence and Education*. London: Temple Smith.

GOLDBERG, M. L. (1970) Sociopsychological issues in Education. In DAVITZ, J. R. and BALL, S. (eds.) *Psychology of the Educational Process*. New York: McGraw-Hill.

GRAY, S. W. and KLAUS, R. A. (1965) An experimental pre-school program for culturally deprived children. *Child Developm.*, **36**, 887–98.

GRAY, S. W. and KLAUS, R. A. (1970) The Early Training Project: a seventh year report. *Child Developm.*, **41**, 909–24.

HALSEY, A. H. (1972) *Educational Priority. Vol. I: E.P.A. Problems and Policies*. London: HMSO.

HEBER, R. (1971) *Rehabilitation of Families at Risk for Mental Retardation: a Progress Report*. Madison, Wis.: Rehab. Res. and Trg. Centre in Ment. Retard.

HEBER, R. and GARBER, H. (1971) An experiment in prevention of cultural-familial mental retardation. In PRIMROSE, D. A. (ed.) *Proc. 2nd Congr. Internat. Assoc. Scient. Stud. Ment. Defic.*, 31–5. Warsaw: Polish Medical Publishers; Amsterdam: Swets & Zeitlinger.

HEBER, R. and GARBER, H. (1974) Progress Report II: An experiment in the prevention of cultural-familial retardation. In PRIMROSE, D. A. (ed.) *Proc. 3rd Congr. Internat. Assoc. Scient. Stud. Ment. Defic.* Warsaw: Polish Medical Publishers (in press).

HEBER, R., GARBER, H., HARRINGTON, S., HOFFMAN, C. and FALENDER, C. (1972) *Rehabilitation of Families at Risk for Mental Retardation*. Madison: Rehabilitation Research and Training Center in Mental Retardation, Univ. of Wisconsin.

HEBER, R., DEVER, R. and CONRY, J. (1968) The influence of environmental and genetic variables on intellectual development. In PREHM, H. J., HAMERLYNCK, L. A. and CROSSON, J. E. (eds.) *Behavioural Research in Mental Retardation*. Eugene: School of Education, Univ. of Oregon.

HESS, R. D. and SHIPMAN, V. C. (1965) Early experience and the socialization of cognitive modes in children. *Child Developm.*, **36**, 869–86.

HINDLEY, C. B. (1965) Stability and change in abilities up to five years: group trends. *J. Child Psychol. Psychiat.*, **6**, 85–99.

HUNT, J. MCV. (1961) *Intelligence and Experience*. New York: Ronald Press.

HUSÉN, T. (1951) The influence of schooling upon IQ. *Theoria*, **17**, 61–88.

JARVIK, L. F. and ERLENMEYER-KIMLING, L. (1967) Survey of familial correlations in measured intellectual functions. In ZUBIN, J. and JERVIS, G. A. (eds.) *Psychopathology of Mental Development*. New York: Grune & Stratton.

JENSEN, A. R. (1969) How much can we boost IQ and scholastic achievement? *Harvard educ. Rev.*, **39**, 1–123.

JENSEN, A. R. (1970a) Hierarchical theories of mental ability. In DOCKRELL, W. B. (ed.) *On Intelligence*. London: Methuen.

JENSEN, A. R. (1970b) A theory of primary and secondary familial mental retardation. In ELLIS, N. (ed.) *International Review of Research in Mental Retardation*, 4, 33–105. London: Academic Press.

JENSEN, A. R. (1971) Note on why genetic correlations are not squared. *Psychol. Bull.*, 75, 223–4.

JONES, D. C. and CARR-SAUNDERS, A. M. (1927) The relation between intelligence and social status among orphan children. *Brit. J. Psychol.*, 17, 343–64.

KIRK, S. A. (1958) *Early Education of the Mentally Retarded*. Urbana: Univ. of Illinois Press.

KOLUCHOVA, J. (1972) Severe deprivation in twins: a case study. *J. Child Psychol. Psychiat.*, 13, 107–14.

LABOV, W. (1972) The logic of nonstandard English. In GIGLIOLI, P. P. (ed.) *Language and Social Context*. Harmondsworth: Penguin.

LAWTON, D. (1968) *Social Class, Language and Education*. London: Routledge & Kegan Paul.

LENNEBERG, E. H. (1964) The capacity for language acquisition. In FODOR, J. A. and KATZ, J. J. (eds.) *The Structure of Language: Readings in the Philosophy of Language*. Englewood Cliffs, NJ: Prentice-Hall.

LERNER, I. M. (1968) *Heredity, Evolution and Society*. San Francisco: W. H. Freeman.

LEVENSTEIN, P. (1969) *Cognitive Growth in Preschoolers through Stimulation of Verbal Interaction with Mothers*. Paper presented at the 46th Annual Meeting of the American Orthopsychiatric Association, New York.

LORGE, I. (1945) Schooling makes a difference. *Teach. Coll. Rec.*, 46, 483–92.

MCCLEARN, G. E. (1970) Genetic influences on behavior and development. In MUSSEN, P. H. (ed.) *Carmichael's Manual of Child Psychology* (3rd edn), Vol. I. New York: Wiley.

MASON, M. K. (1942) Learning to speak after years of silence. *J. speech hear. Dis.*, 7, 245–304.

MAXWELL, J. (1961) *The Level and Trend of National Intelligence*. Scottish Council for Research in Education, No. 46. London: Univ. of London Press.

MITTLER, P. J. (1971) *The Study of Twins*. Harmondsworth: Penguin.

NEWMAN, H. H., FREEMAN, F. N. and HOLZINGER, K. J. (1937) *Twins: a Study of Heredity and Environment*. Chicago: Univ. of Chicago Press.

ODEN, M. H. (1968) The fulfilment of promise: 40-year follow-up of the Terman Gifted Group. *Genet. Psychol. Monogr.*, 77, 3–93.

OUTHIT, M. C. (1933) A study of the resemblance of parents and children in general intelligence. *Arch. Psychol.* (N. York), No. 149, 60.

OWENS, W. A. (1953) Age and mental abilities: a longitudinal study. *Genet. Psychol. Monogr.*, 48, 3–54.

PENROSE, L. S. (1972) *The Biology of Mental Defect* (4th ed.). London: Sidgwick & Jackson.

President's Committee on Mental Retardation (1972) *Entering the Era of Human Ecology*. Publ. No. (OS) 72–7. Washington, DC: Dept of Health, Education and Welfare.

REED, E. W. and REED, S. C. (1965) *Mental Retardation*. Philadelphia: W. B. Saunders.

ROE, A. (1952) A psychologist examines sixty-four eminent scientists. *Scient. Amer.*, **187**, 21–5.

SCHACHTER, S. (1963) Birth order, eminence and higher education. *Amer. sociol. Rev.*, **28**, 757–68.

SCHAEFER, E. S. (1970) Need for early and continuing education. In DENENBERG, V. H. (ed.) *Education of the Infant and Young Child*. London: Academic Press.

SCHOOLER, C. (1972) Birth order effects: not here, not now! *Psychol. Bull.*, **78**, 161–75.

SHIELDS, J. (1962) *Monozygotic Twins*. London: Oxford Univ. Press.

SKEELS, H. M. (1966) Adult status of children with contrasting early life experiences: a follow-up study. *Monogr. Soc. Res. Child. Developm.*, **31** (105), 3.

SKEELS, H. M. and DYE, H. B. (1939) A study of the effects of differential stimulation on mentally retarded children. *Proc. Amer. Assoc. ment. Defic.*, **44**, 114–36.

SKODAK, M. (1968) Adult status of individuals who experienced early intervention. In RICHARDS, B. W. (ed.) *Proc. 1st Congr. Assoc. Scient. Stud. Ment. Defic.*, 11–18. Reigate: Michael Jackson.

SKODAK, M. and SKEELS, H. M. (1949) A final follow-up study of one hundred adopted children. *J. genet. Psychol.*, **75**, 85–125.

SONTAG, L. W., BAKER, C. T. and NELSON, V. L. (1958) Mental growth and personality development: a longitudinal study. *Monogr. Soc. Res. Child Developm.*, **23** (68), 2.

STEVENSON, H. W. (1972) The taxonomy of tasks. In MÖNKS, F. J., HARTUP, W. H. and DE WIT, J. (eds.) *Determinants of Behavioural Development*. New York and London: Academic Press.

VANDENBERG, S. G. (1966) *The Nature and Nurture of Intelligence*. Paper presented at Conference on Biology and Behaviour, Rockefeller University, New York.

VERNON, P. E. (1957) Intelligence and intellectual stimulation during adolescence. *Indian Psychol. Bull.*, **2**, 1–6.

VERNON, P. E. (1960) *Intelligence and Attainment Tests*. London: Univ. of London Press.

WHITE, S. H. (1965) Evidence for a hierarchical arrangement of learning processes. In LIPSITT, L. P., and SPIKER, C. C. (eds.) *Advances in Child Development and Behaviour*, Vol. 2. New York: Academic Press.

5

J. Tizard

Longitudinal studies: problems and findings

Introduction

Interest in longitudinal and follow-up studies of the retarded derives from several sources. Parents, physicians and administrators are interested in the expectation of life of persons suffering from particular diseases or handicaps, or from conditions which manifest themselves in mental handicap. Teachers want to know how many of the skills taught at school are retained, and what use is made of them. The effect on social competence of education and training is of obvious importance to those responsible for planning training programmes, and decisions about when to recommend institutional care, and under what circumstances to grant leave from institutions, must clearly be influenced by what has happened in the past to other mentally retarded persons. Concern has also been shown over the dysgenic implications of mental defect, and more recently, over the mentally subnormal as parents. In much of the literature these problems have not been treated separately so that the total picture is a confusing one.

Some of the sources of this confusion can be spelled out. Longitudinal studies of the mentally handicapped cannot be interpreted unless they take into account: (a) biological differences between so-called high-grade and low-grade defectives; (b) differences between 'pathological', 'clinical' or 'organic' mentally handicapped people on the one hand, and 'aclinical', 'endogenous' or 'subcultural' retardates on the other; (c) the distinction between low intelligence and mental retardation; (d) what is known of the epidemiology of mental handicap, and in particular of the systematic biases that result when generalizations from data relating to samples of diagnosed or 'ascertained' cases of mental retardation are applied to mentally retarded persons not so ascertained.

High-grade and low-grade retardates

The differences between those with handicaps associated with severe (or low-grade) mental defect on the one hand and mild or high-grade mental handicap on the other have been reviewed in Chapters 2 and 3. The severely retarded tend to be stunted physically as well as mentally; their handicaps are often recognizable at birth or during early infancy; they are much more backward in development throughout childhood, and usually remain dependent upon others throughout life; they have a greatly reduced expectation of life; they are rarely fertile; almost all of them suffer from gross structural damage to the brain. However, their relatives tend either to be normal in development or to suffer from severe mental and physical handicaps. Parents of the severely retarded are drawn from all classes of the population and not mainly from one depressed social group.

In all of these respects the mildly retarded differ from the severely retarded and there are indeed very strong reasons for the belief that the two classes of handicap are caused by different agents, and that they necessarily have very different outcomes.

For present purposes the importance of these distinctions lies in the different prognosis of persons diagnosed as either mildly or severely retarded.

In view of the importance of grade (i.e. severity) of mental handicap as a determinant of behaviour it would be valuable for clinical, as well as for statistical, purposes to specify the dividing lines which separate the two groups. There is however no single indicator, no sharp dividing line, and in 'borderline' cases the differential diagnosis is a matter of judgment. The best single indicator is IQ, but since the distribution of IQs in the population forms a continuum, to take any particular IQ as marking the boundary must be to some extent arbitrary (Tizard, 1972a; Chapter 2). In IQ terms earlier writers (e.g. Lewis, 1929) specified an IQ of 45–50 as marking the boundary of severe mental handicap in the case of children; for adults it was placed at about 40 points, though a small number of adults with mental ratios (IQs) in the border zone of 40 to 50 were diagnosed as imbeciles 'because they suffered from serious additional temperamental disabilities, for example, dangerous outbursts of temper'. More recently authorities have tended to use a definition expressed in terms of standard deviation units from the mean. Thus the AAMD Classification (Heber, 1961) has as its cut-off point a level more than 3 standard deviations below the mean (i.e. an IQ of 54 or less on Wechsler Scales or of 51 or less on the revised Stanford Binet Test of Intelligence). This boundary line is also adopted in the eighth revision of the *International Statistical Classification of Diseases, Injuries and Causes of Death* (WHO, 1968). On the other hand, the fifteenth WHO Expert Committee on Mental Health which considered the organization of services for the mentally retarded (WHO, 1968) recommended a cut-off point at IQ 50 (3·3 standard deviations from the mean on a Wechsler scale) and it seems likely that this will be adopted in the ninth revision of the ICD.

Inasmuch as diagnosis is based upon IQ alone, these differences in criteria will result in the same individual being differently classified by different authorities. The problems of classification are further complicated by sampling errors, the use of different tests and assessment procedures, and by the problems of IQ standardization and calibration, particularly as these affect scores which deviate markedly from the mean (see Chapter 2). Despite these uncertainties, there is none the less a substantial measure of agreement among clinicians as to the diagnosis of *severe* mental handicap. Moreover, prevalence rates show a remark-able degree of agreement from one survey to another. By far the most difficult problems arise in regard to the mildly handicapped.

The major reason why it is not meaningful to generalize about the prognosis of the mildly retarded is that the term mental retardation is an administrative one applied to persons who are both intellectually retarded and socially incompetent. This is explicitly recognized in the AAMD Classification of Mental Retardation (Heber, 1961). The Association has devised both behavioural and medical classifications. A critical factor in the AAMD concept of mental retardation is inclusion of the *dual* criteria of reduced intellectual functioning *and* impaired social adaptation. 'It is the impairment of *social* adaptation which calls attention to the individual and determines the need for social or legal action on his behalf as a mentally retarded person; it is the below-average *intellectual* function which distinguishes mental retardation from other disorders of human efficiency.'

As explained in Chapter 2 the phrase 'sub-average general intellectual func-tioning' is defined as performance more than 1 standard deviation below the mean of the standardization sample on the general test of intelligence. Approxi-mately 16 per cent of the population will demonstrate sub-average general intellectual functioning as defined in these terms, 'a figure far exceeding our usual prevalence estimates'. However the Association points out that the majority of those near the cut-off score will not demonstrate significant impairment in adaptive behaviour; where this is found, the sub-average general intellectual functioning is considered to be at least a contributive factor in the adaptive im-pairment. For clinical purposes the use of dual criteria is entirely appropriate, whether or not one regards an IQ of less than 85 as a satisfactory cut-off point to define sub-average general intellectual functioning – see Chapter 2 (WHO, 1968; Tizard, 1972a). Since, however, only one of these criteria, namely intelligence, is as yet measurable – and that imperfectly – it is only in cases of *severe* mental handicap, in which there is a high correlation between adaptive behaviour and measured intelligence, that reliable diagnosis becomes possible.[1]

Recognizing this, psychologists have made a number of attempts – none very successful – to measure social adjustment with the same precision as intelligence is measured. The AAMD classification postulates four levels of impaired adap-tive behaviour and suggests that they be scored in standard deviation units; and a scale to permit this to be done is currently being developed – the AAMD Adaptive Behaviour Scale. To the writer, however, it seems extremely unlikely that psychologists will be any more successful in devising a *valid* 'adaptive behaviour scale' than they have been in devising valid personality measures of traits such as introversion or aggressiveness (see Mischel, 1968, for a critique of attempts to measure traits and states as personality constructs). The problems

[1] In the 1973 Revision of the AAMD *Manual on Terminology and Classification in Mental Retardation* (Grossman, 1973) 'borderline' retardation is no longer recognized; the upper limit of IQ is placed at 2 Standard Deviations below the mean or approximately IQ 70, not IQ 85. See also pp. 30–1.

of assessment of adaptive behaviour are compounded by the fact that the term implies a judgment by others of the character as well as the competencies of the person being judged, and these in the context of a changing social milieu. Barbara Wootton (1959) has discussed the issues that arise in such circumstances in very clear terms:

. . . in a less sophisticated age we should all have said that one of the merits of full employment was that it made it easier for the mental defectives to obtain employment. Now apparently we have to say that it actually reduces the number of such defectives. To appreciate the full significance of this situation we may imagine what would happen if similar reasoning were applied to the analogous case of some incontestable physical disability, such as the loss of a limb. Full employment certainly makes it easier for legless persons to get jobs, but no one in his senses would take it to mean that under full employment there are fewer persons without legs.

She goes on to say:

so long as defectives are subject as they are to legal and other disabilities, the significance of this difference (between criteria dependent and not dependent on social criteria) is more than semantic. If defectives are to be deprived of full civil rights and responsibilities, and even in some cases of their personal freedom, and if the number of defectives varies with the state of the employment market, it follows that some people are liable to lose their status of fully responsible citizens or to be deprived of their liberty merely because employment is bad.

The solution to this problem adopted in the AAMD Classification is that, in assessing mental retardation, *complete* emphasis is to be placed on the present level of functioning of the individual. 'A person may meet the criteria of mental retardation at one age level and not at another; he may change status as a result of "real" changes in level of intellectual functioning; or he may move from retarded to non-retarded as a result of a training programme which has increased his level of adaptive behaviour' (Heber, 1962). This does much to clarify the issues. However, it is important to bear in mind that the limitations inherent in the assessment of intelligence are greatly increased when assessments have to be made of social competence, particularly of persons who do not share, or who only partly share, the cultural background of the clinician. A wealth of experience shows that clinical judgments are usually much more subject to error than are psychometric tests. It follows, therefore, that longitudinal studies of mildly retarded persons are not likely to be very informative, because the initial diagnosis is so subject to error (Tarjan and Eisenberg, 1972).

The social class distribution of organic and subcultural mental handicap

Nearly all severely retarded persons are diagnosable on clinical neurological examination as having abnormalities of function which can reasonably be attributed to organic lesions in the central nervous system. About half of all mentally subnormal children, irrespective of grade of handicap, have definite signs of neurological damage, but this is most frequently found in children with the lowest IQs. Thus, in a major clinical and epidemiological study of mental subnormality in the community, Birch and others (1970) found that three times as many of the children with IQs below 60 had clear evidence of neurological disorder on examination as was the case for mentally subnormal children with IQs equal to or greater than 60. Of 101 mentally subnormal children aged 8 to 10 years in the city of Aberdeen, 50 had signs indicative of organic brain dysfunction. Of these, 36 had IQs below 60 and only 14 had IQs of 60 or more. Among those who did not exhibit central nervous system abnormality upon clinical examination 13 had IQs below 60 and 38 had IQs of 60 or more.

There is also evidence that even among the mildly retarded (those with IQs of 50 or more) children who have demonstrable evidence of central nervous system

TABLE 2. *Social class distribution of mentally subnormal children with IQ $\geqslant$ 50 with and without clinical signs of central nervous system damage (taken from Birch et al., 1970, pp. 69–70)*

Social class of parents	No. of children in population	No. of MS children	
		Without cns damage	With cns damage
Non-manual	2,405	0	1
Skilled manual	3,552	15	10
Unskilled and semi-skilled	2,131	33	14
Total	8,088	48	25

damage do worse educationally than children matched for IQ who do not (Kirk, 1958; Susser, 1968). It is important, therefore, to look at other factors which differentiate between *mildly* handicapped children with and without demonstrable central nervous system damage. Birch *et al.* found, as others have done (Stein and Susser, 1960; Rutter *et al.*, 1970) that not only was there a significant excess of mildly subnormal children contributed by the lower social classes, and a marked under-representation in the upper social classes, but that the distribution of cases with and without clinical evidence of central nervous system damage differed markedly with social class. In Birch's study, *all* mildly retarded children from families in the non-manual social classes had clinical evidence of central nervous system damage. That is, no children with IQs less than 75 who did not also have 'organic' signs were found in the upper social classes. Children with IQs above 50 and with evidence of central nervous system damage were overrepresented in the lower social classes; and in addition, there were three times as many subnormal children among the families of the unskilled and semi-skilled who had no neurological signs. The data are presented in Table 2.

Until recently the differences in the social class distribution of mild mental retardation were explained on a genetical hypothesis: people tend to marry spouses who resemble them in intelligence, and bear children whose intelligence resembles their own (but with some regression to the population mean, see Chapter 7). Stein and Susser (1960), on the basis of findings obtained in the city of Salford, England, which were essentially similar to those obtained later by Birch and his colleagues at Aberdeen, challenged this interpretation. They examined a number of hypotheses to account for their results: a simple genetic theory, a statistical model in terms of regression to the mean, and one based on assortative mating and social mobility. None of these satisfactorily accounted for the data. As Susser (1968) summarizes their argument:

> The social mechanisms of marriage and mobility which might segregate people according to their genes for intelligence, clearly do not have the force to separate the intellectual heritage of the social classes to the degree required to explain the existing distribution. While genetic models alone might conceivably account for much individual variation in intelligence, they cannot be made to account for the gross disparities between the social classes. On the basis of this analysis, one may remain firm in the conviction that most children with mild mental subnormality and with no detectable handicaps to learning suffer from the effects of the environment in which they were reared. The social class gradient of low intelligence is similar to the gradient for those other disorders and attributes that are closely related to social conditions, such as bronchitis, tuberculosis, heights and weights, infant deaths and fertility. A generally accepted interpretation of these social class differences, strongly supported by secular trends, is that they are chiefly the result of social conditions. The improvement in intelligence through time shown in the two Scottish National Education Surveys of 1932 and 1947 leads to the same interpretation (Scottish Council for Research in Education, 1953). These studies show the decline in the percentage of low scorers from 18·7 per cent to 15·4 per cent in a period of 15 years. A similar trend appears in the prevalence of mild mental subnormality in England at periods separated by 30 years. Estimates suggest that in the 1950s there were little more than half as many recognized cases as in the 1920s. Such rapid change must certainly have been the result of changing environment.

Susser believes that it is the non-material rather than the material aspects of culture which are chiefly responsible for this secular trend. The Scottish data indicated that the change was chiefly confined to verbal and scholastic ability and did not affect other abilities. However 'better nutrition, the decline in infectious diseases, and similar factors, cannot easily be dissociated from the non-material aspects of culture. Such factors also vary in accord with the secular changes in low scoring on intelligence tests and with the social class gradient on these tests. For example, children from large families score lower on IQ tests than do children from small families, and even in the 1960s in Britain children from large families eat less well. Nutrition may be connected directly with prematurity, and in turn prematurity has been connected with mental subnormality. Premature births are also associated with poor living conditions and services, so that high rates of prematurity and high prevalence of mild subnormality tend to co-exist. Malnutrition might thus be related to subnormality directly, through a connection with prematurity, or through a coincidental relationship with poverty.'

Birch *et al.* (1970), in an elegant analysis of family characteristics of minimally and borderline subnormal children, looked at size of family, area of residence, degree of crowding, and mother's premarital occupation, singly and in combination, as well as at the sibs of the index cases in their study. They suggest that:

a number of family characteristics distinguish the minimally and borderline subnormal children from other families in social classes IV and V. These characteristics are highly inter-related, and taken together, they identify those groups of the population with low status and aspirations, minimal education, poverty, family disorganisation, and unwillingness or inability to plan the major economic and marital aspects of their lives. Such characteristics serve to identify certain of the families of minimally subnormal children, but by no means all of them.

They postulate a 'micro-environmental setting associated with the highest prevalence of minimally and borderline subnormal children'. However they do not assume that low occupational class, large family size, overcrowding or slum living directly *cause* mental subnormality. Rather,

children born to parents who have themselves been inadequately housed, nourished, and educated, are at risk to a variety of hazards – pre-natal, peri-natal, and post-natal – and the combined weight of such hazards and interaction produces mental subnormality in a substantial proportion of those who survive. Improvements in the standards of medical care must be accompanied by improvement in education and social welfare if we are to reduce the numbers of minimally subnormal children.

These epidemiological studies of mental retardation carried out in Britain give rise to two broad sets of conclusions. First, demographically it is well established that (a) there is a social class gradient in mental retardation which is particularly marked in the case of mild mental retardation; (b) there is an almost complete absence of aclinical or endogenous mental retardation among children of non-manual parents, and a greatly reduced prevalence of organic retardation; (c) prevalence rates both of severe mental handicap (Goodman and Tizard, 1962; Tizard, 1964) and of mild mental handicap have fallen during the last thirty years. Second, case studies of individual retardates show that disproportionately more of them come from certain families and types of family among the unskilled working class (see above, also Heber and Dever, 1970).

There seems little doubt that the first set of findings can be accounted for in environmental terms. As standards of living rise, and as more attention is paid to the health and welfare of mothers and young children, so the proportion of handicapped children decreases. Where living conditions remain poor, and people are ignorant, the cycle of deprivation and handicap recurs. This is true both of handicaps associated with organic signs of central nervous system dysfunction, and of those which lead to a diagnosis of 'endogenous' mental handicap in childhood. There is evidence that the educational progress of children in the two groups differs – but we know much less about differences in adult adjustment.

The second set of problems, as to why it is that within what is in many respects a fairly homogeneous lower working class environment some families appear to be much more vulnerable than others, raises quite different questions. Do individuals select, so to speak, certain types of environment in which they 'find their own level' in society and reproduce their like in conditions which they themselves help to perpetuate? Why should some people and not others be affected in this way? Can anything be done to help them?

There is some evidence that lends support to the view that certain types of vulnerable personality do, in a sense, select particular types of environment. Thus, recent research in another field, namely that of the relations between social class and schizophrenia, has suggested that the high social class gradient (many more schizophrenics among the unskilled working-class population than among those in non-manual occupations) may have been brought about by occupational shifts: the fathers of schizophrenics are a cross-section of the working population, but the index cases 'drift' into unskilled occupations because their illness, or the personality factors which predispose them to their illness, prevent them from making use of available opportunities to improve or maintain their lot (see Birtchnell, 1971, for an excellent treatment of this complex problem). Similarly British studies (Birch *et al.*, 1970; Rutter *et al.*, 1970) which have examined the *grandparents* of educationally and intellectually backward children have shown them to be similar in social class distribution to grandparents of children in a control group. The social differences associated with intellectual retardation and with educational handicap had, in these studies, existed for only a single generation. In the Rutter *et al.* study it was noted that the over-representation of unskilled workers among the fathers of the intellectually and educationally backward was the result of different patterns of intergenerational mobility. There tended to be *downward* occupational mobility among the parents of the children with intellectual or educational retardation, but *upward* occupational mobility among the control group. It was thought possible that educational difficulties in the parents of the backward children might have been responsible for their downward mobility. Compared with the control group, over twice as many of the children with intellectual or reading retardation had parents who reported that they themselves had been backward in their schooling or had had great difficulty in learning to read. Unfortunately, in this study the numbers were

too small to test, within groups, the association of parental difficulties and downward social mobility.

The significance of the Aberdeen and Isle of Wight studies lies in the demonstration that in societies in which geographical and occupational mobility is not
sharply restricted, and in which social conditions are improving, it is not the
case that the majority of the backward come from a 'submerged tenth' of the
population which has remained in the lowest social strata for generations. On the
other hand, short-term, intergenerational effects have been shown.

Detailed studies both of the biomedical and social characteristics of vulnerable
groups of families and of the life histories of individuals who at one point in time
were known to have been 'handicapped' also throw light on specific factors
which influence the course of their development. In doing so they indicate
possible areas for intervention. Birch and Gussow (1970) have for example
reviewed the numerous studies on relations between low birth weight and
subsequent development, and have shown convincingly that seemingly contradictory findings regarding outcome can be reconciled if one looks at characteristics of the low birth weight child's *subsequent* environment. Except in the case
of children with very low birth weights who have suffered organic damage,
where the subsequent environment is benign the children develop normally;
where it is adverse they fall behind their sibs and other children growing up in
similar circumstances. In broad terms there are complex interactions between
adverse biomedical factors at one point in time and subsequent biomedical and
social circumstances which affect development. (Work in progress indicates that
the development of children hospitalized for severe malnutrition in Jamaica
during the first two years of life is similarly influenced by the characteristics of
the environment they return to: if this favours their physical growth – and is
presumably also favourable in other ways – they are, during their years of primary
schooling, similar in IQ and in their educational attainments to their sibs and to
children of the same age in the same classes at school. If however the environment is such that they remain short in stature, they are also stunted intellectually
and educationally.) We have here, then, one group of factors which can be shown
to affect the development of vulnerable children.

Today psychologists are also examining factors in the *social* environment
during infancy and early childhood which may be of crucial significance for
later development. A widely publicized study by Heber and associates (Heber
and Dever, 1970; Heber, 1971) which, however, has not as yet been written up
in any detail in the scientific press, reports striking gains in IQ and in social
competence among *all* of a group of twenty children, of Negro mothers having
IQs of 75 or less, who were subjected to an infant stimulation programme which
began at the age of 3 months. As part of this study an intensive habilitation
programme for mothers was also undertaken. Preliminary data indicate a rapid
acceleration of intellectual development on the part of experimental subjects
whose performance is uniformly high, as contrasted with that of control groups
where only about a fourth of the children test at or above test norms, the

remainder trending towards sub-average performance. The difference between children in the experimental and control groups has increased with time, and it is a matter of the greatest interest to know how these children will fare in school, now that the oldest are reaching the age of school entry (see Chapter 4).

Essentially similar results have been reported, in preliminary form, by Robinson and Robinson (1971), on the basis of work done in an experimental nursery which provided for disadvantaged infants and pre-school children. They found differences between experimental and control groups at 18 months, and at ages 2-4 years Negro children attending the Centre attained a mean Stanford-Binet IQ of approximately 120 as opposed to a control Negro mean IQ of approximately 86. 'The crucial variables of day care, educational and health programmes cannot be identified in a pilot study, but that the "package" made a difference in the lives of the children is unmistakable.' The findings of these two studies are in agreement with Hindley's data (1968) on social class differences in the developing intelligence of young children in middle-class and working-class homes. They are in sharp contrast to those obtained in most Head-Start Programmes in which, however, instruction does not begin normally until the fourth year of life (see Chapter 4).

It is too early to say whether the preliminary findings of Heber and the Robinsons will hold up over time, and if they do, to what extent the improvement will be attributable to specific teaching, better nutrition and health care, or a more benign social environment in which kindly and consistent individual attention is given to children by the same maternal figure. Whatever the reason, if it is found that early intervention can cure or prevent most mild mental handicap, while later intervention is much less effective, the implications for mental retardation will indeed be profound, and the problems of prognosis will be seen in an entirely new light. So far the evidence in favour of this highly attractive hypothesis is by no means substantial; and until much more work has been done, and the findings have been replicated by others, most people will reserve judgment about their generality – without wishing to dismiss them or to deny their importance.

Mental handicap and low intelligence

Finally on this matter it should be added that one conclusion which has been drawn over and over again from longitudinal studies begun in early childhood is that 'intervention' at one point in time is unlikely to have long-term results unless there is 'follow-through' in the ameliorative effort. Eisenberg and Connors (1968), summarizing data on the beneficial effects of Project Head-Start Programmes upon the intellectual development of young children, have put the argument for this point of view succinctly. We are, they say, 'far from convinced that the gains (which they report) will endure, given the over-crowding, educational impoverishment, and generally negative attitudes towards the poor that characterize inner-city elementary schools. We would not, after all, anticipate that a good diet at age five would protect a child against malnutrition at age six. The mind, like the brain, requires alimentation – biochemical, physiological, and cognitive – at every stage of its development.' At present knowledge even about long-term effects of malnutrition and dietary deficiency upon the development of brain tissue is fairly sketchy; knowledge about mental alimentation scarcely exists at all. The real advance that has been made in the developmental sciences during the last decade or so has come from a realization that growth and development cannot be understood without detailed studies of the timing as well as the duration of a multitude of specific factors, interacting in highly complex ways to produce different outcomes. A very similar view is expressed in Chapter 4.

Until we know very much more about the specific determinants of growth and behaviour, firm conclusions about, for example, the relative contribution of hereditary and environmental influences is unwarranted. In short, as Birch and Gussow (1970) put it, 'the genetic inferiority theory which many have found insupportable can more properly be described as presently unsupportable, and non-intervention on the basis of such a theory is therefore clearly unjustified'.

Epidemiological considerations

As has already been indicated, longitudinal studies of children initially ascertained through administrative, educational referral to be 'mentally retarded' represent only a proportion of the numbers who would be so diagnosed if other criteria were uniformly applied to all persons in a population. Ascertained cases are, however, likely to include a higher proportion of the multiply handicapped, and of those with the most severe problems. Results cannot, therefore, be generalized unless it is established how typical such cases are.

The importance of taking these selective factors into account can be seen from the Wessex data and from any study of special school provision and its consequences. Thus Kushlick's study in Wessex showed that even if we consider only severely mentally retarded persons, something like a third of these were unknown to the authorities responsible for planning services. One simply cannot say from what is known about the numbers of ascertained cases what is happening to the others. When we move from severe to mild mental handicap the difficulties of working epidemiologically become insuperable, and usually the best that one can do is to review administratively collected data in the hope that they may provide rough guidelines for future practice, or give an inkling as to factors which might cause us to modify practice in the future. The issues raised here have been more fully discussed in other reviews: see, for example, Gruenberg (1964); Birch et al. (1970); Kushlick and Blunden (1974); Susser and Watson (1962); Susser (1968); Tizard (1972c). A lucid general discussion of methodological issues involved in longitudinal studies is contained in Wall and Williams (1970).

The longitudinal study of mildly retarded persons

Literally hundreds of studies have been published describing the life histories of persons who at one point in their lives have been regarded as mentally retarded. A valuable review has been written by Goldstein (1964) and an annotated bibliography of research up to 1966 has been prepared by Cobb and his associates; the same writers have undertaken an analysis of the literature up to 1969. Together these two reports assemble virtually all that has been published on this problem; they make a definitive statement of the issues which surround it. Because of Cobb's review and because many other, briefer summaries of the literature are readily available it is not proposed to assess the field once again. Instead, some conclusions, taken partly from Cobb but with additional comments, will be presented, together with an Appendix summarizing a few of the major studies, the findings and methods of which are fairly typical of those reported in other but less adequate studies.

Cobb ends his exhaustive review of the 'outcomes' of research with the statement that 'no neat and certain formulae for predicting adult success in the retardate have been achieved. To the contrary, if there is one clear conclusion to be drawn from this array of studies, it is that no simple formula for prediction is possible, that the relationship between predictors and criteria are enormously complex, and that outcome in terms of personal, social and vocational success are the product of manifold interactive determinants.' With this one can only agree. The 'problem' is essentially a practical one; to look for general solutions is misguided.

The main findings of research studies can conveniently be grouped under eight headings.

(1) DIAGNOSIS OF MILD RETARDATION

Identification (or 'ascertainment') of the mildly retarded almost always occurs during the years of compulsory schooling, most commonly with children at an age when the basic educational skills of reading and arithmetic are being mastered and made use of by ordinary children – that is, from the age of 8 or so. The identification of a child as mentally retarded generally follows from school failure. Not all school failures are of course diagnosed as mentally retarded. Moreover, formal ascertainment as retarded may not take place until the years of secondary schooling. In such cases however the child is likely to have been known to his teachers as educationally backward well before he is designated as mentally retarded. Some children are recognized (by parents, doctors, or others) to be developmentally backward, or intellectually slow. These, too, are likely to be later identified as mentally retarded (Illingworth, 1966).

Backward children most likely to be called mentally retarded are those of different ethnic origin, those of low socio-economic status, those living in poor environmental circumstances, and those in large families. Such children tend also to test low on IQ tests. In perhaps a majority of cases retarded children coming from adverse backgrounds suffer from more than one of the associated (from an educational point of view in contemporary Britain or the USA) disadvantages (see Birch *et al.*, 1970; Mercer, 1970; Heber and Dever, 1970; Rutter *et al.*, 1970).

(2) EDUCATIONAL BACKWARDNESS AND MENTAL RETARDATION

Some educationally retarded children, including a higher proportion of those who are most seriously handicapped educationally, are referred for special schooling in special classes or schools. One would expect the results of this special schooling to be unequivocably beneficial, in that the children are taught in smaller classes, and often by specially trained teachers. There is, however, little firm evidence to support the view that special schooling offers great advantages; instead, results of controlled studies are highly equivocal (Goldstein *et al.*, 1965; Blackman, 1967; Dunn, 1954; Goldstein, 1964, 1967; Goldstein *et al.*, 1969; Tizard, 1970). In a comment on this puzzling finding Goldstein *et al.* (1969) pointed out that the majority of investigations into the efficacy of special classes have concerned themselves mainly with actuarial and administrative variables related to special class composition and organization. Child variables are usually confined to traditional psychometric and socio-economic data. Teacher variables are rarely considered. Programme variables, where referred to at all, are stated in rather gross terms. It is assumed that the fact that teachers and children are together in a special classroom implies the presence of an educational programme *relevant* to the development of the children; also, that the presence of a teacher in a special class ensures the competence of the teacher to provide an effective educational programme; and thirdly, that a relevant educational programme and a competent teacher imply that the administration and management of the educational programme is systematic and methodologically appropriate for retarded children.

In practice none of these desiderata have been met. Even if they were, one could still add a fourth criticism of published experimental studies of the effects of special schooling. What is the value of showing – if indeed it can be shown – that specially trained teachers working with special programmes, smaller classes and in an appropriate educational milieu achieve better results than teachers who are not specially trained, who work with much larger classes of children, without special help, and in an educationally impoverished and inappropriate milieu? Demonstration projects can explore the value of new ideas or techniques, but for educational purposes the most useful comparisons are likely to be those which explore alternative ways of employing scarce resources – of specialist teachers, educational psychologists, technical aids and the like. One would like to see, therefore, studies in which equivalent resources were made available to teachers of children in ordinary schools and to teachers in special schools or classes. No such studies have as yet been carried out.

(3) MENTAL RETARDATION AND LOW INTELLIGENCE

A diagnosis of mild retardation implies that the person so diagnosed has a measured IQ which is substantially below the average. However, placement in a special class, as has been mentioned, is made on the basis of *educational* criteria rather than mental test performance. Hence as many as 40 per cent of 'educationally subnormal' children in special classes (in England) may have IQs which are greater than 70. These relatively bright children are however among those who are *educationally* the most backward: that is why they are placed in special classes. Similarly, in England and probably in most other countries, at least three times as many children with IQs less than 70 remain in ordinary classes. Such children are more likely to be girls than boys – in England there are three boys to every two girls in special schools for the educationally subnormal, though the number of girls with IQs below 70 is actually slightly higher than that of boys (Rutter *et al.*, 1970). The reason is clear. Boys give more trouble in school than girls.

This fact raises awkward problems for follow-up studies, since initial diagnosis is likely to be based on a hotchpotch of factors which differ from one place, and from one time, to another.

(4) CONSTANCY OF THE IQ

Low intelligence is a *sine qua non* of mental retardation but, as has been mentioned earlier, low intelligence is not synonymous with mental retardation. In general the IQ is a fairly stable measure over time, but in individual cases the prediction of IQ in adult life from scores obtained in childhood is subject to considerable error (see Chapter 4). Within the mildly subnormal range of IQ intelligence is a poor predictor of adult adjustment.

(5) CRITERIA OF ADULT ADJUSTMENT

Cobb states that the problem of defining and measuring the criteria of adult adjustment has been approached but by no means resolved. Older follow-up studies tended to use rather simple and readily tabulated biographical data: actual employment, marriage and divorce or separation, court convictions, institutional recidivism. Cobb himself is critical of this approach. He seems to regard factor scores based on factor analysis of correlational data as being more likely to provide answers to the 'problems of heterogeneity in the criterion variable'. If, however, we see the problem of prediction of adult adjustment as essentially a practical one, studies such as that by Stevens (1964) in which 'a factor analysis of 80 continuous point scales together with an additional 61 dichotomous variables' is carried out 'in an attempt to define systematically the full range of relevant criteria' look like using a computerized sledgehammer to crack a conceptual nut. In other words, all that can come out of sophisticated correlational analyses of 'criteria' is something we already know, namely that we cannot substitute one for another: people who are well adjusted in employment are not necessarily happily married, and those who are happily married are not necessarily law-abiding citizens. Hence, in sticking to simple and socially relevant criteria, the older studies were, if this view is accepted, working on the right lines. Analyses which substitute indirect measures for direct ones tend on the whole not to be useful.

(6) ACTUAL ADJUSTMENT IN ADULT LIFE

The conclusion to be drawn from studies such as that by Kennedy (1966) and by Baller et al. (1966) which are summarized in the Appendix is that:

> in terms of the criteria of employment, marriage and law abiding behaviour, studies over 50 years have shown that a high proportion of those identified as mildly retarded make satisfactory adjustments. Without any special service or treatment, they tend to disappear into the general lower class population from which they are hardly distinguishable as a social group . . . All of the major longitudinal studies report identifiable shifting from early instability to relatively increased stability over time. Thus, as compared with a non-retarded control group, the retarded show a higher incidence of marital, civic and occupational failure, especially in the early stages. The difference, however, tends to diminish over time. The group identified as retarded still tends to retain a difference in frequency of unsatisfactory adaptations from non-retarded controls, but these frequencies are relatively small and decreasing. (Cobb, 1969)

Cobb, like most writers, points out that this tendency is consistent with a hypothesis of cultural deprivation from which recovery is possible over time and with improvement in environmental conditions. What most psychologists do not also point out is that effects such as these are also consistent with a psycho-biological hypothesis of delayed maturation. There is no necessary contradiction between these two viewpoints – cultural and material poverty could conceivably delay psycho-biological maturation. (The situation is not dissimilar from that which obtains in regard to psychopathy and delinquency – both of these social disorders are most commonly found among young people, and show a decreasing prevalence with age.)

(7) PERSONALITY

The work which has been done on personality factors affecting adjustment is much more inconclusive than the studies of competencies and of intelligence. In general, tests and rating of personality 'factors' have proved of little value (Menolascino, 1970). Behaviour checklists, and factors such as those relating to employment, marriage and delinquency offer much more scope, and are in general more useful predictors of future behaviour.

(8) INSTITUTIONAL STUDIES

A special interest has attached to studies of mentally retarded persons who are or have been in institutional care, because, contrary to the expectations of institution staff, numerous investigations have shown that a high proportion of patients discharged to the community make a reasonably adequate social adjustment there. A painstaking review of published work has been undertaken by Windle (1962), and Cobb's reviews of this literature are as competent as his analysis of the rest of the field. No general interpretation of findings obtained from institutional studies can be given because in most of the early ones the only patients to be discharged were those carefully pre-selected for discharge – or those who escaped from legal detention. The latter group were, not unnaturally, difficult to trace – and if traced they were in any case usually classed as having 'failed' in the community because they were picked up and returned to the institution.

Conclusions

In the changing situation in which nearly all patients admitted to institutional care in Britain, as in some other countries, come in voluntarily and remain as voluntary 'patients', the problem of 'success' following discharge ceases to be of much importance. Readmissions to residential care are common – and why not? Today we see residential care in a different light. We see that whether or not a retardate ever goes into an institution in the first place depends upon a host of factors: the amount of provision available, the admission policy adopted, the alternative provision for care or education in the community, the community attitudes to mental retardates, the state of the labour market, the circumstances both material and social of the retardate's own family, the advice and help that the retardate and his family are given, the retardate's own handicaps both physical and mental. Similarly it has become obvious that how long a patient stays in hospital is also dependent upon a large number of factors, only a few of which relate to the personal qualities of the patient. The discharge or rehabilitation policy may be liberal or conservative; the community services may be generous or inadequate – in the way of opportunities for employment in the open market or in sheltered workshops in the case of adults, or in special classes or schools, or day hospitals, in the case of children or very severely handicapped adults; and the availability of services depends upon their proximity or on the transport which is provided. Furthermore the provision of hostels or alternative forms of residential care outside hospital greatly influences discharge policies, and the amount of social work which is provided profoundly affects the willingness of families to have a mentally retarded person at home on trial, and the extent to which they can cope with his problems. Such casework also assists in the finding of jobs for the retardate and in enabling families to deal with problems which are not related to his presence but which decrease their general efficiency and happiness and thus indirectly make it more difficult for them to cope with him at home.

Likewise, how long a patient stays outside an institution is today seen to be dependent upon constellations of factors which differ for different individuals living in differing environments. To regard the return to the community as 'success' and placement in a hospital or institution as 'failure' leads to the reactionary and absurd conclusions that the fewer beds there are available for the mentally disordered the better a country's health service. Judged by this Spain and Egypt are more advanced than England, and Mexico and Brazil more advanced than the United States.

Baller *et al.*'s study (1966) and that by Kennedy (1948) – see Appendix – and similar investigations carried out of the after careers of institutional defectives, make further purely descriptive studies of little general interest. It can indeed be said that half a century of investigations has done little more than correct the false ideas that have been put forward during the same period. The twentieth century discovered and gave labels to the high-grade retardate; perhaps his problems should now be seen in the wider context of providing adequate medical, social and educational services for all who are disadvantaged or handicapped. High level generalizations about prognosis have been, and are likely to remain, banal. Research can however make a contribution to the elucidation of *specific* problems. A valuable review of factors influencing employment has been prepared by Clarke and Clarke (1972), and similar, analytical studies of factors influencing other aspects of social adjustment are very much needed.

Appendix

LONGITUDINAL STUDIES OF INDIVIDUAL RETARDATES

Comprehensive reviews and summaries of longitudinal studies of persons who at one time or other during the course of their lives were classified as mentally retarded have been published by Goldstein (1964) and Cobb (1966, 1969). The following synopsis of some of the principal studies is intended merely for illustrative purposes: to give examples of some of the more influential studies (including older ones as well as more recent ones). Differences in methodological sophistication, the representativeness of the samples, the opportunities made available to the retardates and the economic situation at the time the investigations were carried out, as well as differences in the problems posed by the researchers, make quantitative comparisons between one inquiry and another unprofitable.

Goddard, H. H. (1910, 1912, 1914)

Goddard's famous studies purporting to show the overwhelming importance of heredity in mental retardation were based on three assumptions: (1) that mental defect could be diagnosed from reports about an individual's conduct;

(2) that the condition was determined wholly by heredity; (3) that it was incurable.

His first study, which was reported in a paper read to the American Breeders' Association in 1910, went into the family histories of a number of mental defectives at the Vineland Institution. Charts were produced showing the presence of mental defect in the families for generation after generation. No comment or conclusion was offered by Goddard, but the material itself strongly suggested to the audience the transmission of defect in a typical Mendelian way (Davies, 1930).

A year later this material was used by Davenport as the basis for formulating a clearly expressed statement about the transmission of mental defect. He says

. . . there are laws on inheritance of general mental ability that can be sharply expressed. Low mentality is due to the *absence* of some factor, and if this factor that determines normal development is lacking in both parents, it will be lacking in all of their offspring. *Two mentally defective parents will produce only mentally defective offspring.* This is the first law of inheritance of mental ability. It has now been demonstrated by the study of scores of families at the Vineland Training School for defectives by Dr H. H. Goddard . . . The second law of heredity of mentality is that, aside from 'Mongolians', probably no imbecile is born except of parents who, if not mentally defective themselves, both carry mental defect in their germ plasm.

In 1912 Goddard published a study of the Kallikak family, purporting to show the transmission of mental defect in one family through five generations. (An earlier work on the Juke family published by Dugdale in 1910, which is also very well known, had been concerned with criminality and destitution rather than with mental defect, but about this time a further history of the family was written up, and the findings reinterpreted in terms of mental subnormality by Estabrook, 1915.)

Goddard published a second volume (1914) in which he presented 327 family histories of feeble-minded persons. This study can be regarded as the first major scientific attempt to discuss the hereditary aspects of mental deficiency in a systematic way. The data were collected by three field workers, and information was obtained about no fewer than 13,711 persons. Attempts were made to check the reliability of the data by having some families visited independently by more than one investigator; mental tests were used for the first time in a social inquiry, and alternative hypotheses to account for the facts were examined. In these respects the investigations were an advance not only over previous studies, but also over many which have followed them. Goddard traced his families back for several generations, deciding in each case whether an individual had been feeble-minded or not:

Three generations back is easy, and six is not impossible. It is not difficult for one versed in the subject to tell whether or not a man was feeble-minded even though he lived 100 years ago, providing he made enough impression upon his time for traditions of him to have come down . . . any person living or dead who was so abnormal that his neighbours or friends or descendants always spoke of him as 'not quite right' is certain to have been decidedly defective. (pp. 28–9)

Following Goddard's example, other investigators added to the list of families such as the Jukes and the Kallikaks (see Louttit, 1947, for reference to these studies). His work thus had a widespread influence on psychologists both in the United States and in this country. It formed a basis for the first article on mental defect to appear in the *Encyclopaedia Britannica* (1919). As late as 1933 Pintner cited the conclusions uncritically in his chapter on feeble-mindedness in Murchison's *A Handbook of Child Psychology*, summing up as follows: 'The chief cause of feeble-mindedness is heredity. Numerous family histories support this contention. A very small proportion of cases is due to disease or accident. There is at present no cure. The care and control of the feeble-minded consists of education, segregation, and sterilization' (p. 838).

As a comment it should perhaps be said that contemporary writing about mental handicap is highly critical of the work of Goddard and his followers: indeed nearly all that has been written since the first world war about the natural history of retarded persons has contradicted or qualified his basic postulates.

Fernald, W. E. (1919)

During the closing years of the nineteenth century and the first quarter of the present one, W. E. Fernald was the most influential medical superintendent of a mental deficiency institution in America. Throughout most of his life his attitude to the patients under his care was primitive and pessimistic. Wolfensberger (1969) has given an authoritative analysis of the mood of the period and an account of Fernald's part in shaping it (see also Davies, 1930; and Kanner, 1964). The following quotation accurately expresses Fernald's views reiterated on many occasions:

The social and economic burdens of uncomplicated feeble-mindedness are only too well known. The feeble-minded are a parasitic, predatory class, never capable of self-support or of managing their own affairs. The great majority ultimately become public charges in some form. They cause unutterable sorrow at home and are a menace and danger to the community. Feeble-minded women are almost invariably immoral and if at large usually become carriers of venereal disease or give birth to children who are as defective as themselves . . . Every feeble-minded person, especially the high-grade imbecile, is a potential criminal, needing only the proper environment and opportunity for the development and expression of his criminal tendencies. (Quoted in Davies, 1930)

In 1919, however, Fernald published the results of a survey he had undertaken of all patients who had left Waverly State School – which he ran – during the years 1890–1914. The findings were 'so much at variance with the then accepted theories dealing with mental deficiency' that he hesitated for two years to publish the results of this study. Fernald's work led others to carry out similar inquiries (reviewed in Goldstein, 1964) which had essentially similar results. The bleak, hostile stereotype of the incurable, irredeemable moron was shown to be false.

Subjects. These were 1,537 retardates who had left the institution between 1890–1914, of whom 612 had been transferred to other institutions and 279 could not be traced.

Method. Letters were sent to friends or relatives of the remaining 646 former patients (176 females, 470 males). A social worker then visited the community and questioned agency personnel, police, ministers of religion and others about the retardate. Findings were tabulated and analysed.

Results. Thirty-five per cent of females had been readmitted to institutional care, 14 per cent had died, and 51 per cent remained in the community. Of these 52 (58 per cent) were not presenting problems: 11 were married and keeping house, 8 were totally self-supporting and independent, 20 worked at home and 13 lived at home without working. There were 38 females (42 per cent) who presented problems: mainly sexual offences, alcoholism and theft. However, only 4 had been sent to prison.

Of the men 24 per cent had been readmitted and 12 per cent had died, while 64 per cent had remained in the community. Only 13 out of the 305 such men had married; wives were judged to be normal as were the 12 children born to them. Of the total group 28 were self-supporting and living independently; 86 were employed but living at home; 77 worked at home; and 55 lived at home but contributed little to the family. Only 32 had been sentenced to prison or detention centre, though during the twenty-five-year period another 23 had been arrested but not sent to prison.

Most of those employed were in unskilled jobs but some were doing skilled or semi-skilled work. In general those who were contributing nothing to their families were among the most retarded, while those in skilled work were among the least retarded.

Community adjustment both of men and women appeared to be related to the amount of guidance and support available either from the retardate's relatives or from others in the community.

Remarks. As Goldstein (1964), from whom the above summary is taken, noted, once this study was published administrators and workers in institutions were faced with a question: If some mentally retarded persons with serious records of misbehaviour, who had been discharged from the institution under protest of the administration, could make adequate adjustment in their communities despite minimal training, chance placement, and chance supervision, what might be expected of those who received relevant training, selective placement and supportive supervision?

The history of rehabilitation and habilitation services over the last fifty years can be viewed as a series of attempts to provide data to answer this question. The following eight studies are representative of the inquiries that have been published.

Bronner, A. F. (1933)

Subjects. Cases referred to Judge Baker Foundation.

Results. Three studies reported. In the first, 189 'defectives' with IQs between 75 and 103 were followed up over at least four years with these results: 53 per cent successful (i.e. regular work and no trouble caused); 21 per cent failures (irregular work, or court records, or placed in institution); 26 per cent doubtful (unstable work record, or caused concern through petty misdemeanour). Second study: 50 defectives, mean IQ 68, all with IQs under 75, matched for age and crime with 50 non-defectives, mean IQ 96, range 90–110. Defectives 20 per cent success; non-defectives 16 per cent success, defined as above. For a group of first offenders, 39 per cent success for defectives; 54 per cent success for non-defectives. Third study: 500 adolescents on probation, of whom 19 per cent were defectives. Five-year follow-up. Of 400 boys, non-defectives 44 per cent success; defectives 40 per cent success; of 100 girls, non-defectives 84 per cent success; defectives 68 per cent success.

General remarks

Summarizing the three independently conducted researches, it seems thoroughly justifiable to conclude that the defective, even the defective who in childhood or adolescence presents a problem serious enough to warrant referral to a guidance centre for study, may be so managed that he stands a fair chance of becoming no great burden to the community . . . equated for type and degree of offence there is little difference in outcome as related to intelligence.

Fairbank, R. F. (1933)

Subjects. These were 122 adults from a group of 166 who had been ascertained as mentally defective seventeen years before. Adjustment compared with that of 90 adults who had been regarded as normal children. Also 173 children of the 'defective' group, of whom 79 were at school and 64 given Stanford-Binet test.

Results. Totally self-supporting: 78 per cent as against 88 per cent for 'normal' group. Remainder: partially self-supporting 5 per cent, receiving family assistance 10 per cent, living with parents 4 per cent, state care or widow's pension 3 per cent. Owned or buying a home: 30 per cent as against 24 per cent for the 'normal' group; and 16 per cent as against 36 per cent were saving money.

More marriages and slightly more sex delinquency among subnormals; more dependence on charitable organizations; living conditions were not so good as those of the 'normals'; more juvenile court records but the police records were about the same; less migration to better parts of the city. Of their children only 3 were defective with a mean IQ of 66; 24 were dull, mean IQ 89; 7 were average, mean IQ 109; 4 were of superior intelligence, mean IQ 118.

General remarks. This study was carried out during the economic depression of the 1930s and ran counter to the predictions of Campbell who had considered that self-support was impossible for 22 of the original group, and a 'dubious probability for the remaining 144'.

Abel, T. M. and Kinder, E. F. (1942)

Subjects. Eighty-four mentally subnormal girls placed in industry over a three-year period, beginning work at age of 17. IQ range 50–90 on Otis Scale.

Method. Trained for from one to two years in adjustment classes in New York City, learning simpler processes of women's garment-making. Placed doing similar work; followed up by placement officer of their school; social worker visited their homes periodically. If not able to be placed on machine work, sent as factory workers doing packing or other unskilled work. Employers not told they were subnormal.

Results. During first year half the girls succeeded in one concern; 35 per cent unable to hold a job for more than two weeks. In third year, 55 per cent worked steadily in one concern, half total number doing work for which trade training was useful, and others doing light packing and factory work; 20 per cent failed. Remainder partially successful, working steadily for less than trade union rates. Factors contributing to success were IQ, other aspects of personality, employers' attitudes, work drive or ambition, home stability and luck.

General remarks. The book gives a useful, mainly qualitative account of the major problems of subnormal adolescent girls during the 1930s, and of the exacerbation of their problems through the economic depression. The authors comment that better placement could have been secured if more time had been given to training.

Ramer, T. (1946)

Subjects. These were 626 special school pupils and 589 control cases in Stockholm, born 1905–17. Purpose: to examine how many had failed in life, had to apply for public assistance, became invalids or were delinquents. S. between 26 and 38 years of age at the time of inquiry. IQs as children mainly 70–84.

Method. Examination of official records concerning outdoor relief, invalid pension, drunkenness, court records, etc. (It should be remembered that Swedish social records are extremely well kept.)

Results. More of the subnormal from broken families or from unstable homes; lower social status on the whole. Higher mortality, lower marriage rate, higher divorce rate, more in unskilled jobs. One in three of special class pupils and one in five of controls had been in receipt of poor relief or invalid pensions. More of subnormal group in institutions. No differences in criminal record or in types of crime. Twice as many of the *controls* in trouble for vagrancy. Little difference in alcholism.

General remarks. ' "Temperament" plays a greater part in criminality than intelligence.' Study very carefully carried out and appropriate statistical comparisons made. Data are not, however, analysed separately for the period of the economic depression and the later period of full employment. A valuable review of European literature given.

Hoyle, J. S. (1951)

Subjects. Mentally defective persons under supervision in the City of Leeds. Comparison made between situation in 1929 and 1949. (Both high-grade and low-grade cases are included.)

Method. Analysis of official returns.

Results. In 1929, of 772 defectives under supervision 12 per cent lived under good home conditions; 79 per cent under fair conditions; and 9 per cent under poor ones. In 1949, the corresponding figures were 66 per cent, 31 per cent, and 3 per cent. In 1929, 12 per cent over 16 years of age were self-supporting; 39 per cent partially self-supporting; 12 per cent useful at home; 29 per cent unemployable; and 8 per cent out of work. Corresponding figures for 1949 were 44 per cent, 20 per cent, 9 per cent, 26 per cent, and 1 per cent. An Industrial Centre employs 53 youths and 30 girls, included in the 'partially self-supporting group'. Full employment and better social services are responsible for the change

Hilliard, L. T. (1956)

Subjects. These were 250 feeble-minded women admitted to the Fountain Hospital between 1946–55, and placed in an eighty-bed hostel.

Method. Of all admissions 152, i.e. 60 per cent, have been discharged from the MD Act, and a further 40 employed in the community on licence – 12 in residential jobs, and 28 in daily employment. Six have been placed under Guardianship. 'Of 250 consecutive feeble-minded patients dealt with in this hospital under the MD Act, more than 75 per cent are living or working in the community.' Of the 152 discharged patients, 21 (14 per cent) subsequently married.

Ferguson, I. and Kerr, A. W. (1955, 1958)

Two studies describe the after-histories of girls and boys who left special schools for educable mentally handicapped (ESN) children in Glasgow.

Subjects. These were 207 women, 22 years of age, who were consecutive school-leavers from special schools for the educationally subnormal in Glasgow six years previously; 225 men aged about 25 who had left similar schools nine years previously.

Method. Study of records, and by interview.

Results.

The final impression left by the performance (of both boys and girls) is one of amazement that they have been so successful in holding jobs, even in their middle twenties, when the mad scramble for juvenile employment has largely passed. With meagre educational equipment, usually without the advantage of a pushing parent and often with all the handicaps of an indifferent home, the great majority have contrived to keep in steady work. Certainly many of the jobs they held were jobs that have to be done, even in this streamlined age. But if the picture from the employment point of view is reasonably satisfactory, the general social condition of many of these young people leaves much to be desired; for many have had little chance in life, little chance to make the most of what talents they have. The police records of these youths can only be viewed with grave concern; it is obvious that many of your young criminals are recruited from the ranks of high-grade mental defectives. Nor is this surprising; for too many are inhibited, dull and simple and find it easy, almost natural, to develop antisocial behaviour through suggestibility and lack of 'insight'. There is no lack of suggestion.

Remarks. This careful study shows the material and cultural poverty still to be found in a welfare state in the middle years of the century, and the distressing social consequences for handicapped young people and their families. The attention paid on the one hand to physical handicaps and on the other to material deprivation make it an unusually informative study.

Saenger, G. (1957, 1960)

Subjects. A carefully constructed representative sample of 520 severely retarded adults who had attended classes for the 'trainable retarded' in New York City between 1929 and 1955. Age range 17–40 years. IQs mainly between 40 and 50 points. Twenty per cent were mongols.

Method. Interviews by trained psychiatric social workers, using interview schedules and check lists. Careful attention paid to training of interviewer, piloting study and checking validity of conclusions.

Results. Most of retarded alert and lively, taking an interest in life around them. One-third markedly self-confident, only 13 per cent lacking in affect, and 7 per cent lifeless and inattentive. Neurotic trends suspected in 20 per cent and psychotic tendencies in 6 per cent.

Secondary physical handicaps in three-quarters; 20 per cent had motor disabilities; 40 per cent speech defects; but 83 per cent able to dress and feed themselves and take care of bodily functions. Two-thirds able to express themselves in complete sentences and one-third able to pick out a car fare and distinguish coins. But only one in nine able to read even simple passages.

Saenger gives a wealth of data on the factors affecting institutionalization, and on family adjustment. One-quarter were in institutions, and 14 per cent had spent some time in an institution. No relation was found between institutionalization and parental income, education, or family size. Nor did secondary handicaps influence placement to any marked degree. Behaviour problems and disturbed family relations were the most important factors.

The adjustment of the defectives in their own families was surprisingly good: 75 per cent of parents reported no major difficulties and only 5 per cent had serious problems. These in general were those commonly found in normal 5–6-year-old children, namely restlessness and tantrums, stubbornness, fears, and overdependence.

About half took responsibility for their own things, and rooms, 20 per cent assumed major housekeeping responsibilities, and an additional third did household chores; 80 per cent were left alone safely, and probably others could have been.

The great majority spent most of their leisure time in the home but went out occasionally. Only about one-half had friends and only half of these had friends of the opposite sex. Only 4 per cent appeared to have had sex relations and only twelve children had been born. Delinquency was extremely uncommon.

The employment data were remarkable: 27 per cent were working for pay, and an additional 9 per cent had worked in the past. Four times as many men as women worked and Saenger believes that the numbers could have been increased, perhaps even doubled.

General remarks. These two monumental studies by Saenger provide data of extraordinary interest and importance regarding the low-grade defectives and their families. They are, moreover, models of research design, and should be studied by anyone contemplating research in this field.

In conclusion three studies of exceptional interest are described. Two of them (by Kennedy, 1948 and 1966; and by Baller, 1936, continued by Charles, 1953, and Baller, Charles and Miller, 1966) are noteworthy in that they included an appropriately matched control group. In both studies the subjects were also followed up on more than one occasion, in order to survey their social adjustment over time, and in both a psychiatric study was made of the children of the retardates.

The other study summarized below (by Edgerton, 1967) looks qualitatively at factors influencing adjustment. In doing so it goes beyond the endlessly repetitive findings of traditional follow-up studies, and opens up new avenues of approach to understanding of the problems and way of life of retardates.

Kennedy, R. J. R. (1948)

Subjects. These were 256 'morons' living in the community (IQs 45–75), and diagnosed as mentally subnormal when at school. Mean age at the time of the inquiry was 24·5 years. Control group of 129 adults of normal IQ matched for age, sex, and socio-economic status.

Method. Careful and comprehensive social investigation. Adequate statistical treatment of results.

Results. Comparing the two groups, morons came from poor backgrounds, with more parental instability. No significant difference in number married or in number of children born to them. Morons with more step- and adopted children and with higher divorce rate. Some tendency for more morons to have an unsatisfactory work record. Little difference in economic adjustment. More morons in trouble with the police. Morons showed less tendency than controls to participate in recreational activities, including cinema, sport, and dancing. They read less and participated less in group activities.

General remarks

In final summary, our study reveals that morons are socially adequate in that they are economically independent and self-supporting; and that they are not serious threateners of the safety of society, but are rather frequent breakers of conventional codes of behaviour . . . The morons we studied are, by and large, successful in their social adjustment within limitations . . . apparently imposed by their inferior mental capacities. Doll's remark . . . that 'they find some humble niche in society which they can fill without becoming such a social menace that society becomes gravely concerned about them', seems to fit the actual situation very well.

This account is remarkable for its detail and thoroughness, and for the inclusion of a control group, and the above summary does less than justice to the mass of detailed information given in it.

Kennedy, R. J. R. (1966)

In 1960 all available subjects (N = 179, 69·9 per cent of the original sample) and controls (102, 79·7 per cent of the original 129) were again followed up, and their children were studied and given intelligence tests.

Results. Marriages: 86 per cent of the retarded and 92 per cent of controls were married. Divorce rate not significantly different (<10 per cent). Mean number of children (2·1) the same; mean IQs 99·5 and 106·6. Children of control subjects were in general doing better at school, children of retarded *mothers* having most difficulties. The economic status of members of both groups had risen over the years and job stability was high. One-third of the retarded group were engaged in skilled work, apparently fairly successfully. There were few differences in regard to unemployment. Retarded persons however had a higher incidence of delinquency – though in 1960 this was only half as high as in 1948.

Remarks. '1. The overwhelming majority of both subjects and controls have made acceptable and remarkably similar adjustments in all three areas: personal, social and economic. The main differences are of degree rather than of kind.' 2. 'In the sphere of personal and familiar behavior, subjects show no striking divergencies from what is generally attained by the normal controls.' 3. Although controls exceeded retarded subjects in a number of criteria of social adaptation, both groups showed an upward mobility in economic functioning. While the retarded subjects showed more irregularity of behaviour than controls, they do not in any respect threaten the safety of society (Cobb, 1969).

Baller, W. R. (1936), Charles, D. C. (1953), Baller, W. R., Charles, D. C. and Miller, E. L. (1966)

The other major study is that begun by Baller in the 1930s and continued through the 1940s and 1950s by Charles, and into the 1960s by Baller, Charles and Miller.

Method. The original sample comprised 206 former pupils of 'opportunity rooms' in Lincoln, Nebraska, all of whom had been classified as mentally deficient because of educational failure, and scored IQs less than 70 on the Stanford–Binet Test of Intelligence. At the time of the study they were aged 21 or more. Each index case was matched by sex, age, race and ethnic origin with a control subject with an IQ on the Terman Group Test of Mental Ability ranging from 100–120. A second contrast group having IQs 75–85 was recruited by Baller (1939). This constituted the 'Middle Group' in the follow-up studies, the index cases making up the 'Low Group' and the normal controls the 'High Group'.

Full data were secured on just over half of each group in the follow-up studies, but the samples appeared to be representative of the groups as a whole. The subjects themselves were interviewed, as were relatives (spouses and children). Where possible intelligence tests were given. Information was obtained from social agencies, the courts and from bureaux of vital statistics.

Results. The Low Group was less geographically mobile than members of the other two groups, 65 per cent as against 45 per cent remaining in or near Lincoln. Only 9 out of 205 members of the Low and Middle Groups were in institutional care and most of these had severe physical handicaps and had been placed in institutions in childhood.

The Low Group had an excess mortality, about one-third having died between the ages of 5–56 years against an expected mortality of one-sixth. The mortality of the Middle Group resembled that of the High Group. Among the Low Group there was in adult life a raised incidence of accidental death, but between 1953 and 1964 (that is, after the subjects were aged 40 or so) only one accidental death occurred. The Low Group were less likely to have married, more had divorced, and in general their marital situation was less stable than was that of the Middle and High Groups. The proportion fully employed rose from 27 per cent in 1935 to 36 per cent in 1951 and 67 per cent in 1964, at which time 80 per cent of the men and 77 per cent of the women were reported to be 'usually employed', as compared with 93 per cent and 96 per cent of the other two groups fully employed. As would be expected, the Low and Middle Groups tended to be in unskilled jobs, though as many as 13 per cent of the Low Group had their own business or were engaged in non-manual commercial employment.

Baller reported in 1936 that breaches of the law were three to seven times as frequent among the retarded groups as among the control group (though the controls had more reported traffic offences). Charles (1953) reported that 40 per cent of the subjects still living in Lincoln, and nearly 60 per cent of the men, had been involved in violation of the law since 1935. One-quarter of the violations were traffic offences, and the rest civil, with drunkenness accounting for half of the civil cases. None of the offences had been serious. From 1951 onwards only two males and no females have been in civil conflict with the law, though fourteen males and two females have had a total of fifty-six traffic offences. A small number (15) tested and retested first on the Stanford–Binet, then on the Wechsler–Bellevue and finally on the WAIS showed IQ rises: the interpretation of this finding is uncertain because of changes of test and of standardization. However the results do demonstrate once again that low IQ in childhood is a poor predictor of adult adjustment, and an imperfect predictor of adult IQ:

> The great variation in the present abilities and achievements of the subjects should dispel any notion that persons who give evidence of low ability in childhood develop and perform according to a rigid stereotype . . . Psychologists, educators and parents may gain encouragement from the knowledge that many children whose test scores and academic performance suggest mental deficiency develop into self-sufficient and desirable citizens as adults. (Charles, 1953, p. 67)

Baller, Charles and Miller believe that the explanation for their findings lies in the cultural deprivation suffered by the retardates as children. Subsequent recovery was slow, but steady; and in the absence of special services to help them:

> . . . they had to learn from experience in society rather than in the home. This necessity forced a slow and fumbling start, and much experience of

failure. This 'slow start' was reflected in the records of many subjects whose adolescent and early adult years were marked by delinquency, dependency on relief, and generally poor adjustment, but whose later adult lives were reasonably satisfactory. (Baller *et al.*, 1966, p. 87)

Edgerton, R. B. (1967)

Edgerton's study is quite different from any of those summarized so far, in that he is concerned not about quantifiable characteristics of a sample of persons judged retarded at some earlier point in their lives but with 'a general description of the lives of mentally retarded persons in the community [proceeding] to a specific discussion of the problems they face, and the techniques they employ, in dealing with their stigma and their incompetence' (Edgerton, 1967, p. xiv). The method is 'anthropological': that is, the material was gathered through repeated non-structured interviews with the respondents. These consisted of fifty-three former patients of Pacific State Hospital who had settled within a fifty-mile radius of the hospital.

Edgerton's thesis is that the dominating feeling governing these persons' lives is 'a single-minded effort to "pass" or "deny" ': to pass as ordinary people with ordinary memories of families, current friends, an ordinary place in a literate, educated world, and to deny their institutional experience, their ignorance and their stupidity. In order to cope most of them are dependent upon 'benefactors' who help them to survive. It is the *stigma* of mental handicap which is their greatest burden, one which leads them to don a *cloak* of competence to try (unsuccessfully) to cover their incompetence. To cope with this problem is, Edgerton believes, an unsolved task for institutional services.

Remarks. Edgerton's study is the only full-length report on *institutionalism* (see Wing, 1962; Wing and Brown, 1970) in mental subnormality presented from the point of view of the patient. Though Edgerton leaves the impression that the feeling is perhaps an inherent part of mental handicap, it is more realistic to regard it as a consequence of a particular pattern of 'treatment'. This issue is discussed more fully in Wing (1962), Wing and Brown (1970), and by the present writer (Tizard, 1964, 1970; King *et al.*, 1971). See also Chapter 13

References

ABEL, T. M. and KINDER, E. F. (1942) *The Subnormal Adolescent Girl.* New York: Columbia Univ. Press.

BALLER, W. R. (1936) A study of the present social status of a group of adults who, when they were in elementary schools, were classified as mentally deficient. *Genet. Psychol. Monogr.*, **18**, 165–244.

BALLER, W. R. (1939) A study of the behavior records of adults who, when they were in school, were judged to be dull in mental ability. *J. Genet. Psychol.*, 55, 365–79.

BALLER, W. R., CHARLES, D. C. and MILLER, E. L. (1966) *Mid-Life Attainment of the Mentally Retarded, A Longitudinal Study.* Lincoln: Univ. of Nebraska.

BIRCH, H. G. and GUSSOW, J. D. (1970) *Disadvantaged Children: Health, Nutrition and School Failure.* New York: Harcourt, Brace, and Grune & Stratton.

BIRCH, H. G., RICHARDSON, S. A., BAIRD, D., HOROBIN, G. and ILLSLEY, R. (1970) *Mental Subnormality in the Community: A clinical and epidemiological Study.* Baltimore, Md.: Williams & Wilkins.

BIRTCHNELL, J. (1971) Social class, parental social class, and social mobility in psychiatric patients and general population controls. *Psychol. Med.*, 1, 209–21.

BLACKMAN, L. S. (1967) Comments on Goldstein's 'The efficacy of special classes and regular classes in the education of educable mentally retarded children'. In ZUBIN, J. and JERVIS, G. A. (eds.) *Psychopathology of Mental Development.* New York: Grune & Stratton.

BRONNER, A. F. (1933) Follow-up studies of mental defectives. *Proc. Amer. Assoc. ment. Defic.*, 38, 258–67.

CHARLES, D. C. (1953) Ability and accomplishment of persons earlier judged mentally deficient. *Genet. Psychol. Monogr.*, 47, 3–71.

CLARKE, A. M. and CLARKE, A. D. B. (1972) Problems of employment and occupation of the mentally subnormal. In ADAMS, M. (ed.) *The Mentally Subnormal: The Social Casework Approach.* London: Heinemann.

COBB, H. V. (1966, 1969) *The Predictive Assessment of the Adult Retarded for Social and Vocational Adjustment: A Review of Research. Part I Annotated Bibliography; Part II Analysis of the Literature.* Dept of Psychology, Univ. of South Dakota.

DAVIES, S. P. (1930) *Social Control of the Mentally Deficient.* London: Constable.

DUGDALE, R. L. (1910) *The Jukes.* New York: Putnam.

DUNN, L. M. (1954) A comparison of the reading progresses of mentally retarded and normal boys of the same mental age. *Monogr. Soc. Res. Child Developm.*, 19, 7–99.

EDGERTON, R. B. (1967) *The Cloak of Competence: Stigma in the Lives of the Mentally Retarded.* Berkeley: Univ. of California Press.

EISENBERG, L. and CONNORS, C. K. (1968) The effect of Head Start on developmental processes. In JERVIS, G. A. (ed.) *Expanding Concepts in Mental Retardation.* Springfield, Ill.: Charles C. Thomas.

ESTABROOK, A. H. (1915) *The Jukes in 1915.* Washington: Carnegie Institution.

FAIRBANK, R. F. (1933) The subnormal child – 17 years after. *Ment Hyg.*, **17**, 177–208.

FERGUSON, T. and KERR, A. W. (1955) After-histories of girls educated in special schools for mentally handicapped children. *Glasgow med. J.*, **36**, 50–6.

FERGUSON, T. and KERR, A. W. (1958) After-histories of boys educated in special schools for mentally handicapped children. *Scot. med. J.*, **3**, 31–8.

FERNALD, W. E. (1919) After-care study of the patients discharged from Waverley for a period of twenty-five years. *Ungraded*, **5**, 25–31. Cited by Goldstein, 1964.

GODDARD, H. H. (1910) Heredity of feeble-mindedness. *Amer. Breeders Mag.*, **1**, 165–78.

GODDARD, H. H. (1912) *The Kallikak Family*. New York: Macmillan.

GODDARD, H. H. (1914) *Feeblemindedness: Its Causes and Consequences*. New York: Macmillan.

GOLDSTEIN, H. (1964) Social and occupational adjustment. In STEVENS, H. A. and HEBER, R. (eds.) *Mental Retardation: A Review of Research*. Chicago: Univ. of Chicago Press.

GOLDSTEIN, H. (1967) The efficacy of special classes and regular classes in the education of educable mentally retarded children. In ZUBIN, J. and JERVIS, G. A. (eds.) *Psychopathology of Mental Retardation*. New York: Grune & Stratton.

GOLDSTEIN, H., MISCHIO, G. S. and MINSKOFF, E. (1969) *A Demonstration Research Project in Curriculum and Methods of Instruction for Elementary Level Mentally Retarded Children*. Yeshiva University Final Report to US Office of Education, Bureau of Education for the Handicapped.

GOLDSTEIN, H., MOSS, J. W. and JORDAN, L. J. (1965) *The Efficacy of Special Class Training on the development of Mentally Retarded Children*. Cooperative Research Project No. 619. Urbana, Ill.: Univ. of Illinois, Institute for Research on Exceptional Children.

GOODMAN, N. and TIZARD, J. (1962) Prevalence of imbecility and idiocy among children. *Brit. med. J.*, **1**, 216–19.

GROSSMAN, H. J. (1973) *Manual on Terminology and Classification in Mental Retardation: 1973 Revision*. American Association on Mental Deficiency Spec. Publ. Ser. No. 2. Baltimore, Md: Garamond Pridemark Press.

GRUENBERG, E. (1964) Epidemiology. In STEVENS, H. A. and HEBER, R. (eds.) *Mental Retardation: A Review of Research*. Chicago: Univ. of Chicago Press.

HEBER, R. (1961) *A Manual on Terminology and Classification in Mental Retardation in the United States of America* (2nd edn). Amer. J. ment. Defic. Monogr. Suppl.

HEBER, R. (1962) The concept of mental retardation; definition and classification. *Proc. Lond. Conf. Scient. Stud. Ment. Defic., 1960*, **1**, 236–42.

HEBER, R. (1971) *Rehabilitation of Families at Risk for Mental Retardation: A Progress Report*. Madison: Rehabilitation Research and Training Centre in Mental Retardation, Univ. of Wisconsin.

HEBER, R. and DEVER, R. B. (1970) Research on education and habilitation of the mentally retarded. In HAYWOOD, H. C. (ed.) *Social-Cultural Aspects of Mental Retardation: Proceedings of the Peabody – NIMH Conference*. New York: Appleton-Century-Crofts.

HILLIARD, L. T. (1956) Discussion on community care of the feebleminded. *Proc. Roy. Soc. Med.*, **49**, 837–41.

HINDLEY, C. B. (1968) Growing up in five countries: a comparison of data on weaning, elimination training, age of walking and IQ in relation to social class from European longitudinal studies. *Developm. med. Child Neurol.*, **10**, 715–24.

HOYLE, J. S. (1951) Home conditions and employment of mental defectives. *Amer. J. ment. Defic.*, **55**, 619–21.

ILLINGWORTH, R. S. (1966) *The Development of the Infant and the Young Child, Normal and Abnormal*. Edinburgh and London: Livingstone.

KANNER, L. (1964) *A History of the Care and Study of the Mentally Retarded*. Springfield, Ill.: Charles C. Thomas.

KENNEDY, R. J. R. (1948) *The Social Adjustment of Morons in a Connecticut City*. Hartford: Mansfield-Southbury Training Schools (Social Service Dept, State Office Building).

KENNEDY, R. J. R. (1966) *A Connecticut Community Revisited: A Study of the Social Adjustment of a Group of Mentally Deficient Adults in 1948 and 1960*. Hartford: Connecticut State Dept of Health, Office of Mental Retardation.

KING, R. D., RAYNES, N. V. and TIZARD, M. (1971) *Patterns of Residential Care: Sociological Studies in Institutions for the Handicapped*. London: Routledge & Kegan Paul.

KIRK, S. A. (1958) *Early Education of the Mentally Retarded*. Urbana: Univ. of Illinois Press.

KUSHLICK, A. and BLUNDEN, R. (1974) The epidemiology of mental subnormality. In CLARKE, A. M. and CLARKE, A. D. B. (eds.) *Mental Deficiency: The Changing Outlook*, 3rd edn. London: Methuen; New York: Free Press.

LEWIS, E. O. (1929) *Report of the Mental Deficiency Committee*, Part IV. London: HMSO.

LOUTTIT, C. M. (1947) *Clinical Psychology of Children's Behaviour Problems*. New York: Harper & Row.

MENOLASCINO, F. J. (1970) *Psychiatric Approaches to Mental Retardation*. New York: Basic Books.

MERCER, J. R. (1970) Sociological perspectives in mild mental retardation. In HAYWOOD, H. C. (ed.) *Social-Cultural Aspects of Mental Retardation: Proceedings of the Peabody – NIMH Conference*. New York: Appleton-Century-Crofts.

MISCHEL, W. (1968) *Personality and Assessment*. New York: Wiley.

MURCHISON, C. (1933) *A Handbook of Child Psychology*. Worcester: Clark Univ. Press.

PINTNER, R. (1933) The feeble-minded child. In MURCHISON, C. (ed.) *A Handbook of Child Psychology*. Worcester, Mass.: Clark Univ. Press.

RAMER, T. (1946) The prognosis of mentally retarded children. *Acta Psychiat., Neurol. Suppl.*, **41**, 1–142.

ROBINSON, H. B. and ROBINSON, N. M. (1971) Longitudinal development of very young children in a comprehensive day care programme: the first two years. *Child Developm.*, **42**, 1673–84.

RUTTER, M., TIZARD, J. and WHITMORE, K. (1970) *Education Health and Behaviour*. London: Longmans.

SAENGER, G. (1957) *The Adjustment of Severely Retarded Adults in the Community*. Albany: New York State Interdepartmental Health Resources Board.

SAENGER, G. (1960) *Factors Influencing the Institutionalization of Mentally Retarded Individuals in New York City*. Albany: New York State Interdepartmental Health Resources Board.

Scottish Council for Research in Education (1953) *Social Implications of the Scottish Mental Survey*. London: Univ. of London Press.

STEIN, Z. and SUSSER, M. W. (1960) The families of dull children: classification for predicting careers. *Brit. J. prev. soc. Med.*, **14**, 83–8.

STEVENS, W. B. D. (1964) *Success of Young Adult Male Retardates*. Ann Arbor, Mich.: University Microfilms Inc. Cited by Cobb, 1969.

SUSSER, M. W. (1968) *Community Psychiatry*. New York: Random House.

SUSSER, M. W. and WATSON, W. (1962) *Sociology in Medicine*. London: Oxford Univ. Press.

TARJAN, G. and EISENBERG, L. (1972) Some thoughts on the classification of mental retardation in the United States of America. *Amer. J. Psychiat.*, **128**, 14–18.

TIZARD, J. (1964) *Community Services for the Mentally Handicapped*. London: Oxford Univ. Press.

TIZARD, J. (1970) The role of social institutions in the causation prevention and alleviation of mental retardation. In HAYWOOD, H. C. (ed.) *Social-Cultural Aspects of Mental Retardation: Proceedings of the Peabody – NIMH Conference*. New York: Appleton-Century-Crofts.

TIZARD, J. (1972a) A note on the international statistical classification of mental retardation. *Amer. J. Psychiat.*, **128**, 25–9.

TIZARD, J. (1972b) Planning and evaluation of special education. In *Proceedings of the European Association for Special Education International Conference 'Teaching the Handicapped Child', Norrkoping, Sweden*.

TIZARD, J. (1972c) Research into services for the mentally handicapped:

science and policy issues. *Brit. J. ment. Subn.*, **XVIII,** Part I, 34, 1–12.

WALL, W. D. and WILLIAMS, H. L. (1970) *Longitudinal Studies and the Social Sciences*. London: Heinemann, for the Social Science Research Council.

WINDLE, C. (1962) Prognosis of mental subnormals. *Monogr. Suppl. Amer. J. ment. Defic.*, **66,** 1–180.

WING, J. K. (1962) Institutionalism in mental hospitals. *Brit. J. Soc. Clin. Psychol.*, **1.**

WING, J. and BROWN, G. (1970) *Institutionalism and Schizophrenia*. London: Cambridge Univ. Press.

WOLFENSBERGER, W. (1969) The origin and nature of our institutional models. In KUGEL, R. B. and WOLFENSBERGER, W. (eds.) *Changing Patterns in Residential Services for the Mentally Retarded*. Washington, DC: President's Panel on Mental Retardation.

WOOTTON, B. (1959) *Social Science and Social Pathology*. London: Allen & Unwin.

World Health Organization (1968) *International Statistical Classification of Diseases, Injuries and Causes of Death, 8th revision*. Geneva: WHO.

World Health Organization (1968) *Organization of Services for the Mentally Retarded*. Tech. Rep. Ser. No. 392. Geneva: WHO.

6

A. M. Clarke and A. D. B. Clarke

Experimental studies: an overview[1]

Introduction

During the last decade there has been a vast increase in experimental studies of subnormal behaviour. More often than not, these have been laboratory-based and short-term in nature. In this chapter, an overview of the main fields of work is offered together with a discussion of some of the methodological difficulties involved. Research on operant learning and behaviour modification is virtually excluded here because of its detailed treatment in Chapter 12. The literature review, for reasons of space, is necessarily selective and attempts to cover recent findings up to and including the year 1970. Discussion of experimental research is not, of course, confined to this chapter.

Theories of subnormal behaviour

In any new scientific field, after a period of large-scale data collection, some general hypotheses or general attitudes arise to which research workers, wittingly or unwittingly, adhere. Currently, three positions with respect to mental subnormality may be outlined. These are as yet embryonic and are perhaps less important in their own right as psychological theories than for the role they play in determining research projects and type of experimental design.

(1) THE DEFECT THEORY

Adherents to this view consider that the mentally subnormal differ from the normal not only quantitatively but qualitatively. The argument rests on the many studies comparing subnormal and normal subjects *matched for MA* which show inferior performance in the former group, and the special difficulties of most subnormals in the area of language development and verbal mediation.

[1] This chapter is based upon part of Chapter 6 in H. J. Eysenck (ed.) *Handbook of Abnormal Psychology* (London, Pitman's Medical Press, 1973), and is reproduced by permission of the editor and publishers. It was written while the authors were in receipt of a generous grant from the Association for the Aid of Crippled Children, New York.

Most defect theorists (Ellis, 1963; Spitz, 1963; Luria, 1961) have elaborated their own physiological models which serve as guidelines in formulating hypotheses for behavioural research. Although their views are sometimes ambiguous, a strong impression is gained that they see the mentally subnormal, regardless of aetiology or level of intellect, as neurologically different from the normal population. As Ellis (1969), one of the chief exponents of this theory, puts it, MA, IQ, or 'developmental level', however defined, are rejected as an *explanation* of behaviour. Given that there are behavioural differences between normals and retardates of equal CA, the primary task for a behavioural science is to describe these differences. In view of Ellis's position it is logical that he believes the term 'defectives' more accurately describes this population than 'retardates', the latter term holding connotations of a developmental lag, which might in time be made good.

(2) THE RETARDATION OR DEVELOPMENTAL LAG THEORY

This states that the cognitive development of the mentally retarded is characterized by a slower progression through the same sequence of cognitive stages as the normal, and by lower limits to full development. Thus, the difference between normal and subnormal is analogous with the difference between the very superior and normal. The developmental position generates the hypothesis that there are no differences in formal cognitive functioning between *familial* (biogenic) retardates and normals, matched on general level of cognition (typically measured by MA). Zigler (1969) has contributed an excellent statement of this position and critique of the defect theory. He (1967) believes that many of the reported differences in performance between normal and mentally retarded individuals of the same MA may be traced to such variables as motivation and experience, rather than to basic cognitive deficiencies.

Although the differences in theoretical position between adherents of these views of subnormality sometimes appear wide, in fact there is considerable overlap, and the most important point of contention probably resides in the question as to whether the broad aetiological classification (biogenic versus pathological) is so basic to a consideration of any problem in mental retardation that research workers are in error to include in one group subjects selected on intellectual level as the sole criterion. Zigler (1969) would have it that a developmental lag theory applies best to the familial/cultural subnormals, reserving the defect theory for the pathological. By contrast, Leland (1969) and others argue that it is not to the scientist's advantage to dichotomize mentally retarded groups on the basis of presumed aetiologies. Most of them are so labelled because of maladaptation and behavioural difficulties. The only serviceable classification system is one that groups individuals by their ability to cope with specific critical demands, and that provides a guide to the modification and reversal of these behaviours.

(3) THE SKINNERIAN POSITION

The latter position has something in common with Skinnerian theory, elaborated for retardation by Bijou (1963 and 1966), which is important not so much for its effectiveness in describing the nature of subnormality, as in focusing the research of its adherents on to the antecedent conditions, and future methods of shaping the behaviours of sometimes profoundly subnormal individuals who might not otherwise be seen as promising material for psychological research. (See section on Operant Learning, and Chapter 12).

Bijou eschews the use of hypothetical mental constructs such as defective intelligence and hypothetical biological abnormalities such as 'clinically inferred brain injury' in the classification of mental retardation. He maintains that, since it is the behaviour that is retarded, correlates must be sought for this retarded behaviour. These must be observable events that clearly limit or control behaviour; antecedent events are grouped in classes such as abnormal anatomical structure and physiological functioning, the consequences of severe punishment, or inadequate reinforcement history. Once the relationship is established the basis for behaviour control is reached.

In summary, the main point of contention in the recent experimental literature on mental subnormality has related to the first two hypotheses outlined above, and frequent references to this issue will be found in the following pages. The recent polemic between Milgram (1969), Zigler (1969), and Ellis (1969) suggests a considerable overlap between the 'defect' and the 'retardation' theories, as well as some misunderstanding by the main protagonists of the others' position. But Ellis now considers that a sharp distinction between developmental and defect approaches lacks substance. Be that as it may, it is clear that much research owes its parentage to one or other of these positions.

Problems of research design

A majority of the experimental studies reviewed in this chapter contrast a group or groups of mentally retarded subjects' performance on a task or tasks with that of normal subjects matched for MA or CA. In both cases, IQ differences between groups will be inevitable and sometimes considerable. With MA matches, up to 50-point IQ differences may be found and with CA matches, 30 points is usual and up to about 70 points has been reported, when retarded children are compared with groups of intellectually superior subjects. Although in many cases of MA-matched groups, psychologists have clearly stated that they were looking for qualitative differences between groups who on intelligence tests had performed similarly, the suspicion arises that, on occasion, inclusion of normal controls in a research design was due to a blind adherence to a fashionable trend. Only recently have scientists looked critically at research designs in common use and at the questions that may legitimately be answered in any particular case.

Zeaman (1965) points out that the psychologist may attack the problems of subnormality in at least two ways, either by finding the laws, principles, or regularities that govern the behaviour of retardates, or by finding the *unique* laws of their behaviour. If the latter is to be attempted, comparisons with normal children are essential, but control in such comparisons is fraught with difficulty. 'If you match for CA, then MA is out of control. It you match for MA, then CA is necessarily out of control. If you assume CA is not a relevant variable and match for MA, then other differences appear to be out of control. Length of institutionalization, home environments, previous schooling, tender-loving-care, and socio-economic status are factors likely to be different for retardates and normals.' To tackle such problems realistically would require heroic investigators matched by heroic budgets, hence, Zeaman and some others confine their interest to laws about subnormal behaviour rather than unique laws.

Baumeister (1967b) discusses in detail the difficulties encountered in comparing subnormals and normals. Obviously, the fundamental problem is one of ensuring that the task is an equivalent measure of the same psychological processes for both groups. If one is investigating some cognitive process, and differences emerge, it is necessary to be able to exclude sensory, motor, motivational, and other differences, but this can seldom be achieved. Obvious violations of this principle occur in studies of institutionalized subnormals and non-institutionalized normals. Zigler (1969) quotes the following example. Rohwer and Lynch (1968) compared the paired-associate learning efficiency of institutionalized retardates (having a mean CA of about 25) with groups of normal children of varying economic strata (having CAs ranging from about 5 to 12). The finding that the institutionalized retardate group did worse than MA-matched normals (and even normals having lower MAs than the retarded) was interpreted as convincing evidence of the erroneousness of the retardation theory. However, in another article in the same journal, Baumeister (1968a) reported a study of paired-associate learning of MA-matched groups of institutionalized retardates, non-institutionalized retardates, and children of normal intellect. There was no difference between the latter two groups, but the institutionalized retardates were inferior to both. Furthermore, there was a significant correlation between length of institutionalization and trials to criterion: the longer the child was institutionalized, the worse was his performance.

Another example of a questionable comparison of groups is provided by some early work on short-term memory in which innumerate severely subnormal children were contrasted with normal schoolchildren of digit repetition.

Transcending the developmental *v.* defect controversy, there is agreement that the essential problem of mentally retarded individuals is their intellectual or cognitive inadequacy. Zigler (1969) reasons that since cognitive functioning lies at the core of retardation phenomena, it is easy to see why, in this particular area, workers have concentrated on cognitive functioning, often totally ignoring the possibility that other factors such as temperament, educational opportunities, motivation, social class, and environmental background might contribute at all to the current status, and consequent task performance of the retardate. Indeed, this chapter is itself testimony to the imbalance of experimental research

in mental deficiency since the interactions of these factors with cognitive development has not been systematically explored. A notable exception is the work of
Zigler and his colleagues (see section on Personality and Motivation).

A few investigators have argued against attempts to match experimentally on
either an MA or CA basis, on the grounds that it is not always a valid assumption
that either of these is the most relevant variable that could be used, and may
lead to the introduction of systematic differences between groups on variables
other than these. Furthermore, experimental matching normally results in biased
selection of subjects due to the necessity for discarding those who cannot be
paired with others, or who alter means of variance on the matching variable.
Stanley and Beeman (quoted by Prehm, 1966b) advocated statistical matching:
subjects should be drawn at random from a specified population, and assigned at
random to the various treatment conditions, a procedure that should result in
subjects varying at random on any antecedent variable. Matching of subjects
could then be accomplished through analysis of covariance. Prehm (1966b)
discussed this suggestion, and adopted it in a study of paired-associate learning
(Prehm, 1966a); however, experimental matching remains the preferred method
by a majority of investigators.

Baumeister argues that comparison of subnormals and normals is most
appropriate where their behaviour is observed as a function of systematic
variations in task or environmental variables; this calls for a multiple factor
design in which subject characteristics are co-manipulated with experimental
factors. The question then posed is not whether the subnormal is inferior but
whether experimental manipulation will produce the same behavioural adjustment in both groups. One is thus no longer concerned with showing that there are
deficits in the subnormal (this is taken for granted) but with determining the
conditions that produce variability in group differences. This procedure does
not assume that the task is exactly the same for the two groups, but that task and
subject characteristics are constant for all values of the experimental variables.
This latter is normally a far safer assumption.

Where after an MA match, performance differences emerge, the researcher has
identified a difference not residing in the MA scores themselves. 'That this
difference is any more fundamental and theoretically meaningful than one which
happens to correlate with test performance is dubious. One might say that such a
result shows that intelligence tests do not measure all adaptive behaviours . . . we
may have done nothing more than to discover another way of diagnosing mental
retardation' (Baumeister, 1968a). Moreover, the MA is itself compounded of
many factors, equal MAs may be reached by several routes, and are a reflection of
an interaction between the content of the test, the experience of the subject and
his 'true' ability. As such, the MA has little explanatory value. Baumeister notes
that far more attention has been devoted to MA than to other variables such as
reinforcement history, comprehension of instructions, and so on. In effect, like
Zeaman, he concludes that to understand the behaviour of subnormals one must
study the behaviour of subnormals, and the study of normal behaviour 'is quite

irrelevant to this purpose'. He does not entirely dismiss the usefulness of comparative studies, but considers that observations of normals will not, of themselves, tell us about the behaviour of subnormals. At best it may raise hypotheses.

'Floor' and 'ceiling' effects are a further source of difficulty in group comparisons, particularly in learning studies. Clarke and Blakemore (1961), for example, compared adults, adolescent and child imbeciles from the same institution on their learning and transfer on various pairs of perceptual-motor tasks. They found that there was greater transfer in the children than in the adolescents and adults. This resulted from a 'ceiling effect' which prevented the adolescents and adults from improving their performance on tasks not especially difficult for them. When Clarke and Cooper (1966) repeated some of this work but adjusted task difficulty to achieve equal starting points for older and younger subnormals, no transfer differences were found.

Ellis (1969) makes a masterly contribution to this whole problem. The apparent rationale of an equal MA match is that this equalizes 'development'. Rarely, however, is the meaning of 'development' scrutinized. There is the additional and already noted problem of whether equal MA scores are based on equal subtest performance, and there is also the possibility that MA may reflect past and present motivational status as well as cognitive factors.

Ellis believes that the equal CA matching procedure is directed to the primary characteristic of subnormality. There are, however, serious problems with this design. Behavioural differences (except for the mildly retarded) are often so great that measurement on the same scale is impossible. 'Floor' and 'ceiling' effects (noted above) are inevitable hazards (Ellis and Anders, 1968). Nevertheless, Ellis argues that for certain purposes CA matches appear to carry more theoretical significance than a comparison of adult mental retardates with normal children on the basis of an MA match.

Finally, Baumeister (1968b), who makes a habit of tackling difficult methodological problems which are easily swept under the carpet, has pointed to the problem of greater performance variability of defective than normal subjects, a matter that must surely have been observed by all research workers who have studied both groups. He reviews the literature, which is not extensive, and concludes that it is almost certain that the two intelligence groups do differ on this characteristic to a significant extent; he suggests, tentatively, that variables related to arousal, attentional, or motivational processes may be implicated in normal-retardate efficiency differences.

These problems have been outlined at some length because, although they permit no easy solution, it seems essential that research workers should be aware of them, since the conclusions derived from much of the early experimental work on mental retardation must be regarded as equivocal, due to a failure on the part of investigators fully to understand the many pitfalls. Furthermore, the fact that in most areas included in this review both results and interpretations by different authors conflict, is acknowledged to be largely due to differing methodological preferences.

Bortner and Birch (1970) review a large number of studies of subnormal and normal children and experimental animals which demonstrate that performance levels under particular conditions are but fragmentary indicators of capacity (or potential). Glaring differences occur in the estimates of potential when significant alterations are made in the conditions for performance. This distinction between capacity and performance, more often implicit in the literature than explicit, has led some workers to start investigating systematically the appropriate conditions, both cognitive and motivational, for maximizing performance.

In considering the following text, which reviews a selection of studies published up to 1970, readers should bear firmly in mind the problems discussed above and, also, that the subjects used in the various experiments range from helpless idiots (see Operant Learning), through imbeciles (often malformed, malcoordinated with severe speech defects) to the mildly subnormal, many of whom in later life are barely distinguishable from members of the normal working population, but who, while young, by virtue of learning difficulties, find their way into special classes, schools, or institutions for the retarded.

Perceptual processes

Although sensory perception may be considered basic to cognitive functioning, psychologists have concerned themselves much less with the operation of sensory and perceptual processes in the mentally subnormal than with problems of learning and memory. Spivack (1963) reviewing this field concluded that the paucity of research data on perceptual processes is striking, and the results are too fragmentary to permit of meaningful integration. 'Too often the "single-shot" study raises more questions than are answered and is rarely followed up by others.' The situation has not changed substantially to date and, with certain important exceptions, there is as yet little theoretical debate of the sort likely to give rise to hypothetico-deductive studies. Moreover, the problem is complicated by the fact that some influential clinical theorists, notably Goldstein and Scheerer (1941), Werner (see Diller and Birch, 1964), Strauss and Lehtinen (1947), and Strauss and Kephart (1955) suggested that cortical lesions interfere with perception and in consequence special training and educational methods have been devised to take account of the effects of brain injury (either demonstrable or assumed). A vast literature exists on the psychological diagnosis of brain damage, and the differentiation of exogenous from endogenous mental defectives. This will not be reviewed here, but the reader is referred to a summary by Diller and Birch (1964), who raise a number of methodological problems that affect interpretation of the data. Haywood (1966), in a discussion of training programmes for the perceptually handicapped, concludes that no definite criteria reliably differentiate the perceptually handicapped (or minimally brain damaged) child from the emotionally disturbed or generally mentally retarded. No systematic research has been conducted to demonstrate the validity of these programmes, and it is suggested that 'perceptual handicap' may be 'an artifact of our ignorance and lack of solid descriptive research' (see also Sternlicht *et al.*, 1968).

The difficulty some brain-damaged children experience with visuo-motor tasks, such as copying a diamond or reproducing a block design, by comparison with controls matched for mental and chronological age, has given rise to a debate as to whether the basic problem is visuo-perceptual or visuo-motor. Bortner and Birch (1960), working with adult hemiplegics and cerebral-palsied children, found that these subjects made many more errors than did control subjects in copying block designs. However, in the vast majority of cases the brain-damaged subjects were able to select the correct design (over their own reproductions and a standard incorrect copy) when the task was presented in multiple-choice version. The investigators concluded that the difficulty of the brain-damaged lies not in the perceptual system but in the perceptual-action system.

Support for this view is provided by Ball and Wilsoncroft (1967) who used the phi-phenomenon to investigate perceptual-motor deficits. The technique used was based on Orlansky's (1940) demonstration that type of form used as stimuli influences phi-thresholds. If two squares are used, a certain threshold is obtained; if a square is paired with a diamond, the threshold changes signifi-nificantly. It is assumed that if a subject obtains thresholds that differ for homo-geneous (two squares) and heterogeneous (square and diamond) forms, it is due to his perceptual ability to discriminate these forms. Three groups, normals, institutionalized retardates, and cerebral-palsied were studied; the latter two groups were tested on the Stanford–Binet task of copying a diamond (MA 7) as well as reproduction of a straight line and a diamond on a peg-board. Since all subjects had MAs over 8, the inability by some to copy or construct a diamond represented a specific perceptual-motor deficit. There were no differences in ability to discriminate form as measured by phi-thresholds among the groups and subgroups studied, although there was a significant difference in overall reactivity to phi motion in favour of the normals. The authors conclude that the results substantiate the position advocated by Bortner and Birch (1960) and are at variance with Kephart's theory which emphasizes the role of perception in accounting for perceptual-motor deficits.

On the other hand, Deich (1968) challenged this conclusion by demonstrating that retardates at two MA levels, matched on the variable with normal children, aged 6 and 8·9 years, were significantly inferior in both reproduction *and* recognition of block designs, although all groups performed better on the latter than the former. Deich believes her results support the view that retardates are perceptually impaired, at least for complex visual stimuli. In this connection, Gaudreau (1968) points to the great difficulty of discriminating between the roles played by perception and those by intelligence when complex problems are used. Krop and Smith (1969) showed that performance by retardates on the Bender-Gestalt test improves with participation in an educational programme, and further improvement resulted from specific instruction in drawing geometric patterns.

A marked contrast to the single-shot studies of perception, deplored by Spivack, is provided by the systematic work on illusions conducted recently over several years by Herman Spitz and his colleagues. Spitz (1963) offers a cogent defence of Gestalt theories in the study of mental retardation; more specifically, the application of Köhler and Wallach's (1944) theory of cortical satiation to the results of experiments on figural after-effects (Spitz and Blackman, 1959), kinesthetic after-effects (Spitz and Lipman, 1961), and perspective reversal (Necker cube) led him to postulate (1964) that cortical changes take place more slowly in retardates than in normals. Therefore retardates should be *less* susceptible to 'physiological' illusions than normal subjects, but *equally* susceptible to 'experiential' illusions, a classification applied to those illusions induced primarily by distorting the stimulus and/or reducing the viewer's observing power, apparently causing the viewer to resort to faulty assumptions and inferences based on past experience (Spitz, 1967).

Mental retardates were found to be less capable than equal CA controls of perceiving visual after-effects, and had a lower reversal rate on the Necker cube. Winters (1965) and Winters and Gerjuoy (1965, 1967) compared college students with high-grade retardates on sensitivity to gamma-movement (the apparent expansion and contraction of a briefly exposed figure) and concluded that, unlike normals, retardates do not perceive gamma at ·2 sec, but that it was possible to induce gamma in retardates by lengthening the exposure time. The authors believe that slower electro-chemical processes in the cortex rather than an attention deficit account for the differences observed between their groups (see section on EEG Studies).

Of the experimental illusions, Spitz (1964) found retardates equally susceptible as normals on the rotating trapezoidal window illusion, and on the distorted room illusion (Spitz, 1967). In the latter study, adolescent retardates were compared with college students on a table model of the Ames distorted room – a trapezoidal room which simulated rectangularity – and a control room that was truly rectangular. Loss of size constancy in judging two unequal circles was the illusion indicator. No significant differences between groups was found on either room. Even under visual restraint retardates maintained as much size constancy as equal CA normals.

Spitz (1965) has also reported *greater* susceptibility on the part of retardates than of normals to a physiological illusion that can be countered by an awareness of the depth cue of interposition (the rotating cube illusion). The results of all these experiments lend support to Spitz's contention that retardates differ from normals in their sensitivity to 'physiological' and 'experiential' illusions.

Winters (1969) took the argument further by postulating that if the only prerequisite for demonstrating physiological visual illusions is that a subject possesses a healthy central nervous system, then young normals (of equal MA to retardates) should demonstrate physiological illusions to the same degree as older normals (matched for CA to retardates), but should differ from older retardates; furthermore, that on a presumably experiential illusion different age-groups will be differentially affected. Winters contrasted perception of gamma-movement (physiological illusion) with two-dimensional size constancy (experiential illusion) using institutionalized male retardates (CA 16·4; IQ 63·7), normal adolescent males (CA 16·7; IQ 103·8) and normal male children (CA 10·8, no IQs available). The retardates did not demonstrate the physiological illusion, whereas both normal groups did, though not differing from each other. All three groups exhibited size constancy, with greater constancy of retardates over equal MA normals reaching only marginal significance. Winters interprets the results as confirming the defect theory of mental deficiency and offering evidence against the retardation theory.

The important question of the interdependence of perceptual and intellectual development was considered by Doyle (1967). Starting with the observation of an adult retardate whose perceptual skills appeared so well developed that by capitalizing on them she was able to perform tasks beyond her intellectual capacity, Doyle advanced the hypothesis that perceptual skill development might proceed independently of intellectual development. One hundred and eight children from special classes for the mentally retarded were allocated to CA groups (at 7, 9, and 11) and MA groups (at 7, 9, and 11) so that each MA level was represented at each CA level, and vice versa. The children's susceptibility to the horizontal-vertical illusion for hearing, sight, and touch was determined by the method of constant stimuli. Susceptibility to the illusion was associated with independently varied MA and CA; (e.g. retarded children in the highest CA group were less susceptible to the illusion than their younger MA counterparts) and the findings were interpreted as supporting the hypothesis. Although this conclusion should probably be accepted with caution until more studies have been conducted, the experimental design might be used to good effect to investigate other aspects of perception.

EEG studies

There is some, but by no means conclusive, evidence that EEG tracings are related to IQ (Ellingson, 1966; Vogel and Broverman, 1964, 1966).

The literature up to and including 1961 has been well reviewed by Berkson (1963), and Clevenger (1966) has provided an annotated bibliography of over 100 references. The former author distinguishes five main parameters of the alpha rhythm that have been studied. These are: (1) the frequency of alpha rhythm; average frequencies for normals and subnormals are closely similar, although there is a suggestion that the range for subnormals is greater; (2) the average amplitude of alpha rhythm; and (3) the proportion of time during a resting period for the subjects, when the rhythm is exhibited. Some studies show a relationship with MA while others do not; (4) and (5) are measures of response to short duration stimuli. If the subject is resting quietly in a darkened room, the alpha rhythm is most pronounced. With the presentation of a short-duration stimulus (e.g. light flash) the alpha rhythm is blocked, and the length of the block has been termed perseveration time. Berkson offers no information on speed of alpha blocking except from an unpublished study where no differences were found between normals and subnormals. The perseveration time of normals was, however, rather longer. Later work by Wolfensberger and O'Connor (1965) failed to confirm this finding. This later study also yielded information that subnormals were slower to block than normals.

Baumeister and Hawkins (1967) note the above discrepancies in the published findings and believe that difficulties may arise when widely disparate intelligence groups are compared. They aimed, therefore, to study the relationship between alpha phenomena and intelligence within subnormal groups, using twenty-one male adult cultural-familial subnormals. One-second duration light stimuli were used during the presence of alpha rhythm for twenty trials. IQ and alpha block duration were not correlated within this group, but the correlation between IQ and number of blocks was significant (·05 level), the more intelligent blocking more frequently. Brighter subjects were also slower to block, and a significant habituation effect was noted, the block duration decreasing over trials. This appeared to be unrelated to other measures. These findings are interpreted as indicating that decreasing intelligence seems to be associated with a reduction in responsiveness to external stimulation, a view that corresponds closely to clinical impressions, which should be considered in conjunction with the conclusions of Butler and Conrad (1964). These authors interpret the EEG findings as indicating an impaired speed of integration of complex sensory information.

Vogel and co-workers (1969) noted the lack of studies of behavioural correlates of abnormal EEG phenomena among the mentally subnormal, and attributed this to a consensual assumption that a group of people with abnormal EEGs will, on average, evidence more cortical pathology and therefore more maladaptive behaviour than those with normal EEGs. They investigated forty-five retardates with abnormal EEGs and an equal number with normal EEGs, matched for age and diagnosis. The groups were compared for test intelligence, school, and occupational performance, personal skills, social behaviours, and psychiatric status for three separate periods: year of admission, year of EEG examination, and current year. EEG abnormality was associated with deficits on intelligence test performance, but not with deficits in broader categories of adjustment. However, mean alpha frequency of EEG was associated with behavioural adjustment as reflected in personal skills (e.g. dressing) and social behaviours (e.g. cooperation with ward staff), as well as test intelligence and classroom performance. The authors suggest that quantitatively derived EEG indices, such as alpha frequency, which are thought to reflect particular underlying neurological processes, relate more effectively to retardates' behaviour than do clinically derived categories such as EEG 'normality' or 'abnormality'.

Reaction time

Studies of reaction time (RT) using mentally subnormal subjects have been carried out by several investigators, particularly Baumeister and Berkson and their associates.

Baumeister and Kellas (1968c), reviewing the literature, concluded that:

1. Intelligence is functionally related to RT, not only when normal and sub-normal subjects are compared (Scott, 1940), but also within the retarded population (Pascal, 1953; Ellis and Sloan, 1957; Berkson, 1960b). Although there has been some dispute on the nature of the function, it is suggested that it can best be described as linear.

2. Intensity of the stimulus influences retardates' response speed more than that of normals (Baumeister *et al.*, 1964; Baumeister *et al.*, 1965a, b). As the intensity of the signal to respond increases, RT correspondingly decreases. However, at stimulus values near threshold, normals and retardates are similarly affected.

3. Compound reaction stimuli appear to decrease RT in a manner similar to intensity. Holden (1965) showed that trimodal stimulation (auditory, visual, cutaneous) yielded faster reactions than any of these stimuli presented singly, possibly implying increased arousal. However, compound warning stimuli did not influence RT (Baumeister *et al.*, 1965c).

4. In conditions of stimulus complexity requiring choice, response speed of normals and defectives are equally affected (Berkson, 1960a, b). Berkson also found that when both stimulus and response complexity were varied, IQ interacted with the latter but not the former. Berkson concluded that IQ is not relevant to making a choice or planning a movement, but is related to the performance of that movement. Hawkins *et al.* (1965) compared college students and retardates on simple and choice RT tasks, using a verbal rather than motor response. Normals were faster than defectives and both groups showed slower choice RTs, but there was no interaction between type of task and intelligence level.

5. Temporal factors are related to the performance of mental defectives; these include the uncertainty, length of warning interval, psychological refractory period, and warning signal duration.

6. Attempts have been made to relate parameters of the alpha rythm to RT of retardates. Since it has been shown that alpha blocks are shorter in defectives than normals (Baumeister *et al.*, 1963; Berkson *et al.*, 1961), it seems possible that EEG responsivity is related to slow RT. Furthermore, reaction signals presented during the period of alpha block are associated in normal subjects with faster RT than stimuli presented during a no block period (Fedio *et al.*, 1961; Lansing *et al.*, 1959). Thus, Baumeister and Hawkins (1967) suggested that retarded subjects whose alpha waves are particularly responsive to visual stimulation might be rapid responders. Their findings failed to support the hypothesis. Hermelin and Venables (1964) used visual warning stimuli of different

duration and a wide range of warning interval. Reaction times to a sound stimulus were equally fast during periods of alpha and during alpha blocks.

7. Incentive conditions have been found to influence speed of RT (Baumeister and Ward, 1967).

8. Within-subject variability of RT is greater in defectives than normal subjects. Berkson and Baumeister (1967), examining variability in RTs of bright and dull subjects, found substantial correlations between medians and standard deviations (see also Baumeister and Kellas, 1968a, b; Baumeister, 1968b). Baumeister believes that greater variability of response generally characterizes the defective individual, and suggests that to determine the source of this variability offers an important subject for future research.

Baumeister, Wilcox and Greeson (1969) used a reaction-time experiment to test the hypothesis that mental retardates are at a particular disadvantage in situations that require rapid adjustment to a complex and uncertain environment. Two experiments were conducted to compare the reaction times of normals and retardates as a function of the relative frequency of reaction signal occurrence, using a buzzer and a light as signals. The results indicated that both groups displayed increased reaction times as the probability of a particular stimulus decreased. Only when the frequencies of stimulus occurrence were markedly different did the interaction between intelligence group and event probability reach significance.

Hyperactivity and distractibility

Clinicians have noted that among the retarded, and particularly severely retarded brain-injured children, many are hyperkinetic and distractible to a point where these characteristics actively interfere with attempts to educate or train them. Strauss and Lehtinen (1947) vividly describe the difficulties presented by such children; recently, research workers have attempted to explore factors affecting activity level and distractibility in the mentally retarded. Cromwell and co-workers (1963) summarize findings and theories concerning activity level, and rightly question whether it can be considered a unitary topic of review. The same point can justifiably be made concerning distractibility, and in consequence only a few very recent studies from these areas are included here.

Tizard (1968a) notes that, although hyperkinesis is a very real phenomenon to parents and teachers, it has proved strangely elusive to laboratory investigation. Neither McConnel et al. (1964) nor Schulman et al. (1965) were able to establish a relation between observers' ratings of overactivity and objective measures (by ballistograph or actometers). On the other hand, Hutt and Hutt (1964), who measured locomotion, found higher movement scores in hyperkinetic than normal children, and suggested that their activity was comparatively unmodifiable by any environmental influence, whether social or otherwise. In a preliminary study, Tizard observed two groups of severely subnormal children, rated very overactive and not overactive, during free play. The overactive children moved about significantly more often than the control children but were not rebuked more often nor did they receive more attention from their teachers. They were not more aggressive than the non-overactive group, but they made significantly fewer friendly contacts. The classical hyperkinetic syndrome was not seen; instead, the overactive children showed a wide range of personality characteristics. There was some evidence that they had suffered brain damage of a different kind from that found in the control group.

Since theories to account for overactivity postulate an inhibitory defect, as a result of which the child is unable to stop attending to, or responding to, irrelevant stimuli, or is slow to habituate, Tizard (1968b) conducted an experiment to determine (a) the effect of stimulus variation on the amount of locomotion, and (b) the effect of increasing familiarity with the environment on the amount of locomotion. Overactive and non-overactive severely subnormal children were tested four times, with and without toys, in an experimental room. There was no significant difference in the movement scores of the two groups and no significant habituation in the amount of movement recorded over four sessions for either group. Stimulus variation did not affect overall movement score, although it did affect the nature of the children's activity. Tizard concludes from the two studies that overactivity is a real characteristic of children designated overactive and one that is difficult to modify, and that delayed maturation or general retardation are inadequate concepts to account for the behaviour studied.

In an attempt to investigate the 'inhibitory defect' theory, Tizard (1968c) tested the responsiveness of overactive imbeciles to auditory stimuli using EEG and skin potential changes as measures of response, and the habituation of these responses while awake and while asleep. Control groups of non-overactive imbeciles and normal children were used. Only the normal children showed habituation of skin potential while awake; while asleep no habituation occurred in any group. There was no difference in the frequency of EEG and skin potential changes in response to sound in the three groups; a difference in alertness while awake was a confounding variable. Tizard (1968d) analysed the all-night EEGs, electro-oculograms, and movement records for the three groups. Apart from clinical EEG abnormalities, few group.differences were found. The overactive group tended to have more but briefer periods of deep sleep, while the normal children tended to have longer waking periods. Over half the imbeciles, and a quarter of the normal children had periods resembling Stage I Rapid Eye Movement sleep without REMs. All groups spent longer in deep sleep, and less time in Stage I REM sleep than adults. Tizard notes with interest that children whose daytime behaviour is very abnormal and severely retarded, and in whom electro-physiological habituation is disturbed, have sleep patterns barely distinguishable from those of normal children.

Turning now to studies of distractibility, the experimental literature suggests that comparisons of the intellectually normal with the mentally retarded (and particularly brain-injured) do not always support the view that the latter are more distractible. Schulman and co-workers (1965) suggest that in view of the wide range of types of brain damage, the failure to differentiate between hetero-geneous groups of brain-injured and non-brain-injured is not surprising. It is also clear that 'distractibility' cannot be viewed as a unitary characteristic, but one that must be seen both in terms of individual differences and situational variables. Ellis and colleagues (1963) compared 'familial', 'subcultural', 'brain-injured', and defectives of unknown aetiology and normal children of equivalent MA on an oddity problem under two kinds of distraction: attention value of stimulus objects and the presence of a large mirror. The main hypothesis, that defective subjects would be more distractible than normal, was not confirmed, and the mirror actually facilitated the normal group's performance. Similarly, Baumeister and Ellis (1963) found that a potential distractor resulted in improved performance in a group of retardates. Girardeau and Ellis (1964) found no effect of various background noises (train noise, buzzer, playground noise, music, conversation, automobile horn, dog barking) on serial and paired-associate learning by normal and mentally retarded children. Sen and Clarke (1968) conducted a series of experiments, using subnormal subjects of two IQ levels, which showed that: (1) subjects' susceptibility to extraneous stimuli designed to act as distractors is clearly related to the level of task difficulty, and (2) not all external stimuli operate as distractors for a given task. In addition it was sug-gested that the following variables are important: (a) nature of the task; (b) its duration; (c) intensity of the distracting stimuli; (d) relevance of the distractors to the task; and (e) in case of conversation or stories, their attention value. The findings of these studies are consistent with the view that retardates, as a group, are more likely to show distractible behaviour than normal subjects (since more tasks will be at a level of difficulty producing distractible behaviour), but also suggest that a blanket description of retardates as distractible serves only to cloud the issue of why and in what circumstances they manifest this behaviour, and how it may be overcome.

Rather similar conclusions were reached by Belmont and Ellis (1968), who studied the effects of extraneous stimulation on discrimination learning in normals and retardates. Bright lights produced a decrement in 2-choice discrim-ination learning of normal subjects, but *facilitated* retardate learning. In two further experiments, retardates learned a series of six 2-choice problems, on which post-response extraneous stimulation (meaningful pictures) was at first found to facilitate learning. The same stimuli distracted the subjects later in the series. It was concluded that current notions regarding distractibility in retarda-tion require serious qualification.

Operant learning

The application of operant conditioning techniques to the mentally subnormal has aroused considerable interest within the last few years, and it is clear that further developments are to be expected. (See Chapter 12 for full details.)

This area is, however, different from the others reviewed, in that no comparative studies have been undertaken, and there has, until recently, been little controversy over method and interpretation of findings. The question raised by the Skinnerians is rarely 'Can a subnormal person learn by operant methods task X as well as a normal person matched on MA or CA?' The orientation is much more that since operant methods have been shown to be useful in shaping behaviour in animals and normal human beings, the same principles should result in efficient shaping in the subnormal at all levels. The evidence suggests that this faith has been justified.

As Dent (1968) indicates in an admirably succinct review, man's interaction with his environment results in the development of both simple and complex forms of behaviour. According to behaviour theory, these behaviours are acquired, altered, or maintained by the reinforcement received from the environment; the frequency of a response is subject to the consequences of that response. Broadly speaking, reinforcement may be positive (pleasant, rewarding) or negative (noxious, punishing). The former is assumed to increase, and the latter to decrease, the frequency of a particular response. There are four simple schedules of reinforcement: fixed ratio; variable ratio; fixed interval; and variable interval. Dent stresses that since society skilfully dispenses its reinforcement on a variable interval schedule, the ultimate goal in training the subnormal is to achieve control of the particular behaviour in such a way that it will eventually be maintained by society. This, in turn, suggests that the desired response should be established by means of a fixed ratio reinforcement schedule (i.e. rewards given in a fixed ratio to the subject's response rate) which is then gradually shifted to variable interval reinforcement; at the same time there should be a shift from primary reinforcers (e.g. edibles) to secondary (e.g. social approval).

Operant techniques are important, since they have often been applied to subnormals with IQs below 35, and in particular to those of idiot grade who are normally regarded as unresponsive to the more usual modes of training. Positive reinforcement is used to create desirable forms of behaviour and negative (e.g. aversive) reinforcement to eliminate undesirable traits such as aggressive, destructive, or self-destructive behaviour. Various studies have concerned the development, by means of operant conditioning, of personal self-care skills and social and verbal skills. Useful and comprehensive reviews have been produced by Watson and Lawson (1966); Spradlin and Girardeau (1966); Watson (1967); and Baumeister (1967a). An Orwellian twist has been provided by Henker, according to Dent (1968). She contends that the mentally subnormal can be trained to apply operant procedures in the training of other subnormals. This will create 'therapeutic pyramids' whereby a small number of professionals train a larger number of subnormals who, in turn, train a still larger number of their peers.

Of the general reviews, the most detailed appears to be that of Watson (1967) to whose work the writers are indebted. He discusses four types of positive reinforcement: edible, manipulatable, social, and token or generalized. In considering a number of studies in which comparisons between different reinforcers were made, he concludes that token reinforcement possesses two major advantages: first, it is possible that a summation effect may occur because of numerous associations with each of the edible, manipulatable, or social reinforcement with which it has been related; and second, it is relatively independent of specific deprivation states. A very useful annotated bibliography with over 100 references has been provided by Gardner and Watson (1969).

Positive reinforcement is not always a sufficient condition for developing certain behaviours while eliminating others, and the use of negative reinforcement at the same time has been found appropriate (Giles and Wolf, 1966; Watson, 1967). Time-out procedures have been used effectively to eliminate head banging, window-breaking, and other aggressive behaviour (Watson, 1967).

Studies have been mainly carried out in the following areas and some examples are given below:

1. Toilet training (Baumeister and Klosowski, 1965; Bensberg et al., 1965; Hundziak et al., 1965; Giles and Wolf, 1966; Watson, 1967).
2. Self-feeding (Gorton and Hollis, 1965; Henriksen and Doughty, 1967).
3. Self-dressing (Bensberg et al., 1965; Gorton and Hollis, 1965; Roos, 1965; Watson, 1967).
4. Self-grooming (Girardeau and Spradlin, 1964; Bensberg et al., 1965; Gorton and Hollis, 1965).
5. Social play behaviour (Girardeau and Spradlin, 1964; Bensberg et al., 1965; Watson, 1967).
6. Undesirable behaviour (Girardeau and Spradlin, 1964; Giles and Wolf, 1966; Hamilton et al., 1967; Watson, 1967; Wiesen and Watson, 1967).
7. Speech (Kerr et al., 1965; Doubros, 1966; Hamilton and Stephens, 1967; Sloane and MacAulay, 1968). See also section on Language.
8. Work skills (Girardeau and Spradlin, 1964; Bensberg et al., 1965).

In controlling undesirable behaviour, Gorton and Hollis (1965) and Bensberg et al. (1965) found that, with few exceptions, operant procedures were effective in maintaining desirable behaviour without the aid of tranquillizers, energizers, or sleeping medication. As Watson and Lawson (1966) put it, 'instrumental learning research is providing the basis for a new, effective technology of educating and training mental retardates, with both academic and social implications. ... Of significance is the fact that ... (these conditioning techniques) ... have succeeded with the severely and profoundly retarded, where other training methods have failed.'

Despite the large number of studies reported, Watson (1967) concluded that, although they indicate that severely and profoundly retarded children can develop skills when systematic training procedures are used, it is not clear what variables are responsible for the success of these programmes and which are either irrelevant or possibly even interfering. Gardner (1969) examined the methodology and results of operant conditioning techniques, and concluded that to some extent all the studies have violated one or more of the following require-ments of good experimental design: (1) exact specification of *all* relevant inde-pendent variables; (2) proper sampling techniques; (3) use of adequate controls; (4) proper assessment of the dependent variable; and (5) evaluation of long-term gains. Gardner recommends: (1) direct and indirect measures of both specific and general changes in behaviour; (2) individual as well as group presentation of results; (3) pre- and post-treatment evaluations, including periodic assessment to measure long-term gain; and (4) multivariate manipulation of the independent variables, particularly specific techniques. Progress in elucidating these problems can confidently be expected.

Learning sets and transfer of learning

As Deese (1958) puts it, 'There is no more important topic in the whole of the psychology of learning than transfer of training. Nearly everyone knows that transfer of training is basic to educational theory. Practically all educational and training programs are built upon the fundamental premise that human beings have the ability to transfer what they have learned from one situation to another.' The question at once arises whether the subnormal in addition to his deficiencies in acquisition is also defective in the extent to which previously learned responses may be generalized to new situations.

The first part of this section is concerned with learning set formation in the mentally subnormal; studies of transfer of training among problems of disparate classes, and the effects of special programmes of instruction upon test perfor-mance are reviewed later.

LEARNING SET ACQUISITION

A learning set (Harlow, 1949) is acquired through practice on problems that have a common basis for solution. Once the solution is apparent, performance on subsequent problems of the same type changes from a trial-and-error response pattern to one approximating single-trial learning. Learning set acquisition is based on a history of discrimination experience and represents a particular kind of transfer of training, transfer among many problems of a single class. The main variable of interest is, thus, interproblem learning as opposed to intraproblem learning.

Watson and Lawson (1966) provide a detailed review of the vast number of experiments using mentally retarded subjects on the Wisconsin General Test Apparatus, most of which have been concerned with object-quality discrimina-tions, reversal learning and oddity learning. Only a highly compressed summary of some of the findings will be included here.

The relation between mental age and speed of acquisition of an object-quality learning set was one of the first problems to be investigated. Ellis (1958) investi-gated object-quality discrimination at 'low' (5·05) and high (8·02) MA levels.

Ten successive problems were given and on each the subject had to reach a criterion of twenty successive correct responses ('finding the marble'). While both MA groups developed discrimination learning sets, the higher made fewer errors per problem and acquired learning sets more rapidly. Efficiency in learning set formation thus appeared to be a function of MA but, as Watson and Lawson point out, the possible effect of IQ was not partialled out. Stevenson and Swartz (1958) carried out a somewhat similar study but comparing two not greatly different MA groups. The lower of these (MA 4·1) failed to develop a set. Ellis and colleagues (1962), however, were able to show that even those with lower MAs were in some circumstances able to form object-quality discrimination sets. It seems probable that discrepancies between the findings of different studies can be accounted for by such factors as the nature of the discriminanda, number of problems, length of training, learning criterion, background experience, and type of reinforcement offered, as well as to such factors as MA (see also Wischner et al., 1962). Kaufman (1963) and Girardeau (1959) also point to the influence on discrimination of factors other than MA. Hayes and co-workers (1953) believed that learning set acquisition is a joint function of trials-per-problem and level of performance.

Studies of reversal discrimination learning show that, in general, the subnormal learn a position discrimination reversal most easily, followed in order of difficulty by intradimensional reversal shift and extradimensional reversal shift (Watson and Lawson, 1966). Subnormals with MAs as low as two years were able to master reversal position problems (House and Zeaman, 1959). Some studies have found no difference between the reversal performance of retardates and equal MA normals (Plenderleith, 1956; Stevenson and Zigler, 1957). There appears to be little relationship between MA and position reversal performance, but there may be a relationship between MA and stimulus reversal, particularly where an extradimensional shift is required.

Oddity discrimination learning has been shown to be related to MA. The general finding is that subnormals with MAs below five years do not form oddity learning sets, but above this level, speed of learning set acquisition is related to MA (Ellis and Sloan, 1959; Ellis et al., 1963; House, 1964).

Watson and Lawson point out that all conclusions concerning the relationship between MA and discrimination learning are open to the alternative interpretation of an IQ relationship, since both MA and IQ control procedures were not used. Furthermore, it is possible that institutionalized retardates, who were the subjects of these studies, may by virtue of the restricted environment be specifically deficient with respect to learning visual discriminations. These authors also conclude that the learning set acquisition is a function of the particular method employed. For maximizing the possibility of a low MA subnormal acquiring, for example, an object-quality set it is necessary to: (1) use many trials per problem or a high learning criterion; (2) employ a non-correction stimulus presentation technique; and (3) present the negative stimulus only on the first trial of each new problem.

Zeaman and House (1963) have provided an important theory of retardate discrimination learning that distinguishes two responses: (1) attending to the relevant stimulus dimension, and (2) approaching the correct cue of that dimension. From a large amount of data on visual discrimination learning in severely retarded subjects, they plotted the forward learning curves of sub-groups of subject homogeneous with respect to the number of trials taken to reach criterion of learning. From this it emerged that slow learners stayed close to chance performance for varying numbers of trials, but once performance started to improve, it moved relatively fast. Plotting the same data as backward learning curves (Hayes, 1953) showed that the final rates of all groups, fast or slow, were similar. It was concluded that the difference between fast and slow learning was not so much the rate at which improvement takes place *once it starts*, but rather the number of trials taken for learning to start. It was concluded that the difficulty retardates have in discrimination learning is related to the attention phase of the dual process, rather than to approaching the correct cue of the relevant stimulus dimension. Those who are familiar with studies of animal discrimination learning will note the similarity of this theoretical formulation with that of Sutherland (1964) and Mackintosh (1965). Zeaman and House present a number of stochastic models organized by the dual process theory and demonstrate the application of these to discrimination experiments with lower-level retardates, including original learning, reversals, effects of intelligence, stimulus factors, schedules of reinforcement, and transfer operations.

The discrimination reversal problem has been used to test verbal mediation deficiency hypotheses in mental retardates; these studies are reviewed in the section on Verbal Mediation.

Shepp and Turrisi (1966) have provided an important review (forty-six references) of work on learning and transfer of mediating responses in discrimination learning. In addition to discussing individual papers as well as methodological problems, these authors offer some general process laws. As already noted, intra-dimensional shifts are learned faster than extra-dimensional and this is held to support the proposition that the mediating process is dimensional in nature. Subjects learn to respond to a discriminative cue common to a class of stimuli, and they can transfer these responses to subsequent discriminations. Secondly, intra-dimensional shift performance improves with increasing amounts of overtraining, this being directly implied in the theories of Sutherland and Zeaman and House. These state that the strength of a relevant mediator approaches its asymptote slower than does the strength of an instrumental response. 'Consequently, with a weak criterion or just a few overtraining trials, the relevant mediator may be weak, and any intradimensional and extra-dimensional shift difference may be attenuated. With increasing amounts of overtraining, the strength of the relevant mediator increases, and the probability of this response approaches unity. There is also some evidence that extra-dimensional shifts become progressively more difficult with increases in amount of overtraining. This finding also supports the notion that the relevant mediator becomes stronger as a function of overtraining' (Shepp and Turrisi, 1966).

A third and much less certain 'law' is related to the type of irrelevant dimension presented during original learning (Shepp and Turrisi, 1966). In most experiments that have shown dimensional mediating-response transfer, the irrelevant dimension during training was presented with a variable-within arrangement. In one study, however, the irrelevant dimension was constant and there was subsequently no intra- or extra-dimensional shift difference and no evidence for mediating response transfer. Now mediating-response theories have not specified the variable-within irrelevant condition as a prerequisite for the acquisition of a mediating response. This poses an important theoretical question, and the authors suggest that the two types of shift should be compared with constant irrelevant and variable irrelevant dimensions to settle the question of whether the acquisition of a mediating response requires a variable irrelevant dimension during training.

RETENTION OF LEARNING SETS

Wischner and colleagues (1962) used a large number of problems (12 a day for 10 days) with mildly subnormal subjects, to study the formation of object-quality learning sets. The authors studied retention 6 months later, using an additional 2 days of practice on 12 3-trial problems a day. For those who had reached criterion in the earlier learning, the additional practice was sufficient to restore performance to its final level. For those who had earlier learned less well, however, performance was only a little above chance at the end of the 2 days of practice.

Clarke (1962) reported that a group of adult imbeciles, retested on the learning of the 4 Minnesota formboards 7 years after initial learning (32 trials), showed greatly enhanced performance, particularly on the first board. This could not be attributed to maturation but may, however, have resulted from the reinforcement provided by perceptual-motor experience in industrial workshops. However, Clarke and Cookson (1962) showed impressive retention of perceptual-motor learning by child and adult imbeciles over 6 months and 1 year, respectively, of non-reinforcement. In both these studies learning had been taken to asymptote, and motivation was apparently very high indeed.

Kaufman (Kaufman and Prehm, 1966), however, carried out a study on retention by mongols of three-trial object-quality problems. This experiment was marred by an institutional epidemic but limited findings failed to indicate retention by this group.

Much more information is needed on the degree to which learning sets may be retained. Apart from the nature of the tasks, at least two powerful factors seem to be involved. Firstly, the amount of learning and overlearning undertaken is clearly relevant, and secondly, the degree to which the ordinary life experience of these subjects possesses relevant reinforcers or makes direct use of the induced sets. (See also the section on Memory.)

TRANSFER OF TRAINING

Despite the acknowledged importance of transfer effects on all human activities, surprisingly little systematic research has been conducted in this area using mentally retarded subjects. In their comprehensive review, Kaufman and Prehm (1966) point to the diversity of work in this area and to the difficulty of coming to any precise conclusion concerning the conditions under which retardates will show positive (or negative) transfer.

An illustration of the importance of method to experimental outcome and thus to conclusions, is given in a later section on the Role of Input Organization in Memory. Gerjuoy and Alvarez (1969) failed to find any effect on amount recalled or amount of clustering one week after a single training session of five trials in which material to be recalled was presented clustered. By contrast, the present authors, using a different design, a long-term training procedure, and only one day between the end of training and initial transfer tests, did find significant effects. Both types of experiment are clearly necessary if the precise conditions in which transfer will occur are ever to be specified.

In the absence of data on which to base an analysis of transfer effects in the subnormal, this section will be confined to a summary of the only two long-term programmes of research on transfer reported in the literature, apart from the already discussed and monumental work by Zeaman and House on learning sets. This will be followed by discussion of three attempts to alter test behaviour on the basis of widely based programmes of instruction.

Using pairs of perceptual-motor learning tasks of equal difficulty, each of which made similar demands but had a different content from the other, Clarke and Blakemore (1961) showed that transfer, using a time score for twenty trials, was easily demonstrated, particularly among the younger imbeciles. Subsequent work suggested that this latter result was due to a ceiling effect for the adults. Clarke and Cookson (1962), using similar tasks and the same subjects, showed that earlier easier learning transferred six months later to more difficult learning, without intervening practice. Clarke and Cooper (1966) evolved a method for directly comparing adult and child imbeciles on the same tasks. Either the difficulty of the task pairs could be increased for the adults so that the time taken for initial performance was equal to that of the children, or difficulty could be decreased for the children so that their starting point was the same as for adults. Both methods gave similar results, showing that adults and children in these tasks exhibited similar learning and transfer curves. More importantly, it seemed that task complexity might, within limits, facilitate transfer. This notion was now tested by Clarke *et al.* (1966) who evolved a new experimental design, and, holding age constant, gave matched groups of imbeciles training on conceptual sorting tasks of different complexity. It was found that: (1) transfer was related to training task complexity; (2) it occurred across tasks that possessed no identical elements other than that they were conceptual problems; (3) differential effects of differing degrees of complex training were subsequently persistent over ten trials of the transfer task; and (4) the amount of overlearning of the complex training task was also relevant. This work was replicated, with rather more striking results on normal pre-school children (for review of these studies see Clarke *et al.*, 1967a).

The question of the nature of transfer between different conceptual tasks using normal pre-school children was then studied by Clarke *et al.* (1967b). Among other findings, it seemed that improved performance did not result from an increased arousal arising from exposure to a difficult problem, but rather from the practice of relatively unpractised processes – in this case the reduction of stimulus variability by categorization. The authors interpreted these and some later findings in terms of the subject's increased sensitivity to the categorical properties of the stimuli (Clarke *et al.*, 1970) a process not normally high in the hierarchy of preferred responses for these populations.

Bryant (1964) used apparently simple discrimination tasks and tested the ability of his severely subnormal subjects to abstract. Half were given verbal instruction on the first task, while the others were not. Against Bryant's expectancies, it emerged that verbal instruction heavily impeded transfer. A later experiment (Bryant, 1965a) showed that verbalization had interfered with the component on which imbeciles tend to base their transfer in discrimination learning, namely, learning to avoid the irrelevant dimension. Nevertheless, verbal instruction improved learning at the time when the instruction was given.

Subsequent work by Bryant (1967a) was aimed at elucidating the effect of verbal instruction: first, on the response about which instruction was being given, and second, on the response about which no instruction was given. Subjects were required to sort cards of two different colours into different boxes. Without verbal instructions, errors were equal for both. With instruction, errors were reduced but equal; and with instruction about one colour, errors were reduced for that colour, but for the other, errors remained equal to the earlier situation where no instruction was given. A transfer post-test showed many more errors with unfamiliar than the familiar colours. It seems, writes Bryant (1968) that learning strategies adopted by subnormals might be maladaptive to the introduction of language.

The author raises the question whether verbal instruction improves learning by direct attention or by affecting memory processes. His preliminary investigations (1965b, 1967b) suggested that memory is improved only when verbal labelling relates to a verbal problem, and that attentional processes are affected only when the stimulus array is a complex one.

The effects of specific, fairly long-term programmes of instruction, as measured by standard tests, have been explored in three recent studies.

Rouse (1965) found significant changes in educable retarded children after exposure to a special curriculum aimed at enhancing productive thinking. The training programme for the 47 experimental subjects comprised 30 half-hour lessons over a period of 6 weeks, and included a wide range of carefully specified activities; members of a control group meanwhile attended their regular classes.

Budoff and colleagues (1968) repeated the experiment, but their subjects failed to show gains on the Minnesota Tests of Creative Thinking commensurate with those previously reported; the authors were unable to offer precise reasons why the outcome of the two experiments differed.

Corter and McKinney (1968) conducted an experiment on flexibility training with educable retarded and bright normal children. Although much work on the alleged rigidity of the subnormal can be found in the literature, the authors were unable to identify any previous attempts to improve flexibility.

The major purpose of the study was to develop a process-oriented programme of training designed to provide subjects with reinforced practice in making cognitive shifts. The effectiveness of this training was then evaluated on 'flexibility tasks', the Binet scale, and five tests developed by the authors selected from a larger number by factor analytic techniques.

Training employed a large number of different exercises involving a variety of materials. Three general areas, perceptual, conceptual, and spontaneous flexibility, were sub-divided into two kinds of exercises for each. The perceptual area, for example, involved figure-ground reversal and embedded figures. The conceptual exercises used similarities-differences and concept shifting. For spontaneous flexibility, exercises included tasks in both structured and con-structured fluency such as class naming, rhymes, and cancellation. Efforts were also made to teach appropriate verbal concepts such as 'figure', 'ground', 'part', 'whole', 'alike', and 'different'.

The subjects were 32 mildly subnormal children attending special education classes and 32 normal children in kindergarten, matched for MA and sex, and allocated randomly to teaching or control conditions. The experimental groups received cognitive flexibility training for 20 days in sessions that lasted between 30 and 45 minutes. Control groups participated in their usual classroom activities. At the conclusion, experimental and control groups were retested on the Stanford–Binet and with the Cognitive Flexibility test battery. The Stanford-Binet retests were carried out by 3 experienced examiners, who had not pre-tested the same children and had not taken part in the training programme.

Results indicated that for the experimental groups the mean change in flexibility score between pre- and post-test was highly significant ($p < \cdot 001$). The mean change for the retarded controls was not significantly different from zero, although the normal controls had achieved significantly higher scores ($p < \cdot 001$). Mean IQ increases for experimental groups were as follows: for retarded, 6·25 and for normals 10·19, these both being significant. For the controls, however, non-significant gains were reported.

The authors consider that their results support earlier findings of greater difficulty in concept shifting in retardates as compared with normals, but, as they indicate, their normals were 'bright' and the two groups were not matched for social class so that such results are somewhat equivocal. However, the training programme was effective in producing significant increases in flexibility, and it is of interest that a hypothesis that retardates and normals would respond differentially was unsupported. The IQ increases were significantly greater for the trained than the controls, and this appeared to indicate generalization from training to other areas of cognitive functioning. However, the authors properly list the limitations of their study and are cautious in their interpretations. An important point emerging from this study is that, although retardates may gain significantly from a training programme, it is likely that normal children, subjected to the same programme, will gain more, particularly if, as in this case, they are above average in intelligence.

The present authors conclude with Kaufman and Prehm (1966) that there is a need for greatly increased research activity on transfer of training. It is difficult to see how efficient programmes for use in schools and rehabilitation centres can be evolved without a great deal more knowledge of factors underlying the generalization of learning in the subnormal.

Memory

Studies of memory in the mentally retarded have focused attention on the problem of identifying deficits in short-term memory, long-term memory, and the role of input organization, usually by contrast with normal control groups, matched for MA or CA. Most of the studies on short- and long-term memory have used rote memory or rote learning techniques and either digits, letters of the alphabet, or conceptually unrelated words or pictures. Those interested in input organization have used word lists or picture displays in which the stimulus material can be grouped into common conceptual categories.

SHORT-TERM MEMORY (STM)

The importance of short-term memory is emphasized in a number of psychological theories (e.g. Broadbent, 1958; Miller *et al.*, 1960) which assume that if information cannot pass from STM into permanent storage, learning will not occur. It should follow that where the major distinguishing feature of a group is their inability to learn as efficiently as others of similar age, the key to their deficiency might well be found in the process underlying STM.

Ellis (1963) elaborated a theory embodying two constructs, stimulus trace and central nervous system integrity, to account for the behavioural inadequacies of the mentally retarded. The stimulus trace is a hypothetical neural event or response which varies with the intensity, duration, and meaning of the stimulus situation. CNS integrity is defined by indices of adaptability such as intelligence test score, and serves as a limiting function for the stimulus trace. The central hypothesis is that the duration and amplitude of a trace are diminished in the subnormal organism. Ellis further hypothesized that the apparent learning deficit in the subnormal organism is due to noncontinuity of events as a result of an impoverished stimulus trace. He presents an account of his physiological model and cites evidence in support of it from a wide range of behavioural research with mental defectives. These included the areas of serial verbal learning, paired associate learning, reaction time, EEG studies, and factor analytic studies of intelligence test profiles.

Further support for this theory is provided by Hermelin and O'Connor (1964; O'Connor and Hermelin, 1965), whose evidence suggested that recall deficits in STM might be due to both memory decay and input restriction, and Madsen (1966) who reported a series of five experiments involving the assessment of the recall performance of normal and retarded subjects for a single paired associate, under different conditions. Performance of the retarded subjects was consistently inferior to that of the normal controls. On the other hand, Butterfield (1968a) investigated several predictions from the stimulus trace theory concerning serial learning in normal and retarded subjects, and concluded from a review of the research literature that these predictions had not been supported. In order to determine whether the central organismic variable of stimulus trace theory (i.e. neural integrity) was more closely related to MA or IQ, Butterfield (1968b) compared digit span performance of groups who were matched on either MA or CA but who differed in IQ. Differences were found between normal, borderline, and retarded IQ groups matched on CA, but not between those matched on MA. It was concluded that stimulus trace theory may best be regarded as a developmental rather than a defect approach to mental retardation. Further experimental studies on STM are reported by Ellis and Munger (1966), Ellis and Anders (1968), and Baumeister *et al.* (1967).

Neufeldt (1966) conducted a series of experiments to investigate STM in mental retardates using the dichotic listening technique initiated by Broadbent (1954). The experiments were devised to discover whether STM *capacity* and/or *strategy of encoding information* would account for some of the differences between retardates and normals. Four groups of subjects were compared: two groups of retardates (IQ range 53 to 79), one Organic and one Cultural-Familial in aetiology; a normal group matched for MA, and a second normal control group matched for CA. The evidence indicated that STM capacity was indeed an important difference between retardates and CA controls, but not between retardates and MA controls. The most important differences lay in the superior strategies manifested by both normal control groups, who, by comparison with the retardates, demonstrated a marked degree of flexibility in their adaptation of different recall strategies to various rates of informational input, and an ability to use more ambiguous strategies; familial defectives were somewhat better in this respect than organic retardates. The differences between the two normal control groups (of different ages) were indicative of the degree to which both memoric capacity and ability to apply useful strategies develops in normal individuals over time. The discussion and interpretation of these findings is consistent with the 'developmental lag' theory of familial retardation.

Kouw (1968) investigated the stimulus trace construct as an explanatory mechanism in retardate STM. He argued that (a) the capacity of retarded subjects to perform a delayed response task will vary as a function of CNS integrity; and (b) their delayed response capacity will vary as a function of both the intensity and duration of the pre-delay stimulus as well as the interaction of these variables. Using the Knox Cubes Test to classify 181 retardates as high or low on STM adequacy, he found that stimulus intensity affected delayed response as predicted, but that stimulus duration had no effect on performance. The author does not accept the latter results as necessarily conclusive, suggesting refinements in the technique for further investigation. He concludes that the limitations imposed on behavioural adequacy in STM functioning in organisms with subnormal CNS integrity were shown to change in the direction of greater adequacy, and this change was greatest for those with the lowest degree of CNS integrity. He concurs with Ellis's (1963) suggestion that the investigation of learning difference between retardates and normals must focus attention on the acquisition aspects, rather than long-term retention.

Gordon (1968) showed how stimulus presentation rate may both enhance and hinder recall of stimuli, depending on the interacting effects of stimulus complexity and the level of intellectual competency of the subjects. Using mildly subnormal and normal adults, three levels of stimulus complexity and three rates of presentation (40, 60, or 120 units per minute) he showed that: (a) subnormal subjects were inferior to normals in all conditions; (b) while normal subjects recalled simple concepts at a high level under all rate conditions, subnormal performance was adversely affected by high-speed presentation; (c) the normal group curve of performance was positively decelerated with increasing stimulus complexity, while the retarded group curve was negatively decelerated; (d) the variance in normal performance decreased with increase in presentation rate, while the opposite occurred for the retarded; and (e) that the error pattern for the two groups differed, suggesting differences in both accuracy of perception and in the ability to organize, encode, or associate what has been perceived.

Scott and Scott (1968) in reviewing a vast literature on STM, comment on the importance of Ellis's theory in providing a focal point for investigation in this area, and suggest, further, that two relatively new experimental techniques show promise of major theoretical importance. These are Broadbent's dichotic listening technique used by Neufeldt (1966) and the miniature experiment technique elaborated by House and Zeaman (1963), which are seen as providing an essential bridge between research on attention and memory and the relations between these two processes.

Latterly, Ellis and his colleagues, E. A. Holden and K. G. Scott, have reported important methodological advances, experimental results and theoretical models (Ellis, 1970; Holden, 1971; Scott, 1971), which give promise of a comprehensive account of retardate memory processes within the context of a general theoretical model of memory. Although there are differences in approach, the major conclusion of these writers is the complexity of human memory processes and the potential importance of rehearsal strategies. Since the projects and the thinking underlying the three statements are ambitious and as yet in tentative form, no attempt will be made to summarize them as a whole. Ellis's own position (1970) may, however, be briefly stated. Two processes are involved in the short-term storage of supraspan messages; one is Primary Memory, a limited capacity system, capable of retaining transiently only a few items. Rehearsal strategy is seen as the mechanism whereby information is passed to the Secondary Memory and Tertiary Memory (equivalent to LTM, see pp. 176-7). It is assumed that the latter is normal in retardates. Active rehearsal strategies are essential for one of the short-term storage processes but not the other. When the Primary Memory system is maximally loaded, the Secondary Memory serves to store the 'overload'. It is this which is weaker in retardates while Primary Memory is assumed to be normal. But the main reason for this weakness is seen as a probable failure of rehearsal mechanisms. As Ellis indicates, this model suggests the need to investigate the role of language in rehearsal strategies, and studies are planned to attempt to teach retardates how to rehearse.

SERIAL ANTICIPATION AND THE MCCRARY–HUNTER HYPOTHESIS

If a list of items is learned to perfection and the number of errors made in the course of learning is plotted for each item in the series, according to its position, a bow-shaped curve is obtained. The degree of bowing may be influenced by several conditions such as distribution of practice, rate of presentation, familiarity of material, and individual differences in learning ability. McCrary and Hunter (1953) showed that, if the curve is plotted in terms of *percentage* of total errors occurring at each position, the effect of differing conditions and subject differences disappears and the distribution of errors remains invariant.

Lipman (1963) reviews many of the studies of this hypothesis using contrasted groups of subnormals and normals. Subsequent work by Girardeau and Ellis (1964), McManis (1965), and Sen and Sen (1968) has confirmed the invariance hypothesis, using subjects of different intellectual levels under various conditions of learning. Butterfield (1968a) reviewing studies of serial learning in mental retardates, points out that the McCrary–Hunter procedure does not take account of learning efficiency, and suggests that a correction be made to subject's percentage error scores prior to evaluating the relation between learning rate and the shape of the serial curve. He re-analysed data and found a significant interaction between rate of learning and serial position, reflecting the fact that slow learners made relatively more errors in the middle positions of the list. Butterfield points to the growing body of evidence showing the inadequacy of trace-interference explanations of the serial position curve, and suggests that strategy analysis might provide a testable framework within which to study individual differences in rate of learning and relative position errors.

The von Restorff effect has been investigated in mental retardates by McManis (1966), Sternlicht and Deutsch (1966), and Sen *et al.* (1968), with results that are consistent with the view that while serial learning performance in the subnormal is inferior to the normal, the effects of varying experimental conditions operate in a similar way in both groups. McManis (1969a), however, obtained results that supported a stimulus and response generalization explanation of the isolation effect for normals but not for retardates.

In summary, the findings in the area of short-term memory and serial learning generally support the thesis that comparisons of mental retardates with normally intelligent subjects, whether matched for CA or, in some cases, MA, is likely to result in a demonstration of inferior performance on the part of the mentally subnormal, but that the effects of varying conditions operate in a similar way for both groups. Any precise theoretical interpretation of these findings must await the resolution of some of the methodological problems that bedevil this area, and that were discussed earlier in this chapter.

LONG-TERM RETENTION

Although learning ability in the subnormal is typically impaired, their retention of learned material is usually found to be as good as that of normal subjects. Haywood and Heal (1968) provide the following succinct review of the literature:

> Experimenters have typically failed to find differences in long term retention between retardates and non-retardates of comparable mental age (MA) (Cantor and Ryan, 1962, relearning of picture paired associates; Johnson, 1958, recognition, recall, and relearning with nonsense syllables learned serially; O'Connor and Hermelin, 1963a, recall of word paired associates; Plenderleith, 1956, reversal learning with picture paired associates). Furthermore, experimenters have failed to find differences in retention between retardates and non-retardates of comparable chronological age (CA), provided adjustments were made for differences in learning level (Klausmeier, Feldhusen, and Check, 1959, savings in reworking simple arithmetic problems; Lance, 1965, savings scores with nonsense syllable paired associates; Pryer, 1960, savings scores with words in a serial anticipation task; Vergason, 1964, 30-day savings scores with picture paired associates). Only Heber, Prehm, Nardi and Simpson (1962, relearning with nonsense syllable paired associates adjusted for original learning by co-variance) and Vergason (1964, 1-day savings scores with picture paired associates) have reported poorer retention by retardates than by non-retardates of comparable CA when adjustments were made for original learning level.

Nevertheless, interpretation of these data must take account of a number of methodological problems, discussed in detail by Belmont (1966), who considers the literature in the light of critical analyses made by Underwood (1954, 1964) and Keppel (1965). Belmont abstracts certain principles considered essential to the construction of a viable experiment:

(a) level of learning, defined as probability of performance, must be equalized for all subjects, especially where subject variables are studied independently;
(b) the optimum level of learning must be less than maximal at the beginning of the retention interval; and

(c) there must be a criterion against which retention test performance will be judged. This criterion should take the form of a reliable evaluation of what subjects would have done had there been no retention interval, thus permitting an evaluation of the retention interval *per se*.

Implicit in this analysis are two further principles: the original learning phase must be regulated to yield sufficient acquisition data for all subjects, while avoiding asymptotic performance, and the retention test conditions must be identical to the conditions prevailing at the time of immediate memory assessment. Belmont reviewed twelve studies of retention in the mentally retarded and found that most suffered in varying degree from one or more methodological weakness, principally failure to demonstrate equal original learning and problems of floor versus ceiling effects. The single study (by Klausmeier *et al.*, 1959) which seemed to overcome these problems found that normals and retardates were equal in long-term memory.

Haywood and Heal (1968) conducted a retention experiment in the light of the foregoing analysis, taking account of the important methodological principles arising from it.

Experimentally naïve institutionalised retardates at four IQ levels were trained in a group procedure by the study-test technique over 15 presentations of a visual code task. Each IQ level was divided into the top, middle, and bottom thirds according to the number of codes correctly recalled during the 15 acquisition trials. Retention tests were given all Ss at post-training intervals of one hour, 24 hours, one week, two weeks, and four weeks. There were no differences among IQ levels in either training or retention performance. Those in any IQ group who made more correct responses during acquisition retained the learned associations best and appeared to forget them at a slower rate.

THE ROLE OF INPUT ORGANIZATION

Miller's (1956) paper on memory and the storage of information is too familiar to need summarizing. Suffice it to say that considerable research investment in the general area of input and storage organization has subsequently been made.

A further stimulus had been provided by Bousfield (1953) who studied associative clustering in free recall. Words from the same category tend to be recalled consecutively even though they may have been presented randomly. Recall of word lists is improved where categorizable words are included. Tulving (1962, 1964, 1966) took matters further by demonstrating the presence of organizing activities even with apparently unrelated words. It seems clear that this organizational process takes place at or during memory storage.

Turning to the field of subnormality, Osborn (1960) carefully selected two groups of 'organic' and 'familial' mildly subnormal institutionalized patients, together with normal MA-matched school controls. Using pictures, rather than words, as experimental material, no significant differences were found between 'organics' and 'familials', both groups recalling and organizing them in recall as efficiently as the controls. Osborn draws attention, however, to some qualitative differences that might be the result of inappropriate learning habits.

Rossi (1963) compared the clustering of normal and subnormal children using a list of 20 stimulus words, 5 from each of 4 categories, randomized in 5 different ways. Each subject was given 5 trials with the same words arranged in different order to minimize serial learning order effects. The words were almost identical with those employed by Osborn (1960). Using 3 PPVT MA levels for normal children (4–6; 7–3; and 10–0), he matched 3 subnormal groups, finding that there was no significant difference between normals and subnormals in amount of recall. The normals showed a superior clustering performance only when a special clustering measure which eliminated categorical intrusions was employed. Practice effects as well as MA were associated with clustering within each diagnostic group.

Evans (1964) used Rossi's methods with adult subnormals, which he divided into two intelligence groups with mean WAIS IQs of 69 and 47, respectively. Each was subdivided into subgroups with or without material incentives. This latter had a negligible effect, but the brighter subjects tended to recall more words than the duller. Neither main group differed on clustering. Evans also discusses the problem of intrusions in relation to indices of clustering.

Gerjuoy and Spitz (1966) review the literature and in the findings point to inconsistencies that may result from the use of two different measures of clustering. Moreover, neither measure takes into account the number of words recalled by the subject. The investigation summarized here had as its aims the study of the growth of clustering and free recall as a function of age, intelligence, and practice, as well as an elucidation of the relationship between clustering and free recall. Five populations were used: 20 middle-grade subnormals (mean IQ 53), 20 high-grades (mean IQ 72), 19 matched normal MA subjects (mean IQ 107), 14 matched CA subjects (mean IQ 117) and finally, a group of 20 college students.

The experimental material consisted of 20 nouns, 5 from each of 4 categories (animals, body parts, clothing, and food). Using an identical procedure to that of Rossi (1963), 5 separate randomizations of this test were used.

Two measures of clustering were used; the first was the amount of clustering above chance. Chance clustering, or expected repetitions was defined as follows:

$$E(R) = \frac{m_1^2 + m_2^2 + m_3^2 + m_4^2 - l}{n}$$

where m_1, m_2, m_3, and m_4 are the number of items recalled from the categories, and n the total number of items recalled. Observed repetitions, $O(R)$, were defined as the number of times a stimulus word was followed by one or more stimulus words from the same category. Categorical or irrelevant intrusions, and perseverations were not counted. The amount of clustering of each subject was defined as the difference between expected and observed repetitions.

The authors developed a second measure of clustering: the observed/maximum ratio, which again takes into account the number of stimulus words recalled. Maximum possible clustering, Max (R), was defined as $(m_1 - 1) + (m_2 - 1) + (m_3 - 1) + (m_4 - 1)$. The observed/maximum ratio formula is:

$$\frac{O(R) - E(R)}{\text{Max}\,(R) - E(R)}$$

which indicates the amount of above chance clustering achieved in relation to the maximum possible clustering based on the number of stimulus words recalled.

Data for middle- and high-grade subnormals were pooled since there were no significant differences between them on recall or amount of clustering. Comparison of the subnormals with the other populations was made by means of a Lindquist Type I analysis of variance. Significant Population and Trial effects (both with $p < \cdot 001$) with nonsignificant interactions were demonstrated. There were no significant differences between the two lower MA groups, nor between the two higher MA groups. The latter, however, both recalled more words than the former.

Subnormals and their MA matched controls clustered very little, and only on Trial 5 for the subnormals were the scores significantly above chance. Equal CA normals clustered significantly on Trials 4 and 5 ($p < \cdot 02$), and college students on Trials 3, 4 and 5 ($p < \cdot 001$). Significant correlations between clustering and recall were found only for equal CA normals on Trial 5 ($r = \cdot 55$, $p < \cdot 05$) and for college students on Trials 4 ($r = \cdot 81$, $p < \cdot 01$) and 5 ($r = \cdot 85$, $p < \cdot 01$).

A second experiment was planned to determine whether conditions designed to increase clustering would aid the recall of the retarded. Two different methods were used: the Presented Clustered (PC) method where the stimulus words were presented in categories, and the Requested Clustered (RC) method where the experimenter requested the words by category name. Fifteen institutionalized subnormals were randomly assigned to each condition, and the same stimulus material was used as earlier. For the first group (PC), however, 5 new orders of the 20 stimulus words were produced with the 5 words of each category placed consecutively but with the order of categories, and the order of words within categories, randomized.

The recall data were compared with those from the subnormals in the first experiment. There were significant effects of Treatment ($p < \cdot 005$), Trials ($p < \cdot 001$), and Treatment $\times$ Trials ($p < \cdot 005$). Results from the two induced clustering groups did not differ significantly but induced clustering significantly increased the recall of both of these groups and produced steeper learning curves.

The clustering data were equally interesting. The PC group on Trial 1 clustered almost twice as much as the subnormals in the first experiment, and significantly above chance. On Trial 4 the correlation between clustering and recall ($r = \cdot 63$, $p < \cdot 05$) was significant, decreasing to a non-significant $\cdot 39$ on

Trial 5. The observed/maximum clustering scores on the PC group were ·72, ·35, ·19, ·24, and ·26 for the five trials, respectively.

Irrelevant intrusions were few in all three conditions, but categorical intrusions were somewhat higher. The RC group gave significantly more categorical intrusions that the first experiment or PC subjects.

Spitz (1966) offers an important review of the literature and concludes that subnormals are primarily deficient in the categorization and chunking of incoming information rather than in simple memory. In a sense this notion is supported by much work on long-term memory which indicates that this process may be specifically less defective than some others.

Madsen and Connor (1968) investigated the extent to which high-grade subnormals categorize verbal material during the storage process in comparison with college students. Small groups were selected and given pre-training in the coding of 18 categories of 4 words each. They were then tested for the free recall of lists of 12 words which differed in the amount and type of categorization. With increased degrees of categorization in the lists, an increased recall score by both groups was apparent. When an uncorrected categorization score was used, the students showed a significantly higher rate than the subnormals. When, however, the score was based on the number of words recalled, there were no significant differences. These results are in marked contrast with those of Gerjuoy and Spitz (1966) and may result from the pre-training procedure used by Madsen and Connor, which ensured that the categories and words were available to the subjects. It is clear that the mildly subnormal can use clustering processes and information reduction under the above-stated conditions.

Gerjuoy and Alvarez (1969) failed to produce a set to cluster in educable retarded adolescents (CA 15·2 years, IQ 59·4) and normal children matched for MA, using 1 training session of 5 trials and a transfer session one week later. Two lists of 20 familiar words were used, 5 words from each of 4 categories. Half the subjects in each population received List 1 during training and List 2 for transfer, and the other half had the converse. Half the subjects were trained with randomized word lists, while the other half were given clustered presentation; all subjects had randomized lists in the second (transfer session). Both populations exhibited increased clustering and recall when the list was presented in a clustered, rather than a randomized order, thus confirming previous findings. Neither practice and familiarity with the task, nor experience with a clustered list aided performance at the second session.

By contrast, Clarke and co-workers (1970) found significant effects of a learned set on the free recall of retarded adults (mean PPVT IQ 60). Two groups of subjects matched for score on a pictorial similarities test and ability to recall unrelated words, were trained as follows: the Blocks Group was required to recall a list of 16 words, 4 in each of 4 categories, presented in clusters (i.e. 'blocks'), twice every day until a criterion of 4 consecutive scores of 15 or 16 out of 16 words was reached, or they had completed 24 trials. The orders of words within clusters, and position of clusters within the list, were systematically changed from trial to trial. The Random Group was required to recall a list of 16 unrelated high-frequency words (Thorndike-Lorge) to the same criterion, the order of presentation of words varying from trial to trial. Both groups were subsequently presented with the same new list of 16 words, 4 words in each of 4 categories in which no 2 conceptually related words were ever juxtaposed, and neither words nor categories were common to either of the 2 training lists. There was a significant difference in *amount* recalled ($p < \cdot 025$) on the first 2 trials of transfer, favouring the Blocks Group, but neither group showed much tendency to cluster; on Trials 3 and 4 the differences between the groups in terms of amount recalled was reduced to non-significance, but there was a significant difference ($p < \cdot 05$) in cluster index (taking account of score) in favour of the Blocks Group. A further study by the authors, using memory for pictures as the transfer task, and groups of subjects, including an equal number of educable and trainable (imbecile) adolescents, showed a significant difference in score only between Blocks and Random Groups on Trials 1 and 2 of transfer, and no difference whatever in clustering, educable subjects in both groups clustering above chance, and the imbeciles showing little tendency to cluster. It was concluded that if categorical relations among words are repeatedly demonstrated by clustered presentation, a set to perceive inter-item associations develops. This is available for use with new categorizable material so that the categorical relations are perceived at the input-coding stage with consequent augmentation of total output (recall score). Clustering at any significant level is a reflection of organization of input material in store, and is an activity that occurs after at least two repetitions of a list, predominantly among subjects of higher intelligence. The results point to the importance of total recall score as a measure of categorization, in addition to clustering, which latter may well depend on different psychological processes.

Language, verbal mediation, and conceptual behaviour

LANGUAGE

The proposition that language development in the mentally subnormal tends to fall below the general level of their abilities has commanded almost universal support for many years. Recently, Alper (1967), analysing the WISC test results of 713 institutionalized children aged 5 to 16, found performance IQs were significantly higher than verbal IQs; within the verbal scale the Comprehension and Similarities subtests were consistently higher than Arithmetic and Vocabulary, while within the performance scale Picture Completion and Object Assembly tended to be high and Picture Arrangement and Coding lower. Belmont and colleagues (1967) compared WISC performance of a total population sample of home-based educable mental retardates aged 8 to 10, in Aberdeen, with the performance of normal children. The subtest profile for the subnormal group differed from that of the normal, the outstanding feature being their lack of verbal facility, with Vocabulary the lowest subtest score. The factorial organization of intellectual patterning also differentiated the groups and led to the suggestion that the limited level of functioning in the retarded children may be directly related to their less-developed verbal skills and to the non-availability of such skills in the service of perceptual-motor performance.

As in other areas of research, however, two divergent positions, the 'developmental lag' and the 'defect' theories, have been used to account for such findings; Luria (1961) and Luria and Vinogradova (1959) have been the chief exponents, along with other Pavlovian 'defectologists', of the latter view. Thus, Luria has contended not only that speech and thinking are intimately related, and that speech plays a vital part in the regulation and integration of normal behaviour, but that in the retarded there is a pathological inertia of the nervous processes. Unlike the normal child, the subnormal also suffers a dissociation between speech and motor signalling systems. These facts are said to account for 'the extreme difficulties with which their training is connected'.

Luria's approach has involved ingenious experimentation but there remains some doubt about his methodology. In the famous Luria and Vinogradova (1959) experiment, for example, it was shown that imbeciles generalized to homonyms, while normal children generalized to synonyms. It is, however, unclear whether the words used were equally familiar to the subnormals as to the normals. If the words were not understood very well by the former, the results are entirely to be expected.

Work on language has been well reviewed by O'Connor and Hermelin (1963b) who also outline their own experiments. While these authors find some merit in the approach of Luria they believe the prediction that the dissociation between speech and motor behaviour cannot be overcome to be too pessimistic. Part of the subnormal's incapacity to handle symbols comes from a reluctance to use them. Thus, 'a verbal disinclination as well as a verbal disability seems to be present' (1963b).

Lenneberg (1967), unlike Luria, espouses a developmental view of language. Recognizing that each disease giving rise to retardation has its typical manifestations, he nevertheless states that: 'the development of language, insofar as it occurs at all in these patients, follows some general laws of evolvement which may be traced among all of these conditions, and which, indeed, are not different in nature from the unfolding of language in healthy children. Among the retarded the entire developmental process is merely slowed down or stretched out during childhood and is regularly arrested during the early teens.' Support for this view is provided by Lenneberg et al. (1964) who studied over a three-year period sixty-one mongoloid children reared in their own homes. The children were visited periodically, and data consisted of psychological test results, tape recordings of spontaneous utterances during play, performance on an articulation test and a sentence-repetition test, assessments of vocabulary, understanding of commands, and nature of vocalization. Lenneberg points out that the IQ threshold for language development is quite low, and that above it, chronological age is the better predictor for language development. In this sample, the sequence of learning phases and the synchrony of emergence of different aspects of language was normal; progress in one field of language learning was well correlated with progress in all fields other than articulation. Poor articulation seemed to be to some extent a motivational factor and not primarily due to structural abnormalities.

Two important review papers on language functions in mental retardation have been published by Spreen (1965a, b). In the first, evidence is presented on the relationship between intellectual and language development and consideration is given to specific types of retardation and to factors identified as contributing to the severity of language handicaps. The second concentrates on the role of language in higher intellectual functions such as abstraction, concept formation, learning, and verbal mediation.

Spreen indicates that language dysfunction occurs in 100 per cent of those below IQ 20, in 90 per cent of those between IQ 21 and 50, and in around 45 per cent for the mildly subnormal. It is also argued that the abstract-concrete dimension in vocabulary definitions is of some value in differentiating subnormals matched for mental age with younger normals, and there is some indication that the brain damaged are more handicapped in abstraction ability than familial subnormals.

In Spreen's second paper, attention is again directed to the work of Luria, and to the broad question of verbal mediation. He reviews the Dissociation Hypothesis as put forward by Luria, where, in the final stage (about the age of 6 in the normal child) spoken language becomes more and more replaced with inner language which 'constitutes the essential component of thought and volitional action'. If this is so, the fact that subnormals are on the average markedly deficient in language in comparison with their other deficiencies, may be particularly significant. That this view is at least oversimple has been shown in the work of Furth and Youniss (1964) and Furth and Milgram (1965). All that can be repeated with certainty is that there tends to be a particular language deficit in the subnormal, and this may have a bearing on the rest of their cognitive development. Spreen concludes his review of this complicated problem by suggesting that although some of the evidence points to a specific innate verbal deficit in the retarded, the effects of environment and interpersonal communication, and the effects of general anxiety and motivation are probably important additional factors in determining the retardate's poor performance in this area.

Blount (1969) has reviewed studies of language in the more severely retarded, below IQ 50. He points to the dearth of research in this area and draws attention to the important work of Lyle (1959, 1960a). Lyle (1960b), in collaboration with Tizard, studied the experimental manipulation of environment and its effect on verbal development in a sample of imbecile children. In this, the Brooklands experiment, a control group was left in impoverished institutional surroundings while the experimental group was moved to a small 'child centred' family unit. Over a two-year period very significant verbal gains (e.g. on the Minnesota

Pre-School Scale) were demonstrated in the experimental group. Later work (Lyle, 1961) also supported the findings of Karlin and Strazzulla (1952). The more severely retarded are delayed in language development but follow the same sequence as normals. Poor home environments as well as the restricting effects of institutionalization are among the relevant factors. Other important descriptive studies have been provided by Mein and O'Connor (1960), Mein (1961) and Wolfensberger *et al.* (1963).

Beier and co-workers (1969) studied vocabulary usage in 30 institutionalized mentally retarded male subjects aged 11 to 24, IQ range 23 to 75, who were known to talk and whose articulation was good. Data on normal children, aged 12 and 16, IQ range 90 to 110, were available from a previous study. The subnormal group spoke more slowly than normals; used more positive words such as 'yes' and 'okay', and used more self-reference words. There was very little difference between the samples in extent of vocabulary: both had a vocabulary of about 40 words which comprised 50 per cent of their language; the same high agreement was true for the 10 most frequently used words. The authors conclude that the deficit in mental retardation is not so much in vocabulary as in conceptualization, organization, language structure, grammar, and syntax usage.

It would be surprising if some degree of language remediation were not possible with the mentally retarded. Indeed, Lyle's (1960b) experiment showed that considerable gains could be induced in a deprived imbecile group. A much shorter five months' programme by Kolstoe (1958) with a mongol group was, however, largely unsuccessful. On the other hand, a two-year study by Harvey *et al.* (1966) showed highly significant improvements. In the present writers' view, a major research attack on the question of remediation of verbal deficiencies is now overdue; these need to be explored in much the same way as did earlier experimental work on manual skills. In particular, the question of length of training as well as the most appropriate methods need to be evaluated. It seems probable that if significant effects are to be obtained, training programmes will have to be carried out over long periods of time.

VERBAL MEDIATION

Since there is general agreement that the mentally subnormal tend to be particularly handicapped in the area of language development, a number of experimental studies have been undertaken to determine whether they can use verbal mediators to facilitate learning, and whether, as suggested by Jensen and Rohwer (1963) and Jensen (1965), retardates have a specific deficit in this ability. The methods used have commonly been reversal and non-reversal shift learning and paired-associate learning.

O'Connor and Hermelin (1959) found that 11-year-old imbeciles were greatly superior to 5-year-old normal subjects (matched for MA) on a reversal shift, although the groups had not differed on the original discrimination. However, the normal children would verbalize the principle, while the imbeciles would not.

A second group of imbeciles, required to verbalize their choices on the initial discrimination, showed no facilitation on reversal, resembling the normal controls in that discrimination and reversal scores were equal. A possible interpretation is that the original learning was not under verbal control in the retarded subjects and, consequently, they did not have to inhibit a strong pre-experimental verbal set in the reversal situation, as did the normal children.

Balla and Zigler (1964) replicated this experiment, and found no difference in discrimination or reversal learning between retardates and normals at MA levels 5 and 6. They challenged the view that the cognitive functioning of retarded subjects is inherently different from normal children of equivalent MA.

Milgram and Furth (1964) compared normal and educable retarded children at two MA levels on a variety of reversal, non-reversal, and control shift conditions. They found evidence for the mediational deficiency hypothesis in significant age and IQ differences on dimension reversal, the greater difficulty of non-reversal over reversal shift, and in the relation of retrospective verbalization about relevant cues with age and task variables.

The finding reported by Kendler and Kendler (1959, 1960) and others that reversal shifts are easier than non-reversal shifts for normal elementary school-children was confirmed by Sanders *et al.* (1965). Retarded children of similar MA, however, performed equally well on each problem, thus presenting ambiguous data for a theory that proposes presence or absence of verbal mediation as the basis for the difference in ease of learning the two types of problem.

Heal and colleagues (1966) compared retarded children (MA 6·4, CA 14–8) with normal children (MA 6·5, CA 5–4) on three reversal problems. While the groups did not differ on original learning, the retardates were inferior to the normals in overall reversal, results discrepant with those of O'Connor and Hermelin (1959). The authors suggested two deficits in retardates: inability to inhibit a previously acquired habit, and susceptibility to disruption by novel stimuli, and speculated that increasing mental age may be associated with increasing retardate inferiority on a discrimination reversal.

The data on reversal shifts are thus to some extent inconsistent, and it seems unlikely that this method will yield crucial evidence on possible mediational deficiencies in retardates (see also section on Learning Sets).

Evidence on mediation in retardates from studies of paired-associate learning is more extensive, and excellent summaries are provided by Prehm (1966a, b), Goulet (1968), Mordock (1968), and Baumeister and Kellas (1971).

Of those early workers who matched subjects for CA, Eisman (1958), Akutagawa and Benoit (1959), and Vergason (1964) failed to find significant differences between their retardates and normals. Berkson and Cantor (1960) compared normal and retarded children matched for CA in a three-stage mediation paradigm, where the mediator was based on laboratory acquired associations. They found no difference between the groups for mediated facilitation, but the normal subjects learned the test stage faster than the retardates. Blue (1963), Carrier *et al.* (1961), Madsen (1963), and Ring and Palermo (1961) also found differences between groups on rate of initial learning. Of those workers who matched on MA, Cantor and Ryan (1962), Girardeau and Ellis (1964), and Vergason (1964) found no differences between normal and subnormal groups, while Blake (1960) and Heber *et al*. (1962) did find retardates significantly inferior.

Lipman (1963) suggested that the meaningfulness of the stimulus material was a major variable in determining outcome of experiments such as these; the less meaningful the material, the greater would be the performance deficit in retardates. Evidence in support of this notion comes from Noble and McKeely (1957), Cieutat *et al*. (1958), Lance (1965), and Prehm (1966a). Mordock (1968), commenting on these findings, points out that although there is empirical support for Lipman's contention, the relationship between decreasing meaningfulness and deficit in retardates is not linear, since both Lance and Prehm imply that at certain levels decreases in meaningfulness do not further handicap the subnormal.

The effect of different exposure times and anticipation intervals is considered to be another possible source of variation among reported results (see section on Reaction Time). Recently, Penney and colleagues (1968a) used a similar experimental design to that of Berkson and Cantor (1960), but matched their subjects on MA. They found that the retardates were mediationally deficient relative to normal children when a relatively short anticipation interval was used during the mediation test. Lengthening the interval facilitated mediation in the former group but was detrimental to the latter.

The nature of the stimulus and response items and their relative similarity or dissimilarity is also relevant to the outcome of comparative studies of paired-associate learning. It is suggested by Mordock that since subnormal subjects have weaker associative strengths to the same words than have average subjects (Evans, 1964; Silverstein and McLain, 1966), it is possible that stimulus differentiation will be more difficult for them. Furthermore, if subnormal and average subjects are differentially affected by stimulus similarity, then they should differ in R–S recall. Rieber (1964) found that subnormal subjects do not differ from average in learning simple verbal responses to stimuli but they do differ considerably in their ability to use these responses; this suggests a relative inability in the retardate to acquire mediating responses, and a greater rigidity once these have been established.

Milgram has investigated the mediational deficiency hypothesis in a series of studies. A comparison of educable and trainable retardates of comparable MA with young normal children at two age levels on paired associate learning with response competition, showed a relationship between susceptibility to interference and a combination of MA and IQ variables (Milgram and Furth, 1966). Retardates were found to be inferior in long-term retention of a mediational set (Milgram, 1967), although they had benefited significantly from verbal mediation instructions. Milgram draws attention to Maccoby's (1964) distinction between *production deficiency* (failure to employ verbal statements that are potentially available and useful) and a genuine *mediation deficiency* (actually producing these verbalizations without using them to elicit effective covert mediating responses) and suggests that his data support a production deficiency in retardates (see also section on Concept Learning). This line of argument is further elaborated by Milgram (1968) in a study of verbal mediation in paired-associate learning in severely retarded subjects compared with 4-year-old children. Mediational facilitation was of borderline significance for the retardates, but was effective in the young normals. However, Milgram, drawing on a great deal of evidence, suggests that as yet the question of production versus mediational deficiency has not been resolved.

Prehm (1968) gives the following summary of a series of experiments by Martin and his associates (Martin *et al.*, 1968; Berch, 1967; Bulgarella, 1967; Hohn, 1967; Van der Veen, 1967):

Martin, Boersma and Bulgarella studied the use of associative strategies (mediators) by retarded and normal adolescents. Using a seven-level schema for classifying subjects' verbal reports about how they learned pairs of dissyllables developed in a previous study (Martin, Boersma, and Cox, 1965), they found that significantly more normal than retarded subjects used high-level, and fewer normal than retarded subjects used low-level, strategies. Both groups used intermediate-level strategies to a comparable degree. Hohn provided groups of retarded and normal subjects with associative strategy aids and found that, although the provision of aids facilitated the performance of the retarded subjects, their acquisition performance was still below that of unaided normal subjects. Berch found that the performance of retarded subjects who were made familiar with stimulus elements was superior to the performance of subjects who were familiar with the entire stimulus. Bulgarella found that retarded subjects could be conditioned to use high-level strategies and that acquisition performance of subjects so conditioned was superior to control subjects.

Baumeister and Kellas (1971) present a model of acquisition strategies in paired-associate learning based on studies of normal and retarded subjects. There are four main features: (1) *strategy selector* – the one chosen probably depends on (a) meaningfulness level of task items, (b) the amount to be learned, (c) response required, (d) rate of presentation, (e) subject's pre-experimental history, and (f) ongoing self-evaluation of own performance; (2) *coding*, including visual imagery and mediational techniques (e.g. clustering, chunking, rhyming); (3) *rote repetition*, the coding product is itself subject to rote repetition; and (4) *feedback loop*, involving hypothesis testing and possible change of strategy by the subject.

Evidence that mental retardates can be persuaded to use mediators, granted the appropriate learning opportunities, is provided by two recent papers. Borkowski and Johnson (1968) replicated the Berkson and Cantor (1960) experiment, but used an MA control group as well as a CA control. Furthermore, the control paradigm in the three-stage chaining experimental model differed from the mediational paradigm in stage II rather than in stage I to prevent the occurrence of differential stimulus familiarity in stage III learning. The paired-associate learning of retardates was inferior to that of MA and CA controls when mediators were not available. However, when mediating links were provided, retardates used these associations in learning as well as the MA control group though not as efficiently as the CA controls. Furthermore, comparison of higher IQ levels with lower, within the retarded group, showed that the beneficial effects of mediation were not restricted to the former.

In a further carefully controlled study, again using a three-list paired-associate task, Penney et al. (1968b) explored the possibility of creating a set to mediate, by giving half their mentally retarded subjects a learning set task, while the other half were given an operant task. Both groups were then again given the three-list paired-associate task as a post-test of their mediational ability. The results showed that learning-set training enhanced mediation, while operant condition-ing retarded mediation; the former result is consistent with the emerging notion that mentally retarded subjects can learn to organize behaviour verbally and to use mediators. The latter result, which was unexpected, is, however, difficult to explain.

The important question of the retention of mediational sets in retardates has not as yet been adequately explored; thus, this remains a crucial area for investi-gation, with the probability of major theoretical and practical implications.

Gallagher (1969) used a variant of the three-stage chaining paradigm to in-vestigate with normal and retarded subjects (MA 8·76, CA 15–16) the influence of free association strength (FAS) as an *inferred* mediator between word pairs that are non-associated according to normative data (e.g. table-chair: A–B stage chair–sit: B–C stage; both normal associations, should lead to table-sit: A–C faster than a control condition, A–D, where no associative links are available). Each subject received a list of six pairs. Two pairs had high FAS between both the A–B and B–C links; two pairs had low FAS between these links, and two pairs were non-associated. As predicted on the basis of previous work with normal subjects, paired-associate learning was a function on the multiplicative value of the FAS values from stages A–B and B–C for both normal and retarded subjects. Normals learned faster than retardates for both types of A–C pairs (high and low multiplicative FAS values), and for the A–D control pairs. The findings are further evidence that retardates use verbal associations to facilitate learning, although dependence on their natural repertoire may result in less efficient learning than laboratory controlled associations (Berkson and Cantor, 1960; Borkowski and Johnson, 1968).

STUDIES OF CONCEPTUAL BEHAVIOUR

The material to be reviewed in this section overlaps to a considerable extent with much of the foregoing research data on verbal mediation, and organization of input for memory storage. The chief difference lies in the type of problem studied, being less dependent on rote learning or memory components (as in paired-associate learning) and more dependent on spontaneous processes of abstraction. Useful summaries of some of the evidence are provided by Rosenberg (1963) and Blount (1968).

An important study by Miller and associates (1968) sought to determine a hierarchy of problems that might differentiate the mentally retarded from normal controls. The investigation is unique in that it employed a repeated measures design and used films in presenting 9 different tasks to 96 retarded adolescents, 100 normal adolescents of similar CA, and 109 normal children of similar MA to the retarded. The tasks included: paired-associate learning, discrimination learning, probability learning, incidental learning, concept of probability, conservation of volume, age estimation, verbal memory, and ability to construct anagrams. All subjects were non-institutionalized and testing took place in school classrooms.

The results offer clear evidence of less effective performance in learning and problem solving tasks by retarded subjects than by normal people of either similar CA or MA. The only task in which retarded subjects performed at a higher level than normals was probability learning (confirming previous findings by Stevenson and Zigler, 1958); on paired-associate and discrimination learning the differences failed to reach the ·05 level of significance; on all other tasks, significant inferiority of performance by the retarded, as compared with CA or MA matched peers, was demonstrated. The authors conclude that the ability of the retarded to organize verbal material, and to apply conceptual schemes to its analysis, is more drastically impaired than is their ability to modify their responses in a learning task as a consequence of the information they receive. A very important subsidiary finding lay in the difference between normals and retardates in their pattern of relations between IQ and performance on the 9 tasks. The correlations for the 2 groups of normal subjects were consistently positive and significant for the majority of tasks. By contrast, few significant correlations between IQ and performance were found for the retarded subjects. The authors suggest that variables other than intelligence, possibly motivation and attention (see Zigler, 1967), play a greater part in retardate than normal performance.

The results of Miller *et al.* (1968) lead to the proposition, which many assume tacitly, that if out of a number of tasks (given in the same circumstances to groups of normal and retarded subjects) some differentiate between the groups better than others, those that differentiate will be: (a) more difficult, and (b) have a larger verbal/conceptual component than those that do not. A study by Milgram and Furth (1963) is important in showing that these two factors are not always correlated. They compared retarded schoolchildren in the IQ range 50–75 with normal children matched by CA to subgroups of MA 6, 7, 8, and 10 (approximately) on 3 tasks previously used by Furth (1961) in a study of deaf children. The Sameness task involved discrimination between 2 identical geometrical figures and 2 different shapes; the Symmetry task required discrimination between symmetrical and asymmetrical figures (both these tasks were assumed to be predominantly perceptual); the Opposition task, which was assumed to involve language-mediation, required choosing the opposite to 1 exemplar among a series of objects varying (on any one occasion) in size, volume, length, member brightness, position, and texture. Size opposition was used as the standard, subjects being required to reach a criterion of 6 consecutive correct choices; the others (1 trial each) were used as transfer tasks. Trials to a given criterion were used as the measure to compare groups, which did not differ on the Sameness discrimination task, differed in favour of the retarded on Symmetry ($p < \cdot 05$), and differed very significantly in favour of normal subjects ($p < \cdot 001$) on Opposition. Further analysis of the data, however, revealed that this latter task was much the *easiest* of the 3 for both retarded and normal subjects. The authors interpret their findings as showing that the retarded are not adept at the discovery and application of a language-relevant concept within their realm of comprehension, but do as well as normals in (more difficult) problems where perceptual rather than verbal modes of solution might be more appropriate.

An important theoretical point arises from the work of Furth on concept learning in the deaf, elaborated by Furth and Milgram in studies using mentally retarded subjects of different levels of ability. Furth and Milgram (1965) challenge the commonly held assumption that thought and language are so inextricably related as to be to all intents and purposes identical. While not disregarding the presumed interaction of language and cognitive behaviour, they believe that many views about the relationship of the two are oversimplified and potentially confusing, and point out the dangers inherent in procedures adopted by Piaget, Vigotsky, and Kendler which rely on verbal operations as mechanisms for advanced stages of conceptual ability. It might be added that the hazards involved in demanding a verbal response as evidence even of verbal comprehension (let alone potential non-verbal concepts) are underlined by Lenneberg (1962) who described a case which he claims is typical of a larger category of patients, where an organic defect prevented the acquisition of the motor skill necessary for *speaking* a language but the patient showed evidence of a complete *understanding* of language.

In an attempt to explore non-verbal and verbal classificatory behaviour, Furth and Milgram (1965) constructed a pictorial similarities task. Eighteen sets of 7 pictures were presented, and from each set the subject was required to select 3 (out of 7) which belonged together (*picture sorting*). The subjects were presented with the 18 sets of 3 conceptually related pictures and asked to explain why they belonged together (*picture verbalization*); the material was presented verbally, i.e. 18 sets of 7 words (*word sorting*); and subjects were given 3 related words and asked to verbalize the basis for the relation (*word verbalization*). In the first of a series of experiments, 38 non-institutionalized retardates (CA 12 years, IQ 70, MA 9 years) were compared with 38 normal schoolchildren (CA 9·1). Half the children in each group were used for the first 2 tasks, and half for the latter. For both groups the 2 word tasks were more difficult than the picture tasks;

there was no difference between the groups on picture sorting; retardates were, however, significantly inferior to the normals on the remaining 3 verbal tasks.

In a further experiment the authors used lower CA–MA groups: 16 retardates (CA 9·2; IQ 66·9; MA 6) and 16 normal children (CA 6·1). As before, the groups were equal on picture sorting; they were also similar on picture verbalization, a fact interpreted as showing with normal children that, developmentally, verbal formulation lags behind cognitive behaviour at the 6-year level. A statistical analysis of the data from both experiments showed a significant IQ × CA × Modality (pictures/words) interaction, suggesting that retardates improve (from MA 6 to 9) significantly less than do normals on the verbalization task by contrast to the sorting task.

Milgram (1966), using the same procedure, compared severely retarded (trainable, institutionalized), mildly retarded (educable, non-institutionalized) and normal groups of similar MA (6) but with an IQ difference of 30 points between adjacent groups. No difference was found among the three groups on picture sorting, but the severely retarded were significantly inferior to the other two groups with respect to verbalization. As before, at this MA level, the mild retardates and normals did not differ on verbalization. Milgram concludes that the greater the severity of mental defect, the greater the deficiency in verbal formulation of adequate conceptual performance.

Somewhat different results are reported by Stephens, who conducted a series of investigations into the presence and use of categories by mentally retarded schoolchildren. He (1964) compared 30 mildly subnormal (mean IQ 60) boys with 30 normals (mean IQ 101) using a CA match. Cards, each containing 7 pictures, 4 of which represented a particular category, were presented to the subjects. The experimenter named the category and the boy was required to point out the 4 exemplars. The normals gave significantly more correct responses than the subnormals and could identify all exemplars of more categories.

Stephens (1966a) repeated the earlier study, using CA matched groups. The subnormals were selected in three CA ranges: 90 to 101 months; 102 to 113 months; and 114 to 126 months. On this occasion, the cards were demonstrated twice. First, the subject was asked to point out which 4 pictures went together and why; and second, with the same instructions as in the earlier experiment. The normals were able to indicate more of the exemplars of categories, and could also label more of the correctly identified categories under both experimental conditions. It appeared that the concepts were present but were poorly delineated in the subnormals, with, for example, not all exemplars being correctly identified.

In a further study (Stephens, 1966b) subnormals did not differ from MA controls, both these groups being significantly less efficient than CA controls. All subjects were more effective when the category was named by the experimenter than when they had to discover the category for themselves.

Stephens (1968) studied the linguistic deficiencies of mentally subnormal children by investigating the types of errors they exhibited when required to provide verbal labels for concepts they had used successfully. Seven types of error were discovered, ranging from over- or undergeneralization to inability to state a category by name. Further support is thus provided for the view that it is possible successfully to use categories for problem solving without being able to provide an appropriate verbal label (see Furth and Milgram, 1965). The author suggests two possible conclusions. 'On the one hand, there may exist a developmental sequence in concept learning and utilization which begins with no knowledge of a concept, proceeds to a functional ability to use the concept, and is concluded by the higher level development of the ability to label the concept appropriately, as well as to employ it correctly.' The second possibility is that it may be 'easier, and less threatening, to respond to a labelling task by citing a series of low level descriptive features of the stimuli than by risking failure'. This reference to a possible problem of motivation is reminiscent of O'Connor and Hermelin's (1963b) conclusion that there is a disinclination on the part of the subnormal to use speech. Allen and Wallach (1969) found that educable retardates (IQ range, 41 to 77) were considerably less efficient at word definition than recognition on the PPVT (with the recognition score corrected for guessing) and conclude that the major functional weakness of this population is verbal encoding.

The relative importance of the alternative explanations will be determined only after a great deal more experimental work has been undertaken contrasting retarded groups with normal (IQ 90 to 110) and normal with superior (IQ 130 and above), at all ages, including adults.

A series of experiments on conceptual behaviour has been reported by Griffith and his colleagues. Griffith and Spitz (1958) presented 8 groups of 3 nouns each, requiring institutionalized retarded subjects (IQ 66, CA 17 years) to state the relationship of the words in the triad, i.e. to abstract. An additional vocabulary test included 18 of the 24 words already used, and the subject was asked to define these. The definitions of each word in the triad were checked for the presence of identical characteristics having been stated which might serve as a common abstraction. The data were then compared with results from the other test (order of presentation having been controlled). Subjects who defined at least 2 of the triad words by mentioning a common characteristic were 10 times more likely to offer the abstraction common to the triad. Conversely, if they defined less than 2 words with a mention of common characteristics, they were unlikely to offer the abstraction common to the words in the triad. Had the subnormals been 'testing hypotheses', only one abstraction suitable to relate the constituents of the triad would need to appear in the definitions; hence, the authors concluded that they were not testing hypotheses. Moreover, the subnormals, while offering adequate definitions, found it difficult to produce adequate abstractions.

Griffith and colleagues (1959) used a similar procedure with institutionalized retardates but added normal MA matched controls. Their purpose was to cast light on the relationship between concept formation and the availability of mediators. Retardates and normal 7-year-old children were not very successful in concept attainment unless they defined at least two words in terms of an acceptable abstraction. Normal 9-year-olds, however, were relatively successful even when they defined only one word in terms of an abstraction. The authors consider that conceptual tasks are sensitive indicators of retardation.

Further work by Griffith (1960) aimed to establish whether retarded subjects' performance in reporting similarities depended on their defining a threshold number or some constant proportion of the presented stimulus words in terms of an appropriate similarity for the entire set of presented words. Subjects were required to respond to 3- and 6-word sets of stimulus words. Those with IQs below 65 showed little success unless they could define, in terms of a possible abstraction, approximately two-thirds of the words. The results for those of IQ 65 and above did not clearly support either hypothesis.

Miller and Griffith (1961) studied the effect of a brief period of training (three sessions) upon abstraction. Social reinforcement appeared to exercise little influence on abstraction performance, but training produced significant conceptual effects on materials used in training. This did not transfer to new material. The conclusion that any improvement in the conceptual behaviour of retardates, effected through training, may be limited to the materials used, must, however, be viewed in the context of the short duration of these experiments.

Concept attainment by induction and deduction was investigated by Blake and Williams (1968) using retarded, normal, and superior subjects, all from state schools. Two sets of subjects were used, one equated for MA (approximately 11), and the other for CA (approximately 14), with the same group of retardates in each set. The task was concept-identification with object-level words from 4 categories used as specific instances to be associated with 2-digit numerals, which served as category labels. Subjects were allocated to the following conditions: induction-discovery, induction-demonstration, or deduction. No significant groups effect was shown in the equal MA comparison; it was, however, significant in the equal CA comparison (where analysis of covariance was used to adjust for a superior group younger than the retarded group). In this comparison the superior group exceeded the normal and the retarded, while the normal exceeded the retarded. Furthermore, the difference between the superior and the normal was larger and more significant than that between the normal and retarded. Although the authors do not comment on it (perhaps because the groups were statistically rather than experimentally matched for age), this finding raises the question of whether differences between superior and average 'normal' children may be as great as differences between mildly retarded and normal (see Osler and Fivel, 1961; Osler and Trautman, 1961), an important point in considering the 'defect' versus 'retardation' view of mental subnormality. The methods of concept attainment did not differentially affect the relationships among the groups. Deduction was the most effective method for all three types of subject; induction was less effective, and no difference was found between the discovery and demonstration methods. The authors rightly suggest, in view of findings with normal populations, that the lack of qualitative difference should be interpreted with caution, and may not hold with different tasks and different material.

Gozali (1969) investigated cognitive style in mental retardates, using a method devised by Kagan (1966) for normal children. A circular version of Kagan's Matching Familiar Figures test was administered to eighty educable retardates and measures of response latency, number of errors and order of errors were obtained. The findings were similar to those reported for normal children: subjects with long time response latencies and few errors (reflective children) made consistent efforts to solve test items; subjects with short latencies and high error scores (impulsive) tended to employ a position response set. The findings are important in showing the lack of homogeneity in behaviour among a retarded group which was representative of a limited age range (8 to 10·5 years), IQ range (55 to 78) and drawn from special classes within one city.

The question of some variables affecting the development of relative thinking by retardates has been explored by McManis (1968), using a technique designed by Piaget (1928) and investigated with normal children by Elkind (1961, 1962). The 'right-left' test and 'mother-sister' test both assess a subject's ability to handle certain abstract relations without a necessary reference to himself. Thus, questions in the former test range from concrete, 'Show me your left hand, show me your right hand', to the abstract connotation of spatial relations between three objects *opposite* to the subject; in the latter test, questions range between 'How many brothers have you, how many sisters?' to 'Ernest has three brothers: Paul, Henry, and Charles. How many brothers has Paul? Henry? Charles?'

The subjects were 140 institutionalized subnormals with an IQ range of 30 to 60, CA 7 to 8 to 21 to 11, and MA from 5–0 to 8–11. The normal controls were provided from Elkind's data. A succinct description of the results has been provided by McManis. 'Retardate MA and normal CA correspondence was good for concrete understanding of both concepts. Abstract right-left understanding was CA related (low IQ retardates > high IQ retardates > normals). Abstract understanding of kinship, however, was not a simple function of either MA or CA (high IQ retardates > normals > low IQ retardates). Understanding of the class concept of brother-sister was a function of IQ (normals > high IQ retardates > low IQ retardates).

Commenting on these results, McManis points out that his data support the view that relative thinking development is hierarchically ordered. Success at the abstract-relative level was invariably associated with success with the concrete problems but the reverse relationship was not found.

In a study of mass, weight, and volume conservation, McManis (1969b) found conservation to be MA rather than CA related, and more or less in the expected order of difficulty, although there were several reversals. Conservation of volume was poor for both groups, and both failed to show MA related improvement on this task. In a further study, McManis (1969c) showed that retardates attained transitivity of weight and length considerably later than normals. Conservation developed prior to transitivity, with more retardates between MA 7 and 10 being in a transitional stage of the sequence.

In view of the recent plethora of Piagetian studies on normal children, one must expect this fashionable trend to extend to the field of subnormality. It is to be hoped that experimenters will not be content with describing Piagetian stages in relation to MA, CA, and IQ, but will also conduct rigorous, long-term learning experiments to establish the conditions in which conservation, transitivity, and other processes may be acquired.

Evidence already exists to suggest that neither the hierarchical sequences nor the developmental ages at which these types of thinking occur can be regarded as anything like as clear and predictable as has been claimed by Piagetian enthusiasts.

Personality and motivation

The emphasis of this chapter is on research connected with aspects of cognitive functioning, and important problems such as the general motivation, need achievement, or anxiety level of subjects taking part in the many experiments have largely been ignored. Writing on personality disorders and characteristics of the mentally retarded, Heber (1964) stated:

Despite the generally acknowledged importance of personality factors in problem solving there has been relatively little experimental work relative to personality development and characteristics of the retarded. Not one of such commonly purported attributes of the retarded as passivity, anxiety, impulsivity, rigidity, suggestibility, a lack of persistence, immaturity, withdrawal, low frustration tolerance, unrealistic self-concept or level of aspiration can be either substantiated or refuted on the basis of available research data.

It is beyond the scope of this chapter to summarize research findings in the area of personality assessment; we will confine ourselves to a brief outline of two related theories of personality and motivation which in each case have served as a focus for systematic investigation. Both Cromwell and Zigler have been concerned to analyse the motivational effects of failure experiences and failure expectancies; Zigler has concentrated on the outcome of general deprivation suffered by most retardates in institutions.

Cromwell (1963) summarizes his social learning theory, emphasizing the critical role of failure experience and generalized expectancies for failure which typically characterize the retardate. Based on careful studies over many years he concluded that retardates: (1) enter a novel situation with a performance level which is depressed below their level of constitutional ability, (2) have fewer tendencies to be 'moved' by failure experience than normals, and (3) have fewer tendencies than normals to increase effort following a mild failure experience. Evidence was also obtained which gave partial support to the notion of separate approach and avoidance motivational systems. Stronger avoidance tendency was sometimes, but not always, shown by retardates. From this research there gradually developed a theoretical formulation that posited a success-approach and failure-avoidance motivational system which was separate from the hedonistic system typically described in terms of primary and secondary drives.

Zigler and his colleagues believe that many of the reported differences between the retarded and their normal MA matched controls may arise from a variety of differences in their motivational systems, associated with their impoverished experience and social deprivation. Zigler's interest arose in connection with a careful testing of the 'rigidity' hypothesis first advanced by Lewin and Kounin, a typical 'defect' theory of subnormality. This hypothesis was rejected, and in its place a social deprivation motivational hypothesis proposed (Zigler, 1966). Differences in 'rigidity' between the subnormal and their MA matched controls may be related to motivational differences for obtaining adult contact and approval. Those in institutions are likely to suffer a degree of deprivation and be more highly motivated to seek contact and approval. This view was supported by experimental evidence and led to an extension of the hypothesis that 'the greater the amount of pre-institutional social deprivation experienced by the feeble-minded child, the greater will be his motivation to interact with an adult, making such interaction and any adult approval or support that accompany it more reinforcing for his responses than for the responses of a feeble-minded child who has experienced a less amount of social deprivation' (1966, p. 85). For example, 60 retarded children were divided into 2 groups, high and low socially deprived, but matched on all other relevant variables. The study employed a 2-part satiation game and 3 out of 4 predictions were confirmed. The more socially deprived children: (1) spent a greater amount of time on the game; (2) more frequently made the maximum number of responses allowed; and (3) showed a greater increase in time spent on part 2 over that on part 1 of the game. The predictions that the more socially deprived would make fewer errors, however, reached only borderline significance.

Zigler pursued the point by demonstrating significant differences in performance of institutionalized retardates by comparison with home-based retardates and normal children matched for MA, the latter two groups showing no difference in performance; further, he found similar differences between institutionalized children of normal intelligence, by comparison with non-institutionalized controls (summarized in Zigler, 1966).

Butterfield and Zigler (1965) studied two institutions in the same state, having identical admission policies, but very different social climates in terms of staff attitudes to rehabilitation of their charges. In one institution, all except the most severely retarded were regarded as potentially capable of returning to the community, granted adequate preparation; in the other, a custodial attitude predominated. Butterfield and Zigler found that retardates in the latter institution had a greater need for social reinforcement than had those in the former (see also, Butterfield, 1967).

Additional research yielded data supporting the following hypotheses:

(1) Institutionalized retarded children tend to have been relatively deprived of adult contact and approval, and hence have a higher motivation to secure such contact and approval than do normal children.

(2) While retarded children have a higher positive-reaction tendency than normal children, due to a higher motivation to interact with an approving adult, they also have a higher negative-reaction tendency. This higher negative-reaction tendency is the result of a wariness which stems from retarded children's more frequent negative encounters with adults.

(3) The motive structure of the institutionalized retardate is influenced by an interaction between pre-institutional social history and the effects of institutionalization. This effect is complicated by the fact that institutionalization does not constitute a homogeneous psychological variable. Instead, institutions differ, and underlying psychological features of the particular institutions must be considered before predictions can be made concerning the effects of institutionalization on any particular child.

(4) The positions of various reinforcers in a reinforcer hierarchy differ as a function of environmental events. Due to the environmental differences experienced by institutionalized retarded children, the positions of reinforcers in their reinforcer hierarchy will differ from the positions of the same reinforcers in the reinforcer hierarchy of normal children.

(5) Institutionalized retarded children have learned to expect and settle for lower degrees of success than have normal children.

(6) An inner- versus outer-directed cognitive dimension may be employed to describe differences in the characteristic mode of attacking environmentally presented problems. The inner-directed person is one who employs his own thought processes and the solutions they provide in dealing with problems. The outer-directed person is one who focuses on external cues provided either by the stimuli of the problem or other persons in the belief that such attention will provide him with a guide to action. The style which characterises the individual's approach may be viewed as a result of his past history. Individuals whose internal solutions meet with a high proportion of failures will become distrustful of their own efforts and adopt an outer-directed style in their problem-solving. Since retardates unquestionably experience a disproportionate amount of failure, they are characterized by this outer-directedness. Many behaviours that are thought to inhere in mental retardation, e.g. distractibility, may be a product of this cognitive style. (Zigler, 1966)

Zigler's position must not be misconstrued as denying cognitive deficiencies of varying degree and quality in the mentally subnormal. He is, however, persistent in his assertion that factors other than 'pure' cognition determine performance in most behavioural situations, and that research workers should attempt some control of these factors in selecting groups for comparison (Zigler, 1969). He has shown that the institutionalized retarded, when confronted with an experimental task, tend to look for cues and solutions provided by others, rather than relying on their own judgment, as the intellectually normal tend to do (Turnure and Zigler, 1964; Sanders *et al.*, 1968).

The emphasis by both Cromwell and Zigler on failure experiences as an important motivational factor find support in Zeaman's (1965) summary of his research on discrimination learning sets. 'We have, on the other hand, observed *failure sets*. Prolonged failure on difficult problems leads to an inability to solve even the easiest problems, ordinarily solved in a trial or two' (p. 112).

Gardner (1968), in a careful review of research on personality characteristics, notes the paucity of systematic studies (other than those by Cromwell and Zigler), and that the results reported in the areas of self concept and anxiety level are conflicting and inconclusive. He can see no reason why personality characteristics in the subnormal should not be studied in an objective and meaningful fashion provided that the special problems of measurements in a population characterized by language deficits can be overcome.

Overview

If the reader of this chapter expected to gain clear knowledge from experimental studies of the precise nature and extent of the retardate's deficiencies and the methods by which these can be ameliorated, he will have been disappointed. In almost every area in which the methods of experimental psychology have been applied, apparently conflicting results have been reported. The wide range of subject and situational characteristics (including age, intellectual ability, and social background), experimental techniques, stimulus material, and criterion measures that have been employed, makes a critical evaluation of the literature exceedingly difficult, and it would at present be unwise to attempt to draw many firm conclusions. There is, however, an increasing awareness of methodological problems, and an increasing sophistication in the planning of experiments, which, combined with the differing attitudes of experimenters towards the problem of subnormality should, it is to be hoped, bring about a deeper understanding of this branch of psychology during the next decade.

The evidence summarized leads the authors to the following selective evaluation:

1. The question of whether the mentally subnormal is qualitatively deficient, due to general CNS impairment, or a retarded normal, remains to be resolved, if indeed it is susceptible of resolution. The fact that a large section of institutionalized populations are known to be the victims of chromosomal or metabolic defects, or conditions involving brain injury, makes the defect position tempting. There are, however, two problems: first, the fact that there is by no means clear evidence that the behaviour of diagnosed organically impaired retardates differs from matched groups in whom no impairment can be demonstrated (Haywood, 1966; Sternlicht *et al.*, 1968; Zeaman, 1965); second, that the few comparisons

made of normal with super-normal children tend to show similar differences to those between normals and the mildly subnormal (Osler and Fivel, 1961; Blake and Williams, 1968; discussed on p. 193). If the hundreds of studies comparing retarded with normal subjects were repeated, but comparing normal children (preferably from orphanages or other institutions) with superior children, it might be concluded that on the whole people with IQs above 130 are qualitatively superior to those with IQs of 100, and that the latter were inferior in CNS functioning to the former. Such a (hypothetical) conclusion might be entirely valid, but would invalidate suggestions that the majority of the mentally subnormal are to be regarded as a race apart.

Despite the persuasive evidence presented by Spitz (1967) and Winters (1969) suggesting that normal and subnormal subjects differ with respect to their perception of 'physiological' but not to 'experiential' illusions (pp. 156-7), the present authors conclude with Zeaman (1965) that the emphasis of psychological research is best directed to an examination of the laws governing the retardate's behaviour, rather than a search for unique laws (p. 151). In this connection, there is no systematic evidence suggesting that the laws governing learning, including language acquisition, or retention, are essentially different from those underlying these processes in normal human beings, or, in some cases, other animals. Zeaman and House's analysis of discrimination learning in the subnormal bears a striking similarity to that of Sutherland (1964) and Mackintosh (1965) in the field of animal behaviour. The principles of operant learning, successfully applied in many cases to the subnormal, all originated in the animal laboratory.

Baumeister and others found that, although RT is functionally related to intelligence, alteration of experimental conditions similarly affected reaction times of normals and subnormals (pp.159-60); Sen and Clarke showed within a defective population that susceptibility to external distractors was related to task difficulty, as previously demonstrated with normal subjects (p. 162); factors affecting verbal mediation, such as meaningfulness, exposure time and free-association strength (pp.186-7) appear on balance to apply similarly to retardate behaviour and to the normal population. Blake and Williams (p. 193) showed that methods of concept attainment did not differentiate superior, normal, and mildly retarded subjects, although there was a clear difference in levels of performance. Baumeister and Kellas (1971) have concluded that differences in verbal learning behaviour across IQ levels seem to be quantitative rather than qualitative and are best understood in terms of a developmental rather than a pathological conceptualization. Other examples could be cited from the text.

2. Altogether too much of the evidence concerning different aspects of behaviour in the subnormal is based on institutionalized samples. Since a majority of the subnormal never go to an institution, and those who do must be regarded as an unrepresentative sample (see Introduction) there is a danger that inaccurate generalizations may be made.

There is sufficient evidence suggesting that institutionalized retardates differ from non-institutionalized retardates of similar level (Kaufman, 1963, learning sets; Baumeister, 1968a, paired-associate learning; Lyle, 1959, 1960a, language; Zigler, 1966, personality and motivation) to render suspect any conclusions relating to cognitive difference based on differences between institutionalized retardates and normal subjects. Fortunately, this point seems at last to have been taken, and recent studies have tended to compare normal and subnormal children in the same schools, or retardates of different levels in the same institution or workshop.

3. Zeaman and House's (1963; Zeaman, 1965) careful analysis of retardate discrimination learning have led them to conclude that this process is mediated, not by verbal behaviour, but by attention. Discrimination learning involves a chain of at least two responses, the first being that of attending to the relevant dimension, the second being to approach the positive cue of that dimension; it is in the former aspect that retardates are deficient (this behaviour being MA-related) rather than in the latter. Learning and extinction, once the process starts, do not appear to be related to intelligence (p. 167).

4. Although studies of short-term memory greatly outnumber those on long-term retention, and there is no consensus as to whether retardates generally are inferior to MA-matched controls, as they clearly are to CA-matched on short-term memory (pp. 172–3), there do seem to be reasonable grounds for tentatively concluding that the acquisition of new material is the chief area of deficit in the subnormal, while retention of well-learned material is good (pp. 176–7).

5. The fact that subnormals often show variability of performance (Baumeister, 1968b), low degree of intercorrelation among tasks, and low correlation with intelligence test performance (Miller et al., 1968) suggests either a lack of a firmly based, well-ordered repertoire of response tendencies enabling the subject to select an appropriate strategy when first confronted with a task, or fluctuating motivation to succeed, or both in combination.

Work on verbal mediation (Borkowski and Johnson, 1968; Penney et al., 1968b; Gallagher, 1969) suggests that mental retardates can be shaped in the laboratory to use mediators, but the strong possibility exists that without long-term over-learning they would quickly lapse back into their lower-order response habits. Milgram (1967) found that retardates, although benefiting significantly from verbal mediation instructions, were inferior to normal controls in their long-term retention of a mediational set.

6. There is impressive evidence that retardates are particularly handicapped with respect to verbal and higher-order conceptual abilities (Alper, 1967; Belmont et al., 1967; Miller et al., 1968). This is to be expected, almost by definition, and may reasonably be accepted as evidence of constitutional deficits. It should, however, be immediately apparent that differences between the sub-normal and normal in these respects find a direct parallel in differences between the average and intellectually gifted, and the entire nature-nurture controversy (which will not be elaborated here) can be applied to the findings (see Introduction). It has been suggested that, even among the severely retarded,

environmental factors significantly influence the level attained (Lyle, 1959, 1960a, b).

It is equally clear from the work of many investigators, and particularly Furth and Milgram (pp. 190–1) that even fairly low-grade subnormals are not wholly devoid of conceptual categories, but that the greater the severity of defect, the greater the deficiency in *verbal formulation* of conceptual activity.

Bortner and Birch (1970) make the important point that the performance of a subnormal or normal child in a particular experimental situation does not necessarily give an accurate indication of his capacity, or of his potential for learning. These authors assert that 'it is clear that we have but begun to explore the universe of conditions for learning and performance which will facilitate most effectively the expression of the potentialities for adaptation which exist in mentally subnormal children'.

Granted that the subnormal are impaired in their ability to learn, verbalize, and abstract, the question remains open concerning the extent to which they can be made more competent in these respects. Such evidence as is available suggests that they might. On the other hand, the criticisms voiced by Watson (1967) and Gardner (1969) of studies of operant learning would with profit be borne in mind by any potential researcher in this area. Neither short-term periods of specific instruction nor blunderbuss educational programmes are likely to lead to the detailed understanding of how verbal and conceptual training of the retarded should most effectively proceed. Obvious, but frequently overlooked problems, are 'Hawthorne' effects and the personal qualities of the instructor. Both of these should be controlled in the experimental design, in addition to other variables. Research on higher cognitive processes, to be of any value, will probably need considerable financial support, and the services of a team of scientists; it seems to the present writers that it offers a most challenging and potentially interesting area for endeavour – whatever the outcome.

References

AKUTAGAWA, D. and BENOIT, E. P. (1959) The effect of age and relative brightness on associative learning in children. *Child Developm.*, **30**, 229–38.

ALLEN, M. R. and WALLACH, E. S. (1969) Word recognition and definition by educable retardates. *Amer. J. ment. Defic.*, **73**, 883–5.

ALPER, A. E. (1967) An analysis of the Wechsler Intelligence Scale for Children with institutionalized mental retardates. *Amer. J. ment. Defic.*, **71**, 624–30.

BALL, T. S. and WILSONCROFT, W. E. (1967) Perceptual-motor deficits and the phi-phenomenon. *Amer. J. ment. Defic.*, **71**, 797–800.

BALLA, D. and ZIGLER, E. (1964) Discrimination and switching learning in normal, familial retarded, and organic retarded children. *J. abn. soc. Psychol.*, **69**, 664–9.

BAUMEISTER, A. A. (1967a) Learning abilities of the mentally retarded. In BAUMEISTER, A. A. (ed.) *Mental Retardation: Appraisal, Education and Rehabilitation.* London: Univ. of London Press.

BAUMEISTER, A. A. (1967b) Problems in comparative studies of mental retardates and normals. *Amer. J. ment. Defic.*, **71**, 869–75.

BAUMEISTER, A. A. (1968a) Paired-associate learning by institutionalized and non-institutionalized retardates and normal children. *Amer. J. ment. Defic.*, **73**, 102–4.

BAUMEISTER, A. A. (1968b) Behavioral inadequacy and variability of performance. *Amer. J. ment. Defic.*, **73**, 477–83.

BAUMEISTER, A. A. and ELLIS, N. R. (1963) Delayed response performance of retardates. *Amer. J. ment. Defic.*, **67**, 714–22.

BAUMEISTER, A. A. and HAWKINS, W. F. (1967) Alpha responsiveness to photic stimulation in mental defectives. *Amer. J. ment. Defic.*, **71**, 783–6.

BAUMEISTER, A. A. and KELLAS, G. (1968a) Distributions of reaction times of retardates and normals. *Amer. J. ment. Defic.*, **72**, 715–18.

BAUMEISTER, A. A. and KELLAS, G. (1968b) Intrasubject response variability in relation to intelligence. *J. abn. Psychol.*, **73**, 421–3.

BAUMEISTER, A. A. and KELLAS, G. (1968c) Reaction time and mental retardation. In ELLIS, N. R. (ed.) *International Review of Research in Mental Retardation*, Vol. 3. New York: Academic Press.

BAUMEISTER, A. A. and KELLAS, G. (1971) Process variables in the paired-associate learning of retardates. In ELLIS, N. R. (ed.) *International Review of Research in Mental Retardation.* New York: Academic Press.

BAUMEISTER, A. A. and KLOSOWSKI, R. (1965) An attempt to group toilet train severely retarded patients. *Ment. Retard.*, **3**, 24–6.

BAUMEISTER, A. A. and WARD, L. C. (1967) Effects of rewards upon the reaction time of mental defectives. *Amer. J. ment. Defic.*, **71**, 801–5.

BAUMEISTER, A. A., HAWKINS, W. F. and HOLLAND, J. M. (1967) Retroactive inhibition in short-term recall in normals and retardates. *Amer. J. ment. Defic.*, **72**, 253–6.

BAUMEISTER, A. A., HAWKINS, W. F. and KELLAS, G. (1965a) The inter-active effects of stimulus intensity and intelligence upon reaction time. *Amer. J. ment. Defic.*, **69**, 526–30.

BAUMEISTER, A. A., HAWKINS, W. F. and KELLAS, G. (1965b) Reaction speed as a function of stimulus intensity in normals and retardates. *Percept. mot. Skills*, **20**, 649–52.

BAUMEISTER, A. A., HAWKINS, W. F. and KOENINGSKNECHT, R. (1965c) Effects of variation in complexity of the warning signal upon reaction time. *Amer. J. ment. Defic.*, **69**, 860–4.

BAUMEISTER, A. A., SPAIN, C. J. and ELLIS, N. R. (1963) A note on alpha block duration in normals and retardates. *Amer. J. ment. Defic.*, **67**, 723–5.

BAUMEISTER, A. A., WILCOX, S. and GREESON, J. (1969) Reaction times of retardates and normals as a function of relative stimulus frequency. *Amer. J. ment. Defic.*, **73**, 935–41.

BAUMEISTER, A. A., URQUHART, D., BEEDLE, R. and SMITH, T. E. (1964) Reaction time of normals and retardates under different stimulus intensity changes. *Amer. J. ment. Defic.*, **69**, 126–30.

BEIER, E. G., STARKWEATHER, J. A. and LAMBERT, M. J. (1969) Vocabulary usage of mentally retarded children. *Amer. J. ment. Defic.*, **73**, 927–34.

BELMONT, I., BIRCH, H. G. and BELMONT, L. (1967) The organization of intelligence test performance in educable mentally subnormal children. *Amer. J. ment. Defic.*, **71**, 969–76.

BELMONT, J. M. (1966) Long term memory in mental retardation. In ELLIS, N. R. (ed.) *International Review of Research in Mental Retardation*, Vol. I. New York: Academic Press.

BELMONT, J. M. and ELLIS, N. R. (1968) Effects of extraneous stimulation upon discrimination learning in normals and retardates. *Amer. J. ment. Defic.*, **72**, 525–32.

BENSBERG, G. J., COLWELL, C. N. and CASSEL, R. H. (1965) Teaching the profoundly retarded self-help activities by behavior shaping techniques. *Amer. J. ment. Defic.*, **69**, 674–9.

BERCH, D. (1967) *Comparison of Training Methods in Effective Utilization of High-Level Associative Strategies.* Unpubl. paper presented at the 91st Annual Convention, Amer. Assoc. on Ment. Defic., Denver, Colorado.

BERKSON, G. (1960a) An analysis of reaction time in normal and mentally deficient young men. II. Variation of complexity in reaction time tasks. *J. ment. Defic. Res.*, **4**, 59–67.

BERKSON, G. (1960b) An analysis of reaction time in normal and mentally deficient young men. III. Variation of stimulus and of response complexity. *J. ment. Defic. Res.*, **4**, 69–77.

BERKSON, G. (1963) Psychophysiological studies in mental deficiency. In ELLIS, N. R. (ed.) *Handbook of Mental Deficiency*. New York: McGraw-Hill.

BERKSON, G. and BAUMEISTER, A. A. (1967) Reaction time variability of mental defectives and normals. *Amer. J. ment. Defic.*, **72**, 262–6.

BERKSON, G. and CANTOR, G. N. (1960) A study of mediation in mentally retarded and normal school children. *J. educ. Psychol.*, **51**, 82–6.

BERKSON, G., HERMELIN, B. and O'CONNOR, N. (1961) Physiological responses of normals and institutionalized mental defectives to repeated stimuli. *J. ment. Defic. Res.*, **5**, 30–9.

BIJOU, S. W. (1963) Theory and research in mental (developmental) retardation. *Psychol. Rec.*, **13**, 95–110.

BIJOU, S. W. (1966) A functional analysis of retarded development. In

ELLIS, N. R. (ed.) *International Review of Research in Mental Retardation*, Vol. 1. New York: Academic Press.

BLAKE, K. A. (1960) Direct learning and transfer. In JOHNSON, G. O. and BLAKE, K. A. (eds.) *Learning Performance of Retarded and Normal Children*. New York: Syracuse Univ. Press.

BLAKE, K. A. and WILLIAMS, C. L. (1968) Induction and deduction and retarded, normal and superior subjects' concept attainment. *Amer. J. ment. Defic.*, **73**, 226–31.

BLOUNT, W. R. (1968) Concept usage research with the mentally retarded. *Psychol. Bull.*, **69**, 281–94.

BLOUNT, W. R. (1969) Language and the more severely retarded: a review. *Amer. J. ment. Defic.*, **73**, 21–9.

BLUE, C. M. (1963) Performance of normal and retarded subjects on a modified paired-associate task. *Amer. J. ment. Defic.*, **68**, 228–34.

BORKOWSKI, J. G. and JOHNSON, L. O. (1968) Mediation and the paired-associate learning of normals and retardates. *Amer. J. ment. Defic.*, **72**, 610–13.

BORTNER, M. and BIRCH, H. G. (1960) Perception and perceptual-motor dissociation in cerebral palsied children. *J. nerv. ment. Dis.*, **130**, 49–53.

BORTNER, M. and BIRCH, H. G. (1970) Cognitive capacity and cognitive competence. *Amer. J. ment. Defic.*, **74**, 735–44.

BOUSFIELD, W. A. (1953) The occurrence of clustering in the recall of randomly arranged associates. *J. gen. Psychol.*, **49**, 229–40.

BROADBENT, D. E. (1954) The role of auditory localization in attention and memory span. *J. exp. Psychol.*, **47**, 191–6.

BROADBENT, D. E. (1958) *Perception and Communication*. Oxford: Pergamon.

BRYANT, P. E. (1964) The effect of a verbal instruction on transfer in normal and severely subnormal children. *J. ment. Defic. Res.*, **8**, 35–43.

BRYANT, P. E. (1965a) The transfer of positive and negative learning by normal and severely subnormal children. *Brit. J. Psychol.*, **56**, 81–6.

BRYANT, P. E. (1965b) The effects of verbal labelling on recall and recognition in severely subnormal and normal children. *J. ment. Defic. Res.*, **9**, 229–36.

BRYANT, P. E. (1967a) Verbal labelling and learning strategies in normal and severely subnormal children. *Quart. J. exp. Psychol.*, **19**, 155–61.

BRYANT, P. E. (1967b) Verbalisation and immediate memory of complex stimuli in normal and severely subnormal children. *Brit. J. soc. clin. Psychol.*, **6**, 212–19.

BRYANT, P. E. (1968) Practical implications of studies of transfer. In RICHARDS, B. (ed.) *Proc. 1st Congr. Internat. Assoc. Scient. Stud. ment. Defic.*, 865–8. Reigate: Michael Jackson.

BUDOFF, M., MESKIN, J. D. and KEMLER, D. J. (1968) Training productive thinking of E.M.R.'s: a failure to replicate. *Amer. J. ment. Defic.*, **73**, 195–9.

BULGARELLA, R. (1967) *Conditionability of Associative Strategies among Educable Retardates.* Unpubl. paper presented at the 91st Annual Convention Amer. Assoc. on Ment. Defic., Denver, Colorado.

BUTLER, A. J. and CONRAD, W. G. (1964) Psychological correlates of abnormal electroencephalographic patterns in familial retardates. *J. clin. Psychol.*, **20**, 338–43.

BUTTERFIELD, E. C. (1967) The role of environmental factors in the treatment of institutionalized mental retardates. In BAUMEISTER, A. A. (ed.) *Mental Retardation: Appraisal, Education and Rehabilitation.* London: Univ. of London Press.

BUTTERFIELD, E. C. (1968a) Serial learning and the stimulus trace theory of mental retardation. *Amer. J. ment. Defic.*, **72**, 778–87.

BUTTERFIELD, E. C. (1968b) Stimulus trace in the mentally retarded: defect or developmental lag? *J. abn. Psychol.*, **73**, 358–62.

BUTTERFIELD, E. C. and ZIGLER, E. (1965) The influence of differing institutional social climates on the effectiveness of social reinforcement in the mentally retarded. *Amer. J. ment. Defic.*, **70**, 48–56.

CANTOR, G. N. and RYAN, T. J. (1962) Retention of verbal paired-associates in normals and retardates. *Amer. J. ment. Defic.*, **66**, 861–5.

CARRIER, N. A., MALPASS, L. F. and ORTON, K. D. (1961) *Responses of Bright, Normal, and Retarded Children to Learning Tasks.* Office of Education Co-operative Project No. 578. Carbondale: Southern Illinois Univ.

CIEUTAT, V., STOCKWELL, F. and NOBLE, C. (1958) The interaction of ability and amount of practice with stimulus and response meaningfulness (m, m') in paired-associate learning. *J. exp. Psychol.*, **56**, 193–202.

CLARKE, A. D. B. (1962) Laboratory and workshop studies of imbecile learning processes. *Proc. Lond. Conf. Scient. Stud. Ment. Defic.*, **1**, 89–96.

CLARKE, A. D. B. and BLAKEMORE, C. B. (1961) Age and perceptual-motor transfer in imbeciles. *Brit. J. Psychol.*, **52**, 125–31.

CLARKE, A. D. B. and COOKSON, M. (1962) Perceptual-motor transfer in imbeciles: a second series of experiments. *Brit. J. Psychol.*, **53**, 321–30.

CLARKE, A. D. B. and COOPER, G. M. (1966) Age and perceptual-motor transfer in imbeciles: task complexity as a variable. *Brit. J. Psychol.*, **57**, 113–19.

CLARKE, A. M., CLARKE, A. D. B. and COOPER, G. M. (1967a) Learning transfer and cognitive development. In ZUBIN, J. and JERVIS, G. (eds.) *Psychopathology of Mental Development.* New York: Grune & Stratton.

CLARKE, A. M., CLARKE, A. D. B. and COOPER, G. M. (1970) The development of a set to perceive categorical relations. In HAYWOOD, H. C. (ed.) *Social-Cultural Aspects of Mental Retardation.* New York: Appleton-Century-Crofts.

CLARKE, A. M., COOPER, G. M. and CLARKE, A. D. B. (1967b) Task complexity and transfer in the development of cognitive structures. *J. exp. Child Psychol.*, **5**, 562–76.

CLARKE, A. M., COOPER, G. M. and HENNEY, A. S. (1966) Width of transfer and task complexity in the conceptual learning of imbeciles. *Brit. J. Psychol.*, **57**, 121–8.

CLEVENGER, L. J. (1966) Electroencephalographic studies relating to mental retardation. *Ment. Retard. Abstrs.*, **3**, 170–8.

CORTER, H. M. and MCKINNEY, J. D. (1968) Flexibility training with educable retarded and bright normal children. *Amer. J. ment. Defic.*, **72**, 603–9.

CROMWELL, R. L. (1963) A social learning approach to mental retardation. In ELLIS, N. R. (ed.) *Handbook of Mental Deficiency*. New York: McGraw-Hill.

CROMWELL, R. L., BAUMEISTER, A. A. and HAWKINS, W. F. (1963) Research in activity level. In ELLIS, N. R. (ed.) *Handbook of Mental Deficiency*. New York: McGraw-Hill.

DEESE, J. (1958) *The Psychology of Learning*. New York: McGraw-Hill.

DEICH, R. (1968) Reproduction and recognition as indices of perceptual impairment. *Amer. J. ment. Defic.*, **73**, 9–12.

DENT, H. E. (1968) Operant conditioning as a tool in the habilitation of the mentally retarded. In RICHARDS, B. (ed.) *Proc. 1st Congr. Internat. Assoc. Scient. Stud. Ment. Defic.*, 873–6. Reigate: Michael Jackson.

DILLER, L. and BIRCH, H. G. (1964) Psychological evaluation of children with cerebral damage. In BIRCH, H. G. (ed.) *Brain Damage in Children*. New York: Williams & Wilkins.

DOUBROS, S. G. (1966) Behavior therapy with high level, institutionalized retarded adolescents. *Except. Child.*, **33**, 229–33.

DOYLE, M. (1967) Perceptual skill development – a possible resource for the intellectually handicapped. *Amer. J. ment. Defic.*, **71**, 776–82.

EISMAN, B. (1958) Paired associate learning, generalization, and retention as a function of intelligence. *Amer. J. ment. Defic.*, **63**, 481–9.

ELKIND, D. (1961) Children's conception of right and left: Piaget replication study IV. *J. genet. Psychol.*, **99**, 269–76.

ELKIND, D. (1962) Children's conception of brother and sister: Piaget replication study V. *J. genet. Psychol.*, **100**, 129–36.

ELLINGSON, R. J. (1966) Relationship between E.E.G. and test intelligence: a commentary. *Psychol. Bull.*, **65**, 91–8.

ELLIS, N. R. (1958) Object-quality discrimination learning sets in mental defectives. *J. comp. physiol. Psychol.*, **51**, 79–81.

ELLIS, N. R. (1963) The stimulus trace and behavioral inadequacy. In ELLIS, N. R. (ed.) *Handbook of Mental Deficiency*. New York: McGraw-Hill.

ELLIS, N. R. (1969) A behavioral research strategy in mental retardation: defense and critique. *Amer. J. ment. Defic.*, **73**, 557–66.

ELLIS, N. R. (1971) Memory processes in retardates and normals. In
ELLIS, N. R. (ed.) *International Review of Research in Mental
Retardation*, Vol. 4. New York: Academic Press.

ELLIS, N. R. and ANDERS, T. R. (1968) Short-term memory in the mental
retardate. *Amer. J. ment. Defic.*, **72**, 931–6.

ELLIS, N. R. and MUNGER, M. (1966) Short-term memory in normal
children and mental retardates. *Psychon. Sci.*, **6**, 381–2.

ELLIS, N. R. and SLOAN, W. (1957) Relationship between intelligence and
simple reaction time in mental defectives. *Percept. mot. Skills*, **7**, 65–7.

ELLIS, N. R. and SLOAN, W. (1959) Oddity learning as a function of
mental age. *J. comp. physiol. Psychol.*, **52**, 228–30.

ELLIS, N. R., GIRARDEAU, F. L. and PRYER, M. W. (1962) Analysis of
learning sets in normal and severely defective humans. *J. comp. physiol.
Psychol.*, **55**, 860–5.

ELLIS, N. R., HAWKINS, W. F., PRYER, M. W. and JONES, R. W.
(1963) Distraction effects in oddity learning by normal and mentally
defective humans. *Amer. J. ment. Defic.*, **67**, 576–83.

EVANS, R. A. (1964) Word recall and associative clustering in mental
retardates. *Amer. J. ment. Defic.*, **69**, 413–18.

FEDIO, P. M., MIRSKY, A. F., SMITH, W. J. and PARRY, D. (1961)
Reaction time and E.E.G. activation in normal and schizophrenic
subjects. *Electroencephalog. Clin. Neurophysiol.*, **13**, 923–6.

FURTH, H. G. (1961) The influence of language on the development of
concept formation in deaf children. *J. abn. soc. Psychol.*, **63**, 386–9.

FURTH, H. G. and MILGRAM, N. A. (1965) The influence of language on
classification: a theoretical model applied to normal, retarded and deaf
children. *Genet. Psychol. Monogr.*, **72**, 317–51.

FURTH, H. G. and YOUNISS, J. (1964) Colour-object paired-associates in
deaf and hearing children with and without response competition. *J.
consult. Psychol.*, **28**, 224–7.

GALLAGHER, J. W. (1969) Mediation as a function of associative chains in
normal and retarded children. *Amer. J. ment. Defic.*, **73**, 886–9.

GARDNER, J. M. (1969) Behavior modification research in mental retardation: search for an adequate paradigm. *Amer. J. ment. Defic.*, **73**, 844–51.

GARDNER, J. M. and WATSON, L. S. (1969) Behavior modification of the
mentally retarded: an annotated bibliography. *Ment. Retard. Abstrs.*, **6**,
181–93.

GARDNER, W. I. (1968) Personality characteristics of the mentally retarded:
review and critique. In PREHM, H. J., HAMERLYNCK, L. A. and
CROSSON, J. E. (eds.) *Behavioral Research in Mental Retardation*.
Corvallis: Oregon State Univ.

GAUDREAU, J. (1968) Interrelations among perception, learning ability and
intelligence in mentally deficient school children. *J. learning Dis.*, **1**,
301–6.

GERJUOY, I. R. and ALVAREZ, J. M. (1969) Transfer of learning in associative clustering of retardates and normals. *Amer. J. ment. Defic.*, **73**, 733–8.

GERJUOY, I. R. and SPITZ, H. H. (1966) Associative clustering in free recall: intellectual and developmental variables. *Amer. J. ment. Defic.*, **70**, 918–27.

GILES, I. K. and WOLF, M. M. (1966) Toilet training institutionalized, severe retardates: an application of operant behavior modification techniques. *Amer. J. ment. Defic.*, **70**, 766–80.

GIRARDEAU, F. L. (1959) The formation of discrimination learning sets in mongoloid and normal children. *J. comp. physiol. Psychol.*, **52**, 566–70.

GIRARDEAU, F. L. and ELLIS, N. R. (1964) Rote verbal learning by normal and mentally retarded children. *Amer. J. ment. Defic.*, **68**, 525–32.

GIRARDEAU, F. L. and SPRADLIN, J. E. (1964) Token rewards in a cottage program. *Ment. Retard.*, **2**, 345–51.

GOLDSTEIN, H. (1964) Social and occupational adjustment. In STEVENS, H. A. and HEBER, R. (eds.) *Mental Retardation*. Chicago: Univ. of Chicago Press.

GOLDSTEIN, K. and SCHEERER, M. (1941) Abstract and concrete behavior: an experimental study with special tests. *Psychol. Monogr.*, **53**, 25–42.

GORDON, M. C. (1968) Some effects of stimulus presentation rate and complexity on perception and retention. *Amer. J. ment. Defic.*, **73**, 437–45.

GORTON, C. E. and HOLLIS, J. H. (1965) Redesigning a cottage unit for better programming and research for the severely retarded. *Ment. Retard.*, **3**, 16–21.

GOULET, L. R. (1968) Verbal learning and memory research with retardates: an attempt to assess developmental trends. In ELLIS, N. R. (ed.) *International Review of Research in Mental Retardation*, Vol. 3. New York: Academic Press.

GOZALI, J. (1969) Impulsivity-reflectivity as problem solving styles among educable mentally retarded children. *Amer. J. ment. Defic.*, **73**, 864–7.

GRIFFITH, B. C. (1960) The use of verbal mediators in concept formation by retarded subjects at different intelligence levels. *Child Developm.*, **31**, 633–41.

GRIFFITH, B. C. and SPITZ, H. H. (1958) Some relationships between abstraction and word meaning in retarded adolescents. *Amer. J. ment. Defic.*, **63**, 247–51.

GRIFFITH, B. C., SPITZ, H. H. and LIPMAN, R. S. (1959) Verbal mediation and concept formation in retarded and normal subjects. *J. exp. Psychol.*, **58**. 247–51.

HAMILTON, J. W. and STEPHENS, L. Y. (1967) Reinstating speech in an emotionally disturbed, mentally retarded young woman. *J. speech hear. Dis.*, **32**, 383–9.

HAMILTON, J., STEPHENS, L. and ALLEN, P. (1967) Controlling aggressive and destructive behavior in severely retarded institutionalized residents. *Amer. J. ment. Defic.*, **71**, 852–6.

HARLOW, H. F. (1949) The formation of learning sets. *Psychol. Rev.*, **56**, 51–65.

HARVEY, A., YEP, B. and SELLIN, D. (1966) Developmental achievement of trainable mentally retarded children. *Training School Bull.*, **63**, 100–8.

HAWKINS, W. F., BAUMEISTER, A. A., KOENINGSKNECHT, R. A. and KELLAS, G. (1965) Simple and disjunctive reaction times of normals and retardates. *Amer. J. ment. Defic.*, **69**, 536–40.

HAYES, K. J. (1953) The backward curve: a method for the study of learning. *Psychol. Rev.*, **60**, 269–75.

HAYES, K. J., THOMPSON, R. and HAYES, C. (1953) Discrimination learning sets in chimpanzees. *J. comp. physiol. Psychol.*, **46**, 99–104.

HAYWOOD, H. C. (1966) Perceptual handicap: fact or artifact? *Ment. Retard.* (Canada), **16**, 9–16.

HAYWOOD, H. C. and HEAL, L. W. (1968) Retention of learned visual associations as a function of I.Q. and learning levels. *Amer. J. ment. Defic.*, **72**, 828–38.

HEAL, L. W., ROSS, L. E. and SANDERS, B. (1966) Reversal and partial reversal in mental defectives and normal children of a comparable mental age. *Amer. J. ment. Defic.*, **71**, 411–16.

HEBER, R. (1964) Personality. In STEVENS, H. A. and HEBER, R. (eds.) *Mental Retardation*. Chicago: Univ. of Chicago Press.

HEBER, R., PREHM, H., NARDI, G. and SIMPSON, N. (1962) *Learning and Retention of Retarded and Normal Children on a Paired-Associate Task.* Paper read at the Annual Meeting, Amer. Assoc. on Ment. Defic., New York.

HENRIKSEN, K. and DOUGHTY, R. (1967) Decelerating undesired meal time behavior in a group of profoundly retarded boys. *Amer. J. ment. Defic.*, **72**, 40–4.

HERMELIN, B. F. and O'CONNOR, N. (1964) Short-term memory in normal and subnormal children. *Amer. J. ment. Defic.*, **69**, 121–5.

HERMELIN, B. F. and VENABLES, P. H. (1964) Reaction time and alpha blocking in normal and severely subnormal subjects. *J. exp. Psychol.*, **67**, 365–72.

HOHN, R. (1967) *Facilitation in Associative Learning Ability among Educable Retardates.* Unpubl. paper presented at the 91st Annual Convention, Amer. Assoc. on Ment. Defic., Denver, Colorado.

HOLDEN, E. A. Jr. (1965) Reaction time during unimodal and trimodal stimulation in educable retardates. *J. ment. Defic. Res.*, **9**, 183–90.

HOLDEN, E. A. Jr. (1971) Sequential dot presentation measures of stimulus trace in retardates and normals. In ELLIS, N. R. (ed.) *International*

Review of Research in Mental Retardation, Vol. 5. New York: Academic Press.

HOUSE, B. J. (1964) The effect of distinctive responses on discrimination reversals in retardates. *Amer. J. ment. Defic.*, **69**, 79–85.

HOUSE, B. J. and ZEAMAN, D. (1959) Position discrimination and reversals in low-grade retardates. *J. comp. physiol. Psychol.*, **52**, 564–5.

HOUSE, B. J. and ZEAMAN, D. (1962) Reversal and non-reversal shifts in discrimination learning in retardates. *J. exp. Psychol.*, **63**, 444–51.

HOUSE, B. J. and ZEAMAN, D. (1963) Miniature experiments in the discrimination learning of retardates. In LIPSITT, L. P. and SPIKER, C. C. (eds.) *Advances in Child Development and Behavior*. New York: Academic Press.

HUNDZIAK, M., MAURER, R. A. and WATSON, L. S. (1965) Operant conditioning in toilet training of severely mentally retarded boys. *Amer. J. ment. Defic.*, **70**, 120–4.

HUTT, S. J. and HUTT, C. (1964) Hyperactivity in a group of epileptic (and some non-epileptic) brain damaged children. *Epilepsia J.*, **5**, 334–51.

JENSEN, A. R. (1965) Rote learning in retarded adults and normal children. *Amer. J. ment. Defic.*, **69**, 828–34.

JENSEN, A. R. and ROHWER, W. D. (1963) The effect of verbal mediation on the learning and retention of paired-associates by retarded adults. *Amer. J. ment. Defic.*, **68**, 80–4.

JOHNSON, G. O. (1958) *Comparative Studies of Some Learning Characteristics in Mentally Retarded and Normal Children of the Same Mental Age.* Syracuse, NY: Syracuse Univ. Press.

KAGAN, J. (1966) A developmental approach to conceptual growth. In KLAUSMEIER, H. J. and HARRIS, C. W. (eds.) *Analysis of Concept Learning.* New York: Academic Press.

KARLIN, I. W. and STRAZZULLA, M. (1952) Speech and language problems of mentally deficient children. *J. speech hear. Dis.*, **17**, 286–94.

KAUFMAN, M. E. (1963) The formation of a learning set in institutionalized and non-institutionalized mental defectives. *Amer. J. ment. Defic.*, **67**, 601–5.

KAUFMAN, M. E. and PREHM, H. J. (1966) A review of research on learning sets and transfer of training in mental defectives. In ELLIS, N. R. (ed.) *International Review of Research in Mental Retardation,* Vol. 2. New York: Academic Press.

KENDLER, T. S. and KENDLER, H. H. (1959) Reversal and non-reversal shifts in kindergarten children. *J. exp. Psychol.*, **58**, 56–60.

KENDLER, T. S., KENDLER, H. H. and WELLS, D. (1960) Reversal and non-reversal shifts in nursery school children. *J. comp. physiol. Psychol.*, **53**, 83–8.

KEPPEL, G. (1965) Problems of method in the study of short-term memory. *Psychol. Bull.*, **63**, 1–13.

KERR, N., MEYERSON, L. and MICHAEL, J. (1965) A procedure for shaping vocalizations in a mute child. In ULLMAN, L. P. and KRASNER, L. (eds.) *Case Studies in Behavior Modification.* New York: Holt, Rinehart & Winston.

KLAUSMEIER, H. J., FELDHUSEN, J. and CHECK, J. (1959) *An Analysis of Learning Efficiency in Arithmetic of Mentally Retarded Children in Comparison with Children of Average and High Intelligence.* Madison: Univ. of Wisconsin Press.

KÖHLER, W. and WALLACH, H. (1944) Figural aftereffects: an investigation of visual processes. *Proc. Amer. Phil. Soc.,* 88, 269–357.

KOLSTOE, O. P. (1958) Language training of low grade mongoloid children. *Amer. J. ment. Defic.,* 63, 17–30.

KOUW, W. A. (1968) Effects of stimulus intensity and duration upon retardates' short-term memory. *Amer. J. ment. Defic.,* 72, 734–9.

KROP, H. D. and SMITH, C. R. (1969) Effects of special education on Bender-Gestalt performance of the mentally retarded. *Amer. J. ment. Defic.,* 73, 693–9.

LANCE, W. D. (1965) Effects of meaningfulness and overlearning on retention in normal and retarded adolescents. *Amer. J. ment. Defic.,* 70, 270–5.

LANSING, R. W., SCHWARTZ, E. and LINDSLEY, D. B. (1959) Reaction time and E.E.G. activation under alerted and non-alerted conditions. *J. exp. Psychol.,* 58, 1–7.

LELAND, H. (1969) The relationship between 'intelligence' and mental retardation. *Amer. J. ment. Defic.,* 73, 533–5.

LENNEBERG, E. H. (1962) Understanding language without ability to speak. *J. abn. soc. Psychol.,* 65, 419–25.

LENNEBERG, E. H. (1967) *Biological Foundation of Language.* New York: Wiley.

LENNEBERG, E. H., NICHOLS, I. A. and ROSENBERGER, E. F. (1964) Primitive stages of language development in mongolism. In *Disorders of Communication,* Vol. XLII. Res. Publ. Assoc. Res. Nerv. Ment. D.B.

LIPMAN, R. S. (1963) Learning: verbal, perceptual-motor, and classical conditioning. In ELLIS, N. R. (ed.) *Handbook of Mental Deficiency.* New York: McGraw-Hill.

LURIA, A. R. (1961) *The Role of Speech in the Regulation of Normal and Abnormal Behaviour.* Oxford: Pergamon.

LURIA, A. R. and VINOGRADOVA, O. S. (1959) An objective investigation of the dynamics of semantic systems. *Brit. J. Psychol.,* 50, 89–105.

LYLE, J. G. (1959) The effect of an institution environment upon the verbal development of imbecile children: I. Verbal intelligence. *J. ment. Defic. Res.,* 3, 122–8.

LYLE, J. G. (1960a) The effect of an institution environment upon the verbal development of imbecile children: II. Speech and language. *J. ment. Defic. Res.*, **4**, 1–13.

LYLE, J. G. (1960b) The effect of an institution environment upon the verbal development of imbecile children: III. The Brooklands residential family unit. *J. ment. Defic. Res.*, **4**, 14–23.

LYLE, J. G. (1961) A comparison of the verbal intelligence of normal and imbecile children. *J. genet. Psychol.*, **99**, 227–34.

MCCONNEL, T. R., CROMWELL, R. L., BIALER, I. and SON, C. D. (1964) Studies in activity level VII. *Amer. J. ment. Defic.*, **68**, 647–51.

MCCRARY, J. W. and HUNTER, W. S. (1953) Serial position curves in verbal learning. *Science*, **117**, 131–4.

MACKINTOSH, N. J. (1965) Selective attention in animal discrimination learning. *Psychol. Bull.*, **64**, 124–50.

MCMANIS, D. L. (1965) Relative errors with serial lists of different lengths. *Amer. J. ment. Defic.*, **70**, 125–8.

MCMANIS, D. L. (1966) The von Restorff effect in serial learning by normal and retarded subjects. *Amer. J. ment. Defic.*, **70**, 569–75.

MCMANIS, D. L. (1968) Relative thinking by retardates. *Amer. J. ment. Defic.*, **73**, 484–92.

MCMANIS, D. L. (1969a) Intralist differentiation and the isolation effect in serial learning by normals and retardates. *Amer. J. ment. Defic.*, **73**, 819–25.

MCMANIS, D. L. (1969b) Conservation of mass, weight, and volume by normal and retarded children. *Amer. J. ment. Defic.*, **73**, 762–7.

MCMANIS, D. L. (1969c) Conservation and transitivity of weight and length by normals and retardates. *Developm. Psychol.*, **1**, 373–82.

MACCOBY, E. E. (1964) Developmental psychology. *Ann. Rev. Psychol.*, **15**, 203–50.

MADSEN, M. C. (1963) Distribution of practice and level of intelligence. *Psychol. Rep.*, **13**, 39–42.

MADSEN, M. C. (1966) Individual differences and temporal factors in memory consolidation. *Amer. J. ment. Defic.*, **71**, 501–7.

MADSEN, M. C. and CONNOR, K. J. (1968) Categorization and information reduction in short-term memory at two levels of intelligence. *Amer. J. ment. Defic.*, **73**, 232–8.

MARTIN, C. J., BOERSMA, F. J. and BULGARELLA, R. (1968) Verbalization of associative strategies by normal and retarded children. *J. gen. Psychol.*, **78**, 209–18.

MARTIN, C. J., BOERSMA, F. J. and COX, D. L. (1965) A classification of associative strategies in paired associate learning. *Psychon. Sci.*, **3**, 455–6.

MEIN, R. (1961) A study of the oral vocabularies of severely subnormal patients: II. Grammatical analysis of speech samples. *J. ment. Defic. Res.*, **5**, 52–9.

MEIN, R. and O'CONNOR, N. (1960) A study of the oral vocabularies of severely subnormal patients. *J. ment. Defic. Res.*, **4**, 130–43.

MILGRAM, N. A. (1966) Verbalization and conceptual classification in trainable mentally retarded children. *Amer. J. ment. Defic.*, **70**, 763–5.

MILGRAM, N. A. (1967) Retention of mediation set in paired-associate learning of normal children and retardates. *J. exp. Child Psychol.*, **5**, 341–9.

MILGRAM, N. A. (1968) The effect of verbal mediation in paired-associate learning in trainable retardates. *Amer. J. ment. Defic.*, **72**, 518–24.

MILGRAM, N. A. (1969) The rational and irrational in Zigler's motivational approach to mental retardation. *Amer. J. ment. Defic.*, **73**, 527–31.

MILGRAM, N. A. and FURTH, H. G. (1963) The influence of language on concept attainment in educable retarded children. *Amer. J. ment. Defic.*, **67**, 733–9.

MILGRAM, N. A. and FURTH, H. G. (1964) Position reversal versus dimension reversal in normal and retarded children. *Child Developm.*, **35**, 701–8.

MILGRAM, N. A. and FURTH, H. G. (1966) Response competition in paired associate learning by educable and trainable retarded children. *Amer. J. ment. Defic.*, **70**, 849–54.

MILLER, G. A. (1956) The magical number seven, plus or minus two: some limits on our capacity for processing information. *Psychol. Rev.*, **63**, 81–97.

MILLER, G. A., GALANTER, E. and PRIBRAM, K. (1960) *Plans and the Structure of Behavior*. New York: Holt, Rinehart & Winston.

MILLER, L. K., HALE, G. A. and STEVENSON, H. W. (1968) Learning and problem solving by retarded and normal Ss. *Amer. J. ment. Defic.*, **72**, 681–90.

MILLER, M. B. and GRIFFITH, B. C. (1961) The effects of training verbal associates on the performance of a conceptual task. *Amer. J. ment. Defic.*, **66**, 270–6.

MORDOCK, J. B. (1968) Paired associate learning in mental retardation: a review. *Amer. J. ment. Defic.*, **72**, 857–65.

NEUFELDT, A. H. (1966) Short-term memory in the mentally retarded: an application of the dichotic listening technique. *Psychol. Monogr.*, **80**, 1–31.

NOBLE, C. E. and MCKEELY, D. A. (1957) The rôle of meaningfulness (m') in paired-associate verbal learning. *J. exp. Psychol.*, **53**, 16–22.

O'CONNOR, N. and HERMELIN, B. F. (1959) Discrimination and reversal learning in imbeciles. *J. abn. soc. Psychol.*, **59**, 409–13.

O'CONNOR, N. and HERMELIN, B. F. (1963a) Recall in normals and subnormals of like mental age. *J. abn. soc. Psychol.*, **66**, 81–4.

O'CONNOR, N. and HERMELIN, B. F. (1963b) *Speech and Thought in Severe Subnormality*. Oxford: Pergamon.

O'CONNOR, N. and HERMELIN, B. F. (1965) Input restriction and immediate memory decay in normal and subnormal children. *Quart. J. exp. Psychol.*, **17**, 323-8.

ORLANSKY, J. (1940) The effect of similarity and difference in form on apparent visual movement. *Arch. Psychol.*, **246**, 85.

OSBORN, W. J. (1960) Associative clustering in organic and familial retardates. *Amer. J. ment. Defic.*, **65**, 351-7.

OSLER, S. F. and FIVEL, M. W. (1961) Concept attainment: I. The rôle of age and intelligence in concept attainment by induction. *J. exp. Psychol.*, **62**, 1-8.

OSLER, S. F. and TRAUTMAN, G. E. (1961) Concept attainment: II. Effect of stimulus complexity upon concept attainment at two levels of intelligence. *J. exp. Psychol.*, **62**, 9-13.

PASCAL, G. R. (1953) The effect of a disturbing noise on the reaction time of mental defectives. *Amer. J. ment. Defic.*, **57**, 691-9.

PENNEY, R. K., SEIM, R. and PETERS, R. de V. (1968a) The mediational deficiency of mentally retarded children: I. The establishment of retardates' mediational deficiency. *Amer. J. ment. Defic.*, **72**, 626-30.

PENNEY, R. K., PETERS, R. de V. and WILLOWS, D. M. (1968b) The mediational deficiency of mentally retarded children: II. Learning set's effect on mediational deficiency. *Amer. J. ment. Defic.*, **73**, 262-6.

PIAGET, J. (1928) *Judgement and Reasoning in the Child*. London: Routledge & Kegan Paul.

PLENDERLEITH, M. (1956) Discrimination learning and discrimination reversal learning in normal and feeble minded children. *J. genet. Psychol.*, **88**, 107-12.

PREHM, H. J. (1966a) Associative learning in retarded and normal children as a function of task difficulty and meaningfulness. *Amer. J. ment. Defic.*, **70**, 860-5.

PREHM, H. J. (1966b) Verbal learning research in mental retardation. *Amer. J. ment. Defic.*, **71**, 42-7.

PREHM, H. J. (1968) Rote verbal learning and memory in the retarded. In PREHM, H. J., HAMERLYNCK, L. A. and CROSSON, J. E. (eds.) *Behavioral Research in Mental Retardation*. Corvallis: Oregon State Univ.

PRYER, R. S. (1960) Retroactive inhibition in normals and defectives as a function of temporal position of the interpolated task. *Amer. J. ment. Defic.*, **64**, 1004-11.

RIEBER, M. (1964) Verbal mediation in normal and retarded children. *Amer. J. ment. Defic.*, **68**, 634-41.

RING, E. M. and PALERMO, D. S. (1961) Paired associate learning of retarded and normal children. *Amer. J. ment. Defic.*, **66**, 100-7.

ROHWER, W. D. and LYNCH, S. (1968) Retardation, school strata, and learning proficiency. *Amer. J. ment. Defic.*, **73**, 91-6.

ROOS, P. (1965) Development of an intensive habit training unit at Austin State School. *Ment. Retard.*, **3**, 12–15.

ROSENBERG, S. (1963) Problem-solving and conceptual behavior. In ELLIS, N. R. (ed.) *Handbook of Mental Deficiency*. New York: McGraw-Hill.

ROSSI, E. L. (1963) Associative clustering in normal and retarded children. *Amer. J. ment. Defic.*, **67**, 691–9.

ROUSE, S. T. (1965) Effects of a training program on the productive thinking of educable mental retardates. *Amer. J. ment. Defic.*, **69**, 666–73.

SANDERS, B., ROSS, L. E. and HEAL, L. W. (1965) Reversal and non-reversal shift learning in normal children and retardates of comparable mental age. *J. exp. Psychol.*, **69**, 84–8.

SANDERS, B., ZIGLER, E. and BUTTERFIELD, E. C. (1968) Outer-directedness in the discrimination learning of normal and mentally retarded children. *J. abn. Psychol.*, **73**, 368–75.

SCHULMAN, J. L., KASPAR, J. CHARLES and THRONE, F. M. (1965) *Brain Damage and Behavior. A Clinical-Experiment Study*. Springfield, Ill.: C. C. Thomas.

SCOTT, K. G. (1971) Recognition memory: a research strategy and a summary of initial findings. In ELLIS, N. R. (ed.) *International Review of Research in Mental Retardation*, Vol. 5. New York: Academic Press.

SCOTT, K. G. and SCOTT, M. S. (1968) Research and theory in short-term memory. In ELLIS, N. R. (ed.) *International Review of Research in Mental Retardation*, Vol. 3. New York: Academic Press.

SCOTT, W. S. (1940) Reaction time in young intellectual deviates. *Arch. Psychol.*, **36**, 1–64.

SEN, A. K. and CLARKE, A. M. (1968) Some factors affecting distractibility in the mental retardate. *Amer. J. ment. Defic.*, **73**, 50–60.

SEN, A. K. and SEN, A. (1968) A test of the McCrary-Hunter hypothesis in mentally retarded subjects. *J. ment. Defic. Res.*, **12**, 36–46.

SEN, A. K., CLARKE, A. M. and COOPER, G. M. (1968) The effect of isolating items in serial learning in severely retarded subjects. *Amer. J. ment. Defic.*, **72**, 851–6.

SHEPP, B. E. and TURRISI, F. D. (1966) Learning and transfer of mediating responses in discriminative learning. In ELLIS, N. R. (ed.) *International Review of Research in Mental Retardation*, Vol. 2. New York: Academic Press.

SILVERSTEIN, A. B. and MCLAIN, R. E. (1966) Associative process of the mentally retarded: III. A developmental study. *Amer. J. ment. Defic.*, **70**, 722–5.

SLOANE, H. and MACAULAY, B. (1968) *Operant Procedures in Remedial Speech and Language Training*. Boston: Houghton-Mifflin.

SPITZ, H. H. (1963) Field theory in mental deficiency. In ELLIS, N. R. (ed.) *Handbook of Mental Deficiency*. New York: McGraw-Hill.

SPITZ, H. H. (1964) A comparison of mental retardates and normals on the rotating trapezoidal window illusion. *J. abn. soc. Psychol.*, **68**, 574–8.

SPITZ, H. H. (1965) The effect of a single monocular depth cue deficit on retardates' perception of the rotating cube illusion. *Amer. J. ment. Defic.*, **69**, 703–11.

SPITZ, H. H. (1966) The rôle of input organization in the learning and memory of mental retardates. In ELLIS, N. R. (ed.) *International Review of Research in Mental Retardation*, Vol. 2. New York: Academic Press.

SPITZ, H. H. (1967) A comparison of mental retardates and normals on the distorted room illusion. *Amer. J. ment. Defic.*, **72**, 34–49.

SPITZ, H. H. and BLACKMAN, L. S. (1959) A comparison of mental retardates and normals on visual figural aftereffects and reversible figures. *J. abn. soc. Psychol.*, **58**, 105–10.

SPITZ, H. H. and LIPMAN, R. S. (1961) A comparison of mental retardates and normals on kinesthetic figural aftereffects. *J. abn. soc. Psychol.*, **62**, 686–7.

SPIVACK, G. (1963) Perceptual processes. In ELLIS, N. R. (ed.) *Handbook of Mental Deficiency*. New York: McGraw-Hill.

SPRADLIN, J. E. and GIRARDEAU, F. L. (1966) The behavior of moderately and severely retarded persons. In ELLIS, N. R. (ed.) *International Review of Research in Mental Retardation*, Vol. 1. New York: Academic Press.

SPREEN, O. (1965a) Language functions in mental retardation: a review I. Language development, types of retardation, and intelligence level. *Amer. J. ment. Defic.*, **69**, 482–94.

SPREEN, O. (1965b) Language functions in mental retardation: a review II. Language in higher level performance. *Amer. J. ment. Defic.*, **70**, 351–62.

STEPHENS, W. E. (1964) A comparison of the performance of normal and subnormal boys on structured categorization tasks. *Except. Child.*, **30**, 311–15.

STEPHENS, W. E. (1966a) Category usage by normal and mentally retarded boys. *Child Developm.*, **37**, 355–61.

STEPHENS, W. E. (1966b) Category usage of normal and subnormal children on three types of categories. *Amer. J. ment. Defic.*, **71**, 266–73.

STEPHENS, W. E. (1968) Labelling errors of mentally subnormal children in a concept attainment task. *Amer. J. ment. Defic.*, **73**, 273–8.

STERNLICHT, M. and DEUTSCH, M. R. (1966) Cognition in the mentally retarded: the von Restorff effect. *J. ment. Defic. Res.*, **10**, 63–8.

STERNLICHT, M., PUSTEL, G. and SIEGEL, L. (1968) Comparison of organic and cultural-familial retardates on two visual-motor tasks. *Amer. J. ment. Defic.*, **72**, 887–9.

STEVENSON, H. W. and SWARTZ, J. D. (1958) Learning set in children as a function of intellectual level. *J. comp. physiol. Psychol.*, **51**, 755–7.

STEVENSON, H. W. and ZIGLER, E. F. (1957) Discrimination learning and rigidity in normal and feeble minded individuals. *J. Personal.*, **25**, 699–711.

STEVENSON, H. W. and ZIGLER, E. F. (1958) Probability learning in children. *J. exp. Psychol.*, **56**, 185–92.

STRAUSS, A. A. and KEPHART, N. C. (1955) *Psychopathology and Education of the Brain Injured Child. Vol. II, Progress in Theory and Clinic.* New York: Grune & Stratton.

STRAUSS, A. A. and LEHTINEN, L. E. (1947) *Psychopathology and Education of the Brain Injured Child.* New York: Grune & Stratton.

SUTHERLAND, N. S. (1964) The learning of discriminations by animals. *Endeavour*, **23**, 148–52.

TIZARD, B. (1968a) Observations of over-active imbecile children in controlled and uncontrolled environments: I. Classroom studies. *Amer. J. ment. Defic.*, **72**, 540–7.

TIZARD, B. (1968b) Observations of over-active imbecile children in controlled and uncontrolled environments: II. Experimental studies. *Amer. J. ment. Defic.*, **72**, 548–53.

TIZARD, B. (1968c) Habituation of E.E.G. and skin potential changes in normal and severely subnormal children. *Amer. J. ment. Defic.*, **73**, 34–40.

TIZARD, B. (1968d) A controlled study of all-night sleep in over-active imbecile children. *Amer. J. ment. Defic.*, **73**, 209–13.

TULVING, E. (1962) Subjective organization in free recall of 'unrelated' words. *Psychol. Rev.*, **69**, 344–54.

TULVING, E. (1964) Intratrial and intertrial retention: notes towards a theory of free-recall verbal learning. *Psychol. Rev.*, **71**, 219–37.

TULVING, E. (1966) Subjective organization and effects of repetition in multi-trial free-recall learning. *J. Verb. Learn. Verb. Behav.*, **5**, 193–7.

TURNURE, J. and ZIGLER, E. (1964) Outer-directedness in the problem solving of normal and retarded children. *J. abn. soc. Psychol.*, **69**, 427–36.

UNDERWOOD, B. J. (1954) Speed of learning and amount retained: a consideration of methodology. *Psychol. Bull.*, **51**, 276–82.

UNDERWOOD, B. J. (1964) Degree of learning and the measurement of forgetting. *J. Verb. Learn. Verb. Behav.*, **3**, 112–29.

VAN DER VEEN, C. (1967) *Verbalization of Associative Learning Strategies among Educable Retardates and Normal Children.* Unpubl. paper presented at the 91st Annual Convention, Amer. Assoc. on Ment. Defic., Denver, Colorado.

VERGASON, G. A. (1964) Retention in retarded and normal subjects as a function of amount of original learning. *Amer. J. ment. Defic.*, **68**, 623–9.

VOGEL, W. and BROVERMAN, D. M. (1964) Relationship between E.E.G. and test intelligence: a critical review. *Psychol. Bull.*, **62**, 132–44.

VOGEL, W. and BROVERMAN, D. M. (1966) A reply to 'Relationship between E.E.G. and test intelligence: a commentary'. *Psychol. Bull.*, **65**, 99–109.

VOGEL, W., KUN, K. J., MESHORER, E., BROVERMAN, D. M. and
    KLAIBER, E. L. (1969) The behavioral significance of E.E.G.
    abnormality in mental defectives. *Amer. J. ment. Defic.*, **74**, 62–8.
WATSON, L. S. (1967) Application of operant conditioning techniques to
    institutionalized severely and profoundly retarded children. *Ment.
    Retard. Abstrs.*, **4**, 1–18.
WATSON, L. S. and LAWSON, R. (1966) Instrumental learning in mental
    retardates. *Ment. Retard. Abstrs.*, **3**, 1–20.
WIESEN, A. E. and WATSON, E. (1967) Elimination of attention seeking
    behavior in a retarded child. *Amer. J. ment. Defic.*, **72**, 50–2.
WINTERS, J. J. (1965) Gamma movement: a comparison of normals and
    retardates. *Amer. J. ment. Defic.*, **69**, 697–702.
WINTERS, J. J. (1969) A comparison of normals and retardates on physio-
    logical and experiential visual illusions. *Amer. J. ment. Defic.*, **73**, 956–62.
WINTERS, J. J. and GERJUOY, I. R. (1965) Gamma movement: field
    brightness, series, and side of the standard. *Psychon. Sci.*, **2**, 273–4.
WINTERS, J. J. and GERJUOY, I. R. (1967) Gamma movement: a
    comparison of normals and retardates under several temporal conditions.
    Amer. J. ment. Defic., **71**, 542–5.
WISCHNER, G. J., BRAUN, H. W. and PATTON, R. A. (1962) Acquisition
    and long-term retention of an object quality learning set by retarded
    children. *J. Comp. Physiol. Psychol.*, **55**, 518–23.
WOLFENSBERGER, W. and O'CONNOR, N. (1965) Stimulus intensity and
    duration effects on E.E.G. and G.S.R. responses of normals and
    retardates. *Amer. J. ment. Defic.*, **70**, 21–37.
WOLFENSBERGER, W., MEIN, R. and O'CONNOR, N. (1963) A study of
    the oral vocabularies of severely subnormal patients. *J. ment. Defic. Res.*,
    7, 38–45.
ZEAMAN, D. (1965) Learning processes of the mentally retarded. In OSLER,
    S. F. and COOKE, R. E. (eds.) *The Biosocial Basis of Mental Retarda-
    tion.* Baltimore, Md.: Johns Hopkins Press.
ZEAMAN, D. and HOUSE, B. J. (1963) The rôle of attention in retardate
    discrimination learning. In ELLIS, N. R. (ed.) *Handbook of Mental
    Deficiency.* New York: McGraw-Hill.
ZIGLER, E. (1966) Research on personality structure in the retardate. In
    ELLIS, N. R. (ed.) *International Review of Research in Mental
    Retardation*, Vol. 1. New York: Academic Press.
ZIGLER, E. (1967) Familial mental retardation: a continuing dilemma.
    Science, **155**, 292–8.
ZIGLER, E. (1969) Developmental versus difference theories of mental
    retardation and the problem of motivation. *Amer. J. ment. Defic.*, **73**,
    536–56.

7

N. O'Connor and B. Hermelin

Specific deficits and coding strategies

Introduction

Failure to learn is the basic psychological characteristic of subnormality and Binet and Simon (1909) first drew attention to this problem in his classical studies of Parisian schoolchildren. His development of the concept of capacity, as distinct from acquisition, set the tone for subsequent work on intelligence and intelligence testing. Binet was, of course, reflecting a viewpoint that had already gained support in the nineteenth century. Galton (1892) held that individuals differed from each other in their physical and mental abilities and he maintained that the effects of training had strict limits. He was easily able to confirm both hypotheses, and indeed such opinions might be regarded now as commonplace. By drawing on statistical records, Galton was able to show that many characteristics were distributed in a relatively static population in a fairly constant way. Spearman (1904) was already correlating mental and physical characteristics and discussed the concept of intelligence in terms of proficiency and native capacity rather as Binet was to do. He estimated intelligence in terms of the relationship between achievement and chronological age. However, he also pointed out that many tests correlated together when individual scores on different kinds of performance were compared. (See also Chapter 8.)

Perhaps the most important observation made by Spearman which relates to our present subject is that which he made concerning the part played by general ability in different activities. At one point he suggests that a 'central function, whatever it may be, is hardly anywhere more prominent than in the simple act of discriminating two nearly identical tones'; in other words, even in such an apparently simple function as discrimination, central ability was thought to be playing a vital part. The extent to which 'g' (General Ability) contributed to specific functions varied in Spearman's view from dominant to subsidiary. The same idea has been expressed in a similar way by Vernon (1950), but other opinions also referred to by Vernon such as that of G. H. Thomson (1939) have a rather different character. Thomson suggested that the fact that many test scores correlate positively and may be represented by a single factor does not prove that this factor corresponds to any unitary faculty in the mind. His theory of multiple bonds, reflexes and associations allows that any one task or test might call into play a number of such bonds. These might appear to have the character of factors, but should not be thought of as faculties or organs.

All these authors, therefore, and others such as Burt (1937) and Thurstone (1935) have propounded views of intelligence of a more or less hierarchical character mostly distinguishing performance at any one time from native ability and mostly attributing some degree of acquisition in specific functions to a central general ability probably inherited. Hebb (1949) discussed the question of intelligence in terms of inherited potential, the state of the nervous system (Intelligence A) and the actual functional performance or comprehension of the person (Intelligence B). He points out that 'An innate potential for development is not logically a guarantee that the development will occur.' He argues on the basis of deprivation experiments that experience is essential to development. Both this kind of argument and questions concerning damage to the central nervous system, therefore, become of some importance when we try to account for the subnormals' cognitive incapacity. Duncan (1942) and others have remarked on brain injury as shown in patterns of performance on IQ tests. The verbal versus performance differences shown by subnormals could be of significance in examining specific deficits and their relationship to more general defects.

Specific disabilities and neuropsychology

The continued finding of different verbal and performance levels in the subnormal has led to such investigations as those of Sylvester (1966) and Blundell (1966), which point to the existence of localized lesions in addition to generalized damage in severe subnormality. Workers like Kirk and McCarthy (1961) have drawn attention to patterns of psychological response and their presumed neurological basis, and Strauss and Lehtinen (1947) noted the possible consequences of specific or more general lesions when found in the subnormal. However, despite attempts made by Reitan (1966) and his colleagues, a developed neuropsychology of subnormality does not exist. The problems of neuropsychology, as seen by Teuber (1959) and Teuber and Liebert (1958), deal with phenomena which are characteristic of lesions occurring at particular stages of development, and in this sense might be relevant to studies of subnormality. As has been shown, notably by Crome (1954) but also in much of the clinical literature, brain damage in the severely subnormal is diffuse and has general consequences which make the detection of specific effects more difficult.

Clearly, therefore, the detection of behavioural patterns in subnormality has to be set against the presence of widespread neurophysiological maldevelopment. Patterns of behaviour are not clearly associable with neurological lesions as they sometimes can be shown to be in adults suffering from dysphasias, short-term memory loss or disturbance of spatial perception.

The dilemma presented by Binet has been dealt with in part by the concept of islets of intelligence in autism as suggested by Creak (1961). It has also been considered by Binet and Simon (1909) himself and by subsequent workers such as Scheerer, Rothman and Goldstein (1945) in the concept of the *idiot savant*. However, despite clear evidence for unusual memories, and some evidence for *grands calculateurs*, e.g. Binet (1894) and Hunter (1962), examples are infrequent. They are clearly insufficient in number to provide a convincing case in favour of patterns of cognitive behaviour in subnormality as examples of specific abilities or deficits.

Specific theories of learning deficit

None the less, in recent years a number of attempts have been made to explain the subnormals' failure to learn, in terms of the weakness of a specific cognitive process. Such attempts have ignored the problem of neurophysiology or accepted a general theory of a molecular kind, in other words, a model with a presumptive neuroanatomy. Amongst these theories which, in a sense, oppose wholistic 'intelligence' type explanations, and which try to explain the learning problems of the subnormal in terms of specific deficits, are those of Ellis (1963, 1970) and Zeaman and House (1963) and Luria (1961). Ellis and his colleagues have suggested that a state of low cortical arousal which might be characteristic of subnormals results in a poor or weak trace in short-term memory (STM) and a consequent failure to establish events in long-term memory (LTM) in a more categorized form. This early form of a 'trace decay' hypothesis has been criticized by O'Connor and Hermelin (1965) and by Belmont and Butterfield (1969). Belmont and Butterfield have summarized material which shows that most results would accord with our own views of the importance of processes occurring at the input phase of learning. More recently, Ellis (1970) has examined STM in a theoretical framework which concedes the normality of LTM and discusses STM in terms of primary and secondary systems. Adopting different stimulus presentation rates, Ellis notes that subnormals differ from normals in material requiring rehearsal, e.g. the earlier items in a series of digits. Failure to rehearse is therefore advanced as an explanation of normal, subnormal differences in STM. Whatever the theoretical and practical variations of this short-term memory deficit as an explanation of failure to learn in the subnormal, it is given here as an example of a specific deficit hypothesis. It tends to advance failure to rehearse and hence failure of the secondary part of short-term memory as the reason for learning failure in the subnormal subject.

Another example of the specific type of hypothesis is that advanced by Zeaman and House (1963). This two-stage learning model assumes deficits in an attentional rather than in an S–R process, and in this respect resembles the dimensional theories advanced by Estes (1959) and Sutherland (1959). It is basic to such attentional theories that connection forming or the formation of stimulus response relations is rapid once the subject understands what is the nature of the stimuli. However, he must first have the capacity to orient his attention in the direction of the appropriate dimension within any one modality, for example, shape rather than size, within the visual modality. Some support for this view is contained in the studies of subnormal transfer carried out by Bryant (1965). (See also Chapter 6.)

Some criticisms of specific hypotheses

However, although this theory appears to be a specific hypothesis, it may prove to be more closely allied with a more general developmental view of the sub-normals' failure to learn. For example, Zeaman and House (1963) have them-selves suggested that dimensional orientation varies with development and may follow a definite emergent order. The evidence for the emergent nature of orientation to dimensions with development is questionable in view of evidence summarized by Pick and Pick (1970) concerning the primacy of modalities and the results of Bower's (1967) studies concerning infants' perception of form. However, more damaging to the specific character of the Zeaman and House hypothesis may be an observation made by Folkard (1971) as a result of vigilance studies carried out with normal and subnormal adolescents on a signal detection basis. He suggests that in their analysis of subnormal learning, they assume that the low probability of observing one dimension entails the high probability of observing another. This view is based on the assumption that probabilities must sum to unity, which in turn requires that only factors within the learning situa-tion are being attended to and that subnormals, like normals, can restrict their attention to one dimension. If subnormals are distractible, Folkard argues, they might be unable to focus attention at all, rather than failing to attend to the correct dimension. This would substitute an arousal hypothesis for one concern-ing lack of attention to specific dimensions. Such an arousal hypothesis would be a neurologically general one, rather than a specific theory.

Even if Folkard's objection did not apply, it could be argued that the emergence or orientation towards particular perceptual dimensions is a developmental hypothesis, and that developmental arrest as an explanation of failure to learn is like Woodward's (1963) adaptation of Piaget's (1953) and Piaget and Inhelder's (1969) theories, a general account of learning failure, applying to all types of performance, rather than to just one function such as dimensional orienta-tion.

Luria's (1961) very well known and brilliant exposition of verbal difficulties in the subnormal is based on the work of Vygotsky (1962) and also draws on Luria's (1961) extensive knowledge of neurology. The claim of his theory of verbal deficit in subnormals to account for their failure to learn is based on the important assumption that language, or in Pavlovian terms, the second signal system, is a more efficient medium for the acquisition of knowledge and in some situations the only one. As the theory of language as the initiator of thinking is one which may underlie some of Luria's arguments concerning subnormality, and as this view has been disputed, notably by Binet and Simon (1909) and Piaget

(1970), it is of interest to determine whether or not this relatively specific theory can be accepted as an explanation of learning failure. To some extent our own previous investigations in this field noted the failure of subnormals to use words effectively in learning procedures, and Bryant's studies of transfer showed that words had not the significance for subnormals in aiding transfer as they had for normals. However, as Bryant's studies also showed, the same was true of the use of signs by severely subnormal children. To express this differently, not only words but all symbols lacked generality when used by the subnormal.

The question of the primacy of thought or language is a subject on which Binet, Piaget and Vygotsky have each expressed views. Piaget's ideas are perhaps too well known to need emphasis, but Binet's (1909) are seldom quoted. He gives examples of single word answers to questions such as 'Have you read this book?' A negative word such as 'No' is a general negative and in no way indicates a particular answer to such a particular question, Binet argues. Even if we suppose that the answer is a series of words such as 'No, I have not read the book about which you speak', it could be shown by reference to imbeciles who lack more than a few words of speech that equally meaningful one-word answers can be evoked by questioning. In a similar fashion, Binet argues that an image such as one we might have in thinking about a planned expedition is inadequate fully to express the thought, just as words are. We think neither of the future, nor of the expedition, but often just of one aspect of the proposed journey. Binet concludes his discussion as follows: 'All this comes back to the conclusion that the thought is distinct both from the image and from the word, that it is quite another thing, that it constitutes a different element.'

Vygotsky (1962) expresses remarkably similar views concerning the way in which thought and language come to be related: '1. In their autogenetic development, thought and speech have different roots. 2. In the speech development of the child, we can with certainty establish a pre-intellectual stage, and in his thought development, a prelinguistic stage.' Vygotsky believes, however, that at a certain stage the two streams become one, whereas Binet obviously does not.

From the point of view of the subnormal person his failure to learn cannot always be explained in terms of a specific verbal deficit as many of Binet's examples suggest. Our own suggestions concerning language and thinking in the subnormal were that cross-modal coding was inadequate because subnormals often do not verbally describe the operations which they can none the less perform correctly, and hence are not able to carry out similar operations in a different context without further instruction. This original observation is subject to the findings made by Bryant subsequently, that failure to transfer is a product of failure to observe the general character of any signal whatsoever.

A number of explanations for learning deficiency have been listed and described above, and in each case we have attempted to offer reasons why such accounts are inadequate. If our arguments are valid, the general nature of the learning deficit in subnormal and severely subnormal people would have received some confirmation because of the failure to establish a strong case for a specific cause for failure to learn. Even had the theories reviewed made a very strong case, they would still face the logical objection that the presence of a particular deficit does not exclude the possibility of a general deficit in addition. Thus, for example, Down's syndrome children are known to have poorly-developed cerebella, but in addition to the poor stereognosis to which this gives rise, they suffer from widespread CNS damage and maldevelopment which impairs their general ability in other respects.

What, then, is undifferentiated subnormality?

The problem presented by Binet, therefore, and examined by his factorist successors, remains with us. What is the nature of the deficit which appears to affect a variety of measures of performance in the subnormal? What is the effect of retarded development which most characterizes subnormality and distinguishes it from the syndromes which show obvious specific deficits?

Our previous attempts to answer similar questions have led us to favour two main hypotheses, one arising from experiments concerned with subnormal and one arising from experiments with autistic children. The first offered an explanation in terms of a failure of coding at the input phase (O'Connor and Hermelin, 1965), and the second favoured an explanation in terms of a central logical deficit (Hermelin and O'Connor, 1970). In both series of experiments, the basic cognitive problem of these two groups was seen as a failure of categorizing or coding following immediate perception or short-term storage.

From such a standpoint we could criticize such views as those advanced by Ellis (1963) and Zeaman and House (1963) because they make use of concepts of formal descriptive faculties such as perception, learning and memory, without at the same time analysing the process common to these operations. Previous work of our own could also be criticized for an incompletely clear appreciation of the underlying unity of these processes.

Being led to analyse perceptual, associative and retrieval processes in this way, investigators have also concentrated on specifying deficits in such operations as if they were operations isolated in themselves and differing one from another. As a result there has been a tendency to look for diagnostically based and specific deficits. Diagnostic groups have been examined because of the presumed specificity of localized defects, as for example, in Down's syndrome (motor defects) or autism (language deficiency).

However, although such an approach is not without merit and effectiveness, it does fail to analyse the organizing process which underlies each such specific operation. Our own attempts to analyse cross-modal coding brought us towards such an appreciation of a common element in all learning operations, but did not, at that time, lead us to a definitive statement of its nature. Though we examined cross-modal coding in a variety of studies with subnormals, we did not propose that coding was an element basic to all processes connected with the acquisition of knowledge. Cognate problems have been discussed elsewhere by O'Connor and Hermelin (1971b).

A new attitude to cognitive deficits

Coding might be defined as the translation of an item from one sign system to another. Each sign stands for a class or category of items or an individual member of such a class. It appears to us that the process of learning includes in any operations such as perception, recall and recognition in each of which coding, either on input or at a later stage, plays an important part. It is possible to go further and suggest that the classification of any particular input, and its appropriate tagging for reference, constitutes the basic operation in perception, learning or recall and that this operation is coding. Therefore coding plays a central part in learning, and if subnormals fail to learn, the factors possibly affecting coding need careful examination.

Another reason for examining factors affecting coding is to test what might seem to be a possible example of Hebb's (1949) phase structure theory of learning. This theory posits that learning cannot occur in the absence of one of its basic stages. If a step in the process is missed out, normal development is arrested. The experiments of many of Hebb's colleagues such as Bexton, Heron and Scott (1954), and others whom he quotes such as Riesen (1947) and von Senden (1932), were directed towards showing that lack of experience led to developmental arrest. Many other workers tried to extend the theory to higher mammalian and to human behaviour, for example, Harlow (1958) and Spitz (1945). In general, so far as humans are concerned such experiments have not been too successful. However, Hebb's theory, in providing an explanation of learning failure, may also offer a behavioural theory of intellectual deficit and to some degree an account of the nature of (low) intelligence.

In examining coding, therefore, we might be considering a function which is basic to learning. In considering specific deficits which might affect coding, we would be examining the relationship between specific and general impairments. Therefore we began to consider cross-modal coding and the effect of specific sensory impairments on this process. It could be the case that some aspects of coding are supra-modal and dependent on a kind of operation which is either independent of, or common to, all modalities. Other coding functions may be modality specific. Questions of this kind concerned us when we began recent studies which are now described.

CODING OF TEMPORAL AND SPATIAL SEQUENCES

Many authors have drawn attention to the significance of coding as an operation which might be affected by cognitive handicap. Our own studies with sub-normals, reported in O'Connor and Hermelin (1963) and with autistic children (Hermelin and O'Connor 1970) yield examples of such findings of coding deficits.

Whether the deficit in coding operations is confined to cross-modal coding, or to problems of feature extraction, or of sequential ordering, remains undecided at this stage. It is possible that different deficits involved in the process could be associated with different diagnostic conditions.

We attempted to examine the effects of blindness and deafness on coding operations. Our concern with coding was to determine whether it was affected by restriction of input modality. We also wished to determine whether it was a supra-modal operation or one which was specific to each modality. In general, we could examine the effect of restriction of input modality, i.e. a specific restriction on a presumedly more general function.

This aim determined our selection of subject groups: blind and deaf groups in whom input was presumably restricted, normal hearing and sighted controls whom we sometimes temporarily deprived of sight or hearing, subnormals in whom deficit was supposedly general rather than specific. The experiments reported below are concerned with the discrimination of temporal interval and with temporal or spatial-sequential coding. The former topic serves merely as an introduction to the latter.

DISCRIMINATION OF DURATION

In the first of these experiments, we tested cross-modal coding and temporal discrimination (O'Connor and Hermelin, 1971c).

Evidence on cross-modal transfer with children is inconclusive. Smith and Tunick (1969) carried out an experiment with retarded children where discrimination had to be transferred from touch to vision and vision to touch. When the same cues or stimulus objects were used, transfer was achieved across modalities. Blank and Bridger (1966) reported positive transfer of discrimination between sounds and lights provided that there was adequate verbalization during training. Blank, Altman and Bridger (1968) subsequently demonstrated positive transfer between touch and vision even in children unable to name the stimuli. While Birch and Belmont (1965) have reported deficits in matching auditory with visual patterns in cerebral palsied children, Rudel and Teuber (1968) found brain damaged and retarded children not to be different from controls in visual-tactile and tactile-visual shape recognition. In view of the contradictory evidence, it seemed appropriate to consider cross-modal transfer in terms of developmental deficits, associated with diffuse brain damage, and also in relation to such lasting impairment as might arise as a result of blindness or deafness. We therefore selected deaf, blind, subnormal and normal children matched for mental age.

Blind, normal, subnormal and deaf children were taught to discriminate between touch stimuli lasting either 6 seconds or 2 seconds. Appropriate motor responses to the long and the short stimulus were taught to each subject. The learning task involved discriminating between a rotary probe in the palm of the hand which lasted for 6 seconds and another which lasted for 2 seconds.

When the basic touch task had been learned, the subjects were asked to do a transfer task. The transfer stimuli were two touch signals of a different kind from that in the learning task, air puffs, and sounds or lights for the blind and deaf and their control groups respectively. Stimuli were of 2 seconds or of 6 seconds.

The results showed that the initial touch discrimination transferred to another kind of touch stimulus, but not to light or to sound. Absence of speech was no special handicap as the deaf did at least as well as other groups. Analysis of variance of transfer error scores showed that transfer was greatest within the modality and least across modalities. Differences between groups were not significant. Thus cross-modal transfer of a learned discrimination was not affected by restriction of sensory input. In the experiment reported above we had used successively presented stimuli in a temporal discrimination task. The relative failure of the subjects to judge two durations as being either the same or different may have been specifically related to the stimulus modality used, or to the successiveness of the exposures. Thus stimuli in another sense modality, or a simultaneous rather than a successive stimulus exposure, might yield different results.

It has been argued that hearing is a process which integrates successive stimuli. Although Savin (1967) suggests that the results of many experiments tend to confirm such a view, simultaneous sounds are also obviously integrated by the auditory system, as, for example, in the appreciation of harmony or the recognition of different speech accents. Conversely, though the eye deals with a wide visual field which presents information simultaneously, successive focusing on different points also occurs. The experiment reported below was designed to investigate the effect of simultaneous and successive presentation of stimuli on temporal and non-temporal discriminations when stimuli were presented in either the visual or auditory modality. Eighty 5-year-old children were asked to examine visual and auditory displays. The visual displays consisted of lines of different lengths (5, 10 or 15 cm) which could remain on for durations of 2, 4 or 6 seconds. The auditory display consisted of high,- medium- and low-pitched tones (1,200, 500 and 400 Hz) which could vary in duration from 2 to 4 or 6 seconds.

The procedure was designed to compare the effect of stimuli presented either simultaneously or successively, in either the visual or auditory modalities, and in terms of the dimensions of space or pitch, as compared with time. In all conditions 24 pairs of stimuli were presented to the subjects who had to judge whether these stimuli were the same or different. Each correct response was reinforced by the experimenter saying 'good' and each incorrect one was followed by the experimenter saying 'no'. The pairs of stimuli were either visual or auditory and varied in one of two ways. Either they varied in duration or alternatively they varied in another dimension, e.g. length in the case of visual and pitch in the case of auditory stimuli. When duration was invariant, this second dimension varied, and when the alternative dimension was invariant, duration was varied from trial to trial. When duration was invariant, exposure time was always 4 seconds, but when it was variable, stimuli were either both exposed for 2 seconds or both for 6 seconds, or one for 2 seconds and one for 6 seconds. A similar rule applied to the constancy or variation of length and pitch. When duration was varied, an intermediate length (10 cm) or pitch (800 Hz) was used. When the non-temporal dimensions were variable, combinations of the extremes (5 and 15 cm; 400 and 1200 Hz) were used, while duration was held constant at 4 seconds.

Instructions were always similar, e.g. 'Two lights (tones) will come up here and there. Watch (listen to) them carefully and when they have gone, tell me whether they were the same or different.' Successive displays were separated by a 5 second gap. Simultaneous displays always commenced at the same time, and the visual stimuli appeared one above the other, with a 5 cm gap between them.

Results showed that durational judgments were more difficult than the non-durational ones, though this difference was more marked when lights rather than when sounds were the stimuli.

Durational judgments were more efficient when the stimuli were exposed together than when one followed the other, and this was true with lights as well as with sounds. The patterns of responses for durational judgments were very similar for both stimulus modalities, indicating similar response strategies. In contrast to one of the previously advanced hypotheses, simultaneous presentation of stimuli varying in duration resulted in better performance with auditory as well as with visual signals.

These results also showed clearly that the relationship between modality of stimulus, manner of presentation and tendency for temporal or non-temporal coding needed further investigation. The results had shown that, particularly with visual stimuli, orientation towards the temporal dimension was not readily obtained. On the other hand, they had failed to provide evidence that successive stimulus presentation facilitated temporal orientation. The next series of studies further tested temporal and non-temporal coding when the material was either visually or auditorily presented.

INPUT MODALITY AND TEMPORAL AND SPATIAL CODING

For the following study we adopted a technique originally used by Attneave and Benson (1969) who tested the coding of tactile information. This consists of stimulating the finger ends of both hands and associating each separate tactile stimulus with a spoken word. After learning to associate a word with a stimulated finger, hand positions are reversed for the second part of the experiment. With sighted subjects, association between a word and a particular location in space were stronger than those between words and fingers. McKinney (1964), in a study of hand schema in blind children, concluded that these children relied on tactual cues as a guide to a spatial schema. We were interested to know whether the blind or children temporarily deprived of sensory input would use spatial schemes which differed from those of sighted children.

Blind and autistic children were matched on chronological age with sighted children, one group of whom were blindfolded for the experiment. Another group of blindfold adults was added to obtain further information. The autistic children had been diagnosed by a psychiatrist and had an onset before 18 months of age. Their mean IQ was 85. The blind were either totally blind from birth or had only light, without pattern vision. Their IQs had a mean of 118 and a range from 100 to 142 on the Williams (1950) test.

Ss were tested individually. They were first told that they had to learn four words. These were: 'run', 'sit', 'walk', 'stand'. The index and middle fingers of each hand were then placed on a 6 × 16·5 inch board in the position illustrated in Fig. 2.

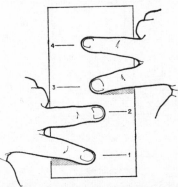

Fig. 2 A test of the coding of tactile information:
association of tactile stimulus with the spoken word.

Half the children began with the right hand extended in front of the left, and for the other half these positions were reversed. The top of a finger was then lightly brushed with a toothbrush while E said, 'This is "run"', or while touching another finger, 'This is "sit"', etc. Care was taken not to indicate whether 'this' referred to the stimulation of a particular finger or its particular position.

After this demonstration the subject had to learn to respond to stimulation with the brush by uttering the correct word. Stimulation was administered in a predetermined random order. After the association had been learned to a criterion of 19 out of 20 trials the position of the hands was reversed, and E said, 'We will just go on.'

Results show that location or absolute spatial responses were predominant in those who carried out the task using touch and vision, and that finger responses were more common in those who carried out the task using touch alone. For example, 10 blind children gave 276 finger responses out of 400, whereas sighted children gave only 158. Oddly enough, blindfold adults gave no location responses and autistic children behaved as did the sighted normal. Neither chronological age nor psychiatric diagnosis affected this clear finding that space schema vary according to input restriction. If an input-independent concept of visually represented space were built up only gradually by experience, one might expect adults to respond more frequently than children in accordance with such an internal visual schema. This did not occur in the present experiment, where blindfolded adults gave more rather than fewer consistently finger-determined responses than did blindfolded children. The results showed that the absence of sensory input might have an effect on coding. Also, modality restriction appeared to be more important than handicap and for both these reasons we decided to use an input restriction paradigm in further experiments.

The method of the experiment to be reported next was developed from a study of short-term memory by Murdock (1969). In our study, subjects who

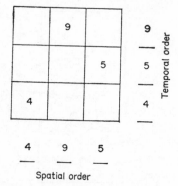

Fig. 3 A test of spatial v. temporal coding.

were either blind, deaf or normal were presented with 3 digits, either visually on a display panel or auditorily through three loudspeakers arranged in a semi-circle to the left, in front and to their right. The 3 digits were presented successively in such a way that their temporal sequential order differed from their left to right spatial order. An example might be presented as in Fig. 3 where the temporal sequential order is shown vertically and the left-right order is shown horizontally.

After each presentation the subject was asked to name or write down 'the middle number'. The question is ambiguous and the answer depends on whether the subject processes the digits in temporal sequence or left-right sequence. If a subject coded temporally his answer to the above example would be '5', and if spatially his answer would be '9'.

The hypothesis to be tested was that modality of presentation was the critical factor which would determine the choice of strategy. It was predicted, therefore, that blind children would respond temporally because receiving auditory input, and deaf children spatially, because their input would be visual. Normal children with auditory presentation were expected to respond temporally and normals with visual input were expected to code spatially, as would the deaf.

Eighty children took part in the experiments. In the first 10 deaf children and 2 groups of 10 normal children matched for digit span and chronological age were tested with visual material. One group of normal children wore earmuffs which restricted hearing. Ten blind children of a similar chronological age, and 2 groups of 10 normal children, one of them blindfolded and matched for chronological age, were tested with auditory material. The children were all chosen from average groups in their school classes, so that their mental ages would be approximately equal to their chronological ages. No tests of intelligence were made. The chronological ages of the groups were between 13 and 14 years and simple analysis of variance showed the groups to be statistically equal in age. The digit spans for each group exceeded the total length of the presentations by at least 2 digits.

The 3 digits were presented over a 2 second period, and the average pause between any 3 digits was 8 seconds, range 6 to 12 seconds. The results were that in the deaf and in both the 2 normal control groups, organization of visual items was predominantly spatial, as the spatially central digit was chosen as the middle one in an overwhelming number of instances. In the blind and the two control groups, with auditorally presented digits, the chosen central or 'middle' digit was predominantly a temporal one.

Results from this experiment are so clear that conclusions can be stated very simply. In an ambiguous situation, modality of presentation determines whether stimuli will be organized spatially or temporally. Thus an auditory presentation determines that subjects will regard the temporally central digit as the 'middle one' rather than the spatially central. A visual presentation determines that subjects will select the spatially central digit and ignore the temporal one. The fact that blind children always choose the temporal middle and deaf children the spatial is a result of the fact that their input is confined to auditory and visual modalities respectively. This is demonstrated by the response of the control groups. In nearly all cases they showed results characteristic for modality of presentation. The blind and deaf children responded in a manner like that of the hearing and sighted in their functioning modality.

Essentially our results indicate that modality of input induces either a temporal or spatial set: that is, the nature of the intuition, to use the terminology of Kant (1781), influences the selection of one or other category or concept. The term 'dimensions' as used by Sutherland (1959) and Zeaman and House (1963) might be mentioned. One could say that the input modality was the trigger which switched on the appropriate dimension for coding the stimuli. Thus the nature of the input to a great degree determines the code used to organize it.

The selection of one 'middle' digit was a task which could be accomplished without drawing on memory, and was in itself a decision and not a recall function. If instead of a decision process recall was required, it might be possible to emphasize and increase the frequency of sequential responses. We therefore modified the task of the previous experiment to ask for the recall of all 3 digits instead of the selection of the 'middle one'.

The experiment was carried out with normal children aged about 9 years who either spoke or wrote down the 3 digits presented. Results as predicted were entirely sequential even with visual presentation. However, when the same technique was used with normal IQ deaf children of the same CA, recall was not temporal-sequential but, in the case of most children, spatial. This result would appear to accord with theoretical expectations and would be explicable in terms of the failure of the deaf to rehearse or recall presented digits verbally. We were interested also in the behaviour of subnormal subjects and believed that their recall of 3 digits would be sequential because of their relatively normal verbal development at least to a limited mental age. We therefore tested severely subnormal adults of IQ 50 to 60, and with mental ages of 8 or 9 years. Responses, unexpectedly, were spatially ordered. This result cannot be easily explained in terms of a simple verbal deficit, unless this were such a deficit as that mentioned by Ellis, namely a rehearsal incapacity in the presence of a reasonable vocabulary.

Recognition scores confirmed the recall findings. For recognition the digits were presented in the same manner as for recall. Then the subjects were shown on some trial series the temporal sequence along with the same digits arranged randomly. On another trial series they were shown the spatial or left-right sequence along with an alternative random arrangement of the same digits. Both 3 digit numbers were presented together on a card and the subject was asked to point to the one he had just seen on the display panel.

Deaf children chose the spatial rather than the random series in 130 out of 160 trials, but gave responses on a chance level when asked to recognize temporal sequence. Normals on the other hand chose the temporal rather than the random sequence 114 times out of 160, but failed to recognize spatial order. Scores for the autistic children were closely similar to those for the deaf, and subnormal children behaved similarly but their bias was less marked.

Thus both in recall and in recognition a differential pattern of input processing occurred in which group differences were marked. Normal children, given a visual input, noted the temporal sequential order of the items, and recalled or recognized this order, whereas deaf, autistic and many subnormal children noted and recalled or recognized the spatially ordered sequence. These results differ from those found in the experiment concerned with the choice of the middle digit. In that case, modality of presentation appeared to determine the elective strategy, whereas in this case the results would appear to be divided according to groups. As the most obvious difference between normals and the other three groups is verbal competence, an explanation should perhaps be sought in these terms.

Specific deficits and general functions

The experimental findings described in the preceding section fall into several distinct patterns of results. In the first two studies, i.e. those concerned with cross-modal coding (O'Connor and Hermelin, 1971c), and with the judgment of duration (Hermelin and O'Connor, 1971a), neither different modalities of stimulus presentation, nor different groups of subjects used, gave differential result patterns. Thus the processes investigated by these studies, i.e. cross-modal coding and durational judgments, seem to be independent of both modality and diagnostic factors.

In the second set of experiments concerned with spatial and spatial-temporal coding (Hermelin and O'Connor, 1971b; O'Connor and Hermelin, 1971a), the crucial variable which affected response patterns was that of presentation modality. Auditory stimuli gave rise to temporal and visual signals to spatial organization of the stimuli. These experiments used single item selection tasks, in which a particular strategy, once adopted, would determine the set of subsequent responses. Thus, while response strategies may be elective in single item selection tasks, there are suggestions in the literature that short-term memory for verbal material is temporally organized, regardless of the mode of its presentation. Thus Tulving and Madigan (1970) state that 'information about the temporal data of the occurrence of an item is an absolutely necessary condition for the recall or recognition of this item'. Similarly, Murdock (1969) also supports this view.

We thus predicted that, with normals at any rate, visually presented digits which had to be recalled or recognized would be temporally rather than spatially coded. This, in fact, was what occurred, and though normal children had selected a spatially central digit as the middle one in the previous experiment, they ordered the same digits temporally when they had to recall them. Deaf, autistic and some subnormal subjects, on the other hand, recalled and recognized the digits in a spatial left-to-right order, ignoring temporal sequence. However, the level of recall and recognition obtained did not differ between the groups, demonstrating that memory could be effectively organized in a non-temporal manner.

An explanation of the difference between the decision or 'middle' experiment and the 3-digit recall and recognition studies requires us to assume that in the case of normal subjects recalling 3 digits after their visual display, some verbal coding occurred either at input, during storage or at retrieval. If the input stage is favoured as an explanation, evidence could be adduced in support of the likelihood of some subnormals failing to use verbalization at this stage, including studies by Luria (1956), O'Connor and Hermelin (1959), and Bryant (1967). Subnormals notoriously do not verbalize or describe in words the input which they may be receiving. This is obviously true of the deaf and may be true of autistic children. As not all subnormals coded spatially in the 3-digit recall task, it must be assumed that only some fail to code verbally. If an explanation in terms of spontaneous verbal coding is acceptable as an account of the difference between the two sets of results, the 'middle' results should be reversible in the case of normal subjects if they vocalized the 3 digits before deciding which was the middle one. This hypothesis remains to be tested. Thus whether because of the modality of input, or because of failure to code verbally, coding strategy is affected. While, therefore, we cannot say that a specific impairment has led to a general deficit, it has led in some cases to a higher level coding strategy effect. In the case of each of the last three sets of experiments, some aspect of the nature of specific input has affected the subject's conceptual schema, whether spatial in the 'run, sit, walk, stand' experiment, the concept of 'middle' in the auditory and visual presentation experiment, or the choice of spatial or temporal sequential coding in the last experiment. These effects on coding must be considered as general effects although, of course, they are not in any sense deficits. The conclusion must be therefore that in certain instances specific impairments result in conceptual schemas which differ from the schemas characteristic of normals.

Conclusions

Such results, therefore, while not confirming a theory of phase sequence in the sense advanced by Hebb (1949), would be an example of limitation of sensory input affecting the operation of a process which, because supra-modal, must be seen as general. The theories of the mode of operation of specific deficits given at the beginning of the chapter were judged to be unsatisfactory in some respects as accounts of failure to learn. The examples we have given may also be inadequate in so far as they show not so much how children fail to learn, but how they tend to observe or record one event or series of events rather than another. However, these experiments may suggest ways in which learning patterns could diverge and lead to different conceptual frameworks in case of specific input handicap. They also show that subnormals, perhaps because they notoriously do not verbalize input, may provide examples of temporal coding deficit. Our results show that not all, but only some, subnormals behave as do deaf and autistic children. The reason for their failure to code temporally requires further study.

In a previous paragraph we referred to earlier attempts on our part to explain learning failure in handicapped groups in terms of a failure of coding at input. The results reported above tend to confirm this conclusion and show further the mechanisms by which characteristics of coding may be affected.

References

ATTNEAVE, F. and BENSON, L. (1969) Spatial coding of tactual
    stimulation. *J. exp. Psychol.*, **81**, 216–22.
BELMONT, J. M. and BUTTERFIELD, E. C. (1969) The relations of short-
    term memory to development and intelligence. In LIPSITT, L. P. and
    REESE, H. W. (eds.) *Advances in Child Development and Behaviour*,
    Vol. 4. New York: Academic Press.
BEXTON, W. H., HERON, W. and SCOTT, I. H. (1954) Effects of
    decreased variation in the sensory environment. *Canad. J. Psychol.*, **8**,
    70–6.

BINET, A. (1894) *Psychologie des Grands Calculateurs.* Paris: Hachette.

BINET, A. and SIMON, T. H. (1909) A scheme of thought. In *The Intelligence of the Feeble-minded. L'Année Psychologique*, 1–147. Reprinted 1966, Baltimore, Md.: Williams & Wilkins.

BIRCH, H. G. and BELMONT, L. (1965) Auditory-visual integration in brain damaged and normal children. *Developm. med. Child. Neurol.*, **7**, 135–44.

BLANK, M. and BRIDGER, W. H. (1966) Conceptual cross-modal transfer in deaf and hearing children. *Child Developm.*, **37**, 29–38.

BLANK, M., ALTMAN, L. D. and BRIDGER, W. H. (1968) Cross-modal transfer of form discrimination in pre-School children. *Psychon. Sci.*, **10**, 51–2.

BLUNDELL, E. (1966) Parietal lobe dysfunction in subnormal patients *J. ment. Defic. Res.*, **10**, 141–52.

BOWER, T. G. R. (1967) Phenomenal identity and form perception in an infant. *Perception and Psychophysics*, **2**, 74–6.

BRYANT, P. E. (1965) The transfer of positive and negative learning by normal and severely subnormal children. *Brit. J. Psychol.*, **56**, 81–6.

BRYANT, P. E. (1967) Verbalisation and immediate memory of complex stimuli in normal and severely subnormal children. *Brit. J. soc. clin. Psychol.*, **6**, 212–19.

BURT, C. (1937) *The Backward Child.* London: Univ. of London Press.

CREAK, M. (1961) Schizophrenic syndrome in childhood: progress report of a working party, April 1961. *Cerebral Palsy Bull.*, **3**, 501–4.

CROME, L. (1954) Some morbid-anatomical aspects of mental deficiency. *J. ment. Sci.*, **100**, 894–912.

DUNCAN, J. (1942) *The Education of the Ordinary Child.* London: Nelson.

ELLIS, N. R. (1963) The stimulus trace and behavioural inadequacy. In ELLIS, N. R. (ed.) *Handbook of Mental Deficiency.* New York: McGraw-Hill.

ELLIS, N. R. (1970) Memory processes in retardates and normals. In ELLIS, N. R. (ed.) *International Review of Research in Mental Retardation*, Vol. 4. New York: Academic Press.

ESTES, W. K. (1959) The statistical approach to learning theory. In KOCH, S. (ed.) *Psychology: A Study of a Science*, Vol. 2. New York: McGraw-Hill.

FOLKARD, S. (1971) *Attentional Deficits in ESN Children.* Unpubl. Ph.D. thesis, Univ. of London.

GALTON, F. (1892) *Hereditary Genius.* London: Macmillan.

HARLOW, H. F. (1958) The nature of love. *Amer. Psychol.*, **13**, 673–85.

HEBB, D. O. (1949) *The Organisation of Behaviour.* London: Chapman & Hall.

HERMELIN, B. and O'CONNOR, N. (1970) *Psychological Experiments with Autistic Children.* Oxford: Pergamon.

HERMELIN, B. and O'CONNOR, N. (1971a) Children's judgements of duration. *Brit. J. Psychol.*, **62**, 13–20.

HERMELIN, B. and O'CONNOR, N. (1971b) Spatial coding in normal, autistic and blind children. *Percept. mot. Skills*, **33**, 127–32.

HUNTER, I. (1962) An exceptional talent for calculative thinking. *Brit. J. Psychol.*, **53**, 243–58.

KANT, I. (1781) *Kritik der reinen Vernunft*. Riga. J. F. Hartknoch. 1933 edn, transl. N. Kemp Smith, London: Macmillan.

KIRK, S. A. and MCCARTHY, J. J. (1961) The Illinois test of psycholinguistic abilities – an approach to differential diagnosis. *Amer. J. Ment. Defic.*, **66**, 399–412.

LURIA, A. R. (1956) Problems of the higher nervous activity of normal and abnormal children. *Acad. Pedagog. Sci.* Moscow: RSF SR.

LURIA, A. R. (1961) *The Rôle of Speech in the Regulation of Normal and Abnormal Behaviour*. Oxford: Pergamon.

MCKINNEY, J. P. (1964) Hand schema in children. *Psychon. Sci.*, **1**, 99–100.

MURDOCK, B. B. (1969) Where or when: modality effects as a function of temporal and spatial distribution of information. *J. Verb. Learn. Verb. Behav.*, **8**, 378–83.

O'CONNOR, N. and HERMELIN, B. (1959) Discrimination and reversal learning in imbeciles. *J. abn. soc. Psychol.*, **59**, 409–13.

O'CONNOR, N. and HERMELIN, B. (1963) *Speech and Thought in Severe Subnormality*. Oxford: Pergamon.

O'CONNOR, N. and HERMELIN, B. (1965) Input restriction and immediate memory decay in normal and subnormal children. *Quart. J. exp. Psychol.*, **XVII**, 323–8.

O'CONNOR, N. and HERMELIN, B. (1971a) Seeing and hearing and space and time. *Perception and Psychophysics* (in press).

O'CONNOR, N. and HERMELIN, B. (1971b) Cognitive deficits in children. *Brit. med. Bull.*, **27**, 227–31.

O'CONNOR, N. and HERMELIN, B. (1971c) Inter and Intra-modal transfer in children with modality specific and general handicaps. *Brit. J. soc. clin. Psychol.*, **10**, 346–54.

PIAGET, J. (1953) *The Origins of Intelligence in the Child* (transl. M. Cook). London: Routledge & Kegan Paul.

PIAGET, J. (1970) *Genetic Epistemology* (trans. E. Duckworth). New York: Columbia Univ. Press.

PIAGET, J. and INHELDER, B. (1969) *The Psychology of the Child* (transl. H. Weaver). London: Routledge & Kegan Paul.

PICK, H. L. and PICK, A. D. (1970) Sensory and perceptual development. In MUSSEN, P. (ed.) *Carmichael's Manual of Child Psychology*. New York: Wiley.

REITAN, R. M. (1966) A research programme on the psychological effects of brain lesions in human beings. In ELLIS, N. R. (ed.) *International Review of Research in Retardation*, Vol. I. New York: Academic Press.

RIESEN, A. H. (1947) The development of visual perception in man and chimpanzee. *Science*, **106**, 107–8.

RUDEL, R. and TEUBER, H. L. (1968) Pattern recognition within and across sensory modalities in normal and brain-injured children. *Annual Report, MIT Dept of Psychology*.

SAVIN, H. B. (1967) On the successive perception of simultaneous stimuli. *Perception and Psychophysics*, **2**, 479–82.

SCHEERER, M., ROTHMAN, E. and GOLDSTEIN, K. (1945) A case of 'idiot savant': an experimental study of personality organization. *Psychol. Monogr.*, **58**.

SMITH, J. and TUNICK, J. (1969) Transfer of discrimination by retarded children. *J. exp. Child Psychol.*, **7**, 274–84.

SPEARMAN, C. (1904) 'General intelligence': objectively determined and measured. *Amer. J. Psychol.*, **115**, 201–92.

SPITZ, R. A. (1945) Hospitalism: the inquiry into the genesis of psychiatric conditions in early childhood. In EISSLER, R. S., FREUD, A., HARTMANN, H. and KRIS, E. (eds.) *The Psychoanalytic Study of the Child*, Vol. 1. New York: Internat. Univ. Press.

STRAUSS, A. A. and LEHTINEN, L. E. (1947) *Psychopathology and Education of the Brain-injured Child*. New York: Grune & Stratton.

SUTHERLAND, N. S. (1959) Stimulus analysing mechanisms. In *Proceedings of Symposium on the Mechanisation of Thought Processes*, Vol. 2, 575–609. London: HMSO.

SYLVESTER, P. E. (1966) Parietal lobe deficit in the mentally retarded. *J. Neurol. Neurosurg. Psychiat.*, **29**, 176–80.

TEUBER, H. L. (1959) Some alterations in behaviour after cerebral lesions in man. In *Evolution of Nervous Control*. Washington, DC: Amer. Assoc. Adv. Sci.

TEUBER, H. L. and LEIBERT, R. S. (1958) Specific and general effects of brain injury in man. *Arch. Neurol. Psychiat.*, **80**, 403–7.

THOMSON, G. H. (1939) *The Factorial Analysis of Human Ability*. London: Univ. of London Press.

THURSTONE, L. L. (1935) *The Vectors of the Mind*. Chicago: Univ. of Chicago Press.

TULVING, E. and MADIGAN, S. A. (1970) Memory and verbal learning. *Ann. Rev. Psychol.*, **21**. Palo Alto: Annual Review Inc.

VERNON, P. E. (1950) *The Structure of Human Abilities*. London: Methuen.

VON SENDEN, M. (1932) *Raum und Gestaltauffassung bei operierten Blindgeborenen vor und nach der Operation*. Leipzig: Barth.

VYGOTSKY, L. S. (1962) *Thought and language*. New York: MIT and Wiley.

WILLIAMS, M. (1950) *Williams' Intelligence Test for Children with Defective Vision*. Birmingham: Univ. of Birmingham Institute of Education.

WOODWARD, M. (1963) The application of Piaget's theory to research in mental deficiency. In ELLIS, N. R. (ed.) *Handbook of Mental Deficiency.* New York: McGraw-Hill.

ZEAMAN, D. and HOUSE, B. J. (1963) The role of attention in retardate discrimination learning. In ELLIS, N. R. (ed.) *Handbook of Mental Deficiency.* New York: McGraw-Hill.

8

A. M. Clarke and A. D. B. Clarke

Severe subnormality:
capacity and performance[1]

Introduction

This group of people are those most easily recognized as mentally handicapped in any community. The vast majority owe their condition to one or other of a variety of unusual genetic or environmental events which render them permanently damaged organisms, who will never be capable of leading a properly independent existence in the community. In societies with a high rate of child mortality, relatively few survive to adulthood; in advanced societies providing good medical care their survival may present a considerable problem to their families. Probably about a third live permanently in hospitals or other institutions, and about two-thirds are reared by their parents, but will by virtue of their handicaps require some form of supervised residential provision all their lives.

The recognition that many severely retarded children and adults are susceptible to training, and in later life can contribute to varying extents to their own support in sheltered conditions, has been one of the major advances in the study of the mentally subnormal.

With the greater understanding of the potential adverse effects of the large institution on the subnormal (Lyle, 1959, 1960a, b; Tizard, 1960; Morris, 1969), there is an increasing tendency to keep the severely retarded in the community. This implies a requirement to provide skilled teaching from a very early age and at least into late adolescence in order to normalize the child (Grunewald, 1969). Considerable advances have taken place in the educational technology required to develop social, language and vocational skills in the severely retarded, and it is no longer considered desirable for a majority either to 'put them away' from society or to keep them occupied with leisurely activities such as painting and dancing.

Until the early 1950s there had been little interest in the psychology of moderately and severely retarded persons. Clinical descriptions in textbooks

[1] Partly based upon a paper presented to the Ciba Foundation and Institute for Research into Mental Retardation, Study Group No. 5, London, December 1971. Published in P. J. Mittler (ed.) *Psychological Assessment of the Mentally Handicapped* (London, Churchill, 1973). Reproduced in part by kind permission of the editor and publishers.

concentrated upon what they *cannot* do rather than what they might achieve with training. The view of various authors can be summarized as follows:

1. At best they find it extremely difficult to concentrate and, more typically, seem capable only of involuntary and momentary attention.
2. They are incapable of comparing and discriminating even on the simplest plane, and of appreciating the relationship between cause and effect.
3. They are quite incapable of adapting themselves to anything out of the ordinary.
4. They are only able to perform the simplest routine tasks under constant supervision.
5. All this makes them unable to contribute appreciably towards their own support.

The traditional concepts referred to above were sanctified by repetition as recently as 1956 in the ninth edition of Tredgold's well-known text (Tredgold and Soddy, 1956), as the following excerpt indicates:

Imbeciles, as a class, stand above the idiots in that they can be taught to understand and protect themselves against many common physical dangers. For instance, they will not deliberately walk into a pond or put their hands into the fire, and they will attempt to get out of the way of a motor-car. They stand below the feeble-minded in that, whilst many of them can be trained to perform simple routine tasks under supervision, they are incapable of earning their living or of contributing materially towards their support. Most of them can wash, dress, and feed themselves under supervision. They are markedly defective in educational capacity, and as a class they cannot be taught to read beyond words of one syllable, to spell more than a few two- and three-letter words, or to do simple mental addition and subtraction beyond the smallest units. They can tell their name, say whether it is morning or afternoon, winter or summer. They can recognize and name common objects, and can say for what they are used, but they cannot give a description of them.

It is increasingly recognized that these negatives have much validity for the institutionalized severe subnormal who has not enjoyed an active training programme, but that they seriously underestimate, in their general tone, the possibilities of remediation. Indeed a review of only fifteen studies in the first edition of this book forced us in 1958 to conclude that:

. . . in this neglected field of imbecile learning, it is clear that much more research is needed and that the investigations reported have merely laid a basis for later work. Even so, there is little doubt that already some traditional concepts of imbecile abilities and trainability are in need of qualification or revision; consequently this must also apply to our methods of helping and training the low-grade patient.

This view was further documented in the second edition written in 1964. During the intervening years there had been something of an explosion of interest in this field and our review had become necessarily selective. In rewriting this chapter in 1972 it was obvious that even greater selectivity would be required, for a detailed coverage of the literature would demand a book in its own right. Thus we propose to organize the discussion around two broad topics, first, the psychometric, and second, the experimental approach to severe subnormality. In so doing we shall merely sample the considerable literature. It should, however, be stated at the outset that we believe that modern research gives guidance on some broad general principles of remediation. It seems to us that the most important general deficits in the severely subnormal are, firstly, a *severe inability to learn spontaneously from ordinary life experience* which includes social contacts with parents, peers and the community at large; secondly, there is almost always a severe language impairment; and thirdly, there is a considerable slowness in learning. Thus, if they are merely exposed to normal social and educational situations they will, on the whole, fail to profit from them. If, however, a situation or task is analysed for them and their attention directed to the relevant aspects by means of *structured training*, a very different picture will emerge, granted a sufficiently lengthy period (Clarke and Clarke, 1973). Thus the older generalizations noted above are true of those who have not been exposed to programmes of directed training with adequate rewards; they tend initially to be very bad at any task. However, the starting level (unlike that of normal people) bears little or no relationship to the final level after training, and, furthermore, on *simple* tasks they are usually able to achieve the same speed and quality as normals, but the time taken to reach this standard is very much longer.

Limitations of the psychometric approach

Psychometric assessment has four main functions:

1. to describe the individual as he is at a particular point in time, upon intellectual, social, emotional, educational or other variables with reference to a normative or contrast population;
2. to predict the individual's probable status at later points in time;
3. to provide a behavioural profile of assets and deficits as a starting point for remedial programmes;
4. to provide an objective means of checking progress of an individual or a group.

These categories of assessment in mental subnormality are intimately related to the services society provides, and thus to the demands for different types of information made upon the psychologist. If, for one reason or another, only custodial care is offered and no attempts at remediation, then assessment will only be concerned with the establishment of a clear borderline, related to the amount of provision, the estimated demands and the degree of handicap. In such a situation an individual intelligence test and an assessment of social competence will be essential. If, on the other hand, an adequate remedial service becomes available, then assessment becomes a starting point for action and a means for evaluating its results.

Most assessment procedures aim as far as possible to give an indication of native ability or capacity. It is nowadays recognized that it is impossible to measure 'pure' ability, unaffected by life experience, which must be largely unknown to the psychologist. On the whole, however, the vast literature on psychological assessment in the normal population is generally interpreted as indicating that properly standardized measures of ability or aptitude are at least useful in helping to predict achievement granted 'normal' life experience and 'normal' educational experience without any special remedial element. Two *caveats* are, however, increasingly accepted: that prediction is strongly affected by (1) the age at which it is undertaken, the earlier the measure the lower its predictive power; and (2) the length of time over which predictions are made, the longer the period, the less the accuracy. It has recently been argued that these generalizations apply not only to intelligence but also to personality measurements and attainment tests. Moreover, examination of data suggests that in the mildly subnormal, average and supernormal populations there is much more variability in growth than has been accepted. The contrary view results from a misunderstanding of the implications of correlation coefficients between repeated measurements over time. Even a ·9 correlation describes a situation in which a minority may make considerable changes of status, and in longitudinal studies one is normally dealing with much lower relationships and thus considerably greater proportions of significant individual change. Such an analysis is borne out by all really long-term studies (e.g. Baller *et al.*, 1967; Oden, 1968). In brief, predictive assessment is in general less accurate over the long term than is generally assumed (Clarke and Clarke, 1972). There is, however, a lack of long-term data on the severely subnormal but a consensus that, under conditions of minimal remediation, there will be little achievement. Global predictions are thus possible and probably fairly accurate.

The main argument of this chapter is that assessment, as outlined in the first three headings (and particularly in the first two), is of limited value in the field of subnormality. In Britain it has been classically regarded as the main contribution of psychologists. As currently employed it appears more often as an epiphenomenon keeping them busy, stimulating often unprofitable research and leading to a perpetual quest for the philosopher's stone (better and better tests) which will ensure more and more accurate predictions. It will be argued that, for a number of reasons, such hopes are misguided and that more profitable alternatives already exist.

THE BACKGROUND – AN OVERVIEW

Post-war research on severe subnormality began with the work of Tizard and his colleagues Gordon and Loos. This showed that, granted individual attention and training in simple and not-so-simple laboratory tasks, the traditional picture of the behaviour of the severely subnormal needed substantial revision. For example, good motor dexterity and good spatial judgment could be achieved within a reasonable period of training, the skills gained were retained, and learning transfer could be demonstrated as a powerful function on some tasks. Within a few years Clarke and Hermelin showed that the results of these laboratory studies could be replicated in sheltered 'real life' industrial working conditions. Later still it was concluded that the combination of typically poor starting points yet subsequently good learning, both on laboratory and industrial tasks, could only be explained by postulating a relative inability in these subjects to learn spontaneously from ordinary life experience (Clarke and Cookson, 1962).[1] It was thus easy to understand the traditional view of the lack of capacity in the severely subnormal; Tredgold and others had taken initial performance as a sample of potential learning ability, and therefore that the SSN were incapable of learning, full stop.

There are two sources of learning which may interact with the biologically determined potential of any developing human organism: (1) unstructured situations, the majority, and (2) structured learning situations, the minority. As we see it, the highly intelligent 'spontaneous' learner will profit greatly from the former, as well as from the latter, the less gifted will rely increasingly on the latter, and the severely subnormal will profit rather little from unstructured situations. The notion that the best learning is self-generated has for years been the basis of 'progressive' education, associated in this country with the names of A. S. Neill and Bertrand Russell among others. It has become a major article of faith in Colleges of Education, and has become logically attached to the developmental theory of Piaget. Teachers in training are encouraged to use informal assessment of Piagetian stages to discover whether their pupils are 'ready' to learn certain concepts, or, indeed, certain skills like reading. Since what they are assessing is the spontaneous acquisition of certain elaborate behaviours based upon innate abilities interacting with the environment in an unknown way over an unknown period, by the time the child shows 'readiness' he requires little formal teaching. If one assesses the severely subnormal in Piagetian terms (as in any other terms) one will be likely to conclude that he is not ready to learn.

It appears that the severely subnormal child may lose out under both headings mentioned above. First, there is an obvious constitutional deficit which imposes severe limits upon his development, and includes, if we are correct, a relative inability spontaneously to structure ordinary experience. Moreover, as a mainly passive baby and child, his role in the dyad with his parents will tend to evoke

---

[1] It is difficult to define spontaneous learning ability without embarking on a discussion of the nature of intelligence. However, it includes the ability to organize or code incoming stimuli in a variety of ways and to build up schemata appropriately which enable the individual both to respond selectively and to embark upon the next stages of learning. It includes the ability to perceive relationships and make deductions without the intervention of another human agent. We are not arguing that the SSN have no spontaneous learning ability, merely that it is very greatly impaired.

less responsiveness and thus less stimulation. Second, the current move away from structured situations, already referred to, avoids the conditions which for him are almost the sole possibility of learning.

The early background work can be summarized by stating in more modern terms that in the severely subnormal there is a profound gap between psychological capacity and initial performance, a gap which has its origin in constitutional factors on the one hand, and mode of handling on the other.

SOME DETAILED EVIDENCE

Assessment usually involves a one-trial measure on a particular variable, and hence indicates initial performance. Brief evidence has already been offered on the inadequacy of initial performance as a predictor, and hence on the inadequacy of normal assessment methods for prediction in this population. It may, however, help to put some flesh on the bare bones of the argument, to select for purposes of illustration a stream of work which illustrates the theme and with which Tizard and ourselves have been concerned. For this we take the Minnesota Spatial Relations Test, normally an industrial selection test, but used as a learning task on several occasions in the last twenty years. This consists of 4 very large form-boards each containing 58 holes into which the corresponding 58 pieces have to be fitted, these being first set out in a pre-determined order. The boards comprise 2 pairs, A and B, and C and D. For each pair, a single set of pieces is common although the corresponding holes are in very different places in each board. For efficient performance on this difficult task, not only is it necessary accurately to perceive form, but clustering behaviour, involving the selection of sets of 3 or 4 identical shapes (differing in size), aids the speed and efficiency of solution, these being the test criteria.

The classic assessment approach might raise the following problems:

1. How good or bad is the individual on a spatial relations task (i.e. *on 1 trial of 1 board*)?
2. On the basis of the test (i.e. single trial), can we predict the subject's suitability for, e.g., industrial training?
3. From his performance can we predict his future status on this task?

The inadequacy of these questions will be obvious from what follows. With hindsight, it can be assumed that the individual's spatial ability is to varying extents damaged, that prediction of future status on the basis of initial test score is very limited, that however poor his initial performance, he will respond to training, that the degree of his disability will only affect the speed of responsiveness and that therefore a specific individual programme is hardly necessary. Let us see how learning experiments built up this somewhat different picture.

Tizard and Loos (1954) showed that a group of SSNs selected as being thought virtually unemployable in an institution workshop with average IQs of about 35 exhibited exceedingly poor performance (averaging about 20 minutes) on Trial 1 of the first board (the normal average being about 4 minutes). Their learning curves were impressive and over the succeeding 3 boards they showed considerable transfer. Time scores for correct solutions were used, and by Trial 32 had reduced to 3 or 4 minutes, the average Trial 1 score for normals. This work was confirmed and amplified by Clarke (1962), Clarke and Cooper (1966) and Radon and Clarke (1971).

In an oversimplified way some of these findings may be summarized: (1) initial (i.e. assessment) score bears no relationship to final score; (2) while initial scores are very poor and vary widely between individuals, final scores after 32 trials are very homogeneous and good (i.e. the 'funnel effect'); (3) learning transfer takes place between boards and is an impressive function; (4) over very long periods of time without direct practice, a retest indicates that initial scores are greatly improved probably because of exposure to other industrial tasks involving spatial relationships; (5) clustering behaviour, which ordinarily occurs poorly but spontaneously can be differentially increased by a particular type of training.

These facts being established for this type of perceptual-motor activity, single trial assessment of spatial ability together with individual predictions, or selection on this basis, are misconceived. Rather, the more economical assumption with the SSN subject is that he will show initial inadequacy and thus a programme to overcome it needs to be prescribed.

Of course it may well be that the work on the Minnesota Test, which has been summarized, by chance capitalized upon particular potential assets and the findings might not, for example, apply to a complicated language programme. All one can say, however, is that on initial performance (i.e. test assessment) one scarcely gained the impression that these gravely damaged subjects had any spatial assets at all. But certainly in this area at least, the total inadequacy of assessing 'spatial ability' or 'clustering ability' by exposure to a single trial or even a few trials is obvious. Indeed, had Tizard and Loos (1954) merely used this task for its usual purpose, a 1-trial assessment test, and had we then accepted this as a predictor, the course of subsequent work might have been very different. It was this difference between Trial 1 prediction and outcome that stimulated Clarke and Hermelin (1955) to undertake experiments on industrial work. Using *the same subjects* as Tizard and Loos in a recently created industrial unit, these authors sought to establish whether the laboratory findings would be confirmed, and whether more complex skills might be taught. They employed 3 tasks: (1) the use of a guillotine to cut insulated wire to exact lengths; (2) the soldering of 4 different coloured wires to the correct terminals of an 8-pin television plug; and (3) the assembly of a bicycle pump, involving 9 operations which had to be performed in the correct order.

The table overleaf summarizes some of the findings.

The Guillotine data, based on only 2 hours of training, separated by a week of non-practice, show very considerable improvement which no doubt would have continued had the minimal training been prolonged. The relation of initial to final scores for 6 subjects was: 35–46; 23–33; 40–52; 36–56; 16–48; 15–57.

The Television Plug results show widely different starting points and great improvement, leading to very similar endpoints (the 'funnel effect').

The Bicycle Pump Assembly data indicate precisely similar results to the above.

In all cases, Trial 1 performance (the typical assessment device) is very poor, nor is it any guide to ultimate level of improvement, nor is it correlated with ultimate level. The authors concluded that the main difference on simple tasks between the ability of these subjects and normals was not so much the endpoint as the time taken to achieve it. Had Trial 1 been used for assessment purposes, it would have been concluded that these subjects were below all norms, and that they were therefore unsuitable for any sort of industrial work, which would also have been predicted from Trial 1 of the Minnesota Test. Data from these two

TABLE 3 . *Some basic data*

	Initial range	*Final range*	*Duration of training*
Guillotine	15–40 wires cut per 5 min.	33–57 wires cut per 5 min.	2 × 1-hour periods
Television plug	4 min.–19 min. per plug	1 min. 42 sec.– 3 min. 30 sec. per plug	34 trials
Bicycle pump	4 min. 20 sec.– 10 min. 45 sec. per assembly	54 sec.– 1 min. 50 sec. per assembly	30 trials

experiments have been presented in some detail because they appear to offer the key to understanding the inadequacy of most assessment methods in this population.

Let us also consider another example, namely some very recent work which, on the face of it, appears to contradict the argument advanced so far but which, in reality, probably supports it. This is some very careful work by Grant (1971) whose concern includes the problem of prediction of workshop industrial ability. Some 13 industrial assessment tests were given to a sample of trainees in an Adult Training Centre, and from these 17 predictor variables were identified. These scores were correlated with performance on 8 industrial tasks on the average of the first 3 successful trials. The findings indicated that a far greater proportion of the tests produced significant correlations with job performance for males than females. 'A tentative explanation for this', writes Grant, 'would be that the previous work experience of males and females has been so different over the years that attributes such as those measured have developed differentially between the sexes.' This notion, which seems entirely reasonable, implicitly supports the view of Ferguson (1954) that specific abilities arise from, among other things, overlearning of typical sequences. The second main finding of Grant was that, on the whole, the correlations were of moderate to high value. Thus, for the males 56 out of 136 correlations were ·70 or above, and for the females, 37 out of 136.

These data appear to yield quite impressive relationships and suggest the possibility of developing a more refined test battery for the accurate prediction of industrial performance. However, as the author seems implicitly aware, the outlook may well be less rosy, because what he has in effect done is to correlate initial performance on assessment tasks, themselves designed to sample the basic perceptual-motor processes involved in industrial work, with initial performance (on the average, the first five trials) on industrial tasks. That initial industrial-type performance correlates quite well with initial industrial performance, while interesting, does not necessarily imply that these devices would in any sense predict final achievement levels after training.

As a further example, the work of Cobb (1969) can be cited. He has provided in two volumes a summary of the research literature on the predictive assessment of the adult retarded for social and vocational adjustment. He reaches thirteen conclusions, of which three will be alluded to here. His views in this particular field bear striking similarity with some of the more general points we have made.

1. The most consistent and outstanding finding of all follow-up studies is the high proportion of the adult retarded who achieve satisfactory adjustments, by whatever criteria are employed. This is, of course, especially true of those at mild level, on whom most of the studies have been done; but it also holds for the retarded at moderate and even severe levels. This should guide the counselor to the adoption of more generally optimistic expectation than has generally prevailed in the past. Indeed, the evidence suggests that it is more appropriate to make an assumption of positive adaptation on some meaningful criteria of employability and social integration until negative evidence appears rather than to assume a poor prognosis until positive evidence appears. The latter attitude, which has been highly prevalent in the past, has the general effect of creating its own proof by failing to provide available means for facilitating successful adaptation. Every follow-up validation of predicted successes and failures has shown a higher rate of false negatives than of false positives. . . .

3. Evidence from the major follow-up studies indicates that adult adaptation of the retarded may take considerable time, especially when retardation is related to social and cultural deprivation. The movement from instability to stability may take years but it may be greatly facilitated by flexible, open-ended programs of social-vocational training. Failure at any point should never be taken as conclusive. The general principle, supported throughout the research literature, is that predictions of adaptive success are generally more reliable than predictions of failure. This might lead a counsellor who is interested only in building a good record of successful closures to concentrate

all his attention on the clearly positive cases and exclude all the 'risk' cases. But it will lead the counsellor who is really client-centered to be very cautious in accepting negative prognosis as final evidence of unfeasibility. . . .

6. Of particular significance to case workers is the finding from Parnicky's research that predictive validity decreases rapidly over time and over the stages of training. This finding suggests that we are on much firmer ground in using predictive measures more as estimates of preparation for the *next step* in training or placement than as determiners of the longer-range future.[1]

In this section some brief attention has been devoted to spatial ability, industrial performance and to social and vocational adjustment. To round off this survey, a short account will be given of a different area, namely 'clustering', a higher-order cognitive ability in which it might reasonably be expected that subnormals would be clearly deficient. Gerjuoy and Spitz (1966) studied clustering and free recall as a function of age, intelligence, and practice. Five populations were used: 20 middle-grade subnormals (mean IQ 53), 20 high-grades (mean IQ 72), 19 matched normal MA subjects (mean IQ 107), 14 matched CA subjects (mean IQ 117) and finally, a group of 20 college students.

The experimental material consisted of 20 nouns, 5 from each of 4 categories (animals, body parts, clothing, and food). Using an identical procedure to that of Rossi (1963), 5 separate randomizations of this test were used, together with 2 different measures of clustering. Data for middle- and high-grade subnormals were pooled since there were no significant differences between them on recall or amount of clustering. Comparison of the subnormals with the other populations showed significant Population and Trial effects (both with $p < \cdot 001$) with non-significant interactions. There were no significant differences between the 2 lower MA groups, nor between the 2 higher MA groups. The latter, however, both recalled more words than the former.

Subnormals and their MA matched controls clustered very little, and only on Trial 5 for the subnormals were the scores significantly above chance. Equal CA normals clustered significantly on Trials 4 and 5 ($p < \cdot 02$), and college students on Trials 3, 4 and 5 ($p < \cdot 001$). Significant correlations between clustering and recall were found only for equal CA normals on Trial 5 ($r = \cdot 55$, $p < \cdot 05$) and for college students on Trials 4 ($r = \cdot 81$, $p < \cdot 01$) and 5 ($r = \cdot 85$, $p < \cdot 01$). The implications are clear; no clustering above chance levels for the subnormals on the first 4 trials. Traditional assessment using Trial 1 would thus confirm a total deficiency in this area. However, a second experiment was planned to determine whether conditions designed to increase clustering would aid the recall of the retarded. Two different methods were used: the Present Clustered (PC) method where the stimulus words were presented in categories, and the Requested (RC) method where the experimenter requested the words by category name. Fifteen institutionalized subnormals were randomly assigned to

---

[1] Here Cobb is really stating that initial performance at any stage correlates with initial performance at the next step.

each condition, and the same stimulus material was used as earlier. For the first group (PC), however, 5 new orders of the 20 stimulus words were produced with the 5 words of each category placed consecutively but with the order of categories, and the order of words within categories, randomized.

The recall data were compared with those from the subnormals in the first experiment. There were significant effects of Treatment ($p < \cdot 005$), Trials ($p < \cdot 001$) and Treatment + Trials ($p < \cdot 005$). Results from the 2 induced clustering groups did not differ significantly, but induced clustering significantly increased the recall of both of these groups and produced steeper learning curves.

The clustering data were equally interesting. The PC group on Trial 1 clustered almost twice as much as the subnormals in the first experiment, and significantly above chance. On Trial 4 the correlation between clustering and recall ($r = \cdot 63$, $p < \cdot 05$) was significant, decreasing to a non-significant $\cdot 39$ on Trial 5. The observed/maximum clustering scores on the PC group were $\cdot 72$, $\cdot 35$, $\cdot 19$, $\cdot 24$, and $\cdot 26$ for the 5 trials, respectively.

Irrelevant intrusions were few in all three conditions, but categorical intrusions were somewhat higher. The RC group gave significantly more categorical intrusions than the first experiment or PC subjects. This second experiment therefore indicates that under certain conditions clustering can be induced.

Yet another experiment underlines what has been said about duration of training. Thus Gerjuoy and Alvarez (1969) failed to produce a set to cluster in educable retarded adolescents (CA 15·2 years, IQ 59·4) and normal children matched for MA, using 1 training session of 5 trials and a transfer session 1 week later. Two lists of 20 familiar words were used, 5 words from each of 4 categories. Half the subjects in each population received List 1 during training and List 2 for transfer and the other half had the converse. Half the subjects were trained with randomized word lists, while the other half were given clustered presentation; all subjects had randomized lists in the second (transfer session). Both populations exhibited increased clustering and recall when the list was presented in a clustered, rather than a randomized order, thus confirming previous findings. Neither practice and familiarity with the task, nor experience with a clustered list aided performance at the second session.

By contrast, Clarke and co-workers (1970) found significant effects of a learned set on the free recall of retarded adults (mean PPVT IQ 60), all members of an Adult Training Centre. Two groups of subjects, matched for score on a pictorial similarities test and ability to recall unrelated words, were trained as follows: the Blocks Group was required to recall a list of 16 words, 4 in each of 4 categories, presented in clusters (i.e. 'blocks'), twice every day until a criterion of 4 consecutive scores of 15 or 16 words was reached, *or* they had completed 24 trials. The orders of words within clusters, and position of clusters within the list were systematically changed from trial to trial. The Random Group was required to recall a list of 16 unrelated high-frequency words (Thorndike-Lorge) to the same criterion, the order of presentation of words varying from trial to trial. Both groups were subsequently presented with the same new list of 16 words, 4 words in each of 4 categories in which no 2 conceptually related words were ever juxtaposed, and neither words nor categories were common to either of the 2 training lists. There was a significant difference in *amount* recalled ($p < \cdot025$) on the first 2 trials of transfer, favouring the Blocks Group, but neither group showed much tendency to cluster; on Trials 3 and 4 the differences between the groups in terms of amount recalled was reduced to non-significance, but there was a significant difference ($p < \cdot05$) in cluster index (taking account of score) in favour of the Blocks Group. A further study by the authors, using memory for pictures as the transfer task, and groups of subjects, including an equal number of ex-ESN and ex-JTC adolescents in an Adult Training Centre, showed a significant difference in score only between Blocks and Random Groups on Trials 1 and 2 of transfer, and no difference whatever in clustering, the ESN subjects in both groups clustering above chance, and the JTC Ss showing little tendency to cluster. It was concluded that if categorical relations among words are repeatedly demonstrated by clustered presentation, a set to perceive inter-item associations develops. This is available for use with new categorizable material so that the categorical relations are perceived at the input-coding stage with consequent augmentation of total output (recall score). Clustering at any significant level is a reflection of organization of input material in store, and is an activity that occurs after at least two repetitions of a list, predominantly among subjects of higher intelligence. The results point to the importance of total recall score as a measure of categorization, in addition to clustering, which latter may well depend on different psychological processes.

It is clear that both types of experiment, that by Gerjuoy and Alvarez (1969) and Clarke *et al.* (1970) with their negative and positive results, respectively, are important in delineating the conditions which favour or inhibit the development of a higher order activity. In the latter investigation, those of very low intelligence failed to profit by this type of training, while those of higher ability did. It may be that the use of conceptual categories in the organization of randomly pre-sented verbal material, in contrast with the growth of clustering on the Minnesota Form boards, cannot be achieved by those with severe verbal impairment but this for us remains an open question.

Alternatives to the psychometric approach

We have perhaps laboured the point that initial performance on any task is an inadequate predictive device. It should also be stressed that in our experience structured training diminishes individual differences, so that from rather heterogeneous initial performance a group will tend to reach a more homogeneous final performance. It will be apparent below how this limits prediction by the more usual psychometric methods, although not by the third method we outline. The 'funnel effect' to which we have already referred (i.e. decreasing variability as learning improves) is also implicitly supported by the work of House and

Zeaman on 'backward learning curves' first suggested by Hayes (1953). These workers show that in discrimination learning there are apparently wide differences in performance. The plotting of backward learning curves shows, however, that once learning has commenced, the curves are very similar for different individuals.

For useful predictive assessment there are three normative possibilities, the first two of which are essentially psychometric: (1) a considerable dispersion of initial scores; (2) a considerable dispersion of final scores after, e.g. training or a mere lapse of time. If these two criteria are met, then a correlation coefficient is a short-hand way of expressing the predictive ability of the assessment, although, as already noted psychologists seldom understand the implication of such coefficients and are easily led up the garden path by them. It has already been indicated, however, that the second possibility is seldom fulfilled, and this is a roundabout way of restating the main argument. There must in the vast majority of cases be low correlations between initial performance and final attainment after training. We now come to point (3), however. The learning experiment, of which we have given a few examples earlier, can examine any aspect of any function both *ab initio* and also its modification by particular forms of structured training. It is then possible to specify the endpoint, together with its rather limited dispersion of scores, and hence the training objective. Subsequently the effect of different forms of training, different durations and reinforcements will provide a technology of remediation, a process which has barely begun. Rather similar conclusions have been reached by Bortner and Birch (1970) who have surveyed the scattered literature from mainly cognitive fields in their important paper on cognitive capacity and cognitive competence. In summarizing their survey, they state that:

Our consideration of the relation between cognitive capacity and cognitive performance in mentally subnormal children, as well as in normal children and experimental animals, permits a general conclusion. It is clear from all these data that performance levels under particular conditions are but fragmentary indicators of capacity. Possessed concepts and skills, and particular conceptual abilities, as well as levels of learning when manifested in performance, all reflect the interaction between possessed potentialities and the particular conditions of training and task demand. Glaring differences occur in the estimates of potential when meaningful alterations are made in the conditions for performance. It is clear that we have but begun to explore the universe of conditions for learning and performance which will facilitate most effectively the expression of the potentialities for adaptation which exist in mentally subnormal children. Clearly, the most effective facilitation of development will be dependent on the ingenuity with which such conditions are elaborated. It is hoped that placing this question in the broader context of psychology will contribute to the invention of more effective strategies for training and for the maximization of competence.

It appears that the severely subnormal person is initially to some extent a *tabula rasa*; his limited achievements are directly and almost solely related to the structured and directed training, whether social or vocational, he has undergone, together with its subsequent reinforcement, and to the demands made upon him and to their motivational consequences. These rather simple ideas have as yet made virtually no impact upon practice, as Grant (1971) has clearly indicated. In his experiment, for example, he demonstrated eight industrial tasks to each supervisor, who was himself encouraged to try the assembly. He was then asked to estimate (1) whether each trainee could learn each of the tasks, and (2) how many trials would be required for the successful trainee to reach the criterion standard. As the author indicates, supervisory predictions were emphatic, but when compared with the actual mimimal training outcome, large numbers turned out to be successful job performers who appeared to have been written off as failures by their supervisors. Further, the abilities of the females were underestimated to a far greater extent by their supervisors. Failure sets apparently do not only apply to the mentally handicapped: '. . . many supervisors must be unaware of much latent ability, and this attitude is probably in part accountable by the simplicity of work normally undertaken in centres' (Grant, 1971). And, one might add, lack of awareness of the points to which this chapter is devoted.

Discussion

So far the inadequacy of predictive assessment of potential achievement has been presented in the context of attempts at remediation. To give an overall picture, however, it must be noted that predictive assessment will be highly accurate on any task if one knows that the individual is not subsequently to be exposed to structured learning opportunities and good incentive conditions. This is perhaps stating the obvious but this is justified when varying claims for prediction are made without reference to their context. This point was well recognized even in the mid-1950s when the British Psychological Society gave evidence before the Royal Commission on the Law relating to Mental Illness and Mental Deficiency, 1954–7. Responsiveness to training was then suggested as a main predictive device. It is possible that some measure might be developed to predict the time period necessary for the subject to achieve a given level of proficiency.

Across the Atlantic the Skinnerians have got into gear, and the impetus in research on developing socially adaptive skills in the severely subnormal has shifted from Britain to America. Mittler (1973) expresses concern that psychologists in this country are not being involved in the establishment and day-to-day running of new diagnostic units in hospitals, clinics and schools. Since virtually all recent knowledge on perceptual and cognitive processes in the subnormal has been developed by psychologists, as well as all the major programmes of educational remediation in the last half century, it is indeed curious and sad that this should be so.

We would like to suggest that one reason is that British psychologists, both theoretical and applied, have concerned themselves too much with assessment and too little with learning processes. Possibly the success of the Skinnerians with the subnormal has been due in large measure to their (otherwise unfortunate) disinclination to make assumptions about internal processes, but instead to manipulate observed behaviour in a systematic way.

Kirk and McCarthy's (1961) construction of the ITPA was aimed not primarily at producing a better diagnostic test for predictive purposes, but rather as an attempt to provide a more detailed guide for the design of remedial education programmes. Marianne Frostig advocates the use of a battery of tests for a similar purpose. On the other hand Tyson (1970) points out that in connection with the design of remedial programmes for people above the level of severe subnormality:

> Having stated that an essential pre-requisite . . . is first of all a clear diagnosis of the child's difficulties, it is necessary now to qualify this statement in that, given the crudity of some of the psychological tools available at present, it may not be possible initially to pin-point the exact area of disability. In this case, to an even more important degree than in more clear-cut diagnosis, *the teaching itself carries the burden of diagnosis*, in that the pay-off from different approaches gives some indication as to where difficulties lie; but some general idea at least of the area of difficulty must be available in order to establish the initial teaching techniques that are to be employed. (our italics)

Neither Heber (1971), Bereiter and Engelmann (1966) nor Gray and Klaus (1970) (all of whom work with the socially deprived mildly subnormal) have shown much interest in assessment procedures, except as an essential tool for evaluating changes in their experimental subjects. They are all involved in the much more interesting task of modifying behaviour.

We fail to see what purpose can be served by applied psychologists carrying out detailed and elaborate assessment procedures in new diagnostic units, unless they can offer some prescription for remediation. Furthermore, we are strongly inclined to the view that developmental and cognitive psychology will be entirely rewritten on the basis of the research, as yet to be carried out, of psychologists who become involved in the systematic modification of behaviour at different intelligence levels over a long period of time.

Few psychologists would consider that Skinner has elaborated a satisfactory theory of human behaviour. Perhaps this is because he and his colleagues have ignored a detailed description of the constitutional differences that exist among animals. On the other hand, Piaget, who essentially describes elaborated behaviour, and psychologists such as Hermelin and O'Connor (1970) who conduct brilliantly creative experiments, shedding light on important constitutional differences, seem to pay little attention to the fact that the behaviour they observe has, by the time they observe it, been shaped to an unknown extent by several years of interaction with the physical and social environment, and might (or might not) be modifiable.

Surely the time has come for more psychologists to address themselves to bridging this gap. It seems obvious to us that children with different constitutionally determined assets and deficits interact (probably from birth) differently with their environment, and no adequate theory of behaviour can be developed until these interactions are (a) observed and (b) controlled.

Conclusions

Both for reasons of constitutional deficits and, to an as yet unknown extent, inappropriate handling, the severely subnormal exhibit an initial performance which often appears well below their capacity. While a careful description of the individual on a particular variable may be found helpful, if that individual is then to be exposed to structured learning opportunities, its main function will be merely to mark the start, at a particular point in time, of a remedial process. As a check upon progress, this initial assessment will be essential, and this takes us back to the fourth function of assessment, described at the outset, and indeed the only one about which no reservations have been expressed in this paper.

In the past, and to an extent still at the present time, the function of assessment has all too frequently been solely administrative, and the direct benefit to the individual has more often than not been dubious resulting all too often in deprivation of liberty or of learning experiences. The assessment movement, from Galton and Binet onwards, has depended upon single-shot sampling of an area of behaviour, and from this an estimate of capacity inferred. From all that has been said it is clear that in the severely subnormal this approach can offer little useful long-term guidance, nor indeed can very short-term experimental approaches do so. The alternative is the long-term carefully-conceived prospective experimental study which can outline the 'artificial' development of processes which otherwise will lie dormant, either because ordinary experience fails to stimulate their emergence, or because of failure sets or other factors. It is clear that we are coming to the end of the period of sterile psychometrics and are at the threshold of something of greater interest both theoretically and practically. In summary, there are at least three major variables which must be taken into account in the prediction of achievement: (1) the constitution of the subject, (2) the nature of the task, and (3) the nature, demands and duration of the learning experience, with its motivational consequences. At the present time prediction should be based upon knowledge of the development of a process following remediation rather than upon test results related to initial performance. Capacity can only be inferred when the limits to performance have been reached by systematic, prolonged and structural training.

References

BALLER, W. R., CHARLES, D. C. and MILLER, E. L. (1967) Mid-life attainment of the mentally retarded: a longitudinal study. *Genet. Psychol. Monogr.*, **75**, 235–329.

BEREITER, C. and ENGELMANN, S. (1966) *Teaching Disadvantaged Children in the Preschool*. Englewood Cliffs, NJ: Prentice-Hall.

BORTNER, M. A. and BIRCH, H. G. (1970) Cognitive capacity and cognitive competence. *Amer. J. ment. Defic.*, **74**, 735–44.

CLARKE, A. D. B. (1962) Laboratory and workshop studies of imbecile learning processes. In RICHARDS, B. W. (ed.) *Proc. Lond. Conf. Scient. Stud. Ment. Defic.*, **1**, 89–9. Dagenham: May and Baker.

CLARKE, A. D. B. and CLARKE, A. M. (1972) Consistency and variability in the growth of human characteristics. In WALL, W. D. and VARMA, V. (eds.) *Advances in Educational Psychology*. London: Univ. of London Press.

CLARKE, A. D. B. and COOKSON, M. (1962) Perceptual-motor transfer in imbeciles: a second series of experiments. *Brit. J. Psychol.*, **53**, 321–30.

CLARKE, A. D. B. and COOPER, G. M. (1966) Age and perceptual-motor transfer in imbeciles: task complexity as a variable. *Brit. J. Psychol.*, **57**, 113–19.

CLARKE, A. D. B. and HERMELIN, B. F. (1955) Adult imbeciles: their abilities and trainability. *Lancet*, **ii**, 337–9.

CLARKE, A. M. and CLARKE, A. D. B. (1973) What are the problems? An evaluation of recent research relating to theory and practice. In CLARKE, A. D. B. and CLARKE, A. M. (eds.) *Mental Retardation and Behavioural Research*. Edinburgh: Churchill Livingstone.

CLARKE, A. M., CLARKE, A. D. B. and COOPER, G. M. (1970) The development of a set to perceive categorical relations. In HAYWOOD, H. C. (ed.) *Social-Cultural Aspects of Mental Retardation*. New York: Appleton-Century-Crofts.

COBB, H. V. (1969) *The Predictive Assessment of the Adult Retarded for Social and Vocational Adjustment*, Parts I and II. Vermillion: Psychology Dept, Univ. of Dakota.

FERGUSON, G. A. (1954) On learning and human ability. *Canad. J. Psychol.*, **8**, 95–112.

GERJUOY, I. R. and ALVAREZ, J. M. (1969) Transfer of learning in associative clustering of retardates and normals. *Amer. J. ment. Defic.*, **73**, 733–8.

GERJUOY, I. R. and SPITZ, H. H. (1966) Associative clustering in free recall: intellectual and developmental variables. *Amer. J. ment. Defic.*, **70**, 918–27.

GRANT, G. W. B. (1971) *Some Management Problems of Providing Work for the Mentally Disordered with Particular Reference to the Mentally Handicapped*. Unpubl. M.Sc. thesis, Univ. of Manchester Institute of Science and Technology.

GRAY, S. and KLAUS, R. A. (1970) The Early Training Project: a seventh year report. *Child Developm.*, **41**, 909–24.

GRUNEWALD, K. (1969) *The Mentally Retarded in Sweden*. Stockholm: National Board of Health and Welfare.

HAYES, K. J. (1953) The backward curve: a method for the study of learning. *Psychol. Rev.*, **60**, 269–75.

HEBER, R. (1971) An experiment in prevention of 'cultural-familial' mental retardation. In PRIMROSE, D. A. (ed.) *Proc. 2nd Congr. Internat. Assoc. Scient. Stud. Ment. Defic.* Warsaw: Polish Medical Publishers; Amsterdam: Swets & Zeitlinger.

HERMELIN, B. F. and O'CONNOR, N. (1970) *Psychological Experiments with Autistic Children.* Oxford: Pergamon.

KIRK, S. A. and MCCARTHY, J. J. (1961) The Illinois test of psycho-linguistic abilities – an approach to differential diagnosis. *Amer. J. ment. Defic.*, **66**, 399–412.

LYLE, J. G. (1959) The effect of institution environment upon verbal develop-ment of imbecile children: I. Verbal intelligence. *J. ment. defic. Res.*, **3**, 122–8.

LYLE, J. G. (1960a) The effect of an institution environment upon the verbal development of imbecile children: II. Speech and language. *J. ment. defic. Res.*, **4**, 1–13.

LYLE, J. G. (1960b) The effect of an institution environment upon the verbal development of imbecile children: III. The Brooklands residential unit. *J. ment. defic. Res.*, **4**, 14–22.

MITTLER, P. (1973) *Psychological Assessment of the Mentally Handicapped.* London: Churchill.

MORRIS, P. (1969) *Put Away: a Sociological Study of Institutions for the Mentally Retarded.* London: Routledge & Kegan Paul.

ODEN, M. H. (1968) The fulfilment of promise: 40-year follow-up of the Terman Gifted Group. *Genet. Psychol. Monogr.*, **77**, 3–93.

RADON, M. and CLARKE, A. D. B. (1971) The effects and persistence of different training methods on transfer using the Minnesota formboards. In PRIMROSE, D. A. (ed.) *Proc. 2nd Congr. Internat. Assoc. Scient. Stud. Ment. Defic.* Warsaw: Polish Medical Publishers; Amsterdam: Swets & Zeitlinger.

ROSSI, E. L. (1963) Associative clustering in normal and retarded children. *Amer. J. ment. Defic.*, **67**, 691–9.

TIZARD, J. (1960) Residential care of mentally handicapped children. *Brit. med. J.*, **i**, 1041–6.

TIZARD, J. and LOOS, F. M. (1954) The learning of a spatial relations test by adult imbeciles. *Amer. J. ment. Defic.*, **59**, 85–90.

TREDGOLD, R. F. and SODDY, K. (1956) *A Textbook of Mental Deficiency* (9th edn). London: Baillière, Tindall & Cox.

TYSON, M. (1970) The design of remedial programmes. In MITTLER, P. (ed.) *The Psychological Assessment of Mental and Physical Handicaps.* London: Methuen.

9

P. J. Mittler

Language and communication[1]

Introduction

The ability to use language is obviously closely bound up wtih the development of intelligence, but the relationship between them is far from simple. The fact that a child is mentally subnormal should not be regarded as providing a satisfactory explanation for his inability to speak, nor should failure to learn to speak at the appropriate time be regarded as evidence of mental subnormality.

Many studies have demonstrated the severe language difficulties of the mentally subnormal and suggested that they are underfunctioning in relation to their level of skills in other areas of development. It is therefore important to consider the nature of the difficulties in some detail, since some of these might under certain circumstances be preventable and others might lend themselves to remediation (see Chapter 10).

This chapter will therefore begin with a discussion of some of the skills necessary for normal language functioning and consider implications for delayed or deviant development. This will be followed by an account of some of the more important features of recent work in linguistics and psycholinguistics concerning the structure of language, with special reference to the distinction between competence and performance, and the rule-governed aspects of language, again stressing the implications of such work for subnormality. A separate section is devoted to comprehension, as opposed to production of language, since this has important cognitive and educational implications. This is followed by a review of biological and environmental influences on language development, which stresses their complex interactions in the subnormal. Another section reviews knowledge on the nature and frequency of language difficulties in subnormals, and discusses questions concerned with the relative importance of developmental delay as opposed to specific deficits, and with the role of verbal mediation in thinking and problem solving. Developments in assessment techniques are next considered in some detail, reflecting the shift of emphasis

[1] The preparation of this chapter was supported by a grant from the Social Science Research Council.

from standardized tests towards criterion-referenced observational and developmentally orientated measures, and from a preoccupation with spoken language towards an interest in receptive skills. The final section is devoted to a full discussion of the principles and techniques which have been applied in the teaching of language skills to subnormal individuals, with special reference to the use of systematic teaching methods derived from behaviour modification.

Communication skills

In order to be able to use and understand language, an individual needs to develop a number of skills which can be separately identified and which may be differentially sensitive to subnormal intellectual functioning. One well-known attempt to isolate some of these skills is found in the Illinois Test of Psycholinguistic Abilities (Kirk *et al.*, 1968), which has been discussed above (see section on 'Assessment'). But assessment is by no means limited to psychometric approaches and tests alone cannot sample more than a small part of the communication system of which language is only one part. The processes involved can usefully be considered in terms of information processing strategies which are not unlike those required for perceptual stimuli. Thus, for language functioning to be effective, according to Eisenson (1966), the subject has to:

(a) be able to receive stimuli produced in sequential order;
(b) maintain a sequential impression of the message so that its components can be integrated into a pattern;
(c) scan the pattern from within to categorize the data and compare it with an existing store;
(d) respond differentially to perceptual impression.

Some of these are the very abilities that have been shown to be severely impaired in the mentally subnormal. Experimental studies have consistently indicated that they have particular difficulties in dealing with incoming sensory information, and that many of their learning difficulties can be regarded as stemming from a disorder of attention. Information processing of auditory material is particularly difficult but is also seen in dealing with visual material (O'Connor and Hermelin, 1963; Denny, 1964; Baumeister, 1968). It is therefore important to try to differentiate between a large number of deficits, all of which could result in apparent language impairment, but some of which might be due to basic perceptual and attention disorders. It is not easy to make such a differentiation with the crude assessment techniques currently available, but an experimental analysis can often be suggestive. Needless to say, a programme of language therapy often needs to begin by teaching the child to attend, listen, discriminate and respond selectively to auditory and other material (Bricker and Bricker, 1970a).

Language skills may concern phonology, morphology, syntax and semantics and are defined as follows by Carroll (1967).

(a) Phonology: the specification of the units of sounds (phonemes) which go to compose words and other forms in the language.
(b) Morphology: the listing of the words and other basic meaningful forms (morphemes) of the language and the specification of the ways in which these forms may be modified when placed in various contexts.
(c) Syntax: the specification of the patterns in which linguistic forms may be arranged and of the ways in which these patterns may be modified or transformed in varying contexts.
(d) Semantics: the specification of the meanings of linguistic forms and syntactical patterns in relation to objects, events, processes, attributes and relationships in human experience.

Research and theory are currently emphasizing possible forms of interaction between these different components, particularly the relationship between syntax and semantics, but principles of skills analysis can be fruitfully applied to the study of language.

In an extensive discussion of this topic Herriot (1970) stresses the parallels between motor and language skills by drawing attention to certain common elements. In the first place, language is probably hierarchically organized within as well as between skills; some skills are essential prerequisites for the development and use of others; thus certain minimal articulatory skills are normally prerequisites of syntactical or grammatical skills. Some qualification is necessary in the case of subnormals, however, because the developmental sequence of language acquisition may occasionally be different. Thus, as we shall see, although comprehension normally precedes production, the order may be reversed on occasion; as a corollary, a child may have an advanced level of language comprehension, but have relatively undeveloped productive skills, due to damage to the peripheral speech mechanisms or even because of a primary expressive aphasic disturbance (Lenneberg, 1962).

The second aspect of skills analysis discussed by Herriot is that of feedback. The speaker needs to be able to monitor his own performance in relation to his 'plan' or intention in each instance, and to modify his utterance accordingly. But this process may be faulty in subnormals. For example, a subnormal person may be aware that what he is trying to communicate is being severely disrupted by inadequate articulation or inappropriate syntax or semantics. In other words, the speaker is to a greater or lesser degree aware that his language performance does not match his thought or communicative intent. A second aspect concerns the subnormal person's ability to assimilate feedback information from others. In the two-person communication situation, he may not be as aware as a normal person of feedback information such as lack of comprehension, boredom, embarrassment, etc. Furthermore, the normal listener may in fact suppress such signals and pretend a polite interest for the sake of encouragement and courtesy to the subnormal speaker, thus depriving him of essential cues which might otherwise help him to accommodate to the requirements of the listener.

A third aspect of language skill is automatization, which concerns the skill of emitting chains or sequences of behaviour without the need for fully conscious control. Spoken language is organized in sequences of this type, both at a phonological and also at a grammatical level. Thus, a child rapidly learns that certain sequences are 'permissible' while others are not; for example, that words can begin with g + 1 and k + 1, but not d + 1; similarly, syntactic sequencing normally requires the adjective to precede the noun ('big boy', not 'boy big' etc.). The extent to which automatization occurs must depend to a large extent on the size of the units which can be stored in short-term memory; subnormals may therefore be at a disadvantage in acquiring such skills because of shortcomings both in short-term memory and in ability to chunk or cluster both input and output. Furthermore, studies using the ITPA suggest that subnormals have specific deficits in both auditory and visual sequencing tests (see below).

Fourthly, Herriot draws attention to anticipation as a feature of language skill. The listener needs to be able to anticipate what the speaker is going to say, and in doing so uses a variety of linguistic as well as non-linguistic cues. Some of these derive from the context in which the utterance is made, others are related to the syntactic and semantic organizations of the utterance. Anticipation is also an essential element in planning one's own utterances. It is apparent, however, that subnormals are likely to be at a disadvantage in planning and anticipation, since these skills depend heavily on general intelligence.

Hierarchical organization, feedback, automatization and anticipation may be regarded as essential aspects of language skill which lend themselves to analysis in much the same way as comparable motor skills. Notable advances have been made in the fine grain analysis of motor skills both for normals and subnormals which have led directly or indirectly to remedial programmes designed to overcome specific deficits in one or other aspect of motor skill (Annett, 1971; Whelan, 1973). One task that awaits the research worker is the application to the field of language, of principles of skills analysis as detailed as those which have characterized studies of motor function. This may in time lead not merely to an increase in our understanding of specific language impairments in subnormal individuals, but to the formulation of soundly based remedial strategies.

LANGUAGE AND SPEECH

Carroll (1953), writing as a linguist, defines language as a 'structured system of arbitrary vocal sounds and sequences of sounds which is used, or can be used, in interpersonal communication by an aggregation of human beings, and which rather exhaustively catalogues the things, events and processes in the human environment'. In a later discussion, he stresses the distinction between language and speech in relation to mental handicap: 'when we talk therefore about the *language* of mental retardates, we are talking . . . about the *system* that they have learned. When we refer to the *speech*, of mental retardates we are referring . . . to the actual behaviour of these individuals in using language' (Carroll, 1967).

The distinction between speech and language is not accepted by all authorities in this field but is generally adopted as a matter of convenience. It is a useful distinction in the study of deviant or delayed development, because speech and language may be differentially affected in such cases. To take an extreme example, an articulate and intelligent adult may receive a cerebral injury, such as a gunshot wound, which destroys or impairs speech but leaves his ability to understand language and to write books relatively unaffected. Similarly, a severely retarded child may be able to speak without difficulty, but his language may be primitive and undifferentiated in so far as he has only a minimal grasp of the system of language (in Carroll's sense). In other words, speech and language represent different aspects of verbal behaviour which sometimes get out of step with one another. Hydrocephalus is often quoted as an example of a condition in which the sufferer appears to be able to keep up a continuous chatter despite gross brain damage and physical handicap but whose use of language as a system of rules reflecting ideas and concepts is rudimentary (see Parsons, 1971, for a comprehensive review).

A survey of the literature suggests that more studies have been concerned with speech than with language abilities of the mentally handicapped, and have typically described the nature and incidence of disorders of voice, respiratory coordination (hesitation, stammer etc.), or speech sound production due to demonstrable dysfunction or structural abnormalities of the tongue, lips, teeth or palate. Such disorders are frequent and severe, though precise estimates are not available on account of the difficulty of defining criteria (but see Webb and Kinde, 1968; Fawcus, 1965 and this volume; and Schiefelbusch *et al.*, 1967, for useful accounts of earlier work).

Language structure

The last twenty years have witnessed a complete reorientation in the field of language research. While these changes have been productive of much theory and of further research, their impact on people concerned with handicap and remediation has so far been slight. Nevertheless, it is hardly possible to consider actual or potential developments in language studies in mental subnormality without at least a brief examination of some of the main issues that have been raised by psycholinguistics. Only the bravest or the most fool-hardy research worker would now design a study concerned with language which took no account of this work.

It would not be appropriate to characterize, let alone summarize, the nature of the revolution that has taken place in language studies, since the publication of Miller's (1951) *Language and Communication*, if only because it has now been ably done by many others (e.g. Brown, 1965; Hayes, 1970; Herriot, 1970; Olson, 1970; McNeill, 1970a). But it may be useful to single out a few distinctive features, which have influenced psychologists and educators both positively and negatively, and which will need to be taken into consideration in the planning of future work.

COMPETENCE AND PERFORMANCE

The distinction between competence and performance is fundamental to much recent research and theory in the area of language development, though its implications for grossly delayed or deviant development have not been adequately explored.

Competence relates to a child's knowledge of a language which will enable him to understand and generate an infinite number of grammatical sentences, and no non-sentences of that language. Performance refers to the actual use made of that knowledge. It is widely agreed that competence is influenced and distorted by performance factors, but cannot itself be directly measured. In this respect it is similar to Hebb's concept of Intelligence A, i.e. physiological and genetic aspects of intelligence which are not directly measurable but which form the basis of Intelligence B, intelligence as used in everyday life, and Intelligence C, which is what is measured by the appropriate tests. Although linguists treat the competence-performance distinction as fundamental to an understanding of language, more empirically orientated psychologists tend to regard it as an interesting theoretical construct which does not of itself lead to many testable hypotheses (e.g. Herriot, 1970). Chomsky (1957, 1965) and his followers postulate the existence of an *ideal* speaker-listener', but it is clear that such an abstraction is of doubtful relevance in the field of mental handicap. One can only hope that a study of language pathology in the broadest sense may eventually lend a wider perspective to psycholinguistics.

Chomsky's original concept of competence has been considerably developed and refined by later writers, some of whom have drawn distinctions between different aspects of competence and performance, which have some bearing on applications to language pathology. Recent writings by Campbell and Wales (1970) may be taken as a convenient example. They tend to dismiss as 'nonessential' the kind of limitations to the expression of language competence which might be imposed by short-term memory or the 'various low-level sensori-motor capacities involved in the perception and production of speech' (p. 246). This aspect of competence, characterized for their purposes as 'weak', might well be considered as more significant for the student of language pathology, since it is often at this level that impairment is found. A significant degree of hearing impairment or structural abnormalities of the speech organs are cases in point. The second aspect of competence is characterized as communicative competence, the area with which psycholinguistics has so far been largely concerned and which has been discussed above. It includes such traditional areas of enquiry as linguistic and psychological aspects of the relationships between speaker and listener, and ways in which these are modified in different contexts and situations. Recent work has also placed more emphasis on interactions between syntactic and semantic aspects of language. Campbell and Wales criticize many studies of syntactic development for failing to take account of situational variables, and stress the importance of studying the context within which speech occurs with the same thoroughness as the speech samples themselves. This is particularly important in studying the language of subnormal populations or individuals, since many of their utterances are so primitive that a knowledge of context is necessary to clarify meaning. It is also necessary to create particular contexts for eliciting specific types of utterance – e.g. objects varying in size are essential for eliciting comparative forms.

RULES OF LANGUAGE

It has been said that the task of the linguist is to discover the system of rules which a speaker appears to be using; similarly, the task of the speech pathologist or student of language disorders is to try to assess the extent to which these rules operate in the child's understanding and use of language. It is also important to try to determine at what point the child's use of rules is faulty, and to try to help him to master them.

One of the rule systems that has been studied concerns morphology, in particular the ability to provide appropriate inflectional endings to signal plurals, tenses, comparatives and superlatives etc. The most influential study is that of Berko (1958) who presented children with drawings purporting to illustrate nonsense words and then asked questions designed to elicit specific inflections. For example, a drawing named as a 'wug' was shown to fifty-six children at each age between 4 and 7 years; two further examples of the same picture were then shown to elicit the plural, which was always given as 'wug/z.' Similarly, the past tense was elicited from nonsense syllables such as 'spow', 'rick', 'gling', etc. In general, there were rather few age differences in the range which she studied, suggesting that regular rule systems were fairly well established at the age of 4. That this does not apply to irregular constructions is suggested by her own and a number of later studies, and is also a matter of common observation. The child who says 'digged', 'gooses', 'mans' etc. is presumably misapplying a rule for forming the past tense and for pluralization; he is unlikely to be imitating.

These rules continue to be misapplied for quite some time after children have acquired considerable linguistic proficiency. They are not merely misapplied to nonsense words but also appear to be implicit in their production of phrases and constructions which they are unlikely to have heard – phrases which represent a new construction involving grammatical rules wrongly applied to exceptional instances – 'wented', 'breaked', 'betterdn't we?' etc.

The Auditory Vocal Automatic subtest of the Illinois Test of Psycholinguistic Abilities is designed to sample morphological skills in children between the ages of 3 and 10. Instead of nonsense words, the test employs lexical items and appropriate pictures, and the child is required to complete a statement with an inflected word ('Here is a man: here are two –'; 'The thief is stealing the jewels; here are the jewels he – '). In a study of 100 normal 4-year-olds, only 19 per cent could correctly pluralize 'man' and fewer still could provide irregular past inflections, such as 'wrote', 'hung' or 'stole'. Irregular comparatives and super-latives were also found difficult (Mittler, 1970a). This test appears to be particu-larly sensitive to social class differences; children from social classes I and II differed by the equivalent of thirteen months of language development from those in classes IV and V. (See also Giebink *et al.*, 1970; George, 1970; Howard *et al.*, 1970.)

Subnormal children seem to show marked difficulty or at least a delay in acquiring morphological rules. In a study comparing the performance of three groups of normal, ESN and SSN children on the revised ITPA, this subtest (now renamed Grammatic Closure) discriminated strongly between normal and both subnormal groups, even though all groups were equated for EPVT vocab-ulary age (Marinosson, 1970). Similar studies using adaptations of the original Berko material indicate that subnormal children perform at a consistently inferior level compared to both CA and MA matched controls (Lovell and Bradbury, 1967; Blake and Williams, 1968; Dever and Gardner, 1970).

These studies suggest that an analysis both by tests and by structured observa-tions of a child's ability to use morphological rules may provide valuable insight about competence as well as performance. But we can do little more at this stage than speculate about possible reasons for the relative inferiority of subnormal children in these tasks.

Even normal children, however, strongly resist attempts made by adults to modify their own idiosyncratic version of the rules of the language. Ervin (1964) reports one unsuccessful attempt to replace a child's '*Nobody don't like me*' with '*Nobody likes me*'. The correct version was presented to the child eight times. At the ninth attempt, the child brightened and said, 'Oh, I see: *nobody don't likes me.*' Children also tend to preserve the word order of their own telegraphic utterances, even though the mother regularly expands them, and do not seem to be able to expand the length of their utterances beyond a specific number of morphemes, even under considerable adult pressure. Thus the child's imitations do not increase as a function of the length of the adult's sentence, but a pattern of regularity is maintained in which nouns, main verbs and adjectives appear to be retained, while articles, prepositions, auxiliaries and the final '-ing' form tend to be omitted.

The fact that children's utterances cannot easily be expanded or made gram-matically more advanced should not necessarily be taken as evidence for a biological or maturational view of language development. Even if such a model satisfactorily accounted for most of what we now know about language develop-ment, we would not be justified in withholding educational or language therapy programmes designed to accelerate development. Examples of such teaching programmes are discussed later in this chapter ('Language Teaching').

Comprehension

Most parents and teachers seem to identify language with what a child says rather than with what he understands. This is a curious placing of the developmental cart before the horse, since it is generally thought that comprehension precedes production of language and is an essential foundation for further development. The implications for remediation are obvious; it may be important to begin a language facilitation programme by assessing and then furthering the child's comprehension of spoken language rather than concentrating exclusively on expressive aspects. The factors that prevent a child from speaking are not necessarily the same as those which prevent him from understanding. There may be biological and neurological obstacles to the development of speech, including abnormalities or disorders of the tongue, lips or palate (see Fawcus and Fawcus, Chapter 10). The processes involved in language comprehension are probably more directly cognitive in nature, and include listening, auditory discrimination, reference to store and interpretation.

In an important discussion of this topic, Friedlander (1970) stresses other important psychological differences between listening and speaking, chiefly those relating to control and also to divergence and convergence. The speaker has

> total freedom to control the formulations of his message, while the listener must accommodate his information processing tactics to the requirements of the message . . . speech is generative, egocentric, essentially unconstrained in the possibilities over which it may range, unlimited in its options, and subject to continual branching off in new directions. Listening is fundamentally reconstructive, constrained to processing the speech of others, operates towards the progressively more limited options of interpreting inputs, often must select among inputs from two or more message sources at the same time, and is directed towards the attainment of specifiable objectives. Speech is open-ended in its possibilities while listening is closed-ended in its constraints. (p. 22)

These considerations appear to be of particular relevance to the mentally subnormal, since they frequently lack the social and behavioural skills which would allow them to indicate to the speaker that he was not being understood, thus depriving the speaker of the kind of cues which would enable him to modify his utterance accordingly. A normal child learns as he gets older to send out signals of non-comprehension: he frowns or looks puzzled, or asks for something to be repeated, just as a person in a foreign country may ask the speaker to speak more slowly or more distinctly. These are essential social skills in a communication situation, which the normal child may acquire without conscious effort, but which may have to be systematically taught to the subnormal child.

If comprehension is to a large extent a matter of guesswork, then the less intelligent child will be at a disadvantage; not only does he lack a sufficiently wide range of experience against which to match new utterances, but he may be less receptive to the minimal and sometimes quite subtle cues which form part of the communication situation, and which facilitate the discriminations on which adequate comprehension depends.

A normal child between the age of 18 and 24 months knows from frequent examples the context within which a large number of single words is normally spoken, but this is not to say that he is equal to the task of decoding a long and syntactically complex sentence, even though he may know each individual word in the sentence. The child who goes to sit at the dinner table in response to the mother saying 'get ready for your dinner' is not really proving that he has understood the mother's statement. He needs to understand no more than the word 'dinner', and might have reacted similarly (though perhaps with some surprise) if she had said 'dinner your for ready get', or produced some other low order approximation to English. A parallel may be drawn here with a child with a partial hearing loss who hears only vowels and very few consonants but can follow what is being said by using the minimal cues that are available.

It is important to remember that cues are not only verbal but also non-verbal. Mothers and teachers are not always aware of the extent to which they use gestures, or hand and eye pointing; it is instructive to observe the effect on the child of complete elimination of all gestural and situational cues, leaving him with nothing but the verbal component of the instruction. By doing this on one or two occasions, the mother can make a more realistic appraisal of her child's comprehension. It is one thing to understand language when it is supported by numerous other cues, and another thing to react appropriately to language without situational context. A teaching programme based on such a simple experiment might begin by providing the child with a large number of non-verbal cues, including gesture, pointing, eye contact and other redundant information; these prompts would then be faded one by one, leaving him at the end of the programme responding to the verbal message alone, divorced as far as possible from pragmatic expectation or visual or personal cues.

When a subnormal child fails to carry out a 'simple request' it is often assumed that he has not 'understood'; by this we imply that he is unable to cope with the demands which are being made on his limited intelligence, whereas it is possible that a careful rephrasing of the same request may reveal that it is syntactic or semantic rather than the cognitive aspects of the instruction that are responsible for his difficulty. In either case, it would be useful to equip the child with a non-verbal signal to indicate that the message has not been understood. Such signs exist in the Paget system which has been widely used with the deaf; modifications have been developed by Levitt (1970) with SSN spastic children. Needless to say, it is not enough to teach the system; the child has also to learn the social conventions governing its use. It is not only normal children but also highly intelligent adults who may be reluctant to admit that they are having comprehension difficulties.

The use of gesture need not be dismissed as a recourse to 'primitive' methods of communication, but should be seen as an important step in a graded teaching programme, to be discarded as soon as the child can dispense with it. It is important for teachers of the subnormal to avoid the controversies between 'oral' and 'manual' methods which have divided teachers of the deaf for so many years (Lewis, 1968), and to try to relate teaching techniques to the particular developmental needs of the child rather than to the requirements of fashion or theory.

Processes underlying comprehension of language are difficult to isolate, but appear to have a strong cognitive component. The child needs to be able to attend, listen, discriminate between sounds, and later to adapt to the sequential aspects of incoming language, and to appreciate the significance of different word orders. Linguists and psychologists have very recently begun to construct provisional models of the processes involved in language comprehension, but it is still too early to work out the educational implications of these theories (Herriot and Lunzer, 1971; Olson, 1972; Trabasso, 1972). We might suggest, however, that the cognitive processes that have been implicated are precisely those in which subnormal children have been shown to have specific difficulties and deficits. We know from the experimental literature that they have particular difficulties in information processing generally, not merely in language, but also in tasks where they have to discover and attend to the relevant as opposed to the irrelevant features of a visual stimulus display (Zeaman and House, 1963). It has also been suggested that one of their characteristic difficulties lies in their inability to profit from 'incidental learning' (Denny, 1964). A difficulty in learning spontaneously and without specific guidance would be likely to handicap a child in a situation where he has to attend to a wide spectrum of cues, both of a verbal and a non-verbal nature.

The fact that psychologists have isolated a number of specific cognitive deficits which appear to be critical to comprehension of language does not mean that they are unamenable to remediation. We might try to help a child to improve basic skills, such as attention, discrimination between sounds, words and sentences of gradually increasing length and complexity. For example, the child might need to be taught to listen to loud, simple and meaningful sounds which would first be paired with significant events (the rattle of a spoon on a cup to precede food), and then as part of a series of increasingly complex discriminations between different sounds. Such techniques are not uncommonly used by teachers, but they are rarely part of a graded programme and often begin at too advanced a level. At one point it might be possible to teach a child that reward always follows the quieter of two sounds, or the highest of two notes. It is important not to keep the child as a passive listener, but to try wherever possible to allow him to produce the sounds himself.

Particular emphasis has been placed on language comprehension and on possible means of developing receptive skills in children, since these seem to be of a more cognitive nature, and may lend themselves to the design of an appropriately designed remedial programme based on research findings. In fact, recent work in psycholinguistics has been closely concerned with language comprehension and has largely proceeded on the assumption that comprehension might provide a fruitful means of studying 'competence'. But the assessment of language comprehension is no easy matter, either for the research worker or the applied psychologist, and presents particular difficulties with subnormal children, to be further discussed later (p. 284).

Biological and environmental influences

The work of Chomsky and his associates has richly influenced students of language and psychology, but has made less impact in educational circles, partly perhaps because teachers have understandably reacted against the notion of an innately determined Language Acquisition Device (LAD), and also against a biologically orientated and strictly maturational model of language development. It is sometimes objected that by the time Chomsky and (*a fortiori*) Lenneberg (1967) have finished, there is precious little left for the teacher (or parent) in providing environmental variables, such as appropriate teaching or a 'stimulating language environment'. In the same way, Piaget is sometimes criticized for providing the intellectual foundations of over-rigid 'readiness' notions in teaching number, scientific or moral concepts etc. It is true that both groups emphasize the unfolding of maturationally determined potentialities, and tend to characterize development by reference to distinct stages; it has been left to others to devise means of facilitating progress from one stage to the next, and to investigate the contribution of experiential and learning factors to development.

But to describe the stages of growth is not necessarily to describe the process. Thus, the existence of well defined and frequently validated stages of development need not inhibit the teacher from trying to accelerate the child's progress from one stage to the next. Such attempts need not necessarily be unacceptable to theorists and model-builders, most of whom might be prepared to adopt some kind of interactionist position rather than placing exclusive emphasis either on a biological-maturational or an environmental-learning view. We should surely have learned enough from the nature-nurture controversies of the 1930s to know that heredity cannot operate outside an appropriate environmental context, or vice versa. But although we pay lip service to interactional processes, we have not made much progress in understanding them. Biological and genetic factors may set the limits to development, but environmental factors may also retard growth (Mittler, 1971).

Although biological factors obviously play a crucial role in both speech and language disorders, they must be seen as interacting with environmental variables. A child with severe articulation difficulties is likely to suffer secondary language disorders in addition to his primary speech disorders; his efforts at communication are often unsuccessful, he will be misunderstood or even ignored, and may come to regard his attempts at communication as inefficient and not worthwhile. In this situation he may resort to non-verbal means of communication, such as gestures and mime, and hope that his needs will be understood without the use of language.

It is important not to polarize biological and environmental accounts of language development, and to avoid the danger of treating as irreconcilable two theories which to some extent are concerned with different stages as well as different processes of language development. Skinner's (1957) theory is an attempt to explain the development of speech on a selective reinforcement basis; a baby exposed to and also initially producing a wide range of human speech sounds learns to associate certain regularly occurring patterns with specific perceptual or personal situations (such as feeding). Thus a conditioned stimulus (the word 'dog') comes to be associated with the unconditioned stimulus (a dog, or picture of a dog) and eventually comes to evoke the appropriate conditioned response in the child. This has been likened to a classical conditioning paradigm, whereas the child's own speech is explained in terms of operant conditioning, the strength of the operant response being regarded as a function of the strength of the positive reinforcement.

In his celebrated review Chomsky (1959) accused Skinner of 'complete naïveté with respect to grammatical mechanisms', of ignoring the whole problem of 'meaning', and of circularities in defining stimulus, response and reinforcement. From a psychological point of view, Osgood (1963) concluded that Skinner was 'not false but insufficient'. He agrees with linguistic criticisms that there is nothing in Skinner's model about the meaning of signs or about semantic generalization and adds that decoding processes are also not adequately catered for.

These two points of view are not as irreconcilable as they seem. In the first place, each theory concentrates on a different stage of language development. Learning theories seem to concentrate on the earliest stages of *speech* development, whereas generative grammarians and most psycholinguists concentrate on the acquisition of early *grammars*, beginning with two-word utterances, and have relatively little to say about pre-grammatical language such as babbling or the origins of single-word responses. This is obviously an over-simplification, especially since neo-behaviourists such as Staats (1968) have begun to work with child grammars. The dispute is moreover a real one in so far as it concerns possible models or processes which might affect language growth.

Secondly, language skills almost certainly comprise both innate and learned components; only the most extreme theorists would now claim that the two were mutually exclusive.

Finally, it is worth emphasizing that a language skill can be facilitated or taught even if it can be shown to be a 'linguistic universal'.

One difficulty arises from the use of the term 'environment' as a global term, denoting a set of amorphous and ill-defined forces. No one could possibly deny a general statement along the lines that 'environment' affects 'language'; the problem is to break down these global terms and to study the exceedingly complex interactions between them. For example, we know far too little about the nature of the language used by mothers to their normal children in everyday situations, or in guided play situations, though we do have some preliminary evidence of social class differences in conversational and maternal teaching strategies (Hess and Shipman, 1965; Robinson, 1971). It is far from easy and perhaps not altogether desirable to specify what kind of language stimulation is most conducive to language development in the child. Even if we could do this with some confidence for normal children, would the same conclusions necessarily apply to mentally handicapped children?

INSTITUTIONALIZATION

A further example can be taken from studies comparing institutionalized children with those living at home. Almost without exception, such studies document the inferiority of the institutionalized group (Schlanger, 1954; Lyle, 1960; Muller and Weaver, 1964). The consistency of the findings does not easily allow the data to be dismissed as a mere selection artefact. The adverse effects of institutionalization are neither irreversible nor inevitable, as Tizard's (1964) Brooklands experiment demonstrated. Substantial increments in verbal and social development took place when children were removed from hospital and cared for in family groups along modern 'child-centred' lines. No improvements were apparent in non-verbal tests – confirming other evidence which suggests that performance on non-verbal tasks might be more genetically determined than on verbal or social tests (Vandenberg, 1968). Nor was improvement maintained when the children were eventually returned to the original hospital conditions (Tizard, personal communication).

The example of institutionalization is well known, but illustrates the difficulty of penetrating beyond a 'global' conception of environment. We know at a general level that 'environment' or even 'institutionalization' adversely affects language, but we need to identify the critical characteristics in any given situation, and proceed from there to conduct experiments in which these independent variables are systematically manipulated so that the effects of such manipulations on language can be examined. Few such studies are available, though recent work by Barbara Tizard (1971) carries some interesting implications. She found that merely increasing the staff/child ratio did not by itself lead to better language performance, since adults were likely to spend more time talking to each other, and did not necessarily spend more time with the children in their care. Her study also stresses that it is not institutionalization as such which affects language development, but the type of child care practices to which the child is exposed.

In the absence of experimental data, we can do no more than formulate the problem in terms of more or less plausible models. Spradlin (1968), for example, invokes a learning theory approach by emphasizing (no doubt rightly) that the hospital environment tends to reinforce non-verbal rather than verbal behaviour. 'If the retarded child lines up and follows the other children, he may end up in the dining-room or the picture show. If he imitates the verbal responses of a peer, it is unlikely that anything very dramatic will occur.' Put in cognitive terms, we might say that he has little opportunity to differentiate relevant foreground from irrelevant background. The constant background of radio or piped music during the day and the tranquillizing use of television from late afternoon till bedtime present him with a problem of differentiating 'signal' from 'noise'. Adults rarely talk to him from close quarters, and he tends to hear language addressed to others rather than to him individually. The existence of a set routine reduces the need for communication, and the best way to gain adult attention is often non-verbal. It is extremely difficult to set up an institutional environment that reinforces rather than discourages language.

We should also note that some aspects of language are more likely to be affected by some aspects of environment than others. It is possible, for example, that an institutional environment may be more deterimental to language production than to language comprehension, or, as a corollary, that children brought up at home might be less competent at understanding than at speaking. Even if this were so, we should still need to try to isolate which aspects of a particular environment were critical.

SOCIAL CLASS AND FAMILY INFLUENCES

Many studies have examined socio-economic status or social class as a crude index of environment. Although massive social class differences have been found in children's language development (McCarthy, 1954; Lawton, 1968), it is not clear whether these represent real differences in language abilities or merely social class differences in general intelligence. Few studies have attempted to partial out or control for IQ (see also Chapter 4).

Although social class differences have been consistently reported for normal populations, it is possible that these are more marked for some language abilities than for others. This possibility was examined in a recent study in which the ITPA was administered to a sample of 100 normal children who were all within four weeks of their fourth birthdays (Mittler and Ward, 1970). Social class differences were highly significant, but were stronger on the auditory-vocal than on the visual-motor channel. This finding can be compared with a parallel study in which the ITPA was administered to 100 twin pairs of the same age. Twins showed an average retardation of 6 months of language development at 48 months; their performance on non-verbal tests was within the average range, so that the language retardation could not be attributed to general intellectual retardation alone (Mittler, 1970b). Comparisons between identical and fraternal pairs in the context of a classical twin study design suggested that genetic factors (expressed in terms of heritability) accounted for a greater proportion of the variance on visual-motor than on auditory-vocal tests (Mittler, 1969). Thus, the findings of the twin study provide the corollary of those on the normal controls, and suggest that tests on the auditory-vocal channel are heavily influenced by environmental variables (expressed in terms of social class), whereas tests on the visual-motor channel appear to carry a stronger genetic loading. These findings are broadly consistent with findings from behaviour genetics and twin studies in suggesting that some cognitive skills are more environmentally determined than others (Mittler, 1971).

There have been surprisingly few studies which have concerned themselves with social class influences on the severely mentally retarded, though the critical role of socio-economic variables on the mildly subnormal (ESN) pupil is better documented (e.g. Tizard, 1970). The few studies that have examined this question have not found any consistent social class differences. In a study of over 2,000 admissions to mental retardation treatment centres in Ontario, Singer and Osborn (1970) could not find any clear-cut or consistent social class differentials in respect of IQ scores. A detailed longitudinal study of forty-seven mongol babies in the London area (Carr, 1970) using the Bayley mental scales showed no difference between working-class and middle-class children at any age between 6 weeks and 2 years. In fact, the middle-class children were somewhat worse, though this was largely accounted for by two very low scorers. Normal controls, howeyer, showed clearcut social class differences at all ages. Results on the motor tests of the Bayley scale showed that middle-class mongols were slightly better than working-class mongols at 6, 10 and 15 months, but this was reversed at the age of 2 years. In the case of the normal controls, working-class children remained consistently above middle-class children on the motor scale.

We can do no more than speculate on possible reasons why the social class differentials which in normal children operate strongly in favour of middle-class children do not appear to produce the same effects in the case of the severely subnormal. The lack of clear-cut differences in language development between middle- and working-class subnormal children has still to be properly established, but a number of possibilities suggest themselves. In the first place, the finding may be no more than an artefact of the association between language and general intelligence. We would not necessarily expect middle-class SSN children to score higher on intelligence tests, partly because the impairment of general intelligence is largely a result of biological factors. Since language and general intelligence are closely associated, both developmentally and psychometrically, the absence of social class differential on language tests is hardly surprising. But we are still justified in asking what aspects of 'environmental stimulation' are critical to the development of language skills in the mentally handicapped, and whether these differ in any essential sense from those which apply in the case of normal children.

Unfortunately, we have few guidelines from research to help us towards the answers to these questions. We know very little about how parents or teachers actually talk to subnormal children. A number of studies have demonstrated how adults typically restrict the range and diversity of their utterances when talking to retarded children (Spradlin and Rosenberg, 1964) and that the more retarded a child is perceived to be, the less people talk to him (Rosenberg et al., 1961). The effect of this is to remove language stimulation from the child who needs it most. Moreover, since many subnormal people are underfunctioning in respect of language skills, their lack of language may give others the impression that they are more subnormal than they really are, thus further reducing the language stimulation from the environment.

It would be useful to have more information about ways in which mothers and teachers actually talk to and interact verbally with subnormal children in everyday situations, and to study adult utterances in terms of their communicative efficiency and their relevance to the language skills of the retarded person. Jeffree and Cashdan (1971) reported a tendency for mothers of subnormal children to fire a constant barrage of questions at them in order to get them to talk, and that most of these questions were of the 'what's this called?' type – i.e. calling for one word answers, usually nouns. This behaviour occurred in a situation in which mothers were asked to take their child round a model zoo, and talk to them about the various animals and situations in the same way as if they were visiting a real zoo. A previous study of mothers of normal nursery school children had shown substantial social class differences (Adkins, 1969); however, mothers of subnormal children of comparable levels of development differed significantly in their behaviour from mothers of normal children. 'They failed to set the scene or to explain what was happening, or to feed in information or fantasy.' Instead, they tended to fire simple questions at the child. Further work is needed to establish whether they would use similar language at home, and the extent to which findings such as these might be due to a special artefact of the testing situation.

However, even if parents are intent on providing a rich and complex language environment, this is not necessarily appropriate for a language retarded child. To a child with a severe comprehension difficulty the use of long sentences or of an elaborated type code may be meaningless and confusing, and may succeed only in teaching him that adult language is best ignored. A programme of language therapy, whether formally planned or informally administered, needs to take note of the child's ability to benefit from the kind of adult language stimulation which is generally considered appropriate for normal children (Rutter and Sussenwein, 1971). Similarly, it is of little use exposing a child to a stimulating verbal environment such as a normal nursery school on the assumption that he will learn from other children. The consensus of research evidence indicates that language is best learned from individual interaction with adults rather than from mere exposure to other children. On the other hand, one should be cautious about advising parents to 'keep talking to him', since they might then maintain a continuous chatter which is largely unintelligible to the child and which will lead him to regard adult language as unrewarding, and eventually to stop listening (Rutter and Mittler, 1972).

Language disorders in subnormals

Our knowledge of language development in the mentally handicapped is lamentably limited; in fact, there is little that we can assert with confidence, beyond the much-documented truisms that language develops late and that it remains primitive and undifferentiated. We lack detailed longitudinal studies of language development in subnormal populations; even the numerous cross-sectional and survey type studies have tended to concentrate on global estimates of language development and have so far made little use of the kind of detailed and fine-grain measures which would clarify whether some aspects of language considered as a group of skills were more impaired than others.

INCIDENCE

We shall confine ourselves in this section to a brief consideration of surveys of language as distinct from speech disorders. The distinction is obviously not a hard and fast one, but will follow the lines proposed at the beginning of this chapter. Even so, many of the surveys express their findings in global fashion ('difficulties of communication'), and do not differentiate at a detailed level between different aspects of language functioning.

In a review of earlier studies, Spreen (1965a) documents the expected relationship between IQ and both speech and language disorders. The frequency of language disorders is 100 per cent below IQ 20, around 90 per cent in the IQ range 21–50, and about 45 per cent in mildly retarded groups. These figures are based on a large number of reports, but definition criteria and survey methods obviously vary widely. Problems also arise on account of overlap in item content between intelligence tests and language measures; many IQ test items are verbal, and many items in language tests are similar to those found in intelligence tests. That some measure of independence does exist, however, is suggested by factorial studies and by studies which correlate items of low redundancy. Although it would be unrealistic and meaningless to demand 'pure' measures of either language or intelligence, some attempt to differentiate between them is necessary, partly because of the possibility which exists both for individual subjects and for populations that language functions are specifically depressed in relation to other aspects of development. If this is the case, there is justification in designing remedial compensatory measures.

It seems probable that some aspects of language are more affected than others. For subnormals who have developed some degree of language ability, there appears to be little difference in size of vocabulary between normals and subnormals matched on MA; in fact, a study of Thompson and Magaret (1947) suggested that subnormals were better. On the other hand, they were substantially inferior on higher level language skills. Lyle (1961) reported that subnormals scored lower than matched normals on naming of familiar objects, word definitions, grammatical accuracy and complexity of utterances, and also used much more jargon, sign language and irrelevant remarks. Mein (1961), on the basis of interviews and semi-structured picture descriptions of institutionalized subnormal adults, suggested that they tended to rely unduly on nouns, and that this was particularly marked in mongols, who were not otherwise impaired in word production or fluency. Other studies have noted discrepancies based on measures of sentence length, relative to normative data reported by Templin (1957). However, O'Connor and Hermelin (1963), on the basis of experiments on noun, verb and adjective usage, could not find differences between normal and subnormals in respect of language structure.

In general, the evidence suggests that subnormals are likely to show specific difficulties or protracted delay in the structural aspects of language, particularly in respect of sentence length, and syntax and sentence complexity (for other reviews see Jordan, 1967; Webb and Kinde, 1968; Schiefelbusch, 1963, 1972; and Schiefelbusch *et al.*, 1967. Relevant recent studies include those by Saunders and Miller, 1968, and Beier *et al.*, 1969).

LANGUAGE AND DOWN'S SYNDROME

Mongols appear to show a pattern of inferiority on some aspects of language, and also to be particularly vulnerable to the effects of institutionalization (Lyle, 1960; Schlanger and Gottsleben, 1957). In Lyle's study, there was a difference corresponding to nine months of verbal MA between mongols and non-mongols, but this discrepancy was not significant in comparable samples living at home and attending training centres. But he also showed that much depended on the level of language development attained by the child prior to hsopitalization. Children who had acquired some language skills adjusted better to hospital than those who had failed to do so. In a recent longitudinal study of mongol children living at home, Carr (1970) showed that 'motor' development was consistently ahead of 'mental' development, as measured by the Bayley scales.

A number of ITPA studies have suggested a specific mongol profile on this test, characterized by outstandingly high scores on motor encoding (use of gesture), poor performance on the auditory-vocal channel (particularly the auditory-vocal automatic subtest concerned with morphology) and relatively high scores on the visual-motor channel (Bilovsky and Share, 1965; McCarthy, 1964). Their language development is also markedly slow compared to other aspects of development. In Thompson's (1963) sample no child showed language skills commensurate with mental age.

We cannot in the present state of knowledge easily relate deficits of the kind described to specific physiological or biological deficits. Even if it were possible to demonstrate a link between a specific clinical syndrome and a characteristic pattern of language function, we still need to examine the extent to which environmental variables constitute contributory factors. This is a relevant question for research using groups, but is even more pertinent when we are considering an individual child. Although the relative contribution of biological and environmental factors to language development cannot be precisely assessed even in the individual case, the educator will clearly be concerned with environmental influences which may have unduly prevented or further retarded language development, and will also try to mobilize environmental resources as effectively as possible in order to facilitate further development, whatever the cause of the previous failure. (See Evans and Hampson, 1968, for a review.)

DELAYED OR DEVIANT?

It is sometimes asked whether subnormal children are merely very slow developers, or whether they show specific deficits in one or other aspect of language skill over and above what might be expected on the basis of their mental subnormality. This sounds a reasonable question, but we have no proper basis on which to answer it, and what evidence we have suggests that both developmental delay and specific deficit can be held responsible. On a developmental view, the mentally handicapped person is held to pass through the same stages of development as a normal person, but at a slower rate and with a reduced likelihood of reaching the stages attained by normal children at the age of about 8. A defect position is supported if it can be shown that subnormals are inferior on a learning task or language skill compared with normal children matched for mental age. It will be apparent that the issue revolves largely around mental age matching procedures. But the assumptions behind MA matching have now been questioned for a variety of reasons (e.g. Baumeister, 1967) and the contrast between developmental and deficit positions may be more apparent than real. (See also Chapter 6.)

A number of studies have provided preliminary if not conclusive evidence. The study by Lenneberg et al. (1964) is usually quoted in support of a developmental position, but it is open to more than one interpretation. They examined the language development of sixty-one mongol children living at home, between 3 and 22 years of age, and with IQs ranging between the 20s and 70s. A strong relationship was found between language and motor development – especially age of walking, dressing and feeding independently. In general, language development was more strongly related to chronological age than to IQ. Moreover, mongols seemed to go through the same stages of development as normal children in respect of babbling and early one-word utterances, though articulation disorders were frequent. However, language development stopped far short of that reached by normal children; the rate of progress was slowed down as the children became older, so that they seemed to lag further behind the older they became. Thus, what begins as a developmental disorder in childhood finishes as a deficit at maturity.

It is also relevant to ask not merely whether language is developmentally delayed, but the extent to which it is delayed. Evidence on this question is hard to find, partly because it is difficult to estimate the level of language development that should be expected in a subnormal person or population with given characteristics. But it is reasonable to assume that many mentally handicapped persons are underfunctioning in so far as their language development is well below what might be expected from a knowledge of their level of development in other areas of development. For example, it is not at all uncommon to encounter patients in hospitals for the subnormal with a mental age around 5 years whose language development is well below a 3-year level. The normal 2-year-old has a vocabulary of several hundred words and is rapidly mastering the rules of syntax and morphology, but few subnormal children can expect to reach the level of linguistic competence reached by the normal child of 5 or 6. In a study of an institutionalized population, Blanchard (1964) found few patients whose level of language development went beyond a 4-year level. An unpublished study by Webb (cited in Webb and Kinde, 1968) showed that 70 per cent of a sample of adults in a sheltered workshop scored 2 years below MA on ITPA total Language Age scores.

Unfortunately, we do not precisely know the level of language development that can be expected at any particular stage of intellectual development. Clearly, there is cause for concern about a child whose mental and social development corresponds to a 4- or 5- year level but whose language development is well below a 2- year level. But what about a child with a mental age of 5 and a 'language age' of 4 years? Discrepancies as small as this may be of little real significance, and may be no more than measurement artefacts. Moreover, we have no basis for assuming that there should be a one-to-one relationship between intellectual development on the one hand and language development on the other. Even if the test results were reliable and accurate, we could not assume that a child with a mental age of 5 and a language age of only 4 was necessarily 'under-functioning'. Similar problems occur at a later stage in considering the equally complex relationship between mental age and reading age (cf. Graham, 1967; Burt, 1967).

Although it seems likely on the whole that a considerable degree of underfunctioning is to be found in the mentally subnormal, the precise amount is difficult to determine and will, in any case, vary considerably depending on individual circumstances. Thus, developmental delay can be seen not only in relation to normal populations, but also by comparison with other aspects of the subnormal person's own development. The existence of both developmental disorders and specific deficits is suggested in the comparative study by Marinosson (1970) in which the revised edition of the ITPA was administered to 30 normal, 30 educationally subnormal (ESN) and 30 severely subnormal (SSN) children, carefully matched for vocabulary age on the English Picture Vocabulary Test. Although all the groups had a VA between 5–0 and 6–0, the normal children were consistently superior on all the ten subtests, the SSNs lowest, while the ESN children showed intermediate scores. The profiles of the three groups were on the whole parallel, suggesting that the pattern of linguistic organization was similar. Both groups of subnormal children showed substantial underfunctioning in relation to the normal controls. However, the subnormal children showed specific impairments on the two sequential memory tests; both ESN and SSN children produced very low scores on the visual sequential memory test, whereas the impairment on auditory sequential memory was less marked for the ESN subjects.

Some groups of children also seem to have particular difficulty in structuring incoming auditory material. Autistic children, for example, are in some respects at least quite different from SSN children. Although they show exceptionally good immediate rote memory, and do not show the characteristic deficits of sequencing found in the SSN, they seem to be extraordinarily unselective in what they remember, and perform equally well if they are asked to recall unstructured nonsense strings as they do when presented with structured and meaningful sentences (Hermelin and O'Connor, 1970; Hermelin, 1971; Frith, 1971). This suggests specific deficiencies in coding and categorizing processes which are relatively more marked in autistic than in matched subnormal or normal controls .

It is worth recalling in this connection that factorial studies on the Wechsler scales tend to suggest the presence of a short-term memory factor which is present in subnormals but not in normals (Baumeister and Bartlett, 1962a, b).

LANGUAGE AND PROBLEM SOLVING

A further example of a possible specific deficit arises from work on the verbal regulation of behaviour. A subnormal person may show deficiencies in language functions when these are analysed in terms of communication or skills analysis, but may be relatively proficient in the use of language in problem solving situations. At these times he may be making use of what has been described as 'inner' or 'covert' language. That such a language system exists is suggested by a substantial body of research with intelligent but profoundly deaf subjects (Furth, 1966).

The nature of the relationship between language and thinking has preoccupied philosophers and psychologists for a long time. Luria (1961, 1963) and other Soviet psychologists have developed Pavlov's later distinction between first and second signalling systems. Luria has described four stages in which behaviour comes under increasing control of the second signalling system. His experimental situation required the child to press (or not to press) a button on the appearance of a particular signal, usually a light or buzzer, though this basic paradigm has been extensively varied.

In the first stage, any utterance by the experimenter (E) causes the subject (S) to press, regardless of whether E says 'Press' or 'Don't press'. This is essentially the *orienting* phase, the words primarily serving to attract the child's attention. In the second stage, the child can inhibit pressing in response to E's 'Don't press'. This is described by Luria as the *releasing* or *impulsive* function of language which seems to cue the child to do what he was already going to do. Thirdly, the child tells himself aloud what to do, and can be heard quietly rehearsing 'Press', 'Don't press', or 'Yes', 'No'. At this stage, language has acquired a *selective* function. The final stage consists primarily of covert self-instruction (preselection) in which the child can respond appropriately to an instruction in the form 'Press if the red light comes on, but don't press if the green light comes on'. This stage is not normally reached until around 5 years. Even at this stage, the child may repeat the instructions to himself more or less verbatim, but later comes to condense them to telegraphic form. Luria particularly stresses the role of language in *inhibiting* behaviour, and argues that subnormals have a particular deficit in this respect. A small number of normative and experimental studies have been reported in recent years which suggest that Luria's model is potentially of diagnostic as well as theoretical significance (Burland, 1969; Schubert, 1969; Hogg, 1973) though a study by Miller *et al.* (1970) failed to confirm the increasing use of verbal mediation with age.

The effects of language on thinking and problem solving are usually demonstrated by studying the effects of labelling or other verbal cues on a discrimination learning task. A study by Barnett *et al.* (1959) demonstrated that subnormal subjects who learned names of objects on a delayed recall task performed significantly better than those who did not, and that this effect was equally marked for both higher and lower MA levels. This subject was also extensively investigated by O'Connor and Hermelin (1963), in a series of studies in which the contribution of verbal mediation was systematically varied in tasks involving generalization, transfer and cross-modal coding. A brief summary of this and later research is contained in a recent review (O'Connor and Hermelin, 1971). It appears that subnormal children could perform certain visual discriminations without verbal labelling, but they were not retained. They tend not to use verbal labels spontaneously, as normal children do, but can be helped to acquire and use them under certain conditions. Thus, the original formulation of Soviet psychologists in terms of a dissociation between first and second signalling systems was not supported, and one cannot any longer confidently assert that subnormals suffer from a 'specific verbal mediation deficiency', over and above what would be expected for the MA level.

Different results were obtained in tasks calling for cross-modal coding. The necessity for verbal coding in translating a stimulus from one modality to another seemed to facilitate learning, though this was less effective in conditions in which the verbal coding was difficult.

Later work by Bryant (1967) has indicated that verbal labelling at the initial learning phase does not necessarily make for transfer. He also showed that while verbal labelling facilitates recall, there are no clear effects on recognition, though matched normal subjects demonstrated effects on both recall and recognition. Similar lack of transfer in subnormals is shown as a result of providing specific verbal instructions about the relevant dimension in a discrimination learning task.

Absence or deficiency in verbal mediation may be a positive advantage in those cases where self-imposed verbal mediation strategy may provide misleading information. This has also been suggested in some studies of highly intelligent children in concept attainment tasks (e.g. Osler and Trautman, 1961). An example of such a situation occurs in a non-reversal learning shift situation: in a study reported by Sanders *et al.* (1965) subnormals were actually found to be superior to MA matched normals (see Reese and Lipsitt, 1970, for a fuller discussion of this question). It has also been suggested that verbal mediation may not be the most parsimonious explanation, and that the problem may take the form of a production deficiency in which children have the necessary cognitive skills but can neither make use of them nor produce verbal formulations of the reasons for their solutions (Flavell *et al.*, 1966).

From a practical point of view, it is important to stress that the degree of meaningfulness of the material is a particularly critical variable for subnormals. Weir and Stevenson (1959) showed that learning was facilitated if the subject had to name the stimulus before responding, while Jensen and Rohwer (1963) showed that mediators provided in the form of a sentence were superior to mere labelling, though long-term retention did not seem to show any benefit.

Spreen (1965b) summarizes the conditions that must be fulfilled if learning is to be furthered by verbal mediation: (i) the discrimination stimuli must be similar enough to allow generalization to occur initially; (ii) the responses to be learned must be discrete; (iii) the names learned during pre-training must be distinctive; (iv) the names must all be learned to a high criterion. Even Kendler and Kendler (1967), the most dedicated proponents of verbal mediation theory, have now conceded that a mediator need not necessarily be verbal. In fact, any response, whether implicit or a motor act, may have the effect of adding distinctiveness or signalling properties to cues, and thus enhance learning. The systematic use of non-verbal cues both by teachers and by subnormals themselves seem to be an important development in compensatory education for this population, but has not yet been tried on any scale. The most promising work has in fact been done on chimpanzees (Gardner and Gardner, 1969; Premack, 1970).

Assessment

Although adequate assessment procedures are essential both for the subnormal individual and for research, priorities have recently shifted from assessment to teaching. This is partly due to dissatisfaction with currently available assessment tests, and partly to a greater appreciation of what can be achieved by teaching. But the Skinnerian precept, 'Don't test, teach,' might be rephrased as 'Don't teach without testing', since it is difficult to evaluate the effects of teaching without previously assessing the child's language skills. But there is considerable uncertainty at the present time both about the strategy and the tactics of testing, not only in language but in relation to other aspects of cognitive development. Doubts are being expressed about the rationale of using normative instruments which compare the subnormal with the normal population on which the test has been standardized, about the reliance on such measures for the planning of remedial programmes (Mittler, 1970a, 1973a) and about the assumption that a test adequately samples 'real' skills and abilities as reflected in ordinary situations. Moreover, existing tests are often unsuitable for subnormal individuals with only limited language development; the ITPA, for example, although standardized on a normal population ranging in age from $2\frac{1}{2}$ to 10, suffers from 'floor' effects and is difficult to use below a 4-year level of language development. Finally, a formal test involving language skills may be inappropriate for motivational reasons in a subnormal population.

Increased emphasis is therefore being placed on assessment techniques which rely on observational methods. Samples of language can be collected in various real-life situations – in school, on the ward and at home, as well as in free play situations in an assessment class or clinic. The degree of sophistication which is then applied to the analysis of the data depends on the specific interests of the investigator. Greater use is also being made of developmental scales completed by someone who is familiar with the child. This includes parents as well as professionals.

OBSERVATIONAL METHODS

Reliable sampling of a child's language in everyday situations presents fewer problems with retarded children who say relatively little during the course of a single observational session than in the case of a larger class of normal pre-school children. A teacher in an assessment class would not be able to listen to more than one child during a session but it should not be impossible for her to record everything the child says during a given period of time. Observation and recording of language in 'real life' situations has advantages over the artificial sampling of language skills in a formal test situation, but the interpretation of the data collected presents more problems. Analysis of utterances can obviously range in sophistication from a simple count of the number of words spoken (assuming we can agree on the definition of 'word') to a complex analysis of the generative transformational complexity of the child's grammar. Whatever the level of analysis used, it is essential that the data be systematically collected, otherwise the observations and the time spent on them will be wasted. The data can be kept in cumulative record form merely for the teacher's own information, so that a regular check on the nature or complexity of the child's utterances is available. At the simplest level it need be little more than a slightly more systematic version of the kind of language diary which many mothers keep on their own children at the earliest stages of language development. If a full record is kept of everything that the child says in a fifteen-minute session over one or more days, together with comments on the general context in which the utterances took place, it should be possible to note changes in length or complexity of utterances over a period of time.

The way in which language data is analysed clearly depends on the purposes to which the analysis is put. Although it is useful to keep the analysis to a simple level for ordinary purposes, it is also important to be aware of somewhat more complex though time-consuming methods. One of the earliest but most useful indices of language maturity is based on the mean length of utterance over a given period. This method was used by earlier investigators such as McCarthy (1954), Davis (1937) and Templin (1957) who collected a great deal of data on utterance length as a function of age, sex, social class, etc. Rules for the use of this method are clearly described by Templin (1957). Mean length of response appears to be a sensitive index of language development; Shriner and Sherman (1967) reported that this was the most useful of several other measures, including mean of five longest responses, number of one-word responses, the number of different words and a structural complexity score. A more complex system has been developed by Miner (1969).

Length of utterance is by itself a fairly limited criterion of language development, and needs to be supplemented by an analysis of level of linguistic complexity. Such measures are influenced by recent work in developmental psycholinguistics. Lee and Canter (1971) have recently reported a procedure for estimating the complexity of the sentence structure used by children between 3 and 7 years. Although percentile norms are provided for this particular age range, the method is not a standardized test and still depends on collecting the language samples in natural play situations. Developmental Sentence Scoring (DSS) provides a method of estimating the extent to which a child has learned grammatical 'rules' concerned with the use of indefinite and personal pronouns, verbs, negatives, conjunctions, interrogative reversals and 'wh-' questions. Suggestions are given for ways in which the teacher or speech pathologist can plan a series of teaching situations which introduce such structures in an appropriate sequence.

Teachers of very young or severely handicapped children may feel that these methods assume a more advanced level of language development than that shown by children in their class. It is therefore necessary to devise assessment techniques, whether based on formal tests or systematic observation, which are relevant to much earlier stages of development. To cater for this need, Lee (1966) devised a Developmental Sentence Type Chart to estimate the child's ability to use two-word utterances, simple phrase structure rules and transformations of kernel sentences. Going back further still, it is possible to carry out a straightforward classification of single-word utterances by dividing them into different 'parts of speech' – e.g. nouns, verbs, adjectives, interjections, etc. Note should also be taken of whether the utterance is in response to another person, whether it is a repetition of what someone has just said, and whether it is spoken to someone else or to no one in particular.

DEVELOPMENTAL SCALES

Most of the examples already considered refer to children whose language development has reached the point where they have a vocabulary of at least single words or where they have already started to combine two words meaningfully. Many mentally handicapped children have not yet reached either of these stages, particularly the younger ones who are increasingly being admitted to special schools or observation units. It is often a case of assessing the 'language' abilities of a child who does not yet have any meaningful speech. This is not a contradication in terms, since language comprises many skills, only some of which concern expressive language. These skills can be tentatively assessed by comparing the child's performance with approximate sequences of normal development.

The value of normative data should not be underestimated. Although there are still many gaps in our knowledge, a great deal of research has been done on the development of language in the normal child with the result that we know a good deal about the stages or sequences of development. It seems reasonable to assume, at least as a preliminary basis for study of an individual or group, that the stages will be similar for normal and subnormal children, provided we bear in mind that individual discontinuities and distortions will occur in many cases. For example, a stage or step may be omitted; this is not uncommon in physical development, when we find that a child progresses to the walking stage with little or no time spent crawling. Similarly, one occasionally hears anecdotal evidence about a child who suddenly begins to speak in long sentences, having previously been heard to speak only in single-word utterances. Such cases are rare, and few have been adequately documented, but it is worth bearing in mind that they may exist. Unevenness of development may also occur horizontally as well as vertically; Down's syndrome children are commonly relatively more advanced in physical than in language development, and in one aspect of language compared with another (Evans and Hampson, 1968).

But the normative approach has certain limitations. These can best be illustrated by an examination of published scales of language development. In the first place, many of the items on such a scale are difficult to interpret and score ('Quieted by voice', 'Searches for sound with eyes', 'Shouts for attention', etc.). Secondly, the scales assume agreement on the meaning of 'the word' as a stage of development. Darley and Winitz (1961) after an exhaustive review of the numerous studies investigating 'age at first word' concluded that 'children begin to speak when their parents think they do'. In the case of subnormal children, it is particularly difficult to know whether a certain sound is consistently used in the context of a particular situation or object; it is all too easy to attribute meaning or consistency to a sound, when it may exist in the ear of the listener rather than in the mind of the child. Furthermore, the scales are lacking in detail after the age of about 12 months and tend to be confined to a few items only (e.g. one clear word at 12 months, three at 13 months etc.).

In addition to the normative approach, it is useful to attempt an assessment which, while still being roughly developmental in character, is based on an attempt to describe the development of specific language skills from a criterion point of view. Such an attempt was made in the context of a workshop for parents of young mentally handicapped children, which had as one of its objectives the training of parents in a form of developmental assessment of their own child, based on observation and the use of specially prepared developmental schedules (Cunningham and Jeffree, 1971). The chart was designed to help parents and others to structure their observations, and to consider different aspects of language, including the growth of vocabulary, the use of language for communication, sentence structure, comprehension and imitation. It was also hoped that the chart would highlight specific needs and hence lead to a programme of structured play and language stimulation. Parents appeared to welcome the opportunity to carry out an assessment of their own child's development, and generally succeeded in filling in the charts, once ambiguities and difficulties had been clarified in small tutorial-type discussion groups. The profile approach enabled them to understand the unevenness of development both between and within areas of development. Thus, a young mongol child may be relatively advanced in imitation, but may be poor at understanding instructions or in vocalization. Parental assessment was not compared with that carried out by 'experienced testers', but the aim was not so much accuracy of normative placement as the sharpening of observational skills.

A number of published scales are now available which consist of a more or less detailed check list of skills and abilities reached by normal children at different ages. Some are rapid screening devices containing only a few items, others are longer and more comprehensive schedules with many items at each period. Among the shorter American scales are the Denver Developmental Screening Test (Frankenburg and Dobbs, 1967), the Utah Test of Language Development (Mecham et al., 1967), the Houston Test for Language Development (Crabtree, 1958). Relevant British scales that include but are not exclusively concerned with language have been prepared by Sheridan (1973) and Gunzburg (1966).

A final limitation of developmental charts is that many aspects of behaviour may be critical to the development of a skill but are difficult to place on a scale. One example of this concerns the importance of play as a precursor to language. The child whose play is representational or symbolic, who shows, for example, that he is able to make one thing stand for another, is laying essential foundations for language development.

LANGUAGE COMPREHENSION

The importance of comprehension in language acquisition has already been discussed, but it may be useful to refer to methods of assessing comprehension, since this is clearly essential in the case of people whose expressive language skills are limited or non-existent. It is frequently claimed that a child 'understands everything you say', but such statements should be treated with caution, since he is likely to be using a wide variety of non-verbal, contextual and situational cues, and it is difficult to distinguish these from the processes involved in understanding language itself.

How then can we assess comprehension? It is not difficult to test for comprehension of single words, and standardized tests are available for this purpose. Perhaps the best known is the Peabody Picture Vocabulary Test (Dunn, 1959). This test merely requires the child to point to one of four pictures in response to a stimulus word spoken by the experimenter. The number of words correctly identified can be compared against available norms, and expressed in terms of a vocabulary age, percentile equivalent or IQ. The test begins at a 21-month level, and usually presents few difficulties of administration, since the child merely has to be able to select one of four pictures by pointing. It is a useful test to administer at the beginning of an assessment session, though results must be interpreted with caution. Although the test shows acceptable levels of reliability, it does not always correlate well with other language tests such as the Illinois scales (Carr *et al.*, 1967) or with a test of general intelligence such as the Wechsler (Shaw *et al.*, 1966). To use it as an intelligence test may therefore be misleading; it is, however, of interest as a simple measure of vocabulary recognition, yielding a vocabulary age. Shortened English versions are also available, though only from a 3-year level upwards (Brimer and Dunn, 1965).

One of the difficulties of tests of the Peabody type is finding visual referents which provide an equal amount of information to the child. The very young or the very handicapped child may point to the most interesting picture of the four, or the one that provides the most novelty. It is almost impossible to hold visual variables constant, so that one picture does not prove to be more salient or prominent to the child than any other. If the child is correct, then we can safely assume that he knows the word being tested: if he points to the wrong picture, or appears to be pointing quite randomly, then we do not really know whether this is because he does not know the word, or because he cannot carry out the visual search operations necessary to enable him to look at each picture successively; furthermore, he might be unable to integrate the visual scanning task with the verbal signal from the examiner: in other words, he might have difficulties in cross-modal coding, or in short-term memory. Most commonly, however, the very young child tends to point to the picture that first captures his attention, and sometimes does so even before the examiner has had a chance to say the stimulus word.

The Peabody test is merely the most obvious instance of our ignorance of the psychological processes underlying what appears at first sight to be a commonplace task. In fact, we have not begun to study all the relevant variables involved in tests of this kind, and there is reason to be dissatisfied with most tests that purport to measure comprehension of language but which depend heavily on the need to scan visual material, and then to make fairly complex discriminations in which the relative prominence of auditory and visual cues is difficult to control.

Similar problems arise when we ask a child to carry out comprehension tasks using small toys and other three-dimensional material. Here again, such items as 'put the spoon in the cup' or 'Give me the car' are highly predictable, and are just the kind of actions which the child might carry out even if no instructions had been given. Toys have the additional disadvantage of being too interesting, so that a child might become so absorbed in playing with them that he is not really listening to the examiner asking him to carry out certain actions. He might therefore be correct because most of the commands might be guessed by chance, or he might be wrong for any of the reasons discussed earlier but also because the test has become too much of a play situation for him.

These sources of error or bias must not be exaggerated, but it is also important not to assume that a child's failure is due to lack of comprehension when other variables may be involved which have not been adequately controlled in the test, and which generally remain uninvestigated. For this reason, it is necessary to ask the child to carry out fairly unexpected actions with the test material, though this too may have the disadvantage of violating too many pragmatic expectations. If, for example, one is investigating the child's comprehension of prepositions, he may not expect you to say 'Put the spoon *under* the cup', and conclude that you must obviously be asking him to 'Put the spoon *in* the cup'.

It is apparent therefore that the listener trying to understand a message is dealing not only with the language used by the speaker but also with a very large number of communication cues. If we want to assess the extent to which a child understands language, we should try as far as possible to exclude as many non-linguistic cues as possible. To some extent this is bound to be an artificial exercise, since the child normally has so many non-linguistic cues available to help him. But these cues will obviously vary considerably from one situation to another, so that it seems important to try to differentiate between linguistic and non-linguistic information, and in particular to vary the nature of the linguistic input in a systematic manner.

Work is now in progress in the Hester Adrian Research Centre to develop a sentence comprehension test. This test was originally devised with Angela Hobsbaum at Birkbeck College, London, and has now undergone various modifications (Hobsbaum and Mittler, 1971). The child is presented with 4 examples of 15 types of sentence of varying complexity and grammatical structure. His task is to identify which of 3 or 4 pictures corresponds to the sentence spoken by the examiner. Each picture illustrates an alternative grammatical interpretation. Thus, in response to the sentence '*The cat is sleeping*', the child is shown pictures of a *dog* sleeping, and also of a cat *playing* with a ball of string, i.e. the noun and the verb have been systematically varied. Similarly, in response to the sentence '*The girl is cutting the cake*', the child is shown the following pictures:

The girl is cutting the cake (stimulus)
The *boy* is cutting the cake (subject varied)
The girl is *eating* the cake (verb varied)
The girl is cutting the *loaf* (object varied)

Other sentence types tested include comparatives and superlatives, past and future tenses, passives, negatives, plurals, prepositions and embedded clauses.

Data are now available on 150 normal nursery school children between 34 and 54 months; the test has also been administered to 200 SSN children matched for mental age with the normal controls (mean MA 3–7). Order of difficulty was very similar for normal and subnormal children (rho = ·78), suggesting that the test is measuring comparable processes in the two groups. It also shows acceptable levels of test reliability (Mittler and Wheldall, 1971; Mittler *et al.*, 1974).

Other attempts to assess sentence comprehension have also been reported in recent years. Carrow (1968) presents a useful table (reproduced in Berry, 1969) showing the approximate ages at which 60 per cent of normal children understand specific grammatical structures, such as nouns, verbs, adjectives, adverbs, prepositions, tenses and genders. The North West Syntax Screening Test (Lee, 1969, 1970) consists of 20 sentence pairs to be identified respectively by picture selection, and 20 comparable pairs to be produced in response to stimulus pictures. Norms for both receptive and expressive skills are presented in percentile graphs, but as the name implies, the test provides only a rapid screening measure yielding a global total score, and is not intended as a detailed grammatical analysis of receptive language.

These tests are still at the research stage, and are mentioned mainly in order to illustrate the difficulty in differentiating between comprehension of language and the child's response to the total communication situation of which language forms only one element. It is important to bear in mind that failure on a test is no proof of inability to perform a cognitive task; it is possible that the child has not adequately understood what is required of him, that he has been distracted by an irrelevant feature of the test situation or that he is in a general sense inattentive to the task. When dealing with mentally handicapped children, we cannot assume, as we usually do for normal children, that they are attending to or understanding our instructions, or that they are interested in carrying them out. In this sense, we need to pay special attention to the complexity of the language which we use in testing or talking to children with intellectual or linguistic handicaps.

STANDARDIZED TESTS

Perhaps the best known and certainly the most ambitious test of language abilities is the Illinois Test of Psycholinguistic Abilities (ITPA). An experimental edition of the test was published in 1961 (McCarthy and Kirk, 1961) and a revised edition is now available in Britain (Kirk *et al.*, 1968; Paraskevopoulos and Kirk, 1969). The test is based on a model of communication processes first proposed by Osgood (1957). Basically, the model distinguishes between channels of communication, levels of organization and psycholinguistic processes. The model aims to provide a specification for all the processes and all the levels that appear to be involved in both understanding and speaking a language, but the test itself only samples ten features of the model. Each test purports to assess a different aspect of language functioning, and can be scored in terms of raw score, language age and standard scores. A total language score can also be derived.

A substantial literature has now grown up around the experimental edition (Bateman, 1965, 1968; Kirk, 1968; Kirk and Kirk, 1971). The test was initially enthusiastically received in North America, but its reception in Britain has been more conservative.

The need for a multifactorial test of language should be seen in the context of a reaction against the traditional monopoly enjoyed by intelligence tests such as the Binet and Wechsler scales, and a growing interest in attempts to identify and isolate specific cognitive skills, not only in respect of language abilities, but also in the area of perception, memory, learning and intelligence itself. It was hoped that a 'profile' approach would yield an analysis of specific strengths and weaknesses which could then be used as the basis of a remedial programme tailor-made to the needs of the individual child. In other words, the test was designed to be diagnostic, but did not confine itself to mere classification.

Nevertheless, the test has latterly come under increasing criticism, partly on technical grounds, and partly as a result of a growing disenchantment with formal tests in general. Technical criticisms throw doubt on the claim to have identified specific language abilities; factorial studies suggest that a substantial proportion of the variance is accounted for by general linguistic ability (Mittler and Ward, 1970; Smith and Marx, 1971). In a review of eighteen factorial studies, Ryckman and Wiegernink (1969) found little consistency of factor structure between age-groups, but showed an increase in the number of factors as age increased. At younger ages the test appears to function in a more global manner, presumably because language abilities have not been or cannot be differentiated at these early stages of development. Technical and psychometric criticisms have also been made by Weener et al. (1967).

The ITPA represented a useful development when it was first developed in the 1950s, but now suffers from having been overtaken by events. The model of language on which it was based now seems outmoded in the light of the developments that have taken place in psycholinguistics. Apart from a brief reference to the work of Berko (1958), the test owes little or nothing to models of language structure developed by Chomsky or to theories of the language acquisition process proposed by some of his followers (e.g. McNeill, 1966, 1970a; Menyuk, 1969; Slobin, 1971a). Osgood himself has modified the original (1957) model on which the ITPA was based towards one more influenced by transformational generative grammar (Osgood, 1968), but these developments are not reflected in the test.

Nevertheless, the ITPA represents an important advance and deserves some (if not all) the popularity which special educators and psychologists have bestowed on it. It has helped us to take a more multifactorial view of language, with the result that we are now more cautious in using global shorthand in describing handicapped children. But it should not be thought that the ITPA provides a comprehensive or relevant analysis of language skills. It is too far removed from 'real life' language behaviour, and is not based on any attempt to analyse minimum language requirements for a child in a given community. Such a requirement is particularly relevant for the older mentally handicapped child whether he is living in the community or being considered for discharge from residential care. The very success of the ITPA may, in fact, have hindered the development of more functionally orientated assessment techniques (Rosenberg, 1970). It may also have prevented psychologists and educators from subjecting recent language research to critical scrutiny of its possible practical significance.

OTHER LANGUAGE SCALES

Mention should also be made of a number of other scales which have become available in recent years.

(1) *The Reynell Developmental Language Scales* (*Reynell, 1969*)

The Reynell Scales have normative data based on children between the ages of 6 months and 6 years, but were designed from the outset with the needs of handicapped children in mind. They distinguish between receptive and expressive aspects of language. The Verbal Comprehension scale (A) requires mainly a simple pointing response or the manipulation of appropriate play materials. The child is required to point to objects or pictures which have to be identified or manipulated according to instructions of gradually increasing complexity. There is an alternative form of the Comprehension Test (B) for use with physically handicapped children who cannot pick up or even point to toys. The expressive tests aim to elicit samples of the child's spoken language in free conversation and in response to standard materials, and to score these in terms of structure, content and vocabulary. The RLDS is of particular value in the assessment of children whose language development is immature or uneven, and for whom more precise information is needed than that provided in general tests of language development. The distinction between receptive and expressive skills is a particularly important contribution towards assessment. It has not been available long enough for validation or subpopulation studies to be carried out on a large scale, but a dissertation by Rogers (1971) suggests that mongol children produce substantially lower receptive than expressive scores.

(2) *Renfrew Language Attainment Scales* (*Renfrew, 1971*)

The Renfrew Scales are primarily designed to help speech therapists and other experienced examiners to assess relevant aspects of language and speech in children between 3 and 7 years.

They consist of the following tests:

(i) *Articulation Attainment Test.* This test is designed to 'provide a standardized estimate of the extent to which use is made of all the English consonants'. The test makes use of 38 words containing 100 consonants, and is phonetically balanced in so far as each consonant is represented with the same frequency as in everyday speech. Spontaneous naming of the objects in pictures is required, as well as serial counting and imitation of phrases.

(ii) *Word Finding Vocabulary.* This scale assesses the ability of children to find words, as distinct from recognizing them in association with pictures (as in the Peabody tests). The items are modified from those originally used by Watts (1944), and call for the identification of parts of the body, the naming of objects and shapes, the use of common and proper nouns, verbs, prepositions and other parts of speech.

(iii) *Action Pictures.* This test is designed to stimulate the child to give short samples of spoken language for purposes of a simple grammatical analysis. The child is shown nine pictures illustrating common activities, and asked questions designed to elicit the use of present, past and future tenses in regular and irregular forms, singular and plural nouns and simple and complex sentence constructions. The test is separately scored in terms of information and grammar.

(iv) *A Test of Continuous Speech.* A sample of continuous speech is elicited by first telling the child an interesting story, illustrated by suitable pictures (e.g., 'The Bus Story'), and then asking him to tell the story to the examiner. Scoring criteria are in terms of information and sentence length.

Some of the Renfrew tests have been under constant development and modification for a period of years, and data are available on a large number of children tested in various parts of Britain. Although problems of scoring and interpretation remain, the tests promise to be a useful addition to the better known and more ambitious scales already described.

(3) *Michigan Picture Language Inventory (Lerea, 1958; Wolski, 1962)*

The Michigan Inventory represents an early ingenious technique for the separate assessment of receptive and expressive skills, using identical linguistic content. Lerea, who originally devised the test, used the 'missing word' technique which is also found in the Grammatic Closure Test of the ITPA, and is intended to elicit specific grammatical constructions from the child, including regular and irregular nouns and verbs, different tenses, demonstratives, articles, pronouns, etc. The limitations of this method have been criticized elsewhere (Mittler, 1970a), but it is now widely agreed that knowledge of morphological rules may provide a sensitive reflection of linguistic competence. Berko's (1958) original study of morphological skills has given rise to a number of psychometric instruments (e.g. Blake and Williams, 1968; Berry and Talbot, 1966; Berry, 1969).

(4) *Sentence Repetition Tasks*

Elicited imitation has until quite recently been neglected as an assessment device, partly because imitation was thought to be a purely mechanical or perceptual-motor skill, and partly because such tasks were conventionally associated with memory testing. It is now becoming apparent that imitation involves the structuring and at least partial comprehension of the material, and that a detailed analysis of the imitation strategies and the exact type of errors made can provide a means of assessing linguistic maturity. The advantage of imitation as an assessment technique lies in the element of control which can be exercised over input, so that the complexity of the utterance can be made progressively more difficult, while keeping length and memory load constant as far as possible. It also has the advantage of being reasonably interesting to the child, as long as the test is not too long and is played almost as a game. Unfortunately, the use of imitation tasks is still in its infancy. Work is now in progress in Manchester on the construction of an imitation test for subnormal children (Berry, 1971; Mittler *et al.*, 1974).

Conclusions

In considering the status of language assessment techniques, we need to strike a sensible balance between clinging to tests merely because they provide scientific respectability or because we happen to be familiar with them, and abandoning them in favour of an enthusiastically but perhaps indiscriminately planned and applied teaching programme. According to one view, assessment for assessment's sake is educationally sterile and there is neither psychological nor indeed ethical justification for subjecting an individual to tests unless it can be shown that the procedures are designed to help him. In the case of a handicapped child, this would limit the use of tests largely to situations in which a remedial programme was to be designed on the basis of test findings.

It is also questionable whether the monopoly of testing traditionally enjoyed by psychologists is not now something of an anachronism. It has been argued elsewhere (Mittler, 1970c, 1973a) that intensive courses of training should be established for special educators in the principles and practice of psychological assessment, with the objective of having in each special school at least one teacher (not necessarily the head teacher) who is trained not merely in testing but in the use of assessment procedures to plan remedial programmes. School psychologists should by this means be freed from much of what is now called 'routine testing' in order to act as specialists and consultants in problem cases. There will always be complex or experimental tests which should be restricted to psychologists – perhaps ITPA was (or still is) in this category – but many other tests are comparatively simple and straightforward to administer, score and interpret.

Language teaching

STIMULATION AND STRUCTURE

In view of the evidence of serious underfunctioning, delay or deficit in language abilities, the question of teaching assumes added importance. Until quite recently, however, the fashion has been to rely on 'exposure' methods to a rich and linguistically stimulating environment, in the hope that the subnormal child will acquire language partly by 'learning from others', partly by listening to stories, and partly by needing to communicate his needs and thoughts in a social situation. This is presumably the rationale underlying the use of normal nursery schools for speechless or language disordered children. We have argued elsewhere that this may be more an act of faith than judgment unless specific efforts are directed to obtaining the desired verbal interaction (Rutter and

Mittler, 1972; Mittler, 1973b). A lively and stimulating environment is no doubt valuable, but it may not be enough. Some children have to be helped or even taught to adapt to such an environment, and may need to begin at an earlier developmental level by learning language at 'mother-distance' (Sheridan, 1964). Schiefelbusch *et al.* (1967) draw attention to certain prerequisites of language development which may have to be taught or recapitulated in the case of sub-normal or severely language disordered children. These essentially concern stages in social development, and include sensory stimulation and smiling, attachment, word acquisition and social exploration, and lastly language acquisi-tion and experience.

A further disadvantage in relying exclusively on exposure and stimulation is that such methods do not take account of the difficulties which subnormals appear to experience in spontaneous or incidental learning (Denny, 1964; Clarke and Clarke, 1973a) or in discriminating the relevant from the irrelevant in a learning situation. If these are 'real' deficits which are likely to occur with high frequency in a subnormal population, then the design of an appropriate learning environment both for the individual and for the group will need more careful thought than has so far been forthcoming. A wide variety of methods is in use, but very little research has been devoted to their effectiveness or to long-term results. Bereiter and Engelman (1966) advocate highly structured formal language lessons, designed to teach children to exploit the grammatical and syntactical possibilities of language to the full. Other workers have described less formal approaches, which place less reliance on drills and try to help the child to develop language skills in the context of enjoyable and relevant play and learning experiences (e.g. Klaus and Gray, 1968; Gahagan and Gahagan, 1970).

At this stage the problem appears to be one of finding a balance between stimulation and structure, and of realizing that they do not represent incom-patible educational objectives or philosophies. But stimulation by itself is probably not enough for the majority of subnormal children, though it provides an essential background against which more structured approaches may be developed. It may be useful to think in terms of designing a series of graded environments which would provide for the needs of the individual child at various stages of his development. This might involve initially teaching him in fairly quiet conditions, in short sessions by himself or with only one or two others, and then gradually introducing him to progressively more stimulating and demanding situations. In other words, the relative prominence of stimulating or structured methods should be determined by the stage of development and the needs of the child, and this in turn can only be discovered as a result of syste-matic assessment.

What, then, do we mean by a rich and lively language environment, and what is it that constitutes stimulation?

THE LANGUAGE ENVIRONMENT

The child is in some form of language environment the moment he enters the classroom. The modern 'child-centred' approach to education is one of activity and movement, and encourages conversation between children, and between children and teachers. Inevitably and appropriately, it is likely to be noisy. But some children cannot tolerate what to them may be excessive stimulation, just as others react adversely to individual contact with an adult, even for a brief period. In the first group are children who can be seen to put their hands over their ears in conditions that would not strike an outsider as particularly noisy, or who retreat into a corner to pursue their own interests or to do their work. In the second group are children who are reasonably active and busy until an adult makes an individual approach or begins to make demands, when they avert their eyes or move away. Individual differences such as these exist in most classrooms and may be based on 'real' differences of personality or biological constitution. But this does not mean that they are necessarily resistant to modification. Some children may need to be taught or helped to function intellectually as well as socially in a group, while others may need help to allow them to cope with the demands of a one to one relationship.

It is also relevant to consider the function of adult utterances to children. Some of our utterances are in the form of commands ('Come here', 'Sit down', etc.) and some are merely offered as a running commentary or as a general encouragement ('That's a nice picture'). The running commentary is a powerful means of focusing the child's interest and helping to create a link between his own activity and the teacher's verbal formulation ('Oh, I see, you're making a train with your bricks, here's the engine, and here's the guard's van', etc.). Similarly, the teacher can try to extend the range of a child's representational play. If a pile of bricks is being used to make a train, she can ask (or ask the child to show) what else they can be used for – e.g. to make a station, a signal etc. The use of language in such circumstances comes as second nature to many teachers, and it is hardly necessary to provide a psychological rationale. Other teachers and many parents, however, tend to get discouraged if the child does not answer them, and may reduce the amount of verbal interaction with such a child without being fully aware of it. This is understandable, since we are conditioned by years of contact with normal children and adults to expect a reply and an interchange sooner or later, and some mothers in particular feel embarrassed by talking to a child who does not reply and who may not even show that he is understanding her.

Once a child does begin to say a few words, the teacher will obviously consider ways in which she can not only encourage him to extend his present level of language functioning, but also talk to him in ways that will help him to attain the next stage. For example, a child's spoken language may be confined to a small number of single words, all of which happen to be nouns. The teacher may want to introduce more nouns, in order to reinforce the principle that 'things' have 'names' – a breakthrough which may be as dramatic and as significant as it was in the case of Helen Keller and Miss Sullivan. At the same time, she may be considering how to introduce him to verbs, by using and perhaps encouraging him to use verb forms to describe his own activities ('eating', 'painting', 'running' etc.). Chalfant (1968) has reported a kind of 'do and say' programme for young mongol children, who are encouraged to use a single verb or verb phrase in the form of a pacing commentary on their own activities. (See also Mittler *et al.*, 1974.)

It is also instructive to listen to a tape recording of an adult with a group of retarded children, and then to carry out a simple analysis of the kinds of questions which children are asked. Many questions are phrased in such a way as to make it almost impossible to answer in anything other than single words, most of which are likely to be nouns. It is natural for adults to encourage children to talk by asking questions, but these need not be exclusively of the 'What's this called?' or 'What colour is it?' variety. In fact, a good deal of what is said to retarded children seems to take this form. At the very least, it should be possible to phrase questions so that the child has to make a choice ('Would you like milk or juice?' 'Shall we go for a walk now or later?'). More open-ended questions follow at a slightly later stage ('What shall we buy at the shops?' 'What are you going to do now?'). The skilled teacher knows how to talk to the child at his own level and in the natural context of his play or other activities without appearing to turn the conversation into a formal language lesson, so that the child learns that language is not only a natural accompaniment to play but can help to extend and develop it. If language experiences are relevant and enjoyable, the child may adopt a more positive attitude to more formal or structured approaches which may be introduced at a later stage.

There are, of course, some practical limitations to the introduction of more structured language programmes, the chief of these being shortage of staff, since most of the methods that have been reported involve a one to one working relationship between teacher and child. This need not present insuperable obstacles to the teacher wishing to experiment with these methods. In the first place, a structured approach calls for a carefully considered definition of short-term and long-term objectives for each child, and for detailed planning of how these aims can be met. Secondly, it may only be appropriate to carry out such a programme for a relatively short period. Few would advocate that structured teaching should take place all day and every day, though critics of these methods sometimes talk as though this was all that happened in such a classroom. The important principle is to know what one's objectives are, and to exploit every possible teaching opportunity to achieve them. This calls for an alert sensitivity to the child's language needs, and to his particular developmental pattern. Children develop in ways and at a speed that we do not necessarily expect; a systematically planned teaching programme should be flexible enough to be modified or abandoned in the light of cues provided by the child.

It is also worth emphasizing that teachers and even administrators in special education are working towards the principle of the two-teacher class. Once we achieve this objective, or even approach it by having at least a second adult such as a nursery nurse in each special school classroom, one teacher will be free to devote parts of the day to individual teaching, while the other is concerned with the rest of the group. Ideally, this principle involves an architectural innovation in special schools: the addition of a small room for individual teaching alongside each main classroom. This is hardly ever found.

EVALUATING RESULTS

Although a number of attempts at language improvement have been reported, the studies are often poorly controlled and of short duration. Earlier studies were well reviewed by Spradlin (1963) in the context of a critical discussion of the methodological problems which arise in designing and evaluating language teaching programmes. More recent studies have been brought together in two publications by Schiefelbusch (Schiefelbusch *et al.*, 1967; Schiefelbusch, 1972). Characteristic of the more recent work is a broadly behavioural approach to both assessment and teaching, with an emphasis on functional as opposed to psycho-metric analysis of language behaviour, followed by the systematic use of principles of programming and reinforcement (Sloane and Macaulay, 1968). Most of these studies deal with small samples and use the individual as his own control, whereas earlier workers tended to use pre- and post-test measures, often with a control or contrast group. Summarizing group studies of this type, Spradlin (1963) indicated that seven out of twelve reported some improvement in language skills, and an eighth was inconclusive. The four studies that reported insignificant or negative findings all used a form of control, though these were not regarded as satisfactory either. Only four of the seven studies among those reporting successful treatment included an element of control in the experimental design. One is reminded of an earlier parallel in the field of drug trials in psychiatric populations; Foulds (1958) showed that most of the studies reporting positive effects were poorly designed or statistically inadequate, whereas those characterized by proper control tended to report negative findings.

The difficulty of evaluating change is partly one of constructing appropriate control groups, and partly one of choosing relevant measures of language behaviour. The former difficulties are now more widely recognized, and investigators appreciate the problems of matching groups for comparison purposes, whether the match is based on a test score or on a specific criterion, such as being on a waiting list (Baumeister, 1967; Clarke and Clarke, 1973b). The second group of problems derives from the uncertain status of currently available measures of language functioning (see section on 'Assessment'). The fact that scores on a test such as ITPA change in an upward direction following a programme of language teaching cannot necessarily be ascribed to the teaching programme. At the lowest level of explanation, it may be due to the unreliability of the tests for the particular group under investigation. In other cases, the nature of the teaching is so closely based on a test-based diagnosis of the language difficulties that it is sometimes questionable whether the programme has done more than teach the children to do the tests more effectively. However, the reliability of standardized language tests is at least known with some measure of confidence. This is not usually the case with observations by skilled or un-skilled observers of the child's language in everyday situations, though proper attention to time sampling and to observer reliability should make it possible to objectify such observations, and to reduce unreliability to the minimum. At least naturalistic observation eliminates the artificiality of a formal test, usually carried out by a stranger who is often required by the conventions of research to be not only unfamiliar with the child but ignorant of the 'treatment' he has received.

Methodological problems of evaluation of the effects of language teaching can be illustrated by reference to a study by Kolstoe (1958) which is frequently cited as an example of a successful programme. An experimental group of fifteen institutionalized mongol children receiving speech therapy was individu-ally matched on Kuhlmann MA with a no-treatment control group. The treat-ment, which was based on principles of verbal and social reinforcement, was given in forty-five minutes sessions five days a week over a period of over five months, and used a variety of methods, including pictures, mechanical toys, films and records. The results indicated a loss on the Kuhlmann for both groups, though the experimental group lost fewer points than the controls, and children with higher IQs stood to gain more from the programme than those with lower IQs. It is possible that the largely negative findings of this study were due to the fact that the IQ of both groups was in the low 20s. Other measures also failed to reflect any significant benefit, but the experimental group did show higher scores after treatment on the Differential Language Facility Test – an early version of the experimental edition of the ITPA. Spradlin con-siders that this is one of the few studies with an adequate design; but it is a pity that the control group did not receive an equal amount of adult attention.

A study involving a more elaborate design and using children of greater ability was reported by Lassers and Low (1960), whose subjects were between 7 and 15 and had IQs ranging between 40 and 79. Two experimental groups were created, one receiving traditional speech therapy with an emphasis on sound discrimina-tion and production in a 'clinic' setting, the other being encouraged by means of simulated 'real life' situations to increase their language skills. A control group was also used. After fifteen weeks of therapy, differences between the three groups were shown only on an articulation test, and not on a sound discrimina-tion test or on the San Francisco Inventory of Communicative Effectiveness. Spradlin points out that even on the articulation test there was a confounding between examiners and treatments which might have resulted in bias. Treatment studies are also reported by Schlanger (1953), Strazzula (1953), Mecham (1955), and Johnson et al. (1960).

One feature of most of the studies reviewed by Spradlin and also characteriz-ing a number of later reports lies in the absence of detail concerning the aims and objectives of therapy, and the exact techniques used by the therapists. A considerable variety of aims and methods seem to have been involved, so that it is difficult to know whether improvements should be related to one part of the programme rather than another. Similarly, more success might have been achieved if the therapy had been restricted to specific aspects of language ability.

BEHAVIOUR MODIFICATION: PRINCIPLES

Since the mid-1960s an increasing number of workers in this field have been using a variety of techniques and models which are based to some degree on principles of behaviour modification. Some are undoubtedly strictly operant and neo-Skinnerian in character, while others make use of one or other principle or technique based on operant theory. For example, a number of workers employ systematic reinforcement, but without necessarily subscribing to a consistent theoretical framework, or basing their treatment on a preliminary functional analysis of behaviour.

Work in this area owes much of its impetus to advances made over a wide front in abnormal psychology in treating individuals with disorders of behaviour, both in building up new behaviours and in removing undesirable or unadaptive behaviours. In the field of language, it derives from the premise that language is in principle no different from other aspects of behaviour in being subject to modification as a consequence of the applications of systematic reinforcement. Different workers might disagree, however, about the limits of what can be achieved by such methods.

It would not be appropriate here to embark on a full exposition of the principles of behaviour modification. These can be found in chapter 12 of this volume, and also in Gardner (1971), Kiernan (1973), Weisberg (1971), and many others. A useful volume summarizing operant work in relation to speech and language disorders has been brought together by Sloane and Macaulay (1968). Bricker's work represents perhaps the most consistent theoretical as well as practical approach to the teaching of language skills to the mentally retarded, and is also notable for the attempt to relate behaviour modification to cognitive and developmental psychology in general and to psycholinguistics in particular (Bricker and Bricker, 1970a, b, 1973; Bricker, 1972).

Operant theory regards a retarded person as characterized by a limited repertoire of behaviour, and as being in a sense a product of his reinforcement history (Bijou and Baer, 1967). The practical question confronting the therapist concerns the principles and techniques which should underlie a systematic attempt to increase the retarded person's repertoire. In order to do this, it is necessary to begin with a functional analysis and assessment. This, according to Kiernan (1973), involves (i) a clear definition and description of the behaviour, (ii) an attempt to specify the precise stimulus conditions which appear to be related to the occurrence or non-occurrence of the behaviour under study (i.e.

stimulus and setting conditions), and (iii) specification of the events which are acting as reinforcers. This analysis is the foundation of the treatment programme, in so far as the treatment provides for a manipulation of the stimulus and setting conditions in relation to specific target behaviours. Indeed, as Kiernan points out, it is only through the attempt to modify behaviour which arises out of functional analysis that the appropriateness of the analysis can be examined.

It is worth pointing out, however, that functional analysis is more appropriate for some language skills than for others. In many cases, the therapist is confronted by a total absence of language or even vocalization, so that it is hardly possible to specify the conditions under which the child vocalizes or not. It may be necessary in such cases to implement a form of 'diagnostic therapy' by embarking directly on a course of treatment, by means, for example, of shaping techniques, with the object of finding out whether the individual's vocalizations can in any specifiable sense be brought under operant control. On the other hand, a view of language which was not simply confined to expressive aspects allows a programme of treatment to consider what kind of skills are necessary to the development of speech, to apply a functional assessment to these skills and to plan an appropriate regime of treatment to compensate for deficiencies in areas which are deemed critical to development. We have already discussed the importance of receptive skills, and suggested that it may be important at certain states of development to assess and if necessary further listening and receptive language. It has also been suggested that imaginative and representational play forms an important foundation to language development, since the ability to play in such a way as to make one object or activity stand for another is the precursor of learning not only that things have names, but that language can be used creatively and generatively.

It is in this connection that a hierarchical model of language development becomes relevant, in the sense that it may be necessary to assess and develop looking, listening, sound discrimination, word recognition and finally sentence discrimination before embarking on a speech and language programme.

The importance of planning a language training curriculum in the context of a consistent theoretical and procedural framework is repeatedly stressed in Bricker's writings. He uses the device of a procedural lattice to specify the terminal states which he wishes to reach in specific and individual areas of language skill, and the training sequences which will be necessary to achieve these aims. Fig. 4 provides a convenient illustration of his approach (Bricker and Bricker, 1973).

The lattice specifies a number of programme steps in a language training curriculum and also shows how they are related in time and in order. Boxes above the diagonal represent various terminal behaviour states, those below the diagonal specify the subprogrammes that are likely to be needed to achieve these goals. The lattice begins on the left with initial behaviour control and attention training achieved through reinforcement procedures, and proceeds through stages such as discrimination, memory, vocabulary, imitation, articulation, syntax and morphology. Furthermore, more detailed procedural lattices

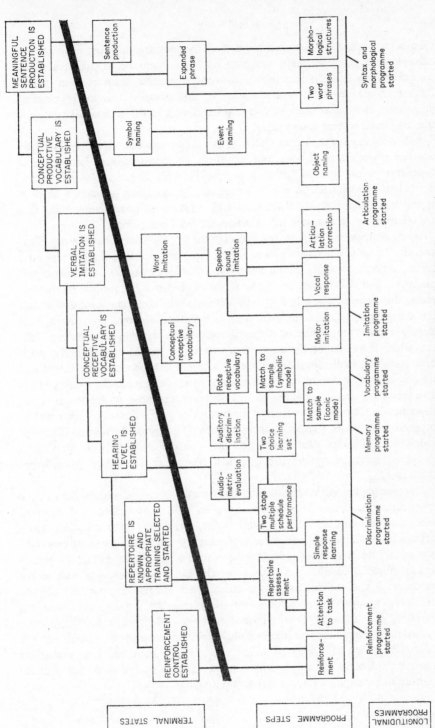

Fig. 4 Language Training Lattice (from Bricker and Bricker, 1973).

have been worked out for specific parts of the language training programme; examples are given for steps and methods that might be used to teach the comprehension and production of two-word utterances, such as 'want milk'. Bricker emphasizes that the key feature of this model is that as the training progresses, each subsequent step involves a change in the antecedent stimulus, the reinforced response, or both.

A disadvantage of the lattice system is that it can only be used by professionals who are already trained behaviour modifiers, since it assumes a knowledge of operant terminology and techniques. The Brickers also describe the use of flow charts which can be used with relatively untrained personnel, since it specifies in detail both the antecedent and the subsequent stimulus events that are regarded as necessary to move behaviour from one point to another.

It will be apparent from the discussion of the principles of behaviour modification that some of the techniques to which these principles have given rise offer certain advantages both in the design and implementation of treatment programmes, and also in relation to the problem of evaluating results. In the first place, this approach largely dispenses with the need for standardized tests and for comparison of an individual with a hypothetical population average. It largely replaces the traditional normative test with a criterion-referenced evaluation which is focused on the question of whether or not the individual is capable of a particular skill. Secondly, it forges a direct link between assessment and treatment, so that the response to treatment partly determines the validity of the assessment. Thirdly, it allows the individual's response to treatment to be described in relation to the level of his own prior performance. In other words, progress is evaluated in relation to an objectively established baseline. Using the individual as his own control also provides a partial solution to the problem of designing matched control groups when comparing the effects of different treatments.

In principle there is no reason why these methods cannot be combined with a more traditional form of evaluation, including analysis of variance and 'repeated measures' designs. In an important paper, Gardner (1969) criticizes many behaviour modification studies in subnormality for failing to specify or take account of important independent variables such as age, duration of institutionalization, physical condition, diagnosis, psychometric test scores, as well as the nature, type and schedule of reinforcement used. He also criticizes the absence of control groups, biased samples, imprecise measures even of the dependent variable, and absence of long-term follow-up. A similar article evaluating behaviour therapy with children includes a table showing the very small number of studies which have adopted at least some of the more stringent evaluation criteria available (Pawlicki, 1970). It seems likely that future studies will increasingly combine individual and group designs.

BEHAVIOUR MODIFICATION: PRACTICE

After the foregoing discussion of principles, a few examples of application will now be considered, though these are intended merely as illustrations of a rapidly growing area of work. The most comprehensive recent summary of operant studies has been compiled by Sloane and MacAulay (1968); an unannotated bibliography up to 1968 has been prepared by Peins (1969), and a section of speech and language is regularly included in *Mental Retardation Abstracts*.

The importance of imitation as the foundation for a language teaching programme has already been emphasized. Before a child can begin to imitate or produce speech, he must clearly be able to interact with the teacher and be sufficiently responsive to commands and cues to enter a language programme. But many children need first to be taught to imitate, and a number of workers have reported in detail on methods that have been employed to this end. Peterson (1968) summarizes a series of studies originally carried out at the University of Washington (e.g. Baer and Sherman, 1964; Sherman, 1965; Risley, 1966). Later work on generalized imitation and specific setting events is reported by Peterson and Whitehurst (1971) and Peterson *et al.* (1971).

The technique frequently adopted in these studies is to begin by trying to establish a simple imitative behaviour which can be physically prompted. For example, the teacher taps the table, takes the child's hand and taps the table and provides immediate reinforcement. The physical prompt of holding the child's hand is then gradually faded, while continuous reinforcement is provided for responding. At this stage, some workers introduce the discriminative stimulus 'Do this', following this by the behaviour to be imitated. In order to establish a hierarchy and to avoid entering the programme at too advanced or complex a level, it is common to begin with gross movements such as standing, sitting, jumping, clapping, and then to begin to localize imitation to the head (head shaking and nodding), and finally to the mouth, tongue, lips and throat. Here again, it is useful to introduce a verbal discriminative stimulus by saying 'Do this: stand up', etc., in order to maintain control at later stages. A number of relevant movements of the mouth and tongue can be imitated by this means: opening and shutting the mouth, tongue in and out, tongue in various placements (on lower lip, behind teeth, tongue click), blowing, hissing, an aspirated 'h', 'ppph' and 'fff', etc. It may be necessary to produce prompts in the form of guidance of the child's lips, tongue and mouth, or to put the child's hand on the teacher's throat to feel the vibrations produced by vocalizations and to provide a discriminative stimulus to the child that a voiced response is required. Similarly, a hand placed in front of the mouth will enable the child to feel voiceless plosive or fricative sounds. Phonetic placement procedures are discussed by MacAulay (1968) following Van Riper (1954).

At this point the most difficult stage of imitating voiced sounds has been reached, and failure is frequently encountered. Sherman (1965) suggests a backdown and chaining procedure to try to overcome this. It involves pairing a verbal response (e.g. 'ah') with a previously learned motor response. Thus, standing up might be paired with 'ah'; the child is more likely to produce the verbal imitation if it is chained to a previously learned motor response, which can then in turn be faded (see also Nelson and Evans, 1968, for a useful account of a collaborative project between a psychologist and a speech therapist).

MacAulay (1968) describes her teaching procedures in detail, and reports results in a series of individual case studies. The teaching programme incorporates a number of stages: individual sounds, blending sounds into words, a naming vocabulary and, where possible, word phrases. She makes systematic use of colour cues, employing black alphabet cues for consonants and a different colour for each of ten vowel sounds. The colour cues consisted originally of rectangles, but these were later 'shaped' to the appropriate letters of the alphabet.

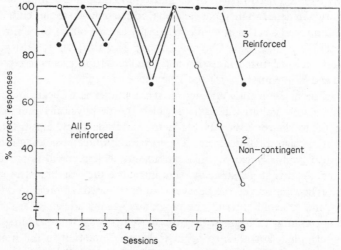

Fig. 5 Effect of reinforcement on accuracy of tacting (from Sloane *et al.*, 1968).

A particular feature of her method lies in her use of similar principles to teach both speech and basic reading skills. Her subjects ranged in IQ from 27 to 92, but most of the detailed case studies in her report are in the severely subnormal range. Five of her eleven subjects were originally mute and had previously not responded to speech therapy. All of these children learned to produce sounds and in some cases words. Improvements in articulation were also reported, and the graphs show a substantial rise in the percentage of sounds which came under discriminative control. She reports that most children acquired a full repertoire of speech sounds within four to six months while being seen only twice a week. One wonders whether results could have been achieved more quickly if daily sessions had been used.

MacAulay's study did not include formal control procedures, either through control groups, by using the individual as his own control, or by experimentally removing contingent reinforcement. A more controlled design was used by

Sloane *et al.* (1968), who measured the effects of non-contingent reinforcements. An example is provided in Fig. 5.

The child was required to name five pictures and was reinforced with ice cream for each correct response. After the sixth session, reinforcement was provided for only three of the pictures, and ice cream was given on a non-contingent basis for the remaining two. Accuracy of naming for the two pictures fell from 85 to 25 per cent, but remained at 85 per cent for the other three. Unfortunately, no data are given for a return to the experimental condition for

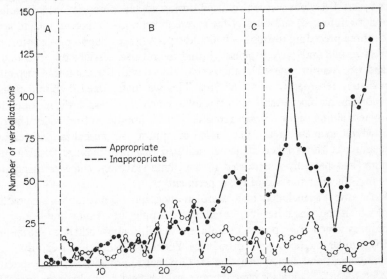

Fig. 6 A record of appropriate and inappropriate verbalization (from Hall, 1970). A = Baseline period prior to contingent reinforcement. B = Reinforcement period, verbalizations reinforced by food, play materials and the E's attention. C = Reversal period, return to baseline conditions of non-contingent reinforcement. D = Second reinforcement period, return to procedures of contingent reinforcement.

the two pictures, though it is likely on the basis of other studies that near 85 per cent accuracy would have been restored. Use was also made of 'time out' from reinforcement immediately after inappropriate behaviour or incorrect responding, though this was rarely needed after the initial sessions. A notable feature of this report is the involvement of mothers as co-therapists. The mothers were initially trained in the laboratory by being cued over an intercom when to start, reinforce, correct errors, etc. These prompts were gradually removed, and the training continued in the home, with frequent reports to staff, first in person, and then by telephone.

The importance of experimentally reversing and reinstating reinforcement contingencies is also illustrated in a single case study reported by Hall (1970), illustrated in Fig. 6.

The subject of Hall's study was a 6-year-old boy who had been diagnosed as brain damaged and autistic, and suffering from moderately severe mental retardation. Although he could produce a few words of appropriate speech, most of his utterances consisted of jargon and nonsense syllables, and he barely responded to verbal direction. Following three baseline sessions in which a mean of 3·3 appropriate verbalizations were recorded, reinforcement was provided only for appropriate verbalization, though this did not produce a marked improvement for about sixteen sessions. Nevertheless, the mean rate of responding rose 20·0 per session during the reinforcement periods. At this point three reversal sessions were introduced during which appropriate verbalizations were not reinforced, and bites of food were given non-contingently. Compared to the three preceding sessions in which the percentage of appropriate responses were 48·3, 44·8 and 53·7, responses during the reversal sessions dropped to 9·6, 6·7 and 1·6. Reinforcement was then reintroduced with the result that responses immediately returned to a rate of 43·7. This was maintained despite a change from continuous to a variable ratio of reinforcement, and despite the introduction of a new training regime which required him to imitate and produce 'I want'. The overall increase in the percentage of appropriate verbalizations reached 78·5, and recordings taken at home indicated that the language training programme had partially generalized to the home situation, and was mantained three months after the end of the experiment.

Hall's study is included in a useful monograph (Girardeau and Spradlin, 1970) which contains other highly relevant examples of training and evaluation procedures which are reported in sufficient detail to allow others to repeat and modify similar methods (see particularly Yoder and Reynolds, and important methodological and review chapters by Girardeau and Spradlin and Spradlin and Girardeau). Significant contributions to this field have also been made by Hewett (1966), Kerr et al. (1965), Lovaas (1966), Risley and Wolf (1967), Johnston (1968) and many others. One of the most exhaustive accounts of a language training programme has recently been reported by Buddenhagen (1971) who incorporated recent developments in phonetics into his teaching of four profoundly language-retarded mongols. His monograph is also notable for its highly critical discussion of the implications (or lack of them) of psycholinguistics in general and of the work of Chomsky in particular for language teaching of the mentally subnormal. Reference should also be made to a growing tendency to combine behaviour modification principles and teaching techniques with formal methods of evaluation of the results, including pre-and-post testing of experimental and control groups on standardized tests (even including Binet IQ) and observational studies of language behaviour in both free and structured situations (e.g. Talkington and Hall, 1970; MacCubrey, 1971).

A number of recent studies have incorporated, but also modified, models and theories derived from developmental psycholinguistics. The work of Bricker and his associates is the most notable example of an attempt to use both operant techniques and a systems analysis approach in order to try to teach young subnormal children to reach the stage of using two-word utterances of the 'pivot-open type' (Bricker and Bricker, 1973). 'Pivots' are words which occur with high frequency on which a larger number of 'open' class words are hung. Thus 'allgone' might be a pivot preceding open class words such as 'dinner', 'potty', 'Daddy', etc. According to linguists (e.g. Slobin, 1971b; McNeill, 1970a) the pivot-open structure is an innately determined linguistic universal, and part of the 'Language Acquisition Device' common to all known languages. But this does not necessarily debar the educator from trying to teach children to acquire it; indeed, as Bricker (1972) points out, this constitutes a powerful challenge to the educator. There are also important implications for cognitive development in the acquisition of two-word structures, since the child equipped with even a small number of two-word utterances can begin to express increasingly complex intentions and meanings (e.g. no dinner, my car, more dinner, etc.). He has progressed from the stage of labelling, using mainly nouns, to his first statements about situations and relationships.

A small study designed to teach pivot-open structures has recently been completed in Manchester (Jeffree *et al.*, 1973). Two 4-year-old mongol boys who were developmentally equated and who were both using only single-word utterances were used in a design involving both within subject and between subject control procedures. Both boys were initially taught the appropriate use of ten nouns, as well as the participle 'gone'. Play for the experimental child was then structured with the help of appropriate apparatus and teaching with a view to eliciting pivot-open utterances, using five of the ten nouns, together with 'gone'. The control child had identical conditions but no pivot-open models were given. When criterion level was reached for the first child, he was exposed to the second five nouns, suggesting that some generalization had occurred. At this point, the control child who had not previously produced two-word utterances was switched to the experimental condition, and quickly learned both to imitate and generalize the appropriate pivot-open construction.

A study by Fygetakis and Gray (1970) is of considerable interest for its close attention to programming variables and its systematic attempt to teach linguistic constructs. The subjects were three children with severe language disorders which mainly took the form of distorted and inadequate syntactic constructions reflecting inability to differentiate between singular and plural subject or between present and past tense. They did not demonstrate usage of many of the transformation rules for reordering and changing the underlying deep structure into the appropriate surface structure. Consequently they did not make the word order changes necessary in forming questions. The paper then describes a form of 'programmed conditioning' designed to develop the base structure rules involved in using *is* in sentences with a singular noun phrase and a verb phrase containing either an adjective or prepositional phrase. The subjects not only learned the task, but were able to use it in free play and conversation outside the experimental situation. In addition, considerable success was obtained in a second programme designed to teach transformational rules involved in the reordering of words in question form.

Although the authors of this study argue that they have directly taught competence, this issue will be regarded as theoretical by many; even those who subscribe to a theory of linguistic universals would not necessarily object on principle to remedial measures which are designed to develop linguistic skills, whether these are related to competence or performance. But the question is not as theoretical as it might seem, since some skills may lend themselves more easily to remediation than others. Educators and behaviourists have been applying themselves to a wide range of language behaviours, including simple noun-labelling responses, two-word utterances and more complex and elaborate syntactic skills. Major advances have also been made in the technology of establishing communication systems with chimpanzees. By careful use of pro-grammed techniques, chimpanzees have been taught both to understand and to produce three-dimensional representations of fairly complex syntactic con-structions – including statements of the form 'Sarah, put the banana into the pail and the apple into the dish' (Premack, 1970). In addition, components of the American Sign Language for the Deaf have been taught to chimpanzees who learned to use and maintain a form of conversational behaviour (Gardner and Gardner, 1969).

Without in any way adopting an extremist behaviourist position that anything is teachable if properly taught, it is rarely justifiable to conclude that the failure of a teaching programme is necessarily due to the fact that the child is not 'maturationally ready' or that he is 'too dull to benefit', or to withhold treatment on the grounds that a specific deficit is 'constitutional'. Nor is it enough for psychologists merely to demonstrate that subnormals have specific deficits in this or that cognitive or linguistic skill; they could usefully continue their studies by considering whether the deficits that they have demonstrated yield in any measure to specific programmes of remediation designed with the same detail as the experiment which demonstrated the deficit in the first place. Such remedial programmes can be short term or long term; in other words, they can be begun in the 'laboratory', as one of the experimental conditions, and developed by gradual stages into a classroom teaching programme. The important point here is that we should not conclude that initial performance on a learning task is necessarily predictive of how the individual will respond to a programme of teaching, or that failure to learn is necessarily due to 'innately low intelligence', 'laziness', 'psychosis' or any other quality in the individual (Clarke and Clarke, 1973). Such variables may impose limits on the amount that can be learned, and the time that will be taken to learn, but much can also be achieved by careful attention to teaching methods.

A survey of the work now proceeding on the teaching of language skills to the mentally subnormal gives good ground for optimism. In particular, the principles and practice of behaviour modification appear to be productive, not only in the hands of psychologists but also when systematically taught and applied by nurses, teachers and, most significantly of all, by parents. However, both prin-ciples and the practice are not without their limitations, and many of the studies

reported are still inadequate in conception, badly carried out and unsystematic-
ally reported. Behaviour modifiers have on occasion not taken account of knowledge in related fields, including linguistics, phonetics and even developmental
psychology, in selecting target behaviours which they wished to teach. Should
one, for example, begin by shaping and developing sounds that are already in the
child's repertoire, or start with sounds which we know from studies of normal
speech development are the earliest or the easiest in the developmental sequence?
How far should the therapist be guided by the child's interests and how far by
the demands of the teaching regime in, for example, determining the criteria
for 'time out' or the length of the sessions? In reporting the results of language
training programmes, is it necessary to concentrate largely on single case-
studies, or can we in future incorporate stricter methods of design and statistical
evaluation?

Systematic attempts to improve language skills in the mentally subnormal
have hardly begun, but seem to offer reasonably promising prospects. It may
therefore be premature to come to any firm conclusions about the ultimate level
of language skill that a mentally subnormal child may be expected to reach at
adulthood. It would be equally unrealistic to exaggerate what could be achieved
even if the best teaching methods were more widely available.

Conclusions

Both parents and professionals agree on the central importance of language in
the development of the child, but we know more about the language deficiencies
of the mentally handicapped than about ways of tackling them. Much of the
recent psycholinguistic research has taken the form of theorizing and model
building, and has on the whole discounted the role of environmental factors in
language development. Educational practice has in its turn tended to be influenced by a maturational orientation which has resulted in a somewhat un-
critical reliance on techniques that have been developed with younger normal
children. It might have been hoped that psychology would play a mediating
role between psycholinguistic research and educational practice; instead, many
psychologists have tended to concentrate on the development of assessment
techniques, and on perfecting techniques of demonstrating deficits.

Nevertheless, there are encouraging signs of a more positive approach. Research
and practice are coming closer together, though the gap between them is still
uncomfortably wide. Research into the structure of language and a growing
interest in normal language acquisition have resulted in an interest in the underlying processes of development, and in the variables associated with growth
from one stage to another, rather than in descriptions of the stages themselves.
This process-orientated approach has in its turn led to attempts to isolate specific
skills and abilities. Global concepts identifying language exclusively with the
spoken word are being replaced by a growing appreciation that some aspects of
language may be less affected than others both in the individual and in groups.

Experimental techniques have been applied to clinical populations to describe characteristic strategies of dealing with language input, and useful parallels have been drawn both with motor skills and with models of information processing. The emphasis of recent psycholinguistic research on the structure of language has led to a greater awareness of the complexity of language input both at a semantic and a syntactic level. Techniques which have so far been used mainly in the laboratory seem likely to be adapted for the classroom and for assessment purposes in order to assess the degree to which an individual is able to impose order and structure and to extract relevant features from incoming information. More emphasis is also being placed on the extent to which spoken language is understood, and on the interaction between non-verbal and verbal cues both in speaking and in listening.

It is becoming apparent that the emphasis which has recently been placed on maturational components of development do not necessarily deny the contribution of environmental factors. Biological and environmental variables are now seen as interacting in a complex relationship which is only partly understood and certainly under-investigated. Most of the research studies have been concerned with one or other group of variables, but the interaction between them does not easily lend itself to systematic study, though its existence seems theoretically plausible.

Perhaps the most positive development in recent years can be found in a more positive approach to teaching and remediation. With a growing awareness of the central importance of language skills in the total development of the child, a number of teachers and research workers have been adopting an increasingly systematic approach to teaching, and have been less inclined than in the past to wait for language to develop spontaneously or to limit themselves to providing an appropriately stimulating environment. Some teaching programmes have been based on theories and models of language structure and language processes derived from cognitive psychology and psycholinguistics, and have therefore concentrated on attempts to help the child to acquire basic skills connected with morphology, syntax and appropriate language use. But the most substantial body of work has depended heavily on learning theory and on principles of behaviour modification, including functional analysis, and the use of a graded programme involving shaping, successive approximation and consistently applied schedules of reinforcement.

There can now be little doubt that behaviour modification techniques constitute a powerful therapeutic weapon in the teaching of language and other cognitive skills. While it would be dangerous to exaggerate what might be achieved, it would be even more shortsighted to neglect the potential contribution which systematic teaching can make in this field. Many reports have now been published which testify to the effectiveness of these methods, and it is likely that they will be increasingly applied in educational programmes in the future. An immediate problem arises from the shortage of staff who are trained in the use of behaviour modification techniques, and who can in their turn train not merely psychologists, but other professional and paraprofessional groups, including teachers, nurses and nursing assistants, and above all parents. Results obtained so far certainly justify some degree of optimism in experimenting with new approaches to the teaching of language skills.

References

ADKINS, S. (1969) *The Language Addressed by Mothers to their Three and Four Year Old Children.* Unpubl. dissertation, Univ. of Manchester.

ANNETT, J. (1971) Acquisition of skill. *Brit. med. Bull.,* **27,** 266–71.

BAER, D. and SHERMAN, J. A. (1964) Reinforcement control of generalised imitation in children. *J. exp. child Psychol.,* **1,** 37–49.

BARNETT, C. D., ELLIS, N. R. and PRYER, M. W. (1959) Stimulus pre-training and the delayed reaction in defectives. *Amer. J. ment. Defic.,* **64,** 104–11.

BATEMAN, B. (1965) *The Illinois Test of Psycholinguistic Abilities in Current Research: Summaries of Studies.* Urbana: Univ. of Illinois Press.

BATEMAN, B. (1968) *Interpretation of the 1961 Illinois Test of Psycholinguistic Abilities.* Seattle: Special Child Publications.

BAUMEISTER, A. A. (1967) Problems in comparative studies of mental retardates and normals. *Amer. J. ment. Defic.,* **71,** 869–75.

BAUMEISTER, A. A. (1968) Learning abilities. In BAUMEISTER, A. A. (ed.) *Mental Retardation: Appraisal, Education, Rehabilitation.* London: Univ. of London Press.

BAUMEISTER, A. A. and BARTLETT, C. J. (1962a) A comparison of the factor structure of normals and retardates on the WISC. *Amer. J. ment. Defic.,* **66,** 641–6.

BAUMEISTER, A. A. and BARTLETT, C. J. (1962b) Further factorial investigations of WISC performance of mental defectives. *Amer. J. ment. Defic.,* **67,** 257–61.

BEIER, E. G., STARKWEATHER, J. A. and LAMBERT, M. J. (1969) Vocabulary usage of mentally retarded children. *Amer. J. ment. Defic.,* **73,** 927–34.

BEREITER, C. and ENGELMANN, S. (1966) *Teaching Disadvantaged Children in the Pre-School.* Englewood Cliffs, NJ: Prentice-Hall.

BERKO, J. (1958) The child's learning of English morphology. *Word,* **14,** 150–77.

BERRY, M. F. (1969) *Language Disorders of Children.* New York: Appleton-Century-Crofts.

BERRY, M. F. and TALBOTT, R. (1966) *Exploratory Test of Grammar.* Cited in Berry, 1969.

BERRY, P. (1971) *Imitation of Language in Subnormal Children.* Unpubl. M.Ed. thesis, Univ. of Manchester.

BIJOU, S. W. and BAER, D. M. (1967) Operant methods in child behaviour and development. In BIJOU, S. W. and BAER, D. M. (eds.) *Child Development: Readings in Experimental Analysis*. New York: Appleton-Century-Crofts.

BILOVSKY, D. and SHARE, J. (1965) The ITPA and Down's Syndrome: an exploratory study. *Amer. J. ment. Defic.*, **70**, 78–82.

BLAKE, K. A. and WILLIAMS, C. L. (1968) *Use of English Morphemes by Retarded, Normal and Superior Children Equated for CA*. Athens: Univ. of Georgia.

BLANCHARD, L. (1964) Speech pattern and etiology in mental retardation. *Amer. J. ment. Defic.*, **68**, 612–27.

BRICKER, W. A. (1972) A systematic approach to language training. In SCHIEFELBUSCH, R. L. (ed.) *The Language of the Mentally Retarded*. Baltimore, Md: Univ. Park Press.

BRICKER, W. A. and BRICKER, D. D. (1970a) A program of language training for the severely language handicapped child. *Except. Child.*, **37**, 101–11.

BRICKER, W. A. and BRICKER, D. D. (1970b) Development of receptive vocabulary in severely retarded children. *Amer. J. ment. Defic.*, **74**, 599–606.

BRICKER, W. A. and BRICKER, D. D. (1973) Behaviour modification programmes. In MITTLER, P. (ed.) *Assessment for Learning in the Mentally Handicapped*. London: Churchill Livingstone; Baltimore, Md: Williams & Wilkins.

BRIMER, M. A. and DUNN, L. M. (1965) *English Picture Vocabulary Test*. Bristol: Educational Evaluation Enterprises.

BROWN, R. (1965) *Social Psychology*. New York: The Free Press.

BRYANT, P. E. (1967) Verbal labelling and learning strategies in normal and severely subnormal children. *Quart. J. exp. Psychol.*, **19**, 155–61.

BUDDENHAGEN, R. G. (1971) *Establishing Vocal Verbalizations in Mute Mongoloid Children*. Champaign, Ill.: Research Press.

BURLAND, R. (1969) The development of the verbal regulation of behaviour in cerebrally palsied (multiply handicapped) children. *J. ment. Subn.*, **15**, 85–9.

BURT, C. (1967) Capacity and achievement. *Education*, 198–201.

CAMPBELL, R. and WALES, R. (1970) The study of language acquisition. In LYONS, J. (ed.) *New Horizons in Linguistics*. Harmondsworth: Penguin.

CARR, D. L., BROWN, L. F. and RICE, V. A. (1967) The PPVT in the assessment of language deficit. *Amer. J. ment. Defic.*, **71**, 937–40.

CARR, J. (1970) Mental and motor development in young mongol children. *J. ment. Defic. Res.*, **14**, 205–20.

CARROLL, J. B. (1953) *The Study of Language: A Survey of Linguistics and Related Disciplines in America*. Cambridge, Mass.: Harvard Univ. Press.

CARROLL, J. B. (1967) Psycholinguistics in the study of mental retardation. In SCHIEFELBUSCH, R. L., COPELAND, R. H. and SMITH, J. O. (eds.)

Language and Mental Retardation. New York: Holt, Rinehart & Winston.

CARROW, M. A. (1968) The development of auditory comprehension of language structure in children. *J. speech hear. Dis.,* **33**, 99–111.

CHALFANT, J. (1968) Systematic language instruction: an approach for teaching receptive language to young trainable children. *Teaching except. Child.,* **1**, 1–13.

CHOMSKY, N. (1957) *Syntactic Structures.* The Hague: Mouton.

CHOMSKY, N. (1959) Review of Skinner's *Verbal Behavior. Language,* **35**, 26–58.

CHOMSKY, N. (1965) *Aspects of the Theory of Syntax.* Cambridge, Mass.: MIT Press.

CLARKE, A. D. B. and CLARKE, A. M. (1973a) Assessment and prediction in the severely subnormal. In MITTLER, P. (ed.) *Assessment for Learning in the Mentally Handicapped.* London: Churchill Livingstone; Baltimore, Md: Williams & Wilkins.

CLARKE, A. M. and CLARKE, A. D. B. (1973b) What are the problems? In CLARKE, A. D. B. and CLARKE, A. M. (eds.) *Mental Retardation and Behavioural Research.* London: Churchill Livingstone; Baltimore, Md: Williams & Wilkins.

CUNNINGHAM, C. and JEFFREE, D. (1971) *Working with Parents: Developing a Workshop Course for Parents of Young Mentally Handicapped Children.* Manchester: National Society for Mentally Handicapped Children, North-West Region.

CRABTREE, M. (1958) *The Houston Test for Language Development.* Houston Test Co.

DARLEY, F. L. and WINITZ, H. (1961) Age of first word: review of research. *J. speech hear. Dis.,* **26**, 272–90.

DAVIS, E. A. (1937) *The Development of Linguistic Skill in Twins, Singletons and Sibs and Only Children from 5–10.* Inst. Child Welf., Monogr. No. 14. Minneapolis: Univ. of Minnesota.

DENNY, M. R. (1964) Research in Learning and Performance. In STEVENS, H. A. and HEBER, R. (eds.) *Mental Retardation: A Review of Research.* Chicago: Univ. of Chicago Press.

DEVER, R. B. and GARDNER, W. I. (1970) Performance of normal and retarded boys on Berko's test of morphology. *Language and Speech,* **13**, 162–81.

DUNN, L. (1959) *The Peabody Picture Vocabulary Test.* Minneapolis: Amer. Guidance Service Inc.

EISENSON, J. (1966) Perceptual disturbances in children with central nervous system dysfunctions and implications for language development. *Brit. J dis. Comm.,* **1**, 21–32.

ERVIN, S. M. (1964) Imitation and structural change in children's language. In LENNEBERG, E. H. (ed.) *New Directions in the Study of Language.* Cambridge, Mass.: MIT Press.

EVANS, D. and HAMPSON, M. (1968) The language of mongols. *Brit. J. dis. Comm.*, **3**, 171–81.

FAWCUS, M. (1965) Speech disorders and therapy in mental subnormality. In CLARKE, A. M. and CLARKE, A. D. B. (eds.) *Mental Deficiency: the Changing Outlook* (2nd edn). London: Methuen.

FLAVELL, J. H., BEACH, D. R. and CHINSKY, J. M. (1966) Spontaneous verbal rehearsal in a memory task as a function of age. *Child Developm.*, **37**, 283–300.

FOULDS, G. A. (1958) Clinical research in psychiatry. *J. ment. Sci.*, **104**, 259–65.

FRANKENBURG, W. K. and DOBBS, J. B. (1967) *Denver Developmental Screening Scale.* Denver: Univ. of Colorado Medical Center.

FRIEDLANDER, B. Z. (1970) Receptive language development in infancy: issues and problems. *Merrill-Palmer Quart. Behavior Developm.*, **16**, 7–51.

FRITH, U. (1971) Spontaneous patterns produced by autistic, normal and subnormal children. In RUTTER, M. (ed.) *Infantile Autism: Concepts, Characteristics and Treatment.* London: Churchill Livingstone.

FURTH, H. (1966) *Thinking without Language: Psychological Implications of Deafness.* New York: The Free Press.

FYGETAKIS, L. and GRAY, B. B. (1970) Programmed conditioning of linguistic competence. *Behavior Res. Therapy*, **8**, 153–63.

GAHAGAN, D. M. and GAHAGAN, G. A. (1970) *Talk Reform: Explorations in Language for Infant School Children.* London: Routledge & Kegan Paul.

GARDNER, J. M. (1969) Behavior modification research in mental retardation: search for an adequate paradigm. *Amer. J. ment. Defic.*, **73**, 844–51.

GARDNER, R. A. and GARDNER, B. T. (1969) Teaching sign language to a chimpanzee. *Science*, **165**, 664–72.

GARDNER, W. I. (1971) *Behavior Modification in Mental Retardation.* Chicago: Aldine Atherton.

GEORGE, R. ST. (1970) The psycholinguistic abilities of children from different ethnic backgrounds. *Austral. J. Psychol.*, **22**, 85–9.

GIEBINK, J. W., NEVILLE, A. R. and DAVIDSON, R. E. (1970) Acquisition of morphological rules and usage as a function of social experience. *Psychology in the Schools*, **7**, 217–22.

GIRARDEAU, F. L. and SPRADLIN, J. E. (1970) *A Functional Analysis Approach to Speech and Language.* ASHA Monogr. No. 14. Washington, DC: American Speech and Hearing Association.

GRAHAM, C. (1967) Ability and attainment tests. *Education*, 902–3, 948–9, 1000–2.

GUNZBURG, H. C. (1966) *Progress Assessment Charts.* London: Nat. Assoc. Ment. Health.

HALL, V. R. (1970) Reinforcement procedures and the increase of functional speech by a brain-injured child. In GIRARDEAU, F. L. and SPRADLIN, J. E. (eds.) *A Functional Approach to Speech and Language.* ASHA

Monogr. No. 14. Washington: American Speech and Hearing Association.

HAYE, J. R. (1970) *Cognition and the Development of Language*. New York and London: Wiley.

HERMELIN, B. (1971) Rules and language. In RUTTER, M. (ed.) *Infantile Autism, Concepts, Characteristics and Treatment*. London: Churchill Livingstone.

HERMELIN, B. and O'CONNOR, N. (1970) *Psychological Experiments with Autistic Children*. London: Pergamon.

HERRIOT, P. (1970) *An Introduction to the Psychology of Language*. London: Methuen.

HERRIOT, P. and LUNZER, E. (1971) *Comprehension and Cognitive Development*. Paper delivered to Research Workshop on 'Language Comprehension and the Acquisition of Knowledge', Durham, North Carolina, April 1971.

HESS, R. D. and SHIPMAN, V. (1965) Early experience and socialisation of cognitive modes in children. *Child Developm.*, **36**, 869–86.

HEWETT, F. M. (1966) Teaching speech to an autistic child through operant conditioning. *Amer. J. Orthopsychiat.*, **35**, 927–36.

HOBSBAUM, A. and MITTLER, P. (1971) *Sentence Comprehension Test. Experimental Edition*. Hester Adrian Research Centre, Univ. of Manchester.

HOGG, J. H. (1973) Personality assessment of the subnormal as the study of learning processes. In MITTLER, P. (ed.) *Assessment for Learning in the Mentally Handicapped*. London: Churchill Livingstone; Baltimore, Md: Williams & Wilkins.

HOWARD, M. J., HOOPS, H. R. and MCKINNON, A. J. (1970) Language abilities of children with differing socio-economic backgrounds. *J. learning Dis.*, **3**, 32–9.

JEFFREE, D. and CASHDAN, A. (1971) Severely subnormal children and their parents: an experiment in language improvement. *Brit. J. educ. Psychol.*, **41**, 184–94.

JEFFREE, D., WHELDALL, K. and MITTLER, P. (1973) The facilitation of two word utterances in two Down's syndrome boys. *Amer. J. ment. Defic.*, **78**, 117–22.

JENSEN, A. R. and ROHWER, W. D. (1963) The effect of verbal mediation on the learning and retention of paired associates by retarded adults. *Amer. J. ment. Defic.*, **68**, 80–4.

JOHNSON, G. O., CAPOBIANCO, R. J. and MILLER, P. Y. (1960) Speech and language development of a group of mentally deficient children enrolled in a training program. *Except. Child*, **27**, 72–7.

JOHNSTON, M. (1968) Echolalia and automatism in speech. In SLOANE, H. N. and MACAULAY, B. D. (eds.) *Operant Procedures in Remedial Speech and Language Training*. New York: Houghton Mifflin.

JORDAN, J. E. (1967) Language and mental retardation. In SCHIEFELBUSCH, R. L., COPELAND, R. H. and SMITH, J. O. (eds.) *Language and Mental Retardation*. New York: Holt, Rinehart & Winston.

KENDLER, T. S. and KENDLER, H. H. (1967) Experimental analysis of inferential behavior in children. In LIPSITT, L. P. and SPIKER, C. S. (eds.) *Advances in Child Development and Behavior*. New York: Academic Press.

KERR, N., MEYERSON, L. and MICHAEL, J. (1965) A procedure for shaping vocalisation in a mute child. In ULLMAN, L. P. and KRASNER, L. (eds.) *Case Studies in Behavior Modification*. New York: Holt, Rinehart & Winston.

KIERNAN, C. K. (1973) Functional analysis. In MITTLER, P. (ed.) *Assessment for Learning in the Mentally Handicapped*. London: Churchill Livingstone; Baltimore, Md: Williams & Wilkins.

KIRK, S. A. (1968) The Illinois Test of Psycholinguistic Abilities: its origins and implications. In HELLMUTH, J. (ed.) *Learning Disorders*, Vol. 3. Seattle: Special Child Publications.

KIRK, S. A. and KIRK, W. (1971) *Psycholinguistic Learning Disabilities: Diagnosis and Remediation*. Urbana: Univ. of Illinois Press.

KIRK, S. A., MCCARTHY, J. J. and KIRK, W. (1968) *Illinois Test of Psycholinguistic Abilities. Revised Edition*. Urbana: Institute for Research in Exceptional Children.

KLAUS, R. A. and GRAY, S. W. (1968) The early training program for disadvantaged children. *Monographs of the Society for Research in Child Development*, **33**, 120.

KOLSTOE, O. P. (1958) Language training of low grade mongoloid children. *Amer. J. ment. Defic.*, **63**, 17–30.

LASSERS, I. and LOW, G. (1960) *A Study of the Relative Effectiveness of Different Approaches of Speech Therapy for Mentally Retarded Children*. Report to Office of Education on Contract 6904. (Cited in Spradlin, 1963.)

LAWTON, D. (1968) *Social Class, Language and Education*. London: Routledge & Kegan Paul.

LEE, L. (1966) Developmental sentence types: a method for comparing normal and deviant syntactic development. *J. speech hear. Dis.*, **31**, 311–30.

LEE, L. L. (1969) *The Northwestern Syntax Screening Test*. Evanston, Ill.: Northwestern Univ. Press.

LEE, L. L. (1970) A screening test for syntax development. *J. speech hear. Dis.*, **35**, 104–12.

LEE, L. and CANTER, S. (1971) Developmental sentence scoring: a clinical procedure for estimating syntactic development in children's spontaneous speech. *J. speech hear. Dis.*, **36**, 315–40.

LENNEBERG, E. H. (1962) Understanding language without ability to speak: a case report. *J. abn. soc. Psychol.*, **65**, 419–25.

LENNEBERG, E. H. (1967) *Biological Foundations of Language*. New York: Wiley.

LENNEBERG, E. H., NICHOLS, I. E. and ROSENBERGER, E. F. (1964) Primitive stages of language development in mongolism. In *Disorders of Communication*, XLII. New York: Assoc. Res. nerv. ment. Dis.

LEREA, L. (1958) Assessing language development. *J. speech hear. Res.*, 1, 75–85.

LEVITT, L. M. (1970) *A Method of Communication for Non-speaking Severely Subnormal Children*. London: Spastics Society.

LEWIS, M. M. (1968) *The Education of Deaf Children: the Possible Place of Finger Spelling and Signing*. London: HMSO.

LOVAAS, I. (1966) A program for the establishment of speech in psychotic children. In WING, J. K. (ed.) *Early Childhood Autism: Clinical, Social, and Educational Aspects*. London: Pergamon.

LOVELL, K. and BRADBURY, B. (1967) The learning of English morphology in educationally subnormal special school children. *Amer. J. ment. Defic.*, 71, 609–15.

LURIA, A. R. (1961) *The Role of Speech in the Regulation of Normal and Abnormal Behaviour*. London: Pergamon.

LURIA, A. R. (1963) *The Mentally Retarded Child*. London: Pergamon.

LYLE, J. G. (1960) The effect of an institution environment upon the verbal development of institutionalised children. *J. ment. Defic. Res.*, 4, 1–23.

LYLE, J. G. (1961) Comparison of the language of normal and imbecile children. *J. ment. Defic. Res.*, 5, 40–50.

MACAULAY, B. D. (1968) A program for teaching speech and beginning reading to nonverbal retardates. In SLOANE, H. N. and MACAULAY, B. D. (eds.) *Operant Procedures in Remedial Speech and Language Training*. New York: Houghton Mifflin.

MCCARTHY, D. (1954) Language development. In CARMICHAEL, L. (ed.) *Manual of Child Psychology*. New York: Wiley.

MCCARTHY, J. J. (1964) Research on the linguistic problems of the mentally retarded. *Ment. Retard. Abstrs.*, 2, 90–6.

MCCARTHY, J. J. and KIRK, S. A. (1961) *Illinois Test of Psycholinguistic Abilities. Experimental Edition*. Urbana: Inst. for Research in Exceptional Children.

MACCUBREY, J. (1971) Verbal operant conditioning with young institutionalised Down's Syndrome children. *Amer. J. ment. Defic.*, 75, 696–701.

MCNEILL, D. (1966) Developmental psycholinguistics. In SMITH, F. and MILLER, G. A. (eds.) *The Genesis of Language*. Cambridge, Mass.: MIT Press.

MCNEILL, D. (1970a) *The Acquisition of Language: The Study of Developmental Psycholinguistics*. New York and London: Harper & Row.

MCNEILL, D. (1970b) The development of language. In MUSSEN, P. H. (ed.) *Carmichael's Manual of Child Psychology* (3rd edn). New York and London: Wiley.

MARINOSSON, G. (1970) Language abilities of normal, ESN and SSN children: a comparative study. In MITTLER, P. (ed.) *The Work of the Hester Adrian Research Centre: A Report for Teachers*. Monogr. suppl., *Teaching and Training*, **8**, 17–21.

MECHAM, M. J. (1955) The development and application of procedures for measuring speech improvement in mentally defective children. *Amer. J. ment. Defic.*, **60**, 301–6.

MECHAM, M. J. and JEX, J. L. (1962) *Picture Speech Discrimination Test.* Provo, Utah: Brigham Young Univ. Press.

MECHAM, M. J., JEX, J. L. and JONES, J. (1967) *Utah Test of Language Development.* Salt Lake City: Communication Research Associates.

MEIN, R. (1961) A study of the oral vocabularies of severely subnormal patients. II. Grammatical analysis of speech samples. *J. ment. Defic. Res.*, **5**, 52–9.

MENYUK, P. (1969) *Sentences Children Use.* Cambridge, Mass.: MIT Press.

MILLER, G. A. (1951) *Language and Communication.* New York: McGraw-Hill.

MILLER, S. A., SHELTON, J. and FLAVELL, J. H. (1970) A test of Luria's hypotheses concerning the development of verbal self-regulation. *Child Developm.*, **41**, 651–65.

MINER, L. E. (1969) Scoring procedures for the length-complexity index: a preliminary report. *J. Comm. Dis.*, **2**, 224–40.

MITTLER, P. (1969) Genetic aspects of psycholinguistic abilities. *J. Child Psychol. Psychiat.*, **10**, 165–76.

MITTLER, P. (1970a) The use of morphological rules by four year old children; an item analysis of the Auditory-Vocal Automatic Test of the ITPA. *Brit. J. dis. Comm.*, **5**, 99–109.

MITTLER, P. (1970b) Biological and social aspects of language development in twins. *Developm. med. Child Neurol.*, **12**, 741–57.

MITTLER, P. (1970c) *Psychological Assessment of Mental and Physical Handicaps.* London: Methuen.

MITTLER, P. (1971) *The Study of Twins.* Harmondsworth: Penguin.

MITTLER, P. (1973a) *Assessment for Learning in the Mentally Handicapped.* London: Churchill Livingstone; Baltimore, Md: Williams & Wilkins.

MITTLER, P. (1973b) The teaching of language. In CLARKE, A. D. B. and CLARKE, A. M. (eds.) *Mental Retardation and Behavioural Research.* London: Churchill Livingstone; Baltimore, Md: Williams & Wilkins.

MITTLER, P. and WARD, J. (1970) The use of the Illinois Test of Psycholinguistic Abilities with English four year old children: a normative and factorial study. *Brit. J. educ. Psychol.*, **40**, 43–53.

MITTLER, P. and WHELDALL, K. (1971) Language comprehension in the severely subnormal. *Bull. Brit. Psychol. Soc.*, **24**, 227A (abstr.).

MITTLER, P., JEFFREE, D., WHELDALL, K. and BERRY, P. (1974) *Assessment and Remediation of Language Comprehension and Production in Severely Subnormal Children.* Final Report to Social Science Research Council (unpubl.). Hester Adrian Research Centre, Univ. of Manchester.

MULLER, M. W. and WEAVER, S. J. (1964) Psycholinguistic abilities of institutionalised and non-institutionalised trainable mental retardates. *Amer. J. ment. Defic.*, **68**, 775–83.

NELSON, R. O. and EVANS, I. (1968) The combination of learning principles and speech therapy techniques in the treatment of non-communicating children. *J. child Psychol. and Psychiat.*, **9**, 111–24.

O'CONNOR, N. and HERMELIN, B. (1963) *Speech and Thought in Severe Subnormality.* London: Pergamon.

O'CONNOR, N. and HERMELIN, B. (1971) Cognitive deficits in children. *Brit. med. Bull.*, **27**, 227–31.

OLSON, D. R. (1970) Language acquisition and cognitive development. In HAYWOOD, H. C. (ed.) *Social-Cultural Aspects of Mental Retardation.* New York: Appleton-Century-Crofts.

OLSON, D. R. (1972) Language use for communication, instruction and thinking. In CARROLL, J. B. and FREEDLE, R. (eds.) *Language Comprehension and the Acquisition of Knowledge.* Washington, DC: Winston.

OSGOOD, C. E. (1957) A behavioristic analysis. In OSGOOD, C. E. (ed.) *Contemporary Approaches to Cognition.* Cambridge, Mass.: Harvard Univ. Press.

OSGOOD, C. E. (1963) Psycholinguistics. In KOCH, S. (ed.) *Psychology: Study of a Science*, Vol. 6. New York: McGraw-Hill.

OSGOOD, C. E. (1968) Towards a wedding of insufficiencies. In DIXON, T. R. and HORTON, D. L. (eds.) *Verbal Behavior and General Behavior Theory.* Englewood Cliffs, NJ: Prentice-Hall.

OSLER, S. F. and TRAUTMAN, G. E. (1961) Concept attainment. II. Effect of stimulus complexity upon concept attainment at two levels of intelligence. *J. exp. Psychol.*, **62**, 9–13.

PARASKEVOPOULOS, J. N. and KIRK, S. A. (1969) *The Development and Psychometric Characteristics of the Revised Illinois Test of Psycholinguistic Abilities.* Urbana: Univ. of Illinois Press.

PARSONS, J. G. (1971) *Aspects of Verbal Behaviour in Hydrocephalic Children.* Unpubl. Ph.D. thesis, Univ. of Sheffield.

PAWLICKI, R. (1970) Behavior therapy research with children: a critical review. *Canad. J. behav. Sci.*, **2**, 163–73.

PEINS, M. (1969) *Bibliography on Speech, Hearing and Language in Relation to Mental Retardation 1900–1968.* Washington, DC: US Dept of Health, Education and Welfare.

PETERSON, R. F. (1968) Imitation: a basic behavioral mechanism. In SLOANE, H. N. and MACAULAY, B. D. (eds.) *Operant Procedures in Remedial Speech and Language Training.* New York: Houghton Mifflin.

PETERSON, R. F. and WHITEHURST, G. J. (1971) A variable influencing the performance of generalised imitative behaviors. *J. appl. Behav. Anal.*, **4**, 1–9.

PETERSON, R. F., MERWIN, M. R. and MOYER, T. J. (1971) Generalised imitation: the effects of experimenter absence, differential reinforcement and stimulus complexity. *J. exp. child Psychol.*, **12**, 114–28.

PREMACK, D. (1970) A functional analysis of language. *J. exp. Anal. Behav.*, **14**, 107–25.

REESE, H. W. and LIPSITT, L. P. (1970) *Experimental Child Psychology.* New York: Academic Press.

RENFREW, C. E. (1971) *Renfrew Language Attainment Scales.* Oxford: Churchill Hospital.

REYNELL, J. K. (1969) *The Reynell Developmental Language Scales.* London: NFER.

REYNOLDS, L. J. (1970) Reinforcement procedures for establishing and maintaining echoic speech by a nonverbal child. In GIRARDEAU, F. L. and SPRADLIN, J. E. (eds.) *A Functional Approach to Speech and Language.* ASHA Monogr. No. 14. Washington, DC: American Speech and Hearing Association.

RISLEY, T. (1966) *Establishment of Verbal Behavior in Deviant Children.* Unpubl. Ph.D. thesis, Univ. of Washington. (Cited by Peterson, 1968.)

RISLEY, T. and WOLF, M. (1967) Establishing functional speech in echolalic children. *Behav. Res. Therapy*, **5**, 73–88.

ROBINSON, W. P. (1971) Social factors and language development in primary school children. In HUXLEY, R. and INGRAM, E. (eds.) *Language Acquisition: Models and Methods.* London and New York: Academic Press.

ROGERS, M. G. H. (1971) *A Study of Language Development in Severe Subnormality.* Unpubl. dissertation, Institute of Child Health, Univ. of London.

ROSENBERG, S. (1970) Problems of language development in the retarded. In HAYWOOD, H. C. (ed.) *Social-Cultural Aspects of Mental Retardation.* New York: Appleton-Century-Crofts.

ROSENBERG, S., SPRADLIN, J. and MABEL, S. (1961) Interaction among retarded children as a function of their relative language skills. *J. abn. soc. Psychol.*, **63**, 402–10.

RUTTER, M. and MITTLER, P. (1972) Environmental influences on language development. In RUTTER, M. and MARTIN, A. (eds.) *The Child with Delayed Speech.* London: Spastics Society and Heinemann.

RUTTER, M. and SUSSENWEIN, I. (1971) A developmental and behavioral approach to the treatment of preschool autistic children. *J. Autism and Childhood Schizophrenia*, **1**, 376–97.

RYCKMAN, D. B. and WIEGERNINK, R. (1969) The factors of the Illinois Test of Psycholinguistic Abilities: a comparison of 18 factor analyses. *Except. Child.*, **36**, 107–13.

SANDERS, B., ROSS, L. E. and HEAL, L. (1965) Reversal and non-reversal shift learning in normal children and retardates of comparable mental age. *J. exp. Psychol.*, **69**, 84–8.

SAUNDERS, E. and MILLER, C. J. (1968) A study of verbal communication in mentally subnormal patients. *Brit. J. dis. Comm.*, **3**, 99–110.

SCHIEFELBUSCH, R. L. (1963) Language studies of mentally retarded children. Monogr. Suppl., *J. speech hear. Dis.*, **10**, 1–108.

SCHIEFELBUSCH, R. L. (1972) *Language of the Mentally Retarded.* Baltimore, Md.: Univ. Park Press.

SCHIEFELBUSCH, R. L., COPELAND, R. H. and SMITH, J. O. (1967) *Language in Mental Retardation.* New York: Holt, Rinehart & Winston.

SCHLANGER, B. B. (1953) Speech therapy results with mentally retarded children in special classes. *Training School Bull.*, **50**, 179–86.

SCHLANGER, B. B. (1954) Environmental influences on the verbal output of mentally retarded children. *J. speech hear. Dis.*, **19**, 339–43.

SCHLANGER, B. B. and GOTTSLEBEN, R. H. (1957) Analysis of speech defects among the institutionalised mentally retarded. *J. speech hear. Dis.*, **22**, 98–103.

SCHUBERT, J. (1969) The V.R.B. Apparatus: an experimental procedure for the investigation of the verbal regulation of behavior. *J. genet. Psychol.*, **114**, 237–52.

SHAW, H. J., MATTHEWS, C. G. and KLOVE, H. (1966) The equivalence of WISC and PPVT IQs. *Amer. J. ment. Defic.*, **70**, 601–4.

SHERIDAN, M. D. (1973) *Developmental Progress of Infants and Young Children.* London: NFER.

SHERIDAN, V. (1964) Development of auditory attention and the use of language symbols. In RENFREW, C. and MURPHY, K. (eds.) *The Child Who Does Not Talk.* London: Spastics Society and Heinemann.

SHERMAN, J. A. (1965) Use of reinforcement and imitation to reinstate verbal behavior in mute psychotics. *J. abn. soc. Psychol.*, **70**, 155–64.

SHRINER, T. H. and SHERMAN, D. (1967) An equation for assessing language development. *J. speech hear. Res.*, **10**, 41–8.

SINGER, B. D. and OSBORN, R. W. (1970) Social class and sex differences in admission patterns of the mentally retarded. *Amer. J. ment. Defic.*, **75**, 160–2.

SKINNER, B. (1957) *Verbal Behaviour.* London: Methuen.

SLOANE, H. N. and MACAULAY, B. D. (1968) *Operant Procedures in Remedial Speech and Language Training.* New York: Houghton Mifflin.

SLOANE, H. N., JOHNSTON, M. K. and HARRIS, F. R. (1968) Remedial procedures for teaching verbal behavior to speech deficient or defective young children. In SLOANE, H. N. and MACAULAY, B. D. (eds.) *Operant Procedures in Remedial Speech and Language Training.* New York: Houghton Mifflin.

SLOBIN, D. I. (1971a) *Psycholinguistics.* London: Scott Foresman.

SLOBIN, D. I. (1971b) Universals of grammatical development in children. In FLORES D'ARCAIS and LEVELT, W. (eds.) *Advances in Psycholinguistics*. Amsterdam: North Holland.

SMITH, P. A. and MARX, R. W. (1971) The factor structure of the revised edition of the Illinois Test of Psycholinguistic Abilities. *Psychology in the Schools*, 8, 349–56.

SPRADLIN, J. E. (1963) Language and communication in mental defectives. In ELLIS, N. R. (ed.) *Handbook of Mental Deficiency*. New York: McGraw-Hill.

SPRADLIN, J. E. (1968) Environmental factors and the language development of retarded children. In ROSENBERG, S. and KOPLIN, J. H. (eds.) *Developments in Applied Psycholinguistics Research*. New York: Macmillan.

SPRADLIN, J. E. and ROSENBERG, S. (1964) Complexity of adult verbal behavior in a dyadic situation with retarded children. *J. abn. soc. Psychol.*, 68, 694–8.

SPRADLIN, J. E. and GIRARDEAU, F. L. (1970) The implications of a functional approach to speech and hearing and therapy. In GIRARDEAU, F. L. and SPRADLIN, J. E. (eds.) *A Functional Approach to Speech and Language*. ASHA Monogr. No. 14. Washington, DC: American Speech and Hearing Association.

SPREEN, O. (1965a) Language functions in mental retardation: a review. I. Language development, types of retardation and intelligence level. *Amer. J. ment. Defic.*, 69, 482–94.

SPREEN, O. (1965b) Language functions in mental retardation: a review. II. Language in higher level performance. *Amer. J. ment. Defic.*, 70, 351–62.

STAATS, A. W. (1968) *Language, Learning and Cognition*. New York: Holt, Rinehart & Winston.

STRAZZULA, M. (1953) Speech problems of the mongoloid child. *Pediatrics*, 8, 268–73.

TALKINGTON, L. W. and HALL, S. M. (1970) Matrix language program with mongoloids. *Amer. J. ment. Defic.*, 75, 88–91.

TEMPLIN, M. C. (1957) *Certain Language Skills in Children*. Minneapolis: Univ. of Minnesota Press.

THOMPSON, M. M. (1963) Psychological characteristics relevant to the education of the preschool mongoloid child. *Ment. Retard.*, 1, 148–51.

THOMPSON, C. W. and MAGARET, A. (1947) Differential test responses of normals and mental defectives. *J. abn. soc. Psychol.*, 42, 285–93.

TIZARD, B. (1971) Environmental effects on language development: a study of residential nurseries (paper delivered to Annual Conference of The British Psychological Society, Exeter, April 1971). *Bull. Brit. Psychol. Soc.*, 24, 232.

TIZARD, J. (1964) *Community Services for the Mentally Handicapped*. London: Oxford Univ. Press.

TIZARD, J. (1970) The role of social institutions in the causation, prevention and alleviation of retarded performance. In HAYWOOD, H. C. (ed.) *Social-Cultural Aspects of Mental Retardation.* New York: Appleton-Century-Crofts.

TRABASSO, T. (1972) Mental operations in language comprehension. In CARROLL, J. B. and FREEDLE, R. (eds.) *Language Comprehension and the Acquisition of Knowledge.* Washington, DC: Winston.

VANDENBERG, S. G. (1968) *Progress in Human Behavior Genetics.* Baltimore: Johns Hopkins Univ. Press.

VAN RIPER, J. (1954) *Speech Correction: Principles and Methods.* Englewood Cliffs, NJ: Prentice-Hall.

WATTS, A. F. (1944) *Language and Mental Development of Children.* London: Harrap.

WEBB, C. E. and KINDE, S. (1968) Speech, language and hearing of the mentally retarded. In BAUMEISTER, A. A. (ed.) *Mental Retardation.* London: Univ. of London Press.

WEENER, P., BARRIT, L. S. and SEMMEL, M. I. (1967) A critical evaluation of the Illinois Test of Psycholinguistic Abilities. *Except. Child.,* **33,** 373–84.

WEIR, M. and STEVENSON, H. W. (1959) The effects of vocalisation in children's learning as a function of chronological age. *Child Developm.,* **30,** 143–9.

WEISBERG, P. (1971) Operant procedures with the retardate: an overview of laboratory research. In ELLIS, N. R. (ed.) *International Review of Research in Mental Retardation,* Vol. 5. New York and London: Academic Press.

WHELAN, E. (1973) Developing work skills: a systematic approach. In MITTLER, P. (ed.) *Assessment for Learning in the Mentally Handicapped.* London: Churchill Livingstone; Baltimore, Md: Williams & Wilkins.

WOLSKI, W. (1962) *The Michigan Picture Language Inventory.* Ann Arbor: Univ. of Michigan Press.

YODER, D. (1970) The reinforcing properties of a television presented listener. In GIRARDEAU, F. L. and SPRADLIN, J. E. (eds.) *A Functional Approach to Speech and Language.* ASHA Monogr. No. 14. Washington, DC: American Speech and Hearing Association.

ZEAMAN, D. and HOUSE, B. J. (1963) The role of attention in retardate discrimination learning. In ELLIS, N. R. (ed.) *Handbook of Mental Deficiency.* New York: McGraw-Hill.

M. Fawcus and R. Fawcus

Disorders of communication

Introduction

A disorder of communication may be described as any chronic limitation of an individual's ability to engage in social behaviour involving verbal and sometimes non-verbal processes.

Breakdown in communication may occur at any point in the complex sensori-motor cycle and in some cases will occur at several stages. A retarded child, for example, frequently has any deviant articulatory pattern blamed upon his low intelligence. Whilst this may possibly be responsible for the slow development of language, the suggestion ignores the likelihood of sensori-motor dysfunction, hearing loss and unfavourable environmental factors.

Intellectual abilities have a bearing on many features of both learning and performance of communication skills. The normal infant may be expected to achieve considerable control of the necessary perceptual, semantic and syntactic phonological skills over a remarkably short period. Within the group of children of normal and superior intelligence there is, as might be anticipated, considerable variation in the rate of development of the integral skills. The principal feature of the linguistic development of the subnormal child is a delay in semantic and syntactic processing which may or may not be accompanied by a delay in phonological skills.

The acquisition and performance of linguistic skills involves a high level of information processing and represents the most complex universally observable area of skilled behaviour. Vowels, diphthongs and continuant consonants (w, m, n, ng, l, r, y) consist of complex patterns of harmonics achieved by momentary postures of the upper respiratory tract. The variable resonance chambers modulate the laryngeal tone to produce such diverse information as dialectal differences, intonation patterns and affective states.

Plosive, fricative and affricative consonants play a major part in providing a phonological skeleton in most languages. Voiceless consonants (p, t, k, f, v, th, s, sh, ch) generally consist of characteristic high frequency patterns differentiated by duration, mode and place of production. The frequency range of this group is from 1,000 Hz to the upper limits of the audio frequency range.

The voiced counterparts of this group are formed by combining the high frequency elements with the low frequency larynx output (*b, d, g, v, th, z, j*). Complex perceptual processing is obviously vital to the development of communication. The auditory channel is of primary importance in all except children with a severe hearing loss. At higher levels of cerebral function, the neural analogues of acoustic information are correlated with stored previous inputs to achieve semantic matching.

The output stage of language demands the selection of specific neural information with as much, if not greater, precision than the input process. Generation of a speech sound, a syllable or a chain of syllables requires the organization of a series of major and minor feedback loops. Although hearing is of singular importance during the development of language, it is the kinaesthetic feedback channel which is pre-eminent in the performance. A child with little or no useful hearing may go on to learn reasonably fluent intelligible speech whilst a mature speaker may lose his hearing completely and yet retain a fluency and accuracy only a little below his previous performance.

Incidence and prevalence

Two facts emerge very clearly from studying the literature on the prevalence of speech disorders in the mentally subnormal: firstly, that there is a very much higher incidence of communication problems than amongst the normal population, and secondly that, not surprisingly, the incidence increases as the IQ decreases. Surveys have also shown (Schlanger and Gottsleben, 1957; Blanchard, 1964) that there is a particularly strong link between mongolism and communication disorders. This is perhaps not surprising when one considers some of the physical abnormalities associated with Down's syndrome. These will be discussed later under articulation and voice. Only one area of conflicting findings seems to exist, and this is in the prevalence of stuttering.

One of the problems in any 'head-counting' survey is the fact that criteria will obviously differ in deciding whether or not there is a communication problem. For example, dialectal variants with which one is not familiar may render speech unintelligible. Within the subject's own 'speech environment', however, no such problem exists. In such circumstances it is very easy to label speech as 'poor' or 'deviant' when it is the listener's ear which should really be considered at fault. Taking these factors into account, however, there seems little doubt that a great many subnormal subjects have handicapping communication problems which probably prevent them functioning at their highest potential level.

A statistical survey carried out in London by Burt in the 1920s (Burt, 1951) showed that 'severe defects of speech' occurred in just over 1 per cent of normal children (the control group); in over 5 per cent of backward children; and in nearly 11 per cent of those children considered to be mentally deficient. Burt also mentions the results of a survey carried out by Lloyd in Birmingham at the same time, in which severe speech defects were found in ·5 per cent of the (normal) control group, in just over 5 per cent of the backward, and in nearly 15 per cent of the mentally deficient. In the London survey, and taking mild defects into account, Burt estimated that nearly one-quarter of mentally deficient children surveyed showed some defect of speech. It is interesting to compare these figures with those of Wallin (1949) who states that in St Louis over 26 per cent of pupils in special schools had defective speech, compared with 2·8 per cent in 'the regular elementary and high school grades'. Wallin also showed that there are a higher number of articulatory disorders among the mentally deficient children examined than among the normal group – just over 81 per cent of all defects in the former and 57 per cent in the latter.

A more recent survey carried out by Schlanger and Gottsleben (1957) among 516 residents at The Training School, Vineland, New Jersey, showed that no less than 79 per cent had 'varying types and levels of speech defectiveness'. They comment, 'It is interesting to note that practically all the subjects with voice and stuttering defects had, in addition, some degree of articulatory impairment.' The authors attempted to discover the incidence of defective speech amongst the different aetiological groups which come under the broad heading mental retardation. They found that the greatest incidence occurred in the mongol group (of whom 95 per cent had defects of articulation, 72 per cent had voice disorders, and 45 per cent stammered). In the organic group, defective articulation occurred in 84 per cent, 56 per cent had a voice disorder, and 18 per cent stammered. They discovered that the lowest incidence of defective speech was in the familial group, where 66 per cent had some defect of articulation, 22 per cent had voice disorders, and 10 per cent stammered. The lower incidence amongst the familial group 'is to be expected because of a lesser degree of pathology underlying their retardation'. Schlanger and Gottsleben themselves suggest that the very high incidence of defective speech at The Training School is in part due to the fact that only 12 per cent of the school population come in the familial group. In addition, both authors have training and considerable experience in speech pathology and therapy, and their criteria are therefore probably more strict in deciding what constitutes defective speech.

Although there have been several studies of the incidence of speech defects amongst the mentally retarded, not all of these have shown the relative incidence in what were recognized as the three main grades. Kennedy (1930) attempted such a survey, and found that 42 per cent of 249 feeble-minded patients had speech disorders ranging from slight to severe; 71 per cent of 27 imbeciles had speech defects; and none of the 32 idiots examined showed meaningful speech. The age range of the group studied was 5 to 38 years.

In a study of 2,522 institutionalized patients, Sirkin and Lyons (1941) found that 31 per cent of patients with IQs over 69 had speech defects; 47 per cent of the feeble-minded group showed defective speech; and 74 per cent of the imbecile group. Sachs (1951) in a study of 210 feeble-minded and imbecile patients (aged 10–20 years) reported that 57 per cent had defective speech. An analysis of the patients with speech defects showed that 18 per cent of the 'borderline' group had speech defects, 44 per cent of the feeble-minded group, and 79 per cent of the imbecile group.

Three more recent studies have all confirmed earlier findings on the prevalence of communication problems amongst the institutionalized retarded. Saunders and Miller (1968) assessed 1,005 patients at the Manor Hospital, Surrey: 482 males between the ages of 5 and 82 years, and 523 females between 7 and 80 years. They looked at comprehension and use of spoken language, intelligibility of speech, fluency and voice quality. The patients' verbal communication was assessed, and the results examined according to sex, chronological age and intelligence. They concluded that 'normal speech did not occur in more than 42 per cent of any of the groups and a large number of patients were considered to have inadequate verbal communication'.

Of 216 patients examined at Porterville State Hospital (Sheehan *et al.*, 1968) 50 per cent had no speech at all or else severely delayed language development. They found that dental abnormalities and articulation disorders were common, and only 12 per cent of the patients seen had normal speech. This was followed up by a further study (Martyn *et al.*, 1969) at Camarillo State Hospital, California. 'Individual diagnostic speech evaluations' were made on a total of 346 patients. In this study, more than a third of the patients had articulation disorders and almost a third showed lack of or delayed language development.

Two further studies amongst the educable mentally retarded show widely differing results: Donovan (1957) found that 8 per cent of 2,000 educable children had severe defects of articulation, whilst Steinman, Grossman and Reece (1963) considered that 53 per cent of 1,000 children examined had defective speech. As Matthews (1957) points out, 'Variations in the incidence figures are probably due to differences in criteria of what constitutes a speech defect, and to differences in the composition of the retarded group studied.' This high incidence of speech defects would seem to suggest that mental deficiency is the *cause* of many of these disorders of speech and language. As Kastein (1956) has pointed out, however, 'The child's label of gross (mental) impairment does not necessarily indicate the cause for his language and speech deficiency.'

Matthews (1957) has said, 'In view of the high incidence of speech and hearing problems among mentally retarded children, it is not surprising that communication disorders are often thought to result from mental deficiency.' He goes on to say, 'The well-trained speech and hearing therapist should recognize that there may be many explanations of delayed or defective speech which have no relation to intellectual retardation.'

Becky (1942), in a study of fifty children with delayed speech, found that there were a number of constitutional, environmental, and psychological factors, other than mental retardation, to explain the retardation of speech. Matthews (1957) lists brain injury, glandular dysfunction, emotional disturbance, and hearing loss as aetiological factors of speech disorders in mental deficiency.

Berry and Eisenson (1956) are in agreement with these findings and point of view. They say,

> Despite the very high incidence of speech defects among the feeble-minded, low intelligence is probably not a direct cause of defective speech production, though it is undoubtedly directly associated with poor linguistic ability. There are many organic conditions, such as cretinism, mongolism and brain damage, which are responsible at once for both the lowered intelligence and the defective speech of the individual. The amount of intelligence needed for the correct production and control of speech sounds is not great.

These writers emphasize the point that there may be a common aetiological factor (or even factors) underlying both the mental deficiency and the speech or language problem. Furthermore, it will be shown that the speech disorder itself may be largely or in part responsible for the retarded intellectual development.

The efficacy of remedial measures

Because of the generally pessimistic view of achieving any lasting improvement, the field of subnormality was not a popular area with many speech therapists. As some of the early therapists came from the field of speech training, the emphasis tended to be on improving articulation. For a number of reasons, such procedures generally proved to be unproductive: treatment periods were too widely spaced, the children were frequently too immature and therapists lacked the necessary knowledge of learning theory and training procedures. Over the past two decades, however, attitudes have changed and many therapists are now working with both the mildly and severely subnormal. Too many of these appointments are still on a very limited sessional basis, but in the United Kingdom there are now a number of full-time appointments in institutions for the more severely handicapped. A number of influences have been responsible for this change – including work by Clarke and Clarke (1953) and others, showing that the IQ was not so constant a factor as had been imagined, and the increasing awareness of the adverse effects of poor environment on intellectual development. In addition it has been increasingly realized that many retarded children and adults are not functioning at their highest potential level because of communication problems.

There is still a continuing shortage of speech therapists, and often a lack of funds to provide an adequate establishment in centres for the subnormal. The question of training aides has been discussed and Aronson (1968) has reported on their successful use with severely subnormal children at North Jersey Training School. She found a marked improvement in both language development and IQ (from 10–20) at the conclusion of a two-year training programme. Guess, Smith and Ensminger (1971) have also reported favourably on the use of former psychiatric aides as 'language developmentalists'.

The use of speech therapy aides is naturally a controversial one, but speech therapists are realizing the need to cooperate more closely with parents, teachers and others in developing language and improving every aspect of communication. Where a speech therapist has only one or two sessions in training schools for the subnormal, then it would seem to be a more realistic goal to work in an advisory capacity with parents and teachers, rather than try to see a handful of the children needing speech therapy for a single half-hour session each week.

Without speech as an adequate means of self-expression and communication, the child's intellectual and emotional development will suffer, and the resulting anxiety and frustration may produce behaviour problems. Regarding the effect of defective speech on education, Burt (1951) has this to say: 'The handicaps imposed by defective articulation are most easily seen in oral and linguistic subjects. More particularly it is liable to hinder the child's early efforts at phonic analysis, and so prevent him from learning to read as quickly as the rest.' Defective speech may, in fact, be a considerable factor in producing backwardness and, further still, in preventing the child from benefiting from special educational or training programmes available.

Nisbet (1953) has made an interesting contribution on the relationship between environment, verbal ability, and intellectual development. He says,

> Previous studies have shown from the testing of children from institutions, of only children, and of twins, that lack of contact with adults results in retardation of verbal development; and there is substantial evidence to suggest that ability with words is of importance not only in verbal tests but in all abstract thinking.

He quotes Terman and Merrill (1937), who say, 'Language, essentially, is the shorthand of the higher thought processes, and the level at which this shorthand functions is one of the most important determinants of the level of the processes themselves.'

While it is generally recognized that there is an intimate connection between thought and language, what is not always appreciated is the effect of language deprivation on the thought processes of a child, for example, the deaf mute. It is obvious that thought must use symbols of some sort, or what Pavlov (1941) termed 'the signals of signals'. Clearly the deaf mute builds up some sort of process of symbolization, but words are the most obvious, the most flexible, discriminative, and the widest in range of all possible symbols. Nisbet (1953) quotes Ballard's (1934) conclusion: 'Admitting frankly that thought can function without language, we must also point out that it cannot function well without it, and that though it can do without it, it very rarely does.' Thus speech deprivation may not only restrict communication and experience, but depending upon its degree, may even limit the development of the thought processes, and hence intelligence.

The now famous study of twins of normal intelligence by Luria and Yudovich (1959) is relevant in this context. A pair of twins were studied who, at the age of 5 years, communicated only with one another, possessing a very limited vocabulary. Their comprehension was also limited, and they showed no interest in listening to stories. 'While our twins understood perfectly speech that was directly related to an object or action which preoccupied them, they were not in a position to understand speech when it was not directly connected with a concrete situation and took a developed narrative form.' Their play was primitive and monotonous. There was no constructional play, and any meaningful or creative activities were rare. They were unable to draw or model in clay. Speech which consisted mainly of exclamations was, as Luria described it, 'locked in activity', and was not used in any way to organize or direct activity. After an initial period of observation, the two children were removed from the twin situation, and were each placed in a separate kindergarten group. This separation rapidly resulted in an improvement in play activity and the development of constructional activity, with the ability to formulate a project. Instead of scribbles, the children's drawings became, to use Luria's words, 'Goal driven, differentiated and objective'. 'Even more significant', he said, 'was the fact that the whole structure of the mental life of the twins was simultaneously and sharply changed. Once they acquired an objective language system, the children were able to formulate the aims of their activity verbally, and after only three months we observed the beginnings of meaningful play.'

Furthermore, language training in one twin resulted in increased perception of speech and certain intellectual operations, such as the ability to classify. Hermelin and O'Connor have commented, 'The role of language may be decisive for the degree of efficiency with which imbeciles may be able to master problems as distinct from acquiring skills' (1963).

Schneider and Vallon (1955) have published the results of their work with mentally retarded children at the Westchester School for Retarded Children, and have concluded that

There is definitely a place for speech therapy in the educational or training programmes for the moderately and severely retarded child, and that not only can speech therapy be successfully integrated into almost any training programme for such children but that inherent in such a programme are potential values that challenge the imagination.

Supporting their contention that speech therapy has a place in the rehabilitation of the defective child, they say,

Those children who proceeded to develop the ability to communicate verbally have gained considerably more than can be measured by the number of words they have learned. The mere ability to express one's wants or needs in a socially acceptable manner, let alone the facility of fulfilling one's wants or needs through verbal communication, is indeed an invaluable asset to the child on an intellectual, an emotional, and a social level. . . . With greater facility in verbal expression seemed to come a reduction in anxiety-producing situations, which in turn led to a reduction in a-social behaviour, and has, in many instances, made for a happier and better adjusted individual.

Rittmanic (1958) reported a noticeable improvement as a result of a three-month oral language programme, in which a group of institutionalized but educable mentally retarded children were seen five times a week for a period of fifteen to twenty minutes. Kolstoe (1958) found that language training with low-grade mongoloid children resulted not only in an increase in language abilities, but also in a statistically significant increase in IQ. Of 169 institutionalized patients selected for a three and a half year therapy programme (mean length of treatment five months), Sirkin and Lyons (1941) reported that 52 per cent of the total benefited. Divided into categories, improvement was shown in 79 per cent of the borderline, 59 per cent of the educationally subnormal, and 26 per cent of the moderately subnormal group.

Encouraging reports on the results of speech and language therapy with mentally retarded children have also been published by Schlanger (1953a, b) and Strazzulla (1953).

A successful response to speech therapy may be predicted, provided that:

1. the patient has sufficient ability to cooperate with the therapist in carrying out simple instructions;
2. the patient's attention can be gained and then maintained for a reasonable period of time;
3. rapport between patient and therapist has been established, so that the patient has confidence in the therapist and will cooperate with her;
4. anxiety has been eliminated from the learning situation, enabling the patient to function at his highest intellectual level;
5. all distracting stimuli have been removed, such as noise and unwanted equipment;
6. the patient is adequately motivated;
7. the material used is meaningful, and so presented that the patient's interest is stimulated;
8. stages in treatment are so graded that the patient may always succeed at one stage before the next is attempted;
9. speech correction can be carried out at frequent intervals (at least two or three times a week), or else followed up by regular and wisely supervised practice periods;
10. the cooperation of parents, teachers, and all those responsible for the patient's welfare has been gained;
11. the physical handicaps are such that they may to some extent be overcome.

Where the prognosis is in any doubt when the patient is first assessed, a trial period of speech therapy may provide the answer to the question, 'Can this child benefit from treatment?' As Kastein (1956) says, 'The child's response to integrative language and speech therapy should be taken into consideration before his mental potential can be assessed with any degree of accuracy. His response to such therapy is, in fact, an index of his potential.' The same may be said to be true of the adult patient. As Berry and Eisenson (1956) comment, 'Low intelligence undoubtedly is responsible for many cases of delay in speech, but speech delay also is the cause for much apparent low intelligence.' Furthermore,

> There is some evidence to the effect that when children are taught to speak there is a concomitant increase in their IQs. Whether this increase results directly from the ability of the child to use language in a conventional manner, or whether the child who speaks generally makes a more adequate adjustment to his environment, and to the taking of intelligence tests, is not certain.

Hubschman (1967) used behavioural shaping techniques and reinforcement procedures in a daily programme of language stimulation for nine institutional-ized mongols, matched for age, sex, IQ and mental age with a control group. No improvement was reported after a period of six months, but by eighteen months there were significant increases in mental age, intelligence quotient and social quotient.

With the improvement in language assessment techniques, the measurement of response to therapy is becoming a more reliable procedure. Guess, Smith and Ensminger (1971) describe the use of the Illinois Test of Psycholinguistic Abilities (McCarthy and Kirk, 1961) and the Mecham Verbal Language Development Scales (Mecham, 1958) in assessing the results of an eighteen-month language programme. Small groups of moderately and severely retarded children responded encouragingly to 'systematic and intense language training'. Discussing the results, the authors comment, 'the type of low functioning, fairly old and in some cases, multiply handicapped children included in the programme have traditionally been considered a difficult group with whom to work effec-tively'.

Let Matthews (1957) have the final word: 'In making a decision it would be well to remember that in a high-grade defective adequate speech may make the difference between self-sufficiency and dependency – between a lifetime in an institution at tax-payers' expense and vocational adjustment in society.'

With increasing awareness of the importance of differential diagnosis in all communication problems, and with improvement in assessment techniques, there is far less chance of a child being labelled 'mentally deficient' and other causative factors being overlooked. What we must always be on the alert for are discrepancies in test results which may indicate that the child's verbal ability is not in line with his mental age. It is still all too easy, in a child who obviously 'hears', to overlook quite handicapping degrees of high frequency hearing loss. Having labelled a child as mentally defective, then all communication failures may be blamed on his lack of intelligence when, in fact, his overall performance may be depressed by his verbal limitations. There seems little doubt that, if programmes are of sufficient intensity and duration and are planned on appro-priate lines, then significant improvement in language and social skills does take place. It also seems clear that the progress made cannot be measured in terms of language achievement alone, but also in terms of increased confidence and social adjustment.

Disorders of language

(a) DEVELOPMENTAL DELAY

Speech therapists are frequently asked to advise the parents of pre-school children who exhibit no evidence of neuromuscular or perceptual dysfunction, are of normal intelligence with no serious behavioural problems who may be delayed up to two years in either understanding or production of language (Greene, 1967).

The introduction of more sensitive assessments of language has resulted in a substantial improvement in the service which speech therapists can offer to teachers, psychologists, paediatricians and parents. The ITPA is at present employed by a few therapists working in close conjunction with psychologists. The RDLS (Reynell, 1969) is more commonly employed. It is faster to administer and consists of items which are interesting and attractive to the vast majority of children for whom it was designed. The age range is from 18 months to 6 years, and an alternative form of receptive language assessment is specially provided for children with severe physical handicaps.

(b) THE EFFECTS OF LOW INTELLIGENCE

A useful distinction may be drawn between the different conditions which prevail in the familial and pathological groups of subnormal children. The child in the familial group is usually required to learn linguistic skills with a relatively normal but slowly developing sensori-motor mechanism, below average intellectual capacity and an environment in which neither the necessary interest nor skill in teaching language is likely to be present. The child with a history of pathology may have to develop in a similar milieu with the added problems of a damaged sensori-motor system and even less intellectual capacity. Many of the latter group, however, are born into families where both interest and some skill in language teaching are clearly in evidence.

Vocabulary acquisition may be impeded by environmental factors, retarded conceptual development or disordered processing at either peripheral or central stages.

Brook (1966) and Mein and O'Connor (1960) give details of the vocabulary of different populations of institutionalized severely subnormal individuals. Brook comments that:

> The usual tests of vocabulary, the general approach and strategy employed by the speech therapist in schools and general hospitals and so forth, are not valid in such an institution. To illustrate, a 'sister' is no longer a relative, but is the female nurse in charge of a ward. Words in everyday use outside such as 'bus', 'grocer' and 'Father' are found to have few practical associations for these patients. On the other hand words such as 'Charge Nurse', 'stocktaking' and 'injection' are familiar words full of real meaning.

In cases of gross intellectual deficiency the patient is unlikely ever to develop meaningful speech. He may acquire a vocabulary of a few familiar words, and even understand simple commands, but he will not use speech as a means of communication in any real sense. In some low-grade defectives 'there may be an excessive flow of words, but the thought content is elementary, frequently irrelevant, and the vocabulary is limited' (Morley, 1957). Of 32 profound subnormals examined, Kennedy (1930) found that 20 were mute, 10 'jabbered' with an occasional intelligent word, 1 showed echolalia, and 1 had irrelevant speech.

Various investigators have shown that the age at which children first begin to use words and sentences is directly related to intelligence, and general mental retardation is probably the most common single factor in speech retardation. However, only in cases of gross intellectual deficiency would it be true to say that mental retardation is responsible for failure to develop speech at all.

The moderately subnormal vary considerably in their language ability, and much will depend on the stimulation provided by their environmental background. They show a very marked delay in the acquisition of speech: Wallin (1949) found that they used their first words at 2 years 3 months, and their first sentences at 3 years 7 months on the average. They will be unable to comprehend complex commands, and will experience difficulty in formulating sentences for narrative purposes – in describing a picture for example. Attempts may be telegrammatic in form, but they can communicate, and may 'converse' on a simple, concrete level. Vocabulary is limited to words within their more immediate physical environment.

Educationally subnormal children (mild) may use normal sentence construction, but may always prove to be linguistically inadequate in giving complex explanations. Onset of first words and sentences may be retarded, but much of their later verbal limitations may be the result of a restricted language background. This is particularly true where the familial group is concerned.

(c) HEARING LOSS

If hearing loss is sufficiently profound, and is either congenital or acquired before the development of speech, then speech and language will fail to develop once the babbling stage has passed. The child may learn to lip-read and understand simple and familiar speech without special training, but will be able to communicate himself solely through gesture and sublinguistic utterances. Should speech fail to develop, then the possibility of hearing loss should be investigated as early as possible. Unfortunately, deafness may not be detected, so that the most critical period for listening to and learning speech may be lost (Fry and Whetnall, 1964). Once again, the importance of early investigation and careful differential diagnosis cannot be over-stressed – not only because of the importance of early auditory training, but also because of the danger of incorrectly labelling the child as mentally defective. This is particularly true of the child with high-frequency deafness (Foale and Paterson, 1954).

Ives (1967) has outlined the specific tests available for the assessment of conceptual and linguistic development in children with disorders of hearing.

(d) APHASIA

Developmental aphasia is a rare disorder of language or symbolization in which the child fails to comprehend the spoken or written word (receptive or sensory aphasia), or is unable to express himself through language (expressive or motor aphasia). Few cases show an isolated receptive or expressive disturbance, and most patients show some impairment of other language faculties, such as reading (dyslexia) or writing (dysgraphia). Aphasia is a not uncommon condition in the middle-aged and elderly, associated with cerebral vascular lesions, but it is symptomatic of any infective or traumatic lesion involving appropriate areas of the cerebral cortex. Associated with these disturbances of language is a condition known as apraxia. Russell Brain (1952) defines apraxia as 'an inability to carry out a purposive movement, the nature of which the patient understands, in the absence of severe motor paralysis, sensory loss, and ataxia'.

In mental deficiency, and in considering delay or failure in speech development, we are naturally much more interested in developmental aphasia. Mykelbust (1957) mentions anoxia, Rh incompatibility, rubella, cerebral haemorrhage due to birth injury, and encephalopathic diseases such as meningitis and encephalitis, as the most common aetiological factors in aphasia in children. Aphasia may or may not be associated with mental retardation. Receptive aphasia is believed to be an uncommon condition in children, but varying degrees of expressive aphasia may be more common than is realized. The possibility of aphasia should be considered where a child shows an atypical or patchy performance on intelligence tests, performing well on performance tests, but showing a markedly lower score on verbal tests. West (1957) has said, 'The striking thing about the aphasic is the disparity between his language associations and the rest of his mental processes; his power to associate experiences is relatively normal, except for those which have only arbitrary and symbolic meanings.' He continues, 'He thinks in terms of real objects. Words are abstractions; they constitute a type of association with which he cannot deal.'

(e) LACK OF STIMULATION AND MOTIVATION

Cases are sometimes referred for treatment where speech has failed to develop in the absence of any apparent mental retardation, organic cause, or emotional disturbance. Such cases may occur when the young child is left alone a great deal, and generally deprived of human contact. On the other hand, the need for speech may never be created if parents are over-solicitous and anticipate the child's every need. As Van Riper (1952) says, 'The law of least effort is a rather fundamental determinant of human effort, and when children can get their wishes fulfilled without employing speech, they never acquire this all-important tool.'

Deprivation of affection and maternal care (such as may result in the case of children from institutions and large families) may be a very potent factor in the delayed acquisition of speech. The deprived child has little stimulation or motivation to acquire speech, and may therefore be very backward in learning to talk. Nisbet (1953) has already been quoted in this chapter on the relation of family size to verbal ability, and he also mentions the verbal retardation of institutionalized children.

Ainsworth (1962) has said: 'The specific aspects more seriously affected by continuing deprivation have been found repeatedly to be in language and social development.' The whole question of deprivation and its effect on language, and in turn the possible effects on intellectual growth, suggests the importance of a comprehensive and systematic programme of language training. (See Chapter 4.)

Remedial measures

Treatment will obviously depend on the aetiological factors involved in each case. The importance of making a careful differential diagnosis has already been stressed, not only because it is all too easy to blame mental retardation for delayed or inadequate language development, but also because a failure to recognize the real cause may deprive the child of the appropriate treatment or training he needs.

The speech therapist, working in the ESN School or Training School, will usually spend far more time on language stimulation and development than on speech correction of articulatory defects. Indeed, it is in encouraging the development and use of language that there is most possibility of achievement. Irwin (1959) stated that, 'For the mentally defective child the improvement of language is a much more realistic goal than the correction of specific sound defects', and she recommends a programme in which 'improvement in language should take precedence over the correction of specific sounds'.

In the Hospital Service similar emphasis has been placed on the educational nature of the 'therapy' and the importance of language. The speech therapist, whether working in the hospital or in the community, will typically be engaged in:

(a) *An advisory role* in relation to parents of very young retarded children. Medical advice is rarely explicit and frequently terse and pessimistic. Advice could also be given by psychologists, but their knowledge of language development and language stimulation techniques is usually more rudimentary than a speech therapist's.

(b) *Demonstration and training* for parents or surrogates. Demonstration is far more useful than even a series of talks. The vast majority of parents and surrogates tend to know what to do but are anxious about 'doing the wrong thing' when attempting to help with language stimulation. Sociolinguists have underlined class differences in language teaching practices. Normally, it is found that unless domestic and possibly psychiatric factors are extremely burdensome, parents will usually cooperate (Cashdan, 1969). Observation of differences in parental cooperation would suggest that the affective state of the mother will have a profound effect on the enthusiasm with which she engages in language training. Precise delineation of goals and careful encouragement will greatly assist parents or ward staff in their efforts to help the child.

(c) *Intensive training*. Some speech therapists consider that it is important to augment advice and demonstration by brief intensive periods of language stimulation. These are particularly valuable if:

(i) the child has apparently reached a plateau (e.g. six months with no observable change in language or intelligibility) – the most cooperative and capable of parents will often become discouraged if no improvement is evident;

(ii) no parental or substitute assistance is forthcoming. So far only very limited domiciliary facilities are available, but with many families this would provide the only answer to overwhelming domestic difficulties. Peripatetic teachers visit pre-school children diagnosed as suffering from hearing loss and there would appear to be no reason why parents of children with other communication handicaps should not receive this type of assistance.

(d) *Behaviour modification*. The achievement of such basic steps as encouraging the child to listen or to concentrate for any period is of primary importance. Traditional methods whether employed by parents, teachers or therapists have consisted of establishing a relationship with the child and gradually attempting to increase both the duration and depth of concentration. Spradlin (1968) and Yule and Berger (1971) describe behavioural modification techniques designed to remove the 'hit or miss' element from language teaching techniques with the subnormal. Although the reinforcing stimuli may be identical with those employed by parent or therapist, the basic difference lies in the systematic mode of presentation and the careful recording of the subject's responses. Wing (1966) suggests that individuals in the environment of the subnormal or autistic child should be given specific training in behaviour modification techniques in order to facilitate language development. This approach is described in great detail in Chapter 12.

(e) *Language stimulation*. In the case of the physically neglected and emotionally deprived child, every effort should be made so to adjust the environment that his physical and emotional needs are satisfied. The therapist can do much to help parents provide home conditions which will facilitate the optimum development of language within the framework of the child's mental ability and his level of physical maturation. Parents need an acceptance and understanding of the child's limitations, and an awareness of his need for additional stimulation and encouragement. He must be treated as a 'belonging' member of the family unit, in which he may feel loved and secure. He needs an environmental background in which he is exposed to (but not bombarded by) rich and varied sensory experience. He needs, far more than the normal child, to be played with and talked to and must experience success at his own level of attainment. His speech attempts, however poor and late these may be, must be received with pleasure and approval if further attempts are to be made. The therapist must help the critical and demanding parents to accept their child's limitations, and to realize how much their attitude is responsible for the child's lack of speech attempt.

Goda (1960) has given an interesting account of very early sound and language stimulation in non-speaking children, and says, 'Speech stimulation methods for each of these children should be consistent with his or her level of development.'

The therapist may work with these children individually, or in small groups matched for chronological and mental age, and for the type of language difficulty presented. A group has the advantage of simulating a more natural social situation; it creates a greater need for speech; and the therapist may make good use of the competitive element inherent in it.

Where the environment provides little stimulus for speech (e.g. in an institution) the therapist must endeavour to create a need for speech; help build the vocabulary and language to meet this need; and give adequate praise and encouragement when speech is attempted, however inadequate that attempt may be. Within the confines of the institution she must be responsible for increasing the child's experience as far as possible (by taking him shopping, or for a bus ride).

Where the child has been subjected to too much pressure to acquire speech, she must be undemanding in her approach. Once he recognizes that no demands are being made on him, and that his speech attempts, however poor, are accepted without adverse comment (or even with enthusiasm), then he will begin to explore the possibilities of using speech as a means of communication.

The possibility of deafness should of course always be investigated. The responsibility for the development of language and the teaching of speech in the deaf child is normally in the hands of the teacher of the deaf, and there are special schools for the child who is both deaf and mentally deficient. Children may be excluded from these schools, however, having failed to make progress or because of behaviour problems, and sent to residential institutions for the mentally deficient, where they then become a problem for the speech therapist. The therapist working with the born deaf will be primarily concerned with the acquisition of language, and only secondarily with the teaching of speech.

The speech therapist will need to make the greatest possible use of visual aids, and lip-reading will be taught concurrently with language work. As with aphasics, work begins with the association of words with concrete objects and easily demonstrated activities. A great deal of repetition will be necessary in the initial stages, and the associations must be as vivid as possible. New and more abstract words must be explained within the framework of the language the child already knows. As language increases, so the child becomes more accessible, and behaviour problems tend to decrease. Intellectual development is stimulated as language concepts are acquired and the child becomes more capable of abstract thought.

Any residual hearing present should be developed as far as possible, not only by the issue of a hearing aid but also by a thorough and systematic programme of auditory training. Where hearing loss is profound, the teaching of articulate speech will depend on the use of visual and tactile methods of approach. The intelligibility of the speech obtained will be affected by several variable factors, including the degree of hearing loss, the intelligence of the child, and the age at which speech training commences.

In the treatment of developmental aphasia, whether predominantly expressive or with some associated receptive difficulties, progress will inevitably be very slow, and therapy will necessarily extend over a period of several years. It is impossible here to do more than outline treatment. In view of the complexity of the problem, the rehabilitation programme will need to be very carefully planned to cover all aspects of language function. Basically, the therapist aims to build strong and vivid associations between concrete objects or activities, and the verbal symbols or words which we use for them. Rather than bewilder the child with a wealth of auditory stimuli, the therapist aims to establish a small vocabulary of familiar words. The whole speech situation is built up round the new word: for example, 'Give me the ball. Throw the ball. Catch the ball.' Abstractions are avoided, and the initial stages of therapy are based upon the most concrete material. Nouns and verbs are taught first, and only as language begins to develop are more abstract language concepts taught. Lea (1968) describes a comprehensive programme for matching auditory with visual stimuli devised in the course of his work with intelligent developmental dysphasic children.

Emotional conflict or trauma may be responsible for a child's failure to communicate. There are many possible causes of such conflict, which cannot be enumerated here, which careful investigation of the child's background may reveal. A negative attitude towards speech, with a complete refusal to make any speech attempt, may result when a mentally retarded child is over-stimulated by demanding or ambitious parents.

Failure to develop speech, or failure to use speech meaningfully (or to make any attempt at communication), may be symptomatic of autism in children. They may exhibit echolalia, in which the whole or last part of speech addressed to them is echoed without apparent understanding or meaning.

There are many practical problems in making a differential diagnosis between autism and mental deficiency. The subnormal child who has been rejected, or who, through institutionalization, has been emotionally deprived in the early years, may also present a picture of emotional disturbance. If sufficiently severe, this may lead to the problem of non-communication. The autistic child tends to perform at infantile levels of behaviour, which may make accurate assessment of aetiology even more difficult.

O'Connor and Hermelin (1971) describe a range of experiments designed to investigate the basic differences in perception and other capacities between autistic children, normals and the severely subnormal.

Any delay in speech development, or failure to develop adequate language as the child grows older, may be due to a complex aetiology in which two or more physical, intellectual, or emotional factors may be involved. Any of the conditions outlined above may be associated with varying degrees of mental retardation. The label 'mentally defective' may well obscure the child's need for special help with specific language difficulties or emotional problems.

Disorders of articulation

(a) FUNCTIONAL

A disorder of communication may be due to purely social or emotional causes with no direct association with learning problems, anatomical or physiological disorder. It is widely recognized that the majority of stutterers, for example, do not differ significantly from the majority of the normal population in anything but their specifically learned patterns of behaviour.

The effect of any communication disorder, however, is normally to give rise to stress which may exacerbate the original problem. A deviant pattern of articulation in a young mentally handicapped child will often be of more concern to even intelligent parents than the far more serious limitation in language development. This tends to occur because the language problem may be concealed if a child is able to engage in appropriate social responses.

Communication disorders in the subnormal may be the same in essence as those which affect the intelligent or may be derived from the specific condition and environment of individuals with low intelligence. Articulatory skills may be subject to delay in accordance with a total pattern of retarded sensori-motor development. In institutions and some families it may be found that a child conforms to the norms of his peers and is unintelligible to outsiders.

Most of the disorders of articulation prevalent among the subnormal tend to be associated with features of learning. In some cases the deviations are similar to patterns of immature articulation. A statement such as:

[mɪ mʌ̃ 'taʊ mɪ ʔɪ wɔ̃ 'kʌ̃ʔɪ a'mɒwə]

('My Mum told me she wasn't coming tomorrow')

bears a close resemblance to the dialectal forms in use in both the child's ward and the home in which he was brought up. The number of 'errors' or 'defects' to be counted depends completely upon qualitative judgments by the observer.

There is a vast difference between 'careful, polished, precise' articulation and the common patterns of even so-called 'educated speakers'. There is a tendency for all speakers to 'cut corners' physiologically, particularly in natural conversation. Most of the simplifications occur outside the conscious awareness of both speaker and listener and are only obvious to the phonetician or other trained listener. Many dialects abound with assimilations and elisions and successful communication is only achieved by the processes of continual exposure, a limitation of contexts and the general level of linguistic redundancy. Riello (1958) reports on the articulatory performance of a group of boys (N = 55) and girls (N = 45) with mean MA 7 years 9 months and CA 11 years 6 months.

41 per cent had defective articulation.

50 per cent of the deviant patterns were described as substitutions.

28 per cent of the deviant patterns were described as omissions.

19 per cent of the deviant patterns were described as distortions.

Beresford and Grady (1966) insist that this type of analysis ignores the influence of an individual's idiolect and that these phonological deviations must be regarded as features of a total language structure.

(b) ANATOMICAL MALFORMATION

Minor anatomical anomalies of the tongue, soft palate or lips will frequently be compensated for and overcome by children of normal and above average intelligence. The suggestion that this appears to occur less frequently in the subnormal has not been verified but is generally accepted.

Within the normal population there appears to be less successful adaptation to excessively deviant skeletal and muscular structures. The phonetic effects of such obvious features as irregular or missing dentition, disproportion of the mandible, maxilla, or tongue tie are more likely to be an indication of relative tongue mobility and the patency of the sensori-motor pathways (Tulley, 1964; Fawcus, 1969). In the United States intensive research is being directed upon problems of oral sensation and related motor behaviour. Preliminary results suggest that this will continue to be an increasingly important study (Bosma, 1970).

Tredgold and Soddy (1956) state that 'anomalies of teeth are very common' in the mentally deficient, and they go on to say, 'A good set of teeth is rare in mental defectives. Often late to appear, malformed and unhealthy when present, and prone to early decay and disappearance.' Whilst this statement suggests a higher incidence than may be found in actual fact, poor dentition is frequently found amongst the mentally deficient patients referred for therapy. Rather than being a 'stigma of degeneracy', however, these anomalies are more probably due to such factors as poor nutrition, neglect of dental care, and lack of orthodontic treatment, and may also be associated with disease, such as congenital syphilis.

In cases of mongolism, the tongue may appear dystonic and abnormally large in relation to the oral cavity, giving rise to clumsy and indistinct articulation. Macroglossia is not, however, an inevitable concomitant of this condition, and many mongols have surprisingly good speech. Tongue-tie, popularly regarded as the cause of many speech defects, is a relatively uncommon condition, and seldom found in the cases referred for speech correction.

(c) CLEFT PALATE

Figures quoted by Tredgold and Soddy (1956) show that the incidence of cleft palate and lip in mental deficiency is no higher than the incidence among the normal population, and they thus assume that these conditions cannot be regarded as 'stigmata of degeneracy'. (Figures quoted by Morley, 1945, show that cleft palate occurs once in approximately every 1,000 births.) On the other hand, Tredgold and Soddy (1956) show that there is a higher incidence of high, narrow, arched palates amongst mentally deficient patients.

Whilst the chief problem of an unrepaired (or unsuccessfully repaired) cleft of the hard and/or soft palates is excessive nasal resonance, the presence of an incompetent palato-pharyngeal sphincter may also give rise to defective articulation, characterized by nasal escape on consonant sounds, and in some cases sound distortions, omissions, and substitutions. Many of the latter represent the child's attempt to compensate, however inadequately, for the physiologically inefficient mechanism with which he was born. For example, being unable to build up sufficient oral air pressure for plosive consonants such as p and t, he will produce the sound at a level where air pressure can be built up and then released – that is, below the level of the closed glottis, producing the glottal stop sound which is such a characteristic feature of the speech of some cleft palate patients. Fricatives such as (s) and (sh) may also be produced in the larynx.

Other children articulate consonants in the correct position, but due to nasal escape of air and inadequate oral pressure, plosive, fricative, and affricate sounds are weak and even inaudible. Nasal escape may be gross, so that speech is virtually unintelligible. Where nasal escape is less severe, speech will be intelligible, but with marked nasal resonance and characteristic nasal grimace on speaking.

Dental irregularities may also be present, associated with a unilateral or bilateral cleft of alveolus and lip. These will all contribute to the child's difficulties in producing normal patterns of articulation.

(d) NEUROPHYSIOLOGICAL DYSFUNCTION

Dysarthria is a disorder of articulation due to a breakdown in the control and co-ordination of the muscular movements of tongue, lips, jaw, and palate required for speech. There may be a gross disturbance of articulation in cases of ataxic, athetoid, or spastic forms of cerebral palsy. On the other hand, there may be a dysarthria associated with minimal motor disability, or even in the absence of other neurological signs. Morley (1957) has given a comprehensive account of developmental dysarthria, and other disorders of articulation. Dyspraxic dysarthria (Morley, 1957) is a disorder of articulation in which the patient has difficulty in initiating and organizing the complex movements required for speech, in the absence of any muscular paralysis. The degree of difficulty experienced may vary greatly, and may show itself in a tendency for articulation to deteriorate to a marked extent in connected speech, whilst isolated sounds and words may be produced correctly. Ingram (1964) has contested the validity of the diagnosis of dyspraxia for all children who exhibit difficulties in imitation, but considerably more evidence is required before the situation becomes even remotely clear.

(e) HEARING LOSS

Hearing loss must be considered in terms of its effect on language development, the articulatory pattern, and on the pitch, volume, and quality of voice.

The effects of impaired hearing on speech will depend on the type of hearing loss, the severity of that loss, and the age of onset. A congenital high-frequency deafness, for example, will mean that certain sounds (e.g. *s*, *sh*, and *t*) will not be perceived, and will therefore not be incorporated into the speech pattern. The child born with a very profound hearing loss will, in the absence of special training, fail to develop speech at all.

Research undertaken by Foale and Paterson (1954) at Lennox Castle Institution showed that 13 per cent of 100 feeble-minded boys given audiometric tests showed hearing loss sufficient to 'handicap them in ordinary life activities'. They compare these findings with the figure of 6 per cent in Scottish (normal) schools, and from 5·17 per cent to 8·35 per cent as the incidence of all grades of deafness in schools in England and Wales. The same authors quote the investigation of Birch and Matthews (with rather lower grade boys) at Polk State School in the United States. They found an even higher incidence of deafness (32·7 per cent). Foale and Paterson conclude that, 'Impaired hearing may be a contributory factor in low scoring in intelligence tests and a person carrying out psychometric tests should be alert for signs of such impairment, particularly when the subject being tested has an articulatory speech defect.' Of the child with high-frequency deafness, they remark that he is

> most handicapped by his inability to appreciate fully the finer shades of meaning in spoken language. He has to rely more on context and is handicapped in anything which relies on spoken explanation and he, therefore, can become educationally retarded, show inadequate responses to social situations, and have only a limited vocabulary. Handicapped as he is, he may well become emotionally unstable because he is less able to cope with his environment. The clinical picture is thus similar to that found in feeble-mindedness.

Kodman (1958) in a survey of data on hearing loss amongst the mentally retarded says, 'The results agree in one direction; namely, that the incidence of hearing loss amongst mentally retarded children is significantly greater than the incidence of loss among our public school children.' He goes on to predict that 'improved testing techniques and uniformity in reporting the results will find the incidence of 30 *db* or greater losses among the mentally retarded to be three or four times that found in our public school children'. The findings of Lloyd and Reid (1967) would tend to support this suggestion. Pure tone audiometry carried out on 428 institutionalized subjects (age range 6–22 years) indicated a hearing loss present in 138.

Perceptive hearing loss may occur in association with cerebral palsy, mongolism and as a sequala of meningitis. Conductive hearing loss may result from neglect of middle ear infections. As with dental problems, the child with communication difficulties may be unable to indicate the source of his discomfort and can thereby be deprived of available treatment.

Remedial measures

Mental deficiency presents its own special problems in speech therapy which will inevitably affect the prognosis to some extent. Lack of motivation is one of the most important problems to be encountered, and this is particularly true where the patient is institutionalized, or the member of a large family of low social and intellectual status. Conversely, the question of over-stimulation arises where the mentally retarded child has intellectually superior and demanding parents, rendering the child thoroughly negative and unresponsive to all attempts at speech correction.

Far from the mental and physical lethargy popularly associated with mental deficiency, the therapist is often faced with the treatment of an over-active and highly distractible child. In such cases, it may prove extremely difficult to gain and then keep the patient's attention, and it is essential that distracting stimuli should be reduced to the minimum and that optimum conditions for learning should be obtained before therapy is attempted.

Emotional factors, including a tendency to defeatism in many high-grade patients, may make the initial stages of speech correction difficult, but these will tend to become progressively less of a problem as good rapport between therapist and patient is established. Resentment and anxiety may result in a refusal to speak and to cooperate in treatment, or in an exhibition of aggressive behaviour. Whether such problems of behaviour arise will depend to a great extent on the patient's awareness of, and attitudes towards, his mental retardation and/ or speech defect. The adjustment of negative attitudes, with consequent reduction of feelings of inferiority, anxiety, and embarrassment, are very much the therapist's concern, and should, wherever the problem occurs, constitute an essential and major part of therapy.

Finally, the patient's mental and/or physical limitations must be considered. Successful therapy can only be carried out where these limitations are properly understood. Otherwise, the resultant failures in reaching unrealistic goals will produce a state of anxiety and frustration which will adversely affect the patient's performance still further.

Where physical anomalies exist, and are thought to be a contributing factor, patients should be referred for corrective treatment (e.g. orthodontics) wherever possible. Routine hearing tests are always advisable to eliminate the possibility of hearing loss. Where hearing loss is found to be substantial, and felt to be responsible for either the speech disorder or educational retardation, the child should be issued with a hearing aid and, furthermore, be taught how to use it. A thorough programme of auditory training should be carried out, in order that the fullest possible use is made of the child's residual hearing.

The services of a qualified teacher of the deaf are rarely available for the subnormal child. There has been an unfortunate tendency in education to concentrate scarce resources upon the intelligent handicapped child to the detriment of the subnormal child with hearing loss, visual handicap or cerebral palsy.

The challenge of the not uncommon subnormal child with all three handicaps has only begun to be met.

Exercises for muscular control and coordination are only required where there is an obvious impairment of tongue, lip, or jaw movement. Where there is evidence of an articulatory dyspraxia, then visual stimulation through the medium of mirror work will be an essential adjunct to auditory stimulation. Where the patient is able to read, then reading practice may help to establish the correct patterns of movement required for speech (Morley, 1957).

A phonetic assessment of the patient's speech should be made before correction is attempted. The aim of such a speech analysis is to discover which of the speech sounds are omitted, distorted, or have incorrect substitutions – and whether these deviations occur both in isolated words or only in connected speech. With the mentally retarded patient it is advisable to commence correction of a sound which can be both seen and heard, and is therefore comparatively easy to imitate. These patients are easily discouraged, and everything must be done to reward their efforts with success. A patient who experiences constant failure, because speech correction work is too difficult, and beyond the scope of his abilities, will soon become discouraged from making any effort at all. Each step must be so carefully graded that the physical and mental effort required in its attainment are kept to a minimum – failure to do so will result in the rapid onset of fatigue, confusion, and anxiety.

The next important stage in treatment is to make the patient aware of his articulation errors. Providing he is sufficiently intelligent to respond to simple instructions, a fairly intensive programme of auditory training should be undertaken. The aim of such training may be at first to help the patient recognize and discriminate between gross sounds (e.g. money clinking, matches being rattled in a box); secondly, to discriminate between phonically dissimilar speech sounds; thirdly, to hear the difference between acoustically related sounds; and finally, to recognize the difference between errors and the correct pronunciation. Such a training should be fundamental to all speech correction work in disorders of this kind. Providing the patient's attention can be gained, and his interest held, simple hearing training techniques can be very effective. Speech correction, following such auditory training, will tend to proceed far more smoothly and rapidly, and sounds may come spontaneously during this period, even before any direct attempt has been made to elicit them.

Either following on or overlapping with hearing training techniques, the defective or omitted speech sounds must be elicited in isolation. With younger pupils, most of these sounds are obtained through play activities, and it has been found extremely useful to associate speech sounds with some concrete activity or object (thus, *sh* becomes associated with running water for the bath, and *p* is the sound made when blowing out a candle). Such associations help to make the

sounds more vivid in the child's mind, and also make the whole business of
speech correction more pleasurable and interesting for him. The use of a mirror
may prove invaluable in maintaining the mentally deficient child's interest, and
so may the provision of his own 'speech book', in which pictures can be drawn
and credit stars stuck.

More sophisticated feedback devices including storage oscilloscopes, modified
DAF systems and videotape recording are beginning to come into use in a few
clinical centres.

The next step, in which the correct sound is integrated into words, obviously
cannot proceed until the sound can be produced easily and at will in isolation. It
must be stressed that in carrying out speech correction work with the mentally
deficient, each step must be firmly consolidated before the next step is attempted,
otherwise there is a tendency for any achievements to break down under the
pressure of new demands made upon it. This is not to say that patient and
therapist should persevere with a new sound until it is absolutely correct, whatever the amount of time and difficulty involved – rather should the therapist
move to a different and easier sound, and when this has been achieved or improved, return to the original sound. Correction should proceed as Greene (1955)
suggests, 'by horizontal strata rather than by vertical sections. This means that
the ground covered must be traversed again and again, each time aiming at a
higher level of attainment, but this gives the patient a sense of achievement and
raises the whole standard of speech in a very short time.' The aim is achievement,
however modest that achievement may be, and it is the therapist's task so to plan
treatment, and modify her methods and approach, that the speech defective has
the satisfaction of making some progress each time he comes for treatment.

Whilst Sommers *et al.* (1970) describe encouraging effects of intensive
articulatory training in the subnormal, they emphasize the difficulties of 'carry-
over' in treatment generally and in the course of a relatively short experiment.

Perseveration presents a particular problem in the treatment of articulatory
defects. It will be found that once a new sound has been elicited and fairly well
established, the patient will tend to perseverate in using it when another consonant is being corrected. For this reason, the correction of two phonically
similar sounds should never be attempted simultaneously or consecutively.

The use of a tape-recorder is an invaluable asset in the treatment of articulation disorders, since the playback of the recording enables the patient to hear and
analyse his defects more objectively. It also provides a useful source of motivation. Van Riper and Irwin (1958) give many valuable suggestions for hearing
training procedures and other remedial techniques for articulation disorders.

Everything possible should be done to make the learning process as vivid as
possible, and to develop the fullest possible use of auditory, visual and kinaesthetic senses in speech correction.

CEREBRAL PALSY

It has been estimated that from 60 to 70 per cent of the cerebal palsied have some type of speech defect. Where there are difficulties in sucking, chewing, and swallowing, and there is incoordination of the movements of respiration, we may well expect phonation to be uncontrolled and speech to be dysarthric. Whilst dysarthia is generally the most obvious and severe speech problem, the speech therapist may find associated language difficulties, and sensory defects affecting speech.

There is a fairly high incidence of deafness associated with cerebral palsy, particularly of the perceptive type, which will obviously have an adverse effect on the acquisition of both language and normal articulation. In some cases, there may be evidence to suggest a developmental aphasia. Language will also tend to be retarded where severe physical handicaps have resulted in a limited environment and consequently limited experience.

Any attempt at speech may precipitate athetoid movements, or the patient may go into spasm, even when passive movements are attempted. Incoordination and phonation will affect the voice. West, Kennedy, and Carr (1947), describing phonation, say, 'The voice lacks flexibility, resonance and control; instead of a well-modulated, even flow of voice, erratic intensity and sudden pitch changes occur irregularly.'

The first aim in treatment is to establish correct feeding habits as fast as possible, since little can be done to improve speech until this has been done. It is also important to correct head and neck posture, and movements of respiration in the early stages of treatment.

Bobath and Bobath (1952) have described the reflex inhibiting postures in which the cerebral palsied child may experience normal muscle tone, and in which movement, active or passive, may be carried out with a minimum of interference by abnormal spasm or involuntary movement. Accounts of the application of this approach in the field of speech therapy have been given by Marland (1953) and Parker (1957). Phelps (1958) has described the Bobath technique as well as other methods of physical therapy in the treatment of cerebral palsy.

General relaxation is also widely used, and the therapist normally works from facilitated or assisted movements of vocalized babbling, so that the child may experience some of the sensations of normal effortless speech.

Cerebral palsy is an extremely specialized field, and speech therapy is always part of a total programme of physical treatment. Many therapists have evolved their own approach to the problems encountered, through clinical practice and their associations with other workers (e.g. physiotherapists and occupational therapists).

Severely subnormal children with physical handicaps have been successfully taught to employ a gestural means of communication where spoken language was not possible (Levett, 1969).

Disorders of voice

Attempts have been made to classify voice disorders by the aspect of voice affected; that is, problems of pitch, volume or quality. In practice, however, it is seldom that one of these facets of voice production is affected without the other two. To give a typical example: in cases of laryngitis, the quality is husky or hoarse, the volume is markedly diminished and the pitch range, particularly for the higher frequencies, is reduced.

It is useful to classify disorders of voice under the broad headings of organic and functional, but even here some overlap may exist. In addition, 'functional' may refer to a problem which reflects psychogenic disturbance or results from a period of habitual misuse of the vocal mechanism.

The only voice disorder which we may regard as 'characteristic' of mental retardation is the hoarse voice sometimes associated with mongolism. Blanchard (1964) found 'a low-pitched harsh monotone' in 29 of 50 mongoloid subjects examined. Schlanger and Gottsleben (1957) found that 72 per cent of the mongols in their study had voice problems. Zisk and Bialer (1967) have listed factors which have been claimed as responsible for the particular voice quality found in a number of mongols, including a higher placement of the larynx, a thicker and fibrotic laryngeal mucosa, lack of proper mutation, incorrect breathing patterns and hypotonia of abdominal muscles. Luchsinger and Arnold (1965), however, say that the 'rough coarse loud voice' is caused by 'the pronounced congestion and chronic swelling of the vocal cords'. Due to a hormonal imbalance, there is a chronic oedema of the mucous membranes of the larynx. They claim that vocal nodules (a benign thickening on the free edge of the vocal cords, occurring bilaterally) may result from continued overuse of the voice in a forced and strained manner.

Vocal misuse and abuse is probably one of the most common causes of functional voice disorder – the resulting dysphonia may be transient (for example, following voice use at high intensity levels in enthusiastic support of a football team), or it may be chronic as a result of habitual misuse. Here the dysphonia is typically associated with the professional voice user; but may result in any case where the voice is used for considerable periods in an inappropriate way (i.e. with excessive laryngeal tension and at improper pitch or volume levels). Furthermore, there may be adverse environmental conditions, such as background noise or chemical irritants. In addition, there may be emotional problems associated with the onset or the continuation of the voice problem.

A profound hearing loss for the lower frequencies of voice (approximately 100–250 Hz) will have an indirect effect on both the volume pitch and intonation of voice, although the larynx itself is normal. The voice of the patient with a severe impairment of hearing is characteristically monotonous, and may show little variation in volume, which is frequently too loud.

Where articulation is affected due to lesions of the central or peripheral nervous system (as in cerebral palsy, or conditions associated with the adult patient such as Parkinsonism and disseminated sclerosis), then we may also find phonation involved giving rise to the condition known as dysarthrophonia. Voice problems may result from endocrine disorders – in fact, dysphonia may be an early diagnostic sign in cases of myxoedema. Cretinism may be associated with dysphonia, varying from slight vocal dysfunction in the subclinical form to a marked dysphonia in more severe degrees of cretinism. The voice has been described as dull and husky and there is a very limited vocal range, from a few semitones to a single octave.

REMEDIAL MEASURES

Voice therapy will be largely determined by the cause of the voice disorder, and in some cases medical and/or surgical treatment is more appropriate than speech therapy. A careful assessment of the individual and his mode of voice use must be made before an appropriate treatment plan is made. Some of the indications may be:

use of voice at appropriate pitch and intensity levels;
improvement of breath control;
correction of poor postural habits;
reduction of laryngeal tension;
optimum use of resonating cavities.

The aim is to achieve optimum voice use with the minimum of effort. Where the voice disorder is associated with dysarthria, and is organically based, treatment is part of a total programme to improve respiration, phonation and articulation.

Voice disorders generally represent a relatively small proportion of the speech therapist's caseload in most settings and it is therefore considered beyond the scope of this chapter to include conditions which are less common and are not particularly associated with mental retardation.

Voice loss of sudden onset, or which is associated with certain communicative situations, indicates a psychogenic voice disorder (sometimes quite inappropriately called hysterical dysphonia). These cases are frequently very amenable to appropriate treatment. One of the most effective approaches is non-directive counselling as described by Rogers (1942). Very quiet use of the voice, which may lead to communication problems where there is background noise, may indicate nothing more than lack of confidence and feelings of inadequacy on the part of the speaker and may be regarded as personality-tied.

On the whole, unless volume is severely affected, voice disorders do not often have a serious effect on communication, and speech therapy is probably seldom indicated where presented by the mentally retarded subject. An exception would be made where faulty voice use is leading to vocal fatigue, strain and discomfort which, if continued, would ultimately lead to organic changes in the larynx, such as chronic laryngitis or vocal nodules. Whether treatment is given or not would

further be determined by the degree of subnormality and the amount of cooperation one might reasonably expect in carrying out a remedial programme.

The successful treatment of voice disorders arising from habitual misuse
demands a high degree of motivation and cooperation on the part of the patient.
Therefore, unless the mentally retarded child or adult is seriously handicapped
by problems of phonation, treatment would not be contemplated.

Disorders of resonance

(a) INSUFFICIENT NASAL RESONANCE

This may occur where some form of nasal obstruction (e.g. adenoids, chronic
catarrh) results in an inadequate airway. This may lead to mouth breathing and
characteristic 'cold in the nose' speech. Not only will the production of the nasal
consonants (*m*, *n*, and *ng*) be difficult, but vowel quality will also be affected.

(b) EXCESSIVE NASAL RESONANCE

This condition has already been discussed at some length under Cleft Palate, but
there are several other causes of the same speech condition: sub-mucous cleft; a
short soft palate associated with a congenitally large pharynx; paresis of the soft
palate associated with a developmental dysarthria (this often occurs in cerebral
palsy); paralysis of the palate following an infective lesion such as bulbar
poliomyelitis.

Excessive nasal resonance may be a temporary, or in a few cases a more
permanent, sequel to adenoidectomy. Occasionally, the presence of a large
adenoid pad makes normal speech possible where the child would otherwise be
unable to make adequate closure between the soft palate and the posterior wall of
the pharynx. Removal of the adenoids in these cases results in a sudden deterioration in speech, with gross nasal escape. Where the adenoid pad has *prevented* full
movement of the palate, and the sphincter mechanism is otherwise adequate, the
nasal escape results from a purely functional condition, and speech should
improve rapidly and spontaneously. Caution should be exercised, however, in
carrying out routine removal of adenoids in association with tonsillectomy,
particularly in cases of successfully repaired cleft palate, or where there is any
evidence of a sub-mucous cleft.

REMEDIAL MEASURES

In cases of insufficient nasal resonance due to enlarged adenoids, surgical treatment will be necessary. In some cases, speech therapy may still be necessary
after the obstruction has been removed, due to the persistence of poor speech
habits, and the continued tendency to mouth breathing.

In the treatment of cases of excessive nasal resonance auditory training is
essential if the patient is to discriminate between his faulty voice production

and that which is required of him. As Morley (1945) says, 'Not only is the ear of the child becoming accustomed to the sound he hears himself producing, but these abnormal auditory images are being inevitably correlated in his mind with the normal sounds he hears around him, and which he is trying to imitate.'

In cases of cleft palate, the speech therapist's work normally begins where the surgeon's ends. When an unrepaired cleft is encountered, the possibilities of surgical repair should be explored. Should operative treatment not be recommended, the patient may be referred for prosthetic treatment. Following an anatomically and functionally successful repair before the onset of speech, normal speech may develop, and therapy prove unnecessary. The speech therapist is therefore concerned with those cases where surgery has failed to provide a competent palato-pharyngeal sphincter, or where a successful repair was carried out after poor speech habits had been established, and which therefore persist post-operatively. Such cases, in addition to audible nasal escape of air during speech, frequently present deviant articulation. The patient, because of nasal escape which he cannot prevent, is unable to obtain sufficient air pressure to produce plosive and fricative consonants correctly. The problem of speech correction in cleft palate cases may be further complicated by the presence of gross dental irregularities and a short and/or immobile upper lip.

The speech prognosis in cases of an incompetent palato-pharyngeal sphincter has, in the past, been considered poor, but Greene (1955) indicates that good results, and even normal speech, may be obtained in such cases, and she outlines an excellent programme of speech rehabilitation. In considering the factors influencing prognosis in these cases, she rates cooperation in treatment higher than intelligence. This observation is of particular significance in connection with the possibilities of achieving results with high-grade defectives.

In cases of excessive nasal resonance, due to an incompetent palato-pharyngeal sphincter, speech therapy aims to: stimulate movement of the soft palate as far as possible; encourage oral breath direction, with the minimum of physical effort, and the consequent elimination of the characteristic nasal grimace; correct excessive resonance on vowel sounds, principally through ear-training, and by encouraging more 'open' production of vowel sounds; and finally, correct articulation of consonants, both by reducing nasal escape of air, and by correcting placement of speech sounds (e.g. where glottal stops and pharyngeal fricatives have been substituted for normal consonant sounds).

Stuttering

Whilst the cause of stuttering is still a subject of considerable controversy, it is now fairly generally held, both in the UK and the USA, that it arises from the normal non-fluencies that occur to a greater or lesser extent in the speech of most young children. Wendell Johnson's very extensive research (1959) indicated that non-fluencies (in the form of effortless prolongations and repetitions) were a feature of the speech of children between the ages of 3 and 4 years. Qualitatively

and quantitatively he considered these non-fluencies to be the same whether manifested by an experimental group of children 'diagnosed' as stutterers by their
parents, or as the 'normal' non-fluencies shown by a matched group of normal
children. From these findings he formulated his semantogenic or diagnosogenic
theory of stuttering, which suggested that these non-fluencies become a problem
only when they are evaluated as stuttering by the anxious parent.

Bloodstein (1969) extended Johnson's ideas and suggested that expectations
of 'speech failure' of various kinds (e.g. articulation errors) might also lead to the
'anticipatory struggle behaviour' which marks the onset of true stuttering. He
states: 'An important source of the stutterer's belief in the difficulty of speech
are the anxieties and demands focused by parents with ranging degrees of
subtlety on the communicative process.' Such a child, Bloodstein feels, is
particularly vulnerable to environmental pressures and he may be 'quick to
accept a concept of himself as a failure'.

With this point of view in mind the findings of Andrews and Harris (1964)
are of particular interest. In a careful survey carried out in Newcastle-upon-Tyne
they found that the speech of a group of 86 stutterers was characterized by a
history of late and poor talking, and that they showed poor attainment on tests of
intellectual ability. IQ tests on 86 stutterers matched with 86 non-stutterers
showed small but statistically significant differences: the experimental group
had an average IQ of 95, whilst the control group had an average IQ of 100.
Taking the positive family history into account, and the poor and late speech
development, they suggested that stuttering may be a question of multifactoral
inheritance – 'genetic loading' plus unfavourable environment 'exceeding a
certain threshold'. In other words, 'certain adverse environmental factors
acting upon a genetic matrix'. Weuffen (1961) reported lower scores for stutterers
in a test of word-finding ability. 'This is of interest, among other reasons,
because of its possible relationship to speech fluency', comments Bloodstein
(1969).

Wendell Johnson's observations that non-fluencies reach their peak between
3 and 4 years suggests that the breakdown in fluency occurs at a stage in speech
development when the child is particularly vulnerable to speech stress or disruption. In the subnormal child, whose acquisition of stable speech skills proceeds
at a much slower rate, there is obviously a much longer period of vulnerability.
We may therefore anticipate a higher incidence of stuttering amongst the
mentally retarded. There is conflicting evidence, however, about the prevalence
of stuttering in the subnormal population. Sheehan, Martyn and Kilburn (1968)
at Porterville State Hospital, California, examined 216 patients, and found only
1 stutterer and 1 clutterer amongst them.

Sheehan, Martyn and Slutz (1969) followed this up by a further study at
Camarillo State Hospital, California. Among 346 institutionalized, retarded
patients, they found 3 stutterers. 'Thus,' comments Sheehan (1970), 'assertions
that stuttering appears more frequently among the retarded, or related to either
end of the distribution of intelligence, appear totally unfounded.'

Schlanger and Gottsleben (1957) in their survey of speech defects at Vineland Training School found that 17 per cent of the 517 residents examined exhibited stuttering. In the aetiological groups considered, the highest incidence was amongst the mongoloid subjects (45 per cent). There were only 10 per cent of stammerers in the familial group, and 18 per cent in the remainder of the organic group. Their findings are supported by those of Schubert (1966) who found 15 per cent of a group of 80 institutionalized mongols stuttered and 8·8 per cent of a group of institutionalized non-mongols, matched for functioning level, chronological age and sex.

Beech and Fransella (1968), surveying the conflicting literature, came to the following conclusion: '. . . while the difficulties of assessment must play some part in determining the different figures for incidence among subnormals, the consistency of the findings strongly suggests that, at lower levels of intelligence, the occurrence of stammer plus intelligence are in some way associated.'

It is not within the scope of this chapter to do more than mention theories which are still current but which are no longer so widely held in the UK and the USA. The two main theories hold that stuttering is (a) symptomatic of an underlying emotional disturbance or conflict, for which symptomatic therapy will be neither appropriate nor effective; or (b) caused by an underlying neurological diathesis, the value of which is not yet fully known or understood.

The 'secondary symptoms' of stuttering develop as the child becomes increasingly aware of his non-fluencies as an embarrassing and sometimes socially penalized piece of behaviour. In place of the effortless repetitions and prolongations we find tense and often voiceless blocks as the stutterer tries to inhibit the non-fluencies. Finding that he has interfered only too successfully with the forward flow of speech, he must now devise a method of forcing his way out of the block he has unintentionally created. One of the most famous quotations in the literature is Wendell Johnson's observation that 'stuttering is what the stutterer does to stop stuttering'.

As the stutterer begins to 'predict' and anticipate feared situations and words, he starts to approach words in an abnormal fashion incompatible with normal speech, so that his prediction is fulfilled and he blocks just as he had anticipated he would. The initial arousal response may be viewed as a type of classical conditioning and the subsequent struggle behaviour as an operant response. He may also develop very effective strategies of word and situation avoidance. Whilst helping to create a superficial fluency, they none the less do little to remove the anxiety of stammering and may severely limit his verbal output and affect his mode of expression.

We may expect that the development of such approaches will depend on the level of intelligence of the subnormal patient and on the amount of adverse environmental reaction he has encountered. Certainly word avoidance, by the substitution of a word similar or identical in meaning, demands a fairly good level of intelligence. Lerman, Powers and Rigrodsky (1965) looked at the stuttering behaviour of subnormal children and found it comparable to that of children of normal intelligence in its early stages. They observed, however, that fears, avoidances and secondary symptoms can and do occur.

Cabanas (1954) regards the hesitances of the mongol as cluttering, since he found no evidence of anticipations, substitutions or other avoidance devices, or even a memory of past blocking. Lack of awareness of non-fluencies is regarded by many as one of the most crucial signs of cluttering as opposed to stuttering.

The approach to therapy will be determined by a number of factors, including the pattern of stuttering presented, the age and intelligence of the stutterer and, most important, his awareness of stuttering. If speech is characterized by non-fluencies not associated with either tension or anxiety, then the aim is to prevent the development of stuttering. This is normally done through careful parent counselling and management of the child's environment. Factors which precipitate or aggravate non-fluencies (such as interruptions or lack of attention on the part of the listener) need to be modified or eliminated. In order to 'canalize' the parents' natural anxiety into useful channels, they can be shown how to develop the child's language ability so that he is better able to meet the demands on his speech skills. This is particularly important in the case of the mentally retarded child who is linguistically at a disadvantage. Finally, social penalties of any kind – which may make the child aware that his non-fluencies are a problem – must be removed.

Where awareness and tension have occurred, then a symptomatic approach may be used to modify any abnormal speech behaviour which has developed. Verbal communication in all speech situations must be encouraged and word and situation avoidance discouraged. Syllable-timed speech (Andrews and Harris, 1964; Brandon and Harris, 1967) has proved to be one of the simplest and most effective techniques in the treatment of stuttering. Clinical observation suggests that this approach will be particularly appropriate with the mentally retarded stutterer.

Conclusions

It is recognized that speech and language are essential to the individual's intellectual and emotional development. Therefore, any impairment of speech and language functions which prevents communication and the satisfaction of his emotional and physical needs will tend to produce maladjustment and behaviour deviations. Furthermore, the absence of linguistic concepts will hinder abstract thought, and prevent the individual from functioning at his highest potential mental level.

The speech therapist's gradual change in emphasis from 'speech and language' to 'communication' has opened a wider range of possibilities within the field of subnormality. Within a generation there has been a growing trend from virtually no provision to a realization that most ESN and SSN children should be assessed by a speech therapist and many should receive specialized help. This may lie in the form of parental advice, collaboration with teachers or direct intervention according to specific circumstances.

Research into linguistic development has begun to influence practical measures designed to overcome communication problems, but can only evolve through close collaboration between psychologists and specialists in linguistics and communication disorders.

References

AINSWORTH, M. D. (1962) *Deprivation of Maternal Care: A Reassessment of its Effects*. Geneva: WHO.

ANDREWS, G. and HARRIS, M. (1964) *The Syndrome of Stuttering*. London: Heinemann.

ARONSON, H. V. (1968) Development of a training and supervisory programme for speech aides at a state institution for the mentally retarded. *Welfare Reporter*, **19**, 25–8.

BALLARD, P. B. (1934) *Thought and Language*. London: Univ. of London Press.

BECKY, R. E. (1942) A study of certain factors related to retardation of speech. *J. Speech Dis.*, 7, 232–49.

BEECH, H. R. and FRANSELLA, F. (1968) *Research and Experiment in Stuttering*. Oxford: Pergamon.

BERESFORD, R. and GRADY, P. A. E. (1966) An investigation into the apparently unintelligible speech of a ten year old boy. In *Speech Pathology: Diagnosis, Theory and Practice. Brit. J. Dis. Communication Suppl.* Edinburgh: Livingstone.

BERRY, M. F. and EISENSON, J. (1956) *Speech Disorders*. New York: Appleton-Century-Crofts.

BLANCHARD, I. (1964) Speech pattern and aetiology in mental retardation. *Amer. J. ment. Defic.*, **68**, 612–17.

BLANCHARD, I. (1968) Diagnostic patterns of articulation. In WALDON, E. F. (ed.) *Differential Diagnosis of Speech and Hearing of Mental Retardates*. Washington, DC: Catholic Univ. of America Press.

BLOODSTEIN, O. (1969) *A Handbook on Stuttering*. Chicago: National Easter Seal Society for Children and Adults.

BOBATH, K. and BOBATH, B. (1952) A treatment of cerebral palsy. *Brit. J. phys. Med.*, **15**, 107–17.

BOSMA, J. F. (1970) *Oral Sensation and Perception*. Springfield, Ill.: Charles C. Thomas.

BRAIN, W. R. (1952) *Diseases of the Nervous System*. London: Oxford Univ. Press.

BRANDON, S. and HARRIS, M. (1967) Stammering: an experimental treatment programme using syllable-timed speech. *Brit. J. dis. Comm.*, **2**, 64–8.

BROOK, J. R. (1966) The spontaneous spoken vocabulary of a group of severely, mentally subnormal children. *Brit. J. dis. Comm.*, **1**, 131–5.

BURT, C. (1951) *The Backward Child* (3rd edn). London: Univ. of London Press.

CABANAS, P. (1954) Some findings in speech and voice therapy among mentally deficient children. *Folia Phoniat.*, **6**, 34–9.

CASHDAN, A. (1969) The role of movement in language learning. In WOLFF, P. H. and MACKEITH, R. (eds.) *Planning for Better Learning*. London: Heinemann.

CLARKE, A. D. B. and CLARKE, A. M. (1953) How constant is the IQ? *Lancet*, **ii**, 877–80.

DONOVAN, H. (1957) Speech programme for the mentally retarded children in the New York City public schools. *Amer. J. ment. Defic.*, **62**, 455–9.

FAWCUS, R. (1969) Oropharyngeal function in relation to speech. *Developm. med. Child Neurol.*, **11**, 556–60.

FOALE, M. and PATERSON, J. W. (1954) The hearing of mental defectives. *Amer. J. ment. Defic.*, **59**, 254–8.

FRY, D. B. and WHETNALL, E. (1964) The auditory approach in the training of deaf children. *Lancet*, **i**, 583.

GODA, S. (1960) Vocal utterances of young moderately and severely retarded non-speaking children. *Amer. J. ment. Defic.*, **65**, 269–73.

GREENE, M. C. L. (1955) The cleft palate patient with incompetent palato-pharyngeal closure. *Folia Phoniat*, **7**, 172–82.

GREENE, M. C. L. (1967) Speechless and backward at three. *Brit. J. dis. Comm.*, **2**, 134–45.

GUESS, D., SMITH, J. O. and ENSMINGER, E. E. (1971) The role of non-professional persons in teaching language skills to mentally retarded children. *Except. Child.*, **37**, 447–53.

HERMELIN, B. F. and O'CONNOR, N. (1963) *Speech and Thought in Severe Subnormality*. Oxford: Pergamon.

HUBSCHMAN, E. (1967) *Experimental Language Programme at the Nursery*. Chicago: American Association on Mental Deficiency.

INGRAM, T. T. S. (1964) Late and poor talkers. In RENFREW, C. and MURPHY, K. (eds.) *The Child Who Does Not Talk*. London: Heinemann.

IRWIN, R. B. (1959) Oral language for slow learning children. *Amer. J. ment. Defic.*, **64**, 32–9.

IVES, L. A. (1967) Deafness and the development of intelligence. *Brit. J. dis. Comm.*, **2**, 96–111.

JOHNSON, W. (1959) *The Onset of Stuttering*. Minneapolis: Univ. of Minnesota Press.

KASTEIN, S. (1956) Responsibility of the speech pathologist to the retarded child. *Amer. J. ment. Defic.*, **60**, 750–4.

KENNEDY, L. (1930) *Studies in the Speech of the Feeble-minded.* Unpubl. Ph.D. dissertation, Univ. of Wisconsin.

KODMAN, F. (1958) The incidence of hearing loss in mentally retarded children. *Amer. J. ment. Defic.*, **62**, 675–8.

KOLSTOE, O. P. (1958) Language training of low grade mongoloid children. *Amer. J. ment. Defic.*, **63**, 17–30.

LEA, J. (1968) Language and receptive aphasia. *Spec. Educ.*, **57**, 2.

LERMAN, J. W., POWERS, G. R. and RIGRODSKY, S. (1965) Stuttering patterns observed in a sample of mentally retarded individuals. *Training School Bull.*, **62**, 27–32.

LEVETT, L. M. (1969) A method of communication for non-speaking severely subnormal children. *Brit. J. dis. Comm.*, **4**, 64–6.

LLOYD, L. L. and REID, M. J. (1967) The incidence of hearing impairment in an institutionalised mentally retarded population. *Amer. J. ment. Defic.*, **71**, 746–63.

LUCHSINGER, R. and ARNOLD, G. E. (1965) *Voice-Speech-Language: Clinical Communicology, its Physiology and Pathology.* London: Constable.

LURIA, A. R. and YUDOVICH, F. I. (1959) *Speech and the Development of Mental Processes in the Child.* London: Staples Press.

MCCARTHY, J. J. and KIRK, S. A. (1961) *Illinois Test of Psycholinguistic Abilities – Examiner's Manual.* Urbana, Ill.: Institute for Research on Exceptional Children.

MARLAND, P. M. (1953) Speech therapy for cerebral palsy based on reflex inhibition. *Speech*, **17**, 65–8.

MARTYN, M. M., SHEEHAN, J. and SLUTZ, K. (1969) Incidence of stammering and other speech disorders among the retarded. *Amer. J. ment. Defic.*, **74**, 206–11.

MATTHEWS, J. (1957) Speech problems of the mentally retarded. In TRAVIS, L. E. (ed.) *Handbook of Speech Pathology.* New York: Appleton-Century-Crofts.

MECHAM, M. J. (1958) *Verbal Language Development Scale: Manual of Item Definitions.* Minneapolis: Amer. Guidance Service Inc.

MEIN, R. and O'CONNOR, N. J. (1960) A study of the oral vocabularies of severely subnormal patients. *J. ment. Defic. Res.*, **4**, 130–4.

MORLEY, M. E. (1945) *Cleft Palate and Speech.* Edinburgh: Livingstone.

MORLEY, M. E. (1957) *The Development and Disorders of Speech in Childhood.* Edinburgh and London: Livingstone.

MYKLEBUST, H. R. (1957) Aphasia in children – diagnosis and training. In TRAVIS, L. E. (ed.) *Handbook of Speech Pathology.* New York: Appleton-Century-Crofts.

NISBET, J. D. (1953) *Family Environment: A Direct Effect of Family Size on Intelligence.* Occasional Papers on Eugenics, No. 8. London: Cassell.

O'CONNOR, N. and HERMELIN, B. (1971) *Psychological Experiments with Autistic Children*. Oxford: Pergamon.

PARKER, L. P. (1957) The preparation for speech in the very young cerebral palsied child. *Folia Phoniat.*, **9**, 54–7.

PAVLOV, I. P. (1941) *Conditioned Reflexes and Psychiatry* (transl. W. Horsley Gantt). New York: International Publishers.

PHELPS, W. M. (1958) The role of physical therapy in cerebral palsy. In ILLINGWORTH, R. S. (ed.) *Recent Advances in Cerebral Palsy*. London: Churchill.

REYNELL, J. (1969) A developmental approach to language disorders. *Brit. J. dis. Comm.*, **4**, 33–40.

RIELLO, A. (1958) *Articulatory Proficiency of the Mentally Retarded Child*. Unpubl. Ph.D. dissertation, New York Univ.

RITTMANIC, P. A. (1958) An oral language program for institutionalized educable mentally retarded children. *Amer. J. ment. Defic.*, **63**, 403–7.

ROGERS, C. W. (1942) *Counselling and Psychotherapy*. Boston: Houghton Mifflin.

SACHS, M. H. (1951) *A Survey and Evaluation of the Existing Interrelationships between Speech and Mental Deficiency*. Unpubl. M.A. thesis, Univ. of Virginia.

SAUNDERS, E. A. and MILLER, C. J. (1968) A study of verbal communication in mentally subnormal patients. *Brit. J. dis. Comm.*, **3**, 99–110.

SCHLANGER, B. B. (1953a) Speech therapy results with mentally retarded children in special classes. *Training School Bull.*, **50**, 179–86.

SCHLANGER, B. B. (1953b) Speech examination of a group of institutionalized mentally retarded children. *J. speech hear. Dis.*, **18**, 339–49.

SCHLANGER, B. B. and GOTTSLEBEN, R. H. (1957) Analysis of speech defects among the institutionalized mentally retarded. *J. speech Dis.*, **22**, 98–103.

SCHNEIDER, B. and VALLON, J. (1955) The results of a speech therapy program for mentally retarded children. *Amer. J. ment. Defic.*, **59**, 417–24.

SCHUBERT, O. W. (1966) *The Incidence Rate of Stuttering in a Matched Group of Institutionalised Mental Retardates*. Paper presented at 90th Annual Meeting of the American Association on Mental Deficiency, Chicago, Ill.

SHEEHAN, J. G. (1970) *Stuttering: Research and Therapy*. New York: Harper & Row.

SHEEHAN, J. G., MARTYN, M. M. and KILBURN, K. (1968) Speech disorders in retardation. *Amer. J. ment. Defic.*, **73**, 251–6.

SIRKIN, J. and LYONS, W. F. (1941) A study of speech defects in mental deficiency. *Amer. J. ment. Defic.*, **46**, 74–80.

SOMMERS, R. K., LEISS, R. H., FUNDRELLA, D., MANNING, W., JOHNSON, R., OERTHER, P., SHOLLY, R. and SIEGEL, M. (1970)

Factors in the effectiveness of articulation therapy with educable retarded children. *J. speech hear. Res.*, **13**, 304–16.

SPRADLIN, J. E. (1968) Environmental factors and the language. In ROSENBERG, S. and KOPLIN, J. H. (eds.) *Developments in Applied Psycholinguistic Research*. New York: Macmillan.

STEINMAN, J., GROSSMAN, C. and REECE, R. E. (1963) An analysis of the articulation of the educable retarded child. *Amer. speech hear. Assoc.*, **5**, 791.

STRAZZULLA, M. (1953) Speech problems of the mongoloid child. *Quart. Rev. Pediat.*, **8**, 268–73.

TERMAN, L. M. and MERRILL, M. A. (1937) *Measuring Intelligence*. London: Harrap.

TREDGOLD, R. F. and SODDY, K. (1956) *A Textbook of Mental Deficiency* (9th edn). London: Baillière, Tindall & Cox.

TULLEY, W. J. (1964) The tongue: that unruly member? *Dent. Practit.*, **15**, 27.

VAN RIPER, C. (1952) *Speech Correction*. New York: Prentice-Hall.

VAN RIPER, C. and IRWIN, R. W. (1958) *Voice and Articulation*. London: Pitman.

WALLIN, J. E. W. (1949) *Children with Mental and Physical Handicaps*. New York and London: Staples Press.

WEST, R. (1947) The neuropathologies of speech. In WEST, R., KENNEDY, L. and CARR, A. (eds.) *The Rehabilitation of Speech*. New York: Harper & Row.

WEST, R., KENNEDY, L. and CARR, A. (1947) *The Rehabilitation of Speech*. New York: Harper & Row.

WEUFFEN, M. (1961) Untersuching der Worfindung bei normal sprechenden und stotternden Kindern und Jugendlichen in Alter von 8 bis 16 Jahren. *Folia Phoniat.*, **13**, 255–68.

WING, J. K. (1966) *Early Childhood Autism*. Oxford: Pergamon.

YULE, W. and BERGER, M. (1971) Applications of behaviour modification principles to speech and language disorders. In RUTTER, M. and MARTIN, J. A. M. (eds.) *Young Children with Delayed Speech*. Clinics in Developm. Med. London: Heinemann.

ZISK, P. K. and BIALER, I. (1967) Speech and language problems in mongolism: a review of the literature. *J. speech hear. Dis.*, **32**, 228–41.

11

H. C. Gunzburg

The education of the mentally handicapped child

Introduction

For a long time there has been an indefensible dividing line between children with IQs above the 50 mark who were given 'education' and those below IQ 50 who were given 'training'. This artificial division served not only administrative convenience but determined the quality of attention given, the qualification of staff and the provisions made. Only quite recently – with the Education (Handicapped Children) Act, 1970 – has it been abolished in England, and all children, irrespective of the degree of their mental disability, are now the responsibility of the Education Authorities. No child will be excluded from the education system, even though its responsiveness to educational stimulation may be regarded as minimal. The dividing line has not simply been placed at a lower level of ability, but has disappeared altogether.

Whilst it must be regarded as an historical advance in English legislation that no child is excluded from educational attention on account of his mental disability, it is necessary to point out that the abolition of an administrative dividing line must not suggest that there are not differences in handicaps, which necessitate different types of programmes and divisions, depending on realistic educational targets for different needs. It would be a retrograde step if education for all were interpreted as meaning the 'same education' to different degrees.

Neale and Campbell (1963) phrased this consideration very neatly when they stated: 'The guiding principle here is, "To each according to his needs", and this is being placed ahead of desert ("To each according to his merit") and capacity ("To each according to his ability").' And they quote Warner et al. (1946) as stating that to treat all pupils alike is like putting little chicks, ducklings, baby swans, kittens and bear cubs all in a pond together and waiting to see how they respond to this 'equal opportunity'. On the other hand, Kolburne (1965) argues that 'academic education is probably the most important phase of a child's life'. Since we live in a democratic society 'a complete educational programme for the trainable mentally retarded should include academic instruction'.

It is, therefore, proposed to discuss the programming for three major levels of educational work, which should be regarded as having no definite borders and which should be applied flexibly as circumstances require. On each of these levels educational and psychological research have made useful inroads.

The first level is characterized by the dominance of 'care problems' and the need for nearly full-time attention to the self-help items, such as toileting, washing, eating, dressing. Most, but not all, children on this level of functioning are profoundly retarded and have IQs below 20. Though their physical care requires the most direct attention, they have emotional problems, they are in need of stimulation and activation to prevent deterioration and can achieve a reasonable level of functioning despite their disability. They will, however, always be high dependency people.

The second level is characterized by the fact that the lowish IQ range (extending up to approximately IQ 55) gives not much indication of the level of social competence that can finally be achieved. 'Academic' achievements, which can be used meaningfully in ordinary life situations, are very meagre or non-existent, but with appropriate education and training a degree of social functioning can finally be achieved which enables many mentally handicapped persons to live comparatively independently and with little assistance by others.

The third level of education has been very widely explored and is most similar to 'normal' education. A large number of children who would benefit by this type of education have been deprived of cultural stimulation or have been emotionally disturbed. Education means, therefore, for them a suitable presentation of normal stimuli, which are well within their mental grasp, and 'academic' work is purposeful on this level. In later adult life a majority of these children merge inconspicuously with the normal population.

The contents of educational work are determined to a large extent by the social future of the mentally handicapped child and the fact that a lower IQ indicates not only a slower rate of learning but also the likely presence of a multitude of additional handicapping factors.

Level 1: The profoundly handicapped child

These children require generally nursing attention, though this can be given by untrained but reasonably careful persons. A number of them, however, e.g. hemiplegia, quadriplegia, are in need of a degree of physical nursing which can in the long run only be met adequately by trained nursing staff. Most of these children are without the ability to look after themselves in the simple skills of toileting, washing, dressing and they are also very unresponsive to stimulation.

The educational objectives are, therefore, primarily concerned with reducing the amount of assistance required in the self-help area and to encourage the child to respond to the environment (Kolburne, 1965).

For quite some time these children were left in the 'back wards' of institutions and Special Care Units, being nursed physically and only by the personal interest of nurses did they ever achieve higher levels of functioning. Recent developments in conditioning methods has resulted in much advance in this area (see Chapter 12).

Operant conditioning in the ward to achieve a higher degree of self-help skills has been described by Colwell and Cassell (1955), Orlando and Bijou (1960), Linde (1962), Hundziak et al. (1965), Bensberg et al. (1965), Whelan and Haring (1966), Hamilton and Allen (1967), Hollis and Gorton (1967), Minge and Ball (1967), Roos and Oliver (1969), and Treffry et al. (1970).

The same approach has also been used for tackling behavioural disturbance in the severely handicapped child (Ellis et al., 1960; Girardeau, 1962; Headrick, 1963; Girardeau and Spradlin, 1964).

These investigations and training schemes are of direct relevance to the child's well-being and are thus of great interest to those who have to evaluate efficient management practices for children with severe handicaps. The nursing press reflects to some extent the successful adoption of similar training programmes by the nurses, often without direct guidance by scientific workers.

Other studies of a more academic nature indicate that there is a capacity of responsiveness even in the severely handicapped child which could be utilized if the right approach can be found and consistently pursued.

Skinner (1965) describes the case of a 40-year-old microcephalic idiot with a mental age of about 18 months, who was partly toilet trained and only able to dress himself with help. This man was taught by carefully programmed instruction to make subtle form discriminations and to use a pencil.

There are now several bibliographical articles on behaviour shaping in mental subnormality (Gardner and Watson, 1969; Nawas and Braun, 1970).

It might be argued that much of the success of the behaviour shaping techniques is due to the attention by staff and consistency of approach rather than the technique itself. Some of the evidence presented is not very convincing on account of methodological inadequacies (Gardner, 1969). However, from the practical point of view, the mere fact that successful guidance in the management of intractable problems has been provided makes it certainly worthwhile to pursue this approach. Little is known yet about the long range effects of such programmes in maintaining the level of behaviour after conclusion of training. Lawrence and Kartye (1971) investigated this aspect in a group of 21 children, aged 8 years to 14 years with IQs ranging from 23 to 36 and SQ (Vineland) from 8 to 42. After a year's training the 14 incontinent children in the sample had been toilet trained and all children were able to feed themselves with a spoon, though none of them had been able to do so at the beginning of the programme. Seventeen children had learned to dress and undress themselves though none of them had originally been able to do this. Training extended to other areas, such as ability to use gestures and to verbalize needs (communication), the ability to perform activities without direction and to carry out peer group activities. After conclusion of the programme there was a four months' period without any formal training, after which a new assessment was made. It was found that the children had regressed significantly in initiative, communication and social skills but not in self-help skills. The authors suggested that the main reason for maintaining the level of competence in this area was due to the daily routine of the ward, which 'provided the residents with opportunities for additional practice and reinforcement in maintaining skills in the area of Self-Help. Dressing, undressing and eating are activities which must be carried out, even in the absence of a formal training program.' This comment reflects the great weakness of the educational approach on this level, when systematic education is only carried out within the framework of a formal training programme, but is not considered as a necessity at all times. The achievements in communication, social skills and initiative could probably have been maintained if staff had provided as many opportunities for these skills as for the self-help items. This is a criticism which applies to this type of exploratory work as well as to much other educational research, which seems to be primarily and solely interested in establishing that a particular method can achieve significant results, rather than in ensuring that it is of a kind which can be applied in practice. There is still a tremendous gap between the laboratory conditions of the research worker and the adoption of his findings in ordinary conditions (Keith and Lange, 1974; Kiernan, 1974).

Many references in modern literature on the very severely disabled child indicate the growing concern for the educational deprivation suffered by these children. Whilst it is clearly recognized that education on that level must be of a fundamentally different character, one feels also that behaviour shaping techniques by themselves will only assist in making the child, and later the adult, more acceptable to others and less dependent on them, but will not be sufficient in encouraging more responsiveness to people and the world around. The two frequently-used key words in this context are stimulation and activation, which are interpreted as ranging from providing coloured balls on a string above the cot of the severely handicapped child to nursery play. Educational efforts for children on that level are mostly seen as providing systematically sensory stimulation in the form of more or less formal exercises, such as following moving objects with eyes, tactile stimulation by presenting various pieces of textures, listening to auditory cues etc.

The child's prolonged unresponsiveness weakens the parents' determination for eliciting responses and the decreased effort in its turn decreases chances for success. It becomes, therefore, important that a stimulation programme is initiated as early as possible to avoid a premature 'setting' due to weak or absent stimulation. Though Heber's investigation (1968, 1971) aims at preventing mild subnormality in children, the methods used may well have relevance to the profoundly handicapped child. Heber reports that babies in this group attended daily special nursery groups with a daily programme of sensory and language stimulation and aiming particularly at problems solving skills and language development. Though the children were not removed from home the mothers were given special training in homemaking and child care skills in order to reinforce the teaching in the nursery. When reassessed at age $3\frac{1}{2}$ the differences in intelligence scores, compared with a control group, were striking. As Heber suggests, 'the trend of our present data engenders the hope that it might prove to be possible to prevent the kind of mental retardation associated with both poverty and parent of limited ability'. Lorenzo (1967) describes a programme in Uruguay designed 'to diagnose and treat at a very early age high risk babies'. This leads to providing 'enriched multi-sensorial stimulation and rich environmental stimulation' to promote a better development of so-called 'high risk babies'. The same author stresses also (1970) that the stimulation required must come from the whole environment and not be limited to set times and places, such as a classroom. This is an important reminder – not only relevant to work with the highly mentally disabled child – that educational work must be extended to all situations, the home, the ward, the nursing staff and the parents, to become really effective. And if sensory stimulation is considered essential in triggering off interest in the surroundings, then it is highly doubtful that either the anaemic, hygienic conditions of a good ward or the barren and dilapidated conditions of a poor ward are conducive to stimulation. One may well think that there could be more enrichment of the severely subnormal child's environment by providing a variety of environmental sensory stimulation for smelling, sensing, hearing and feeling.

Level 2: The moderately handicapped child

Contrary to traditional assessments of the moderately retarded adult's role in the open community, it is now widely accepted that a far larger number of people with intellectual limitations can function outside a protected environment than has been assumed in the past (see Chapter 2). To prepare for the adult role, the education programme will have to be directed primarily towards achieving finally a measure of self-sufficiency and occupational competence.

A careful consideration of the role of education in the social rehabilitation of the subnormal child indicates that objectives have to be formulated not as 'subjects', e.g. reading, writing, arithmetic, but rather as areas of competence. Most modern workers have come to broadly similar conclusions, even though individual preferences often add a quaint note. Generally they have stressed that the subnormal should be taught among other skills:

(a) how to get on with other people;
(b) how to accept the work situation and give reasonable satisfaction;
(c) how to manage money;
(d) how to get about and make use of public services;
(e) how to manage leisure time.

Whilst teaching objectives of the kind mentioned above are realistic and feasible because they are essential for tackling life situations and can be taught within the limits imposed by time and school structure, other educational aims mentioned in the literature appear to be so ambitious as to be unrealistic. 'Acquiring knowledge of, practice in, and zeal for democratic processes; becoming sensitive to the importance of group action in the attainment of social goals;

developing meaning for life' (Nickell, 1951) are statements of aims which seem rather out of place when dealing with mentally subnormal children (Kirk and Johnson, 1951; Ingram, 1953; Kirk *et al.*, 1955; Wallin, 1955; Stevens, 1958; Williams and Wallin, 1959; Gardner and Nisonger, 1962; Kirk, 1962; Gunzburg, 1963).

The fact that the subnormal person's limitations prevent him from achieving normal standards must not prevent the educationalist from striving towards a relative competence within each individual's capability. Only relative degrees of social, personal and economic adequacy can be expected, yet even these limited skills will help the defective to live in the world – in many cases limited to his immediate surroundings – with some confidence and feeling of security (Hudson, 1955; Rosenzweig, 1959).

Educational programmes provide guidance to the many varying and confusing experiences of shopping, of the use of public transport or the telephone, queuing up for buses or at shops, buying little refreshments, etc. Even though teachers realize that knowledge of community demeanour requires experience in the community, the educational classroom situation provides rehearsal and preparation opportunities (Neale and Campbell, 1963; Gunzburg, 1963 ; Stevens, 1971). It is also recognized that the acquisition of the technical skills of social competence eases the mentally handicapped person's adjustment difficulties. The mentally handicapped child tends for various reasons to live a withdrawn and sheltered existence which affects his ability to establish and maintain human relationships. One of the foremost tasks of the educational programme is, therefore, the development of those social skills which encourage cooperation, the give and take of living together, the recognition of authority, the willingness to be directed, the acceptance of rules and property of others – all of which will contribute substantially to a reduction of friction when living in 'normal' society.

Level 3: The mildly handicapped child

The educational literature on the mildly handicapped or educationally subnormal child – ESN(M) – has increased to such an extent that it would be quite unjustified to deal with it in only a few paragraphs. It will therefore be more helpful to discuss in the space available the relative weight of various 'subjects' in the school curricula of the three levels of ability.

Special subjects

Training programmes and their effect on the intellectual and social functioning of severely subnormal children have been described by Francey (1966), Bland (1968), Mitchell and Smeriglio (1970), and Stevens (1971).

Whilst it is nowadays widely accepted that social education must be the prime objective in curriculum planning, there are considerable differences in actual practices regarding how much time should be devoted to that aspect in comparison with the conventional school subjects, such as reading, writing and arithmetic, to which nowadays a new 'subject' tends to be added, namely language development. Some guidance in drawing up curricula and timetables is offered by considering carefully the use a mentally handicapped adult can make of a particular skill, such as reading, and also by assessing its place in the list of needs required for a reasonable adjustment to a particular level of the community.

Reading

(a) THE SEVERELY RETARDED CHILD

It is nowadays generally accepted that the teaching of reading skills should be guided by the practical use to which such an attainment can be put. Though it has been demonstrated by educators, parents and researchers that a reasonable degree of mechanical reading skill, disrespectfully referred to as 'barking at print', can be attained, it becomes a meaningless skill if the reader cannot comprehend what he is reading. There may be, of course, an emotional benefit for the child and the parent, who derive satisfaction from the organization of a technique which is basic to normal school education (Kolburne, 1965); but, it could be argued, a similar feeling of achievement can be obtained by concentrating on competence in number and money skills, which are of immediate practical usefulness.

There seems to be some justification to define the reading targets in accordance with the understanding a child could be expected to have (Kirk, 1940), though it might be dangerous practice to make teaching targets correspond too closely to MA and IQ, which themselves might be affected by reading difficulties (Quay, 1963).

As far as the profoundly and severely mentally retarded is concerned, a prevailing practice is to teach him by sight a vocabulary of cautionary and admonitory words which would help him in daily living (reading for protection).

A list of socially useful words, a social sight vocabulary (Gunzburg, 1968; Bell, 1970), includes, for example: Ladies, Gentlemen, Wet Paint, Danger, No Smoking, No Exit, Entry, etc.

The conventional method of teaching a social sight vocabulary is by exposing flashcards showing the 'word picture' in different sizes and types of print. An interesting variation on this technique is the 'symbol accentuation', developed by Miller (1967). This method refers to 'a motion picture animation technique of integrating spoken and printed language with objects and events in a way that enables those with limited capacity meaningfully to relate words to objects and letters to sounds'.

It is comparatively simple to extend the size of such a sight vocabulary, and Hermelin and O'Connor (1960) found the number of words read by the severely handicapped, with IQs between 35 and 50, ranged from 0–200, with a mean of 45 words read. They also found that there was no significant correlation between the number of words read and the child's IQ, but that mental age and chronological age were significantly correlated with the reading score.

There is, however, a definite danger that a teacher might sacrifice energy and valuable teaching time to the pursuance of a goal which is not necessarily first on the list of priorities for this level of functioning, though it figures as such in 'normal education'.

(b) THE MODERATELY RETARDED CHILD

With the moderately retarded child, reading targets can be set more ambitiously than with the profoundly retarded, but the teacher must still keep in mind that technical mastery of reading will give an illusion of competence which can never exist because the limited mental abilities set a ceiling to the comprehension of the written word. At the same time, it is necessary to remember that within the group will be found many socially deprived children whose academic and intellectual achievements are well below their abilities and require careful encouragement (Dunn, 1968; Tansley and Gulliford, 1960; Bell, 1970; Gulliford, 1971).

On this level, many of the research findings on different methods are of importance. There is now a decided preponderance of work suggesting that mixed linguistic and phonic methods are of greater value than the sight recognition approaches employed with the more disabled child.

As far as the proponents of the sight recognition methods are concerned, they emphasize arguments based on considerations concerning the child's or adolescent's reactions rather than on the efficiency of the learning method itself. Thus, it is suggested that a slow and so far unsuccessful learner – a reading failure – will gain an immediate feeling of success by learning words which he recognizes as being important and useful. Since contents and meaning can be adjusted to individual interests and specific targets, the method is flexible and carries a large factor of inbuilt motivation. It provides a good start, which can gradually merge with the phonics and analytical methods which are required for further development of reading competence. Such a method for mentally retarded non-readers has been described and developed by Gunzburg (1968).

On the other hand, a phonic system represents a systematic step by step approach in which the child is taught a method which can be developed and transferred and is, from this point, far more flexible than an approach based largely on memorizing visual pictures (Daniels and Diack, 1960; Keating, 1962; Chall, 1967).

Within this framework of phonic methods, as used with mentally retarded children, two approaches are of special interest. A linear programme using simultaneous presentation of visual and auditory stimuli was developed by Brown and Bookbinder (Brown, 1967; Brown and Bookbinder, 1966, 1968). Teaching machines and programmed instruction were used by Bijou (1965), Stolurow (1963), though the efficacy of this method has been challenged (Blackman and Capobianco, 1965).

Great interest has been shown in investigating using the phonetic Initial Teaching Alphabet (ITA). This is based on forty-four symbols of sounds and is said to provide an easy introduction to the complexities of conventional English spelling and phonetics. Smith (1966) used this system with eight children (age range 10–12, IQ 53–65), who had reading ages well below their chronological ages. Results after fifteen months indicated significant increases and little difficulty when transferring to ordinary spelling and reading. Similar favourable results were reported by Dunn and Mueller (1966), particularly when combined with a language development programme (Dunn *et al*, 1967), but doubts have been expressed by Labon (1967).

The main purpose of reading on this level is obtaining information and instruction which will help the mentally handicapped child in orientating himself in a world which relies on short written instruction, advice etc.

For this reason classrooms should contain items like telephone directories, railway and bus timetables, newspapers and television programmes. Children should be encouraged to study these and some assignment cards will both give them practice in seeking information and opportunities to follow instructions. Any attempt to link reading with real life situations brings into play the Utility Motive, for children are more likely to see the purpose and relevance of the activity. Opportunities for this type of activity often arise naturally in other subjects of the curriculum. (Bell, 1970)

(c) THE MILDLY RETARDED CHILD

Children whose intellectual abilities and awareness for life around them are near normal are likely to make better and more frequent use of their technical reading facility. In their cases, reading need not only be a laboriously acquired technical tool applied clumsily with little confidence to everyday situations, but can be used with pleasure and advantage in a multitude of situations. Competence in reading on this high 'normal' level will depend not only on technical fluency but on other factors, such as familiarity with the vocabulary, with idioms used, conventions in literary style, ability to discriminate between essentials and inessentials, etc.

There is very little evidence available regarding the actual difficulties in comprehension experienced by children with a mild intellectual handicap when faced with literature apparently suitable for their level.

Gunzburg (1948) investigated the comments on their reading matter made by 14–16–year–old boys in the IQ range 50–75. He found that these children's reading tastes and preferences are very similar to those of normal children. They are attracted by descriptions of fighting, shooting and other dramatic events, descriptions of escapes, last-minute rescues and happy family reunions. However, difficulties are caused by the complexity and unfamiliarity of vocabulary. References to well-known events and persons are not understood, and historical stories using old-fashioned phraseology and vocabulary lead to much confusion. He came to the conclusion that the mentally handicapped does not use his reading skill adequately because of 'disillusionment with his reading matter. He is quite incapable of selecting reading matter which is within his grasp and which is not confusing. Not being of a very persistent nature, he will soon give up the struggle, and a reading skill which has taken years to acquire is left to deteriorate for lack of practice' (Gunzburg, 1968).

These comments suggest that it is essential that teaching should devote systematic attention to the development of aspects which contribute to comprehension of reading matter, and must not take it for granted that fluency in reading itself will encourage adequate use of that skill.

Only a few assessment tools have been developed which will assist in drawing attention to difficulties in reading comprehension. The Neale Test (Neale, 1966a) applies to ages 6–13. Gates (1935) published a diagnostic battery to measure four different aspects of comprehension: (A) to appreciate general significance; (B) to predict the outcome of given events; (C) to understand precise directions; (D) to note details. Other authors (Sangren, 1927; Watts, 1944) followed similar lines, and exercises based on the analysis of the poorly developed aspects of an individual's reading comprehension have been shown to be of considerable help (Duncan, 1942).

Generally speaking, a systematic and well-programmed reading course which attends to reading comprehension appears to be particularly important at this mental level. Reading competence is socially a very approved and appreciated skill, which is taken for granted in normal life, and inadequate competence will make the retarded feel isolated and inferior. Encouraging him in learning to use his reading skill flexibly is, therefore, as much a therapeutic action of gaining his confidence as a purely utilitarian move to make it easier for him to adjust to a literate community.

Gann (1945), who made a careful analysis of the personality of backward, good and average readers on the basis of projective tests, came to the conclusion that the poor readers are 'emotionally less well adjusted and less stable. They are insecure and fearful in relation to emotionally challenging situations and they are socially less adaptable to the group.' She suggested that 'the building of reading adequacy in those who have experienced difficulty with the process would involve, therefore, the resolutions of inhibiting personality forces and negative attitudes, as well as increased interest and skill in reading itself'. It may also happen in some cases, as Burt (1922) has suggested, that the reading matter may be associated with emotionally disturbing memories and thus create a blank leading to miscomprehension and inability to follow the thread of the story. Burt compared these blanks 'to those lapses of speech and memory, the slips of the pen and the trippings of the tongue, which in adults have been shown by psychoanalysis to be so richly symptomatic of the profounder secrets of the individual's mental attitude'.

Though the relationship between emotional maladjustment and reading disability is by now widely accepted, opinions differ whether therapy should precede reading instruction (Axline, 1947; Ewerhardt, 1938), or whether the improvement in reading in itself will lead to better adjustment (Kirk, 1934).

It is often difficult to decide whether emotional disturbance leads to reading failure or the lack of progress in reading causes emotional difficulties. Kirk (1934), investigating the effects of remedial reading on the institutionalized mentally retarded children, noted that progress in reading was associated with better adjustment in the classroom and decreased signs of personality mal-adjustment. On the other hand, Ewerhardt (1938) concluded from his work that the treatment of the emotional problems of retarded children led to better results in reading.

There are now several detailed reviews of work in this field available, which should be consulted (McCarthy and Scheerenberger, 1966; Kirk, 1964; Pope and Haklay, 1970) particularly regarding specific reading disabilities such as 'word blindness', developmental dyslexia, etc.

Number work

It could be argued with much success that it is nearly impossible for a mentally subnormal child or adult to 'get on' in life without some understanding for numbers, even though he might become very successful in the general community without being able to read. Many of the motivational schemes for the very retarded depend to a large extent on the appreciation of comparative sizes of rewards and the wide use of monetary incentives. The attempt to introduce realistic situations into institutions and schools, the aim of training the sub-normal to become a wage earner who can make sensible use of his wage packet, all these require that the subnormal should have a reasonably useful level of competence in this area. Despite its great usefulness fairly little systematic educational work has been published relating to teaching the severely subnormal.

Kirk (1964) summarized the results of research into the relation of arithmetical achievement to mental age as follows: 'Basically, retarded children appear to achieve in harmony with their mental age expectance in arithmetic fundamentals, but are below their expectancy in arithmetic reasoning problems requiring reading.'

(a) THE SEVERELY MENTALLY HANDICAPPED CHILD

There is nowadays much awareness of a need for establishing basic number concepts (Finley, 1962; Thresher, 1962) following a developmental sequence. The work of Piaget has provided guidelines for structuring educational work on a low level, which might have more impact on the subnormal than the more conventional approaches. Many of the devices used in number work may become real obstacles in the development of logical number thinking if the child be-comes impressed with spatial, visual relations and carries those misleading, concrete examples into a later stage, relying on 'visual' rather than logical evidence. Piaget's experiments in 'conservation of quantity', 'ordination' and 'cardination' point to the need to lay far more systematically the foundation for an understanding of numbers before beginning the more formal tasks of teaching number work (Woodward, 1961, 1962a, b).

Woodward (1962a) discusses the use of the usual type of classroom apparatus in relation to Piaget's sequence in development and suggests the correct order of presentation. Richards and Stone (1970) reported significant gains on conservation through a training programme with transfer to related behaviour in a group of 7–12–year–old children with IQs between 44 and 77.

Laying the initial foundations for an adequate understanding of number concepts requires also attention to a number vocabulary (Cruickshank, 1946; Silverstein *et al.*, 1964). Kirk and Johnson (1951) point to the necessity of acquiring a working vocabulary of arithmetical terms encountered in everyday life. It is quite surprising, and a cause of needless misunderstanding, how vague many subnormals are with regard to the meaning of terms concerned with length and distance (inch, foot, yard, etc.), to measurements (quarter, half, dozen, etc.), to amounts (pair, twice, increase, decrease, etc.), to time (day, week, month, etc.), and others. Though they know how to count, the meaning of ordinal figures (first, second, third, etc.) is often unknown.

The limitations imposed by the mental abilities of the pupil, time and educational organization make it imperative to develop a curriculum which deals primarily and perhaps solely with those skills which are of direct use to the defective. As Burns (1961) points out, the introduction of each new arithmetical skill and operation should depend on questions like: 'Is it important enough to teach? If it is to be taught, how can it be introduced in a concrete way? How can the abilities connected with the topic be practised enough to assure real learning?' Nicholls (1963) gives a list of some 200 number words, which is reduced to a more manageable extent by Bell (1970).

(b) THE MODERATELY HANDICAPPED CHILD

This is the child who, when an adult, might have to handle small money transactions in everyday situations. Most of the emphasis of teaching is, therefore, usually placed on encouraging competence in money operations and there is much agreement that 'paper and pencil sums' should give way to actual handling of money, first in mock-up situations and later in practical situations outside the schoolroom.

Brown and Dyer (1963) studied the results of two teaching methods. One group was given coaching in a work situation, where arithmetic problems could be directly related to work in hand. The other group was given conventional teaching in the classroom. The authors showed that there were significant increases in the arithmetical competence of the pupils when taught in a realistic setting.

In the same way as it is necessary to differentiate between the mechanical reading skill (barking at print) and the flexible use made of the skill (comprehension), it will be utterly important in number work to assess the achievements in mere rote memory (e.g. counting of objects) and in number concepts where the child has to apply his knowledge to many different situations (e.g. handing over three objects, counting in threes, reporting that there are three chairs, fetching three books, three children on command etc.). This requires many different types of learning situations for practising (Burns, 1961; Locking, 1966; Ross, 1970).

(c) THE MILDLY RETARDED CHILD

Once the elementary money operations have been satisfactorily mastered, educational targets can be set higher for those who have the innate ability to understand more complex financial operations. With a view to future adult status, more demanding financial situations can be tackled, such as budgeting of a wage packet and the implications of hire purchase arrangements. Programmes suitable for this level of ability are found without difficulty in the literature relating to the teaching of the educationally subnormal child (Duncan, 1942; Tansley and Gulliford, 1960).

Language

Not only do the results of verbal and non-verbal intelligence tests suggest poor verbal functioning, but specific investigation points to the mentally subnormal person's difficulties in verbal expression and understanding. Earl (1961) discussed at great length the language development of mildly and moderately handicapped children. He points out that certain personality aspects typical for the mentally handicapped, such as weakness of drive, simplicity and viscosity affect their ability to express themselves, resulting in a language of their own make, the 'sub-speak'. This is a primitive language with a small vocabulary, little syntax and less grammar, which helps in reinforcing their feelings of being at home in their own world and excluding the adult, normal world, which is beyond the subnormal's grasp.

Various investigations have confirmed the mental defective's difficulties in thinking abstractedly and in manipulating concepts, and it has been pointed out that institutionalization (Papania, 1954; Badt, 1958; Mein and O'Connor, 1960) was in many ways responsible for the low level of abstractness when compared with children of the same ability but receiving home training (Schlanger, 1954; Lyle, 1959): it is usually ascribed to the lack of environmental stimulation in the hospital. Whilst this explanation is generally correct, it must also be remembered that institutions deal probably with the more difficult children because only these tend to be admitted from urgent waiting lists. Mein and O'Connor (1960) studied the oral vocabulary of severely subnormal hospital patients and compared it with that of normal children of approximately the same mental level. The patients used about 1,000 fewer words than did the normal children. Sampson (1964) studied carefully the conversation of severely subnormal children living at home, following up her earlier work (1962) on language development of this type of child. The problems of language and communication have been ably summarized by Spradlin (1963) in the case of the mentally handicapped and by Renfrew and Murphy (1964) for handicapped children in general. Brook (1966) studied the spontaneous speech of severely subnormal institutionalized children, and Beier *et al.* (1969) analysed their vocabulary usage and concluded that 'there is no particular deficit in the type of memory function needed to retain a vocabulary, but that the mentally retarded deficit is likely to be found in conceptualization, organization, language structure, grammar and syntax'.

Major studies in this area are found in Luria (1963), O'Connor and Hermelin (1963), Adler (1964), McCarthy (1964), Mecham *et al.* (1966), Schiefelbusch *et al.* (1967), and Spradlin (1968). They and many others are reviewed in Chapter 9.

Some systematic work in encouraging language competence has been reported (Richardson, 1967), usually as the result of diagnostic assessments of specific language weaknesses, though many educationalists prefer to 'integrate' language activities in a general programme rather than treating them as a subject (Harrison, 1959; Irwin, 1959; Mecham, 1963; Olson *et al.*, 1965; Jeffree and Cashdan, 1971). Generally, the difficulties in communication are tackled in two different ways. Many teachers advocate the need for expanding environmental stimulation by play, activities and discussions. Using informal but natural situations they still attempt to induce a desire for communication in everyday life (Lyle, 1960). There is obviously the danger that the not so expert teacher will miss many teaching opportunities, will be unable to encourage progress and will not remedy in time weaknesses and deficits in language competence. To avoid these possible disadvantages, systematic language training has been advocated to promote the the use of language for thinking, for forming concepts and abstractions. These programmes, usually based on the results of the analysis of language use and understanding, treat language as a subject, following a syllabus step by step (Bereiter and Engelmann, 1966).

(a) THE SEVERELY SUBNORMAL CHILD

Several studies of the language competence of severely subnormal children have been published which have implications on language programmes (Blount, 1968). The language disorders of mongols have attracted particular attention (Lenneberg *et al.*, 1964; Bilovsky and Share, 1965; Evans and Sampson, 1968; Weinberg and Zlatin, 1970) and Jeffree (1971) describes a language teaching programme designed for a particular 8-year-old mongol child. This was an unusually carefully designed programme, which took into account her assets and interests (such as writing, interest in drawing and in humorous pictures), and her immaturities in expressive language (such as short phrases, preponderance of nouns over verbs, preference for gestures, etc.). Five different teaching approaches were developed and the effect of each on both quantity and quality of language was systematically examined. The interaction of language and behaviour in the cerebrally palsied child was described by Burland (1969).

(b) THE MODERATELY RETARDED CHILD

The Illinois Test of Psycholinguistic Abilities (McCarthy and Kirk, 1961) encouraged much systematic classroom work (Kirk and Bateman, 1962; Wiseman, 1965). Smith (1962) reported significant increases in ITPA scores after only thirty-three lessons but also instability of achievement over time (Mueller and Smith, 1964). Kirk (1962) and Kirk and Bateman (1962) give several examples of the use of this test, not only for diagnosis but for suggesting in each individual case a remedial programme to correct the linguistic disability. Language programmes have been described by various educationalists (Dawe, 1942; Harrison, 1959; Irwin, 1959; Mecham, 1963; Olson et al., 1965; Sampson, 1966).

(c) THE MILDLY RETARDED CHILD

Using the Peabody Language Development Kit (Dunn and Smith, 1964), Dunn and his collaborators (Dunn and Mueller, 1966; Dunn et al., 1967) found considerable gains in language ages with socially mildly disadvantaged children, depending on the length of language education. They stress particularly overlearning to facilitate retention, but the approach has been severely criticized by Rosenberg (1970). An example of the classroom use is provided by Carter (1966) who obtained significant gains as the result of an intensive forty-hour programme over ten weeks.

Whilst the dullness of the usual systematic language programme makes it difficult to assess its permanent effect on communication abilities, there is little doubt that this aspect of mental functioning cannot be left to informal and haphazard teaching approaches, which will most likely fail to apply educational pressure on those fronts where it is needed most. It will be essential to stress the language aspect throughout an educational programme, to provide for a variety of experience in other than language lessons, but at the same time adhere closely to a defined programme of language use which is related to the subnormals' interests and life.

Other teaching areas

Compared with the importance of those aspects already discussed, other 'school subjects' assume subordinate and often very minor roles. However, it is very clear that they too, if properly integrated into a programme with clearly defined objectives, can contribute substantially towards its realization. The aim would then be to reinforce learning in the main areas by approaching these objectives in different ways and contexts and presenting the teaching contents in a variety of different situations.

Ross (1970), for example, reports the efficacy of a general programme for teaching basic number concepts and social skills, utilizing table search games, card games, guessing games, board games and active racing. The progress of a group of children was compared with that of a control group in the classroom. It was found that the experimental group obtained higher scores on all measures – rote and rational counting, specific quantitative terms, time, money, shape and colour.

Significant increases in language ability, productivity and good classroom behaviour were the results of an art and movement programme, which aimed to achieve higher competence in self care, language and motor skills as a 'by product' of carefully planned play lessons (Neale, 1966b).

Nature study can provide realistic opportunities for training perception and encouraging sensory discrimination, and Barham (1971) describes such a programme in relation to aspects as measured by the Illinois Test of Psycholinguistic Abilities.

Conclusions

Though some of the educational research has given valuable suggestions and has demonstrated that results can be achieved, the transfer from the laboratory situation to classroom teaching has on the whole been pretty unsuccessful. This is primarily due to a reluctance on the teachers' part to exchange familiar methods and syllabi, hallowed by their long use in 'normal' education, for new, unproven and demanding procedures. It is even more due to the fact that no one has yet 'proved' that the direct teaching of various aspects of social education has substantially increased the mentally handicappeds' prospects of social adjustment, whilst, on the other hand, no one would seriously challenge the value of the basic acquisition of reading, writing and arithmetic. As it is, shifting of emphasis from academic to social education is more an act of faith than the result of demonstrated relevance to the overall aim.

There is also a feeling that thinking of 'adult aims' will violate the right of the severely subnormal child to be treated as a child, who wants to play and to explore. There is really no reason why thinking in terms of a systematic programme of preparation for adulthood should interfere with the need of the child for a stimulating education adjusted to his level. For many, however, the main difficulty is to accept that different final aims may well require different teaching approaches and different teaching contents at comparatively early stages.

References

ADLER, S. (1964) *The Non-verbal Child.* Springfield, Ill.: Charles C. Thomas.

AXLINE, V. M. (1947) Non-directive therapy for poor readers. *J. consult. Psychol.*, **11**, 61–9.

BADT, M. I. (1958) Levels of abstraction in vocabulary definitions of mentally retarded schoolchildren. *Amer. J. ment. Defic.*, **63**, 241–6.

BARHAM, J. (1971) Nature study activities with severely subnormal children. *Forward Trends*, **15**, 29–32.

BEIER, E. G., STARKWEATHER, J. A. and LAMBERT, M. J. (1969) Vocabulary usage of mentally retarded children. *Amer. J. ment. Defic.*, **73**, 927–34.

BELL, P. (1970) *Basic Teaching for Slow Learners*. London: Muller.

BENSBERG, G. J., COLWELL, C. N. and CASSEL, R. H. (1965) Teaching the profoundly retarded self-help activities by behavior shaping techniques. *Amer. J. ment. Defic.*, **69**, 674–9.

BEREITER, C. and ENGELMANN, S. (1966) *Teaching Disadvantaged Children in the Pre-School*. Englewood Cliffs, NJ: Prentice-Hall.

BIJOU, S. W. (1965) Application of operant principles to the teaching of reading, writing and arithmetic to retarded children. In *New Frontiers in Special Education*. Washington, DC: Council for Exceptional Children.

BILOVSKY, D. and SHARE, J. (1965) The ITPA and Down's syndrome: an exploratory study. *Amer. J. ment. Defic.*, **70**, 78–82.

BLACKMAN, L. S. and CAPOBIANCO, R. J. (1965) An evaluation of programmed instruction with the MR utilizing teaching machines. *Amer. J. ment. Defic.*, **70**, 262–9.

BLAND, G. A. (1968) *Education in Hospital Schools for the Mentally Handicapped*. London: College of Special Education.

BLOUNT, W. R. (1968) Language and the more severely retarded: a review. *Amer. J. ment. Defic.*, **73**, 21–9.

BROOK, J. R. (1966) Spontaneous spoken vocabulary of a group of severely mentally subnormal children. *Brit. J. dis. Comm.*, **1**, 131–5.

BROWN, R. I. (1967) A remedial reading program for the adolescent illiterate. *J. spec. Educ.*, **1**, 409–17.

BROWN, R. I. and BOOKBINDER, G. E. (1966) Programmed reading for spastics. *Spec. Educ.*, **55**, 26–9.

BROWN, R. I. and BOOKBINDER, G. E. (1968) *The Clifton Audio-Visual Reading Programme*. Harlow: ESA.

BROWN, R. I. and DYER, L. (1963) Social arithmetic training for the subnormal: a comparison of two methods. *J. ment. Subn.*, **IX**, 8–12.

BURLAND, R. (1969) The development of the verbal regulation of behaviour in cerebrally palsied (multiply handicapped) children. *J. ment. Subn.*, **XV**, 85–9.

BURNS, P. C. (1961) Arithmetic fundamentals for the educable mentally retarded. *Amer. J. ment. Defic.* **66**, 57–62.,

BURT, C. (1922) *Mental and Scholastic Tests* (2nd edn, 1924). London: P. S. King.

CARTER, J. A. (1966) *The Effect of a Group Language Stimulation Program upon Negro Culturally Disadvantaged First Grade Children.* Doctoral dissertation, Univ. of Texas.

CHALL, J. S. (1967) *Learning to Read: The Great Debate, I.* New York: McGraw-Hill.

COLWELL, C. N. and CASSELL, R.H. (1955) Teaching the profoundly retarded self-help activities by behavior shaping techniques. *Amer. J. ment. Defic.*, **69**, 674-9.

CRUICKSHANK, W. M. (1946) Arithmetic vocabulary of mentally retarded boys. *Except. Child.*, **13**, 65-9.

DANIELS, J. C. and DIACK, H. (1960) *Progress in Reading in the Infant School.* Nottingham: Univ. of Nottingham Inst. of Education.

DAWE, H. G. (1942) A study of the effect of an educational program upon language development and related mental functions in young children. *J. exp. Educ.*, **11**, 200-9.

DUNCAN, J. (1942) *The Education of the Ordinary Child.* London: Nelson.

DUNN, L. M. (1968) Special education for the mildly retarded – is much of it justifiable? *Except. Child.*, **35**, 5-22.

DUNN, L. M. and MUELLER, M. W. (1966) *The Effectiveness of the Peabody Language Development Kits and the Initial Teaching Alphabet with Disadvantaged Children in the Primary Grades after One Year.* Nashville: Inst. Ment. Retard. Intellect. Developmt. Sci. Monogr.

DUNN, L. M. and SMITH, J. O. (1964) *The Peabody Language Development Kit.* Minneapolis: Amer. Guidance Service Inc.

DUNN, L. M., POCHANART, P. and PFOST, P. (1967) *The Effectiveness of the Peabody Language Development Kits and the Initial Teaching Alphabet with Disadvantaged Children in the Primary Grades after Two Years.* Nashville: Inst. Ment. Retard. Intellect. Developmt. Sci. Monogr.

EARL, C. J. C. (1961) *Subnormal Personalities: Their Clinical Investigation and Assessment.* London: Baillière, Tindall & Cox.

ELLIS, N. R., BARNETT, C. D. and PRYER, M. W. (1960) Operant behaviour in mental defectives. *J. exp. Anal. Behav.*, **3**, 63-9.

EVANS, D. and SAMPSON, M. (1968) The language of mongols. *Brit. J. dis. Comm.*, **3**, 171-81.

EWERHARDT, P. (1938) Reading difficulties in subnormal children. *Proc. Amer. Assoc. ment. Defic.*, **43**, 188-93.

FINLEY, C. J. (1962) Arithmetic achievement in mentally retarded children. *Amer. J. ment. Defic.*, **67**, 281-6.

FRANCEY, R. E. (1966) Psychological test changes in mentally retarded children during training. In JORDAN, T. E. (ed.) *Perspectives in Mental Retardation.* Carbondale and Edwardsville: Southern Illinois Univ. Press.

GANN, E. (1945) *Reading Difficulty and Personality Organization.* New York: King's Crown Press.

GARDNER, J. M. (1969) Behavior modification research in mental retardation. Search for an adequate paradigm. *Amer. J. ment. Defic.*, 73, 844–51.

GARDNER, J. M. and WATSON, L. S. (1969) Behavior modification of the

GARDNER, W. I. and NISONGER, H. W. (1962) A manual on program development in mental retardation. *Amer. J. ment. Defic. Suppl.*, 66(1).

GATES, A. I. (1935) *Improvement of Reading.* New York: Macmillan.

GESELL, A. (1954) *The First Five Years of Life.* London: Methuen.

GIRARDEAU, F. L. (1962) The effect of secondary reinforcement on the operant behavior of mental defectives. *Amer. J. ment. Defic.*, 67, 441–9.

GIRARDEAU, F. L. and SPRADLIN, J. E. (1964) Token rewards in a cottage program. *Ment. Retard.*, 2, 345–51.

GULLIFORD, R. (1971) *Special Educational Needs.* London: Routledge & Kegan Paul.

GUNZBURG, H. C. (1948) The subnormal boy and his reading interests. *Libr. Quart.*, 18, 264–74.

GUNZBURG, H. C. (1963) *Junior Training Centres: An Outline of the Principles and Practices of Social Education and Training of the Mentally Subnormal Child.* London: National Association for Mental Health.

GUNZBURG, H. C. (1968) *Social Competence and Mental Handicap.* London: Baillière, Tindall & Cassell.

HAMILTON, J. and ALLEN, P. (1967) Ward programming for severely retarded institutionalized retardates. *Ment. Retard.*, 5, 22–4.

HARRISON, S. (1959) Integration of developmental language activities with an educational program for mentally retarded children. *Amer. J. ment. Defic.*, 63, 967–70.

HEADRICK, N. W. (1963) Operant conditioning in mental deficiency. *Amer. J. ment. Defic.*, 67, 924–9.

HEBER, R. (1968) The role of environmental variations in etiology of cultural-familial mental retardation. In RICHARDS, B. (ed.) *Proc. 1st Congr. Internat. Assoc. Scient. Stud. Ment. Defic.* Reigate: Michael Jackson.

HEBER, R. (1971) An experiment in prevention of cultural-familial mental retardation. In PRIMROSE, D. A. (ed.) *Proc. 2nd Congr. Internat. Assoc.*

HERMELIN, B. and O'CONNOR, N. (1960) Reading ability of severely subnormal children. *J. ment. Defic. Res.*, 4, 144–7.

HOLLIS, J. H. and GORTON, C. E. (1967) Training severely and profoundly developmentally retarded children. *Ment. Retard.*, 5, 20–4.

HUDSON, M. (1955) Some theoretical aspects to curriculum building for the severely retarded child. *Amer. J. ment. Defic.*, 60, 270–7.

HUNDZIAK, M., MAURER, R. and WATSON, L. S. (1965) Operant conditioning in toilet training for severely mentally retarded boys. *Amer. J. ment. Defic.*, 70, 120–4.

INGRAM, C. P. (1953) *Education of the Slow-Learning Child*. New York: The Ronald Press.

IRWIN, B. (1959) Oral language for slow-learning children. *Amer. J. ment. Defic.*, **64,** 32–40.

JEFFREE, D. M. (1971) A language teaching programme for a mongol child. *Forward Trends*, **15,** 33–8.

JEFFREE, D. M. and CASHDAN, A. (1971) Severely subnormal children and their parents: an experiment in language improvement. *Brit. J. clin. Psychol.*, **41,** 184–93.

KEATING, L. E. (1962) A pilot experiment in remedial reading at the Hospital School. *Brit. J. educ. Psychol.*, **32,** 62–5.

KEITH, K. D. and LANGE, B. M. (1974) Maintenance of behavior change in an institution-wide training program. *Ment. Retard.*, **12,** 34–7.

KIERNAN, C. C. (1974) Application of behaviour modification in the ward situation. In GUNZBURG, H. C. (ed.) *Experiments in the Rehabilitation of the Mentally Handicapped*. London: Butterworths.

KIRK, S. A. (1934) The effects of remedial reading on the education progress and personality adjustment of high-grade mentally deficient problem children: ten case studies. *J. juv. Res.*, **18,** 140–62.

KIRK, S. A. (1940) *Teaching Reading to Slow Learning Children*. Boston: Houghton Mifflin.

KIRK, S. A. (1962) *Educating Exceptional Children*. Boston: Houghton Mifflin.

KIRK, S. A. (1964) Research in education. In STEVENS, H. A. and HEBER, R. (eds.) *Mental Retardation: A Review of Research*. Chicago and London: Univ. of Chicago Press.

KIRK, S. A. and BATEMAN, B. (1962) Diagnosis and remediation of learning disabilities. *J. except. Child.*, **29,** 73–8.

KIRK, S. A. and JOHNSON, G. O. (1951) *Educating the Retarded Child*. Boston: Houghton Mifflin.

KIRK, S. A., KARNES, M. B. and KIRK, W. D. (1955) *You and Your Retarded Child*. New York: Macmillan.

KOLBURNE, L. L. (1965) *Effective Education for the Mentally Retarded Child*. New York: Vantage Press.

LABON, D. (1967) But does i.t.a. help slow learners? *Spec. Educ.*, **56,** 17–20.

LAWRENCE, W. and KARTYE, J. (1971) Extinction of social competency skills in severely and profoundly retarded females. *Amer. J. ment. Defic.*, **75,** 630–4.

LENNEBERG, E. H., NICHOLS, I. A. and ROSENBERGER, E. F. (1964) Primitive stages of language development in mongolism. *Proc. Assoc. Res. nerv. ment. Dis.*, 119–37.

LINDE, T. (1962) Techniques for establishing motivation through operant conditioning. *Amer. J. ment. Defic.*, **67,** 437–40.

LOCKING, J. R. (1966) An arithmetic programme for the subnormal pupil.

In GUNZBURG, H. C. (ed.) *The Application of Research to the Education and Training of the Severely Subnormal Child.* J. ment. Subn. Monogr.

LORENZO, E. G. C. (1967) Investigation in spontaneous development and development in a group of subjects studied from birth. In RICHARDS, B. (ed.) *Proc. 1st Congr. Internat. Assoc. Scient. Stud. Ment. Defic.* Reigate: Michael Jackson.

LORENZO, E. G. C. (1970) The importance of early stimulation. In PRIMROSE, D. A. (ed.) *Proc. 2nd Congr. Internat. Assoc. Scient. Stud. Ment. Defic.* Warsaw: Ars Polona; Amsterdam: Swets & Zeitlinger.

LURIA, A. R. (1963) *The Mentally Retarded Child.* New York: Pergamon Press.

LYLE, J. G. (1959) The effect of an institution environment upon the verbal development of imbecile children. Part I: Verbal intelligence. *J. ment. Defic. Res.,* **3**, 122–8.

LYLE, J. G. (1960) The effect of an institution environment upon the verbal development of imbecile children. Parts II and III. *J. ment. Defic. Res.,* **4**, 1–23.

MCCARTHY, J. J. (1964) Research on the linguistic problems of the mentally retarded. *Ment. Retard. Abstrs.,* **1**, 3–27.

MCCARTHY, J. J. and KIRK, S. A. (1961) *Illinois Test of Psycholinguistic Abilities: Experimental Edition.* Urbana: Univ. of Illinois Press.

MCCARTHY, J. J. and SCHEERENBERGER, R. G. (1966) A decade of research on the education of the mentally retarded. *Ment. Retard. Abstrs.,* **3**, 481–501.

MECHAM, M. J. (1963) Developmental schedules of oral-aural language as an aid to the teacher of the mentally retarded. *Ment. Retard.,* 359–69.

MECHAM, M. J., BERKO, M. J., GIDEN, F. and PALMER, M. F. (1966) *Communication Training in Childhood Brain Damage.* Springfield, Ill.: Charles C. Thomas.

MEIN, R. and O'CONNOR, N. (1960) A study of the oral vocabularies of severely subnormal patients. *J. ment. Defic. Res.,* **4**, 130–43.

MILLER, A. (1967) Symbol accentuation: outgrowth of theory and experiment. In RICHARDS, B. (ed.) *Proc. 1st Congr. Internat. Assoc. Scient. Stud. Ment. Defic.* Reigate: Michael Jackson.

MINGE, R. and BALL, T. S. (1967) Teaching of self-help skills to profoundly retarded residents. *Amer. J. ment. Defic.,* **71**, 864–8.

MITCHELL, A. C. and SMERIGLIO, V. (1970) Growth in social competence in institutionalized mentally retarded children. *Amer. J. ment. Defic.,* **74**, 666–73.

MUELLER, M. W. and SMITH, J. O. (1964) The stability of language age modifications over time. *Amer. J. ment. Defic.,* **68**, 537–9.

NAWAS, M. M. and BRAUN, S. H. (1970) An overview of behaviour modification with the severely and profoundly retarded. *Ment. Retard.,* **8**, 4–11.

NEALE, M. D. (1966a) *The Neale Analysis of Reading Ability*. London: Macmillan.

NEALE, M. D. (1966b) Perceptual development of severely retarded children through motor experience. In GUNZBURG, H. C. (ed.) *The Application of Research to the Education and Training of the Severely Subnormal Child*. J. ment. Subn. Monogr.

NEALE, M. D. and CAMPBELL, W. J. (1963) *Education for the Intellectually Limited Child and Adolescent*. Sydney: Ian Novak.

NICHOLLS, R. H. (1963) Programming Piaget in practice. *Teaching Arithmetic*, 1(3).

NICKELL, V. (1951) *Educating the Mentally Handicapped in the Secondary School*. Illinois Secondary School Curriculum Program, Bull. No. 12. Springfield: Dept of Public Instruct.

O'CONNOR, N. and HERMELIN, B. (1963) *Speech and Thought in Severe Subnormality*. London: Pergamon.

OLSON, J. L., HAHN, H. R. and HERMANN, A. L. (1965) Psycholinguistic curriculum. *Ment. Retard.*, 3, 14–19.

ORLANDO, R. and BIJOU, S. W. (1960) Single and multiple schedules of reinforcement in developmentally retarded children. *J. exp. Anal. Behav.*, 3, 339–48.

PAPANIA, N. A. (1954) Qualitative analysis of vocabulary responses of institutionalized mentally retarded children. *J. clin. Psychol.*, 10, 361–5.

POPE, L. and HAKLAY, A. (1970) Reading disability. In WORTIS, J. (ed.) *Mental Retardation*. New York: Grune & Stratton.

QUAY, L. C. (1963) Academic skills. In ELLIS, N. R. (ed.) *Handbook of Mental Deficiency*. New York: McGraw-Hill.

RENFREW, C. and MURPHY, K. (1964) *The Child Who Does Not Talk*. London: Heinemann.

RICHARDS, H. E. and STONE, D. R. (1970) The learning and transference of the Piagetian concept of conservation. *Ment. Retard.*, 8, 34–7.

RICHARDSON, S. O. (1967) Language training for mentally retarded children. In SCHIEFELBUSCH, R. L. *et al.* (eds.) *Language and Mental Retardation*. New York: Holt, Rinehart & Winston.

ROOS, P. and OLIVER, M. (1969) Evaluation of operant conditioning with institutionalized retarded children. *Amer. J. ment. Defic.*, 74, 325–30.

ROSENBERG, S. (1970) Problems of language development in the retarded. In HAYWOOD, H. C. (ed.) *Social-Cultural Aspects of Mental Retardation*. New York: Appleton-Century-Crofts.

ROSENZWEIG, L. (1959) How far have we come? *Amer. J. ment. Defic.*, 64, 12–18.

ROSS, D. (1970) Incidental learning of number concepts in small group games. *Amer. J. ment. Defic.*, 74, 718–25.

SAMPSON, O. C. (1962) Speech development and improvement in the severely subnormal child. *J. ment. Subn.*, VIII, 70–7.

SAMPSON, O. C. (1964) The conversational style of a group of severely subnormal children. *J. ment. Subn.*, **X**, 89–100.

SAMPSON, O. C. (1966) Helping the severely subnormal child to develop language. In GUNZBURG, H. C. (ed.) *The Application of Research to the Education and Training of the Severely Subnormal.* J. ment. Subn. Monogr.

SANGREN, P. V. (1927) *The Measurement of Achievement in Silent Reading.* Kalamazoo: West State Teachers' College.

SCHIEFELBUSCH, R. L., COPELAND, R. H. and SMITH, J. D. (1967) *Language and Mental Retardation.* London: Holt, Rinehart & Winston.

SCHLANGER, B. B. (1954) Environmental influences on the verbal output of mentally retarded children. *J. speech hear. Dis.*, **19**, 339–43.

SILVERSTEIN, A. B., AUGER, R. and KRUDIS, B. R. (1964) The meaning of indefinite number terms for mentally retarded children. *Amer. J. ment. Defic.*, **69**, 419–24.

SKINNER, B. F. (1965) The technology of teaching. *Proc. Roy. Soc.*, **162**, 427–43.

SMITH, J. O. (1962) Group language development for educable mental retardates. *Except. Child.*, **29**, 95–101.

SMITH, M. (1966) Right backward pupils and i.t.a. *Spec. Educ.*, **55**, 19–22.

SPRADLIN, J. E. (1963) Language and communication in mental defectives. In ELLIS, N. R. (ed.) *Handbook of Mental Deficiency.* New York: McGraw-Hill.

SPRADLIN, J. E. (1968) Environmental factors and the language development of retarded children. In ROSENBERG, S. (ed.) *Developments in Applied Psycholinguistic Research.* New York: Macmillan.

STEVENS, G. D. (1958) An analysis of the objectives for the education of children with retarded mental development. *Amer. J. ment. Defic.*, **63**, 225–35.

STEVENS, M. (1971) *The Educational Needs of Severely Subnormal Children.* London: Edward Arnold.

STOLUROW, L. M. (1963) Programmed instruction for the mentally retarded. *Rev. educ. Res.*, **33**, 126–36.

TANSLEY, A. E. and GULLIFORD, R. (1960) *The Education of Slow Learning Children.* London: Routledge & Kegan Paul.

THRESHER, J. M. (1962) A problem for educators: arithmetical concept formation in the mentally retarded child. *Amer. J. ment. Defic.*, **66**, 766–73.

TREFFRY, D., MARTIN, G., SAMELS, J. and WATSON, C. (1970) Operant conditioning of grooming behaviour of severely retarded girls. *Ment. Retard.*, **8**, 29–33.

WALLIN, J. E. W. (1955) *Education of Mentally Handicapped Children.* New York: Harper & Row.

WARNER, W. L., HAVIGHURST, R. J. and LOEB, M. B. (1946) *Who Shall Be Educated?* London: Routledge & Kegan Paul.

WATTS, A. F. (1944) *The Language and Mental Development of Children.* London: Harrap.

WEINBERG, B. and ZLATIN, M. (1970) Speaking fundamental frequency characteristics of five and six year old children with mongolism. *J. speech hear. Res.*, **13**, 418–25.

WHELAN, R. J. and HARING, N. (1966) Modification and maintenance of behaviour through systematic application of consequences. *Except. Child.*, **32**, 281–9.

WILLIAMS, H. M. and WALLIN, J. E. W. (1959) *Education of the Severely Retarded Child.* Washington, DC: Government Printing Office.

WISEMAN, D. E. (1965) A classroom procedure for identifying and remediating language problems. *Ment. Retard.*, **3**, 20–4.

WOODWARD, M. (1961) Concepts of number in the mentally subnormal studied by Piaget's method. *J. Child. Psychol. Psychiat.*, **2**, 249–59.

WOODWARD, M. (1962a) The application of Piaget's theory to the training of the subnormal. *J. ment. Subn.*, **VIII**, 17–25.

WOODWARD, M. (1962b) Concepts of space in the mentally subnormal studied by Piaget's method. *Brit. J. soc. clin. Psychol.*, **I**, 25–37.

12

C. C. Kiernan

Behaviour modification

Introduction

The aims of this chapter will be to present a description of the behaviour modification approach to analysis of the behaviour of the mentally handicapped and to discuss representative programmes within this context. It will not attempt an overall critical review of the application of these methods, since the volume of available data is far too extensive. In addition, several reviews have appeared recently which have accomplished this task (e.g. Bandura, 1969; J. M. Gardner, 1971; W. I. Gardner, 1971; Sherman and Baer, 1969). Rather the chapter will aim to develop the approach and to indicate some of its implications.

The application of operant techniques to the behaviour of mentally handicapped individuals began over thirty years ago (Fuller, 1949). Since then its extent has increased at a rapid rate in North America, although in Great Britain and Continental Europe it is lagging several years behind.

The conceptual roots of this application lie firmly in the work of Skinner (1938, 1953). Early use of the term 'behaviour modification' did not tie it specifically to the operant tradition. R. I. Watson (1962) related it to situations which were studies of learning, with a particular intent – 'the clinical goal of treatment'. Among Watson's situations were structured interviews, experimental neuroses and doctor-patient relationships. Krasner and Ullman (1966) focus it further in terms of an elimination of hypothetical constructs, a consequent emphasis on behavioural explanations and an emphasis on social reinforcement. The social learning approach was further developed by Bandura (1969) and by Patterson (1969).

An alternative phrase used in describing the application of operant principles is the 'experimental analysis of behaviour'. The experimental analysis referred to is operant analysis (cf. Bijou and Baer, 1961, 1965, 1967; Keller and Schoenfeld, 1950). This has tended to be used far more precisely but the approach it designates has also been identified by the term behaviour 'modification' (cf. W. I. Gardner, 1971).

One terminological problem is that not all attempts to modify behaviour would be classed under 'behaviour modification' and not all attempts to analyse behaviour experimentally would be classified under the rubric 'experimental analysis of behaviour'.

A further problem is that much work in the applied field does not involve the extensive experimental manipulation of variables which characterizes infra-human experimental analysis of behaviour. The term 'applied behaviour analysis' is preferred by some workers anxious to emphasize the applied orientation as opposed to more analytic studies.

The phrases 'behaviour therapy' or 'behavioural psychotherapy' are rejected by most workers in this field, since they relate to a range of techniques not covered by operant analyses. Furthermore it would be overextending the word 'therapy' to include under it the bulk of work with the mentally handicapped.

The term 'behaviour modification' will be used in this chapter. This usage is a matter of convenience rather than conviction. It reflects an emphasis on the social learning aspects of the application of operant techniques. Much more importantly it reflects an emphasis on the need to re-interpret phenomena described outside the operant tradition in operant contexts. Moreover, it will be interpreted to designate areas of educational, child care and clinical interest rather than restricting it to clinical situations.

The specific argument presented in this chapter will be that operant analysis and operant principles offer a valuable model in the context of which the behaviour of the mentally handicapped may be interpreted and modified. In particular it will be suggested that the model can integrate and systematize diverse approaches to behaviour, including psychological, sociological, bio-logical, education and ecological studies. Many of these disciplines have involved studies which are broadly descriptive in nature and translation of their findings into operant terms serves both to give a unification of theoretical language and to suggest new approaches to the behavioural phenomena involved (Michael, 1970).

It will be evident that this definition of the scope of behaviour modification is broader than other uses quoted. The emphasis on social learning is coupled with an emphasis on environmental modification as a means of effecting change in behaviour through change in the impact of variables isolated as critical within the operant framework.

The first part of this chapter will present a description of the behaviour modification approach with an attempt to show how it develops out of basic principles. Later sections will concern broader factors related to the environment and the curriculum.

The basic approach

The radical behaviourist position represented by behaviour modification has been discussed and analysed fully both in its general application to human behaviour and development (e.g. Bijou and Baer, 1961; Skinner, 1953) and with particular reference to disturbed behaviour or the behaviour of the mentally handicapped (e.g. Bijou, 1966; Spradlin and Giradeau, 1966; Whaley and Malott, 1968; W. I. Gardner, 1971). No attempt will be made here to describe or defend the approach in full. The aim of this section will be to characterize the main outline of the theory and then to examine its chief propositions as they relate to the behaviour of the mentally handicapped.

The fundamental assumptions are that the control and explanation of behaviour are best accomplished in terms of environmental variables which affect behaviour and that therefore this explanation does not require recourse to hypothetical constructs or intervening variables. The heuristic virtues of this approach were outlined by Skinner (1950) in terms of emphasizing the study of behaviour rather than theoretical constructs. In terms of the analysis of human behaviour this emphasis has led to attention being focused on the day-to-day behaviour of the individual, on 'retarded behaviour' rather than on 'retarded mentality' as an abstract entity (Bijou, 1966).

The behaviour of the mentally handicapped is seen within the theory as a function of a number of factors. These include current environmental factors and the history of the individual. Biological variables affecting stimulus reception or response potential are also seen as critical. However behaviour is not 'caused by' biological defects. The defects set the occasion for a failure to learn or for anomalous learning. Similarly environmental factors related to the occurrence of behaviour do not 'cause it'. The attitude of hospital staff does not affect the individual. It is the restriction on the behaviour of the inmate brought about through the behaviour of the staff which is critical (cf. King et al., 1971). Attitudes are critical only in that they correlate with behaviour – behaviour is prime.

In short, biological, sociological and other factors affect the probability of a large number of events. Subnormal behaviour is seen as a failure of learning. Aetiology and history are critical only to the extent that they may affect the formation of stimulus-response relationships. A full analysis of the current behaviour and the factors maintaining it may reveal procedures which will overcome apparent limiting biological factors or lead to a reformulation of arguments relating to the influence of other variables.

RESPONSES AND STIMULI

The basic assumption of behaviour modification is that all responses can be classified in terms of a respondent-operant distinction. Respondents are responses which are elicited by preceding stimulation in a 'reflexive' or 'involuntary' manner. Salivation, pupillary dilation, and patellar responses are all examples of this class. Respondents are seen as being controlled, not by consequences, but rather by antecedent events.

Operants are defined as behaviours which are 'best understood as functionally related to their consequences in the environment' (Bijou and Baer, 1961). These are behaviours which are 'goal-directed', 'purposeful', or 'instrumental' in attaining goals. Antecedent stimulation may set the occasion for operant but the stimulus which controls emission of the operant is the consequent or reinforcing stimulus.

Since the original major statement of the theory (Skinner, 1938) data have accumulated which indicate that responses which would normally be termed respondents may be brought under control of their consequences, i.e. behave as operants. The work of Miller and his associates (DiCara and Miller, 1968; Miller and Banuazizi, 1968; Miller and DiCara, 1967; Trowill, 1967) and others (e.g. Brener and Hothersall, 1967) has demonstrated that responses such as heart rate, vasoconstriction, and intestinal responses may be brought under control of their consequences.

These studies have carefully excluded the possibility that operant components are mediating the observed changes. Thus it is unlikely that heart rate changes are mediated by the subject being conditioned to change skeletal activity in order indirectly to promote the heart rate change (cf. Katkin and Murray, 1968).

These studies do not require any fundamental revision in the operant-respondent distinction. The distinction was always drawn empirically, and in fact it is even arguable that Skinner anticipated the data on operant conditioning of so-called autonomic functions (Skinner, 1938, pp. 112–15). What these studies have stimulated is a further definition of the variables concerned with the operant-respondent distinction (e.g. Catania, 1971). This work is likely to lead in the future to exciting developments but for the moment the critical point is that the operant-respondent distinction can still be meaningfully drawn.

Applications of the theory in the mentally handicapped have tended to deal almost exclusively with operants. In fact, the study of respondents in general have been de-emphasized by the behaviour modification approach. Almost all work of note with the mentally handicapped within this tradition is concerned with operant behaviour.

Stimuli are conceptualized in a variety of ways within the theory. The stimulus may be seen in terms of its physical properties, or in terms of the function it subserves. A stimulus may be measurable physically but may have no function in relation to behaviour. Respondents are elicited by certain classes of stimuli. In relation to operants, the stimulus may serve either a reinforcing or discriminative function. Its reinforcing properties concern its effect on behaviour where it follows a consequence of a response. Consequent stimuli may function to increase the probability of a response, to decrease it or may not affect it.

Consequent events, reinforcing events, may follow a response each time it is emitted. In this case the contingency is termed continuous. However, a contingency may be set up on any one of a wide variety of schedules of reinforcement on an intermittent basis.

The discriminative function of a stimulus refers to the extent to which it will set the occasion for an operant. Thus a green light at a traffic junction and the instruction 'do it if you like' can both function as discriminative stimuli for operants. Discriminative stimuli may be either positive 'go' stimuli or negative 'no-go' stimuli, at any degree of complexity.

A special class of discriminative stimuli, 'setting events', is distinguished by several writers (Kantor, 1958; Bijou and Baer, 1961). A setting event is defined as a stimulus-response interaction which affects a whole set of succeeding events. Physical injury, drugs, deprivation of social contact and some verbal formulations are all seen as such to the extent that they affect a substantial number of subsequent behaviours. Although setting events can be analysed into component stimulus events, it is considered sometimes more convenient and efficient to use the setting concept (Bijou and Baer, 1961). We have already seen that the theory conceptualizes the biological occurrences relating to handicapping conditions in this way.

CONSEQUENCES

The experimental variable most frequently manipulated in behaviour modification is the consequence of the response. As already indicated, operants are seen as being controlled by their consequences. Consequences may be either accelerating, decelerating or neutral, i.e. they may result in the increase or decrease in probability of a response – or they may not affect it. The relationship between a response and its consequences is specified in terms of contingencies, or schedules of reinforcement. Specification of a contingency or schedule of reinforcement indicates when consequences are to be delivered for responses. Lindsley (1970) has pointed out that Skinnerians were at one time the world experts on contingencies. This arose from the fact that responses (pecking or lever pressing) and consequences (grain or rat pellets) were held constant and only contingencies allowed to vary in their studies. Interest in the applied area has broadened the scope of the approach to include greater concern with different types of response and consequence, and also a concern with programmes involving many stimuli, responses, contingencies and consequences. To the extent that behaviour modification is currently involved with shaping new responses, contingencies are often simplified to continuous reinforcement. Certainly the elaborate study of 'schedules' is not evident in the applied field, almost to the point of suggesting that this parameter may not be as important in practice as the initial emphasis of experimental analysis of behaviour would suggest.

The events used as consequences are classified as positive or negative reinforcers. A positive reinforcer is one which, when made to follow a response, leads to an increase in the frequency of that response. A negative reinforcer is defined as an event which results in a decrease in frequency of the response it follows. Thus events are defined by the effects they produce when they are presented as consequences of responding rather than in terms of their apparent 'reward' or 'punishment' value. This serves to emphasize the individualized nature of the approach to behaviour. What is a positive reinforcer for one individual may be negative to another (cf. Bucher and Lovaas, 1968).

The terms positive and negative reinforcer must be understood relativistically in another sense. Premack (1959, 1965) has propounded an influential principle which defines reinforcers in terms of their ability to sustain responding. What Premack has emphasized is that an activity may serve either to reinforce behaviour or be reinforced depending on the alternatives open to the organism at any particular time. Therefore a child may play cooperatively (Event A) if rewarded by adult attention (Event B), when adult attention and cooperative play represent the range of possible events (B reinforces A). The same child may however perform an academic task (Event C) in order to be allowed to play cooperatively if the academic task is less preferred than cooperative play (Event B now reinforces Event C). Therefore the same event, cooperative playing, may be either reinforced or reinforcing depending on the consequences available in the setting (Homme *et al.*, 1963; Spradlin, 1964).

Accelerating consequences may be of two types. Increase in frequency of a response may result from presenting a positive reinforcer or withdrawing a negative. These training procedures are normally termed 'reward training' and 'aversion relief', 'avoidance' or 'escape training'. Decelerating consequences may also be of two types. Decrease in response probability may result from presentation of a negative reinforcer (punishment training) or withdrawal of a positive reinforcer. This latter procedure is usually termed 'time-out' from positive reinforcement and involves the withdrawal of the individual from a situation in which he can attain positive reinforcement, or in which he is being positively reinforced continuously. A variant on time-out, in which the reinforcer is withdrawn completely, is the normal extinction procedure.

The laws governing consequation have been investigated at the human level with mentally handicapped and normal individuals. These studies show a general agreement for basic principles with the more extensive infra-human literature.

The theory argues that the most effective consequence for rapid acquisition of a response will be one which is presented immediately following the response, will be one which is large rather than small, or more intense rather than less intense, and presented on a continuous one-to-one contingency (cf. Hetherington *et al.*, 1964; Schoelkopf and Orlando, 1965, 1966; Ross *et al.*, 1965; Candland and Manning, 1966; Hom *et al.*, 1966; Hom, 1967; Hetherington and Ross, 1967; Piper, 1971).

These empirical laws are seen as holding for both positive and negative reinforcers, i.e. the most effective punishing consequence will be one which follows the to-be-decelerated response immediately, is intense and is presented on a continuous reinforcement schedule (Church, 1963).

Generally speaking, those accelerating consequences which serve to produce maximum rate of acquisition produce maximum rate of loss of response when withdrawn. Thus acquisition of a response is most rapid when each occurrence of the response is rewarded (a continuous reinforcement or *crf* contingency). If responses are rewarded only intermittently during acquisition, the rate of acquisition will be lowered (for example interval or ratio schedules). However, when the consequence is eliminated, decline in rate of responding will be *fastest* following *crf* and delayed under intermittent reinforcement. The same considerations apply with other parameters, for example delay of reinforcement, and to a large extent this generalization holds with decelerative as well as accelerative consequences. Thus recovery of a punished response will be fastest following punishment training on *crf* and slower when punishment has been intermittently presented (Orlando and Bijou, 1960; Bijou and Orlando, 1961; Orlando, 1965; Spradlin *et al.*, 1965).

At their simplest level of statement, these laws would not raise controversy. In complex situations, and especially where 'cognitive' aspects are assumed to be powerful, the laws may require extensive qualification. However, in many of the applications to the behaviour of the mentally handicapped they can be seen to be operating effectively.

METHODOLOGY OF BEHAVIOUR MODIFICATION

Several aspects of the methodology of behaviour modification require special comment. This has been traditionally individual-based (Skinner, 1938). The type of law which has been of interest has concerned the effect of contingencies and consequences on the behaviour of the individual. This led to a rejection of the concepts of Fisherian statistics and the development of an approach which failed to make contact with experimental design in the rest of psychology (Sidman, 1960; Skinner, 1966).

The technique of experimentation developed under the general rubric of applied behaviour analysis has mainly derived from earlier established ones. The basic form of demonstration of the effects of a variable involves a baseline phase in which existent behaviour is assessed, usually over several successive periods and an experimental phase in which the experimental variable is applied and its effects assessed by the extent and pattern of change from the former to the latter phase.

This design suffers several faults, prime among which is the possibility that events other than those manipulated may be changing at the same time as the shift from baseline to experimental operation. Two basic techniques have been developed to deal with this situation (Baer *et al.*, 1968). The *reversal* technique involves the withdrawal of the experimental variable either once or on several successive reversals during the experiment. If the variable is critical, behavioural measures should follow the direction of experimental manipulations. This technique makes the assumption that behaviour is 'reversible', i.e. that baselines can be recovered (Sidman, 1960).

For example Twardosz and Sajwaj (1972) modified hyperactive behaviour in a 4-year-old boy described as retarded. Percentage of time spent sitting during a free play period was recorded over 7 baseline sessions. The child scored zero in each of these sessions. In phase one of the study the child was rewarded for sitting at the table with attention, praise and tokens exchangeable for sweets and trinkets. During the first 8 experimental days the rate of sitting rose to a median of 62·5 per cent of the 30-minute free play period.

During this training phase the teacher's approach to the child shifted from an initial strategy, where she seated the child, to the situation at the end of the 8-day period where the child had to touch the table or chair before being verbally requested to sit and play at the table.

During the reversal phase, attention, praise and tokens were withdrawn and sitting declined virtually to zero. Reintroduction of reward led to recovery of the sitting behaviour.

There are several reasons why reversal procedures may not always be feasible. In particular there may be ethical reasons why a behaviour cannot be reversed, for example, if head-banging has been eliminated by an experimental operation. In addition, new responses may be socially valued. Consequently once they are produced by the subject they may become dependent on the operation of variables in the natural environment. Production of speech or response to requests represent examples of behaviours which would allow the individual to be 'trapped' by the natural environment (cf. Baer and Wolf, 1967; Baer *et al.*, 1968). In the study described above, Twardosz and Sajwaj found that an increase in the amount of sitting was correlated with a decrease in posturing from 81·5 to 18 per cent and an increase in the use of toys and proximity to other children. In this study, reward for sitting was also reward for play and reward for proximity.

A second technique, the *multiple baseline* technique, avoids several of the problems resulting from reversal. This involves the establishment of concurrent baselines for several behaviours which the individual may exhibit. The experimenter then applies the experimental variable to one of these, while continuing to record all. He may note changes in this behaviour with little or no alteration in others. Rather than now removing the experimental variable, he applies it to a second response and observes its effects. If change occurs also in this response, as a function of the experimental variable, there will be evidence of its effectiveness. Clearly the technique can be extended to cover a number of responses. It is advantageous in not involving withdrawal of an experimental variable but it nonetheless allows precise conclusions to be drawn about the effectiveness of these.

Barton, Guess, Garcia and Baer (1970) provide an example of the use of this methodology. Barton and her colleagues worked with a group of severely handicapped hospitalized males. They recorded mealtime behaviours for the group, and isolated several unacceptable behaviours including stealing, inappropriate eating with the fingers, pushing food off the plate, spilling food, and eating spilled food or eating food by mouth directly off the table. These responses were grouped under several headings and then successively eliminated by removing food for 15 seconds on emission of the inappropriate response or, exceptionally, by removing the meal completely (no loss of weight was recorded).

All responses were recorded throughout the 120-meal duration of the study. In general, the results showed that as the contingency was applied to each response that response decreased in frequency without a substantial effect on other responses. However, with a decrease in the use of fingers, there was an increase in the messy use of the spoon. In addition, the authors comment on an apparent cumulative effect of the consequence. As the study progressed, it appeared to become more potent.

The central focus of the reversal and multiple baseline techniques is replication of effects. Replication is on an intra-subject basis with either multiple reversals or with the multiple baseline procedure. Inter-subject replication is achieved by manipulating the same experimental variables with several subjects. Sidman (1960) argued that the number of replications required in order for an effect to be accepted depended on several factors – the main one being the novelty of the effect demonstrated. Thus a demonstration that a subject would avoid an unpleasant event would require only minimal replication. If an *increase* in the possibility of response followed the experience of an unpleasant event this surprising result would require several replications before it would be accepted as a phenomenon and would then need further analysis. Sidman's concern is for the development of a model which would allow experimental results to be evaluated in relation to the extent to which they 'fit' with established phenomena rather than against chance as in the Fisherian model. The concern that the psychological or behavioural significance of data should not be confused with statistical significance is reflected powerfully outside the applied behaviour analysis field (e.g. Bolles, 1962; Lykken, 1968). The need for the adoption of a statistical model which more closely reflects the requirements of behavioural experimentation appears also in the increasing interest in Bayesian statistics (e.g. McGee, 1971).

The methodology of behaviour modification has a basic core of procedures which owe their origin to the Skinnerian tradition. These techniques all involve intra-subject comparisons. This emphasis on single subject designs is almost certainly one reason why behaviour modification has advanced quickly in the research on mental handicap. It represents a rigorous way of dealing with the single subject which is closed to more conventional methodologies.

Workers in applied behaviour analysis are more willing than their colleagues in infra-human research to allow of the desirability of other methodological traditions for the answer to questions concerning the relative value of different educational programmes or services. Inter-group comparisons, in addition to intra-group comparisons, appear desirable if these problems are to receive adequate answer (Baker and Ward, 1971; Kiernan *et al.*, 1971). There is a convergence of methodologies as the requirements of certain problems become clearer in experimental terms (Campbell and Stanley, 1963).

The techniques of behaviour modification experimentation have been developed in the natural environment and have demonstrated the feasibility, if not the ease, of this type of experimentation. In addition, experimentation in the natural environment allows the practitioner to demonstrate that particular experimental variables are not only effective in changing behaviour in the laboratory but also in the 'real life' setting. Put another way, experimentation in the natural environment can demonstrate the effectiveness or power of manipulated variables as they affect behaviour. Thus attention may be focused on potent variables and on variables which actually affect behaviour. This feature is likely to lead to an increased contact between research and practice and increased relevance of research to practice. In this, behaviour modification embraces a theme emphasized by other traditions within psychology over a considerable period of history (Barker and Wright, 1955; Willems and Raush, 1969), but in this case the critical feature is manipulation of variables, which allows decisions on the effectiveness of variables in changing behaviour in the natural environment to be made.

Mention should be made of the 'probe' procedure used in behaviour modification methodology to assess the effects of transfer or generalization of learning. The technique involves the use of a 'test' set of trials which is related in content to the training set, but on which the individual is never trained. Thus in an imitation training study the probe set may involve responses similar to those being trained which are presented for imitation at regular intervals, for instance after each segment of training in which a different type of response has been trained (Garcia *et al.*, 1971).

The probe procedure can be easily adapted for use in the classroom and other 'natural' settings. Here the effects of training are difficult to log on a trial-by-trial basis and the probe procedure offers a method of assessing progress in a standardized way within this type of teaching setting. This approach is characteristic of the use of precision teaching in behaviour modification. (cf. Tharp and Wetzel, 1969; Council for Exceptional Children, 1971).

THE LEARNING SITUATION

Procedures used in behaviour modification are potentially unrestricted in scope. Its central focus is changing behaviour, and any technique which is shown to be effective in this goal may be adopted (Krasner and Ullman, 1966). However, in general, workers in this area proceed on the assumption that the techniques are re-analysed in operant terms before use. The strength of the approach derives from the fact that basic principles can be used to analyse and, potentially, to improve the precision and effectiveness of practices of teaching.

(a) *Establishing responses and response sequences*

At the basis of the most commonly used procedures in behaviour modification is the concept of teaching through successive approximation to target behaviours. In turn the notion of behavioural analysis underlies the use of successive approximation. Successive approximation involves the analysis of behaviour into small steps and the reinforcement of progressively closer approximations to the final behaviour required, the target response, on successive trials.

There are two critical features of this strategy. Firstly, a very clear idea of the target behaviour must be worked out and objectively expressed. Once this task is completed it is possible to break down the steps necessary for achievement of the target response. Here again objective statement allows the teacher to identify appropriate and inappropriate approximations to the target behaviour. The second critical feature of the approach is that, given small enough step sizes, the level of success can be kept to 100 per cent. This question of rate of change of programme requirement is one of the major problems with shaping.

Within the behaviour modification framework these considerations lead in two directions. First, there has been an adoption of techniques used by workers in parallel traditions. These include an extension of educational technology with a particular emphasis on the statement of behavioural objectives, task analysis and systems analysis (Budde and Menolascino, 1971; Davies, 1971). The second direction leads to what may best be called 'art'. Procedures involving interaction between individuals are likely to require changes within the framework of any teaching session which allow for the shift in influence of different variables as a function of previous interactions. Therefore, although basic principles may be clearly stated, the application of these procedures may require moment by moment analysis of the situation concerned and response to this momentary state. Skill in successive approximation will then constitute a sensitivity to the optimal rate of change in requirements for appropriate performance. This aspect may be termed an 'art' since it represents a responsiveness to unique situations, but it must be emphasized that this 'art' is built on principles which can be explicitly stated and taught (Bricker, 1970).

(b) *Forward and backward chaining*

Some behaviours may be seen as single responses; for example, pressing a key on a typewriter or making the sound '*a*'. However, most responses are organized into sequences or chains with a definite temporal ordering. Turning on a water tap involves several responses, including identifying the position of the tap, extending the hand, gripping the tap and then turning it in a specified direction. Single responses within chains can usually be broken down into differently specified response sequences, possibly described in terms of sets of muscular movements.

The level of molarity of description of response sequences used in any programme will depend on the initial pattern of responses, i.e. the capabilities of the subject and the target behaviour aimed at. Whatever the level of specification, the sequence of training of components of the response chain presents a problem.

The behaviour modification approach suggests that behaviour chains should be established by beginning with the response which immediately precedes reinforcement. Once this is established, the second to last response is trained, and so on. Therefore, in putting on a jumper, the last response in the sequence may be pulling the jumper down to the waist, the second last pulling it over the head, etc. The first response trained would therefore be pulling the garment down, the second pulling it over the head. This strategy is termed *backward chaining*. The alternative strategy, *forward chaining*, would involve teaching the individual to pick up the jumper as a first step, then to position it for putting on, etc.

The suggested superiority of backward chaining stems from the fact that this strategy involves the trainee in first learning a rewarded response, then learning another response which leads directly to the already learned response, then a third also leading to learned responses and reward, and so on. In this way the trainee is always working into an already learned behaviour which continues to be rewarded. The learned behaviour is likely also to have conditioned reinforcing properties thus providing immediate reward.

In the forward chaining setting, the individual learns a response which continues to be rewarded only so long as it is the end of the chain. When another response is added, the initial response ceases to be rewarded unless the to-be-learned step follows readily. The effect of this procedure is likely to depend on the probability of the second unlearned step occurring, given the first. If the probability is high, either by the nature of the response or because step two is prompted, forward chaining may be effective. If the probability is low, extinction of the first response in the chain, with the possibility of emotional reactions to the learning situation, may substantially interfere with acquisition. Clearly this type of chaining is at best more 'risky' than backward chaining (but see Mahoney *et al.*, 1971, later).

In the management of learning situations a mixture of forward and backward chaining may be used. W. I. Gardner (1971) describes a situation in which a group of severely handicapped adults were taught a work task involving placing a leather washer on a 4-inch long nail, putting 18 completed units into a box, closing the box and putting it in a basket on the edge of the work bench. These tasks were trained using backward chaining, i.e. the first response trained was stacking closed boxes in the basket. The other responses in the sequence were then added. However, at the beginning of the study the trainees would not sit down at the work table. Therefore, initially they were rewarded for approaching and sitting at the table. This set of responses was rewarded as a separate chain until the work task was acquired at which stage the separate reward for sitting was progressively phased out.

A similar situation occurs in any setting where some responses are pre-requisite for correct performance. For example, in training correct imitation of a model Kiernan and Saunders (1972) found it necessary to teach initially uncooperative severely handicapped children to sit on a chair as a first pre-requisite, secondly to attend to the model on cue, and then to imitate appropriately. This use of forward chaining was necessary because the likelihood of appropriate modelling occurring without both types of pretraining was considered extremely low. The first components were pretrained in order to increase the probability of occurrence of correct responding in the situation of interest.

(c) *Establishing stimulus control*

We have already seen that stimuli can serve several functions within the behaviour modification framework. Stimuli may be discriminative for operants or may reinforce them. A response is considered to be under stimulus control when the probability of the response is high following presentation of the S^D or positive discriminative stimulus and low following the negative discriminative stimulus or S^Δ.

The concept of stimulus control is a very broad one. It encompasses those of generalization and discrimination and may relate to responses as simple as turning the eyes to a sound or light or as complex as delivering a lecture. The stimulus concept here is also broad, ranging from the onset of a simple light, through instructions which may be simple or highly complex, to complicated and subtle situational cues. The use of the term 'stimulus control' stems from the need to distinguish empirical functions of stimuli from process usages of terms like discrimination and generalization (Terrace, 1966).

The strategy for building stimulus control involves the positive reinforcement of appropriate responses in the presence of the S^D and either non-reinforcement or negative reinforcement of responses in S^Δ.

Simple examples of the establishment of stimulus control come from the use of operant techniques in sensory testing. Macht (1971) evaluated visual acuity in a group of 5 non-verbal severely handicapped children and 2 normal adults. The procedure consisted of 4 phases.

In Phase 1 the subject was taught to press a lever with a consumable reinforcer. During this phase the S^D, an illuminated E, was displayed all the time in front of the subject in the darkened test room. Phase 2 was initiated when there was a pause in responding. At this the illuminated display was darkened for 2 to 3 seconds building up to 10 seconds by the end of Phase 2. If lever-pressing occurred during this time the examiner said 'no', gave the subject a slight slap on the responding hand and did not deliver positive reinforcement. Criterial behaviour in this phase was defined as depressing the lever in the presence of E with the lights on, and not pressing the lever at other times.

During Phases 1 and 2 the S^Δ, a reversed E, was covered by a black card. During Phase 3 a reversed E was presented; initially completely covered by a card and then, in 11 steps the reversed E was gradually revealed. Criterion behaviour at the end of Phase 3 involved response in the presence of the correct E and non-response to the reverse E. In Phase 4 Macht assessed acuity by gradually increasing the distance between the subject and the display until responding broke down and it was necessary to move the subject closer in order to re-establish responding.

Macht's procedure is similar to several others developed to assess visual or auditory acuity (Bricker and Bricker, 1969; Spradlin *et al.*, 1969). For example Stolz and Wolf (1969) describe a complex study in which a 16-year-old retarded boy diagnosed as organically blind and treated by those around him as such was taught fine-grain discriminations in a two-choice setting, was taught to make and maintain eye contact on request, and was taught complex self-help skills depending on vision. The Stoltz and Wolf study represents an extensive development of stimulus control in dealing with a single case. Several approaches to establishing control were used, including instructing the subject's responses. It is worth emphasizing that workers in the behaviour modification tradition use verbal instruction and guidance where appropriate, often in conjunction with other procedures. Hence, in this case, the boy's plate was removed for 10 seconds for certain types of inappropriate eating behaviour. When this happened the boy was told the reason.

It is sometimes suggested that behaviour modification techniques are too elaborate for the problems they face. For example it is suggested that, rather than have a complex prompt and fade programme, it would be simpler and more direct to instruct the subject verbally. Clearly, however, verbal instructions are a form of prompt, and in any case the individual has to learn to follow instructions and can be taught to do so using behaviour modification techniques (Whitman *et al.*, 1971).

In practice a behaviour modification programme would include a pre-test phase during which the potentiality of the individual for following such prompts would be investigated.

A further important point concerns stimulus control. Although a stimulus, like the delivery of a consumable, or an event like cuddling a child and smiling, may function primarily as a reinforcement, it will also have discriminative aspects. Spradlin, Girardeau and Hom (1966) present evidence which shows that, after acquisition and extinction of a response, the delivery of free reinforcement leads to the recommencement of responding. In this laboratory study, the response was lever pressing. However, the authors point out that there are possible implications for other responses and settings. If a reinforcer, for example adult attention, has been contingent on undesirable behaviour, then giving attention may lead to recurrence of this behaviour.

This 'priming' function of reinforcement is illustrated in an unpublished study by Kiernan and Burgess (1971). They rewarded upright walking in a severely handicapped blind child. Initially social reinforcement was used but abandoned when it was found to cue the child to circle round on one spot whilst smiling and laughing. Observation outside the experimental setting showed that this behaviour was frequently reinforced by the child being picked up and swung round or cuddled. Use of an alternative reinforcer, the opportunity to ring and throw a hand-bell, produced appropriate walking when the child's name was called from a distance.

In this case the social reinforcer apparently performed a discriminative function for circling and laughing. Similar findings are reported by Stolz and Wolf (1969), by Ayllon and Azrin (1968) with psychiatric patients, and by Bernal (1969) with emotionally disturbed children. Patterson and Reid (1970) provide an interesting theoretical discussion of dyadic interaction in behaviour modification terms. Stolz and Wolf (1969) showed that the appropriate, i.e. non-blind, behaviour of their subject was dependent on the behaviour of those around him. As soon as he was reinforced for single behaviours related to blindness, other behaviours in this class recurred. This setting function of reinforcement is also demonstrated with a blind individual by Brady and Lind (1961) and Grosz and Zimmerman (1965).

Studies by Redd and Birnbrauer (1969) and Redd (1969) demonstrate that normal adults take on discriminative functions for handicapped children which are related to the reinforcement history of the child with the adult. Redd and Birnbrauer used a procedure in which two subjects were positively reinforced for play by an adult who came into the playroom for two 5-minute periods out of a 39-minute session. A second adult dispensed rewards on a non-contingent basis over two separate 5-minute periods. Amount of attention and amount of reward was controlled between adults, the systematically manipulated variable being whether the adult required appropriate play from the children before reward was dispensed. Redd and Birnbrauer showed that the play behaviour of the children did not change when the 'non-contingent' adult came into the room, in fact the children ignored him. When the 'contingent' adult entered the room the children began to play appropriately. In other words the play behaviour of the children was under discriminative stimulus control of the contingent adult, but not of the non-contingent adult despite his free dispensing of reward.

This result indicates the necessity for contingent reinforcement in changing behaviour. It also contrasts with the studies quoted above (Spradlin et al., 1966; Kiernan and Burgess, 1971) in that here the reinforcer did not control behaviour. The behaviour was under control of the adult as a discriminative stimulus probably because the adult was a more reliable predictor of response requirements than the reinforcer.

An extension and replication of this study by Redd (1969) showed the same general effects. In addition however Redd investigated the effects of a 'mixed' régime, i.e. discriminative stimulus properties of an adult who sometimes rewarded contingently and sometimes non-contingently. Redd showed that non-contingent delivery of reward by this adult produced no change in behaviour until he withheld reward. At this point the children began playing in the manner required for reinforcement. In this instance we see a demonstration of the discriminative or setting properties of the adult with appropriate behaviour being cued by the *absence* of reward at the end of the non-contingent session (cf. Spradlin et al., 1966).

This discussion does not exhaust the complexities of considerations raised by the stimulus control concept. It is hoped that the discussion illustrates the short-comings of a simplistic approach. One aspect which will be given more attention later is the consideration of generalization from one setting or teacher to another. What has been said already should serve to illustrate some of the problems with this operation.

(d) *Teaching techniques*

The breakdown of behaviour into steps, the successive approximation of the reinforced response, using a chaining procedure and under particular stimulus control, represents one dimension of the behaviour modification approach. The teaching technique used within this framework represents a further dimension. As with other features of behaviour modification these methods are not novel. They are traditional procedures which are informed by the operant theory.

(i) *Shaping*. Response shaping refers to the procedure whereby a subject is rewarded for successive approximations to the target behaviour with each trial or block of trials requiring a more developed response. Characteristically a backward chaining procedure is used when there is a particular topography of response to be produced. Alternatively, the frequency of a response may be modified through differential reinforcement.

Examples of simple shaping where responses are chained are rare in the literature. The reason is that it is often more economical to use prompts and physical guidance rather than waiting for successive variants of a response to occur. Exceptions are speech sound production where the initial production of some speech sounds may be difficult to prompt completely. Even here, however, the individual may be taught to imitate such responses as opening and shutting the mouth, placing the tongue, blowing out matches, or playing the kazoo, and the child's lips, tongue and mouth may be physically guided (Sloane *et al.*, 1968).

Shaping in terms of increasing the frequency of a response is a more common procedure. In this case the response topography is not deliberately modified. Examples vary from increase in the frequency of lever pressing or panel pushing to responses as complex as social interaction (Orlando, 1965, lever pressing; Hopkins, 1968, smiling; Whitman *et al.*, 1970, social interaction).

Positive reinforcement for non-responding or negative reinforcement for responding as shaping techniques for eliminating behaviour are also fairly commonly used. For example, Paul and Miller (1971) used a procedure in which negative behaviours, including self-destruction, tantrums, spitting and throwing objects including faeces, were reduced by negative reinforcement (time-out) and positive behaviours increased through reinforcement with a consumable reward.

The critical feature of shaping as a training procedure is that the teacher does not intervene in terms of physical guidance, provision of prompts or other props. Other aspects of the procedure, i.e. the use of a graded series of tasks and principles of chaining are shared with other procedures.

(ii) *Prompt and fade.* Two types of procedure are often included under this head. Physical guidance may be given to the handicapped individual, or a verbal or visual prompt may be used. In both cases the individual's behaviour is reinforced when appropriate, regardless of prompting. In both cases rapid withdrawal of the prompt is desirable.

The procedures represent examples of development of stimulus control. In the case of training using physical guidance, the control is transferred from manual or other cues provided by the trainer to the self-generated, proprioceptive or visual cues guiding particular responses. Prompt and fade procedures involving verbal or visual cueing with a gradual fading or modification of the cue by the trainer may not involve a change in the form of response, only of its timing.

Zeiler and Jervey (1968) describe a typical prompt and fade procedure involving guidance. They worked with a 15-year-old severely handicapped institutionalized girl. The child did not feed herself with a spoon; at first her hand was placed on the spoon with an overhard grip. The spoon was loaded with food and brought to her mouth with the teacher moving both spoon and hand and also putting the spoon in the child's mouth for the first few spoonfuls. On subsequent trials, the teacher released the spoon just in front of her lips, the child continuing the movement of the spoon to her mouth without help. In a second session the spoon was released progressively further from the child's mouth until by the end of the session she was moving it from her plate. Other steps were accomplished in subsequent sessions. It will be noted that this procedure involved backward chaining and successive approximation.

Physical guidance and verbal or visual prompting are typically used together in single programmes. Thus a dressing programme may involve a first step of physical guidance and verbal prompting, as skill in putting on individual garments is established. Once individual garments can be put on, the control of initiation of, for example, putting on shoes may be transferred from verbal cues to the sight of feet with socks on and shoes near.

In complex uses of prompt and fade procedures careful task analysis, a graded series of tasks and the principle of backward chaining are typically used (cf. Zeiler and Jervey, 1968).

Prompt and fade procedures are probably the most commonly used methods in behaviour modification studies. This is especially so where new responses are to be established. Here physical guidance is very common. Experience with this suggests the desirability of rapid elimination of prompts, especially of prompts provided at the end of the response sequence. If these are not eliminated rapidly they can become discriminative stimuli for pausing on the part of the trainee until prompted (Kiernan and Saunders, 1972).

A good example of the use of verbal prompting and physical guidance is provided by Whitman, Zakaras and Chardos (1971). They trained two severely handicapped children to follow sets of instructions ranging from 'sit down' to 'put the pencil in the box' or 'put your hands under the table'. Each response was initially physically guided completely but rewarded none the less. Guidance was withdrawn on a backward chaining principle until the children were initiating the responses given only the verbal instruction. The study showed the dependence of correct responding on positive reinforcement and also demonstrated a generalization of instruction – following a set of instructions which were not rewarded. This latter finding suggested that the children concerned were being brought under general stimulus control rather than simply learning a specific set of responses to instructions.

(iii) *Imitation or modelling*. These terms tend to be used fairly interchangeably in behaviour modification literature. They refer to a procedure whereby the to-be-learned response is modelled, usually by a normal adult. Typically the handicapped individual is cued to attend – 'Timmy, look – do this' – the behaviour modelled and then the individual allowed time to imitate before re-presentation of the same or a different model.[1]

Imitation training has been used widely with the mentally handicapped from the time of Séguin and Itard (Ball, 1970). Recently it has received increased attention, partly because of its advantages over shaping as a means of training. Clearly, if a response can be demonstrated and then imitated by the handicapped individual, rate of acquisition can be enhanced very substantially. This strength has led to the development of techniques for training the generalized tendency to imitate, a topic to which we will return later in this chapter.

Modelling or imitation can be seen as a form of prompt and fade procedure. The essential difference lies in the fact that the individual is required to reproduce, not simply to follow, the prompt. However, as in the prompt and fade procedure the prompt may be eliminated in the course of training.

Paloutzian, Hasazi, Streifel and Edgar (1971) provide an example of extensive use of imitation training. The social interaction of twenty children in one ward of an institution was recorded. Ten of these were then randomly assigned to a training group and taught individually to imitate a set of behaviours modelled by an adult. These ranged from folding hands to moving a chair or tugging an ear lobe. During this stage physical prompts were used and all appropriate responses rewarded, regardless of whether they had been physically guided. The next phase of the experiment involved modelling social interaction with other children from the ward. Children were trained in pairs, the exact composition of each pair was changed frequently to promote generalization. The social interaction responses were modelled and physically prompted as necessary. These included walking up to another subject and gently stroking his face, pushing another child in a swing, pulling a peer in a wagon and passing a bean bag. Paloutzian and his colleagues showed a generalization from the off-ward

[1] In fact Bandura's research would suggest that the model ought to be rewarded for his performance in order to demonstrate that reward occurs. Bandura (1965), using normal children, showed that performance was significantly influenced by this factor. The practice has not been followed in behaviour modification work and it is possible that its influence is overridden by reinforcement of the individual trained.

training situation to social interaction on the ward as a result of this training. No change from pre-test to post-test was shown by control subjects. After completion of the study, generalization was assisted by having the ward staff deliver positive social reinforcement, contingent on positive responses in the ward setting. In addition the fact that the children apparently enjoyed the new activities probably significantly assisted the maintenance of the new responses.

Imitation or modelling procedures have been used widely in behaviour modification studies, especially in the area of language understanding and acquisition (cf. Peterson, 1968; Bricker and Bricker, 1970; Buddenhagen, 1971; W. A. Bricker, 1972; D. D. Bricker, 1972). As such they represent potentially powerful procedures for promoting change in the behaviour of the handicapped which unite the strengths of other procedures (Bandura, 1969). However one point about behaviour modification uses of modelling is the relative divorce from general psychological work on imitation (Flanders, 1968). It is to be hoped that valuable features of this research may be explored within a behaviour modification context in the future.

(iv) *Other procedures.* The techniques of training listed above represent the main strategies used in behaviour modification. In the case of the elimination of avoidance behaviour, desensitization through counterconditioning based on the principles of successive approximation, chaining and stimulus control would be one typical strategy (Bandura, 1969; Sherman and Baer, 1969; Kanfer and Phillips, 1970). In this author's experience such studies are rare with the mentally handicapped.

Punishment training and escape training procedures follow the basic principles outlined above. In the case of punishment training, most studies report that shaping procedures are used (e.g. Hamilton *et al.*, 1967). In the very rare documented instances of escape training, shaping was again utilized (Bucher and Lovaas, 1968). In the case of escape training, prompting of the escape response would be likely to speed acquisition.

Implications of behaviour modification

So far, this discussion has been restricted to the presentation and explanation of the basic approach taken by behaviour modification to the behaviour of the handicapped. This has far-reaching implications which will now be considered.

It will be argued that if behaviour modification is accepted as a basic approach, the strategy for modifying the behaviour of the mentally handicapped requires several steps or stages. These are: the initial setting of goals and the assessment of behaviour in relation to these goals both before and after modification; change in the physical layout of the teaching environment in order to maximize the initial probability of responding; change in the structure of interaction between the mentally handicapped individual and the teacher such that the latter provides appropriate discriminative stimuli and immediate appropriate reinforcement for behaviour; and a modification of the social and material environment in which the individual lives in order to maximize the probability of transfer or generalization from the teaching to the living environment.

These stages may be summarized as involving a need to specify goals, a need to modify the teaching environment to allow learning to occur with maximum ease, a need to reinforce appropriately and a need to modify the living environment as necessary, to ensure transfer of new behaviour.

Finally, the approach raises questions concerning the curriculum for the mentally handicapped. It is important to emphasize at this stage that the method does not and cannot dictate the goals of education. Behaviour modification is not a content area – it consists only of a set of procedures to modify behaviour and does not state which behaviours should be modified. The goals of education must be derived from other sources (MacMillan and Forness, 1970). But the approach has important implications for the route by which goals may be achieved.

Assessment may perform a critical role within an administrative framework. For example, a child may be assigned to one type of educational setting or another primarily on the basis of IQ and related assessments. On the other hand, assessment may provide guidance at any degree of specificity within a particular educational framework, right down to the dictation of particular remedial procedures (Clarke and Clarke, 1973).

Within the behaviour modification framework assessment plays a specific role in describing the current state of behaviour. This assessment is normally termed functional analysis since it analyses the effects of variables which are functional in the control of behaviour in any specified setting. It will be readily appreciated that more usual types of assessment do not have this goal, nor can they achieve it since they do not normally involve any systematic evaluation of functional stimuli (Kiernan, 1973a).

There are three steps followed in functional analysis (W. I. Gardner, 1971; Kiernan, 1973a). These are, firstly, the description of behaviour; secondly, the analysis of discriminative stimuli supporting behaviour; and thirdly, the analysis of reinforcing or consequating stimuli (Bijou *et al.*, 1968; W. I. Gardner, 1971; Kiernan, 1973a).

Descriptions of behaviour are in terms of its topography, frequency and any other relevant characteristics. Behaviour is specified at the same level of description which is to be used in modification. Bijou, Peterson and Ault (1968), in describing this approach, emphasize the need to specify the environmental setting in effective terms, to specify the behaviour which is being observed and to define objectively relevant stimuli and responses. These workers distinguish between specific and general observational codes. The former relate to particular problems or sets of problems, e.g. occurrence of spontaneous speech, occurrence of temper tantrums. The latter relate to more general events, for instance, vocalizations or physical contacts. Much behaviour modification with the mentally handicapped requires the development of specific codes for problem behaviours. However, general codes may be used in the training or teaching setting.

For example, a study by Hall and Broden (1967) demonstrated successful modification of rates of play behaviour in brain-injured children through social reinforcement. Up to 5 informal pre-data observation sessions were employed with each child. Then observers and teachers established criteria for the occurrence of the behaviour of interest. Once these criteria were established, and inter-observer reliability was checked, a formal recording sheet was adopted. In this case, a code was evolved which allowed a continuous record of play behaviour of the child, and verbalizations and proximity of the adult, during each 10-second interval of each session.

The initial description of behaviour is likely to generate hypotheses concerning discriminative or setting stimuli. These functional stimuli may be either precise, closely defined stimulus classes or very general setting stimuli. The extent to which a stimulus functions either as discriminative, setting or reinforcing can only be established by manipulating it in the applied setting (Bijou et al., 1968; Kiernan, 1973a). This represents the critical difference between a purely observational form of assessment and one concerned with functional analysis. Manipulation of stimuli in the applied setting in order to investigate their functional properties represents the paradigm of experimental analysis. However, precise analysis of the discriminative and reinforcing functions of stimuli is rare in published literature. This consideration applies particularly to discriminative functions. Most workers appear to rely on a clear specification of the behaviour to be modified, a clear baseline record of this behaviour and the manipulation of potent reinforcing stimuli to change behaviour. The attempt may be made to override any effects of existing discriminative stimuli by eliminating some sources during training and supplying new ones which are then associated with known reinforcers. Generalization back to the natural environment is then ideally graded and carefully controlled.

Rate of reinforcement may be manipulated without a very precise analysis of the nature of the reinforcing event. Thus attention may be made contingent on correct performance when level of relevant attending behaviour on the part of adults has been low (Hall, 1970) or the response of adults may be considered to be maintaining aberrant behaviour, for instance vomiting (Wolf et al., 1970). The experimental procedure in these cases involved paying attention to appropriate behaviour, and withdrawing all reinforcement for inappropriate behaviour. However, no attempt was made in these studies to break down the discriminative stimuli controlling behaviour. In the Wolf study, operant vomiting apparently occurred only in the classroom setting. Although it is possible that particular discriminative stimuli were setting the occasion for vomiting, the intervention strategy involved an increase in the amount of positive reinforcement given during non-vomiting periods and a withdrawal of the usual event of return to dormitory following a vomiting episode without analysis of particular discriminative stimuli.

This approach can be justified in several ways. Firstly, the reinforcers supporting behaviour may be maintaining behaviour on an intermittent schedule and therefore may be relatively difficult to identify (Kiernan, 1973a). Secondly, stimulus control may be loose and based on the individual responding to a highly idiosyncratic discriminative stimulus class (Kiernan and Burgess, 1971).

In fact, it seems most likely that effects such as those described earlier in the section on stimulus control will characterize many real life settings. To try to unravel the effects of a complex reinforcement history may or may not be a useful enterprise. As already noted, most workers appear to adopt a strategy of using settings and reinforcers designed to override preceding history.

Further analysis of discriminative and reinforcing stimuli may be necessary if the attempt at modification fails. Clearly this will be expected and will not appear in the literature unless successful modification eventually occurs, because of the tendency to publish only accounts of successful modification (Gelfand and Hartmann, 1968; J. M. Gardner, 1971).

However, attention needs to be paid to discriminative stimuli in studies of pre-academic or academic performance. For example, the series of studies by Sidman and Stoddard (1967) in circle-ellipse discrimination, the subsequent researches by Sidman and Touchette (e.g. Touchette, 1968, 1969, 1971) and the work of Bijou (1968) on the development of left-right concepts, all show the necessity for sensitive analysis of the discriminative stimuli controlling the individual's behaviour.

Conclusion

The implications of behaviour modification for assessment are that techniques are required which allow a continuity of recording between baseline and experimental procedures. An analysis of the extent to which stimuli in the situation function as discriminative or reinforcing is necessary in order to formulate hypotheses concerning control of behaviour. It has been argued, however, that detailed analysis is not usual provided change occurs. This is likely if potent reinforcers are used as consequences for new behaviour in modified settings with a gradual transfer to the normal living environment or a modification of that setting.

Implications for the establishment of learning situations

In this section, problems arising in the practical implementation of behaviour modification in a natural setting will be considered. These include the selection of reinforcers, and of techniques of training and type of consequence, the reorganization of the learning and living environment and the modification of the behaviour of normal adults in the life-space of the handicapped individual.

First the various types of reinforcer used with the mentally handicapped will be described.

TYPES OF REINFORCERS

An exhaustive listing of possible reinforcers would be impossible. However, certain classifications are perhaps helpful. One class is directly available in the teaching setting. Such reinforcers may be consumable, including the individual's normal diet of food or drink, or extra items like sweets, savouries, ice cream, or drinks of juice. Manipulable reinforcers include toys or trinkets which the individual may be allowed to retain and items which may be available only during training. Sensory reinforcers, flashing lights, vibration, music or other noises are fairly frequently used. Clearly some of these, specifically trinkets, may be stored and removed from the experimental setting. In this case storing may be either enforced by the teacher or may be optional (Bijou and Sturges, 1959).

Rather than supplying consumable, manipulable or sensory reinforcers directly in the experimental setting, whether they are stored or not, the reinforcer can be supplied following training, in exchange for tokens or points gained during teaching. In this case, consumables and other reinforcers function as back-up reinforcers to the generalized conditioned reinforcers, tokens or points. When these latter are exchanged the individual can be given a choice of reinforcers with individuals functioning at an appropriate level. Events like trips out to the cinema or other 'treats' may be traded in exchange for tokens or points.

Positive social rewards can be classed in several ways (Bersoff, 1971). On the positive side, social rewards in the form of attention may be either distal (a smile) or proximal (a cuddle). They may or may not involve verbalization.

Negative reinforcers are equally variable. Non-social sensory reinforcers include the occasional use of brief electric shock, and the more frequent use of withdrawal of the individual from settings where he is experiencing positive consumable, manipulable or sensory reinforcers. In distinction to the positive case, negative reinforcers cannot be 'stored up', except in the situation where tokens or points are used. Here tokens or points may be removed immediately following behaviour and thereby negatively affect availability of back-up reinforcers. This operation, however, corresponds to a simple reduction in amount of positive reinforcement available. Threats of future punishment of a more active kind are, fortunately, not used in behaviour modification programmes.

Negative social reinforcers may again be either distal or proximal and again may or may not involve verbalization. By far the most common form of negative social reinforcement is withdrawal of attention. It may also be the most effective. Simple negative social reinforcement, saying 'no' or, less frequently, slapping, is reported in some studies, often in conjunction with positive reinforcement for desirable behaviour. Other types of negative social reinforcement include the use of holding and 'restitution'. Holding is a technique which has been successfully used in the elimination of problem behaviours like toy throwing and hitting with pre-school retarded children. It consists in holding the child still by the arms until the child ceases to resist being held (Bricker, personal communication). Restitution is described by Azrin and Foxx (1972). This involves the offending individual in 'making good' the situation created by aberrant behaviour. Thus an individual who throws objects would be required to pick them up, to tidy other items in his environment and possibly to calm individuals upset by the throwing. This procedure is clearly more complex as a negatively reinforcing event than are others quoted. Azrin and Foxx claim that this procedure is effective with long-standing problems and it has more positive aspects than most negative reinforcers.

This description of reinforcers is not meant to be either exhaustive or to suggest that all mentally handicapped individuals will respond to all reinforcers. As with other facets of behaviour modification, the question of applicability in the individual case is an empirical one. Reinforcers may be highly idiosyncratic. Recently we came across a child who was rewarded by being allowed to feed the adult with sweets; she herself would not eat them. Considerable ingenuity is required in identifying such reinforcers.

SELECTION OF REINFORCERS

The appropriate selection of a reinforcing event is critical for the success of behaviour modification. It may be suggested that, in general, the problems of the mentally handicapped relate to the fact that their behaviour is not apparently controlled by conventional reinforcers including social, food and drink. Nurses, teachers and parents often point out that it is difficult to find what is a reward or punishment for their charges. Since the success of a behaviour modification programme is dependent on appropriate reinforcer selection, these constraints could be very serious. This is a substantial problem but it is often possible to identify reinforcers which may however be idiosyncratic and clumsy to use.

There are several ways in which reinforcers may be identified. Firstly, adults familiar with the child may be asked to describe events which appear rewarding or punishing and which can be then systematically explored in learning situations. A direct questioning approach may be used with some mentally handicapped individuals (cf. Addison and Homme, 1966; Clements and McKee, 1968) but clearly this would not apply with the severely handicapped. Indirect preference techniques may be used. For example, severely handicapped hospitalized children were presented with five potential rewards, all edibles which they were known to like to some extent. The children were allowed free choice and the order in which the items were selected and the latency of selection were recorded. Repeated testing over a ten-day period showed a very high stability of choices (Riddick and Kiernan, 1972). A review of scaling techniques by Siegel (1968) serves to emphasize the complexity of scaling problems presented by reinforcer selection. What is clear from his review is that if there is an interest in modification of a particular behaviour, it may well be best to select the reinforcer by a technique which examines reinforcement in a setting close to the training setting. In particular, it would appear that the relation between the technique used to establish preference and the type of measure used in training, i.e. rate, error, etc., needs careful consideration. In the study mentioned above there appears to be a close relation between free choice preference and control of rate of performance in simple tasks (Riddick and Kiernan, 1972).

The approach taken by Premack (1959, 1965) to reinforcer selection involves observing the proportion of time spent engaged in different activities, when free choice is allowed in the natural or experimental environment. Premack argues that the longer the duration of time spent in an activity the higher its reward value.

This approach indicates a second technique for selecting reinforcing activities. However, the settings in which handicapped individuals live are often such as to provide very few possible activities in which they can engage. It seems likely that one way round the difficulty of identifying reinforcers in these settings would be to provide an 'enriched' environment which could be 'sampled' by the handicapped individual on a cafeteria basis. The preference hierarchy then observed could be used to identify rewarding behaviours. It seems clear, however, that some individuals may fail to interact with this type of environment and in this case active interventionist tactics may be essential. This may involve a period during which the individual is positively encouraged to touch, taste, feel or see a set of potential reinforcers.

The vagueness of specification of procedures at this level stems from the fact that little is known about the ways in which basic reinforcers develop. This is the phenomenon that Murphy (1947) referred to as canalization, but despite its early description little relevant work appears to be available in the general developmental literature.

A central point so far as the operant approach is concerned is that there may be a need with some individuals to build up rewarding events *before* behaviour modification can be attempted.

THE IDEAL REINFORCER

There are several defining features of the ideal reinforcer which can be deduced from the basic laws of learning taken in relation to the general aims of behaviour modification.

It should be possible to deliver the reinforcer *immediately* following the defined response. Therefore the fact that sweets or other consumables cannot be easily delivered direct into the mouth means that they are not ideal. Similarly, it is often difficult to arrange the environment in such a way that rewarding activities, like playing with a toy, follow immediately on the desired response. The best type of reinforcement from the immediacy viewpoint is a sensory event. Therefore visual displays, sounds, or vibration which can be produced immediately may be ideal (Bailey and Meyerson, 1969; Greene and Hoats,

1969). Conditioned reinforcers, especially verbal social reinforcers, are also excellent in this respect.

A second important defining feature of the ideal reinforcer is that it should be *easy* to deliver and withdraw. In terms of ease of delivery the main problems relate to the bahaviour of the modifier rather than that of the handicapped individual. One can suggest as a 'law' that the less effortful the operation of reinforcement for the behaviour modifier, the more likely he or she is to persist in modification. Once again verbal social reinforcers or tokens, as opposed to edible reinforcers, appear to have an advantage. It 'costs' little in terms of energy expenditure to praise an individual or to hand out a token whereas much effort and organization may be involved in the preparation and delivery of edible or manipulable reinforcers.

A third characteristic of the ideal reinforcer is that it should not interfere with, or interrupt, appropriate behaviour but should still provide an ongoing reinforcement control. Once again the drawbacks of contingently delivered edibles are clear. The use of social reinforcement, or other sensory reinforcement, may also be a problem under certain settings (for example, where the individual is 'distracted' by it), but in general, the use of tokens, points which are given or removed, social and sensory reinforcement are likely to interfere less with ongoing behaviour.

The fourth characteristic of the ideal reinforcer is that it should not be subject to rapid satiation effects. However, little research on satiation has been undertaken within the operant framework. Some types of reinforcer are clearly subject to satiation effects. Prime among these are food and drinks. The evidence provided by Gewirtz (1967) suggests that children may satiate for social reinforcement. Satiation effects within sessions may be minimized if the reinforcers delivered are conditioned ones which are backed up outside the training sessions. Social interaction and tokens or points all fall into this category.

The fifth characteristic appears rather trivial at first sight, but is of substantial importance. Some reinforcers take time to consume, for example sweets or other edibles. Time spent in this way can obviously be cut down by using small quantities and reinforcing frequently. However, their use can be cumbersome. The opportunity to play with toys can produce greater problems. The child usually has to be required to give up the toy after, say, 30 to 60 seconds if the teaching session is not to be infinitely extended. This is likely to be negatively reinforcing for the child or adult concerned. Clearly the optimal reinforcer is one which, when presented, disappears quickly and painlessly, or which is retained by the trainee without on-the-spot 'consumption'. Thus again verbal social reinforcement proves ideal; cuddling or other types of physical contact may present problems of termination if the handicapped individual does not wish to be released. Tokens, points, or edibles which are cumulated during the session and exchanged at the end also satisfy this requirement.

A final critical characteristic of the ideal reinforcer is that it is transituational. In other words, the ideal reinforcer would be usable in a wide variety of settings and by a wide variety of administering individuals. This characteristic is of central importance. If the generalization of trained behaviour is to occur in a variety of non-training situations, there is a serious danger of the handicapped individual learning to discriminate between the settings, and to produce the trained behaviour only in those where reinforcement of a particular type is provided. Thus, if material reinforcers are used consistently in a training situation, transfer to settings where material rewards are not provided is not likely to be complete and may not occur at all.

For example, Kiernan and Saunders (1972) showed that generalization of learned imitation of models, who had not trained the handicapped child, was minimal until the child was reinforced in generalization tests by them. When a prompted response was reinforced, full imitation of a probe set occurred. This evidence suggests that the child was discriminating clearly between settings in which he was reinforced and settings in which this did not occur. This is another example of complex stimulus control (see earlier discussion of stimulus control).

It would seem centrally important to build up reinforcers which can be used transituationally. Clearly social reinforcers meet this criterion most completely. If the individual becomes appropriately responsive to social reinforcement, he has become integrated into the natural reinforcing setting provided by the society (Baer and Wolf, 1967). Time spent in establishing social reinforcers may pay off in terms of more rapid and extensive generalization of responses. This will only occur, however, if the form and scheduling of social reinforcement as well as the frequency of back-up reinforcement is sufficiently similar to the training setting. It is always possible that the reinforcement scheduling provided by the natural environment may not be adequate to support the behaviour of the handicapped individual. Furthermore, handicapped individuals may be less able to provide self-reinforcement than the normal individual and therefore be at a continual disadvantage in a normal setting (cf. Bandura, 1969).

The alternative form of conditioned reinforcement, tokens or points, has strengths and weaknesses similar to social reinforcement. Points or tokens are in addition 'storable' and do suggest the possibility of generalization to the use of normal currency. Again, however, the degree to which generalization to the natural environment can occur will depend on the extent to which the pro-gramme teaches the handicapped individual to work within the contingencies provided by the natural environment and the degree to which the individual's behaviour can be maintained by the contingencies provided in this environment.

MULTIPLE REINFORCEMENT

One practical solution to the difficulties of providing adequate reinforcement is to use several reinforcers concurrently (Logan *et al.*, 1971). This may be done either by using a variety of them on each trial, for example a social reward, immediately delivered, followed by a material reward, offered after 2 or 3 seconds, and another social reward, a cuddle, delivered after 5 to 8 seconds, or by giving a different selection on each trial.

The overall effect of this technique should be to provide both a more powerful overall reinforcement and also a situation in which weak social reinforcers may become more powerful through conditioning effects. Once again the precise nature of these effects needs exploration under controlled conditions in order to investigate the interaction of different positive reinforcers and the additivity of effects.

Intermittent presentation of reinforcers will clearly delay satiation to any single reinforcer. This could be capitalized on by using several different reinforcers at different times during the session. Thus multiple reinforcers would be used but in a successive rather than a simultaneous manner.

In all cases it is likely that the effects of multiple reinforcers offset the defects of less than optimal individual ones in the training setting, but in all cases there is still substantial room for applied research which would investigate interaction effects.

McReynolds (1970) suggests a further dimension. She demonstrated that verbal responses which were not modified early in training by social reinforcers were modified when ice cream was used as reward. These responses could then be maintained by social reinforcement. McReynolds suggests that initial acquisition may require more 'effort' on the part of the subject and hence stronger reinforcers than maintenance of the response once acquired. The author points out that typically speech therapists avoid material reinforcers and indeed the study she describes was on a 4-year-old brain-damaged child who had been 'found unsuitable for speech training'.

MECHANICAL AIDS

A word should be added concerning the use of mechanical aids to deliver reinforcement. These may be of various types, ranging from a switch to turn on a light, or a button to press to produce a sound, up to a complex and expensive reinforcement dispenser. There is a mystique surrounding the use of mechanical aids; such aids are only of use to the extent that they mediate the immediate delivery of reinforcement. To this end they can be of immense value. However, it is clear that they tend to lack generality, they are not likely to be available in a variety of settings, and must therefore serve primarily to provide a means whereby conditioned reinforcement, especially social reinforcement, can be either established or backed up.

CONDITIONED REINFORCEMENT

A good deal has been said in the previous section about the value of conditioned reinforcers, especially tokens or points, and some types of social reinforcement. These are termed generalized conditioned reinforcers since they signify the availability of a wide range of back-up reinforcers (Kelleher and Gollub, 1962).

Ayllon and Azrin (1968) argue that tokens have advantages over other forms of generalized conditioned reinforcers mainly on the grounds that they are tangible and therefore storable, portable, usable in a wide range of contexts and can be durable. In this respect they provide a tangible means of bridging time gaps in a way not possible when social reinforcers only are used.

Kazdin and Bootzin (1972) add that tokens provide a visible record of improvement and facilitate social reinforcement from staff members, as well as self-reinforcement. In effect, they instate all of the values which bank managers urge on their clients.

Despite the obvious parallel with normal money, and the possibility of phasing out tokens and phasing in money as currency, the token system retains a certain artificiality in the ways noted previously. Conditioned social reinforcers are clearly the type more usually dispensed in a face-to-face setting, especially for children. Since part of the problem posed by mental handicap involves adequate integration into natural communities, where social reinforcement is the currency, a direct approach to the establishment of social reinforcers may be more appropriate. Token systems may be more useful where a variety of individuals, no one of whom may have consistent contact with the mentally handicapped individual, have dealings with him. Thus ward-based programmes, with constantly changing staff, may need to run on a token basis in order to overcome problems inherent in each staff member having to develop relationships with each 'patient'. The desirability of this situation represents a separate question. If large, poorly staffed wards exist, it would be inhumane to reject even unsatisfactory part-solutions to their problems.

The establishment of generalized conditioned reinforcers occurs, according to the theory, through a consistent pairing of the initially neutral event with an established reinforcer, the neutral event always preceding the latter. This generalization holds for the establishment of both positive and negative conditioned reinforcers. For example, Locke (1969) showed that the reinforcing value of 'good' was enhanced when it was paired with delivery of a valued token. He also found that precise pairing was not essential for increase in reward value, but that the occurrence of 'good' and the delivery of the valued token in the same setting was essential. Bucher and Lovaas (1968) report that pairing the word 'no' with electroshock for inappropriate behaviour produces behaviour suppression in retarded autistic children. They also report the use of a 'relief' procedure for building positive responsiveness. Here the child could avoid shock for inappropriate behaviour by turning to the adult. Clear indication of the acquisition of reward value was shown by means of a pre- and post-test.

Work at the infra-human level would suggest that the conditioned reinforcer should be uniquely discriminative for established reinforcement (Egger and Miller, 1962). In other words, saying 'good' and following this by pulling out a packet of sweets to give the child one will not necessarily lead to the word good becoming a conditioned reinforcer. Other cues in the situation – reaching to the pocket, the sight of a paper bag etc. – may be much more reliable predictors of reward than the word good. This is especially likely to happen if the child has difficulty in understanding speech. In the establishment of generalized reinforcers the pairing of the reinforcer with a large variety of established reinforcers, each one of which has a different cue pattern preceding delivery, should isolate the conditioned reinforcer as a non-redundant cue (Skinner, 1953).

Once the reinforcer has become established, an intermittent pairing of the reinforcer with back-up reinforcers becomes essential if it is to retain its ability to maintain behaviour (D. W. Zimmerman, 1959; J. Zimmerman, 1963; Findley and Brady, 1965).

Conclusion

Some general conclusions emerge from this discussion. First, it is clear that social reinforcement, and in particular verbal or other distal social reinforcement, meets all the criteria for the ideal reinforcer. This suggests that, in terms of the establishment of an educational programme, first priority should be given to the development of social reinforcers or to their strengthening if they are already partially established. The use of multiple reinforcement procedures is one technique which can be adopted for the establishment of social reinforcers, while maintaining behaviour during training. At first the emphasis in the multiple reinforcement procedure can be placed on known material rewards.

One area which has as yet received very little attention concerns the comparative effectiveness of different reinforcers in the same setting. Part of the reason for this neglect lies in the fact that the value of reinforcers is likely to vary from individual to individual and time to time. However, some work in this direction has already been undertaken within the behaviour modification framework (Burchard and Barrera, 1972). There are interesting possibilities in linking behaviour modification work with studies on social reinforcement in experimental contexts. Of especial potential value is the research of Zigler and his colleagues, indicating a greater responsiveness to social reinforcement of moderately handicapped institutionalized individuals (cf. Zigler, 1968).

SELECTION OF BASIC PROCEDURES AND TECHNIQUES

In general one training procedure, *reward training*, and one training technique, *prompt and fade*, emerge as favoured in teaching in applied work with the mentally handicapped. This holds whether the prime interest is in acquisition of new responses or in the elimination of undesirable behaviour. The precise value of the procedures will obviously also depend on the skill in their application and on the suitability of the technique for the particular handicapped individual. Clearly, if an individual is not able to imitate, the modelling procedure is not going to be effective, and if physical contact is highly aversive, prompt procedures will be rendered less efficient.

(i) *Reward training and other procedures*

There are many reasons why reward training has been favoured over other training techniques. These range from ethical issues to empirical factors. Happily the evidence would suggest that empirical and ethical considerations both indicate the same conclusions. In other words, both suggest the desirability of using reward training as the central procedure.

At the broad level of logic and theory, procedures can be compared on whether they aim primarily at the strengthening or elimination of responses, and the question can be asked as to whether there is a case for eliminating a response rather than trying to shape it into a different form. The behaviour of many severely handicapped individuals tends to involve few response classes, and to try to eliminate any of these seems relatively unacceptable. Thus, on very general grounds, it would seem desirable to build up behaviour rather than trying to eliminate it.

Still at a general level, if any procedure is to be maximally effective it will involve high values of reinforcers. The most rapid acquisition will occur when the rewards are of high value, and conversely the most effective punishment training procedure will involve high levels of punishment (Church, 1963). The same considerations hold for escape training and time-out. Clearly there are substantial ethical problems involved here as well as practical issues of trainer behaviour. Some professionals, having once used punishment, refuse to use it as a procedure again. The dangers of such methods in the hands of non-professionals are obvious.

At the theoretical level, there are contrasts between reward training and escape training as procedures for building up new responses. Reward training will normally involve reinforcement contingent on *completion* of the desired response or response sequence. Therefore the procedure emphasizes the desirability of completing the response as fast as is compatible with correct responding. In escape training, reinforcement follows *initiation* of the response, i.e. the aversive stimulation ceases when the trainee begins to respond – otherwise desired behaviour is punished. Aversive stimulation may begin again when the individual pauses, thus punishing pausing, or reward may follow complete correct performance, but a pure escape training procedure will by its very nature reinforce the initiation rather than the completion of a desired response. This could clearly lead to the situation in which the speed of responding under escape contingencies is very slow and in which performance may be poor. Typically responses based on 'nagging' as a training procedure have these qualities. This would suggest that the only type of response which is suitable for escape training is one which is very brief, for example the response of turning to the adult in order to escape shock used by Bucher and Lovaas (1968).

A related practical issue, concerned with temporal order, is that techniques for eliminating behaviour (punishment training and time-out from reward) should be most effective if they are used at the beginning of the response sequence to be eliminated. Punishment of throwing behaviour will be most effective if it is applied at the beginning of the relevant response sequence than at the end (cf. Skinner, 1953). Similarly time-out for stealing food will be more effective if it follows the beginning of the response sequence leading to stealing than at the end.

These requirements lead to problems concerned with identification of the relevant response sequences. For example, the initial components of the to-be-punished sequence may be common to other desirable sequences. It is likely that the physical arrangement for detection and punishment will be difficult to guarantee and that the individual may be intermittently reinforced, with consequent slowing down of elimination through punishment training. The individual may, alternatively, learn strategies for avoiding punishment. Very fast responding may be acquired if such responding allows the individual to complete the response before punishment or the response may become discriminated. Thus if hitting another person and causing them to cry is reinforcing, a punishment procedure may result in the handicapped person learning to hit only when the punishing adult is not present, or alternatively in learning to hit very quickly, so that the likely reinforcing events of hitting and seeing the other person cry occur despite the punishment. In this case, escalation of punishment or a change in its form are the only solutions.

The considerations so far outlined suggest the general desirability of the use of reward training, largely in terms of an avoidance of the use of negative reinforcement in the punishment or escape training context. This suggests that reward training and time-out from reward would be optimal procedures for building up and eliminating behaviour, respectively.

At this stage it is necessary to introduce a further factor, response competition. This may be said to occur where new responses, which are incompatible with existing behaviours, are rewarded in the presence of particular sets of discriminative or setting stimuli. So throwing toys is replaced by fine manipulation of these toys. It will be argued that response competition lies at the base of the effective use of time-out and punishment training. This concept is also seen as having substantial implications for the arrangement of the teaching and living environment.

(ii) *Development of competing responses – time-out*

The critical feature of a time-out procedure is that there should be a period in which positive reinforcement is not available to the subject following an undesirable response. At this simple level of operation its value has been in doubt in the infra-human literature for some time (Leitenberg, 1961). Studies with mentally handicapped subjects also suggest that unless the environment or activity from which the individual is withdrawn is heavily rewarding, time-out does not lead to elimination of undesirable behaviour.

Time-out has been used most effectively in the feeding situation to control a variety of aberrant behaviours. Several studies report effective control through removal of food for a specified duration of time (Bensberg and Slominski, 1965;

Whitney and Barnard, 1966; Hamilton and Allen, 1967; Zeiler and Jervey, 1968; Stolz and Wolf, 1969; Barton *et al.*, 1970), or by removing the individual from the table at which he is being fed (Barton *et al.*, 1970; Berkowitz *et al.*, 1971). O'Brien, Bugle and Azrin (1972) report a technique in which inappropriate responses were interrupted, and in all cases satisfactory elimination of these was reported. In the feeding situation, appropriate behaviour is positively reinforced with food (if food is not positively reinforcing it is not likely that inappropriate feeding will be the problem shown). Therefore the basis of modification lies in the fact that responses, which may have an initial low level of emission, are strengthened as other responses are punished. The alternative response topographies will be incompatible in this setting. In other situations, the reinforcement for 'other behaviour' may require independent manipulation. Birnbrauer, Wolf, Kidder and Tague (1965) report a study of the interaction of a token system and time-out from a classroom setting. When tokens for good behaviour were withdrawn, two subjects 'competed' to be put into a time-out room separate from the classroom. Birnbrauer suggests that 'removing a child from a classroom is effective to the extent that it is, in fact, time-out from positive reinforcement'.

The bulk of studies have followed this precept and actively built up competing responses which may or may not be topographically incompatible. In some cases, as in the Birnbrauer study just quoted, this may involve an increase in the overall amount of reward delivered. In others the primary shift may be to transfer positive reinforcement from unacceptable to acceptable behaviours, although this is typically not reported. For example, Bostow and Bailey (1969) used time-out in the form of being removed from a chair, placed on the floor and ignored, as a consequence for loud and abusive verbal behaviour on the part of a non-ambulatory hospitalized woman. She remained on the floor for a minimum of 2 minutes, after which a 15-second interval of silence was required before she was put back on to her chair. In addition, she was not allowed to have things she liked until she had been quiet in her chair for a 10-minute period. If the loud and abusive behaviour did not occur she was given a treat, favoured object or attention at least once every 30 minutes. The base rate of positive reinforcement was not reported by Bostow and Bailey, and it is therefore not possible to say whether absolute rate of positive reinforcement was affected. However, they do report consistent improvement with no additional strain on staff resources which suggests that the rate of positive reinforcement necessary to maintain the new behaviour was not substantially discrepant from base rate.

On the other hand, a study by Husted, Hall and Agin (1971) showed reduction in aggressive and self-destructive behaviour during training sessions involving positive reinforcement for acceptable behaviours. The authors found, however, that they could not successfully generalize this behaviour to non-training periods because of a need for high levels of reward. They conclude that time-out programmes are not economical in terms of staff time.

This study raises a critical question. It seems reasonable to suggest that there are environments which are lacking in sources of suitable reinforcement to support appropriate behaviours. The 'back-wards' of institutions possibly represent the clearest examples. In these, the mentally handicapped individual may resort to inappropriate behaviours if these are positively reinforced by custodians or peers (cf. Bostow and Bailey, 1969). Buehler, Patterson and Furniss (1966) gathered data which indicate that delinquent responses are rewarded in a correctional institution. If regular sources of positive social or other types of reinforcement are absent, the result may be that socially un-obtrusive behaviour (e.g. sitting still or mild self-stimulation) may occur. Alternatively, socially obstructive or self-injurious behaviour may result, e.g. shouting, eye-gouging, head-banging, or aggression towards other inmates. If the responses have developed in an environment barren of extrinsic positive reinforcers, 'time-out' in the sense of removal from the environment for un-acceptable behaviour is not likely to be effective. These environments are typically settings in which only certain types of behaviour lead to reward. These behaviours are either independent of the environment – eye-gouging – or completed rapidly – hitting. Removal will clearly not affect the first type. In the second case the individual is moved from his initial situation as a function of his tapping his only source of reward. Since the maintenance and time-out environments are likely to be very similar, time-out may serve only to increase the likelihood of the response on return from time-out. Clearly the only solution in this case is to introduce new forms of positive reinforcement for new behaviours in the living environment. In general, where there are clear sources of positive reinforcement for other behaviour, time-out is effective. This holds whether it takes place in an instructional context (e.g. McReynolds, 1969) or in a more general setting where presence of other members of a group functions as the reinforcer (Peterson and Peterson, 1968; Tyler and Brown, 1967; Pendergrass, 1972).

(iii) *Development of competing responses – punishment training*

Many of the comments made concerning time-out from positive reinforcement can be applied to punishment training. In both cases infra-human research suggests quite clearly that, unless other acceptable responses in the training situation are positively reinforced, punishment training will result in temporary elimination of the punished response (Azrin and Holz, 1966). Lasting elimination only occurs if other competing responses are positively reinforced. The infra-human research also suggests that punishment must be used at high levels from the beginning of training to be maximally effective. Miller (1960) and others have shown that gradually increasing intensity of punishment serves only to habituate the organism to the punishment. This poses clear ethical problems requiring the person administering punishment to be very sure of its value before using it.

Punishment training has been employed mainly in an attempt to eliminate behaviour which is considered to be endangering the health of the individual or others in his environment. Several studies have used electric shock in attempts to eliminate head-banging, ruminating or vomiting (e.g. Insalaco and Hamilton, 1966; Luckey *et al.*, 1968; White and Taylor, 1967). Others have used a variety of punishments including physical restraint (Hamilton *et al.*, 1967) and hair pulling (Banks and Locke, 1966) for self-abusive, destructive or aggressive behaviours. In many of these studies incompatible behaviours have been positively reinforced often on a systematic basis (Mazik and MacNamara, 1967).

One advantage of punishment training over other procedures for the elimination of inappropriate behaviour is that it can be very rapid in its effects. Lovaas quotes several instances in which behaviour which had persisted over long periods of time was eliminated within a very few trials. In one study, Lovaas and Simmons (1969) allowed self-destructive behaviour to extinguish, up to 9,000 self-destructive responses (hitting self) occurring before the criterion was reached. This effect did not generalize to other settings as shown by recordings taken in those settings. A total of twelve 1-second electroshocks over fourteen sessions eliminated hitting completely in that setting. No 'substitute' self-destructive behaviour was observed.

On the other hand, the fact that punishment can eliminate behaviour rapidly can be a disadvantage also. Given time pressure on therapists, there may be a tendency to use punishment because it can produce a rapid change in behaviour, heavily reinforcing to custodians and therapists alike. If, in addition, other approaches require the expenditure of funds, there may be a general pressure to use punishment as a 'coping' procedure. Other disadvantages of punishment were heralded by Skinner (1953) and others. In particular, Skinner suggested that the use of punishment would lead to the individual administering punishment becoming a negative conditioned reinforcer. This danger appears to have been overstressed. The evidence tends not to support the prediction (e.g. Risley, 1968; Whaley and Tough, 1970), and indeed Martin (1963) quotes evidence which suggests that use of positive and negative reinforcers by the same individual may enhance the effects of positive reinforcement (Solomon, 1964). Research on variables affecting identification could clearly be relevant in considering this aspect of the use of punishment.

One finding has emerged fairly clearly in several studies. Punishment effects are likely to be specific to the individual and setting in which training is done (Birnbrauer, 1968; Risley, 1968; Lovaas and Simmons, 1969). This is a parallel result to that seen in reward training but is a more acute problem with punishment since it is less acceptable to recommend it in several contexts. A study by Corte, Wolf and Locke (1971) demonstrated that generalization from one adult to another took place only as several observers independently punished self-injurious behaviour. They also found that setting effects were specific. After behaviour had been suppressed in one setting, it was necessary to punish in a separate setting, in order to attain generalization. They point out the need for a 'planned programme of treating the behaviour under as many different conditions as necessary to produce a generalized effect'.

A related problem is the durability of punishment effects. There are few ethical problems raised by re-programming a natural environment to produce positive reinforcement, but clear difficulties if punishment is to be programmed. Few authors report follow-up. Corte *et al.* (1971) report that one of their four subjects showed a recurrence of self-injurious behaviour within two months.

It would be dangerous to draw any firm conclusions on the advisability or otherwise of punishment training. Where self-destructive behaviour is involved the approach may be most justified but success cannot be guaranteed. Unsuccessful uses of punishment are not likely to be published. On the other hand, there are circumstances where punishment training appears indicated but where other approaches may be equally effective.

As already noted, several studies have used electric shock to eliminate ruminating and/or vomiting behaviour in severely handicapped individuals (White and Taylor, 1967; Luckey *et al.*, 1968). The same type of behaviour has been dealt with successfully by the withdrawal of social reinforcement (Smeets, 1970; Wolf *et al.*, 1970). Similarly, Vukelich and Hake (1971) report a study in which dangerous aggressive behaviour in a severely handicapped institutionalized woman was reduced by a systematic programme involving time-out for aggressive behaviour and initial massive positive social reinforcement for non-aggressive behaviour.

It is clearly foolhardy to attempt a comparison of studies, but one feature which emerges clearly in the latter is that a great increase in attention was necessary especially at first in order to compete out aggressive behaviour. The authors then phased out extra attention but found that when the woman was unrestrained all day and received no extra attention aggressive behaviour recurred. Extra attention at the rate of 6 minutes every 30 minutes phasing down to 6 minutes per hour was programmed during the final phase and successfully controlled her aggression. The authors conclude that 'for severely retarded residents, positive reinforcers are frequently scarce and they may have to be increased by the staff to increase the likelihood of success of treatment programmes . . . that are based on positive reinforcement'. This conclusion is reminiscent of that drawn by Husted, Hall and Agin (1971). Both papers suggest the need for change in the amount of reward given in the environment before procedures can be expected to work. It seems reasonable to suggest that the use of punishment may be avoided if sufficient time can be spent in actively programming for the handicapped individual. However, if this cannot be done, or if the nature of the behaviour is such that it is necessary to eliminate it rapidly, punishment training may be a more humane alternative to restraint or what Baer (1970) has referred to as the 'half-living death of 24-hour-per-day stupor'.

(iv) *Physical organization*

The behaviour modification approach has several implications for environmental organization. It is necessary, first of all, to distinguish between the optimal training environment and the optimal maintenance or living environment.

The optimal training environment, from a behaviour modification viewpoint, can be constructed from a consideration of basic principles; it is one in which the probability of the to-be-trained response is as high as possible in the first instance. This ideal may be reached by eliminating stimuli which would lead to responses which would interfere with the to-be-trained response. Similarly, the environment should be one in which the response made by the individual can be identified precisely as soon as it occurs and reinforced immediately. These considerations suggest a small, simple environment which can be adapted to various needs for modifying different types of response.

The ideal maintenance environment is one which can be geared closely to two factors; firstly, the need to encourage transfer or generalization from the training environment; secondly, the discussion of competing responses in the previous section indicates a further factor. It may be suggested that, without an adequate maintenance environment, the effectiveness of time-out, punishment and especially differential positive reinforcement procedures is likely to be low. We have already suggested that the behaviours usually attacked by these procedures may be a direct function of maintenance environments in which rate of positive reinforcement is chronically low. These environments may be behaviourally toxic or pathogenic in that the only behaviours which lead to positive reinforcement may be either socially obtrusive and unacceptable, self-destructive, or simply result in the individual learning not to respond by sitting and rocking mildly, playing with a piece of material, or many other 'dead' behaviours. If these behaviours are a function of poor environments then the environments must be changed before the behavioural techniques can be expected to operate (cf. Gewirtz, 1968). The approach from behaviour modification would suggest the need for several classes of provision in the ideal maintenance environment. Firstly, the material environment of the living area must provide sources of positive reinforcement from suitable recreational, educational or work settings. This is not simply a 'rich stimulating environment' involving substantial sensory bombardment, but an environment with which the individual actively interacts by producing reinforced overt responses. Martin (1972) describes an environment in which additional cues for behaviour and other supports related to the specific training situation were included.

Secondly, the broader living environment, the community within which the living environment is set, should be capable of complementing the direct living environment to the extent of providing a variety of educational and reinforcing settings. Kiernan (1973b) has discussed this point in relation to a hospital setting and has suggested that if hospitals are to match general communities in the extent of provision of support facilities, the financial expenditure would be very great. Finally, if the individual is to be seen as part of a community of non-handicapped individuals, adequate provision must be made for social interaction resulting in social learning. Newly learned social behaviour should mesh in with, and be trapped by, the reinforcement contingencies provided by the maintenance environment (Baer and Wolf, 1967).

The realization of these ideal environments in the hospital, hostel, school or home setting may require considerable physical and social reorganization. In general it would seem that the more closely the maintenance environment approximates the natural community, the better the chances of habilitation. In fact, in many ways it would appear that segregation from the community is justifiable only if the period of segregation is one in which intensive training related to adjustment is undertaken.

SOCIAL ORGANIZATION

In order to implement behaviour modification programmes it may be necessary radically to reorganize the social setting in which the individual is living.

(i) *Numbers of staff*

It follows from the last section that some programmes require heavy staffing if they are to be implemented. This problem may be acute where all staff have to be hired and paid. One solution adopted by many programmes is to use parents and other members of the individual's family as teachers.

(ii) *Training of change-agents*

There is general agreement amongst behaviour modifiers on two points. Firstly, that training is necessary if effective programmes are to be run (Martin, 1972; Kazdin and Bootzin, 1972). Secondly, it is generally considered that parents, teachers, nurses and other 'untrained therapists' can be taught to be effective behaviour modifiers (Risley and Baer, 1972).

One of the most impressive series of studies is reported by Whalen and Henker (1969, 1971a, b). They taught mentally handicapped adolescents to use behaviour modification techniques with younger children in a hospital setting. The programme was monitored and evaluated. Gains for both trainees and trainers were demonstrated. Many training programmes appear to rely on lectures, reading and examination. There are several training manuals which are designed to assist at this level (e.g. Bensberg, 1965; Larsen and Bricker, 1968; Patterson and Guillon, 1968; Gardner, 1969; Homme *et al.*, 1969; Meacham and Weisen, 1970; Mink, 1970; Hall, 1971; Becker *et al.*, 1971; Kiernan and Riddick, 1972). Lectures, reading and discussion probably affect staff attitudes but may or may not affect behaviour.

Martin (1971) found that staff who were taught to observe behaviour and record it, in addition to being taught basic concepts through examined lectures, discussions and reading, did not in general apply the procedures at all. A second group which, in addition to the experience of Group 1, observed demonstrations and modified one individual's behaviour did rather better. Just under 50 per cent attempted some further work. With a third group the ward was rearranged and cue lights, rules for procedure, etc. were set up in addition to the basic care programme. This group was also required to train a handicapped individual both on and off ward. All of the thirty-one staff in this group subsequently used operant conditioning in the ward setting.

Two points in Martin's account may be emphasized: firstly, the need to have the trainees actually train behaviour with a handicapped individual or at least role play training (cf. J. M. Gardner, 1972); secondly, Martin's stress on the reorganization of the physical and organizational structure of the maintenance environment is echoed elsewhere.

We have already commented on the physical aspects of reorganization. From the viewpoint of job definition other points arise.

The general questions which must be asked are how, and from what sources, the behaviour of the nurse, parent, or other custodian is reinforced. Several possible sources have been suggested. When behaviour changes rapidly, progress of the individual may act as reward or the individual may be rewarded for any efforts he may make, regardless of their value, either by social or financial means. Panyan, Boozer and Morris (1970) argue that, if the individual's progress is slow, additional special reinforcers may be required. Panyan and her colleagues show that, following training, there was a decrease in frequency with which sessions were run in wards. Using a multiple baseline design, Panyan provided feedback to the wards of number of sessions completed beginning at four different dates following the end of training. The results indicate that the effect of feedback from the unit level was to bring about progressive increases in percent sessions completed, from around 25 per cent up to an asymptote of around 95 per cent. Other authors have used more direct forms of reinforcement including trading stamps and videotape records and time off from work (Bricker et al., 1968; Watson et al., 1971; Martin, 1972).

The approach adopted by Panyan, Boozer and Morris involves a redefinition of the job of ward personnel from a custodial to a training role. To this extent, feedback represents a measure for the staff of their effectiveness. In addition the programme described by Panyan and also that described by Watson, Gardner and Sanders (1971) involve staff in making decisions about which behaviours are to be trained and how this is to be done. In other words, autonomy is given to the individual who is to implement the programme. Work in organizational psychology and in the sociology of institutions suggests that this granting of important decision-making functions may be a powerful reinforcer when coupled with feedback on the appropriateness of these decisions (Davies, 1971; King et al., 1971).

The same general considerations apply to parents both in terms of training and motivation. Reported research suggests that effective intervention results when parents are trained in practical application of techniques with feedback on specific programmes. Many factors such as socio-economic status of the parent, crowding in the home and poor physical support may influence effective participation. These variables clearly need investigation but some authors report that as many as 85 per cent of parents participate effectively in training programmes (Terdal and Buell, 1969; Mira, 1970; Fredericks *et al.*, 1971). The development of parent training programmes, especially for parents of pre-school children, represents a potentially important development. It could lead to a situation in which behaviour problems and educational difficulties within adequate pre-school provision could be avoided for many children (Bricker and Bricker, 1972). This type of advance is clearly not necessarily related to the behaviour modification approach. However, the desirability of modifying the behaviour of custodians and the recognition that behaviour change is unlikely to result from half-hour sessions once per week are conclusions which follow from a behavioural model.

Implications for the curriculum

We have already seen that the behaviour modification does not prescribe the goals of education. Behaviour modification represents a set of techniques which can be used to change behaviour, but the direction of modification of behaviour is not dictated. However, several points require discussion concerning the way in which goals may be attained, the feasibility of different types of goals and the types and form of programmes within the behaviour modification framework.

ROUTES OF ACHIEVEMENT OF GOALS

Two points follow from the behaviour modification approach. Firstly, as has already been suggested, if the overall goal is a specified change in behaviour, and if the modifier does not wish to use punishment training, there is an apparent need to use reward training procedures. This, in turn, may require a substantial shift in the provision of material and/or staff in the teaching and maintenance environment.

A second point which follows from an overall learning approach to mental handicap or child development is that it is assumed that such concepts as 'readiness' for particular activities are analysable into component skills and competences each of which may be taught (Gagné, 1968). Consequently, education of the mental handicapped is an active teaching process regardless of the initial abilities of the child. Further, education can and should be started at the earliest possible age. As already noted, the feasibility of this aspect of the approach is currently being investigated at several centres in the United States (Bricker and Bricker, 1972; Eastern Nebraska Community Office of Retardation, 1972).

SPECIFICATION OF GOALS

The behaviour modification approach is predicated on the need to specify the goals of any programme. There are two reasons why these need to be discussed thoroughly. Behaviour modification represents a powerful and, to an extent, prestigious set of techniques. In this context there are considerable dangers inherent in their use; they can be misapplied and employed to achieve goals which are unacceptable. Or, alternatively, practices which are substantially misconceived within the behaviour modification framework may be used in the name of behaviour modification. Any procedures which may legitimatize deprivation of food or drink or administration of punishment clearly require thorough discussion. At a less dramatic, but no less tragic, level the handing out of 'Smarties' and raisins in totally inappropriate ways may do little direct harm, but almost certainly does little good. Furthermore, if behaviour modification techniques are judged in light of such practices, incalculable damage may be done through the failure to allow their development in other areas. What seems essential is that there should be thorough discussion of goals and techniques. In North America these issues have already received considerable public airing resulting in sets of working rules being devised (e.g. Lucero et al., 1968). The main critical considerations are that each individual must be provided with a programme which involves as little use of deprivation or other aversive procedure as is possible, and that where the living environment of the individual can be seen as possibly at fault, this environment is modified (cf. Ulrich et al., 1970, Section 12). Secondly, it has already been indicated that these procedures assume the value of an active structured approach to the education of the mentally handicapped, with active participation by parents, teachers, nurses or other custodians. In addition, these individuals require clear feedback on the success of their efforts in terms of clearly specified goals.

The question then becomes one of who should set the goals. Several possibilities offer themselves. The prime change-agents, the custodians, parents, nurses or teachers, could set goals. The need to motivate change-agents and the fact that these individuals have to deal with the handicapped on a day-to-day basis, and also probably know the individuals concerned better than anyone else, gives them a clear right to participate in goal setting. However, clear problems arise if the prime custodians are to be prime goal-setters. These individuals may not be in a position to judge the relationship between their own short-term needs and the long-term needs of the handicapped individual. For instance, it may appear essential for the disruptive behaviour of a handicapped child to be eliminated within a home, school or hospital environment. But another child who simply sits in a corner and plays with his fingers all day may not be seen as requiring such a high priority of modification. Under situations of environmental stress, or if custodians are poorly trained, the quiet child may be seen as 'no trouble' and allowed to remain undisturbed. The general philosophy of 'readiness' has unfortunately provided legitimatization to this approach. Part of the deteriorative effect of the institutional environment may be the result of this type of factor (Francis, 1970).

Alternative sources of goals are offered by the 'normalization' principle and by work in child development and general psychology. These sources offer two types of alternative: on the one hand, specified goals derived from an analysis of the needs of society, and on the other, suggested sequences of goals through which competency may be developed (Kiernan, 1973a).

The behaviour modification approach would suggest that, if these goals are to be achieved, it is necessary to specify them clearly, to train in specific environments and then to mediate generalization into the final target environment.

One of the most impressive examples of this approach within the relevant literature is the Mimosa C programme run in Parsons, Kansas (Lent *et al.*, 1967). Lent and his colleagues built up a token programme for twenty-seven moderately handicapped adolescent girls (IQ 25–55), in which the target behaviours were designed to allow the girls to integrate in the local community. Aspects of personal appearance, dress, hair styles, gait etc. were analysed, in addition to basic social interactive and adaptive skills including sewing, ironing, leisure time activities, town orientation, cooking, housecleaning and general education. Transfer of new skills into the general community environment was mediated through members of the project staff, who modified behaviour *in situ*. The authors point out that 'on-the-job supervision allowed for gradual, rather than abrupt, shifts of control of the child's behaviour from cottage contingencies to those provided in the community environment'.

Given the goal of adapting the individual to a normal environment it is critical that generalization into the natural community is demonstrated. After reviewing token economy studies, Kazdin and Bootzin (1972) conclude that unfortunately such demonstrations of generalization are rare and although there are several procedures for augmenting generalization and resistance to extinction they have not been used extensively to date.

The use of research findings in child development and general psychology as sources of guidance for programmes in behaviour modification is a relatively recent trend (Kiernan, 1973a). Its basis is to use information derived from studies of normal development or of normal individuals as compared with the handicapped to provide guidance for modification of behaviour. It would seem essential to make use of such information in planning behaviour modification programmes. The limitations on this approach will be explored in the last section of this chapter.

TYPES OF PROGRAMME

The range of programmes which can be implemented using behaviour modification procedures is virtually unlimited. Studies have been reported which have shown modification of basic mobility in profoundly handicapped individuals (Fuller, 1949) on training of self-help skills such as eating, dressing, washing, toileting (J. M. Gardner, 1971; Groves and Carroccio, 1971; Martin *et al.*, 1971; Williams, 1972, for review). Numerous investigations have been reported on the elimination of problem behaviours ranging from self-mutilative actions to the use of foul language (J. M. Gardner, 1970; W. I. Gardner, 1971).

Finally, there are studies showing modification of pre-academic, academic and work behaviours, language and communication, all of which show successful modification of behaviour (W. I. Gardner, 1971; Schiefelbusch, 1972).

Many of these researches can be said to involve 'habit training' in the sense of modification of relatively specific response classes such as washing or responding to instructions. It is often argued that behaviour modification is only suitable for habit-training and that 'rule-learning' cannot be accomplished using these techniques. Secondly, it is often assumed that the behaviour trained in behaviour modification studies lacks flexibility and spontaneity.

Two types of study demonstrate clearly that such techniques can be applied to 'rule-learning'. There are now several studies of generalized imitation which involve mentally handicapped individuals. Baer, Peterson and Sherman (1967) showed that if mentally handicapped children were taught, through prompt and fade procedures with reward, to imitate a number of responses, the children would generalize the tendency to imitate to responses which were not rewarded. The children had not been observed to imitate before training. Baer showed that imitation of non-rewarded responses persisted while other imitated responses were being reinforced, but declined when reinforcement was withdrawn. This, and subsequent experiments, demonstrate that the individual can learn the 'rule' that if he imitates the model he will attain reinforcement (Gewirtz and Stingle, 1968; Sherman, 1971). The inference that a 'rule' has been learned is drawn from the fact that diverse responses which are not reinforced are imitated. This approach follows the basic paradigm of learning set training, i.e. that diverse examples, each illustrating the same 'rule', are taught to the individual. This view of imitation training is not new (cf. Ball, 1970), but current research suggests that the individual learns statements of the rule which are limited by the training set. Thus Garcia, Baer and Firestone (1971) divided training responses into small motor, large motor, and short vocal responses. Training each set separately, Garcia and his colleagues showed that generalization of imitation was limited to the topographical type receiving training or which had previously received training. This study and others suggest that verbal and motor imitation can be seen as separate response classes. The ability to teach rule-following through behaviour modification techniques has contributed substantially to the development of operant language training. Procedures developed for language training involve a progression from generalized motor imitation to head and mouth imitations with a heavier and heavier speech related component and finally to simple vocal imitations. Imitation training is used to establish simple chaining and blending to produce words, at which point control is transferred from the vocal model to named objects. Baer, Guess and Sherman (1972) and others report that at this stage the individual may acquire new labels in a single trial (cf. Bricker and Bricker, 1966; Lovaas, 1967; Risley and Wolf, 1967). Any tendency to maintain imitative behaviour in an inappropriate way is eliminated in these studies by appropriately discriminating settings in which imitation is to occur, i.e. 'do this . . . . . .', and by differential reinforcement of appropriate behaviour (Johnston, 1968; Risley and Wolf, 1967).

Several studies in the language area have demonstrated grammatical 'rule' acquisition. Guess, Sailor, Rutherford and Baer (1968) and Guess (1969) demonstrate the establishment of a generative use of plurals in institutionalized children. Sailor (1971) demonstrated the acquisition of productive plural allomorphs (-s and -z) in two institutionalized handicapped children. The trained allomorph was shown to be generalized to probe items in a manner indicating 'rule' acquisition. Schumaker and Sherman (1970) taught institutionalized children to produce past and present forms of verbs in response to questions like 'Now the man is painting. Yesterday he . . . . . . ' or 'Yesterday the man painted. Now he is . . . . . . '

These studies are clearly only initial demonstrations but they serve to illustrate that surface grammar can be acquired through behaviour modification techniques (Baer *et al.*, 1972).

A second group of studies relates to the question of 'inflexibility' and 'stereotyping' of trained responses. In theory behaviour modification techniques can be used to train any type of behaviour which can be specified, including behaviour which is highly variable. This would be accomplished by selectively reinforcing new responses, or responses which were in general investigative in nature. Goetz and Baer (1971) describe a study in which normal 4-year-old children were reinforced for producing novel constructions with blocks. Juvonen (1972) selectively reinforced 'constructive play' in two severely handicapped pre-school children. Constructive play was defined as involving combining objects together, separating parts, etc. A decline in throwing, banging and other non-rewarded response classes was observed. Both studies showed an increase in 'flexible' and 'spontaneous' behaviours. Morales (1972) taught two severely handicapped children to make simple exploratory responses, for example pushing and shaking objects. Transfer of these newly acquired behaviours to novel objects under conditions of non-reinforcement was demonstrated. This study suggests that the child can acquire responses which may be useful to him in exploring and analysing his environment.

The studies reviewed in this section have been described in order to try to establish two points. First, that behaviour modification techniques can be used to teach 'rules', and second, that the techniques can be employed to teach behaviours which may be termed novel, creative or exploratory. There is no reason why other divergent behaviours, such as decision taking or creative art work, should not be taught using these techniques. Provided criteria can be established for reinforcement, even if the target is specified in an open way, 'a response which the individual has not produced before', the methods can be applied.

At an advanced level the regulation of behaviour by the individual himself through self-reinforcement is an area which is being actively investigated at the present time (Bandura, 1969; Kanfer, 1970). This line of research is clearly exciting in terms of future application with the less handicapped, or as an advanced stage of a curriculum. It also leads to the situation where the individual is offered means of control over his own 'inner' behaviour. Homme (1966) has argued that 'coverants' such as thinking or imagining are amenable to the same general control as operants. This point has been taken up in terms of clinical application by Goldiamond (1965), Cautela (1966), Kanfer and Phillips (1966), and Davison (1968).

FORM OF PROGRAMMES

We turn finally to the question of the implications of behaviour modification for the way in which programmes are set up in practice. Two main issues must be covered, the way in which a complex programme is conceptualized, and the way in which the programmes can be put into practice. There are several reasons why overall planning of a programme is required especially within a behaviour modification context. First, any programme based on an analysis of task requirements (Gagné, 1968; Davies, 1971) will have built into it the logical necessity to establish some competencies before others can be built up. At the fundamental level the individual must be able to walk or crawl independently before he can climb stairs. Similar considerations relate to programmes based on developmental or other theoretical assumptions. These sequences or curriculum components can be highly complex and therefore require some means of overall statement which will allow sequence of steps in training to be delineated.

The second main reason why overall planning is required within the behaviour modification framework is because of the emphasis on goal setting. Within the overall structure of a programme, subprogrammes will represent subgoals. These subgoals are critical in relation to the overall aim of the programme but also serve several other functions which require specific statement. They serve to provide a focus for feedback to the individuals implementing the programme, a factor which we have already argued can be of substantial importance. Secondly, the explicit statement of goals and subgoals is that the behaviour modification approach sees the whole environment as critical, i.e. parents, teachers and nurses are all vital to its success. If these individuals are to be effectively integrated into a scheme, that scheme must be explicitly stated and in a way which is comprehensible to those involved.

The explicit statement of goals requires that the goal-set has been at least seriously considered, i.e. that there is an agreed set of aims for the individual. We have already suggested that the parents, teachers or nurses involved in immediate contact with the individual should play a critical part in deciding on the goals set, but that inputs from a consideration of general long-term adaptation to the normal environment and from child development and psychology are necessary. In this case child development may be taken as an inter-disciplinary area involving both physical and psychological development. Thus inputs from physiotherapy, speech therapy and education as well as psychological and sociological work need to be considered.

The need for an overall assessment procedure to establish the capabilities and progress of the individual is clear. This assessment is also necessary in order to establish priorities of teaching.

The type of assessment required by behaviour modification at this level of analysis is more molar than that involved in functional analysis. What is necessary at this level is an analysis which states the subgoals and major goals of a teaching scheme. An increasing number of workers are using systems analysis, flow chart analysis and parallel schemes to describe this structural aspect of the curriculum and to allow placement of the individual within the system (Davies, 1971). One such analysis is the Lattice Systems Approach (Budde and Menolascino, 1971). The lattice approach involves the breakdown into a logical sequence of a complex problem. For example, Budde and Menolascino (1971) describe an application of it in a vocational rehabilitation setting with severely and moderately handicapped individuals. A simplified version of their Programme Lattice is reproduced in Fig. 7.

The lattice is a summary of a complex training programme involving several subprogrammes. It is read from the left and upwards to indicate progression through training. Base-line cells represent teaching programmes. Cells above the base-line represent developmental modules – signifying completion of base-line programmes. Thus Cell 8B (Social Skills Development Complete) has three base-line cells representing interdependent components (A3, Critical Social Skills Training; A5, Job Related Social Skills Training; A8 Placement Related Social Skills Training). Each of the three base-line cells represents a training programme. Each base-line training programme within this type of system can be broken down into other lattices which can specify particular programme components.

From the assessment viewpoint it is clear that this type of arrangement requires specification of criterion behaviour for each component, and that the individual should not 'graduate' from the programme until all requirements are met. Thus assessment serves to place an individual at the appropriate point on the training lattice and to allow clear decisions on final achievements to be made.

One very ambitious development of the Lattice Systems Approach is the Client Progress System developed by the Nebraska State Office of Mental Retardation in conjunction with the Eastern Nebraska Community Office of Retardation (Falls, 1972). This system of assessment involves forty-five Developmental Ladders covering areas from Attending to Budgeting and including cognitive, social and work skills. Each consists of up to eight or so steps, all defined objectively in terms of acquisition criteria. The system represents a training and assessment scheme for use by attendants, teachers, foster parents and others involved in the care and education of the handicapped. As would be

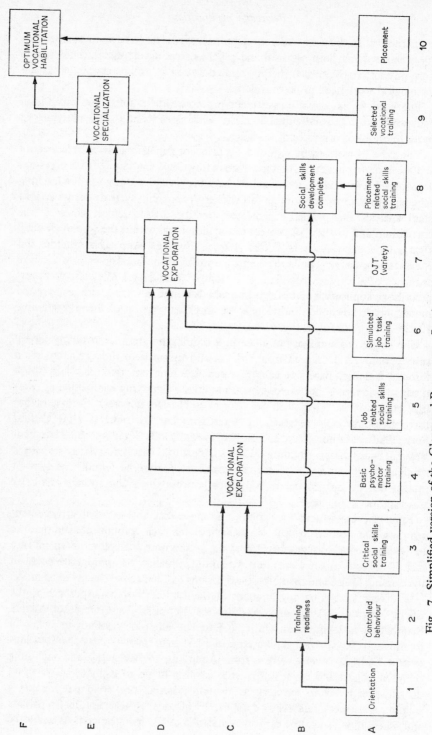

Fig. 7 Simplified version of the Glenwood Programme Lattice (from Budde and Menolascino, 1971).

expected with such an extensive system, data on reliability and validity of the assessment method have not yet been gathered. In addition the extent to which the steps in the training lattices represent a continuous series isolating necessary and sufficient conditions for goal acquisition remains open.

This takes us on to a final point about programme planning, which will arise again in another context, that any programme statement represents a theory about the behaviour concerned. Thus the Glenwood Programme Lattice states a theory of 'optimum vocational rehabilitation'. And, like any theory, programme lattices can be shown to be incomplete or to contain redundant elements. Programme implementation can therefore be likened to theory testing in the natural environment, with the test of theory being the extent of achievement of programme goals.

Studies from two areas of behaviour modification will serve to demonstrate these and other points in practical settings and to complete this analysis of the behaviour modification approach.

One core self-help problem with the severely handicapped and young handicapped individual is toilet-training. There are now a substantial number of studies in the relevant literature which report on toilet-training programmes. As reports have accumulated, successive difficulties in programming have been identified and eliminated and the requirements of the situation more clearly identified.

Following the original statement of the problem in behaviour modification terms by Ellis (1963), two approaches have been taken to toilet training. The individual can be habit trained in the sense that he eliminates appropriately on being placed on the toilet. Several studies have emphasized this (Dayan, 1964; Baumeister and Klosowski, 1965; Hundziak *et al.*, 1965; Kimbrell *et al.*, 1967). The alternative approach aims at the more complex achievement of independent toileting (Bensberg *et al.*, 1965; Giles and Wolf, 1966; van Wagenen *et al.*, 1969; Mahoney *et al.*, 1971; Azrin and Foxx, 1971).

Clearly, the more complex accomplishment is independent toileting. This involves at least the identification of the need to eliminate, walking or in some other way getting to a toilet, removing clothing, eliminating in the toilet, self-cleaning if necessary and replacing clothing. On the other hand, habit training requires far less of the individual especially if assistance is given with removal and putting on of clothing.

Of the studies on toilet training, most have shown gains during training but few give adequate follow-up data, and where it is provided it suggests poor maintenance of behaviour (Rentfrow and Rentfrow, 1969). The obvious explanation of failure to maintain behaviour is that the training programmes have failed to coordinate with the reinforcers available for adequate toileting in the natural environment. Or the reinforcement provided by the natural environment may have been inadequate to maintain any effective toileting.

Mahoney, Van Wagenen and Meyerson (1971) provide an example of training for independent toilet which brings up the main programme planning issues.

They trained a group of 3 young normal children (18–20 months old) and a group of 5 handicapped children (4–9 years old). The procedure involved a pre-test and 6 training phases. During the pre-test phase the children were observed daily for $3\frac{1}{2}$ hours over a 5-day period in order to assess base-line behaviour. During the first major stage of training the child was taught prerequisite toileting behaviour. An auditory signal generator was worn by the child which could be activated either by the subject urinating or by the experimenter. In Phase I when it was turned on the experimenter approached the child and invited and prompted him to go to the potty. Compliance, at first under prompt and subsequently independently, was rewarded with food and social praise. In Phase II the child was taught in addition to lower his pants, again with initial physical prompting. In Phase III the child was taught to sit on the toilet seat or take the proper male stance when facing it. Reinforcement in Phase III was given for sitting or standing appropriately for 30 seconds having approached the toilet and adjusted clothing appropriately.

During these phases no attempt was made to effect actual elimination. The aim had been to teach prerequisite skills. In the second three phases, attention was switched to elimination. In Phase 4 subjects were given 10 ounces of extra liquid during training sessions in order to increase the probability of urination. Clearly the low operant level of elimination makes for problems of programming if the response is to be reinforced. Giving extra liquid is reported as effective in increasing operant levels (Giles and Wolf, 1966; Azrin and Foxx, 1971). During Phase 4 the experimenter generated the auditory signal. If the subject urinated during the 30 seconds at the toilet he was reinforced. Otherwise his pants were pulled up and he was allowed to return to play. If elimination occurred during play the auditory signal sounded. If the child then walked to the toilet and re-started urination he was rewarded. If not he was not rewarded. Wet pants were removed without comment at this stage.

Once the child had urinated successfully in the toilet on one occasion the strategy changed. Now if the child eliminated inappropriately the experimenter said, 'No! Go potty'. Again reward followed urination in the toilet.

The various features of the Mahoney–van Wagenen approach are common to other programmes. Aside from increasing the frequency of response the immediate identification of urination is seen as essential if reinforcers are to be appropriately administered (Mowrer and Mowrer, 1938; van Wagenen and Murdock, 1966; Watson, 1966; Azrin et al., 1971; Azrin and Foxx, 1971). Typically these authors have devised 'trainer pants' worn by the subject during training or have constructed specially wired toilets to detect elimination immediately it occurs appropriately. The other function of these cues is to provide conditioned reinforcers to which internal cues may be conditioned as discriminative stimuli. This immediate detection is likely to be critical. Toileting has in fact got a 'natural' reinforcement sequence built in provided the individual is taught to sit on the toilet. It would be normal under these circumstances to allow the individual off only when he had performed, and it is also likely that the custodian would also initiate social interaction at this stage which would not be present whilst the individual was seated. This sequence was observed as a standard pattern in wards in an institution. It represents a setting in which reward should operate for correct toileting – if the fact that the individual has eliminated is detected. Unfortunately, elimination is characteristically not detected under block treatment unless special cues are developed. In un-modified block treatment appropriate toilet behaviour does not develop.

A third common feature is the joint emphasis on reward for appropriate and punishment for inappropriate behaviour. Azrin and Foxx argue that 'normal toileting is not simply a matter of learning to respond to bladder and bowel pressures by relaxing the sphincter but rather is a complex operant and social learning process that has been hindered (in the institutionalized handicapped individual) by a reduced learning capacity and by institutionalization' (1971, p. 89). They argue that the negative aspects of unsuccessful toileting are critical in control of behaviour. In their study the institutionalized severely handicapped men who served as subjects experienced elaborate consequences for incorrect elimination during training. These included verbal reprimands, an hour of time-out from a heightened level of positive reinforcement, and cleanliness training including being given a tepid shower, changing all his clothes, carrying soiled clothes to the sink, washing them out and hanging them to dry. He also had to clean up all traces of soiling.

The fifth phase of the Mahoney–van Wagenen procedure involved teaching the child to pull up pants. Mahoney and his colleagues hold that the optimal sequence for toilet training is a forward chaining procedure. It will be noted that at each potential problem phase success is assisted by physical prompting thereby minimizing extinction problems. Other authors teach dressing skills as part of the toilet training programme (cf. Giles and Wolf, 1966; Azrin and Foxx, 1971).

The final phase of the Mahoney programme involved the removal of the auditory signal. Mahoney and his colleagues report that by this stage of the study they had learned to identify for each subject specific overt responses which often preceded the act of elimination, for example tugging at pants, or a sudden increase in activity. During this phase the experimenter initiated the auditory signal when the subject showed these signs. The final training component followed when the subject had correctly eliminated three times following the auditory signal. At this time the device was removed. Reinforce-ment was then given for the complete sequence of behaviour without signals or prompts.

In other studies this final transition to independent toileting may begin earlier in training. Azrin and Foxx faded physical prompts for sitting on the toilet from early in training. In their study subjects were on the toilet for much longer periods of time at first (up to 20 minutes of every 30 if appropriate elimination did not occur). Thus isolation of pre-urination behaviour was not as critical. Azrin and Foxx argue that the anticipation of positive reinforcement and the avoidance of disapproval were the basis for toilet approach in their study.

Following basic training, Mahoney and his colleagues ran three days of post-test and then instructed the parents in aspects of the procedures to be continued at home. Follow-up over a period of six months was completed with only two subjects. They showed a low level of inappropriate responses.

Azrin and Foxx instituted a post-training ward maintenance procedure which involved encouragement of proper toileting and social disapproval and cleanliness training for 'accidents'. This procedure was introduced by assigning one

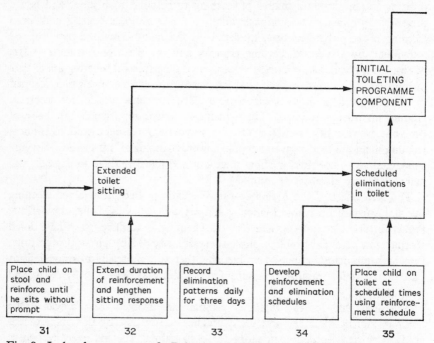

Fig. 8   Isolated component of a Behaviour Modification Training Process Lattice
(from Budde, 1971).

attendant on each shift the responsibility of overseeing the trainees and record-ing behaviour. After one month regular checks were reduced in frequency. This type of modification to the maintenance environment is similar to that discussed by Panyan, Boozer and Morris (1970).

In both the studies discussed, good acquisition of independent toileting was reported. Azrin and Foxx report good maintenance of independent toileting.

Several general points may be made which arise out of this detailed presenta-tion of a programme. Firstly, the environment was modified in order to allow rapid detection and reinforcement of appropriate and inappropriate behaviour. In the Azrin and Foxx study the subjects spent the four days of the training phase actually in the toilet area. Secondly, since the programming was intensive,

TOILET TRAINING

ACCIDENTS

U   BM

TIME

	AM
	PM

MON. AM TRAINER_____ PM TRAINER_____

TIME

	AM
	PM

TUES. AM TRAINER_____ PM TRAINER_____

TIME

	AM
	PM

WED. AM TRAINER_____ PM TRAINER_____

TIME

	AM
	PM

THU. AM TRAINER_____ PM TRAINER_____

TIME

	AM
	PM

FRI. AM TRAINER_____ PM TRAINER_____

TIME

	AM
	PM

SAT. AM TRAINER_____ PM TRAINER_____

TIME

	AM
	PM

SUN. AM TRAINER_____ PM TRAINER_____

Mark a 'U' for urination or 'BM' for bowel movement in the appropriate box.
Mark a '−' if no elimination occurs. Place slash marks (///) in accident column.

PROCEDURE: 1. Children should be placed on the toilet every 2 hours
2. Assign the children to specific stools so that they are toileted in the same place every day
3. Each child should remain on the commode until he urinates and/or defecates, or for 15 minutes
4. The Nurse should be with the children every moment they are on the stool and be in a position to see when elimination occurs
5. The moment a child begins to eliminate, he should be reinforced immediately
6. When the child has had no accidents for 2 weeks, his training is considered successful and a new child should be begun

CRITERION FOR GRADUATION: Three or less accidents per week for 2 weeks. Begin a new child in training at this point

WEEK OF_____ CHILDS NAME_____

Fig. 9   Programming sheet used by ward attendants in a large institution in the United States.

staff, in this case research staff, were assigned specially to training. In these studies ward staff and parents did not participate. In other institutional, pre-school and home settings, parents, teachers or nurses can and do record programmes of the type described (Watson *et al.*, 1971; Boozer, 1972, personal communication; Galloway, 1972, personal communication).

With this type of programme it becomes critical for some form of programme planning of the type offered by the Lattice Systems method to be used in order to establish sequencing. This may be done either through a Lattice Systems Approach or by less formal means. Fig. 8 shows a component of the toilet training programme developed by Budde (1971) which specifies on the base-line several component programmes. Fig. 9 is a programming sheet used by ward attendants in a large institution in the United States (Boozer, 1972, personal communication).

The final point concerning the toilet training programmes is that they clearly differ on some points, in particular on the emphasis on negative reinforcement. These and similar disagreements represent differences in theoretical approach which it is to be hoped will be empirically resolved.

Rather different points concerning programme planning emerge from the consideration of language training. Here there is a greater possibility of deriving programme sequences and structures from linguistic theory or from work on the development of language in normal children.

Normative work on the development of language and other behaviours offers a dubious direct source of programmes. Language scales and other scales of development are normally derived with the explicit aim of isolating behaviours which show differences between different age groups. The implication of this is that, if a behaviour occurs in a particular sequence with other behaviours, but at an unpredictable time, it will not be selected. Thus Behaviour A may characterize the 20-month-old child, Behaviour C the 30-month-old. Behaviour B may occur at any time between 20 and 30 months. In this case it will be a poor item for a developmental test based on age. However B may not be able to occur before A and may be a necessary precondition for C. Thus at a teaching level it may be critical. Scale items are not normally selected in line with any theory of development and scales are not constructed with a view to giving an indication of critical stages of development.

Developmental scales would not be expected to be able to specify all necessary and sufficient steps to the achievement of goals. They therefore represent poor bases for the construction of programme systems (Kiernan, 1973a).

This suggests that either linguisitic or developmental theories, for example Piagetian theory, plus logical analyses of task requirements may offer a better basis for programme construction (Gagné, 1968). This approach also offers a rigorous method of theory testing not usually open to developmental theories. If the theory states all the necessary and sufficient steps towards an achievement, and if these component steps are trained, then the achievement should emerge, given the correctness of the theory.

The unification of linguistic theory and behaviour modification appears in the work of Bricker and Baer (Baer *et al.*, 1972; Lynch and Bricker, 1972). It leads in Bricker's case to the establishment of a complex language training programme (Bricker and Bricker, 1970; Bricker, 1972). The training lattice of this programme is reproduced in Fig. 4 (see p. 299). In this lattice cells below the ridge line all specify programme steps. This programme is highly complex involving a large number of subprogrammes. Each of these can be seen as involving teaching in formal and informal settings or an extensive breakdown into further subprogrammes relevant to the training situation. For example, Fulton (1972) described the development of sets of audiological procedures which include standard puretone audiometry, speech audiometry, 'general' auditory tests and Bekesy audiometry, which would fit into one of the cells of the programme.

In terms of implementation of component programmes in school or home settings, the type of schemes arising from the Lattice Systems Approach may involve a mixture of formal and informal teaching. Thus a motor imitation component may involve the following steps.[1] Firstly, the establishment of reinforcement control in which it is ensured that the subject responds reliably to presentation of reward. Secondly, the subject is assessed for the extent to which he 'attends' in the sense of looking at the teacher when called. This level appears critical for performance in imitation. If the individual does not orient appropriately on around 60 per cent of trials it is desirable to bring behaviour up to this level otherwise test and training is very slow. At this stage motor imitation, with reinforcement for correct responding, is assessed. The test set involves a variety of types of motor responses, i.e. self-oriented, object oriented, gross and fine motor imitation (Kiernan and Saunders, 1972). If the individual does not reach a preset criterion or if performance suggests deficiencies in certain areas of imitation a training programme is introduced. This programme involves either a full twenty minute session once per day with recording of all performances during the training, or a less formal training session with a probe test at the end of each session. In this case the responses to probe may be the only behaviour recorded. In our own case the full sessions are used with nurses. The former approach may be beyond the resources of many parents, teachers or nurses. However, Hall has shown that parents can set up and record not simply single sessions but also full experiments using reversal designs (Hall *et al.*, 1972). The second procedure, involving only recording of responses to probes, tends to be favoured by proponents of precision teaching (Galloway, 1972, personal communication). This method has the obvious virtue of placing less strain on the individual running the teaching session.

Whatever approach is used, this type of individualized teaching can be generalized for all bar research purposes to non-training settings. Thus if motor

[1] These steps are similar to those at present being used in a motor imitation programme for young handicapped children by the author. A debt in the development of this programme is owed to Diane and Bill Bricker whose work suggested many of the steps.

imitation is being trained, reinforcement of appropriate behaviour in the home or classroom would be encouraged. Characteristically this type of casual reinforcement is not recorded.

The training set for individual sessions is devised to cover relevant dimensions of imitation. The individuals running sessions are normally involved in devising such sets. In addition, generalization sets may be introduced to assess degree of acquisition of generalized imitation.

Following achievement of agreed criterion behaviour in training sets re-assessment on the original test set yields a further measure of acquisition of generalized imitation. Progression to the next component in training follows successful acquisition.

Programmes of the type described exist in several centres. What characterizes them is their emphasis on accurate assessment of training needs and then a mixture of formal training and informal training before reassessment.

This type of programme planning clearly differs from that involved in the toilet training programmes. The latter may be classed as total programmes in the sense that they require full-time attention of at least one individual whilst in operation.

Such programmes require more communication between individuals involved in teaching and hence will be more difficult to arrange than individual pro-grammes. In terms of staff economies it may not be possible to run more than one total programme on toilet training or behaviour problems at any one time in a ward, classroom or home. Individual teaching session programmes may be run in addition to a general programme. In this respect specific timetabling of individual sessions appears essential (Kiernan, 1973b). Notices giving instructions to individuals running training, cue lights signifying particular times for events, also assist in programme integration (G. L. Martin, 1972).

Conclusions

The functions of a theory are to allow a systematization of existing data, to make testable predictions, and to provide a more general heuristic framework which stimulates ideas and allows general integration of thinking within an area. This chapter has aimed at presenting the behaviour modification approach in such a way that its potential value in relation to these criteria could be appreciated. No serious attempt has been made to 'evaluate' behaviour modification. The concentration here has been on developing the basic model and indicating what this author feels are its implications for our dealings with the mentally handi-capped.

There are several reasons for adopting this approach. Partly it is conditioned by the large amount of published research.[1] More, it is conditioned by the fact that research and practice are several years ahead of publication. There appears,

[1] See Gardner and Watson, 1969, for a bibliography to that date: *Mental Retardation Abstracts* include behaviour modification research.

therefore, to be a case for selection of studies which exemplify particular important points and indicate apparent trends. Research and practice in this area is progressing beyond basic demonstrations and it is to these areas of development that attention has been directed.

The main emphases in the current position appear to be as follows. As Lindsley (1970) has pointed out there is now a greater emphasis on programmes of education or remediation rather than on individual one-off training (cf. Gelfand and Hartmann, 1968; Gardner, 1969a; Sherman and Baer, 1969). The phase of basic demonstration of effectiveness of reinforcement in changing behaviour in individual cases appears to have passed. As the editor of an international journal has put it, 'many studies have demonstrated that the law of effect has not yet been repealed'. Within this framework three elements dominate: the need to specify clear target behaviours, the need to modify the social and material environment in order to allow the modification and maintenance of behaviour, and finally the emphasis on consequation by whatever reinforcers are effective, be they social or material.

The emphasis on programmes has extended the thinking of workers in the behaviour modification area beyond the specific interaction of the reinforcement event to broader variables which precondition availability of reinforcement. Thus attention in studies within institutions has shifted to institutional reorganization at both the social and material level. The result of this has been to blur edges between different approaches and also to break down the isolation characteristic of operant workers (Krantz, 1971). Baker and Ward (1971), reporting a study in which a behaviour modification programme was implemented on a living unit in an institution, conclude that

> in the last analysis . . . it is not meaningful conceptually to separate the milieu from reinforcement therapy. The availability of reinforcers in the environment, both tangible (as toys or TV) and social (as closer contact with attendants and volunteers) is essential to a total reinforcement therapy program. The reinforcement model becomes helpful in designing the physical milieu so as to provide opportunities and meaningful rewards for learning, along with formal contingencies introduced within that milieu. (1971, p. 133)

Similar blurring appears necessary across disciplines. Michael (1970) has pointed out that behaviour modification can offer a common set of procedures covering several areas including medical and vocational rehabilitation. One can extend the list to include methods used by parents, teachers, nurses, speech therapists, occupational therapists, physiotherapists, music therapists, art therapists, and so forth. These workers have diverse goals but they are all directly concerned with behaviour change. While it has been emphasized that the goals of education are not necessarily the business of behaviour modification, the routes to achievement of these goals could be a matter of concern. Michael (1970) suggests a role of 'primary authority in the arrangement of the environment so as to produce, maintain, or eliminate behaviour' (1970, p. 54). The essence of the argument is that behaviour is a unitary phenomenom which may not be happily split along professional lines which have arisen in the West largely through historical chance.

The broadening of the scope of practice of behaviour modification makes it necessary to ensure that the pure research on which it is based is well founded. In addition studies on the effectiveness of programmes are essential.

Common basic criticisms have been expressed by J. M. Gardner (1968, 1969a, 1971), Gelfand and Hartmann (1968) and Sherman and Baer (1969). No attempt will be made to detail these but it is essential to state the main problems outlined and to comment on issues raised. Gardner (1969) has pointed out that many independent variables are inadequately specified in behaviour modification research, and in a surprisingly large number of cases potentially important variables such as age, diagnostic category, physical condition and test scores are omitted. He and other authors have also drawn attention to the large number of single case studies published (Gelfand and Hartmann, 1968). It has already been noted that the danger here is that only successful cases will be reported. The fact that the 'worst' subjects in institutions were selected especially in earlier studies does not circumvent this difficulty. Even when a sample of subjects are used there is still the likelihood that the samples involved will be biased (Bricker, 1970). Gardner also criticizes the failure to specify relevant experimenter variables including attitude and training in behaviour modification. On the dependent variable side, again the failure to specify the precise effects of a programme and also its more generalized effects is emphasized.

These criticisms reflect problems which are in some ways a function of the behaviour modification approach itself and in others are general problems. For example, the specification of general behaviour before and after modification requires efficient assessment procedures. Some workers have used existing cognitive tests and have shown that these can detect change as a result of behaviour modification programmes. Thus, Sachs (1971) showed WISC score changes resulting from the operation of a token economy. However, these tests are likely to be too gross and insensitive as methods of assessing behaviour change. Gardner's criticisms relate in part to the failure to provide the type of assessment described above in context of programme planning, i.e. a system which allows an extensive specification of progress towards target behaviours. J. M. Gardner (1971) describes a check list system which provides such a frame (Gardner and Hoffman, 1969). Kiernan, Donoghue and Hawks (1971) describe the use of a checklist system devised by Williams and Kushlick (1970).

An interesting further development at a research level which relates to Gardner's main thesis is the appearance of studies in which several dependent variables are assessed simultaneously, usually in an attempt to detect the 'side-effects' of behaviour modification. These investigations have produced some interesting results, all bar one study show positive effects – and in the study showing adverse effects, in addition to positive side-effects, the adverse results were brought under control with an extension of the procedure (Buell *et al.*,

1968; Risley, 1968; Sajwaj *et al.*, 1972). This type of study is too rare in the behaviour modification literature.

The problem of single case studies is partly a function of the methodology of operant research, coupled with problems concerned with the time required to complete researches of this type. Although the numbers of subjects run in most studies is remarkably low, most reports of programme research involve larger numbers of subjects and, in these, negative findings can be and are reported. For example, many of the studies reported by Kazdin and Bootzin (1972) on token economies include discussion of programme failures. Clearly these data are critically important in improvement of programmes if other relevant data are also available which will allow hypotheses related to failure to be formulated. Non-representativeness of samples raises other issues, prime among which is, representative of what? At one level, studies based on epidemiologically representative samples of the population are necessary, and again it is to be hoped that these will be reported from centres in which programmes are being developed. At another level, it would appear that behavioural techniques have been shown to apply to at least some individuals with all degrees of handicap from the most severe.

Another criticism made by Gardner and others is that behaviour modification research fails to report relevant situational variables. This criticism is especially important if the extension of the behaviour modification model to situational variables is to be taken seriously (Baker and Ward, 1971). In addition, as already noted, many studies specify discriminative stimuli generally, if at all. Again, part of the problem facing the behaviour modifier is the availability of relevant measuring instruments. Kiernan, Donoghue and Hawks (1971) used a combination of direct observation, questionnaires on basic ward data, such as number of ambulant children, plus the Child Management Schedule devised by King, Raynes and Tizard (1971), a questionnaire which gives data on management procedures shown relevant to development. There appears to be a clear need for studies which examine the effects of ecological factors on behaviour in relation to the behaviour modification approach.

A critical problem mentioned by all reviewers is the lack of studies showing adequate follow-up, and this raises particular issues for behaviour modification. The approach asserts that behaviour is responsive to environmental change, and therefore environmental changes are used to modify behaviour. However, it also follows that if the contingencies which support new behaviour are removed or reversed the behaviour may well follow. It has been argued throughout this chapter that generalization to non-training conditions must take into account the contingencies in that environment. Successful maintenance of behaviour will then reflect at least two factors: the extent to which training has been geared to the non-training environment and the extent to which the latter has been adapted to accommodate the new behaviour. To expect the techniques to produce lasting change without allowing for this consideration is to test the theory beyond its boundary conditions. The studies by Azrin and Foxx (1971) and Vukelich and Hake (1971) reported earlier exemplify this approach. In both cases maintenance of behaviour was programmed by modifying the environmental setting to ensure sources of check and reinforcement.

Similar considerations apply to the use of conventional control groups. Within the behaviour modification approach the concept of no-treatment control is meaningless. Similarly, alternative approaches to behaviour modification programmes would be expected to be analysable in terms of procedural or content variables. These could be studied in terms of behaviour modification techniques and content, a strategy which may reveal important new content or procedures. But there is no one behaviour modification approach; each programme may be well or poorly carried out, have good or poor content (Kuypers *et al.*, 1968), and therefore the comparison of any particular package with another is a false one. What does seem both valuable and essential is the comparison of different procedures, for example modelling as opposed to verbal prompting in the teaching of particular content, or the comparison of different programme content with procedures held at a common level of efficiency in the achievement of set goals.

The behaviour modification approach provides a challenging and hopeful trend in work with the mentally handicapped. Its main strengths appear to lie in the fact that it is applicable to very young and very severely handicapped individuals to whom little has been offered by other methods. In fact the emphasis on external control of behaviour in the behaviour modification approach as it is currently developed may make it particularly applicable to these individuals. It offers exciting prospects in the active testing of theory in practice. Its emphasis on dealing with the whole social and physical environment and of integrating diverse approaches and disciplines is clearly challenging and promises substantial benefits.

References

ADDISON, R. M. and HOMME, L. E. (1966) The reinforcing event (RE) menu. *National Society for Programmed Instruction Journal*, 5, 8–9.

AYLLON, T. and AZRIN, N. (1968) *The Token Economy*. New York: Appleton-Century-Crofts.

AZRIN, N. H. and FOXX, R. M. (1971) A rapid method of toilet training the institutionalized retarded. *J. appl. Behav. Anal.*, 4, 89–99.

AZRIN, N. H. and HOLZ, W. C. (1966) Punishment. In HONIG, W. K. (ed.) *Operant Behavior: Areas of Research and Application*. New York: Appleton-Century-Crofts.

AZRIN, N. H., BUGLE, C. and O'BRIEN, F. (1971) Behavioral engineering: two apparatuses for toilet training retarded children. *J. appl. Behav. Anal.*, 4, 249–53.

BAER, D. M. (1970) A case for selective reinforcement of punishment. In NEURINGER, C. and MICHAEL, J. L. (eds.) *Behavior Modification in Clinical Psychology.* New York: Appleton-Century-Crofts.

BAER, D. M. and WOLF, M. M. (1967) The entry into natural communities of reinforcement. In ULRICH, R., STACHNIK, T. and MABRY, J. (eds.) *Control of Human Behavior. Vol. Two: From Cure to Prevention.* Glenview, Ill.: Scott, Foresman.

BAER, D. M., GUESS, D. and SHERMAN, J. A. (1972) Adventures in simplistic grammar. In SCHIEFELBUSCH, R. L. (ed.) *Language of the Mentally Retarded.* Baltimore, Md.; Univ. Park Press.

BAER, D. M., PETERSON, R. F. and SHERMAN, J. A. (1967) The development of imitation by reinforcing behavioral similarity to a model. *J. exp. Anal. Behav.,* **10,** 405–16.

BAER, D. M., WOLF, M. M. and RISLEY, T. R. (1958) Some current dimensions of applied behavior analysis. *J. appl. Behav. Anal.,* **1,** 91–7.

BAILEY, J. and MEYERSON, L. (1969) Vibration as a reinforcer with a profoundly retarded child. *J. appl. Behav. Anal.,* **2,** 135–7.

BAKER, B. L. and WARD, M. H. (1971) Reinforcement therapy for behavior problems in severely retarded children. *Amer. J. Orthopsychiat.,* **41,** 124–35.

BALL, T. S. (1970) Training generalized imitation: variations on a historical theme. *Amer. J. ment. Defic.,* **75,** 135–41.

BANDURA, A. (1965) Influence of model's reinforcement contingencies on the acquisition of imitative responses. *J. Pers. soc. Psychol.,* **1,** 589–95.

BANDURA, A. (1969) *Principles of Behaviour Modification.* New York: Holt, Rinehart & Winston.

BANKS, M. and LOCKE, B. (1966) *Self-injurious Stereotypes and Mild Punishment with Retarded Subjects.* Working Paper No. 123. Parsons State Hospital and Training Centre.

BARKER, R. G. and WRIGHT, H. F. (1955) *Midwest and its Children.* New York: Harper & Row.

BARTON, E. S., GUESS, D., GARCIA, E. and BAER, D. M. (1970) Improvements of retardates' mealtime behaviours by timeout procedures using multiple baseline techniques. *J. appl. Behav. Anal.,* **3,** 77–84.

BAUMEISTER, A. and KLOSOWSKI, R. (1965) An attempt to group toilet train severely retarded patients. *Ment. Retard.,* **3,** 24–6.

BECKER, W. C., ENGELMANN, S. and THOMAS, D. R. (1971) *Teaching: A Basic Course in Applied Psychology.* Chicago: Science Research Associates.

BENSBERG, G. J. (1965) *Teaching the Mentally Retarded.* Atlanta, Ga: Southern Regional Education Board.

BENSBERG, G. J. and SLOMINSKI, A. (1965) Helping the retarded learn self-care. In BENSBERG, G. J. (ed.) *Teaching the Mentally Retarded.* Atlanta, Ga: Southern Regional Educational Board.

BENSBERG, G. J., COLWELL, C. N. and CASSEL, R. H. (1965) Teaching the profoundly retarded self-help skill activities by behavior-shaping techniques. *Amer. J. of ment. Defic.*, **69**, 674–9.

BERKOWITZ, S., SHERRY, P. J. and DAVIS, B. A. (1971) Teaching self-feeding skills to profound retardates using reinforcement and fading procedures. *Behav. Therapy*, **2**, 62–7.

BERNAL, M. (1969) Behavioural feedback in the modification of rat behaviours. *J. nerv. ment. Dis.*, **148**, 375–85.

BIJOU, S. W. (1966) A functional analysis of retarded development. In ELLIS, N. R. (ed.) *International Review of Research in Mental Retardation*, Vol. I. New York: Academic Press.

BIJOU, S. W. (1968) Studies in the experimental development of left-right concepts in retarded children using fading techniques. In ELLIS, N. R. (ed.) *International Review of Research in Mental Retardation*, Vol. 3. New York: Academic Press.

BIJOU, S. W. and BAER, D. M. (1961) *Child Development 1: A systematic and Empirical Theory.* New York: Appleton-Century-Crofts.

BIJOU, S. W. and BAER, D. M. (1965) *Child Development II. Universal Stages of Infancy.* New York: Appleton-Century-Crofts.

BIJOU, S. W. and BAER, D. M. (1967) *Child Development: Readings in Experimental Analysis.* New York: Appleton-Century-Crofts.

BIJOU, S. W. and ORLANDO, R. (1961) Rapid development of multiple-schedule performances with retarded children. *J. exp. Anal. Behav.*, **4**, 7–16.

BIJOU, S. W. and STURGES, P. T. (1959) Positive reinforcers for experimental studies with children consumables and manipulables. *Child Developm.*, **30**, 151–70.

BIJOU, S. W., PETERSON, R. F. and AULT, M. H. (1968) A method to integrate descriptive and experimental field studies at the level of data and empirical concepts. *J. appl. Behav. Anal.* **1**, 175–91.

BIRNBRAUER, J. S. (1968) Generalization of punishment effects – a case study. *J. appl. Behav. Anal.*, **1**, 201–11.

BIRNBRAUER, J. S., WOLF, M. M., KIDDER, J. D. and TAGUE, C. E. (1965) Classroom behaviour of retarded pupils with token reinforcement. In SLOANE, H. N. and MACAULAY, B. D. (eds.) *Operant Procedures in Remedial Speech and Language Training.* Boston: Houghton Mifflin.

BOE, E. E. and CHURCH, R. M. (1968) *Punishment: Issues and Experiments.* New York: Appleton-Century-Crofts.

BOLLES, R. C. (1962) The difference between statistical hypotheses and scientific hypotheses. *Psychol. Rep.*, **11**, 639–45.

BOSTOW, D. E. and BAILEY, J. B. (1969) Modification of severe disruptive and aggressive behaviour using brief time-out and reinforcement procedures. *J. appl. Behav. Anal.*, **2**, 31–7.

BRADY, J. P. and LIND, D. L. (1961) Experimental analysis of hysterical blindness. *Arch. Gen. Psychiat.*, 4, 331–9.

BRENER, J. and HOTHERSALL, D. (1967) Heart rate control under conditions of augmented sensory feedback. *Psychophysiol.*, 4, 1–6.

BRICKER, D. D. (1972) Imitative sign training as a facilitator of word-object association with low-functioning children. *Amer. J. ment. Defic.*, 76, 509–16.

BRICKER, D. D. and BRICKER, W. A. (1972) *Toddler Research and Intervention Project. Report Year One.* Nashville, Tenn.: IMRID, Peabody College.

BRICKER, W. A. (1970) Identifying and modifying behavioral deficits. *Amer. J. ment. Defic.*, 75, 16–21.

BRICKER, W. A. (1972) A systematic approach to language training. In SCHIEFELBUSCH, R. L. (ed.) *The Language of the Mentally Retarded.* Baltimore, Md.: Univ. Park Press.

BRICKER, W. A. and BRICKER, D. D. (1966) The use of programmed language training as a means for differential diagnosis and educational remediation among severely retarded children. In *Peabody Papers in Human Development.* Nashville, Tenn.: Peabody College.

BRICKER, W. A. and BRICKER, D. D. (1969) Four operant procedures for establishing auditory stimulus control with low functioning children. *Amer. J. ment. Defic.*, 73, 981–7.

BRICKER, W. A. and BRICKER, D. (1970) A program of language training for the severely language handicapped child. *Except. Child.*, 101–11.

BRICKER, W. A., MORGAN, D. and GRABOWSKI, J. (1968) Token reinforcement of attendants who work with low-functioning children. *Abstracts of Peabody Studies in Mental Retardation 1965–8*, 4.

BUCHER, B. and LOVAAS, O. I. (1968) Use of aversive stimulation in behaviour modification. In JONES, M. R. (ed.) *Miami Symposium on the Prediction of Behaviour, 1967: Aversive Stimulation.* Coral Gables, Fla.: Univ. of Miami Press.

BUDDE, J. F. (1971) *The Lattice Systems Approach: A Developmental Tool for Behavioural Research and Program Models.* Working Paper No. 250. Parsons, Kans.: Parsons Research Centre.

BUDDE, J. F. and MENOLASCINO, F. J. (1971) Systems technology and retardation: applications to vocational habilitation. *Ment. Retard.*, 9, 11–16.

BUDDENHAGEN, R. G. (1971) *Establishing Vocal Verbalization in Mute Mongoloid Children.* Champaign, Ill.: Research Press Company.

BUEHLER, R. E., PATTERSON, G. R. and FURNISS, J. M. (1966) The reinforcement of behaviour in institutional settings. *Behav. Res. Therapy*, 4, 157–67.

BUELL, J., STODDARD, P., HARRIS, F. R. and BAER, D. M. (1968) Collateral social development accompanying reinforcement of outdoor play in a preschool child. *J. appl. Behav. Anal.*, 1, 167–73.

BURCHARD, J. D. and BARRERA, F. (1972) An analysis of timeout and response cast in a programmed environment. *J. appl. Behav. Anal.*, **5**, 271–82.

CAMPBELL, D. T. and STANLEY, J. C. (1963) Experimental and quasi-experimental designs for research. In GAGE, N. L. (ed.) *Handbook of Research on Teaching.* New York: Rand, McNally.

CANDLAND, D. K. and MANNING, S. A. (1966) Elementary learning patterns in mental retardates. *Training School Bull.*, **63**, 57–99.

CATANIA, A. C. (1971) Elicitation, reinforcement and stimulus control. In GLASER, R. (ed.) *The Nature of Reinforcement.* New York: Academic Press.

CAUTELA, J. H. (1966) Treatment of compulsive behaviour by covert sensitization. *Psychol. Rec.*, **16**, 33–41.

CHURCH, R. M. (1963) The varied effects of punishment on behaviour. *Psychol. Rev.*, **70**, 369–402.

CLARKE, A. M. and CLARKE, A. D. B. (1973) What are the problems? An evaluation of recent research relating to theory and practice. In CLARKE, A. D. B. and CLARKE, A. M. (eds.) *Mental Retardation and Behavioural Research.* London: Churchill Livingstone.

CLEMENTS, C. B. and MCKEE, J. M. (1968) Programmed instruction for institutionalized offenders: contingency management and performance contacts. *Psychol. Rep.*, **22**, 957–64.

CORTE, H. E., WOLF, M. M. and LOCKE, B. J. (1971) A comparison of procedures for eliminating self-injurious behaviour of retarded adolescents. *J. appl. Behav. Anal.*, **4**, 201–13.

Council for Exceptional Children (1971) *Teaching Exceptional Children* (Special Issue on Precision Teaching). Arlington, Va.

DAVIES, I. K. (1971) *The Management of Learning.* London: McGraw-Hill.

DAVISON, G. C. (1968) The elimination of a sadistic fantasy by a client-controlled counterconditioning technique: a case study. *J. abn. Psychol.*, **73**, 84–90.

DAYAN, M. (1964) Toilet training retarded children in a state residential institution. *Ment. Retard.*, **2**, 116–17.

DICARA, L. V. and MILLER, N. E. (1968) Changes in heart rate instrumentally learned by curarized rats as avoidance responses. *J. comp. physiol. Psychol.*, **65**, 8–12.

Eastern Nebraska Community Office of Retardation (1972) *General Information Papers.*

EGGER, M. D. and MILLER, N. E. (1962) Secondary reinforcement in rats as a function of information value and reliability of a stimulus. *J. exp. Psychol.*, **64**, 97–104.

ELLIS, N. R. (1963) Toilet training the severely defective patient: An S-R reinforcement analysis. *Amer. J. ment. Defic.*, **68**, 98–103.

FALLS, C. W. (1972) *Client Progress System.* Lincoln: Nebraska State Office of Mental Retardation.

FINDLEY, J. D. and BRADY, J. V. (1965) Facilitation of large ratio performance by use of conditioned reinforcement. *J. exp. Anal. Behav.*, **8**, 125–9.

FLANDERS, J. P. (1968) A review of research on imitative behaviour.
Psychol. Bull., **69**, 316–37.

FOXX, R. M. and AZRIN, N. H. (1972) Restitution: a method of eliminating
aggressive-disruptive behavior of retarded and brain damaged patients.
Behav. Res. Ther., **10**, 15–27.

FRANCIS, S. H. (1970) Behaviour of low-grade institutionalized mongoloids:
changes with age. *Amer. J. ment. Defic.*, **75**, 92–101.

FREDERICKS, H. D. B., BALDWIN, V. L., MCDONALD, J. J., HOFFMAN, R.
and HARTER, J. (1971) Parents educate their trainable children.
Ment. Retard., **9**, 24–6.

FULLER, P. R. (1949) Operant conditioning of a vegetative human organism.
Amer. J. Psychol., **62**, 587–90.

FULTON, R. T. (1972) A program of developmental research in audiological
procedures. In SCHIEFELBUSCH, R. L. (ed.) *Language of the Mentally
Retarded.* Baltimore, Md.: Univ. Park Press.

GAGNÉ, R. M. (1968) Contributions of learning to human development.
Psychol. Rev., **75**, 177–93.

GARCIA, E., BAER, D. M. and FIRESTONE, I. (1971) The development of
generalized imitation with topographically determined boundaries.
J. appl. Behav. Anal., **4**, 101–12.

GARDNER, J. M. (1968) The behaviour modification model. *Ment. Retard.*,
6, 54–5.

GARDNER, J. M. (1969a) Behaviour modification research in mental retardation: Search for an adequate paradigm. *Amer. J. ment. Defic.*, **73**, 844–51.

GARDNER, J. M. (1969b) *The Training Proficiency Scale: Manual.*
Columbus, Ohio: Columbus State Institute.

GARDNER, J. M. (1971) Behaviour modification in mental retardation:
a review of research and analysis of trends. In RUBIN, R. D.,
FENSTERHEIM, H., LAZARUS, A. A. and FRANKS, C. M. (eds.)
Advances in Behaviour Therapy. New York: Academic Press.

GARDNER, J. M. (1972) Teaching behaviour modification skills to
nonprofessionals. *J. appl. Behav. Anal.*, **5**, 517–21.

GARDNER, J. M. and HOFFMAN, D. (1969) *The Resident Comprehensive
Behaviour Check List: Manual.* Columbus, Ohio: Columbus State
Institute.

GARDNER, J. M. and WATSON, L. S. (1969) Behaviour modification of
the mentally retarded: An annotated bibliography. *Ment. Retard. Abstrs.*,
6, 181–93.

GARDNER, W. I. (1969) Use of punishment procedures with the severely
retarded. *Amer. J. ment. Defic.*, **74**, 86–103.

GARDNER, W. I. (1971) *Behavior Modification in Mental Retardation.*
Chicago: Aldine, Atherton.

GELFAND, D. M. and HARTMANN, D. P. (1968) Behavior therapy with children: a review and evaluation of research methodology. *Psychol. Bull.*, **69**, 204–15.

GEWIRTZ, J. L. (1967) Deprivation and satiation of social stimuli as determinants of their reinforcing efficacy. In HILL, J. P. (ed.) *Minnesota Symposia on Child Psychology*, Vol. 1. Minneapolis: Univ. of Minnesota Press.

GEWIRTZ, J. L. (1968) On designing the functional environment of the child to facilitate behavioural development. In DITTMAN, L. L. (ed.) *Early Child Care: The New Perspectives*. New York: Atherton.

GEWIRTZ, J. L. and STINGLE, K. G. (1968) Learning of generalized imitation as the basis for identification. *Psychol. Rev.*, **75**, 374–97.

GILES, D. K. and WOLF, M. M. (1966) Toilet training institutionalized, severe retardates: an application of behavior modification techniques. *Amer. J. ment. Defic.*, **70**, 766–80.

GOETZ, E. N. and BAER, D. M. (1971) Descriptive social reinforcement of 'creative' block building by young children. In RAMP, E. A. and HOPKINS, B. L. (eds.) *A New Direction for Education: Behavior Analysis*. Laurence; Univ. of Kansas.

GOLDIAMOND, I. (1965) Self-control procedures in personal behavioural problems. *Psychol. Rep.*, **17**, 851–68.

GREENE, R. J. and HOATS, D. L. (1969) Reinforcing capabilities of television distortion. *J. appl. Behav. Anal.*, **2**, 139–41.

GROSZ, H. J. and ZIMMERMAN, J. (1965) Experimental analysis of hysterical blindness: a follow-up report and new experimental data. *Arch. gen. Psychiat.*, **13**, 255–60.

GROVES, I. D. and CARROCCIO, D. F. (1971) A self-feeding programme for the severely and profoundly retarded. *Ment. Retard.*, **9**, 10–12.

GUESS, D. (1969) A functional analysis of receptive language and productive speech: acquisition of the plural morpheme. *J. appl. Behav. Anal.*, **2**, 55–64.

GUESS, D., SAILOR, W., RUTHERFORD, G. and BAER, D. M. (1968) An experimental analysis of linguistic development: The productive use of the plural morpheme. *J. appl. Behav. Anal.*, **1**, 297–306.

HALL, R. V. (1970) Reinforcement procedures and the increase of functional speech by a brain-injured child. In GIRARDEAU, F. L. and SPRADLIN, J. E. (eds.) *A Functional Approach to Speech and Language*. ASHA Monogr. No. 14. Washington, DC: American Speech and Hearing Association.

HALL, R. V. (1971) *Behaviour Management Series. Part I: The Measurement of Behaviour. Part II: Basic Principles. Part III: Applications in School and Home*. Kansas City, Miss.: H. & H. Enterprises.

HALL, R. V. and BRODEN, M. (1967) Behaviour changes in brain-injured children through social reinforcement. *J. exp. Child Psychol.*, **5**, 463–79.

HALL, R. V., AXELROD, S., TYLER, L., GRIEF, E., JONES, F. C. and ROBERTSON, R. (1972) Modification of behaviour problems in the home with a parent as observer and experimenter. *J. appl. Behav. Anal.*, 5, 53–64.

HAMILTON, J. and ALLEN, P. (1967) Ward programming for severely retarded institutionalized retardates. *Ment. Retard.*, 5, 22–4.

HAMILTON, J., STEPHENS, L. and ALLEN, P. (1967) Controlling aggressive and destructive behavior in severely retarded institutionalized residents. *Amer. J. ment. Defic.*, 71, 852–6.

HETHERINGTON, E. M. and ROSS, L. E. (1967) Discrimination learning by normal and retarded children under delay of reward and interpolated task conditions. *Child Developm.*, 38, 639–47.

HETHERINGTON, E. M., ROSS, L. E. and PICK, H. L. (1964) Delay of reward and learning in mentally retarded and normal children. *Child Developm.*, 35, 653–9.

HOM, G. L. (1967) Effects of amount of reinforcement on the concurrent performance of retardates. *Psychol. Rep.*, 20, 887–92.

HOM, G. L., CORTE, E., SPRADLIN, J. E. and MICHAEL, J. (1966) Effects of amount of reinforcement on the performance of mildly retarded adolescent girls. *Psychol. Rep.*, 19, 1191–4.

HOMME, L. E. (1966) Perspectives in psychology – XXIV. Control of coverants, the operants of the mind. *Psychol. Rec.*, 15, 501–11.

HOMME, L. E., CGANYI, A., GONZALES, M. and RECHS, J. (1969) *How to Use Contingency Contacting in the Classroom*. Champaign, Ill.: Research Press.

HOMME, L. E., de BACA, P., DEVINE, J. V., STEINHORST, R. and RICKERT, E. J. (1963) Use of the Premack Principle in controlling the behaviour of nursery school children. *J. exp. Anal. Behav.*, 6, 544.

HOPKINS, B. (1968) Effects of candy and social reinforcement, instructions, and reinforcement schedule learning in the modification and maintenance of smiling. *J. appl. Behav. Anal.*, 1, 121–30.

HUNDZIAK, M., MAURER, R. A., and WATSON, L. S. (1965) Operant conditioning in toilet training severely mentally retarded boys. *Amer. J. ment. Defic.*, 70, 120–4.

HUSTED, J. R., HALL, P. and AGIN, B. (1971) The effectiveness of time-out in reducing maladaptive behavior of autistic and retarded children. *J. Psychol.*, 79, 189–96.

INSALACO, C. and HAMILTON, J. (1966) *Modification of Self-Abusive Behaviour with the Use of Punishment and Reward in a Free Operant Situation*. Paper read at the Southeastern Meeting of the American Association on Mental Deficiency, Atlanta.

JOHNSTON, M. (1968) Echolalia and automatism in speech. In SLOANE, H. N. and MACAULAY, B. D. (eds.) *Operant Procedures in Remedial Speech and Language Training*. Boston: Houghton Mifflin.

JUVONEN, L. (1972) *Development of Play Behaviour in Two Severely Retarded Preschool Children.* Unpubl. Master's thesis, Univ. of London Institute of Education.

KANFER, F. H. (1970) Self regulation: research, issues, and speculations. In NEURINGER, C. and MICHAEL, J. L. (eds.) *Behaviour Modification in Clinical Psychology.* New York: Appleton-Century-Crofts.

KANFER, F. H. and PHILLIPS, J. S. (1966) Behaviour therapy: a panacea for all ills or a passing fancy? *Arch. Gen. Psychiat.,* 15, 114–28.

KANFER, F. H. and PHILLIPS, J. S. (1970) *Learning Foundations of Behavior Therapy.* New York: Wiley.

KANTOR, J. R. (1958) *Interbehavioral Psychology.* Bloomington, Ind.; Principia Press.

KATKIN, E. S. and MURRAY, E. N. (1968) Instrumental conditioning of autonomically mediated behaviour. *Psychol. Bull.,* 70, 52–68.

KAZDIN, A. E. and BOOTZIN, R. R. (1972) The token economy: an evaluative review. *J. appl. Behav. Anal.,* 5, 343–72.

KELLEHER, R. T. and GALLUB, L. R. (1962) A review of positive conditioned reinforcement. *J. exp. Anal. Behav.,* 5, 543–97.

KELLER, F. S. and SCHOENFELD, W. N. (1950) *Principles of Psychology.* New York: Appleton-Century-Crofts.

KIERNAN, C. C. (1973a) Functional analysis. In MITTLER, P. (ed.) *Assessment for Learning in the Mentally Handicapped.* London: Churchill Livingstone; Baltimore, Md: Williams & Wilkins.

KIERNAN, C. C. (1973b) Application of behaviour modification in the ward situation. In GUNZBURG, H. C. *Experiments in Rehabilitation of the Mentally Handicapped* (in press).

KIERNAN, C. C. and BURGESS, I. S. (1971) *Shaping Walking in a Profoundly Retarded Blind Child.* Unpubl. manuscript.

KIERNAN, C. C. and RIDDICK, B. (1972) *A Draft Programme for Training in Operant Techniques.* London: Univ. of London Institute of Education.

KIERNAN, C. C. and SAUNDERS, C. (1972) Generalized imitation: experiments with profoundly retarded children. *Second European Conference on Behaviour Modification, Wexford, Ireland.*

KIERNAN, C. C., DONOGHUE, E. C. and HAWKS, G. D. (1971) *A Ward Wide Programme for Profoundly Subnormal Children.* Paper to the 3rd Conference of the Behavioural Engineering Association, Wexford.

KIMBRELL, D. L., LUCKEY, R. E., BARBUTO, P. F. P. and LOVE, J. G. (1967) Operation dry pants: an intensive habit-training program for severely and profoundly retarded. *Ment. Retard.,* 5, 32–6.

KING, R. D., RAYNES, N. V. and TIZARD, J. (1971) *Patterns of Residential Care.* London: Routledge & Kegan Paul.

KRANTZ, D. L. (1971) The separate worlds of operant and non-operant research. *J. appl. Behav. Anal.,* 4, 61–70.

KRASNER, L. and ULLMAN, L. P. (1966) *Research in Behaviour Modification*. New York: Holt, Rinehart & Winston.

KUYPERS, D. S., BECKER, W. C. and O'LEARY, K. D. (1968) How to make a token system fail. *Except. Child.* **35**, 101–8.

LARSEN, L. A. and BRICKER, W. A. (1968) *A Manual for Parents and Teachers of Severely and Moderately Retarded Children*. IMRID Papers V, No. 22. Nashville, Tenn.: IMRID.

LEITENBERG, H. (1961) Is time-out from positive reinforcement an aversive event? *Psychol. Bull.*, **64**, 428–41.

LENT, J. R., LeBLANC, J. and SPRADLIN, J. E. (1967) Designing a rehabilitative culture for moderately retarded, adolescent girls. In ULRICH, R., STACHNIK, T. and MABRY, J. (eds.) *Control of Human Behaviour. Volume Two. From Cure to Prevention*. Glenview, Ill.: Scott, Foresman.

LINDSLEY, O. R. (1970) Procedures in common described by a common language. In NEURINGER, C. and MICHAEL, J. L. (eds.) *Behaviour Modification in Clinical Psychology*. New York: Appleton-Century-Crofts.

LOCKE, B. J. (1969) Verbal conditioning with retarded subjects: establishment and reinstatement of effective reinforcing consequences. *Amer. J. ment. Defic.*, **73**, 621–6.

LOGAN, D. L., KINSINGER, J., SHELTON, G. and BROWN, J. M. (1971) The use of multiple reinforcers in a rehabilitation setting. *Ment. Retard.*, **9**, 3–6.

LOVAAS, O. I. (1967) A behaviour therapy approach to the treatment of childhood schizophrenia. In HILL, J. (ed.) *Minnesota Symposium on Child Psychology*. Minneapolis: Univ. of Minnesota Press.

LOVAAS, O. I. and SIMMONS, J. Q. (1969) Manipulation of self-destructive behavior in three retarded children. *J. appl. Behav. Anal.*, **1**, 143–57.

LUCERO, R. J., VIAL, D. J. and SCHERBER, J. (1968) Regulating operant-conditioning programs. *Hospital and Community Psychiatry*, 53–4.

LUCKEY, R., WATSON, C. and MUSICK, J. (1968) Aversive conditioning as a means of inhibiting vomiting and rumination. *Amer. J. ment. Defic.*, **73**, 139–42.

LYKKEN, D. T. (1968) Statistical significance in psychological research. *Psychol. Bull.*, **70**, 151–9.

LYNCH, J. and BRICKER, W. A. (1972) Linguistic theory and operant procedures: toward an integrated approach to language training for the mentally retarded. *Ment. Retard.*, **10**, 12–17.

MCGEE, V. E. (1971) *Principles of Statistics: Traditional and Bayesian*. New York: Appleton-Century-Crofts.

MACHT, J. (1971) Operant measurement of subjective visual acuity in non-verbal children. *J. appl. Behav. Anal.*, **4**, 23–36.

MACMILLAN, D. L. and FORNESS, S. R. (1970) Behaviour modification: limitations and liabilities. *Except. Child.*, 291–7.

MCREYNOLDS, L. V. (1969) Application of time-out from positive reinforcement for increasing the efficiency of speech training. *J. appl. Behav. Anal.*, **2**, 199–205.

MCREYNOLDS, L. V. (1970) Reinforcement procedures for establishing and maintaining echoic speech by a non-verbal child. In GIRARDEAU, F. L. and SPRADLIN, J. E. (eds.) *A Functional Approach to Speech and Language*. ASHA Monogr., No. 14. Washington, DC: American Speech and Hearing Association.

MAHONEY, K., VAN WAGENEN, R. K. and MEYERSON, L. (1971) Toilet training of normal and retarded children. *J. appl. Behav. Anal.*, **4**, 173–81.

MARTIN, B. (1963) Reward and punishment associated with the same goal response: a factor in the learning of motives. *Psychol. Bull.*, **60**, 441–51.

MARTIN, G. L. (1972) Teaching operant technology to psychiatric nurses, aides and attendants· In CLARK, F. W., EVANS, D. R. and HAMERLYNCK, L. A. (eds.) *Implementing Behavioural Programs for Schools and Clinics*. Champaign, Ill.: Research Press.

MARTIN, G. L., KEHOE, B., BIRD, E., JENSEN, V. and DARBYSHIRE, M. (1971) Operant conditioning in dressing behaviour of severely retarded girls. *Ment. Retard*, **9**, 27–31.

MARTIN, J. A. (1971) The control of imitative and non-imitative behaviours in severely retarded children through 'generalized-instruction following'. *J. exp. Child Psychol.*, **11**, 390–400.

MAZIK, K. and MACNAMARA, R. (1967) Operant conditioning at the training school. *Training School Bull.*, **63**, 153–8.

MEACHAM, M. and WEISEN, A. (1970) *Changing Classroom Behaviour: A Manual for Precision Teaching*. Scranton, Penn.: International Textbook Co.

MICHAEL, J. L. (1970) Rehabilitation. In NEURINGER, C. and MICHAEL, J. L. (eds.) *Behaviour Modification in Clinical Psychology*. New York.: Appleton-Century-Crofts.

MILLER, N. E. (1960) Learning resistance to pain and fear: effects of overlearning, exposure, and rewarded exposure in context *J. comp. physiol. Psychol.*, **60**, 137–45.

MILLER, N. E. and BANUAZIZI, A. (1968) Instrumental learning by curarized rats of a specific visceral response, intestinal and cardiac. *J. comp. physiol. Psychol.* **65**, 1–7.

MILLER, N. E. and DICARA, L. (1967) Instrumental learning of heart rate changes in curarized rats: shaping, and specificity to discriminative stimulus. *J. comp. physiol. Psychol.* **63**, 12–19.

MINK, O. (1970) *The Behaviour Change Process*. Chicago: Harper & Row.

MIRA, M. (1970) Results of a behavior modification training program for parents and teachers. *Behav. Res. Therapy*, **8**, 309–11.

MORALES, I. (1972) *Application of Operant Techniques to Some Aspects of Exploratory Behaviour in Two Severely Retarded Children*. Unpubl. Master's thesis, Univ. of London Institute of Education.

MOWRER, O. H. and MOWRER, W. M. (1938) Enuresis: a method for its study and treatment. *Amer. J. Orthopsychiat.*, **8**, 436–59.

MURPHY, G. (1947) *Personality: a Biosocial Approach to Origins and Structure*. New York: Harper & Row.

O'BRIEN, F., BUGLE, C. and AZRIN, N. H. (1972) Training and maintaining a retarded child's proper eating. *J. appl. Behav. Anal.*, **5**, 67–72.

ORLANDO, R. (1965) Shaping multiple schedule performances in retardates: Establishment of baselines by systematic and special procedures. *J. exp. Child Psychol.*, **2**, 135–53.

ORLANDO, R. and BIJOU, S. W. (1960) Single and multiple schedules of reinforcement in developmentally retarded children. *J. exp. Anal. Behav.*, **3**, 339–48.

PALOUTZIAN, R. F., HASAZI, J., STREIFEL, J. and EDGAR, C. L. (1971). Promotion of positive social interaction in severely retarded young children. *Amer. J. ment. Defic.*, **75**, 519–24.

PANYAN, M., BOOZER, H. and MORRIS, N. (1970) Feedback to attendants as a reinforcer for applying operant techniques. *J. appl. Behav. Anal.*, **3**, 1–4.

PATTERSON, G. R. (1969) Behavioral techniques based on social learning: An additional base for developing behavior modification technologies. In FRANKS, C. M. (ed.) *Behavior Therapy: Appraisal and Status*. New York: McGraw-Hill.

PATTERSON, G. R. and GUILLON, M. (1968) *Living with Children: New Methods for Parents and Teachers*. Champaign, Ill.: Research Press.

PATTERSON, G. R. and REID, J. B. (1970) Reciprocity and coercion: two facets of social systems. In NEURINGER, C. and MICHAEL, J. L. (eds.). *Behavior Modification in Clinical Psychology*. New York: Appleton-Century-Crofts.

PAUL, H. A. and MILLER, J. R. (1971) Reduction of extreme deviant behaviours in a severely retarded girl. *Training School Bull.*, **67**, 193–7.

PENDERGRASS, V. E. (1972) Timeout from positive reinforcement following persistent, high rate behaviour in retardates. *J. appl. Behav. Anal.*, **5**, 85–91.

PETERSON, R. (1968) Imitation: A basic behavioural mechanism. In SLOANE, H. N. and MACAULAY, B. D. (eds.) *Operant Procedures in Remedial Speech and Language Training*. Boston: Houghton Mifflin.

PETERSON, R. F. and PETERSON, L. R. (1968) The use of positive reinforcement in the control of self-destructive behavior in a retarded boy. *J. exp. Child Psychol.*, **6**, 351–60.

PIPER, T. J. (1971) Effects of delay of reinforcement on retarded children's learning. *Except Child.*, 139–45.

PREMACK, D. (1959) Toward empirical behavior laws: 1. Positive reinforcement. *Psychol. Rev.*, **66**, 219–33.

PREMACK, D. (1965) Reinforcement theory. In LEVINE, D. (ed.) *Nebraska Symposium on Motivation.* Lincoln: Univ. of Nebraska Press.

REDD, W. H. (1969) Effects of mixed reinforcement contingencies on adults' control of children's behaviour. *J. appl. Behav. Anal.*, **2**, 249–54.

REDD, W. H. and BIRNBRAUER, J. S. (1969) Adults as discriminative stimuli for different reinforcement contingencies with retarded children. *J. exp. Child Psychol.*, **7**, 440–7.

RENTFROW, R. K. and RENTFROW, D. K. (1969) Studies related to toilet training of the mentally retarded. *Amer. J. occup. Therapy*, **23**, 425–30.

RIDDICK, B. and KIERNAN, C. C. (1972) *Stability of Preferences for Rewards in Profoundly Retarded Children.* Unpubl. manuscript.

RISLEY, T. R. (1968) The effects and side effects of punishing the autistic behaviors of a deviant child. *J. appl. Behav. Anal.*, **1**, 21–34.

RISLEY, T. R. and BAER, D. M. (1972) Operant behaviour modification: the deliberate development of child behaviour. In CALDWELL, B. and RICCIUTI, D. *Review of Child Development Research. Vol III: Social Influence and Social Action.* New York: Russell-Sage.

RISLEY, T. R. and WOLF, M. M. (1967) Establishing functional speech in echolalic children. *Behav. Res. Therapy*, **5**, 73–88.

ROSS, L. E., HETHERINGTON, M. and WRAY, N. P. (1965) Delay of reward and the learning of a size problem by normal and retarded children. *Child Developm.* **36**, 509–17.

SACHS, D. A. (1971) WISC changes as an evaluative procedure within a token economy. *Amer. J. ment. Defic.*, **76**, 230–4.

SAILOR, W. (1971) Reinforcement and generalization of productive plural allomorphs in two retarded children. *J. appl. Behav. Anal.*, **4**, 305–10.

SAJWAJ, T., TWARDOSZ, S. and BURKE, M. (1972) Side effects of extinction procedures in a remedial preschool. *J. appl. Behav. Anal.*, **5**, 163–75.

SCHIEFELBUSCH, R. L. (1972) *Language of the Mentally Retarded.* Baltimore, Md.: Univ. Park Press.

SCHOELKOPF, A. M. and ORLANDO, R. (1965) Delayed versus immediate reinforcement in simultaneous discrimination problems with mentally retarded children. *Psychol. Rec.*, **15**, 15–23.

SCHOELKOPF, A. M. and ORLANDO, R. (1966) Reinforcement delay gradients of retardates with a concurrent discrimination task procedure. *Psychol. Rec.*, **16**, 113–28.

SCHUMAKER, J. and SHERMAN, J. A. (1970) Training generative verb usage by imitation and reinforcement procedures. *J. Appl. Behav. Anal.*, **3**, 273–87.

SHERMAN, J. A. (1971) Imitation and language development. In REESE, H. W. (ed.) *Advances in Child Development and Behavior*. New York: Academic Press.

SHERMAN, J. A. and BAER, D. M. (1969) Appraisal of operant therapy techniques with children and adults. In FRANKS, C. M. *Behavior Therapy: Appraisal and Status*. New York: McGraw-Hill.

SIDMAN, M. (1960) *Tactics of Scientific Research: Evaluating Experimental Data in Psychology*. New York: Basic Books.

SIDMAN, M. and STODDARD, L. T. (1967) Programmed perception and learning for retarded children. In ELLIS, N. R. (ed.) *International Review of Research in Mental Retardation*, Vol. 2. New York: Academic Press.

SIEGEL, P. S. (1968) Incentive motivation in the mental retardate. In ELLIS, N. R. (ed.) *International Review of Research in Mental Retardation*, Vol. 3. New York: Academic Press.

SKINNER, B. F. (1938) *The Behavior of Organisms*. New York: Appleton-Century-Crofts.

SKINNER, B. F. (1950) Are theories of learning necessary? *Psychol. Rev.*, 57, 193–216.

SKINNER, B. F. (1953) *Science and Human Behavior*. New York: Macmillan.

SKINNER, B. F. (1966) Operant behavior. In HONIG, W. K. (ed.) *Operant Behavior: Areas of Research and Application*. New York: Appleton-Century-Crofts.

SKINNER, B. F. (1969) *Contingencies of Reinforcement*. New York: Appleton-Century-Crofts.

SLOANE, H. N., JOHNSTON, M. K. and HARRIS, F. R. (1968) Remedial procedures for teaching verbal behaviour to speech deficient or defective young children. In SLOANE, H. N. and MACAULAY, B. D. (eds.) *Operant Procedures in Remedial Speech and Language Training*. Boston: Houghton Mifflin.

SMEETS, P. M. (1970) Withdrawal of social reinforcers as a means of controlling rumination and regurgitation in a profoundly retarded person. *Amer. Inst. ment. Stud.*, 67, 44–51.

SOLOMON, R. L. (1964) Punishment. *Amer. Psychol.*, 19, 237–53.

SPRADLIN, J. E. (1964) *The Premack Hypothesis and Self-feeding by Profoundly Retarded Children: A Case Report*. Working Paper No. 79. Parson, Kans.: Parsons Research Centre.

SPRADLIN, J. E. and GIRARDEAU, F. L. (1966) The behavior of moderately and severely retarded persons. In ELLIS, N. R. *International Review of Research in Mental Retardation*, Vol. 1. New York: Academic Press.

SPRADLIN, J. E., GIRARDEAU, E. L. and CORTE, E. (1965) Fixed ratio and fixed interval behavior of severely and profoundly retarded subjects. *J. exp. Child Psychol.*, 2, 340–53.

SPRADLIN, J. E., GIRARDEAU, F. L. and HOM, G. L. (1966) Stimulus properties of reinforcement during extinction of a free operant response. *J. exp. Child Psychol.*, **4**, 369–80.

SPRADLIN, J. E., LOCKE, B. J. and FULTON, R. T. (1969) In FULTON, R. T. and LLOYD, L. L. (eds.) *Audiometry for the Retarded: With Implications for the Difficult-to-Test.* Baltimore, Md.: Williams & Wilkins.

STOLZ, S. B. and WOLF, M. M. (1969) Visually discriminated behavior in a 'blind' adolescent retardate. *J. appl. Behav. Anal.*, **2**, 65–77.

TERDAL, L. and BUELL, J. (1969) Parent education in managing retarded children with behavior deficits and inappropriate behaviours. *Ment. Retard.*, **7**, 10–13.

TERRACE, H. S. (1966) Stimulus control. In HONIG, W. K. (ed.) *Operant Behavior: Areas of Research and Application.* New York: Appleton-Century-Crofts.

THARP, R. G. and WETZEL, R. J. (1969) *Behavior Modification in the Natural Environment.* New York: Academic Press.

TOUCHETTE, P. E. (1968) The effects of graduated stimulus change on the acquisition of a simple discrimination in severely retarded boys. *J. exp. Anal. Behav.*, **11**, 39–48.

TOUCHETTE, P. E. (1969) Tilted lines as complex stimuli. *J. exp. Anal. Behav.*, **12**, 211–14.

TOUCHETTE, P. E. (1971) Transfer of stimulus control: measuring the moment of transfer. *J. exp. Anal. Behav.*, **15**, 347–54.

TROWILL, J. A. (1967) Instrumental conditioning of the heart rate in the curarized rat. *J. comp. physiol. Psychol.*, **63**, 7–11.

TWARDOSZ, S. and SAJWAJ, T. (1972) Multiple effects of a procedure to increase sitting in a hyperactive, retarded boy. *J. appl. Behav. Anal.*, **5**, 73–8.

TYLER, V. O. and BROWN, G. D. (1967) The use of swift, brief isolation as a group control device. *Behav. Res. Therapy*, **5**, 1–9.

ULRICH, R., STACHNIK, T. and MABRY, J. (1970) *Control of Human Behavior. Volume Two: From Cure to Prevention.* Glenview, Ill.; Scott, Foresman.

VAN WAGENEN, R. K. and MURDOCK, E. E. (1966) A transistorized signal-package for toilet training of infants. *J. exp. Child Psychol.*, **3**, 312–14.

VAN WAGENEN, R. K., MEYERSON, L., KERR, N. J. and MAHONEY, K. (1969) Field trials of a new procedure for toilet training. *J. exp. Child Psychol.*, **8**, 147–59.

VUKELICH, R. and HAKE, D. F. (1971) Reduction of dangerously aggressive behavior in a severely retarded resident through a combination of positive reinforcement procedures. *J. Appl. Behav. Anal.*, **4**, 215–25.

WATSON, L. S. (1966) Application of behavior shaping devices to training severely and profoundly mentally retarded children in an institutional setting. *Ment. Retard.*, **6**, 21–3.

WATSON, L. S., GARDNER, J. M. and SANDERS, C. (1971) Shaping and maintaining behavior modification skills in staff members in an M.R. Institution: Columbus State Institute Behavior Modification Program. *Ment. Retard.*, **9**, 39–42.

WATSON, R. I. (1962) The experimental tradition and clinical psychology. In BACHRACH, A. J. (ed.) *Experimental Foundations of Clinical Psychology*. New York: Basic Books.

WHALEN, C. K. and HENKER, B. A. (1969) Creating therapeutic pyramids using mentally retarded patients. *Amer. J. ment. Defic.*, **74**, 331–7.

WHALEN, C. K. and HENKER, B. A. (1971a) Pyramid Therapy in a hospital for the retarded: methods, program evaluation, and long-term effects. *Amer. J. ment. Defic.*, **75**, 414–34.

WHALEN, C. K. and HENKER, B. A. (1971b) Play therapy conducted by mentally retarded patients. *Psychotherapy: Theory, Research and Practice*, **8**, 236–45.

WHALEY, D. L. and MALOTT, R. W. (1968) *Elementary Principles of Behavior*. Ann Arbor, Mich; Edwards Brothers.

WHALEY, D. L. and TOUGH, J. (1970) Treatment of a self-injuring mongoloid with shock-induced suppression and avoidance. In ULRICH, R, STACHNIK, T. and MABRY, J. (eds.) *Control of Human Behavior. Vol. Two: from Cure to Prevention*. Glenview, Ill.; Scott, Foresman.

WHITE, J. C. and TAYLOR, D. J. (1967) Noxious conditioning as a treatment for rumination. *Ment. Retard.*, **5**, 30–3.

WHITMAN, T. L., MERCURIO, J. R. and CAPONIGRI, V. (1970) Development of social responses in two severely retarded children. *J. appl. Behav. Anal.*, **3**, 133–8.

WHITMAN, T. L., ZAKARAS, M. and CHARDOS, S. (1971) Effects of reinforcement and guidance procedures on instruction–following behavior of severely retarded children. *J. appl. Behav. Anal.*, **4**, 283–90.

WHITNEY, L. R. and BARNARD, K. E. (1966) Implications of operant learning theory for nursing care of the retarded child. *Ment. Retard.*, **4**, 26–9.

WILLEMS, E. P. and RAUSH, H. L. (1969) *Naturalistic Viewpoints in Psychological Research*. New York: Holt, Rinehart & Winston.

WILLIAMS, P. (1973) Psychological assessment of the mentally handicapped: social skills. In MITTLER, P. (ed.) *Assessment for Learning in the Mentally Handicapped*. London: Churchill Livingstone; Baltimore, Md: Williams & Wilkins.

WILLIAMS, P. and KUSHLICK, A. (1970) *Interview Schedule for the Social Assessment of Mentally Handicapped Children*. Wessex Regional Hospital Board.

WOLF, M. M., BIRNBRAUER, J. S., LAWLER, J. and WILLIAMS, T. (1970) The operant extinction, reinstatement and re-extinction of vomiting behavior in a retarded child. In URICH, R., STACHNIK, T. and MABRY, J. (eds.) *Control of Human Behaviour. Vol. Two: From Cure to Prevention.* Glenview, Ill.: Scott, Foresman.

ZEILER, M. D. and JERVEY, S. S. (1968) Development of behaviour self-feeding. *J. consult. clin. Psychol.*, **32**, 164–8.

ZIGLER, E. (1968) Research on personality structure in the retardate. In ELLIS, N. R. (ed.) *International Review of Research in Mental Retardation,* Vol. I. New York: Academic Press.

ZIMMERMAN, D. W. (1959) Sustained performance in rats based on secondary reinforcement. *J. comp. physiol. Psychol.*, **52**, 353–8.

ZIMMERMAN, J. (1963) Technique for sustaining behavior with conditioned reinforcement. *Science*, **142**, 682–4.

13

J. Tizard

Services and the evaluation
of services

During the last twenty-five years or so, major changes have taken place in attitudes towards the mentally retarded and in administrative policy concerned with their well-being. Throughout the latter part of the nineteenth century and the first half of the present one, mental deficiency services, in virtually all countries which provided them, were governed by legislation which defined mental deficiency in terms of social incompetence 'existing from birth or from an early age' (WHO, 1955). Social incapacity of the sort that led magistrates to 'certify' individuals as mentally deficient was thought to be largely genetic in origin: a direct and inevitable consequence of low intelligence, and one that was largely unmodifiable. The outlook was pessimistic and the concept of mental defect was itself simple minded.[1] This bleak attitude towards the mentally retarded persisted in spite of the fact that the evidence in favour of it was not very strong and despite a good deal of contradictory evidence. Thus Burt (1921) and others pointed out the distinction between low intelligence (a psychological concept) and mental retardation (an administrative one); longitudinal studies gave only weak support to the view that the IQ was constant; cross section studies of relations between IQ and other personal and behavioural characteristics (apart from academic performance at school) resulted in only low correlations; longitudinal studies of the adjustment of persons who at one time or another were classified as mentally retarded indicated that mental handicap was not 'incurable'. Moreover, critics commented that legislation designed ostensibly to protect the liberty of the subject, in practice took away his liberty (a mentally handicapped person could not for example enter a mental deficiency institution as a voluntary inmate, but only on committal by magistrate's order, and once committed he could not in most cases leave of his own free will, nor could his parents have him home again except with the law's consent). Still other critics, in Europe and in the United States, repeatedly attacked the inadequacy and poor quality of the services provided for the retarded. (See also Chapter 2.)

[1] Kugel and Wolfensberger (1969) have written an authoritative account of American experience; a sociological and historical survey of British practice, and of the philosophy upon which it was based, has yet to be undertaken. There is a rich store of primary source material upon which to draw.

Criticisms of the traditional wisdom regarding mental handicap, and of the services provided for them, mounted in many countries after the second world war, and, during the 1950s and 1960s, a rethinking of the basis for services took place (WHO, 1954). In Britain the change was marked by the *Report of the Royal Commission on the Law relating to Mental Illness and Mental Deficiency* (1957), by a new Mental Health Act (1959) and by a recent White Paper, *Better Services for the Mentally Handicapped* (1972). In Denmark, an Act of 1959 laid down a new legal basis for the treatment, teaching and care of the mentally retarded, and ushered in a newly structured national service (Bank-Mikkelsen, 1964, gives a useful historical summary of the development of services in Denmark and an account of the new service). Similar events have occurred in Sweden (Nirje, 1969) and in some other European countries. In the United States in the following year the President's Panel on Mental Retardation, established by President Kennedy in 1961, proposed a 'programme of national action to combat mental retardation'; this, and the subsequent activities of the President's Committee have been highly influential in affecting developments in that country.

All over the world, then, changes were taking place which, in their effects, were as important as those which occurred in the 1840s following the work of Guggenbühl. Séguin's words, applied to that time, are equally applicable to the present one: 'at certain times and eras, the whole race of Man, as regards the discovery of truth, seems to arrive at once at a certain point' (Kanner, 1964).

A good deal of solemn stuff has been written about the principles which underlie the provision of services for the mentally retarded. The matter can, however, be summarized in Bank-Mikkelsen's (1964) rather informal remarks to the International Copenhagen Congress on the Scientific Study of Mental Retardation. We must, he said, regard the mentally retarded person as a fellow human being, one with a handicap and perhaps with more than one handicap – which, however, do not make the mentally retarded individual any more odd than people are in general. Because he is first of all a fellow being, he must as a matter of equality have full rights as a fellow citizen. There is therefore no occasion for a 'special ideology' in the treatment of the mentally retarded. 'If this has been understood the rest is rather easy, because it is only a question of the best treatment of the mentally retarded from a humane and professional viewpoint.' If this is not understood, 'there is a risk of ending simply in sentimental pity, in theories of over-protection, in group discrimination or in something worse. . . . The aim is to give the mentally retarded a normal existence, that is to say to assist with treatment of any kind and ensure living quarters and work in the ordinary community for as many as possible.'

The central importance of epidemiology

To plan services which are adequate to meet needs it is necessary to know the numbers of persons who will make use of them. As Kushlick and Blunden (1974) have pointed out, a number of recent surveys have shown that in industrialized countries prevalence rates for *severe* mental handicap (IQ under 50) can be fairly accurately estimated. The 'peak' prevalence rate among children and young persons is 3·6 to 3·7/1,000. Hence in a population of 100,000, of both sexes and all ages, having a crude birth rate of 18/1,000, in which therefore there are 1,800 births a year, only 6–8 are likely to be children with severe mental handicap. Many of them will have additional handicaps.

No precise figures for the expected numbers of *mildly* handicapped children can be given: the term is an administrative one which lacks clear social and biological definition and in this respect resembles terms such as 'poverty' or 'social deprivation'. There is no doubt that many people are 'poor': but poverty in the United States or in the United Kingdom has a different meaning from poverty in, for example, India. It may be mentioned, however, that many educational systems have found that, in practice, between 1 and 2 per cent of schoolchildren are too backward to be educated in ordinary classes without special help, and for these children some kind of special educational provision, either in the ordinary class or in a special class or school, is needed. To the extent that special provision within the education system is not made for the numbers of children who are officially recognized to need it, there are unmet needs. Whether the educational needs of mildly retarded children are best met in the normal school system or through special classes is a matter of controversy. Kirk (1964) gives a reasoned statement of a case for education in special classes; Dunn (1968) has argued cogently against such provision. The matter is not further discussed here.

One estimate of the numbers of retardates, adults and children for whom further services would have to be provided in a population of 100,000 persons, is given in Table 4 .

The numbers are considerably higher than those reported in most surveys, and are to some extent conjectural. The rates were based partly on data obtained in an earlier survey carried out in London (Goodman and Tizard, 1962), and partly on estimates of what the administrative needs would be in a population of 100,000 which made *adequate* provision for all its mentally retarded. In this sense, they constitute an *administrative* prevalence rate, that is, a rate based on 'the numbers for whom services would be required in a community which made provision for all who needed them' (Tizard, 1964, p. 17). Though they may well be too high to be used as a basis for planning at the present time, the writer believes that numbers of this order will have to be dealt with within the next ten or twenty years. More detailed analyses of the numbers, and handicaps, of retardates actually known to the authorities at the present time in southern England have been prepared by Kushlick and Blunden (1974).

According to the estimate on which Table 4 is based, in a population of 100,000 the diagnostic and treatment services dealing with problems of mental retardation would have to cope with about 90 severely subnormal children, of whom up to 30 might require residential care outside their own homes. About half of those in institutions would be profoundly retarded, or children with gross physical problems who required basic nursing. The figure of 90 does not include 'educable' retarded children (IQ over 50) who would remain in the education system proper and if necessary go to boarding schools, foster care or children's homes which took other children 'deprived of normal home life'.

There would be a further 375 retardates, aged 15 or over, of whom about half (180) would be employable. It is estimated that about 75 of these would be in residential units or in lodgings, while 105 would be at home and would require only occasional supervision and help. Whether these two groups should be regarded as mentally retarded at all is questionable. Their needs can best be considered within a more general social context of providing welfare services

TABLE 4. *An estimate of the numbers of mentally subnormal persons requiring services of various sorts in a city of 100,000 total population.*

Age group	Employable		Ambulant and trainable		Cot and chair and bedfast		Total		
	I	C	I	C	I	C	I	C	T
0–14	—	—	15	45	15	15	30	60	90
15	30	70	15	15	5	10	50	95	145
25	20	20	20	10	5	5	45	35	80
35	15	10	20	5	5	—	40	15	55
45	10	5	25	5	5	—	40	10	50
55	—	—	15	—	10	—	25	—	50
65	—	—	10	—	10	—	20	—	20
Total	75	105	120	80	55	30	250	215	465

I = In institutions. C = At home.

for those who require them. Special difficulties which arise out of the high-grade retardate's *mental* limitations are likely to be few, and on the whole easily dealt with. The psychiatric and other medical problems of the high-grade retarded could, and indeed should, be dealt with by a general community mental health service, since mentally retarded persons do not present *special* psychiatric problems not encountered among other sections of the population.

Of the remaining 195 severely retarded persons aged 15 or over included in Table 26, 140 would be ambulant and trainable, while 55 would be profoundly retarded, or housebound or bedfast. Nearly three-quarters would require residential care (145 out of 195) but their needs would differ considerably according to age and degree of handicap. About half of them are likely to have major physical and mental handicaps, but perhaps only 40 would have disabilities severe enough to warrant the classification of idiocy or profound mental retardation.

The figures given in Table 4 assume rates of residential provision which are higher than those reported in any area known to the writer. They were drawn up several years ago (Tizard, 1964) at a time when it was known that existing services were inadequate to meet expressed need, and when the implications of the increase in mean life span of severely retarded persons were beginning to become apparent. The estimates of numbers of residential places, particularly for younger retardates, may today be somewhat too high, since subsequent experience has shown that if really adequate services are provided for retardates living at home and for their families, the demand for residential care is greatly reduced. This point is currently being made in Britain by *Campaign for the Mentally Handicapped*, a pressure group campaigning on the basis of current knowledge for better services for the mentally retarded; and comprehensive service patterns such as that operated by the Salford (England) Local Authority (Susser, 1968) and by the Eastern Nebraska Community Office of Retardation (Lensink, personal communication) in the United States, have amply demonstrated that as day services improve the pressure on residential services sharply declines.

What is important about Table 4, however, is not so much the figures presented as the method of approach, which is epidemiological. In order to plan comprehensive services we must investigate needs. A first step (logically though not necessarily temporally) is to make estimates of the numbers of persons who have different types of handicap of differing degrees of severity. We can then consider how best to meet their needs.

The organization of services

The organization of *day* services has to be based on the needs of populations residing within easy travelling distance of the facilities they require. In cities and large towns distances are short but travelling time is slow; in more rural areas, the opposite. It is suggested that the *maximum* acceptable area for planning of day services should be one in which any member is within an hour's journey of any centre which he will need to attend frequently. The median travelling time should therefore be very much less than this. For planning purposes, the size of an effective region naturally depends on the density of the population, the administrative boundaries of local government units, and the adequacy of communications. It is obvious that quite different administrative arrangements will be required in the northern half of Sweden, or for the Highlands and Islands of Britain, for example, from those required for Stockholm, Edinburgh or London. In the proposals that follow, a base-line population of 100,000 has been used. For urbanized countries such as Britain, and much of Europe, North America and Australia, in which the majority of the population live in, or near, large aggregates of people, an urban model may be used to give guidelines. Modifications would be required for rural areas and for particular circumstances.

The planning of *residential* services is not closely tied by the constraints that affect the planning of day services. In practice, most residential services have traditionally served much larger catchment areas – populations as large as 1 or even 2 million have been served by a single institution. There is growing dissatisfaction with this system, and over Northern Europe and North America increasing efforts are being made to provide residential services in areas which are coterminous with those for planning day services. The arguments in favour of this policy have been presented elsewhere (Tizard, 1964, 1970).

The following section sketches out one possible model for services which would provide, in a geographically defined population of 100,000 persons, for the needs of all retarded persons and their families without requiring to have recourse to hospital and other facilities outside the catchment area save in quite exceptional instances and for quite specific purposes.

DIAGNOSTIC, COUNSELLING AND EDUCATIONAL SERVICES FOR CHILDREN

The essential elements of the services are that they should be available to all children at risk and their parents – an estimated 1 to 3 per cent – and that the emphasis should be on the full range of diagnostic services coupled with remedial treatment. The remedial aspect should include parent counselling and material support for parents, including constant attendance allowances, free nappy services etc. Remedial services including general education, speech therapy and physical therapy should be available from birth if necessary and should work both through neighbourhood pre-school facilities and through parent training in conjunction with the school where possible. The emphasis of this service must be on massive effective early intervention coupled with accurate diagnosis.

The same basic pattern of diagnostic services linking closely with extensive remedial services should continue at school age. Close collaboration with schools is essential. Psychologists should have special responsibilities for schools and should spend much of their time working with teachers on programmes for individual children.

Schools

A special school with fifty to sixty places would probably prove adequate for trainable (IQ less than 50) children of school age. To this centre would go both the children living in their own homes and those in residential care.

For children whose handicaps were too severe to enable them to profit from the programme provided by the day school, some kind of day hospital or 'special care' unit should be provided. This could usefully be attached to the special school; but it would require special staffing.

Residential places for children

If thirty places are needed, about half would be for the profoundly retarded or for children with severe physical handicaps or behaviour problems, and half for 'trainable' children, capable of attending the special school. The severely handicapped group might be placed in a long stay annexe attached to a children's ward or hospital, while the less severely handicapped imbecile group would be in a special residential home. Alternatively, a single unit, or two units each containing about fifteen children, or four or five smaller units, might be established, each unit having both severely and profoundly retarded children in it. Yet another form of residential provision is foster care. Efforts to get foster homes for severely or profoundly retarded children have not met with great success in the past, possibly because the social workers making the enquiries have themselves been half-hearted about them. More experience is needed in this area.

ADULTS

The services required for adults include vocational guidance and placement for educationally backward school-leavers and others, and where necessary, supervision of those who require it; training courses, sheltered workshops with recreational and other facilities for the more handicapped who cannot easily participate in normal group activities, hostel provision for high-grade defectives who are going out to work and for others who work in sheltered workshops or not at all; homes for old people. With adults, as with children, efforts should be made to find foster homes and family placements.

Sheltered workshops

It is not possible to make more than the most tentative estimate of the number of places required in sheltered workshops for the retarded (140 places have been allowed for in Table 4.) But in spite of uncertainty as to numbers, a great deal is known about how to organize such centres effectively. Both in the United Kingdom and in the Netherlands, as also in other countries, highly successful workshops in which the trainees do simple industrial work have been established. This kind of work appears to be particularly suitable for the subnormal (because they can do it, and do it well), and there is no reason why there should not be, in a sheltered workshop, people with other types of disability also. The numbers of places required would depend on the scope of the service they provide (whether 'high-grade' and 'low-grade' trainees are taken on and whether, for example, some are schizophrenics or adults disabled by epilepsy) and on the prevailing level of employment and the possibility of finding work for marginally employable workers.

The emphasis placed here on work should not be misunderstood. For many centuries the ability to work has been the milestone marking the boundary between childhood and adult life. Handicapped adults who can work, even if only in a limited way, are more likely to be accepted as adults and treated accordingly than are adults who are totally dependent upon others for their subsistence. The handicapped themselves know this – and it is for this reason, and not simply on economic grounds, that the organization of work is stressed here. The dangers to be avoided are, first, that the retardates will be exploited, or made to work in sweatshops; secondly that, out of a laudable desire to maintain efficient workshops, authorities will pay little attention to the social and cultural needs of the retarded who work in them. An adequate programme for young people and handicapped adults must provide for education and make possible a satisfying social life in an environment which is interesting, and which is part of the environment of a wider community.

Residential services for adults

In our supposed population of 100,000, perhaps 15–20 educationally retarded youths would leave school each year. London experience suggests that about 10 would need some kind of special supervision, but that only 2 would require residential care. Hence 2 hostels, with between 10 and 20 places, or an equivalent number of foster homes, would suffice for the needs of adolescents and young adults. English experience suggests that it is desirable to have separate hostels for high-grade retardates who are working out, and for lower grade, dependent retardates. These hostels, it is suggested, should contain both young men and young women. Their function should be to prepare school leavers and young adults for independent living in ordinary lodgings or in their own homes. At the same time they could serve as social centres, to which other young people, living at home, could come.

Long-stay homes for adults

The greatest need for residential accommodation is for long-stay homes for adults who are mentally retarded. In the future these are likely to comprise three-fifths of the total for whom residential care is required. However, very few adult retardates will be severely handicapped, physically or behaviourally. It is suggested that the needs of these people could best be met in small family type units which were separate from but reasonably close to the main sheltered workshops in which many of them would be employed during the day. These hostels should also serve a wider community function, as clubs and meeting places for other retardates who lived at home. There is much room for experiment and innovation here.

PARENTS AND COMMUNITY

The problems that face parents and relatives of the mentally handicapped have already been referred to – but they require special mention since they are seldom dealt with adequately, despite a great deal of knowledge of how to do so.

Few parents to whom a handicapped child is born have any prior knowledge about problems of handicap. Nor are they psychologically prepared for the shock and grief which the birth of a handicapped child brings. They therefore require both to be told about the baby's condition and its implications, and to be helped to come to terms with it. As the baby develops the parents are likely to encounter problems not commonly met by other mothers, so the need for counselling, for practical advice and for practical help continues. These needs persist, though the nature of the problems changes throughout the lifetime of the retarded person.

There has been a good deal of study made of social and family problems associated with mental handicap. For a 'general approach to parents of deformed or ill babies' see Davies *et al.* (1972) who write authoritatively of medical care of newborn babies; Bricker has described the contribution which psychologists can make to parent education and to the development of handicapped children of pre-school age; Carr (1974) gives a detailed account of family and upbringing problems of young children with Down's syndrome, and Hewett (1970) of children with cerebral palsy; the social casework approach to the mentally children with cerebal palsy; the social casework approach to the mentally handicapped of all ages is comprehensively treated in Adams (1971, 1972). Fuller treatments of the problems of organizing community-based *services* for the mentally handicapped are to be found in Tizard and Grad (1961), WHO (1954, 1968), Tizard (1964, 1970), Kushlick (1968), Susser (1968), *Better Services for the Mentally Handicapped* (HMSO, 1971), *Campaign for the Mentally Handicapped* (1972), among other sources. Changing patterns in residential services are comprehensively reviewed by Kugel and Wolfensberger (1969).

Evaluation of services

Today it is fashionable to talk about the evaluation of different types of service for handicapped persons. The subject is complex and is one which presents unusually rich opportunities for research. In mental retardation most studies have been made of the efficacy of various kinds of education in special classes or in ordinary classes (see Chapter 11 of this book) or of projects under the Head-Start Programme (see Chapter 4). Very much less work has been done on the evaluation of other services for mentally handicapped persons and their families.

A model for research on *residential* services has been prepared and is being investigated by Kushlick; the studies which he and his colleagues are carrying out are among the very few large-scale inquiries which both explore the needs of whole communities (i.e. are epidemiologically based) and also attempt to control and investigate the quality as well as the form of the provisions being studied. A brief description of this programme illustrates the types of problems involved and the methods available to deal with them.

Kushlick's starting point was a practical problem facing the Wessex Regional Hospital Board, the Hospital Authority responsible under the National Health Service for providing hospital services (including mental subnormality hospital services) for 2 million total population living in the Wessex region of southern England. The Authority knew that it had a shortage of residential places for mentally retarded persons of the region, but it was uncertain as to the amount of provision it was likely to need in the future, and it was doubtful about the wisdom of adding to the size of existing hospitals. It was in this setting that Kushlick carried out his survey of the prevalence of mental retardation over the whole region.

It emerged from the survey that in every 100,000 of the total population about 25 residential places for severely and profoundly retarded children were required. About 30 per cent of these children were non-ambulant, and 20 per cent were ambulant but had a severe behaviour disorder. The remaining 50 per cent were ambulant and without severe behaviour problems, though two-fifths of them were incontinent.

Instead of building an additional 600-bed hospital to provide for unmet needs, the Board agreed to try experimentally a different pattern of service in parts of the region. There were a number of alternatives to choose from. Two were selected: the traditional all-age hospital, and 20-bed comprehensive units taking *all* severely and profoundly handicapped children in particular areas who required residential care. A number of demographically comparable areas were paired, and children in one half placed in small homes, whereas children in the other half went into, or remained in, the existing hospitals. Extensive data about the children and their families were collected. Progress is being monitored.

So far we have a classical quasi-experimental situation, with several replications, of the traditional sort. A novel feature is, however, now being introduced by Kushlick. He observed, as others have done, that treatment in the hospitals left a good deal to be desired as compared with treatment given to the children in the new residential homes which were established. He is, therefore, persuading the hospital authorities to implement the same operational policy as has been drawn up for the new hostels. (For example, changes in staff ratios, the movement of children whose homes are in the same part of the region into the same ward, the issue of personal clothing to children, and so on.) Thus, the two environments – for the children – are being made as similar as possible, though organizationally of course they remain very different. The interest of the research team is to see whether the environments remain, or can remain, alike – and more important what the effects of the different types of *services* are upon the families, the communities, the staff of the units, and the Regional Hospital Board. What are the administrative problems, what are the costs, what realistically are the benefits and drawbacks of different types of provision when the cards are not all stacked in favour of one type rather than another?

Studies of this sort are extremely difficult to carry out. First, they require an active partnership – which is not easy to establish and maintain – between research workers and bodies responsible for providing services. In this situation the research worker is likely to wish to influence policy, or to suggest alternative ways of doing things, but he cannot as a research worker direct policy. Moreover, if his task is to evaluate the effectiveness of different policies he must remain uncommitted in support of any one of them.

Secondly, field trials of the efficacy of different patterns of service are only possible if the objectives of the service can be specified. In practice this is rarely done: if aims are stated at all, it is usually only in terms of unexceptionable generality. To evaluate success in attaining objectives however it is necessary both to state just what these objectives are, and to devise ways of measuring how far they have been attained – within a specified period of time.

Thirdly, in the design of experimental trials, like has to be compared with like. The subjects (or children or patients or clients) who are studied have to be similar, and the quality of treatment they are offered has also to be, in a specifiable manner, similar. In practice it is often not possible to allocate subjects living in the same geographical area randomly to different treatments; the only practicable procedure is to compare total communities which are in specifiable ways matched and which are then allocated, if possible on a chance basis, one or other form of treatment. In this kind of study it is the community rather than the individual patient that constitutes the element requiring to be replicated.

To specify the quality of treatment is much more difficult than to match communities. There is, however, little point in comparing treatments which differ greatly in quality – for example poorly staffed, grossly overcrowded institutions of one type with generously staffed, well housed institutions of another – if one's interest is to explore differences in the type of institution rather than in, for example, the staff-patient ratios. Kushlick has attempted to get round this problem by working out, with the staff concerned in running the mental subnormality institutions he is studying, an operational policy to which they all subscribe. Moreover the Wessex Regional Hospital Board is attempting to equate staffing ratios and staff workloads in the different types of establishment being studied.

A fourth difficulty in the specification of criteria of effectiveness stems from the fact that there is no *single* objective. In the Wessex studies, for example, use has been made of four types of criteria: the effects on patients, the effects on parents and on the general community, the cost of running different types of service, and problems of management. It may well be that types of care which appear best when viewed from one angle appear worst when viewed from another. If this is so it will pose problems for those responsible for policy decisions: and such problems are substantive not statistical.

Other practical problems in the design of experimental field trials arise from the difficulty in achieving adequate numbers of replications, and from the time scale over which evaluation is possible. In practice it is rarely if ever possible to achieve enough replications for adequate statistical tests to be made of even simple hypotheses. Because in evaluating services the hypotheses are far from simple, and because idiosyncratic features associated with particular establishments account for much of the variance between establishments, conclusions about the relative efficacy of different types of institution have inevitably to be drawn on the basis of inadequate data. Quantitative findings must therefore be supported by assertions based on more or less adequate case studies, or on purely theoretical grounds. Most of those who have carried out evaluative studies have attempted to obfuscate this issue. Often it is difficult for the reader to distinguish between what is asserted and what is statistically validated – and sometimes even the researchers themselves appear to slide from one level of reporting to another without being clearly aware that they have done so. When this happens the results are inevitably suspect.

A factor which makes adequate objective data gathering impossible on a routine replicable scale, is that for many outcome variables (e.g. those associated with the well-being of those for whose benefit the services are ostensibly provided) there are no criteria of quality. This deficiency tends to lead tender-minded researchers to make assertions as though they were based on facts, and tough-minded critics to deny that differences exist because they cannot be measured.

Another type of problem relates to the time scale over which evaluation occurs. For example, critics of current proposals to set up mental subnormality hostels to replace some or all of the large hospitals have argued that they may be all right in the short run, but that over a longer time span they will prove difficult to staff and impossible to run. Equally, however, it can be argued, on the basis of history, that large institutions may be temporarily reformed from time to time but that such places tend inexorably to revert to their ideal type, namely that of the total institution. This view is an explicit part of Goffman's thesis (1961) and Kugel and Wolfensberger (1969) have provided powerful documentary support for it as far as American mental subnormality institutions are concerned. Either or both of these views may be correct; the point is that the time scale argument is one which it is difficult to cope with experimentally. This would not matter very much were it not for the fact that, for planning purposes, it is long-term rather than short-term outcomes which are of crucial importance, because of the long lead-in time between planning and the execution of plans. For this reason policies which permit action to be taken quickly and which do not tie up large amounts of capital resources over long periods of time have much to commend them. This is a fact which should be – though it rarely is – taken into account by planners.

Despite all these limitations, social experiment to help decide issues of urgent practical importance is at least feasible in principle. Moreover studies which have this aim can also explore factors which influence the manner in which institutions differ one from another. In doing so they direct attention to questions of institutional functioning which are of great importance and interest.

Measuring the quality of care

It has been mentioned that for many aspects of care no criteria of quality exist. This has led many investigators to concentrate on matters for which tests or scales already exist (e.g. to measure IQ or educational attainments, or sight vocabulary), irrespective of the relevance of such measures to the problems they are studying. The exploration of other indicators of institutional quality has been remarkably unadventurous, and often very indirect (e.g. through attitude questionnaires to staff rather than direct observations of staff behaviour, and so on). There is however good reason to believe that simple and direct observation of behaviour, and straightforward questions rather than oblique open-ended ones, can go a long way towards exploring differences between types of institutional care. An example taken from the work of our own research group may illustrate the fruitfulness of direct studies of the quality of care.

Our inquiries (King *et al.*, 1971) began with a practical issue which was as follows: institutions differ in patterns of child management. These differences are usually attributed to staff shortages, to staff attitudes, or to the large size of residential institutions. Confident opinions are expressed as to why standards of care differ, but the explanations are often mutually contradictory, and no very clear empirically based description of the ways in which institutions differ had in fact been given. We believed that child management practices were strongly influenced by the manner in which institutions were organized, and we thought that differences in child management practices were therefore likely to be attributable to differences in the organizational structure of institutions which determined staff roles and how they were performed. These differences in child management practices were, in their turn, thought likely to have an influence on the behaviour of children brought up in different regimens. We set out, therefore, to explore a number of hypotheses to account for differences in institutional functioning.

In a series of inquiries lasting over 5 years more than 100 different residential units were examined. In a major study 8 hostels, 5 wards in mental subnormality hospitals, and 3 voluntary homes were investigated. An objective and highly reliable scale of child management practices was devised which enabled us to score patterns of staff behaviour in a quantitative manner which permitted comparisons to be made between one institution and another. Time sampling observations of staff behaviour were carried out, and staff were interviewed using structured interview schedules of predetermined reliability.

There were striking differences in child management practices as scored on the child management scale, with no overlap in scale scores between any of the hostel units and any of the hospital wards. Hospital wards all had high scale scores indicative of institutionally oriented child management practices, whereas hostels had low scores indicative of child-oriented practices. The evidence suggested that differences in child care practices were not due to differences in the handicaps of the children.

Child care practices differed with the size of the institution and the size of the child care units in which the children lived, but differences in unit size did not seem able to account for the differences in child management practices. Nor could differing child care practices be ascribed to differences in assigned staff ratios, though in child-oriented units more staff were available at peak periods.

The organizational structure of child-oriented units was indeed very different, and it was this which appeared to be the principal determinant of differences in patterns of child care.In child-oriented units the person in charge had very much greater responsibility to make decisions about matters which affected all aspects of the unit's functioning. Perhaps because they were accorded greater autonomy, senior staff in these establishments tended to share their responsibilities with their junior colleagues: role differentiation was reduced (e.g. senior staff were more often engaged in child care than were their counterparts in institution-oriented units, who spent far more time on administration and even domestic work, and far less time in child care). Staff stability was also much greater in child-oriented units – partly because staff were not moved from one unit to another to meet crises in units which were short staffed, partly because students in training were not moved about in order to 'gain experience'. Role performances also differed. In child-oriented units staff were more likely to involve the children in their activities. They spoke to them more often, and were more 'accepting' of them, and less often 'rejecting'. Junior staff tended to behave in ways similar to those in which the head of the unit acted.

Though the social organization of the institution appeared to be largely responsible for the differences in staff behaviour, the nature of staff training also seemed important. Trained nurses were in general less child-oriented than were staff with child care training. They were more authoritarian and when the person in charge was a nurse the unit tended to be characterized by sharp role differentiation.

Mentally handicapped children in units which were child-care oriented were significantly more advanced in feeding and dressing skills, and in speech, than were those in institution-oriented units. Though no very adequate study was made of other personality characteristics of the children, fewer of those in child-oriented institutions appeared to be psychiatrically disturbed (Tizard, 1972).

The point about these studies is that they show that there were marked differences between different types of institution: but the factors usually thought to be responsible for differences in the quality of care turned out not to be the significant ones. Thus, by looking directly at particular characteristics of child-care practices which appeared to have beneficial or detrimental effects upon children in residential care at the same time as we examined characteristics of organizational structure in contrasting institutions, we were able to throw light on relationships between organizational structure and organizational function. And in doing this we were also able to examine the effects of specific aspects of child-care practices upon the development of children. It should be added that in a later series of studies carried out by Barbara Tizard (Tizard and Joseph, 1970; Tizard and Tizard, 1971; Tizard et al., 1972) in residential nurseries for normal children deprived of normal home life, strong associations were found between *specific* aspects of the institutional regimen and *specific* aspects of the children's development.

Conclusion

Because mental handicap, at least in its severe form, is an easily identifiable condition, and because services for the mentally retarded have been established for a long period of time, the subject of mental retardation lends itself to social as well as clinical study. Services for the mentally retarded are at present changing and expanding: there is thus opportunity to introduce changes on a planned basis and to explore their consequences. A number of *models* of different types of service have been proposed, some of them well established, others which have been tried out only experimentally in demonstration projects, and still others which have yet to be implemented. Today there is an interest in the evaluation of different types of service, such evaluation forming one of the bases for future policy. Problems of service evaluation are indeed complex. However experience in how to proceed with such studies is rapidly accumulating, and the evaluation of services offers one of the most fruitful avenues for social research.

References

ADAMS, M. (1971) *Mental Retardation and its Social Dimensions.* New York and London: Columbia Univ. Press.

ADAMS, M. and LOVEJOY, H. (1972) *The Mentally Subnormal: The Social Casework Approach.* London: Heinemann.

BANK-MIKKELSEN, N. E. (1964) The ideological and legal basis of the Danish National Service, of the treatment, teaching, training etc. of the mentally retarded, as well as a description of the structure of the National Service. In ØSTER, J. (ed.) *Proceedings of the International Copenhagen Conference on the Scientific Study of Mental Retardation.* Copenhagen: Statens Åndssvageforsorg.

BURT, C. (1921) *Mental and Scholastic Tests.* L.C.C. Rep. No. 2052. London.

Campaign for the Mentally Handicapped (1972) *Even Better Services for the Mentally Retarded.* London: Campaign for the Mentally Handicapped, Central Action Group.

CARR, J. (1971) A comparative study of the development of mongol and normal children from 0–4 years. Unpubl. Ph.D. thesis, Univ. of London.

CARR, J. (1974) The effect of the severely subnormal on their families. In CLARKE, A. M. and CLARKE, A. D. B. (eds.) *Mental Deficiency: The Changing Outlook,* 3rd edn. London: Methuen; New York: Free Press.

DAVIES, P. A., ROBINSON, R. J., SCOPES, J. W., TIZARD, J. P. M. and WIGGLESWORTH, J. S. (1972) *Medical Care of Newborn Babies.* London: Heinemann and Washington: Lippincott, for Spastics International Medical Publications.

DUNN, L. M. (1968) Special education for the mildly retarded: is much of it justified? *Except. Child.,* **35,** 5–22.

GOFFMAN, E. (1961) *Asylums: Essays on the Social Situation of Mental Patients and Other Inmates.* New York: Doubleday.

GOODMAN, H. and TIZARD, J. (1962) Prevalence of imbecility and idiocy among children. *Brit. med. J.,* **1,** 216–19.

HEWETT, S. (1970) *The Family and the Handicapped Child*. London: Allen & Unwin.

HMSO (1957) *Royal Commission on the Law Relating to Mental Illness and Mental Deficiency*. Cmnd 169. London.

HMSO (1971) *Better Services for the Mentally Handicapped*. Government White Paper. London.

KANNER, L. (1964) *A History of the Care and Study of the Mentally Retarded*. Springfield, Ill.: Charles C. Thomas.

KING, R. D., RAYNES, N. V. and TIZARD, J. (1971) *Patterns of Residential Care: Sociological Studies in Institutions for Handicapped Children*. London: Routledge & Kegan Paul.

KIRK, S. A. (1958) *Early Education of the Mentally Retarded*. Urbana: Univ. of Illinois Press.

KIRK, S. A. (1964) Research in education. In STEVENS, H. and HEBER, R. (eds.) *Mental Retardation*. Chicago and London: Univ. of Chicago Press.

KUGEL, R. B. and WOLFENSBERGER, W. (1969) *Changing Patterns in Residential Services for the Mentally Retarded*. Washington, D.C.: President's Committee on Mental Retardation.

KUSHLICK, A. (1968) The Wessex Plan for evaluating the effectiveness of residential care for the severely subnormal. In RICHARDS, B. (ed.). *Proc. 1st Congr. Internat. Assoc. Scient. Stud. Ment. Defic., Montpellier, September 1967*. Reigate: Michael Jackson.

KUSHLICK, A. and BLUNDEN, R. (1974) The epidemiology of mental subnormality. In CLARKE, A. M. and CLARKE, A. D. B. (eds.) *Mental Deficiency: The Changing Outlook*, 3rd edn. London: Methuen; NewYork: Free Press.

NIRJE, B. (1969) The normalization principle and its human management implications. In KUGEL, R. B. and WOLFENSBERGER, W. (eds.) *Changing Patterns in Residential Services for the Mentally Retarded*. Washington, D.C.: President's Committee on Mental Retardation.

SUSSER, M. (1968) *Community Psychiatry*. New York: Random House.

TIZARD, B. and JOSEPH, A. (1970) Today's foundlings: A survey of young children admitted to care of Voluntary Societies in England. *New Society*, **16**, (410), 585.

TIZARD, B., COOPERMAN, O., JOSEPH, A. and TIZARD, J. (1972) Environmental effects on language development: a study of young children in long-stay residential nurseries. *Child Developm.*, **43**, 337–58.

TIZARD, J. (1964) *Community Services for the Mentally Handicapped*. London: Oxford Univ. Press.

TIZARD, J. (1970) The role of social institutions in the causation, prevention and alleviation of mental retardation. In HAYWOOD, H. C. (ed.) *Social-Cultural Aspects of Mental Retardation: Proceedings of the Peabody–NIMH Conference*. New York: Appleton-Century-Crofts.

TIZARD, J. (1972) Research into services for the mentally handicapped: science and policy issues. *Brit. J. ment. Subn.*, **XVIII,** Part 1 (34), 1–12.

TIZARD, J. and GRAD, J. C. (1961) *The Mentally Handicapped and Their Families.* Maudsley Monogr. No. 7. London: Oxford Univ. Press.

TIZARD, J. and TIZARD, B. (1971) The social development of two-year-old children in residential nurseries. In SCHAFFER, H. R. (ed.) *The Origins of Human Social Relations.* London: Academic Press.

World Health Organization (1954) *The Mentally Subnormal Child.* WHO Tech. Rep. Ser., No. 75. Geneva.

Name index

Subject index

5. The double borders at Bramdean House in June

6. Poinsettia patterns in one room of Longwood Garden's Christmas display

7. *Galanthus nivalis* 'Anglesey Abbey' in James Fenton's garden

8. A corner of John Fairey's Peckerwood Gardens

9. *Prunus* 'Tai Haku' by Arabella Lennox Boyd's lake at Gresgarth, Lancashire

10. Spring view in the rhododendron wood, Bowood, Wiltshire

11. The supreme classical scholar, E. R. Dodds, uprooting an anemone in Greece in spring

12. Christopher Lloyd with matching *Verbena bonariensis* at Dixter

13. *Magnolia wilsonii*

14. A happy badger –
on medication?

15. Mixed annual poppies in Le Jardin Plume

16. View to a clipped hornbeam walk at Brécy

Provado range on to all bedding plants and pricked-out seedlings before they leave their boxes and go into open ground. They are then defended against bugs and weevils throughout the season, having taken up the chemical into their system. In my potting shed, there are two non-negotiable allies. Brands based on glyphosate kill couch grass and most of the broad-leaved weeds without any sign of poisoning the soil. Provado reverses the war against lily beetles and teeming female vine weevils.

It was charming to read recently of the writer Candace Bushnell that she likes the country and tells her visitors, 'Honey, we live here and the bugs live here too', so as to stop them complaining about rural infestations of insects. Down my way, honey, the bugs no longer have a chance and it makes no difference if every single one of them is female like yourself. When I drench them, they are dead.

Early Flowering Cherries

Before vine weevils are wriggling in our new spring pot-plants there are weeks when the contrast between town and country gardens is acute. It shows in mid-March when gardens outside the extra warmth of a town are decidedly retarded. They still have crocuses in flower, caught as if in a fridge, whereas southern cities already have flowers on their magnolias and bushes of yellow forsythia.

I would therefore urge anyone with a chilly new country garden to make a strong commitment to prunus. In southern British cities, the first clouds of prunus blossom now open in mid-March, but in the rural mud, country gardeners can enjoy the second flowering on the winter varieties at that time. These flowers are hardly a second best, as the winter cherry, *Prunus* × *subhirtella* 'Autumnalis', is exceptionally pretty. Nearly thirty years ago I picked on it as the finest tree for a flower garden and I see no reason to change my choice. The pinkish-white flowers first open in mid-November and are magnificent when cut and arranged indoors. We expect to see hothouse plants at that time of year, so the simple elegance of this blossom is a charming surprise in a drawing room. It grows anywhere and can sometimes be bought as a bush, not a tree, if space is scarce. The plain form is better than the pink one, which flowers marginally later.

If frost hits the early winter flowers, they re-form on the terminal shoots and then flower in spring all over again. As they eventually fade in mid-March, my next favourite is the neglected *Prunus* 'Okame' with acid pink flowers. This fine tree is wonderfully untroubled by cold weather and flowers strongly even in exposed countryside. 'Okame' has a more vivid rival, *Prunus* 'Kursar', which is less easy to buy but, if anything, is even better. It originated in Central Turkey where it was spotted by the great cherry expert Captain Collingwood Ingram. In later months, the strong pink of its flowers would seem harsh, but it is a bright opening for the rural season and appears to be untroubled by foul weather. Both 'Okame' and 'Kursar' are small trees, the latter reaching no more than twelve feet in height with a modest width. Many country gardens have room for one or both, and they deserve wider recognition. So does the excellent *Prunus* 'Hally Jolivette'. It makes a medium- to large-sized shrub with thin, graceful stems which are covered with semi-double pink-white flowers in late March. It is easy and very pretty, but few gardeners make it a first choice in a new plan, probably because they have never met it. I hope to reverse its neglect, because it is weather-proof, disease-proof and extremely easy to grow.

On dry banks or at the top of a low stone wall, late March then becomes the season for that other vivid shrub, *Prunus tenella*. The common name of this straggly, low bush is dwarf Russian almond. The one snag is that bits of it will sometimes die out, but even so the whole plant is seldom killed and soon covers over its gaps. It likes to fall forwards and cover quite a wide span of ground. The masses of red-pink flowers in the common form called 'Fire Hill' are very heartening during late March and early April. I have learned to grow vigorous forms of alpine clematis at a distance of less than five feet from it and let their stems wind horizontally through the prunus's untidy branches. The blue forms in this group of the clematis family, especially 'Frances Rivis', make a splendid accompaniment. In the wild, these alpine clematises grow flat over low shrubs more often than they try to climb vertically. It is only we who class them as climbers for walls.

As the first blush of hard and reddish-pink flowers on these prunus trees fades, the next wave of blossom needs more thought. Few of us want double-flowered varieties which verge in colour towards blackcurrant ice cream, but I can recommend the semi-double pink flowers of *Prunus* 'Accolade'. It deserves its Award of Merit from the Royal Horticultural Society, as the shade of pink is charming and the trees seem well able to function on poor soil. I have one growing well at a distance of only three yards from a high hedge of the vile Leyland cypress.

By mid-April, the single-flowered 'Umineko' takes over, an upright tree which is good in an avenue and is followed by the arching and spreading white *Prunus* × *yedoensis*. White cherry blossom then comes thick and fast until the final, distinctive flush in mid-May on the excellent *Prunus* 'Shimizu-zakura', popularly known as *longipes*, botanically renamed 'Shagetsu' in recent lists. These whites are a fine threesome, but there are no British festivals of cherry blossom to celebrate them. We do not go out on a public holiday to view the flowers on these cherries or even to become mildly drunk beneath them on picnic rugs. For cherry fiestas we have to go to the Far East. I have longed to see such a festival in action since I first became a cherry-lover at the age of twelve, and used to practise the names of the famous Japanese beauties, 'Shirotae', 'Yoshino', 'Shimizu-zakura', and many others. Recently I saw the flowers in their festival season in the ultimate home of so many wild cherries, Korea.

In Korea the holiday crowds do not set out to become drunk under falling cherry blossom. They turn out in thousands and even take special trains to outlying towns where the flowering cherries are especially good. I chose to avoid a cherry-blossom choo-choo and centred my researches on the capital city Seoul itself. The city scores poorly for green space, but there are magnificent cherries in its expanding perimeter as it leads away to a distant prospect of hills. They surround the city like a ring and tend to escape visitors on business who remain caught in Seoul's stupendous traffic.

I began my historical cherry-trail in the city's Cultural Monument Number One. Changdeokgung is the best restored of the palaces of the Choson dynasty which ruled for five centuries until 1910, the year of Korea's annexation by the Japanese. Cherry blossoms are much in evidence along its outer courtyards, among trees of *Magnolia kobus* with upright flowers of pure white against their bare branches. In earlier times Choson princesses aimed at having a 'garden in every gulley' so as to imitate the mountains around their city. Big trees of *Magnolia kobus* and wild white cherries evoked the mountains and welcomed visiting scholars, as they still do, to the palace's library garden beside a landscaped pond.

From the palace I moved on to two of Seoul's universities and checked for cherries on their campuses. As spring broke on the main avenues of Seoul National and Korea Universities, I walked down long pathways of the fine white cherry, *Prunus × yedoensis*. Justly named the King Cherry, it is a wide-spreading tree which is a superb choice for bigger British gardens too. In Korea, cherry planners do not mix colours or choose varieties with heavy flowers of raspberry-red. The dominant flowers in springtime are white, and two young Korean graduates guided me down their long avenues.

Discreetly, they proposed a final outing to Seoul National Park, and with hindsight, I am ashamed to have feared that they might not know what English visitors expect of a worthwhile garden. With their usual uplifting practicality, Koreans have divided Seoul's National Park into numbered Beautiful Places, and while fearing the worst I was guided to Beautiful Place Number Ten. Among the funfairs and the garden-railway, the world then smiled on us all. Far into the distance, double lines of mature King Cherries exhaled a haze of white blossom onwards and upwards to the blue-grey peaks of the mountains beyond. Korean ladies strolled along cherry avenues wearing eyeshades of green and pink and carrying parasols in matching colours, while a nearby office bus decanted members of the Tax Inspecting Association of Korea for a visit to enjoy the view. For once I wished their profession well, feeling that they, too, had come to be uplifted by the natural world.

Among the publicans and sinners one of my guides then brought me down to earth. 'Cherries mean Japan to us,' she remarked wistfully. Big public plantings of King Cherries were a Japanese initiative during their years of power in Korea, but the results have been so widely imitated that I cannot believe that Koreans look on them all as foreign symbols. So much in their style of gardening was already shared with their temporary Japanese conquerors. These King Cherries are not simply statements of past historical rule. They are among the loveliest avenues in the world.

Let Them Eat Squirrel

From Christmas onwards, while winter cherries brave the winter months, there is a sound of scuttling in the evergreen *Magnolia grandiflora* which has finally reached the top storey of my house. It terrifies overnight visitors, but the noise is caused by squirrels under the gutter: grey, prehensile little nuisances who have stripped the upper branches of the shrub and will be taught a smart lesson if they continue their capers lower down.

While Parliament wastes its time on human ASBOs, daylight robbery by squirrels is allowed to run riot. Up on the roof they sharpen their teeth on the lead and bite holes in it which then leak water through the ceilings of the house. They are a menace to crocus corms and in Chiswick they have developed provocative tendencies. My sister has watched them remove individual bulbs one by one, roll them away for uncertain purposes and replace them with a peanut, impudently pinched from a bird-table, which they drop into each empty hole.

For two decades I have watched the increasing tide of squirrel violence in my Oxford college's garden. In defence we had to fit fine-meshed netting over each window box and nail it into position. We even tried covering the plantings of tulips in open borders with unsightly stretches of green netting until the bulbs' growth showed through. In reply, the squirrels outdid the students by vandalizing the tulips when in bud and leaving fragments as proof of their trespass. It is no use arguing that squirrels should be treated as honourably as people because they share so much of our DNA. If people came into my garden, barked the young beech trees and devastated the tulips, the police would put the offenders in handcuffs.

Self-defence is called for, but culture is an obstacle. We think so fondly of those red squirrels which grey squirrels have now slaughtered as a lesson in unmanaged 'wild life'. We have all been brainwashed by dear Beatrix Potter and her seminal tale of Squirrel Nutkin. How can we punish anything with a brother called Twinkleberry? Here, I am grateful for the front-line experience of a primary schoolteacher in the days when primary schools still taught French. You may remember the seductive picture in Nutkin's story of those squirrels who 'made little rafts out of twigs' and paddled away with their tails held high to visit their ruthless co-predator, Owl. My friend tried teaching French to a primary class from copies of *Noisette L'écureuil*. When she asked a young pupil to translate the passage in which Nutkin's squirrels paddle over the water '*pour ramasser les noix*', the child hesitated and looked at the colour picture. He then went on, 'they paddled away to ram the island'. Try thinking of squirrels as ram-raiders and you will be less sentimental about their habits in flowerbeds.

Trained by politicians, I justify the war as necessary defence. One way of trapping squirrels is to put grain in a squirrel-trap, examples of which are sold in market towns for £29.50 each. Another way is to let a greyhound after them when they are more than fifty yards away from a tree trunk. In country settings I recommend prudent use of the gun. More is at issue than pest control. There is also the chance to enrich the larder.

Here we come to one of our culture's paradoxes. Squirrels are eaten freely in the southern United States but I cannot find a recipe for squirrel stew in my copy of *What Shall We Have Today?* by the great Marcel Boulestin. The artist Toulouse-Lautrec would often eat squirrel in Paris and described the flesh as refreshingly nutty. I have just followed suit, guided by *Classic Game Cookery*, an indispensable book by Julia Drysdale. She knows exactly what she is talking about, and is guided by advice from the Game Conservancy Council. She is accurate on how best to choose a dead rabbit: 'a good young rabbit should have soft ears which are easily torn, and sharp teeth and claws.' She is a practical guide to squirrel cuisine. Think of squirrels as organic, fed on nothing but natural produce and reared within sight of open country. There are no E-numbers in nature's furry tulip-killer. Drysdale's suggestions include an excellent Squirrel in Cider which combines chunks of three squirrels, bits of ham, cream, cider and seasoned flour. Lautrec would love it. It should be put on the national school menu with an accompanying lesson in facts about wildlife in gardens.

In France, they still eat horses. In Italy the best restaurant for horsemeat is in Mantua, within sight of the former stables of the Dukes of Mantua. It is we who draw boundaries around what we will eat and what we will protect. Realistic readers of the *Financial Times* draw realistic boundaries and one of them sent me a variant on Drysdale's Squirrel in Cider from a wartime recipe which was published to ease the problem of rationing in Britain in 1941.

> Kill three squirrels, grey being preferred. Cut off the tails, skin the rest and cut into pieces, soaking them in cold, salted water for 20 minutes. Wipe them dry and dust them with seasoned flour. In a heavy saucepan, brown 100g of diced fat ham. Add the squirrel and brown the pieces in the ham fat. Just cover them with cider and simmer with a lid on until most of the cider has boiled off and the meat is soft. Add two tablespoons of unsalted butter; turn up the heat and brown the pieces again. Transfer them to a warm serving dish; pour 200ml of warmed cream into the remaining juices and stir in the brown bits off the pan. Mix half a tablespoon of plain flour and one tablespoon of butter into a paste. Stir it gradually into the cream and juices. Season with salt and pepper and strain the sauce over the browned nutkins. Display on the centre of your table with the tails arranged around the dish in a neat triangle.

Readers testify that the meat is superior to rabbit and is preferable to the supermarkets' apology for steak. It costs nothing. I presume the tails should retain their fur when displayed.

Spring

Some people like daisies in their turf; others don't. Jean-Jacques Rousseau ascribed pinky eyelashes to the daisy, thought it a general favourite, and called it the robin of flowers. To John Skelton it was 'daisie delectable', Beaumont and Fletcher thought it 'Smell-less and most quaint', incorrectly, for a bunch of daisies has a peculiarly earthy smell, especially when it comes as a hot little gift in the hand of a child. Wordsworth, peering closely, noticed that it cast a shadow 'to protect the lingering dewdrop from the sun'. Tennyson, who was usually extremely accurate about such matters, went very wrong when he claimed for Maud that

> '... her feet have touched the meadows
> And left the daisies rosy,'

for this is simply not true. Enchanted by this idea, I wasted many youthful summer hours stamping on daisies, in fact I still do, but never a daisy has so far blushed beneath my tread.

Fortunately for those who like their turf green and not speckled, it is very easy for them to reverse the old song and give their answer to Daisy. A selective weed-killer will do the trick economically and with a great saving of labour, though it may be necessary to go twice with the lethal watering-can over the ground.

Vita Sackville-West, in
The Observer, *11 March 1956*

Spring begins at an indeterminate moment which even the great pre-war gardener E. A. Bowles took several pages to try to pin down. In Northumberland, spring stirs only in a compressed few weeks from April onwards. In Cornwall camellias give hints of it as early as February. Outside warm London, spring dawns for me when *Magnolia* × *soulangeana* begins to flower, an event which has often come forwards to mid-March in the weather's warmer phase.

Magnolias are the necessary first initiative for any new garden. The work which they repay takes place before they are planted, a time when enthusiasm is running high and no effort seems too much to improve on the garden's previous owners. The planting-hole for a new magnolia should be deeply and widely dug and well manured to improve the soil's texture. A basic fertilizer should be mixed in below the new plant's root-ball to give it the chemicals it will need for swift progress. The plant should not be mulched deeply when it is planted because some of the finer magnolias have been grafted in infancy and a deep mulching may cover over the point of grafting with fatal results. During a new plant's first summers I drench its roots fortnightly with half a watering can of diluted Miracle-Gro. This treatment is not prescribed in other gardening books, but on my quick-draining, poor soil it works wonders. The young plants grow away strongly, leaving others, undrenched, far behind them. With young magnolias, preparation and fertilizing are crucial.

Varieties continue to proliferate and we are now spoilt for choice. Gardens on acid soils are most spoilt, but others have plenty to enjoy too. My top ten include the superb, all-white *Magnolia* × *soulangeana*

'Alba Superba', the loveliest of choices as a shrub against a tall west- or south-facing wall. Two recent forms have flowers of an unusual shape, *Magnolia* 'Manchu Fan' and 'Star Wars'. 'Manchu Fan' is a fan-shaped white flowerer of distinction and 'Star Wars' has the biggest flowers of all, huge rose-pink flushed cups which open to more than a foot in width. Both will grow on lime and 'Star Wars', especially, is vigorous and free-flowering from an early age. Its flowers are so showy.

Gardeners on acid soils are blessed with the option of magnolias whose flowers hang downwards like white lids. *Magnolia wilsonii* is one of the easiest and is sometimes recommended for gardens on lime soils too. It will grow there, but it is usually not happy, and in neutral or acid soils it is three times as good. By contrast all of us can enjoy elegant forms of the excellent *Magnolia* × *loebneri*, with narrow strap-shaped petals which open just before the leaves. I first saw × *loebneri* 'Leonard Messel' thirty years ago as a small tree in the Hillier Gardens in Hampshire, an excellent place for gardeners in the Home Counties to visit in order to view magnolias. It looked far too elegant for my sort of soil, but ten years later I planted one, drenched it with Miracle-Gro as it crawled along and now marvel at it in spring. The flowers have a heavenly pink-rose flush. Its cousin, 'Merrill', is a pure white which impatient gardeners and regular house-movers may prefer. 'Merrill' flowers very freely from a young age and takes the waiting out of wanting.

Once planted, magnolias are no problem. They need no pruning, no training, no weeding. They just develop and improve yearly. They anchor a spring garden which otherwise becomes such a rush for gardeners. Everything is accelerating, and there is so much to sow, plant and weed before the great surge of green growth in May. Before then there is time for just one quick glimpse of spring in the Mediterranean in March or early April and at least one trip to a great collection of old, established rhododendrons in early May. I have, therefore, let my thoughts wander here to two such outings, but Spring is above all the section for activity, in which initiatives multiply and advice could go on forever.

Two observations guide me, one practical, one aesthetic. The practical one concerns the planting of those shrubs and border plants which tempt us every spring in black pots of spongy, dark compost. Many of them have become too dry in the centre or lower half of their root-ball and need forcible watering before they go into their final hole out-doors. If their so-called 'soil' looks anything other than dark black-brown or if the root-ball feels light in the hand, take a hose and ram the tip of it up into the root-ball's underside and let it run until the ball becomes heavy and water is running freely out of its sides. As the weight of the soil increases, so do the plant's chances of surviving hard life outdoors. Its roots will probably be matted and twisted round and round its central ball too. If so, it is worth teasing them out sideways, or scoring them with the upper blade of a pair of secateurs so as to cut into their coiling and twisting and coax them to spread outwards into garden soil. The transition from light, drugged com-post to genuine garden earth will often prove difficult. These plants have been pushed along in artificial compost on artificial food so as to reach a big pot-size quickly and sell at a higher price. They may also have sat for a month or more in a nursery, waiting for a buyer, so that their roots have coiled round their container's circle. When planting, I try to put a light coating of compost round the root-ball to persuade the roots to creep through it and meet the reality of Cotswold soil at one remove. If they are faced with such soil at once, they recoil and continue to twist around in their comfort-zone, their growers' apol-ogy for earth. Thoughtful gardeners even isolate newly bought convalescents and pot them on in a mixture of compost and local soil for another three months before planting.

Visually, spring gives us an array of fresh, invigorating colours, backed by the vivid green of new leaves and grass. So much is written about matching one flower's colour with another and placing plants with care, but in spring, under a clear pale light, this advice seems irrelevant. Everything goes together, set off by vibrant green. I smile wryly when 'guides to gardening' continue to recycle the old 'colour wheel' which the chemical engineer M. E. Chevreul devised in France in the 1860s. It set out the colours of the rainbow in a circle and was used as an argument for placing 'neighbouring' shades side by side in the garden or for combining pairs of colours which were directly opposite each other on the wheel, blue with orange perhaps, or red with green. Such pairing and matching were even believed to have a special stimulation for the 'rods' of vision connected to the human eye. The science of these 'rods' has moved on nowadays and although this wheel suggests one way of matching colours together, there is no reason to consider it the only authoritative way. I am more impressed by art than pseudo-science. When van Gogh looked at the spring flowers in the strong sunlight of Arles in southern France in the 1880s, he was delighted by combinations which the 'wheel' of a previous generation had excluded. He painted orange marigolds with dark maroon scabious or nasturtiums. He liked to use silver, a colour absent from Chevreul's wheel. He loved blue and pink as a pair, and when he found a garden to the north of Paris belonging to the artist Daubigny's widow, he wrote in the last months of his life how he would paint it with green and pink grass, a beech tree with violet leaves, and yellow lime trees, a lilac-coloured bush and 'sky pale green'. The painting still survives, a marvel which ignores the colour wheel's rules. Van Gogh thought carefully about 'entwining colours' and 'colours which cause each other to shine brightly', as he once wrote to his sister, 'which form a *couple*, which complement each other like man and woman'. He found them in pairs which ignored Chevreul's wheel. Increasingly, he looked back to Delacroix for examples of bold colour combinations.

Like van Gogh, the master of colour, gardeners need not be governed by the colour-wheel's rules. They are only one way of combining differently coloured flowers. Even their enthusiasts refer less to them in the bright mêlée of spring. In multicoloured April the wheel seems mysteriously to stop turning.

A Goat Island Garden

The first taste of spring is the sweetest and is usually tasted outside Britain. It is particularly evocative on the isle of Capri, in Italy. In the summer season, Capri is no longer a jewel near the top of informed travellers' wish lists. Too much has been built on it for expatriates in the early twentieth century and too many groups are now shipped across and told to shop and enjoy it. Out of season the island is not exactly a gardener's destination, but in late March I came to Capri on the tracks of a Roman emperor, Augustus' notorious successor, Tiberius. Unexpectedly, the island's flowers took over from its ancient history.

For ten years, between AD 27 and 37, the elderly Tiberius withdrew to Capri and continued to rule the empire from its rocky peaks without going anywhere near Rome. He is said to have owned twelve properties on the island and I wanted to see for myself where he resided, in a big house on the edge of the island. His years of retreat became the subject of gossip so salacious that even two thousand years later it was not translated from its original Latin in texts intended for general readers and schoolchildren. Only recently have editions of Suetonius' *Lives of the Caesars* and Tacitus' *Annals* made the allegations available. They are still strong stuff, of which compulsory sex with babies is only one of the disagreeable items.

I tried to forget the Latin words for swinging threesomes as I took the long uphill track to Tiberius' ultimate refuge, the so-called Villa Jovis, or Villa of Jupiter, on the far western tip of the island. Actually its plan is the plan of a palace, not a villa, at a time when the emperors did not yet have a proper palace in the heart of Rome. There were no signs of orgies, not even when a trio of goats appeared on cue at the path to what the text of the best ancient manuscript of Suetonius calls *'villa Ionis'*, not *'villa Iovis'*. Contemporaries called its grounds the 'old goat's garden', referring to Tiberius' goat-like behaviour with boys and girls in its bushes. I did not follow the goats into the undergrowth.

My thoughts, rather, were historical. How ever did the Roman empire continue to function while the managing director was away for ten years on an island, enjoying the most spectacular view in the Mediterranean without anything so elementary as a phone? Tacitus artfully tells us that some people said the emperor had retired in his sixties because he looked so repulsive: his face was pockmarked and covered in bits of healing plaster. It is as if a British prime minister were to decide to withdraw to Lundy island, off the coast of Devon, for the rest of his term in office. It is interesting to wonder which modern states would function no worse if their leaders pulled out and kept quiet.

Pondering the question, I was not prepared for the exceptional view from the ruined floor of the emperor's residence. Who would ever prefer Rome to this sweeping panorama across the Bay of Naples and its unsurpassable coast? I then looked down, not out, and was even less prepared for the proofs of spring beyond my feet. Whatever may once have happened in the palace and its gardens has done nothing to deter the wild flowers. Down the cliffs and the goat-garden's sea face, flowers tumbled with a message for us all. Small pale-lavender irises were already flowering among the aromatic cistus. There were tufts of good blue flowers on bushes of wild rosemary beside the louche old emperor's bedroom. Above all, single, starry mauve-pink flowers showed by the hundred down cliffs where no goat, old or young, could reach them. Beside them on the crests of the rocks there were bushes of a blue more brilliant than any British forget-me-not. I had hit on the villa's unreported survivors, anemones and lithospermums, in their finest spring flush.

The mauve-pink anemones are the peacock anemones, which are better known in reds and purples on the slopes of stony Greece. I have grown them in Britain but they are best in the related coronaria form, which has flowers in brilliant scarlet, ringed centrally with white. The coloured anemones we use most often in gardens are the heavenly sky blue of *Anemone blanda* and the related pink and white. I began with about a hundred of them some ten years ago but now have ten times more. They have the merit of being unpalatable to British wildlife. In shade, the best choices are the woodland forms of *Anemone nemorosa*, the most delicate member of the family. It is worth paying extra for the best-named forms, including the pale yellow × *lipsiensis*. They are all easy plants, but life on a cliff in Capri is too hot for them.

What is the identity of the palace's deep blue lithospermum? The name is based on the Greek words for 'stone' and 'seed', a pointer to the plant's preferences in the wild. The Capri form is a relation of *Lithospermum diffusum* 'Heavenly Blue', a tempting deep-blue-flowered alpine for pots and low beds. 'Heavenly Blue' needs a lime-free soil and would never colonize arid, limestone cliffs. The modern name of the plant on Capri is *Lithodora rosmarinifolia*, the name by which botanists now call it, as they have dropped the well-known *Lithospermum* from their listings.

On my return home I checked my memories of this plant in one of my older bibles, the manual of the king of alpine plants, W. E. Ingwersen. The manual was published as a book, although it simply reprints the catalogues of Ingwersen's famous Sussex nursery between hard covers. On alkaline soil I have grown the lithospermum's lovely Spanish relation, *Lithodora oleifolia*, without any problems for twenty years. I recommend it, but the rosmarinifolia variety is more brilliant. However, it will not tolerate a chilly British winter.

To my delight, Ingwersen's manual comments simply that rosmarinifolia is 'spectacular on Capri'. Did the great alpine expert once see it there as I have? As I retraced my tracks through the imperial goat-garden, the goats were celebrating spring in a way that Tiberius would have appreciated. They had no interest in flowers which are even more blue than their island's famous Blue Grotto. Tiberius' palace is now a flattened, baffling ruin, better known as the object of ancient gossip, whose twitter makes other societies' tweets seem very tame. Nobody mentions wild flowers among the reasons for the old goat Tiberius' puzzling retreat from Rome. I would like to believe that the anemones diverted him, but somehow I doubt it. As for the blue lithodora, there was never even a word for it in Latin.

Special Spring Shrubs

Back in Britain, early spring shrubs are best in gardens with acid soil which are sheltered from the cold, exposed weather. Warming winters suit them, like their winter-flowering predecessors, but some of the best are still missed by gardeners. When winter's witch hazels have begun to fade, the limelight falls on the family of corylopsis, the witch hazels' botanical relation. If you have acid, leafy ground suitable for camellias, you have an excellent chance of a haze of yellow flowers on corylopsis in mid-March.

Corylopsis is happy in North America and is nowhere better than in the Brooklyn Botanic Garden in New York where it thrives on acid soil. The most impressive variety is a Chinese one, *Corylopsis sinensis*. In Britain sinensis likes light shade and a damp soil with light leaf mould. It grows into a shrub up to eight feet high and covers itself with hanging clusters of yellow, scented flowers on bare branches. In full flush, it is a spectacular sight, the flowers being heavier and more significant than those on its more widely seen relation, *Corylopsis pauciflora*. This one is Japanese and is pretty in lightly shaded acid soil too. Its flowers are a paler yellow in a more delicate shape than those on sinensis, but they have a similar sweet scent. Pauciflora grows about four feet high and when happy spreads outwards into a wider girth.

I covet it but it detests life on my lime soil. A better hope is *Corylopsis glabrescens*, whose flowers hang in heavier bunches. The problem is that it is markedly less hardy, although warmer winters now make it worth a risk. Altogether easier is its fellow Japanese *Stachyurus praecox*, a remarkably obliging shrub with hanging flowers in shades of yellow, this time tending to green-yellow. Its bushes grow taller, up to ten feet eventually, but their hardiness is not in question and I have had happy specimens growing in an exposed north-facing site. Stachyurus is a reliable shrub when competing with rough grass, so long as the underlying soil is damp. It is an easy shrub there and will need no further attention.

Far easier on all soils are the indestructible forms of flowering currant, in the family of ribes. Indoors, they can be enjoyed in very early flower if you pick branches of them in February and bring them directly into a room so that the buds will open early. Outdoors, their great virtue is that they will grow in difficult dry shade, provided that there is sunlight through the canopy early in the year. Their impact is so pleasant, including the currant scent of the leaves and the range of available colours. The best-known forms are red, and I like the deeper shades best, including the later-flowering *Ribes sanguineum* 'King Edward VII'. The good news is there is now an extra-good white form, *Ribes sanguineum* 'White Icicle', which is much brighter than previous white forms and is one to track down. These varieties of ribes are excellent choices for difficult corners along the boundary of a garden where they are tolerant of dry and difficult conditions.

Camellias, by contrast, are not for everyone. Acid soil is their prerequisite, but the easiest group for outdoor gardeners contains the × *williamsii* hybrids, in which there are two excellent varieties from the same breeder in New Zealand. One is a particularly good yellow-centred variety, 'Jury's Yellow', which is compact but upright in growth. It makes an excellent plant in a large pot and, in spring, shows the most beautiful flowers with an outer ring of white petals and a central yellow cluster for contrast. The pair to it, raised by the same Mr Jury, is the unusually weather-proof pink *Camellia × williamsii* 'Debbie'. This mid pink form has several virtues. It starts to flower early and will be fully open in London in mid-January. It stands up relatively well to rain and a touch of frost and, above all, it drops its faded flowers when they are finished. The dying flowers on other camellias have a habit of hanging around for too long, especially on forms of *Camellia japonica*. 'Debbie' is a good choice for a large pot, but like 'Jury's Yellow' must have acid compost only and be kept away from lime, even when watered with tap water.

Denied camellias by my lime soil, I have the early spring varieties of prunus instead and am hoping to see a return from the double pink *Prunus triloba* from China against a wall. Its flowers look almost artificial from a distance and although I had no luck with this plant in open ground, on a wall it is said to be easier. It needs to be pruned hard after flowering and is enchanting if given this minimal attention. The omens look good for *Prunus triloba* 'Multiplex' in only its third year. In pots, meanwhile, there is an excellent new possibility, the single-flowered *Prunus incisa* 'Kojo-no-mai', which is now commonly offered in garden centres. Early March is the time to select plants because they are in delicate flower along their small branches and you can see what you are buying. They have such charm to their flowers and make excellent shrubs for pots in a front garden, where they mark the beginning of longer days and garden-friendly weather. After their spring flowering, you can take the twiggy small bushes away and put them somewhere less prominent. This treatment does not worry them in the least. 'Kojo-no-mai' needs no pruning but has been overlooked until recent years. When we start to think about active gardening again, this early-flowering plant urges us to get out and get on with it.

Harassed by Perpetual Bother

By mid-April, the shrub which many of us still call 'japonica' is start-ing to flower in gardens from Boston across to Rome. To many, it is no more than an admirable shrub for a wall in spring, best grown in a strong red-flowered hybrid form, of which the spreading 'Rowallane' or the flaming red 'Knap Hill Scarlet' are two of the best. They will flower facing north, east, or in tangled clumps if planted as thickets in rougher parts of the garden in order to suppress weeds. The botanists make us call the japonica *Chaenomeles* and even a semi-gardener finds it a difficult plant to kill. There the matter may rest for you, as you bask in hopes of sunshine on a day near Easter. For me, it is the beginning of a deeper story. The red japonica evokes letters, people and a predicament which has changed what I see in its yearly display.

Nobody has been a more straightforward spokesman for the belea-guered British countryside than the nineteenth-century poet John Clare. In his early life in Northamptonshire he would 'watch for hours the little insects climbing up and down the tall stems of wood grass'. He later remarked how 'in my boyhood, Solitude was the most talka-tive vision I met with'. Two hundred years ago, in Northamptonshire, cowslips were still known as paigles and John Clare observed them without botanical training. He loved and knew them nonetheless. Part of Clare's life was spent in the village of Helpston near the stately home of Lord Milton and his head gardener, Joseph Henderson. In 1836, the following exchange of letters took place between these admirable men. 'Will you have the kindness,' asked Clare, 'to give me a few shrubs and flowers, a few woodbines (honeysuckles) and some-thing my wife likes she calls everlasting; have you got a drooping willow and a double blossomed furze? My wife also wants a red japonica . . .'

Joseph Henderson was just the man to cope with this request. He was not a head gardener of the type which colleges produce nowadays, trained in the use of chopped bark and rules about health and safety. He corrected the grammar in one of Clare's most famous poems and hunted down books for him in his employer's antique library. One of the female servants in Lord Milton's big house turned out to know a ballad called 'The Song of All the Birds in the Air'. On Clare's behalf, Henderson promised to copy it from her singing. He duly sent the poet the words.

Henderson was also a dealer in antiquities. Whenever Roman coins were found on Lord Milton's estate, they were brought to Henderson who would pay up to sixpence for 'such as he thinks good' and sell them on to educated collectors. If you wanted a denarius Henderson would see you right. He was well able to meet Clare's request for the red 'japonica', which I assume to have been a variety of *Chaenomeles speciosa*, already known in England for some years before 1836, although its home is in central China. Henderson wrote back to Clare confirming the order and promising to send a man to plant them in. He would be 'including some chrysanthemums, the plants I believe Mrs Clare calls everlasting'.

In mid-April I take cuttings off my chrysanthemums and you may think that this idyllic exchange of letters between two self-taught thoughtful gardeners makes a happy mental accompaniment to the job. It was not, however, as idyllic as it first seems. Clare ended his letter by saying: 'I am hardly able to say more.' The japonica arrived and flowered, but the participants went in different directions. Henderson, the gardener, moved to service in Surrey, but poor Clare was afflicted by mental disorder. It took him first to the asylum in Northampton and then to intensive care, well meant but misguided, at High Beech in Epping Forest. He arrived there about a year after Henderson's gift of the japonica and wrote that he had 'arrived in the land of Sodom where all the people's brains are turned the wrong way . . .' Some of you may recognize your school days, others may think of those nowadays who are still in prisons or in care.

Five years later, Clare was still hoping for news of the drooping willow and the flowers in his abandoned cottage. He then sent the most heart-rending letter which has ever been carried in the post. It went to his wife, whom he pictured in charge of the garden, and told her in simple capital letters: 'My sojourn here has been even from the beginning more than irksome but I shake hands with misfortune and wear through the storm – the spring smiles and so shall I, but not while I am here . . .' With the clarity of long confinement, he then told her: 'It was my lot to seem as living without friends until I met with you and though we are now parted, my affection is unaltered . . . Essex is a very pleasant county. Yet to me "there is no place like home" . . .' The letter cannot have been easy reading for her among her husband's everlasting flowers. It became even more direct. 'For what reason they keep me here I cannot tell, for I have been no other-ways than well a couple of years at the least and I never was very ill, only harassed by perpetual bother . . .'

Out in the country which he loved so well, many of us are 'harassed by perpetual bother' in smaller ways. It is not a bad description of gardening life. I like to think that his wife received the letter, read it by the red japonica and remembered how their life had once been lived before his stability deserted him. 'I would sooner be packed in a slave ship for Affrica than belong to the destiny of mock friends and real enemies . . .' In mid-April *Chaenomeles japonica* comes into flower and as Clare wrote earlier in his life: 'We see a flower not only in its form and colour. Our imagination, too, brings a world of associations adding beauty and interest to the object actually before our eyes.'

Put Them on Prozac

Mid-April ought to be the height of the season for flowering bulbs, but their range in my garden is restricted by uninvited residents. Badgers remain a subject of public debate. Should we cull them or should we cuddle them? Officially, the question is whether or not they spread TB round cattle. During winter and most of the early spring, my garden is battered by badgers who dig holes in the lawn, uproot every tulip and destroy my small-flowered crocuses, planted devotedly over many years. As usual, the government is advancing towards the problem on too narrow a front. We need urgent research not only on badgers' role among cattle but on the crocus-locating facility of the adult badger, which is one of the miracles of the animal kingdom. It might prove to be a discovery as useful as radar. Armed with it, a badger can sense bulbs where they have been sleeping for decades.

Beset by badgers, I have come up with a new solution: put them on Prozac. Why Prozac? I regard it as proof of the lateral thinking for which an Oxford education is famous. In the bathroom I have one of those cupboards which fill up with pills prescribed in emergencies but never consumed over time. Their owners have come and gone in my life and when spring arrives, the urge to clean is in the air. Why not give the pills of absent women to the badgers on the lawn? Here is the logic behind my thinking, based on scraps of badger literature which have explained what may be wrong.

Those of you who work in the public sector will not be surprised to hear that the problem is social. It is not the badger's fault. It is not even that a well-off, middle-class badger would want to eat a crocus out of choice. The problem is the badger's age. When a male badger becomes old, he becomes the most dreadful bore. The rest of the group cannot put up with him and so they expel him from their social circle. A boring badger has to go on the wander and ends up in our gardens, taking disgruntled revenge on the tulips. I recognize this problem because it sometimes afflicts elderly academics of distinction. The years pass and they never fully retire. When they come in for the day from the academic woods they cause younger colleagues to go into hiding at lunchtime. Gone are the days when a king of potential boredom used to send his academic colleagues a courteous postcard, giving details of the days when he would be in Oxford. On it he would write, 'in case you wish to absent yourself'.

Prozac is supposed to cure gloom and isolation, especially as the years pass. If an ageing badger is socially miserable, why not cheer him up? At dead of night I did it. I crushed Prozac in the food mixer and spooned it into lumps of crushed peanut butter which fellow sufferers tell me is the supreme badger-attractor. I put sixteen heaps of the mixture at intervals around the lawn. The next morning they were all gone.

I feel half ashamed and half proud about what happened next. Two days later I returned late at night from work and, with due astonishment, found a badger trotting down the road off which my drive runs. I caught him in the headlights and, obligingly, he swung right up my drive. How fast can a badger run on Prozac? I am sure we were doing twenty miles an hour, but I lack the callous blood-lust of the anti-hunting classes. Every day I pass the road-cull of these liberal opponents of blood-sports who have squashed cock pheasants, rammed a few rabbits and usually left a badger somewhere in their wake. My reason kept telling me that I had a free gift in the headlights, the supreme enemy of the winter garden who was on the run before me. For a hundred yards I could not bear to accelerate but when I finally put on speed, the old boar dodged sideways through the lime trees and vanished from view. I think the Prozac saved him. Full of goodwill and optimistic about the world, he had broken the previous record for a badger sprint.

Many of you may be feeling sympathetic to badgers, but you have been misled by propaganda and those stories that badgers are wise old throwbacks to the pre-Roman era in Britain. A badger in the wrong place is a Class A menace. Why are people sentimental about the species? The Royal Horticultural Society has even teamed up with the Wildlife Trust for a joint initiative for 'wildlife gardens'. What will trusting wildlife gardeners do when a badger cuts loose among the thousands of crocuses recently planted along the Broad Walk in Kew Gardens?

Since the tranquillized peanut butter, there has been a remarkable quiet on my lawn. It is just as well because I am now considering an alternative: the sleeping pill Temazepam. If it was strong enough for Marilyn Monroe, it ought to be strong enough for Mr Brock.

Sow and Scatter

While my badgers bask in a new happiness, the combination of rain, cool temperatures and sun on mid-April days is ideal for sowing hardy annual seeds directly into the ground. Seize the moment and join those who reckon that the results are what make them happy gardeners. Every variety I mention is available from the tireless Chiltern Seeds at Bortree Stile, Ulverston, Cumbria, or from Thompson & Morgan at Poplar Lane, Ipswich, Suffolk.

I will refer only to hardy annuals for which no greenhouse is needed. To sow them you need to have a proper rake, as you will need to smooth over the soil in the beds where you wish to sow. Break the soil up first with a fork of manageable size. Bash any remaining lumps to dissolve them and then rake the surface over to establish a tilth. A tilth is soil with a fine consistency, the sort of consistency which you would get if you put a packet of digestive biscuits into a food processor and scrunched them into crumbs. Water the tilth, if necessary, and leave it to drain for an hour or two. Then with the back of the rake, press a shallow seed-drill in a straight line into the tilth, aiming at a depth of about a quarter of an inch. Into this drill, scatter the contents of the seed packet and then rake the tilth back over it and pat it lightly down with the head of the rake held flat, not at an angle. If the weather turns dry, you will need to water regularly from a can with a fine rose. After three weeks, seedlings should be showing, probably in dense clusters unless you are more deft at sowing pinches of seed than I am. You can thin them out either by discarding the surplus or by transplanting them into the empty spaces which you left between the lines of the seed-drills.

The fun comes in the choice which is available. There is no way that you will be able to buy pre-grown scented mignonette from shops in late May. To enjoy its scent, you have to sow it for yourself, finding it under the name reseda in catalogues. It is extremely easy to grow. So is another of my favourites, the good old pot marigold or calendula. I like all the varieties, including the short, double 'Candyman Yellow', but I recommend a taller double mixture called 'Prince' because it is especially good for picking. These easy flowers give a lift to the garden from July onwards and will often self-seed from year to year. They flourish in all weathers and I recommend them.

I also recommend a prickly little number called silybum. The one to find in the family is the St Mary's thistle, whose leaves are beautifully cut and marked with white spots, attributed to that globally abundant substance, the Virgin's excess milk, flowing freely since her time at Bethlehem. The seeds are very easy to handle and I like to fit a few plants into gravel or the corners of buildings, where their conspicuous spotted leaves become very pretty. The flowers are not interesting, although there is now a white form. Again, St Mary's thistle will not be seen in supermarkets. Nor will the excellent forms of annual sunflower. The name 'helianthus' hides the best available, which grow up to four or five feet and flower in rich colours. They are not as gigantic as the commercial sunflower of Mediterranean farming, and instead of its sunny yellow I recommend the dark crimson-chocolate 'Velvet Queen'. Its flowers enliven the back row of a herbaceous border from late July onwards.

Most gardeners are unaware of two lovely low-growing blue annuals, the rich deep blue *Phacelia campanularia*, which prefers sun, and the sky-blue, white-centred *Nemophila menziesii*, which prefers shade and water. They are easy, charming and too seldom grown, as is the annual blue pimpernel, blue anagallis, which will usually succeed if sown directly outdoors. It, too, is a fine plant for the front row of a flowerbed where its blue flowers continue into the autumn.

Cornflowers are much more familiar in our mind's eye but it will soon be hard to find the colour we really want. Packets of cornflower seed are drifting away into mixtures of blue, off-pink and so forth, whereas the classic blue is the winner and is much better if it has not been miniaturized to a height of six inches. Keep up demand and perhaps we will keep the separated colour of 'Blue Diadem' in the trade. It is the easiest of annuals to sow as its small seeds are like little shaving brushes. It looks so pretty when dotted through flowerbeds of supposedly more distinguished company, or alternatively it can be segregated into a pot and treated as a treasure. It performs very well when pot-grown and catches visitors by surprise for being so straightforward in a special place. I also grow some of the tall varieties for cut flowers and enjoy them in glasses of water indoors.

Even if you are not good at making a tilth, you will succeed with the common forms of annual poppy. Most of the easy ones are forms of *Papaver somniferum*, which have been selected for particular colours and shapes to their petals. I much like the vivid one called 'Red Bombast' which I saw last summer in the garden of an owner who justified the plant's name. There is no missing it as it is such a strong colour. I also like the striped and spotted colouring of the selection called 'Flemish Antique'. They have the look of fine poppies in a Dutch painting and if you thin out the germinated seedlings, the plants will develop strongly, even in dry years. They are obliging as fillers and we do not yet make enough use of them.

We also ignore something so easy and elegant that it ought to be everywhere but never is. The popular name of agrostemma is corn cockle and my favourite is still the one called 'Milas', named after a corner of south-west Turkey where it must have been found as a wild flower. The tall, elegant plants take up very little room and reach about two-and-a-half feet, producing lilac-pink flowers for most of the summer, or a deeper red-pink if you choose 'Milas'. I never tire of them and even in dry summers they will succeed as they succeed in Turkey.

To enjoy these self-raised plants, there is no need for a greenhouse or a cold frame or particular skill. There are dozens more annuals to choose from, all of which give a garden the look of a thoughtfully chosen patchwork which has not been bought ready-grown. They attach us to the process of gardening and make us feel responsible for their generous success.

Harmonious Rhododendrons

When it is warm, green and heavenly in an English spring there is no lovelier time in a landscape. It is particularly lovely if you live on lime-free soil and can grow the great May-flowering trees and shrubs from the Far East. Supreme among such shrubs are rhododendrons, but do they fit into the green nature of Britain when they are at their best? Rhododendrons have their opponents, many of whom do not know the family's full range. They seem to think that all rhododendrons have mauve or purple flowers and are as rampageous as the rampant ponticum form in Sunningdale or Scotland. They also bring up the controversial placing of rhododendrons in natural parks and land-scapes, especially Stourhead in Wiltshire, where they gleam around the historic lake in the eighteenth-century garden.

Recently, I went to a lunch for the rhododendron's friends and experts and saw a setting which refuted the contention about rhodo-dendrons' incompatibility. In Wiltshire, rhododendrons have been sharing another famous landscape with a great design from the eight-eenth century and have not detracted from it at all. At Bowood, home of the Lansdowne family, rhododendrons have had a happy history for more than 150 years. About 200,000 visitors now enjoy Bowood every year, but are slow to hunt out the entrance to its great woodland garden. This separate area of the park can still be enjoyed in fitting tranquillity. It owes its beauty to the family's long involvement with rhododendrons, a relationship whose continuity is unique.

At Bowood the two great elements of the garden are kept separate. From the house, the high point of the landscape is one of the greatest of all lakes by Capability Brown. In the 1760s, the landscape designer was at the height of his powers and his original plan for Bowood's park survives, a tribute to the confidence of the designer and his patron. On it, curving belts of trees are marked in detail for the park's far horizons and a lake is sketched out, placed so as to draw on five natural springs. These springs have never failed, not even in the long drought of 1976. To make room for the lake, a shabby village had to be destroyed and re-sited in a less intrusive position, and its inhabitants had to be transplanted to new homes. In 2007 the foundations of their former village were rediscovered on the floor of Capability Brown's lake, found by members of a sub-aqua diving club from the nearby town of Calne. It was as well that the villagers had moved out. As I walked to this lake past a fine fern-leaved beech tree, I thought how unfair the wits of the eighteenth century had been to Brown. One of them told him that he was fervently hoping to die before him. When Brown asked why, he replied that he was so wanting to see heaven before Brown improved its 'capabilities'. By the lake at Bowood, visitors can feel grateful that if ever they see heaven, they will be seeing it when the lake's designer has had time to reshape it.

Where, then, are the rhododendrons? Their first home, during my visit, was on the tables during lunch. The present Marquis of Lansdowne, the family's ninth, had picked a selection of varieties only a few hours before the party and had put them in vases on his guests' tables. Even the expert Roy Lancaster struggles to identify rare yellow-flowered varieties from Bowood's past. After lunch, we set off in a motor-convoy to a far corner of the park, where Bowood's rhododendrons have been developing since the 1850s. They are not the oldest rhododendrons in Britain, some of which are now classed as 'heritage hybrids' and live on at Highclere Castle near Newbury, where they date back to about 1815. Bowood's plantings are slightly younger but they have had an exceptional continuity in the care of one and the same family. The Lansdownes are still planting new varieties, and their beautifully planted wood should be a first stop in May for the thousands who enjoy the rest of Bowood's magnificent park. It is worth a special trip along the M4 in order to see how rhododendrons will cohabit under a tall canopy of oaks and parkland trees above the most beautiful carpets of English bluebells.

At a rhododendron lunch, always try to sit near an expert so as to keep up with the questions and answers. In a rhododendron plantation, allow the experts to go into a huddle with their breeding books and dispute the inmates' identities. They will even debate the parentage of the pale brown fur, which they call 'indumentum', on the undersides of old varieties, and they debate it especially keenly if the plants have not been labelled since 1854. Bowood has great old specimens which stretch experts to the limit, while the rest of us happily admire the spacing and the colour planning, and recognize old friends like Rhododendron 'Loder's White'.

It is important that these shrubs are generously spaced. Big rhododendrons in banks of flower are easy to accommodate, but they look so much better if sweeps of grass intervene between them and set off their colours. A rhodo-wood is not difficult to maintain if the nettles and other weeds are sprayed from a backpack during their growing season. It is also easier if the soil stays as damp as Bowood's with the help of natural springs. The blue haze of Bowood's mature *Rhododendron augustinii* is a marvel, and even an opponent of rhododendrons would soften before the subtle pale yellow of 'Cool Haven'. When you learn the difference between 'Beauty of Littleworth' and the yellow markings on evergreen 'Glory of Littleworth', you want to grow them both. Dazzled by the colours, I asked the experts which of the strong, clear red varieties they would recommend for amateur gardeners. Their choice was the intense 'May Day', an excellent flowerer which is late enough to miss spring frosts. Their insider knowledge also recommends the later-flowering varieties which carry the season on into July. If you think that rhododendrons are over by mid-June, look out in future for varieties which have been bred in Liverpool and are named after parts of the city. They will flower long after the usual bushes have finished.

Nothing stands safely still in gardens, not even in a mature woodland which has remained in one family's care. In 1990 a storm destroyed one side of the upper canopy in Bowood's rhododendron wood and ruined the shrubs beneath the trees. The line of the damage is still clearly visible, but Bowood's owners continued to replant, adding to the evolution of their great woodland garden. Capability Brown may have gone to heaven and improved it but he died before seeing the rhododendrons whose capabilities have improved his own.

Reappearing Poppies

By late May, gardens are dominated by the colour green, the vibrant green of young leaves on the trees or the fresh green of grass as it accelerates its growth. In his 'green shade' this green seemed 'lovely' and 'amorous' to the poet Andrew Marvell. Thoughtful gardeners consider it overpowering. The classic correction is to send for bright scarlets and reds, a vivid counterweight. Gardeners are no longer so afraid of strong colours in May and early June, and the highest value has come to be set on particular forms of red oriental poppy. These poppies used to be prefaced with apologies. Gardeners had to be warned that their colours could be strong and hard to place and that after flowering they would quickly disappear, leaving unwanted gaps. Nowadays, these vices are seen as virtues. The vibrant reds of the best oriental poppies are an antidote to the excessive green of early summer. Gaps are now seen as a blessing because they allow yet more ingenuity and tightly packed planting which will prolong the season after the early flowerers' disappearance.

Poppies have also prospered mightily on the new wave of garden photography. Perfect colour pictures set the standard for gullible gardeners and few look better than a photo of a poppy, caught in the early morning or late evening without a hint of blackfly or rain damage on its petals. Photographs catch only a brief moment, and the short flowering period of the best poppies is not the photographer's business. Photos of fancy-coloured poppies are deceptive, too, because their shades of grey, brown-maroon or peach-salmon look so much better on film than they do in a living garden. Not long ago a flattering photograph of a poppy called 'Patty's Plum' sent collectors scurrying to south-west England to find stock of this damson-coloured beauty. The price soared upwards and I was grateful to the reader in Taunton who sent me a small plant with her compliments. Two years later I can see why she was willing to be generous. 'Patty's Plum' is an immediate seller at the plant fairs which are organized so nobly in private gardens for charity, but when it flowers off film, it is disappointing, the colour of a muddy tea cloth.

The varieties which deserve acclaim are the ones which used to be avoided because they were too vivid. They have flowers of a blinding scarlet or a deeper red, held on tall stems and opening to a size which makes an impact. I have learned to dot them around the garden at intervals and rely on them to lift it out of excessive greenness in the weeks between the irises and the main showers of roses. Red poppies are also spectacular companions for stretches of roughly mown grass. Here they will compete with a new season's growth among the decaying leaves of daffodils. If the grass is left uncut until late June, the poppies' dying leaves can be cut down at the same time, and year after year the strongest varieties will survive this meadow treatment. By contrast the classic red poppies of cornfields and Impressionist paintings are only annuals. They will not last from year to year unless they happen to seed themselves successfully.

Scarlet-flowered perennial poppies are the ones to work into the setting of a garden. My particular favourites are the strong pink *Papaver orientale* 'Raspberry Queen', the self-supporting 'Brilliant', the tall, deep red 'Goliath', and its upright form 'Beauty of Livermere', whose deep red flowers are wonderfully marked with black. These varieties are extremely easy to grow on dry soil in sunshine, where other late developers can be planted close to them so as to make a tangle from July onwards and cover their decay and disappearance. They are plants to be used individually but they also allow two separate seasons in the same patch of ground. Since Livermere discovered its Beauty, important poppy-breeding has been going on in Europe, as a recent trial of the family at Wisley gardens established. Varieties like pale pink 'Karine' and red-and-black 'Spätzünder' have now proved to be stunning too. Poppies of this quality will not come true from seed and cannot be divided. They put down a long taproot and cannot be split from above, although the clumps of leaves seem to invite an assault in late April. The way to increase them is to take root cuttings, an easy and enjoyable task which is best delayed until late autumn. Root cuttings turn one plant into half a dozen within two years and their method is extremely simple, though it risks being forgotten in this age of supermarket shopping. Dig deeply round an established poppy in autumn and try to lift it from the ground with as much of the taproot as possible. Cut the taproot into pieces about two inches long, laying them out carefully so that you know which end of the cutting came from the upper part of the root when you dissected it. Transfer the cuttings to pots of sandy soil, plant them with the upper part uppermost, water them and put the pots under the staging in a cold greenhouse or on a sheltered area of paving outdoors. If you muddle the ends of the cuttings, you can simply lay them lengthways on a well-watered seedtray of good compost and then scatter another half-inch of well-watered compost on top of them. The miracle then takes place and new shoots will sprout through the soil by the end of the following spring. It is all so easy, but I feel proud when it works. The young plants should be potted on in good, nursery soil and then moved into a permanent place in late summer. They will flower in the following spring, about eighteen months after the start of the operation.

When Connie Met Oliver

Up in Derbyshire, off exit 30 on the M1, a very short drive leads to the gardens at Renishaw Hall, home of the famous Sitwell family for hundreds of years. Their roses are remarkable and in chilly Derbyshire the brilliant blue *Ceanothus* 'Italian Skies' is as prolific as elegant *Magnolia wilsonii* with its hanging flowers. The resident Sitwells still tend and improve the garden with taste and understanding, but the reason for a visit is its history. Renishaw combines two extremes: the formal classical and the seditiously romantic.

The classical extreme connects to a most unusual book, *On the Making of Gardens*, which appeared in 1909, written by the present owner's grandfather, Sir George Sitwell. Its text was the result of painstaking observation and stylistic effort but it was a flop when it first appeared. Even now it is impenetrable, but it has acquired the fascination of a distant time and taste. The book is the literary pair to the backbone of the garden which we now see at Renishaw and it has become an unusual chapter in the history of looking at nature. In the 1890s, Sir George had already been attracted by the green architectural style of the great gardens of Italy. Basically, he had no taste for flowers, thinking them a common distraction. In 1900 his obsessively practical and antiquarian mind had a brief breakdown, after which he travelled, no less obsessively, in Italy, taking careful notes on more than 200 half-neglected formal gardens of the distant Italian past. You might think that he then returned home and laid out his garden on the new principles which this travel had taught him. Not at all. Even before leaving, he had begun the formal design of green yew hedges and geometric patterns which is still one of Renishaw's distinctions. By November 1900, Sir George's garden was already being commended for its 'architectural fitness'. The nervous breakdown, the Italian travel and the book elaborated a taste which he already had. Nine years later, in 1909, the book never mentioned Renishaw, his home. Instead, Sir George tried to establish 'principles of design' and to explain the causes of our pleasure when we look at gardens. His theories are a gold-mine of intellectual debris from the Edwardian past. They link up with a fashion of the time, the Italian style of formal gardening which was being described simultaneously by the novelist Edith Wharton. Another component was the bundle of popularized theories through which Sir George absorbed amateur psychology, evolution and the principles of popular science. He then tried to explain our pleasure in viewing a garden as if it is an echo of our evolutionary history. At the same time, he thought, it exploits more recent elements of our psychology and vision, and more flexible elements of our mental power. His own theory is appealing rubbish and is written in an extraordinary style. His son, the famous Osbert Sitwell, described how Sir George would go to endless pains when trying to research and construct a single sentence. His prose is an unintended tribute to the contrary value of spontaneity.

One of his other sons, Sachie, wrote that 'to have been alive and sentient is the grand experience'. It is, therefore, intriguing to find that Renishaw is not just a classicizing monument. It has had an impact on the literature of life and feeling whose 'grand experiences' are known across the world. Beyond doubt, Renishaw is the model for the great house, Wragby Hall, in D. H. Lawrence's *Lady Chatterley's Lover*. The name 'Wragby' was borrowed from a Lincolnshire village, but Renishaw's house and grounds were the basis for those scenes of sentient life between her ladyship and the gamekeeper at his cottage in the woods.

Walking down Renishaw's fine vistas in search of the cottage, I found myself turning back to Lawrence's erotic masterpiece. Perhaps Lawrence visited Renishaw in September 1926, and certainly he talked with Osbert Sitwell in Italy in the summer of 1927. The disabled Sir Clifford Chatterley owes a debt to Lawrence's impressions of Osbert Sitwell, who was also a baronet's son. Chatterley's house is deliberately described as 'a dreary old house in a defaced countryside, with a rather inadequate income'. It was there that Lady Chatterley found herself dreaming of wild horses and craving the rough kiss of male flesh in the garden grounds.

Lawrence's text survives in several versions, beginning with ones in which Mellors the gamekeeper is called Parkin and there is a greater presence of flowers. After hours of passion in the keeper's hut, Lady Chatterley steadies herself by gardening. She settles down to work with Wragby's housekeeper in a garden which has double lines of auriculas, called 'recklesses', significantly, in Derbyshire dialect. 'For some reason she felt drawn to Mrs Bolton as if she had something in common with her.' Together, the two women 'peg down carnations', a forgotten aspect of modern bedding-out. They also put in 'small plants of flowers for the summer' which turn out to be 'columbines', a most unlikely flower for the summer season as they are aquilegias and would have finished flowering by mid-June. Nonetheless, 'Connie felt a delight in softly putting in the roots into the soft black earth of the borders'. It is one which I am unable to confirm: 'She felt her womb quiver with pleasure, as if something were taking root there, in the same way.'

Floral bedding-out took on a new meaning for her because of her previous bedding-out in the woods. 'Four miles' away from the house, according to Lawrence, lay the gamekeeper's cottage where Connie met Oliver, at least in the book's first version. In his arms, she felt 'like a volcano' at those moments when she 'surged with desire, with passion like a stream of white hot lava'. Flowers, even so, came into the affair. The gamekeeper's cottage was distinguished by the only wild daffodils in the area. When the inmate made love to her on a heap of dry wood, she had the 'grand experience' of 'wonderful rippling thrills and peals of bells'. The steady, silent gamekeeper then admired her ladyship's breasts, 'longish' breasts, according to Lawrence, while her naked skin looked 'faintly golden' like a 'Gloire de Dijon' rose. Nowadays, *Rosa* 'Gloire de Dijon' is somewhat prone to mildew. Afterwards, her ladyship went out naked into the garden and in the first version wreathed those longish breasts with honeysuckle. In the second version of the book, Parkin did it for her and even tucked some 'sprays of fluffy young oak' underneath them. I did not see honeysuckle at Renishaw in early June and I wonder how those oak-sprays stayed in place.

Both of the men in Connie's life were readers, albeit in different ways. Sir Clifford, master of Renishaw, was fascinated by the ancient Greeks, especially by Plato, at least in the novel's first versions. He thought the Greeks were 'sometimes like little boys who have just discovered they can think, and are beside themselves about it'. Thinking, however, was not what his wife wanted. Eventually, Sir Clifford matured from the thoughtful Greeks to material business and started to invest in the local mines. He threw his disabled energy into making them profitable, but his wife, like Lawrence, was horrified. 'A great portion of his consciousness seems to have lapsed, like a flower blown out. And what remained of him was this idolatrous ecstasy to the shrine of Money.' This mania for business struck Lawrence as 'the danger of the Greeks . . . They too had this mad egoism and the insane love of money.' It is not how the famous ancient Greek poets and orators present themselves, but they certainly knew how to make passionate love.

Igniting such passion in a lady was not the gamekeeper's only talent, either. He, too, was a man of unexpected range. As Connie looked round his 'bare little bedroom' in the morning light, at least in the text's later versions, her eye lit on a 'shelf with some books, and some from a circulating library. She looked. There were books about bolshevist Russia, books of travel, a volume about the atom and the electron, another about the composition of the earth's core and the causes of earthquakes: then a few novels: then three books on India. So! he was a reader after all.' When the thoughtful keeper moved away, he became a Communist in a factory.

When ladies say they are 'passionate gardeners', I think of Connie their patron saint planting those columbines in May, a fortnight before they would flower. There were pleasures evoked by Renishaw's gardens for which Sir George's 'evolutionary echo' was much more apt than he realized. As for the patron of thoughtful gardeners, he is not a lecturer in a college of landscape design. He is Parkin the gamekeeper carrying honeysuckle and 'fluffy' oak. 'If only she could stay,' her ladyship yearned, 'if only there weren't the other ghastly world of smoke and iron. If only *he* would make her a world.'

Peonies

What are gardeners gaining from the commercial openness of China? The great plant-hunters of the early twentieth century brought back trees, shrubs and bulbs from east Asia which transformed our plantings in the West. In the 1960s, while a thousand flowers bloomed under the pickaxes of the Revolutionary Guard, the gains for gardeners ceased. Since the 1980s matters have improved, as botanists returned to China and began to discover how much more remained to be introduced to gardens. The first collectors had focused on rhododendrons and other big shrubs, and as smaller plants were less popular with their patrons, these awaited a second wave of discovery. The risk to them is no longer revolutionary. It is the risk of industrialization which diverts water and then dynamites their mountains for stone and metals.

One natural Chinese family has long been known, but has been elusive for Western gardeners who want to acquire and cherish it. The tree peony has had the highest status in Chinese art and culture but until recently it has been difficult to find historic varieties in European nurseries. The most sought-after plant for connoisseurs has been a lovely white form with a dark central blotch on its big, ruffled flowers. *Paeonia rockii* was discovered in the northern mountains of China by the collector Joseph Rock, and its first growers emphasized how unusually tough it was in cold weather, drought and bug-infested gardens. Nonetheless, it almost disappeared from the trade. Ten years ago, my hands shook with excitement when I found two young plants of it in a cold frame in the middle of nowhere. The proprietor quickly took them away and hid them, insisting they would never be for sale. I hope they are setting buds, unscathed each spring.

Back in Imperial China, great peonies had had a restricted circulation too. Essentially, they gravitated to the Emperor's gardens where they were planted in special beds edged with polished stone, the sort of edging which is used in the West round graves in wonderfully vulgar cemeteries. In China, this polished edging was not the kiss of death. Civilized courtiers competed to grow peonies of their own and exhibit them in vast shows which were held in the capital at Luoyang. Spectators would sigh over the richness of the peonies as thousands bloomed in these shows and caused ordinary viewers to envy them as the privilege of the rich and good. Peonies were supporting items of class-superiority before history became a class struggle. As a result, they acquired a touching poetic symbolism. Most of us know classic Chinese poetry only through the romantic veil of Arthur Waley's translations, and I have to take his word for some of the great peony poems of the past. In the Tang era, about AD 890, while Britain was somewhat barbaric, a poet in China was comparing peonies with his lady love. 'My lover is like the tree peony of Luoyang', is how Waley renders his verse. 'And I, like the common willow. Both like the spring wind.'

The poets were not thinking of double-flowered herbaceous peonies, the forms of *Paeonia lactiflora* with names like 'Kelway's Glorious' which are such a stunning sight in late May for gardeners who take the trouble to stake them. Those forms have a different history which traces back to central Asia and the researches of a doctor at the Russian court. Instead, the great Chinese forms are Moutan peonies which grow into woody shrubs about four feet high. They should never be pruned like herbaceous varieties, but they are no more difficult to grow. They can be very long-lived, although in the trade they are grafted so as to give them an accelerated rate of growth. Sometimes, the graft breaks and the main Moutan dies but the fault is its initial grower's, not its own nature.

Where can we buy peonies with such a venerable bloodline? It is a splendid sign of changing times that several British nurseries now import young plants and list them in the *RHS Plant Finder*. Kelways at Langport in Somerset are traditional experts, joined by Binny Plants on the Binny Estate near Broxbourn in Scotland's West Lothian and a good list from Peony Passions at The Old School House, Bracknagh, Rathangan, Co. Kildare in Ireland. All of them cater for orders by post and even the seedsmen Thompson & Morgan offer a range of young tree peonies by mail. We can rush to book plants of the classic *Paeonia rockii*, three- to four-year-old specimens at only £14.99 each. The finest range of all is offered by Phedar Nursery, Bunkers Hill, Romiley, Stockport, Cheshire, who supply some of the best Chinese forms from Gansu province, offering them by mail order. Ultimately, the Chinese peonies still derive from trade sources in Luoyang where they have had such a history for more than 1,500 years, or from Heze in Shandong province which is still crucial for the export trade to Hong Kong and, eventually, to the West. More than 500 tree varieties are kept on sale in these Chinese centres, but only a handful of them have yet come the way of Western gardeners. The annual April peony festivals in these places are spectacular, although nowadays they are a trade fair, not a show of superiority by the upper class.

Chinese tree peonies have had a special relationship with British collectors but they grow very well in the gardens of Britain's European neighbours. On the Continent, an experienced source of the classic tree varieties is Pivoines Rivière at Drôme in south-west France. This nursery now lists up to a hundred different tree peonies, many of which grow well in the hotter climates of French and Mediterranean settings. In dry heat I fondly remember a fine show of tree peonies which I viewed imperiously from horseback in the gardens of the main public square in Ronda in southern Spain. They were lightly shaded by a canopy of tall trees, a reminder that they appreciate shelter in such hot settings and will then grow readily there too.

China's fine peonies also migrated rapidly to Japan, where they found another appreciative audience, this time two-legged. Japanese gardeners called them *bo-tan*, which sounds like Hollywood's version of suncream. The Japanese varieties are excellent garden plants, many of which have the most delicate flowers and again, they are now available from British suppliers in colours which range from shell-pink to the prized, but less subtle, yellows. As a general rule, a *bo-tan* with the letters 'ji' in its name tends to have ruffled double flowers, like the lion which the Japanese word for them signifies. They survive cold winters and ought to outlive us all.

Is there a blue peony out there somewhere? Like Luoyang peonies the thought has haunted Chinese collectors and lovers of women. I am not sure what to make of the idea. Sometimes I drift off to sleep, thinking of that 'last blue mountain barred with snow' which haunts all earthly pilgrims and ought to have blue peonies on its lower slopes. Then, I try to picture one and feel happy that we have found the blotched white rockii instead.

Corona's Imprint

Do owners imprint themselves on their gardens? In their lifetimes, of course they do, as gardening is an art and gardeners are artists who express themselves by what they place and plant. What happens when they die? Sometimes we visit locations which are still marked by the feeling of an absent personality. Their gardener seems to live on. What lies behind this feeling and where does it confront us? It is not ghostly or otherworldly. Gardening is a personal art and for a while it persists, even when its organizing mind is gone. At its best it leaves a sense of its creator, fading as time passes but recoverable for some time after a death. A garden does not acquire a new calm or peace when its owner is recently dead. Instead, there is a period of time when it is deserted and therefore quieter, impressing us all the more with its stillness.

An absentee's post-mortem imprint is best caught soon for reasons which are natural, not supernatural. Fine though the gardens still are at Sissinghurst in Kent, I do not think that they now give us an impression of the lingering presence of their makers, Vita Sackville-West and Harold Nicolson. Too much has had to change and adapt to the ever-increasing numbers of visitors. Gardeners who were most admired for their plants vanish even more quickly. I do not catch the recent presence of Margery Fish or E. A. Bowles in their gardens in Somerset or Middlesex. Too much has died out, although a charming white-flowered sorrel called *Oxalis* 'Bowles's White' still carries its planter's standard in his garden near Enfield.

Instead, I have a strong feeling of an absent presence in an Irish garden in County Carlow to the south-east of Dublin. For about

100 years the gardens at Altamont were fortunate in their family owners. Across two long generations the remarkable sequence of a father and daughter gave this exceptional site the planting and planning it deserved. Since 1999 there has been no heir but the gardens are kept up by four gardeners from Ireland's Office of Public Works. There have been deaths, inevitably, but the main features are so far intact.

By origin, Altamont is a very old garden. Its avenue of beech trees commemorates a community of nuns who once lived on the site and is as fine as only Ireland's beeches can be. In 1923 the owner, Fielding Lecky Watson, began to plant the grounds with shrubs and rhododendrons newly found in the Far East. He made a three-acre lake and surrounded it with ever finer camellias. He was a passionate expert and when his daughter was born he did not name a new rhododendron after her. Instead, he named her after his favourite rhododendron, 'Corona'. In due course Corona married Garry North, but Altamont remained her life-long devotion. Her father had had his big lake dug out by hand in order to give local employment during Ireland's years of depression. In wartime, Corona worked to save his legacy from encroaching weeds and lilies. She would row slowly across her father's lake while cutting away the jungle of weeds, helped by one elderly assistant.

I know her only through others' memories. Tall and blue-eyed, she was a lady with a genius for nature and I like to read that 'when her mother died aged 102, Corona finally moved into the big house'. Herself a widow, she was by then a legendary gardener, working for an apparently free effect which conceals her great skill as a sensitive planter. *Rhododendron* 'Corona' can still be seen in flower in her garden beside a variety which also does her justice, 'White Pearl'. She is remembered as a strong, exceptionally kind and talented lady. It was not only that she mowed her own acres of grass, milked the cows, lived on her own vegetables and dismayed Ireland by 'dying when she was only seventy-seven'. She had begun gardening in her early twenties and continued wholeheartedly until her death, leaving an imprint and an example of sensitive interaction with a place and its context.

Along the main view from its house, the garden at Altamont still has a long central avenue of clipped box with archways of yew whose shapes Corona restored and maintained while adding dense planting on either side. There are still the big, rare rhododendrons around the enchanting lake. Many of the best old roses still flourish, and against the grey stone walls of the house she planted pale pink-white species of rhododendron, including the lovely *triflorum*. The climate is mild enough to allow such Chilean treasures as *Olearia phlogopappa* 'Comber's Pink', and at lower levels she grew excellent scented daphnes, including simple *Daphne collina*. Without ever being too formal, she grouped the white-flowered *Primula pulverulenta* artlessly beside a path but if periwinkles in white and blue ran freely too, she did not interrupt them. She went on planting trees for years, including excellent varieties of oak and an entire meadow of mixed sorbus. Her choice of rhododendrons befitted a lady christened in their honour. She had the right soil for the best flowering cornuses, but it is a joy to meet them in informal clearings where the wild bluebells run beneath a light canopy of trees. The garden is enormous, and a bracing walk round it takes well over an hour, including a climb up a flight of a hundred steps, laid out by Lecky Watson with advice from William Robinson. Its boundary is the magical River Slaney, still a clear-flowing home for migrating salmon. Eventually, the walk circles round and branches off to Corona's most formal feature, a freestanding temple in the green landscape.

Her garden was her universe and she never planted at cross-purposes with it. Away from the house, the two long box-borders on the main axis are planted with sympathetic roses. Her favourite rose was the soft pink 'Celestial' with its grey-green leaves, a choice which helps engage me with her eye. Above all, the setting is Ireland. When she began, one of the only nurseries was Daisy Hill in County Down, which described itself as 'the only nursery in Ireland worth a button and the most interesting nursery probably in the world'. In her later years she and her garden owed much to their sensitive and dedicated neighbour, Assumpta Broomfield. Under Altamont's new Heritage Committee, there is a good nursery now in Corona's own garden, beside two densely planted borders in her memory, though they are not entirely in her style. Despite the divided command, the legacy of the garden's two creators seems unusually strong. From mid-May until mid-June, Altamont deserves a visit as a place with a special presence for thoughtful gardeners. It is given a singular wistfulness by the Irish quality of its gentlemanly house, seemingly left unoccupied in the ten years since Corona's death. I covet it in her wake. Undisturbed by visitors, I stood under a brick-orange *Rhododendron cinnabarinum*, a species brought newly to the garden by Lecky Watson in the 1920s. I then looked past his old camellias to the lake where lily leaves, reflecting the light, were being skated on by a family of ducklings. I thought of Corona, who saved this lake, and of her father and the workers who dug it and how, in a still magical garden, a deeply considered imprint survives its creators.

Digging In

The dead may imprint themselves on gardens, but so do living animals. I am about to apply for a licence to cull. I want to kill a new neighbour who has trespassed and wrecked the garden. He never gets up in the morning and he has amassed an unsolicited heap of rubbish. He is living only fifteen yards from my front door. I can hardly believe what I have to report. After two years of mutual warfare, a badger has built an extension to my house and is living with me.

Throughout the spring, chunks of the lawn went missing, as if somebody had been taking shovelfuls of twigs and rotting leaves. I was slow to realize that they had been piled up between my two prefabricated garages by a badger who had gone to ground. I can smell him but I cannot see him. When I leave for work he is snoozing and when I return to snore, he goes out on the prowl, digging pits in the lawn and rooting round the white-flowered viburnums. Recently, a lady author was interviewed in the *Financial Times* magazine and described herself as 'living alone with the sound of badgers'. I do not believe her. Badgers make no noise at night and only in my dreams do they snarl when disturbed. Scientific teams continue to report to parliamentary committees on whether to consider a cull on badgers because of the risks which they pose to cows. Once again, I beg them to consider the risk to gardeners. I am not bovine and I am not at risk from tuberculosis. My call for a cull is high-minded and horticultural. Badgers have destroyed my spring garden. They have dug up all the crocuses and have chewed up all the tulips. My bulbs now have to be grown in pots which are too high for their paws.

Naturally, I have asked experts at the Chelsea Flower Show but none of them has a clue what to do. One spokesman for wildlife even told me that I must strike immediately because badgers will undermine the foundations of a house and will cause a garden on a hillside to collapse. My badger will have its work cut out. To destabilize me he will have to dig down between two garages whose floors are solid concrete, laid by the village's former GP.

Here the moral menagerie makes its presence felt. My badger is impudent but is it not rather touching that he has had the nerve to choose to live with me? It is even more touching when you remember a badger's stripy habits. In spring, as I have explained, the younger members of a sett become restive and turn on the old boars. I presume they are tired of their conversation. They are fed up with being told to deliver 'teaching outcomes' and 'targeted care' by old boars who have done neither. My badger and I may be boars of a similar kind. The really penetrating question was put by a member of my family who asked if I had given my badger a name. I have, sort of. I tried 'Wedgwood' and 'Benn' and, for a while, 'Boycott' nearly sounded right. His present name is Howard because it suits his pattern of activity. Like Michael Howard, as described by a fellow Conservative MP, he has something of the night about him.

The tale of his arrival may not be quite so heart-warming. I have described how in spring I cleaned out the family medicine cupboard and as I had read that badgers in gardens are unhappy, I hid Prozac in lumps of peanut butter and put the lumps out on the lawn. Is my new friend an addict, hanging around the back door in the hope of another dose? Those to the left of centre refuse to believe this diagnosis. They are adamant that he has come from a failed sett and the only answer is to invade it. The trouble is that I am scared of the inhabitants. If my licence is approved by Defra it will have to be a licence for dogs, spades and a quick cull.

It may be relevant that I live in an old vicarage. Until recently I would simply have turned to Crockford's, that annual bible of ministers of the Anglican faith. You could find anything you wanted among the old-style clergy of the Church of England, except for a bishop who had officially come out. On Sundays, country vicars used to receive the skins of classified vermin from their parishioners and reward them according to a tariff published in the church porch. Badgers were rewarded six times more highly than rabbits. The tariff has gone nowadays, but I live just beside the church and I am sure the congregation would sing a specially adapted hymn for me. 'Brock of Ages . . .' ought to soothe a badger into benignity. In the past I could simply have turned to Parson Russell, a fellow student from Oxford who studied for the Church there in the 1820s. He bought a fine little dog called Trump from the local milkman and bred the badger-hunting terriers which still bear his name. We have one in the family but she has been reared within sight of London's parks and if it comes to an official cull, I will have to shut her in the car and let her watch until Howard is a carcass. I will then turn his skin into a bath mat, his bristles into shaving brushes and I will even consider roasting his haunches, because a reader in Somerset tells me that he used to eat roast badger at his village's annual badger-supper. It tastes like smoked ham, a chance for a Howard's End sandwich.

Am I being heartless? Again the moral menagerie thickens. Young thrusting badgers will never follow an old boar whom they have driven out to live on his own. At his age he has little hope of finding a mate, and as nobody seems interested in stripy partners in our newspapers' sections on Affairs of the Heart, I think I am safe from a disastrous mid-life litter. By keeping the old boar alive I am protecting myself from invasion by his previous partners in horticultural crime. While my garden is his bachelor territory, he will scare off the badgers who expelled him in the first place. I hate to admit it, but I feel I may have to leave him alone. I must be the only man in Britain who is still holding on to Howard for fear of something even worse.

Valerie Finnis

What makes a real gardener? It is certainly not soppiness about badgers. Is it patience or a strong back? Is it firmness of touch, precision and an even temper? An acceptance of the year's rhythms is important, as is a capacity for solitude at short notice. There are many elements but I think they should include a fondness for dogs and an amazing taste in hats.

These two qualities are confirmed for posterity in *Garden People: Valerie Finnis and the Golden Age of Gardening*, by Ursula Buchan, a classic record of great gardeners. Published in 2007, it remains an unmissable book, because it shows photographs taken by the late Valerie Finnis, one of the great gardeners of the past half-century. She was a superb photographer and her pictures have a humanity and eloquence which make them classics. Histories of gardening tend to focus only on the names who wrote most, spent most and made the most fuss, but Valerie Finnis's photographs are the defining record of sixty years of English gardening and the people who really knew what they were doing.

Valerie knew where to aim the camera because she understood the subject so deeply and recognized its true geniuses. She was also exceptionally helpful and generous to younger enthusiasts, as I know from my own experience. In 1964, aged eighteen, I wrote to her when I found her listed as the secretary of my local Alpine Garden Society. My request was not entirely normal. I wished to be appointed to the staff of the alpine section of the Munich botanical garden, which is recognized as the supreme alpine garden in Europe. We had never met, but Valerie wrote back at once and gave me the address of the garden's director, Wilhelm Schacht, a giant of a gardener who had even laid out a big alpine garden for the last-ever king of Bulgaria. She also wrote to him, so when an unsuspecting Schacht received his first-ever request for a job from a pupil at Eton College, he agreed. One reason, he later told me, was a mistake. He mistook the address 'Middleton House' on my family's writing paper for 'Myddleton House', the address of the famous plantsman and gardener E. A. Bowles. He also knew better than to say no to Finnis. A classic photograph in *Garden People* shows Schacht in typically sturdy stockings while focusing his camera tripod on one of the supreme rarities of the Dolomites. Beside him a picture shows the flower in close-up: the sky-blue *Eritrichium nanum* which has been called the king of all mountain plants. By taking these photos at high altitude, Valerie has immortalized the best of plants and the best of men.

Valerie Finnis was born in 1924 and died in October 2006. She loved plants from an early age, a fact which she always relished when she found it shared by other people. Her plant-loving mother, Constance, was a fundamental influence on her but it was in wartime that the young Finnis's future changed. She was sent to Downe House School near Newbury where she befriended one of the gardeners, who had trained at a ladies' college. On leaving school in 1942 she enrolled at her friend's former training ground, the Waterperry Horticultural School for Women near Oxford, under the direction of the inimitable Beatrix Havergal. I have met some unusual women in my life, from Ingrid Bergman to Iris Murdoch, but Miss Havergal is the most extraordinary. At Waterperry she founded, directed and dominated an amazing school for girls, the land girls and female gardeners of the future. Men were excluded. Miss Havergal would stand to command in her trilby hat, while a big stomach-girth held in her dark clothing. When she asked me as a boy to show her if I knew how to hold a trowel, she was wearing green woolly stockings and a green blazer. Fortunately I knew, and so I was treated to a plant in one of the clay pots which were deployed by the thousand in the garden's frames.

Miss Havergal maintained her school by selling the fruit and vegetables which her squadron of digging girls cultivated as part of their practicals. Lessons would stop when the weekly lorry arrived to pick up a load of produce for sale in Oxford and Covent Garden. Much of it grew in the Waterperry greenhouses which were heated and were the girls' responsibility to maintain, whereas the big schoolhouse was left unimaginably cold. In its dormitories, the young Pamela Schwerdt met the young Sybille Kreutzberger, beginning a relationship which has lasted for a lifetime. It was a crucial meeting for the history of British gardening. The two of them went on to work at Sissinghurst in Vita Sackville-West's lifetime and then took on the garden for the National Trust, raising it to the highest standards, so that it was admired by ever more visitors, who thought they were still seeing Vita's own plantings.

Through the Waterperry school Valerie Finnis began to meet the unsung heroes of gardening and, as her eye and skill became known, experts engaged with her on equal terms. Year after year she photographed them: men with their pipes and fox terriers and women with hats so unfashionable that they ought to be donated to *Vogue* magazine. A great lady grower of small bulbs was even photographed with her white Maltese dog sitting happily on the bulb-bed behind her. Such dogs seem to go quite often with gardening genius. So does a sharp, firm tongue but I disagree with Valerie's obituarist that she had 'a knack for engineering and enjoying spectacular fallings-out with people'. I would rather say that they were dramas which she vividly maintained. Her photographs include pictures of the strong-willed Miriam Rothschild, famous scientist, apostle of wild flowers and wearer of white Wellington boots even in her drawing room. In a memoir Valerie describes her as 'the greatest of all human beings, the kindest and the most courageous'. I confess to laughing, because I remember how in my presence she once compared Miriam to a 'bulldozer with a habit of pushing its front bucket into one's face'.

Oddly, the publishers of *Garden People* opted for a picture of the stylish Nancy Lancaster for the cover. She and Valerie were respectful friends, but as I used to garden with Nancy and enjoy her endless wit and sharpness, I asked her about Valerie and heard her describe her as 'all of a tizz'. There was a constant drama but it was Nancy who remarked of Valerie, then unmarried, 'I prefer my whippets to be mated.'

To her surprise, Valerie learned the whippets' lesson and suddenly married, aged forty-six, choosing another supreme gardener, Sir David Scott, who was already in his late seventies. Their friends look on their marriage as the greatest tribute to true love. David had had a sharp eye since boyhood for trees and shrubs, and to his excellent garden beside Boughton House in Northamptonshire Valerie brought an invasion of several thousand small hardy plants. He treasured them all just as he treasured her. Eventually he became confined to the armchair in his sitting-room where he sat, warmed by a blanket, with his copy of the supreme historian, Thucydides the Athenian, on the side table beside his right arm. We would discuss the events of the contemporary world and David would speculate how Thucydides would have analysed their course. Valerie, meanwhile, would set out into the garden, equipped with a long-range mobile radio whose volume, eventually, she learned to control. While David paused to consider Thucydides' view of the Falklands War, a second radio beside him would crackle into action and Valerie's voice would be on it, talking him through the sights of the day in the flowerbeds which they had planted together. 'Have the flowerheads faded yet on the xanthoceras?' he would ask her down the wire, and there would be a lull while she walked up to report on this fine, white-flowered shrub's progress on a south-facing wall. 'Of the gods, we believe, and of men, we know,' David would quote from Thucydides, 'that they rule wherever they can.'

'Twenty-eight flowers on the xanthoceras,' Valerie would report, 'with eleven more buds to come,' and images of the shrub they had planted would soften his bleak thoughts on world affairs, just as Valerie's photos of plants and gardens still soften the edges of a hurried world.

Taking Cuttings

Gardens are idealized, but as Valerie Finnis exemplified, basic gardening is in need of champions. Nothing is more basic than the propagation of garden plants and no champion has been more distinguished over the ages than Augustine, the Christian bishop and thinker. In one of his most civilized moments he wrote: 'Is there any more wonderful sight, any moment when man's reason is nearer to some sort of contact with the nature of the world, than the sowing of seeds and the planting of cuttings? It is as if you could question the vital force in each root or bud on what it can do, what it cannot and why.'

May to July is an excellent time to put Augustine's observations to the test. You may enjoy buying plants in a garden centre, but you are not a gardener who enjoys the full pleasure of the art until you have grown a new generation from your own stock plants. Cuttings are all around us, waiting to be taken and grown at no cost. Here are my six rules for easy entry into this useful skill. The first rule is never to buy a gadget unless you have to. The simplest accessory for the taking of cuttings is an array of empty plastic bottles which once held lemonade, cola and so forth. Cut off their bottoms and gather up some plastic flower pots over which the bottles can be placed like plastic hats. At no cost, you then have your own mini-propagator. When the plants root, you can take off the bottle cap and introduce them gently to fresh air and ventilation.

The second rule is to spend money on a suitable compost. There are endless possibilities here but for easy rooting I have come to trust the widely available J. Arthur Bower's pre-mixed compost for seeds and cuttings, to which I add white perlite to make up as much as 50 per cent of the total mixture's volume. Cuttings prefer an open compost which retains water and the perlite keeps the right texture. It does not decompose when the rooted cuttings are first planted into open soil, but this minor disadvantage does not outweigh its value as a retainer of water, lightness and openness in the soil mixture. I then water my mixture of soil and perlite and put it into small plastic pots. Square pots will sit closely together under a specially bought plastic hat, whereas round pots are best under plastic bottles. It is important to soak the dry perlite and compost thoroughly in advance and leave them to absorb water until the mixture remains slightly damp when squeezed. Do not put cuttings into a dry mixture and then try to water it afterwards, as the watering will dislodge the cuttings.

The third principle is to take a polythene bag whenever you go out on your prowls. You may be prowling at a lunch party with a keen gardening friend or abroad on a sunny holiday. Freezer bags are ideal companions, so I try to travel with a few in the car or my pocket. When you see a plant worth propagating, you can then cut pieces off, with permission if necessary, and put them at once into your personalized plastic holder, adding a few drops of water and sealing the bag. If sealed with water, the cuttings will stay fresh and firm for several days.

Many experts would say that the next rule should be the carrying of a very sharp razor blade or Stanley knife. Perhaps it should, but I have never armed myself as a horticultural teddy boy. A penknife or secateurs usually suffice for taking a strong young shoot off a healthy parent plant where it attaches to older wood. If you pull such a shoot downwards quite sharply, it will come away with a little strip or heel of older wood attached to it and this extra heel will often help it to root. If you are taking soft-stemmed cuttings off plants like dianthus, cut them just below a joint in the stem. Always take unflowered stems and cut as cleanly and sharply as possible so that you do not end up with an outer tube of stem, empty inside. When applied to smaller soft plants, secateurs tend to mash the stem on their lower 'anvil' blade. I see the point of carrying a razor blade for this job, but I am not deft or reliable with one.

The fourth rule is to put the cuttings into a plastic bag at once. Never let them sit in open air or sun, and seal the bag up as soon as possible to keep the maximum freshness. Eventually the bag is taken over to the pots of damp compost and perlite and the plastic bottles, bottom-free, which are waiting to cover them. Use a pencil to poke a hole in the compost which is deep enough to take about 40 per cent of your cutting's length. Take the cutting out of the bag and with a knife or other sharp weaponry, trim off all leaves along the length of stem which will be under or on the soil. Then put the cutting into the hole you have bored, making sure that it rests firmly on the bottom of the hole without an air pocket beneath. If possible, put the cuttings round the edge of the pot, close to the plastic walls, where they will root more easily. Make sure that the soil is very firm around them, adding more soil from a reserve heap of mixture if necessary: pull on the cuttings to test that they are sitting tightly and if they move, firm them in again. Surface the pot with some perlite for appearance and drainage and set a bottom-free bottle over the top of the pot, leaving its plastic cap screwed on. Stand the cuttings in a light, airy place in semi-shade where they will sweat and put a mist over the sides of the bottle. After a week or so you can lift off the bottle, wipe its walls and check that the soil is still damp. If not, add water very gently from a can with a fine rose on it and afterwards check that each cutting is still firmly in the soil. If the water is delivered too hastily it will dislodge the soil-mix and the cuttings. When you see signs of new growth from the tips or joints of a cutting, it is rooted. Unscrew the bottle-top to let a little air in and a few days later you can pot it on to an individual pot of Bower's compost without further perlite. It will grow away and fill its small pot with roots, soon reaching a size for which a nursery would be charging you £2 a plant.

The fifth rule is to begin by taking plants which root easily. Successes do wonders for morale and some of them will be unexpected. In July, hopes of success run high for rooting dianthus, or garden pinks, especially the old laced and striped varieties which make such elegant edgings. However, varieties vary widely in their willingness to root easily. After long experiment my own star is one which I used to name *Dianthus* 'Robin Lane Fox'. I thought it had come from crosses

I had tried in the 1970s, but I now find that it originates from a plant whose label I had lost and its real name is *Dianthus* 'Farnham Rose'. It has rose and white mottled flowers and is extraordinarily vigorous and willing to root. As the *RHS Plant Finder* now lists only two suppliers, it is worth buying a parent plant in the sure knowledge that anyone can turn a single plant into twenty more.

Other worthwhile snippets in late July come off all forms of lavender. If rooted in August, they will make good pot plants for planting out next spring. So, too, will the many varieties of mock orange, or *Philadelphus*, which have just finished flowering. Old plants are covered then in excellent new shoots for rooting, especially the lovely smaller variety 'Sybille' or the large and handsome *calvescens*, which is harder to find in the trade. Other June-flowering shrubs like weigela or kolkwitzia are also apt for cuttings at this same time.

The sixth rule, therefore, is not to be scared of trying cuttings from any shrub or herbaceous plant which sends out soft shoots from a hard central stem. I was surprised to discover that the golden-leaved scented *Daphne odora* will root quickly from cuttings taken in July at points where its growing tips connect to the previous year's growth on the stem. Ever since, I have had plants of this daphne at no expense while the index-cost of daphnes has far outperformed inflation. Young plants now cost as much as £18 in garden centres and even then are prone to virus. Instead, you can root half a dozen cuttings very easily from a disease-free parent in your own keeping.

The Prince of Wales thinks we should talk to our plants, Wittgenstein implies they 'say' things and Augustine wishes we could question them. Mundanely, I recommend being firm with them and keeping their cuttings away from fresh air and strong sunlight. If the good bishop had known about plastic bottles and freezer bags, he might have been even more impressed with the latent power of the natural world.

Mansfield Poke

Have gardening columnists ever been crucial to great literature or art? You would surely think not, unless you have watched one of the BBC's cultural showcases, its film of Jane Austen's *Mansfield Park* which is shown quite often in holiday seasons. It is so hard for fans of Jane Austen to be sure that they remember exact details of her work when the television tests their memory. At a crucial moment in this televised version, a gardening journalist arrives from London and causes great excitement by expressing a wish to write about recent changes to the owner's country garden. His visit precipitates a fine turn in the film's plot. Inside the mansion, the doors are opened upstairs and efforts are made to find the owners to tell them of this unexpected interest in their landscape plans. In one of the bedrooms, the searchers find something altogether more startling. The newly married lady of the house is caught in bed with the visiting bounder Henry Crawford, a suave young gentleman with a Cambridge education who has already been trifling with hearts on screen for more than an hour. Or so the television would have millions of viewers believe. Is it correct?

In the film version of *Mansfield Park* a gardening columnist unwittingly diverts the plot. In the novel whose title the BBC film so proudly bears there is no gardening columnist, no capture of a couple in the act. As always, Jane Austen proceeded more obliquely. Henry Crawford's bad behaviour was announced to the heroine only by letter and was reported as an elopement. Where, then, do the televised inventions stop? What about the startling TV scene in which the owner of Mansfield Park is shown throwing into the fire his sketchbook of black slaves? They are shown suffering tortures and dangling from ropes, but how many of us have read anything about that in the novel? Jane Austen's owner of Mansfield Park had estates in Antigua and in real life her father, a clergyman, was trustee of one such enterprise. In a fine scene in the book, the eighteen-year-old heroine Fanny Price complains that when she raised the topic of the slave trade after dinner on one occasion, the rest of the family was silent. Modern voices have been led by the indiscriminate Edward Said to pounce on this 'silence' about slavery. They even consider it to be political and insist it is a sign of embarrassment. In the text of *Mansfield Park*, it is nothing of the sort. The point there is that the rest of the family dislike serious conversation, although their father, Sir Thomas Bertram, would have liked to talk on the subject, awkward or not.

I have several objections to such televised travesties. The first is entirely ironic. Should we now allow for unmentioned activities by gardening columnists to explain undisclosed items in the plots of other great books we think we know? Did a gardening columnist from the *Petersburg News* first catch Vronsky in the act with Anna Karenin? Did a gardening columnist first warm up the French governess in old Prince Bolkonsky's garden in *War and Peace*? Is that why she fell into the arms of the suitor who had come for the hapless Maria? There is not only the matter of what film-makers put in: there is the important matter of what they leave out. How would viewers ever guess that the text of *Mansfield Park* contains a brilliant interplay of observations on that eternal question, the merits and stupidities of landscape gardening? The issues are still familiar: superfluous improvement at vast expense, designers' egocentricity, and the charms of an existing landscape. Typically, the smooth Henry Crawford claims to have designed his own park while still at school at Westminster and to have added a few touches while at Cambridge before he reached the age of twenty-one. The pretensions of such lavish 'improvements' and the hiring of designer-improvers have never been more sharply punctured than in Chapter six of Jane Austen's novel. She adds an outburst of petty jealousy, touched off in onlookers by the grandiose plans of would-be landscapers. Such rivalry is still with us, but Jane Austen attaches competitive cattiness to the merits of a variety of apricot called 'Moor Park'. Throughout, she implies much sympathy for leaving a well-settled house in the setting which it already has. 'I should not put myself into the hands of an improver,' says the Etonian Edmund Bertram, 'I would rather have an inferior degree of beauty of my own choice, and acquired progressively. I would rather abide by my own blunders than by his.' Competitive gardeners still have their 'Moor Parks' and their social rivalries about plants. Extracts from Chapter six should be printed in red and displayed on the banners at next year's Chelsea Flower Show.

Televisual outrage is also done to the sensibility of Fanny. What TV viewer would guess that Fanny is the first person in literature to realize that by 'passing March and April in a town' she had missed all the pleasures of spring? She lost what we all recognize, 'the earliest flowers in the warmest divisions of her aunt's garden, the opening of leaves on her uncle's plantations and the glory of his woods'. She admires the evergreens in the little wilderness which contains a walk around Mansfield's nearby parsonage. She is a cardinal character in the history of the enjoyment of gardens and it is gruesome that the BBC edited out this aspect of her. Predictably, the fox-hunting in the text is also suppressed. There is not a hint that Henry Crawford liked the sport (he was reduced, however, to three days a week) and that he earned affection by lending Fanny's brother one of his horses for a day with hounds.

The real *Mansfield Park* is a sharp observation of social diversity and its heroine retains a wise judgement and a stillness which many critics have overlooked. Why, then, should we be invited to watch it being violated? In an inclusive age, we are otherwise brainwashed to do verbal justice to any minority of the BBC's choosing. What, then, about the minority of single women who are obliged, like Jane Austen, to live with their brothers and sisters but who happen to give a large part of their life and energy to writing a masterpiece? We do not need a government minister to defend the good name of gardening columnists. We need a minister for authors. Thousands more people are studying English literature than ever before, and among reasons for allowing them to do so, I used to tell myself that a good reason is that their increased knowledge will be good for the future of literature and even for Britain's economy. As practised readers, these graduates will surely understand and do justice to our greatest national assets, the English books which are known and loved more widely across the world than anything produced from British schools of business. Instead, we have ended up with self-willed narcissists who rape the very books they feebly claim to be 'adapting'. Anyone is free to base their own fictions on a masterpiece of the past, but if so they must rename it. *Bridget Jones's Diary* claims to be based in part on *Pride and Prejudice*, but it has never thought of stealing that famous name. Gardeners need to compensate for this televised distortion by reading *Mansfield Park* for themselves. When the BBC screen their film in future, they should be more honest and change the title to *Mansfield Poke*.

Animal Mischief

Gardening in England in late spring is not only unpredictable for the half-hardy bedding. We never know what the weather will do to us. We also do not know what our furred and feathered friends will do next, those busy little sharers of our natural environment. I have had my fill of sprinting and shovelling badgers, but at least in summer there are no snowfalls to reveal the tracks of their animal bloodshed by night. In late May the only tracks are the ones which animals dig so deeply that they last through the night.

On the evidence of these tracks there is continuing mischief in my garden, but the latest round seemed to have begun as an untidy game. Eighty years ago, my long flat lawn was laid out for the noble sport of archery, in the days when its resident vicar took spiritual exercise in hitting a harmless target. On this green and pleasant land, he loosed his arrows of desire and so far as I know, he never hit a parishioner on the church path in the background. At three separate points on the archery-lawn which he laid out for sport, signs appeared recently of someone playing a different game: golf by night. I assume it was golf, because the players forgot to replace the divots. They left plantains and lumps of grass in heaps at three separate points, as if they had taken three separate shots at holing in one into the lilacs. Benignly, I replaced the divots and assumed that it was a round of animal putting. Animals, I believe, play golf like businessmen, except that they play off higher handicaps and make even more of a mess.

After two more nights of animal golf the divots became deeper and thicker and their replacement began to become a bore. At Chelsea Flower Show, I put the problem to experts but once again they were explicit and unhelpful. They told me that the holes were the work of blackbirds, who were digging for worms in the early morning dew. Perhaps there are super blackbirds in those experts' gardens, but they could never have dug holes so deep and round as those in mine. The digging then took on a clear pattern. At each of the three scuffle-points, a small area of scuffling on the surface was accompanied by two deep holes, dug about two feet behind the scuffle and spaced about a foot apart. The holes were becoming deeper, as if the digger was enjoying itself. It was not, I now realized, a game of golf: the answer was much more animal. The scuffle marks and holes were animal signifiers and made sense if gendered by the human eye. The scuffling was plainly the work of a female, mildly enjoying her activity. The spaced-out holes behind her were the foot-holes of a male who was plainly enjoying himself very much indeed. Not long ago, a famous female fund manager told me that her particular talent was anticipation. I asked her if she had anticipated anything special when she first met her husband. 'Yes,' she replied, 'I knew it was really animal.' Since mid-May it has been really animal on my lawn by the light of the moon. The female has scuffled patiently, while the male has discovered that if he digs his hind legs in deeply, he can greatly improve his leverage. Highly leveraged rabbits are not mentioned in my RHS dictionary of pests and diseases. One theory is that there are three pairs of them out there and nightly they take up position at the same three points on the lawn. My personal belief is more economical: there are only two rabbits at work, a heroic young buck and a consenting doe of his choice. He leverages himself up once, recharges while she patters over the next twenty yards and then leverages himself up twice more.

Whatever you may feel about his stamina, the leveraging has to stop. I have tried looking out at 6 a.m., but by then the animal activity is over. I cannot face waking up earlier to throw bricks at the couple while the garden is still dark. Garden centres offer a prevention, but it is beneath my dignity. It is a ferally-correct compound called Renadine, which is said to smell like a fox and to divert unwanted wildlife from its sphere. Unless I Renadine the entire lawn, I will merely displace the partners and encourage them to try their leverage elsewhere.

Those of us who have spent winters chasing the real animal cannot sink to putting artificial fox-scent onto lawns in summer.

Rapid action is needed for an obvious reason. One highly leveraged rabbit will soon lead to many little rabbits, each of whom will be taught that leverage is the route to their future happiness. No doubt they will come and repeat the lesson on my lawn. One Saturday, I resorted to the obvious answer: saucers of sugared milk, heavily laced with weedkiller. I considered using lettuce instead of milk, remembering how lettuce made Beatrix Potter's Flopsy Bunnies feel so soporific. The problem, I reckoned, was that the weedkilling glyphosate would scorch the lettuce leaves before anything could come and eat them. Unfortunately, it rained very heavily on the Saturday night of my initiative. Nonetheless the saucers of laced milk disappeared and Sunday evening was such an animal occasion that it suggested that even rain-diluted poison has a kick. Where there had previously been two foot-holes for a proper grip, there were now four, as if the female was digging in too. In one case I am sure that I counted six. It is wonderful what a cocktail of house poison will do for the nightlife of those who drink it.

I remember a correspondence with a dutiful civil servant in the 1980s when I complained in a gardening column that weedkillers are unnecessarily weak in garden stores and that agricultural chemicals are so much more effective. He defended the labelling and diluting of garden weedkillers on the grounds that the ordinary gardener could not be trusted with strong poison. You never knew, he said, what such a man might do: he might even give it to his wife. On the evidence of last weekend, I can see why a civil servant might be worried. After one saucerful of poison-enhanced milk, Mrs Rabbit starts digging in for better leverage, too.

Where do I go from here? A visitor scared me rigid by suggesting that the players are not rabbits: they are yet more badgers. Has Howard, my back-door badger, invited some young friends in for a stripy pyjama-party? It is no use telling me to set the alarm and use the shotgun. I will never wake up in time and I am much too worried about hitting my best delphiniums on the rebound.

Separate Beds on the Bay

To take the edge off this animal leverage I started to think about grand holiday gardening. It is not an extravagance which began only in the Hamptons. It did not even start on the French Riviera, let alone in Sottogrande. Its roots lie in the unsurpassed landscape of the Bay of Naples, where I went for a walk on the cliffs and found myself thinking about the past and ourselves, about nature and culture and how our ideas of a garden have changed.

The great gardeners on the Bay were ancient Romans, especially the rich and grand contemporaries of the aspiring Cicero in the first century BC. It is no use looking for their gardens along the shores of the modern bay. From the few ruins which remain, you would never guess the scale of their achievement. The best place to begin is in the National Archaeological Museum of Naples, where wall paintings from the region give a better idea of the Romans' capacity for elegant fancy. At first sight, they seem much like the leaders of our age of landscape excess. They undertook gigantic assaults on nature. They built into cliffs and founded densely pillared houses on man-made jetties or on flat promontories levelled from the rocks. Their houses were open to the sun and wind and, at their best, had curved and angled façades. Their designs would still set a fashion on island resorts in the Mediterranean.

I enjoy looking at pictures of these houses in the Museum, but in order to enter their world, we have to read and use our imagination. Our knowledge of Roman gardens depends above all on the letters and poems which were written about them. As I looked across the bay I chose as my couple of the moment a married pair of well-off Romans who were celebrated in florid Latin poems. The poems' author was the admired Statius, who was himself a resident of the Bay of Naples in the latter part of the first century AD. In flattering language he praised the gardens of a couple who had no doubt paid him to praise them, Pollius Felix and his wife Polla. I suspect that Polla paid for the poems because Statius praises her for her youthful grace. At the time she was aged about forty, so some of our aspirations never change.

We can still enjoy a little adventure to find the site where the couple seem to have lived. Their garden is gone but local Italian place names preserve its memory on the road beyond modern Sorrento. The best directions are given in my personal bible, the *Blue Guide: Southern Italy*. Take the road towards Massa Lubrense and head out towards the tip of the Bay of Naples which points in the direction of nearby Capri. There is a marina there whose Italian name derives from Pollius' name, and from there on, you need the *Blue Guide*'s route.

If you read between the lines of Statius' poem, the couple seem like ideal readers of a modern weekend newspaper. Pollius is not short of money. He has had an active life on the council of his local town and is now retired, though the reasons for his retirement are unspecified and may not be entirely of his own choosing. He has taken up poetry, much as retired persons nowadays take to courses in creative writing. He likes to be thought of as a philosopher but not in a strenuous way. He would enjoy the modern books by Alain de Botton. Pollius was an undemanding Epicurean who tried to rise above the ebb and flow of life, and perhaps he succeeded. He did not believe in hell, and he would not take papal edicts on the subject too seriously nowadays. He certainly made a suitable second marriage, because Polla shared his literary interests and appears to have been the daughter of a man who had made a fortune in banking. A rather crude translation of her second name, Argentaria, would be 'Moneypenny'. She is even praised, intriguingly, for keeping a portrait of her first husband over her bed. Pollius was not bothered by it, no more than are those good second husbands who put up with photographs of their predecessor nowadays. It even seems that Polla's first husband was much more famous than Pollius, her second one. First time round, she had married the admired Roman poet Lucan, but he died at the age of twenty-six. It is fun to imagine Pollius and Polla's bedroom, but behind all Statius' flattery I think I catch a hint that in older age they had called a truce and opted for separate beds.

Instead, their energies went into the house and garden on a sheltered sea-cove. From afar, their house looked as if it had a thousand roofs and as if it had been drilled into the face of a resistant cliff. Up to it ran a colonnade which 'creeps zig-zag through the heights, a city's work, mastering the rugged rocks with its lengthy spine'. There were rare marbles all over the house which they had shipped in from Greece and let into the floors or left to glitter as columns. They had even built a vineyard where the cliff met the sea, and in it sea-nymphs were said to enjoy picking the grapes in autumn. How little we change, you might be thinking, but I am not so sure. Visitors to this seaside home were most impressed by the pair of heated bath-houses whose steam rose in clouds on the beach. These houses needed a heavy diet of brushwood and fuel which was cut and supplied by household slaves. The slaves would shock us and ecological gardeners would scowl nowadays too, because the time has passed when saunas were somehow thought 'natural'. Curiously, too, there is no praise in Statius' poems for any of the surrounding flowers. Nor is there emphasis on the natural flora of the local landscape. Instead, Statius' verses congratulate the couple on turning a dry and thirsty cliff into an exotic villa. To correct the picture, I walked down a neighbouring cliff and thought how much they had missed.

On an hour's walk downhill to yet another ancient villa on the bay I found the items which no Roman poet mentions: the last of the blue-flowered grape hyacinths, the first of the wild orchids and several good clumps of local white *Allium neapolitanum*, an easy-growing white-flowered bulb which enjoys a light soil in English gardens. Off-white irises were happy among the rocks and there were dozens of yellow-flowered broom bushes. Between the stones of a shaded wall, there were wild lessons for English gardeners. Hundreds of plants of the little *Cyclamen repandum* were showing their rose-pink flowers and the heart-shaped leaves which are so attractive. The lesson is that this particular variety is happiest out of direct sun and will flower very well in a sheltered wall. Of course there was dark-blue rosemary, yellow sun roses and plenty of myrtle and cistus. In such company, I decided that the owners of the ancient Roman villas were sadly unappreciative of their micro-landscape.

Nowadays we keep a more open mind and carefully cultivate wild flowers. Our bath-houses are not heated with trees from the hillsides and we do not buy and sell slaves. Across the centuries Pollius and Polla seem close to us but from a modern point of view, they have their blind spots. I admire them for that picture of a former husband above their bedsteads, but I doubt if Pollius ever picked a bunch of wild irises and put them on the table beside his wife's bed.

Ways With Wisteria

The end of May sees the end of a clear phase in each English season. From now on, it is time to change the bedding, stake where applicable and try to do battle with ever-present weeds. There are compensations as the season turns: azaleas and rhododendrons on acid soils and wisterias on soils of every type. If you have failed to do the wisteria justice in your garden, you need the first-class guide *Wisterias* by Peter Valder. It was first published in 1995 by Timber Press in America and quickly reached its fourth reprinting. It deserves to be widely read in Britain.

Valder and I disagree on one cardinal principle which he states very clearly: 'Wisterias are almost impossible to kill.' In 2002 I planted eight grafted wisterias, four of which have died. Nobody knows why, as they are all in a similar type of soil. I would blame their grafting, except that they died with the grafts apparently intact. There is no sign of disease, no coral spot or fungus. Vigorous Chinese varieties survived, but others like 'Caroline' and *floribunda* 'Black Dragon' died after only four good years.

In British gardens, the American wisteria tends to be written off as inferior. Thereafter, tastes divide: do we want a Chinese form or a Japanese one? Anyone who looks at an amazing black-and-white photograph from Japan which Valder reproduces will vote for the Japanese. On 6 May 1914 the great plant-hunter E. H. Wilson photographed a forest of poles on which long bunches of Japanese wisteria were flowering as if on pleached trees about eight feet above the ground. This sort of canopy has not been widely imitated in Britain where gardeners think of wisteria tunnels and arches. In Japan, families used to build special terraces for wisteria-viewing, and associated themselves with the exceptional beauty of the flower. Japanese artists represented the long bunches of flower with exquisite skill on early painted scrolls. In China, by contrast, there seems to have been less enthusiasm for the wisteria in early poetry or in art. Recent travellers to China, however, have found spectacular specimens of wisteria growing through the mature trees in temple gardens or spreading sideways over bare ground on lightly cultivated hillsides.

Despite E. H. Wilson's photography, my vote goes to the Chinese varieties. When I planted climbers for four distinctive metal arches, made to resemble gigantic tiaras, I put Chinese wisterias on either side. They rapidly met in the middle, touched tendrils and flowered their heads off, justifying their name of *Wisteria sinensis* 'Prolific'. By contrast, Japanese varieties have very long trusses of flower and although they are recommended as the glory of an average pergola, the flowers on many forms sold in Britain are pale and washy and lack the density and vivid colour which make the Chinese varieties so good. Many gardeners have been saddled with inferior wisterias, raised from seed and distributed round the trade, so it pays to buy a named and guaranteed variety. Valder's book discusses all sorts of named varieties and, in the Chinese section, recommends the darker colour of 'Amethyst' and the wonderful strength of flower on 'Prolific' (which he calls 'Consequa'). The latter, he rightly remarks, is one of the 'great garden plants of all time' when firmly controlled in the space available. Proper control of Chinese wisterias involves the removal of long, weak shoots throughout the growing season and the cutting back of each new shoot to two or three leaves at its base, instead of cutting it out altogether. The weeks after flowering are the best time to attack a Chinese wisteria and keep it within bounds. Bad pruning is a main reason why it may refuse to flower well.

On the Japanese side of the family, the most sensational form is *Wisteria floribunda* 'Macrobotrys' (or 'Multijuga', its latest botanical name). The length of its bunches of flower differs according to season, site and the age of the plant. At its best it is unforgettable. It is highly vigorous and Valder would rate beside it the exquisite white-flowered 'Shiro-noda', which has the particular merit of flowering late. In Britain, therefore, this white wisteria is at less risk from spring frosts. It is one of the four wisterias which have survived life on my tiara-arches, but botanists now name it *Wisteria floribunda* 'Alba', grouping several white-flowerers under this name. These Japanese varieties should be pruned hard, too, when they have finished flowering. A further tidying is then needed in autumn. If you do not already have a wisteria, you might try to imitate a lovely effect which is best seen in south-east Asia. Plant one near an established tree or informal hedge and let it climb to the top without regulation. On the sunny side, it will flower very freely and give years of pleasure. A hedge of feathery Leyland cypress will never look better than in a mantle of vigorous wisteria.

Summer

Half an hour later Nikolay Petrovich went into the garden to his favourite arbour. His thoughts were gloomy. For the first time he recognized how far he and his son had grown apart [. . .]. 'My brother says, We are right,' he thought, 'and setting all vanity aside, I do myself think they are further from the truth than we are, but at the same time I feel they have something which we don't, some advantage over us . . . Youth? No, not just youth. Doesn't their advantage lie in their being less marked by class than we are?' Nikolay Petrovich sunk his head and rubbed his face with his hand. 'But to reject poetry?' he thought again. 'Not to have a feeling for art, for nature . . . ?'

And he looked around him as if trying to understand how it was possible not to have a feeling for nature. Evening was now coming on. The sun had gone behind a small aspen wood which lay a quarter of a mile from his garden and cast its seemingly unending shadow over the motionless fields [. . .] Swallows were flying high; the wind had dropped; lingering bees lazily, sleepily buzzed on the lilac blooms; a column of moths danced above a single protruding branch. 'My God, how beautiful it is,' thought Nikolay and some favourite lines of poetry were about to spring to his lips when he remembered his son Arkady, the book Stoff und Kraft [which the boys had praised], and fell silent. He continued to sit there and continued to indulge in the pleasurable, melancholy sport of solitary reverie. He liked to dream – living in the country had developed that propensity in him.

Ivan Turgenev, Fathers and Sons,
translated by Peter Carson

In his unsurpassed guide to gardening, *Your Garden Week By Week* (first published in 1936, last published 1992), the expert Arthur Hellyer began 'General Work For June' with the instruction, 'Spray Against Pests'. The battle persists and even more pests are arrayed against us, including the recent leaf miner on horse chestnuts which I discuss in this section and badgers and highly leveraged rabbits in the wrong place, on both of which I have expressed new views. Even so, spraying is the least of amateur gardeners' worries. Nowadays summer begins with bedding-out, slides into dead-heading and looks best in August if thoughtful choices prolong the garden's season. June and early July are the easy summer months because roses fall everywhere and love the British climate. I can only select a few of the best here, but I profit from the longer season which well-chosen climbing roses allow, beginning with the fine mauve-pink 'May Queen' and running on into late July with the usefully late 'Paul's Scarlet Climber', worth a place for its delayed season of flower. The art nowadays is keeping up a garden's momentum from mid-July until October, months in which many of the gardens in Britain which open to the public are revealingly closed.

Well-established bedding plants remain colourful until the frosts, but the trick is to establish them smoothly when they first go out. Gardeners with automatic irrigation are not bothered by dry Junes, but the rest of us expect to be watering the new bedding during its first weeks outdoors. From the start I include a dash of artificial fertilizer in the water, beginning with the seaweed-concentrate Maxicrop at half strength. Many annuals grow on poor soils in nature, but they are twice as good in cultivation if they are fertilized every ten days or so. Plants in big pots are especially responsive to this treatment, for which I use the simple diluter from Phostrogen which fits on to the end of a hosepipe, takes in powdered fertilizer and releases it, diluted, as the water passes through its receptacle on the way to water the plants. Watering and fertilizing are thus easily combined.

If dead-headed, the bedding repeats and persists for months. I have devoted one chapter to dead-heading here because it is the essential job in mid-July when other, thoughtless gardens start to go over. Gardeners now have a superb new pair of hardy geraniums, 'Rozanne' and the spreading 'Jolly Bee', which are two necessary plants for every garden, large or small. They flower all summer in a fine combination of mid blue and white and are incomparably the best hardy varieties on the market. They need dead-heading, but not as acutely as all their sprawling relations which are so often recommended as the busy gardener's best friends. Geraniums like pink *endressii*, tall *psilostemon* and all the blue forms of × *magnificum* need to be ruthlessly cut back after flowering, so as to reduce them to their central crown of roots and young leaves. I take barrowloads of debris out of the borders in mid-July and notice how many other gardeners do not.

With the debris out of sight, the eye fastens on clearly coloured perennials from mid-July until autumn. I emphasize in this section the important progress made with agapanthus, but I could say the same of crocosmias in reds, yellows and oranges and even the lovely monardas which used to be sadly short-lived. Crocosmias have turned out to be hardier than expected from their South African origins and many, but not all, will come safely through a frosty winter in open ground. The yellow × *crocosmiiflora* 'Norwich Canary' flowers freely in an excellent shade of clear yellow and the tall, dark red 'Emberglow' is also generous with its striking flowers. There are many intermediate shades, of which red-yellow 'Severn Sunrise' and the fine × *crocosmiiflora* 'Debutante' are particularly good. Crocosmias like full sun, but they also like plenty of water in their growing season, even when they are planted in quick-draining soil.

The improvement of the monarda is excellent news. For years I have wistfully remembered them, not because their native name is bergamot but because they looked so good in gardens in the cooler north of England which I remember from my youth. They always flowered well in their first season and spread into a mat of roots. They brought a fine range of pink, purple-red and deep red flowers to the centre of planned borders at a height of about three feet. The problem was that they lasted for only two or three years. Their weakness was caused by mildew, which attacked the leaves after flowering and was so debilitating that I gave up on the family. Recently, new mildew-resistant forms have been bred and proved their worth in wet summers. 'Squaw' is an excellent strong red and 'Violet Queen' is self-explanatory. These new monardas are robust plants and change the colours with which we can safely play.

These colours, I think, should be restricted to a few, clear tones in particular parts of a border. One-colour beds are boring and there is no need in summer, either, to be bound by the dogma of that 'colour wheel'. Remember Nancy Lancaster and her remark that 'in time, you'll begin to like anything with anything'. I like white, blues and pale yellows in one bed or scarlet-red and white in another ('blood-and-bandages' to fussy flower-arrangers), or in another, shades of burnt orange and yellow shading into each other with occasional spikes of purple-blue *Salvia* × *superba*. In a long border, it is worth repeating a striking patch of colour at intervals down the bed so as to draw a spectator's eye down the full length of it. In a smaller garden or section of a garden it is worth dotting around individual plants of one and the same bold colour so as to give the whole picture a similar highlight. Personally, I exclude rose-carmines and muddy rose-purples, but otherwise I ban nothing, merely limiting particular groups to particular shades, if possible. Too much precision in colour-planning goes wrong nowadays because the weather is so unpredictable. If you try to follow Miss Jekyll's principles of 'colour grading', in which strong colours are carefully approached through paler related shades, the chances are that an early, sunny season will cause all the wrong flowers to open at the wrong times. The academic colleague who asked me if 'all the flowers had been the right colour' was addressing a subject on which I have learned that firm rules merely break down.

Irises on Drugs

Fifty years ago, the thinker and novelist Aldous Huxley stared at a bunch of flowers on his desk and described them in words which many a middle-aged corporate financier would prefer to deny having read in his youth. A purple iris seemed to him to be shimmering with the beauty of eternal life. In his essay *The Doors of Perception*, Huxley described his experience. He had seen 'what Adam had seen on the morning of his first Creation, the miracle moment, the moment of naked creation'. Huxley was out of his mind, having swallowed pills of mescaline, the hallucinatory drug.

Thanks to this class A substance, Chemical Aldous believed that even old Plato had been wrong. Plato, he said, had separated Being from Becoming and had reduced it to an abstract mathematical Idea. In Huxley's view, 'Plato could never, poor fellow, have seen a bunch of flowers shining with this light, all but quivering under the pressure of the significance with which they were charged.' An ordinary purple iris struck him as a 'scroll of sentient amethyst'. Actually, Huxley was the one who was wrong. He was wrong about Plato. He was wrong about the rest of us who look at irises without the help of pills. He is refuted every year in the grounds of my Oxford college garden. He is also refuted by a significant moment which occurred to me in the open air in Paris.

To take Plato first. It is far from clear that Plato would have denied the help of intoxication in order to ascend towards his ideas of higher being. Ideas, however, were divinely beautiful, certainly more beautiful than Chemical Aldous's perception of an iris. On reading his book Plato would have wondered whether Huxley had really approached the ideal Form of an iris, and he would have been sane enough to tell him that he was under distorting influences. So far from seeing more truly, Huxley was out to lunch.

My college garden contains a different lesson. In late May tall bearded irises shimmer down its long borders. It has taken years to build them up, the vibrant yellow *Iris* 'Starshine' which I first saw at Chelsea in 1963, the superb violet-black 'Sable Night', which I owe to the former owner of Scotts Nursery in Somerset, and a fine blue called 'Big Day' which flowers with extraordinary freedom. I doubt if Huxley had ever concentrated on a garden plant before he took his pills. Those who take time to contemplate flowers and plants see as much vibrant beauty as was induced by drugs in his unpractised eyes. It is one thing to see an iris and quite another to contemplate it. Try looking long and hard and spare yourself Huxley's flourish about Adam and Creation. Without it you can apprehend the exceptional beauty and changing grace in these lovely flowers.

In Oxford, we give the drugs to the irises and we like to think that we keep them away from their spectators. On sunny afternoons, those spectators are undergraduates on the lawn, furtively throwing frisbees against a backdrop of iris-beauty. You may wonder if this audience is chemically neutral, but the beauty of the irises exists independently of them. In Oxford, irises owe their beauty to chemical maintenance, not to the chemical enhancement of their viewers.

At the height of the iris season, I verified this point in the great collection of irises in the Parisian garden at Bagatelle on the edge of the Bois de Boulogne. In the mid-May of the fiftieth anniversary year of Huxley's drugged enlightenment, I found myself on a Sunday morning in a garden of pure irises with a beauty which his pills had not been needed to simulate. Behind a hedge and a high wall, Bagatelle's display garden shows a superb collection of modern irises which flower at their best through careful cultivation. While I visited, elderly French couples in grey suits and dark skirts were walking critically between the beds, dressed as if they themselves would never touch a sprinkling of garden compost, let alone a hallucinogenic pill. Together, we wondered at the beauty of the collection, noted down the best varieties and quietly contemplated the display. In Paris, the winners are not irises with French names. 'Rive Gauche' is too fluffy, the one called 'Paris, Paris' is too orange and 'Vin Nouveau' is not the best of dark purples. The winners come from other breeders, most of whom are active in America. 'Dardanus' is an exquisite shade of lemon-yellow, and there cannot be a better sky-blue than 'Proud Fortune' with tall stems. Primeval beauty was all around us, whereupon it began to rain.

At the first drops, the urban French viewers headed for a distant shelter. The rain became a heavy storm, but I continued contemplating in lone contentment until I saw a small group who were doing likewise at the far end of the garden. The irises glowed, Huxley-like, in the rain, and their only other spectators turned out to be English visitors led by the property manager from England's finest garden, Sissinghurst. Ignoring the rain, we compared notes and impressions. How, I asked her, did she bring the best out of the irises at Sissinghurst, many of which are old varieties but which light up the garden in June?

Mescaline does not come into it. Down at Sissinghurst, they put the irises on Dolo Dust every four or five years. This class D substance is powdered limestone from pure Dolomite rock, and is generally available through horticultural wholesalers. On the heavy soil in Kent, they find that irises respond to this extra dressing of grit and lime. Some of the best varieties at Sissinghurst were planted in the very spring when Huxley was playing with drugs, but their beauty has outlasted his perceptions.

In Oxford, we turn on the irises with a well-known dust called Growmore, applied in spring and readily available in garden stores. Huxley, by contrast, described his pills as 'objects of unique distinction', a phrase which government rhetoric now applies to my university colleagues before driving the best of them abroad. Fifty years on, the moral of these observations is simple. Take time, contemplate an iris as bold and beautiful as 'Starshine', and anyone can see a glowing beauty which suspends time and enhances their idea of the natural world. Huxley had his priorities in reverse. The student-spectators are the ones to be kept off chemicals. The irises should be given the drugs instead. Give Dolo Dust to the irises and a wake-up call to the young. Then, stand together and contemplate the consequences of chemical action in the flowerbed.

Six of the Best

After the irises, the high season begins for roses, brought forward by warmer seasons. Perish the thought, but suppose that you only had room for six roses, with another two or three on the walls of a moderate house. At least the restriction would stop you from massing all your roses into one long border, which is never the easiest way to display them. A rose border becomes a tangle and looks wretched in the off-season. It is better to space out a few varieties, stake them carefully and show them off in their profusion.

Which roses would you choose? I am thinking only of older varieties or varieties with an old-fashioned shape to their flowers and a more generous style as shrubs. My two personal winners have remained in the lead for years against all comers. One is the silver-pink 'Fantin Latour', which is a superb rose for spacing down the middle of a mixed border. It can be pruned hard so that it stays relatively upright and it can be clothed with a viticella clematis to give a second season of flower from August onwards. It has no connection with the great French painter of roses, except that his name was given to it in the 1930s by a great English lover of old roses, Nancy Lindsay. We still do not know how or where this miraculous rose originated.

Among the whites, its equal is the equally mysterious 'Madame Hardy'. Its thickly petalled white flowers are folded towards an enchanting central eye of green and the whole flower is scented. Perhaps 'Madame Hardy' is slightly more vigorous than 'Fantin Latour', but it, too, can be fitted in anywhere. It was first recorded back in 1832, and its pedigree is unknown. It has wonderfully fresh green leaves, better than so many old roses', and it has unusual strength on poor, dry soil.

It is a mistake to think that old roses are all big bushes, an idea that encourages those unfortunate borders of roses and nothing else. One of the best for strength and a second season in autumn is the pink-flowered 'Jacques Cartier', which can be pruned and kept to an easy height of about three feet. It grows equally well in dry conditions and its second season of flowers in autumn makes it a first choice for any restricted collection. Its close relation, 'Comte de Chambord', has even fuller and larger flowers, but is slightly less abundant and less willing to flower freely again in autumn.

Stripes and spotting on rose petals are particular fascinations among older varieties, although some of the most vividly striped forms are not easy to keep in good health. The most reliable remains the proven old 'Ferdinand Pichard', which is usually capable of a second crop of flowers in September. Most of its dark rose-red flowers are heavily marked with white and the leaves are a good dark green which stays relatively healthy. 'Ferdinand Pichard' will reach about five feet and is particularly good if supported on three or four strong stakes, pushed well into the ground around it. The long shoots can then be propped or tied on to them to encourage the flowers to stand well clear of the ground.

The most beautiful deep reds among the older varieties are seldom the easiest to keep in good health, and here I would look sideways to *Rosa* 'Geranium'. This hybrid rose (a cross with *R. moyesii*) turned up in Britain in the late 1930s and shows a clear shade of red on its single flowers. Their shape looks as if it has come from an old tapestry and they are followed by brilliant red hips in autumn, which are as bright as a second flowering. 'Geranium' has pretty, light green leaves and a rather upright style of growth to a height of about eight feet. It is a good shrub for a site on its own, perhaps beside the edge of a drive or in isolation against a dark evergreen background.

Shades of pink span a wide range in older roses. I have become fond of the lilac-pink flowers on 'Vick's Caprice', a rose which originated in the 1890s in America and remains an easily managed bush of about three feet with a long season of flower. For the middle-to-front of a big mixed border, a bush or two of the exquisite pinkish-white 'Juno' would also be a classic choice. 'Juno' arches naturally and reaches a height and spread of about four feet, whether or not it is supported on canes. It combines well with almost any border plants in June and is extremely easy to grow.

Perhaps you know and grow these roses already and want one which is less familiar at an odd season. The drier and poorer the conditions, the more I appreciate the pedigree and stamina of particular roses which were bred in America in the 1930s or earlier. The breeders knew that their roses had to survive a tougher life than those in more favoured parts of Europe. Back in 1843, one of them bred a healthy small-flowered climber with clusters of pale and very double cream-pink flowers and called it 'Baltimore Belle'. It is one of those excellent climbers which reaches its best when other roses have faded. It is extremely strong and obliging, but it is seldom seen now, after 150 years on the market. Perhaps there are still a few 'Belles' down in Baltimore, but this child of the 1840s is outstanding up a wall to a height of twelve feet or more.

Lastly, the long-running companion of my life with climbing roses: the heavy-scented 'Climbing Lady Hillingdon,' which has a purple flush to her stems. The flowers are a strong apricot-yellow, the scent is a strong scent of tea, and I have learnt to forgive her ladyship's one failing. In hot weather, 'Lady Hillingdon' does not hold her head up but allows her flowers to droop as they age. Only recently have I discovered her excuse. It was Lady Hillingdon, nearly a century ago, who remarked that she 'shut her eyes and thought of England' whenever Lord Hillingdon began to make love to her. Maybe we will discover a robust red rose in honour of his lordship but meanwhile her ladyship bows her head with her back to the wall in grateful gardens up and down the land.

Head for Herterton

As the old-fashioned roses fade in early July, the north of England is still behind the south. It is there that I have found a haven after the roses, a heavenly English garden which is not unduly big. There are no gardeners except its devoted owners, whose vision it is, their long-pursued aim for more than thirty years. It has not cost a fortune. While other gardeners have been rushing between Chelsea Flower Show and the latest garden centre, Frank and Margery Lawley have been selling home-grown plants to their garden visitors and keeping the weeds off their paths of sand and grit. The *RHS Garden Finder* calls their work a 'modern masterpiece'. I have had the honour of a descriptive tour with the masterminds themselves and as a result I understand so much more than has been written about their work.

Herterton House is a small farmhouse in Northumberland, leased from the National Trust, about twenty-five miles north of Newcastle upon Tyne. The neighbouring village is Cambo, birthplace of the great eighteenth-century landscape gardener Capability Brown. Frank Lawley remarked to me that Capability Brown's descendants are still nearby, but nowadays they are growing leeks. Meanwhile, the Lawleys have been drawing, planting and working their hearts out. Their garden is scarcely an acre big but it falls into four well-proportioned sections. It has no grass area to be mown but it is patterned with harmonious paths which make one forget about lawns. The surfaces are not hard or brutal, as many modern designers would have made them. They have been built up from about a foot's depth of farmers' hardcore, laid by hand and recorded in the photos of the garden's early creation which are preserved in its hand-built gazebo. This core was topped with a mix of dark reddish sand and fine grit from a nearby river and then packed hard and flat. The mixture avoids the mistake of the paths at the National Trust's nearby property Wallington, where yellowish shingle glares at visitors down some of the views. 'How do you manage to poison the weeds?' I asked, as ever inorganic.

'We don't,' Frank replied. 'We never let them start.'

I did not see a start-up weed during my attentive visit.

The first section of the garden is the nursery, where stock plants are grown in long, narrow beds. Reserve stock is dug up from the rich river-soil and sold too when the pick of the day has sold out in the main garden hut. The soil is a lesson to us all. The Lawleys inherited no garden, only a bare farmyard. They laid out their masterplan on paper and waited four years before planting anything. Meanwhile they improved their soil, using rich loam from the nearby rivers, including the poignantly named River Hartburn. To one side of the house, they then laid out a physic garden with small formal beds and herby planting. Its central feature is a formally clipped silver pear and the low edging to each bed is a small form of pink-flowered London pride, probably *Saxifraga* 'Elliott's Variety'. This little garden is pretty and has a good pink Rose 'Great Maiden's Blush' beside it, but it is not the garden's tour de force. Nor is the separate section of garden which fills the space between the house and the small public road, although its main planting cleverly uses topiary yew and box, clipped in the shape of hens, using silver-variegated box to suggest speckled hens. There is something curiously satisfying about the greenery on the far bank of the road here. It, too, has been landscaped, using the unusual variegated woodrush as if it was a wild flower, broken up by architectural plants which are spaced at irregular intervals.

Throughout the flowering seasons, the section of the garden behind the house is the central masterpiece. There is something uplifting and satisfying about the tall greens and trees which frame it. The beds fall into four little bands, with a formal pattern of tall box which hedges them off. I found myself ticking off old favourites, many not seen since the 1960s: prunella, red *Sedum spurium* 'Dragon's Blood', the right sort of bright blue cornflower, smallish inulas and the pretty strain of self-sown Cedric Morris poppies. Frank Lawley traded in oriental carpets to make a livelihood during the garden's early years. I told him that carpet-patterns had surely influenced his design.

Yes, he corrected me: 'but you are looking in too literary a way'. Frank began by studying classics, my own literary subject, but abandoned it at university for art and design. Later he organized and taught a special course in garden appreciation at the adult education centre in Newcastle. The Lawleys then explained why the planting of this section of the garden is so peculiarly appealing. They had pre-planned it so that its colours run through the varying colour-phases of the day. Cream and pale pink evoke the early morning light, captured in old friends like pale *Erigeron* 'Quakeress' and an unusual catmint which is rose-pink and upright. The day colours then show in a central bed of golden yellow and orange to suggest the sun, where they centre on an orange lily which I misidentified. It is *Lilium croceum*, at home on the dykes near the sea in the Netherlands. In each bed beside this flowery sun, the deep blues of adenophora, cornflower, harebells, and so forth suggest the clear blue of a summery sky. Next to them come pearly and grey-shaded poppies, suggesting clouds in late afternoon. Then, dark rare poteriums, purple cirsium and double dark lychnis suggest the darkening light of evening. Carpet-design gave ideas for the planting at the edges, where some beautifully clipped yew and box and specimen golden hazels and elders suggest a sunny frame. They bring light to the average grey of a Northumberland day.

The fine plants here owe much to the Lawleys' years of collecting and selecting, often conducted in the 1960s during visits to the legendary cottage garden of Margery Fish at East Lambrook Manor in Somerset. The crucial influences behind the effect of this garden have been painters. The Lawleys cite the example of Mondrian for the shape and colour-separation and Monet for the pale colours of early day. I thought, too, of Corot for the pearly-greys.

Above a final section and its formal knot-garden, the Lawleys have built a tall gazebo which allows visitors to view this dream from above. On one side are the rising Northumberland fields, but then viewers turn round and look over the garden, a triumph of art over nature. It is heavenly in a way which I have not seen elsewhere in England. The National Trust ought to go and see it and plan to save it, a masterpiece of patience which sums up an artist-vision, the best of thoughtful gardening in the past thirty years.

Not-So-Hot Pokers

In summer gardens like Herterton, flowers of all colours are present but the colours are limited in separate beds for particular effects. In lesser gardens, flowering pokers are a divisive subject. When I first suggested a plan for a border to a young friend I included two groups of red-hot pokers and was nearly sacked. They were too much for rarefied taste. If you look them up in that excellent guide to gardening, *The Small Garden* by Brigadier Lucas Phillips, first published in 1952, you will find that even the old soldier was wary of their strong colour. 'All need careful placing,' he wrote, 'to abate their flamboyance.' He realized that they like a rich soil with good drainage and are not at their best in excessively dry conditions. He recommended them near the seaside, where they duly appear on councils' roundabouts.

A telling history of taste in English gardens could be written around this one unfortunate plant. Its botanical name gave it a bad start, as it was called Kniphofia after an important German professor of botany, Herr Kniphof. I doubt if any other plant name has been so seldom used. It quickly became known as the red-hot poker because of the vivid red colouring at the tips of its flower, and the name did no good to its reputation. By bad luck, the first form to be widely planted was the most flamboyant and the least easy to abate. It is still called *Kniphofia uvaria* and has the over-heated poker look. Meanwhile, dozens of others were being bred, selected and brought to the market, but until about twenty years ago, most of them had been forgotten. The red-hot forms condemned all others.

I can illustrate the change in fashion by my own pokers' progress. In the late 1960s civilized gardens were supposed to be pale, white and ghostly, and pokers were out of the question. I came back to them in 1991 in the excellent garden of a fine connoisseur, John Treasure of Burford House, near Tenbury Wells in Worcestershire, owner of a great collection of clematis. In his declining years, he showed me the most beautiful bed of cream-flowered pokers with toffee-brown tips. He even gave me one, telling me it was called 'Modesta' (it is now 'Toffee Nosed'). I was effusively grateful and then killed it in the next winter because it was one of many pokers which dislike winter wet. During the same visit I must have bought a greenish yellow one called 'Wrexham Buttercup'. It is still with me and is the one which first punctured my poker prejudice. It flowers very freely in August, sending up fat flowers which vary between green and yellow as they age. I bought it because the name was so odd and I recommend it to anyone.

My next adventure was due to my weakness for names with unpromising echoes of Germany. I already had that sparkling red rose, 'Parkdirektor Riggers', and what better to match with that busy little supervisor than a poker which I found labelled 'Star of Baden Baden' in a cold frame? At its best, it too should be green-yellow, but something had gone wrong with the label and I ended up with a fearsome red-tipped poker beneath the flowers of the obliging 'Riggers'. The German aunt of one of my pupils then invited herself to my garden, without warning. The most interesting fact about her visit was that she thought the blazing poker and the blazing rose went so well together. On a fine afternoon, they were the plants she photographed.

After 'Baden Baden', I continued to pussyfoot round the poker family by choosing only those forms which had respectable pale yellow flowers. I bought several called 'Little Maid' and put them along the edges of flowerbeds because they were so small. They were slow to grow there and I never had much luck with them. I learned more from the pale yellow-green 'Maid of Orleans', which still survives and starts flowering in early June. The lesson is that the poker season is far longer than many gardeners realize. Different varieties extend it from May until October and there is even a variety which flowers in winter.

By the mid 1990s I started to notice how gardens were using vivid yellow, orange or pure red pokers in forms which were infinitely better than mine. The National Collection had begun to be gathered at Barton Manor on the Isle of Wight, an excellent source of poker knowledge, and I began to observe how planting plans in old nursery catalogues had used single-coloured pokers with names like 'Bees' Sunset' and 'Johnathan', a very good red. At the same time the rhetoric of civilized gardening was swinging back to favouring strong colours and giving up on ghostliness. This change of tone was not an innovation, as strong colours had been popular before, especially in gardens between 1900 and 1935. In the 1990s we were going back to them after sixty years of pastel doubt. Even so, the true range of pokers fitted brilliantly into this change of fashion. Most pokers do not flower in a hard combination of red and yellow. They glow in a uniform orange, or subtle shades of pink-apricot or red.

Here, I have a cracking success, a famous poker called 'Samuel's Sensation'. It has long, thin spikes of flower which open to a shade of cream-white from orange buds, and if the occasional plant is placed at intervals down a border, the flowers light up the entire composition. This poker grows about three-and-a-half feet high and its flowers twist when they start to die. It is very vigorous and I rate it at the top of the family. It is not in the least red hot.

My other star is 'Tawny King', which is slightly taller. Its flowers stand out in a good shade of cream against brown stems and apricot buds, and although a few plants go a long way, they continue flowering until mid-autumn. They combine well with the earliest blue salvias and are one of the best among the scores of pokers which are now on sale, very few of which combine hard shades of yellow and scarlet. Never confuse the hot colour of a plant's flower with its liking for hot dry soil. Pokers like plenty of damp in summer, although they detest it in winter.

Roses in Dry Places

I like to think of thoughtful gardeners swathed in roses in mid-June and celebrating the magnificent generosity of these wonderful plants. Not too much is made of them in the garden plans of brutal minimalists and eco-planters but they remain the unsurpassed sight of British gardening, smothered in flower and not always ravaged by black spot on their leaves. Nonetheless, about fifteen years ago, fashionable voices started to complain about them, copying the late Christopher Lloyd who had thrown out his old rose garden at Great Dixter amid great publicity. In fact, his roses were old and not very exciting varieties. He was tempted, however, to complain about roses in general, giving a lead to susceptible beginners. I hope that each June he is repenting as he looks through a locked gate in heaven at St Peter's rose garden where there is no black spot and the dead-heading is done miraculously by angels.

So many of the best rose varieties are old, but roses are not standing still or ceasing to be better understood. I have high hopes for a pale yellowish double rose which I noticed only recently in the rococo garden at Painswick in Gloucestershire during a sunny August. Remarkably, Rose 'Princesse de Nassau' was still in full flower, showing fresh leaves and such stamina in late summer that I bought it and put it against a wall and am delighted to discover that its reappearance is owed to that great expert, the late Graham Thomas. The 'Princesse' turns out to be a form of the basic musk rose, *Rosa moschata*, which accounts for its late flowering season. The 'Princesse' will grow about eight feet high, and is thought to be a rediscovery of a lost old variety which was known in the 1820s. Like so many roses, she has been preserved by Peter Beales, one of the princes of rose growing, to whom Graham Thomas sent bits of his rediscovered stock.

Every year, I add new favourites, but I would like to speak up for the long season of the lovely 'Louise Odier'. She makes a bush about five feet high and has full pink-rose flowers in heavy clusters, with the most excellent scent. If she is well treated, she will flower on and off throughout the season after the first flush, refuting unfair critics who believe that old roses all fade within a fortnight. 'Louise Odier' was bred in 1851 and I hope we never lose her.

Roses like 'Louise Odier' flourish in rich, heavy soil, but this sort of soil spoils rose growers for choice. In the Cotswolds it is not mine. Where should you look for infallible shrub roses which remain disease-free even on dry, stony soil? Thoughtful reading of Peter Beales' excellent books gives some answers, including roses of such vigour on poor soil that the problem is how to prune them and keep them under control. The classic duo for dryness are the tall, scrambling 'Rose d'Amour' and the thorny, lower-growing 'Rose d'Orsay'. Again, a clear understanding of these two remarkable roses is owed to Graham Thomas. Both are of North American blood in spite of their French names. They have fresh pink flowers and green leaves which are never troubled by disease or black spot. Their parent is the wild *Rosa virginiana*, which puts up with a dry, light soil in its homeland and has the assets of excellent orange hips and yellow autumn colour. The one complication is that these two roses are very thorny, especially 'Rose d'Orsay'. I shirk the task of pruning them and after fifteen years I cannot say that they seem the worse for neglect. If you can track them down in a nursery list, they are ideal for gardeners on dry soil who want to plant roses and then forget about them, except when enjoying their flowers for no labour at all.

Climbing and rambling roses are more accustomed to dry places because the walls on which they grow are so often dry at their foot. They do not all like this fact of life. The high point of dryness is ground at the bottom of my necessary barriers, the hedges of Leyland cypress which I inherited with my garden's acreage. Here, I have tried several suggestions, all of which have survived, but two of which are outstandingly good.

On advice from an expert in the National Rose Society, I first planted *Rosa helenae*, a thorny single-flowered white climber with good clusters of hips. It has survived and grown quite well, but it has never surmounted a coniferous wall of feathery hedging twenty feet high. Rose 'Seagull' has fared better, but it too is happier when falling forwards off the hedges and making a natural thicket as a reminder that most climbing roses would rather not climb. Far the best has been the natural candidate for life in an old vicarage garden. Rose 'Rambling Rector' is undeterred by the drought at the foot of a high screen of conifers. Up the branches of Leyland cypress the 'Rector' rambles happily, turning the vicarage's hedges into a sheet of white flowers in late June. If you have an old Leylandii in the garden, rector it and turn it into a rose wall. *Rosa* 'Rambling Rector' is sometimes said to be susceptible to frost, but in my garden it is sheltered sufficiently by a supporting hedge and even on its north side, has survived all the cold frosts of the past twenty years. It runs up to the top of a high hedge but has none of the deadly vigour of *Rosa filipes* 'Kiftsgate', whose weight and bulk will overpower any living host.

The one problem with a 'Rambling Rector' is its habit of throwing off long, arching stems above a height at which it is easily pruned. Great rose enthusiasts suggest that these shoots should be anchored back on to the hedging and as they cannot be clipped to feathery conifer-branches, one suggestion is that they should be weighted and thrown back into place. The way to do it, I have been told, is to tie a stone to the end of the outward-facing rose stem and then lob the stone and the stem back into the bulk of the hedge. Weighted by this missile, the rose-stem, supposedly, will stay put. I count this advice to be the most ingenious and the most hopeless that I have received in any walk of life, including cooking. It is almost impossible to fix a stone on a sling to the end of a thorny, arching rose branch and it is impossible to lob it upwards into a twenty-foot hedge of Britain's most feathery conifer without losing the stone, risking the loss of an eye from rose-thorns, and encouraging the hedge's branches to wave around even more freely in contempt.

The 'Rector' is impervious to dry soil and good enough for gardeners to forgive its loose, upper habit. For a tidier effect its only equal on a desiccating Leylandii hedge is an even more beautifully shaped white rose, 'Long John Silver'. Peter Beales' rose catalogue has kept this one in the trade and although it lacks the 'Rector's' extreme vigour, it is a rose of the highest class. Its leaves stay green and fresh, its fully double white flowers appear usefully late in mid-July, and as it is another American-bred rose, it puts up with drought and never causes problems. I am thinking of planting it on every awkward wall in sight. There is a further advantage to it. When its heads of flower are cut and placed in a vase, the rounded white flowers look like a Latour rose-painting at its best. Between a 'Rector' and a 'Long John Silver', even the dreariest hedges and dry places can be given a month of shimmering white beauty.

On the Schynige Platte

In the mountains of southern Europe, mid-June until late August is the prime season for some adventurous and unusual gardens. They lie at high altitudes in the Alps and its outlying ranges and have close connections with nearby botanic gardens and with the surrounding flora of their own Alpine peaks. Munich's great Botanical Garden runs a famous out-station, the Schachengarten in the Bavarian Alps, which I knew as a garden employee more than forty years ago. Similar natural gardens have been laid out or restored in southern France, Austria and Switzerland. They are places for a summer pilgrimage.

On one such pilgrimage I found myself in central Switzerland with a choice of two destinations before me. 'The Top of Europe, please visit our Jungfrau', promised the railway signs in one direction. The Jungfrau is the celebrated ice-maiden of the high peaks above Wengen next to the Eiger. Who better to symbolize the top of modern Europe than a virginal Jungfrau who, by definition, has failed to meet the criteria for convergence? Signs in the other direction pointed to the railway station at Wilderswil. It must be the only station with the words 'Alpine Garden' on its platform's main sign. From Wilderswil, a heroic little train toils up a steep railway, built in 1893, and runs to the Schynige Platte above. Trains run at half-hour intervals throughout the day and move at a slow pace which equals the record set by Network SouthEast into London in those challenging days of 'leaves on the track'. The Wilderswil train can be forgiven its slow progress. It goes directly up a steep mountain to a height of nearly six thousand feet on a breathtaking route, flanked by swathes of wild geraniums, pink-purple campanulas and the bigger forms of gentians in the meadows.

The garden at the railway's end has now celebrated its eightieth anniversary. In 1928, this Alpengarten began to be laid out on the principle that it should display the differing styles of vegetation in the surrounding mountains. Anyone who thinks that ecological gardening was invented by the modern green movement, or that wild gardening is the 'new wave', should study the achievement at Schynige Platte. Its garden was practising them long before modern apostles discovered these styles. A private society of friends of the Schynige Platte cares for it, assisted by the University of Berne which runs the site with sensitivity and science, a combination which often eludes botanic gardens at low levels. The garden is open from mid-June to autumn, although the second week in July is usually the best for alpine flowers.

In Britain, our most familiar wildflowers are nettles and rampant grass, mown by county councils with a budget for 'roadside tractoring'. In the Alps, the natural carpet of flowers is stronger than the local types of grass and the main mowers are the accompanying herds of cows. In Britain, so much is said nowadays about a 'native wildflower' style of gardening and the scope for reinstating the English meadow. Much less is said about the wild style of flowers on Swiss and German mountains, a 'wildflower' style which is wrongly neglected. Its flowers are more varied and beautiful than the limited English flora, and are far more diverse than sweeps of orange rudbeckias and pink poke-weed let loose in imitation of the Midwestern prairies. Alpine meadows and the carpets of flower on Alpine mountains are models for a style which has yet to have its day in England. At its best, it looks like the foreground of a great painting by Bellini, although Bellini never climbed as high as the Schynige Platte to see what nature could do in a foreground of her own.

Up on the Platte, the Alpengarten overlooks a snow-capped perimeter of distant mountains which surround it like icy guardians. The garden's main path runs on a round trip past natural hillsides, each of which is devoted to the ecology of a separate alpine landscape, running from the meadows upwards. The garden's general principle is to allow groups of plants to grow together naturally with the minimum of weeding during the 150 days when the site is not under snow. The labelling is excellent, the grouping is fascinating, and the result is an enchanting wild garden. Anyone who is based at Interlaken and waits for a sunny day to visit the garden by railway will have a day trip to remember. I returned with hundreds of ideas, revitalized by pale yellow-flowered *Hieracium intybaceum* or the white-flowered *Potentilla rupestris* which lingers on in a few British nurseries. A visit suggests a whole new way of gardening by working from botanical seed lists and growing these easy sub-alpine plants from seed at a fraction of the cost of a British nursery's alpine plants. In Britain they would make a small patch of 'meadow' when transplanted outdoors.

On a previous day's walk above Wengen, I had been bluffing to conceal my ignorance of a tall purple-blue flowered plant of the woodlands. It turned out to be the common *Cicerbita alpina*, which is seldom seen in English gardens. Under the trees I misidentified the purple-flowered *Adenostyles* as a *Petasites*, whereas it is a common and easy under-cover for woodland gardens, though never seen in Britain. Spurred on by the Alpine garden, I now picture a garden 'meadow' of mauve thistle-flowered *Rhaponicum scariosum* and a tapestry of campanulas, mixed with rose-pink *Pimpinella major* which resembles a small cow parsley and the white Alpine marguerite, *Leucanthemum adustum*, which is totally hardy. I marvelled at the martagon lilies, coveted the gentians and desired the small, intense flowers of the higher alpines. At these altitudes their beauty is concentrated in the clear sunlight as if it has been reduced by rapid cooking.

The Schynige Platte garden flows beautifully over its natural setting. It is enjoyed by wiry Swiss in the know and botanical enthusiasts from further afield. It merges into meadows which occupy a pleasant day on foot. I think I may apply for a cowbell and go vegetarian during the summer season.

Dreamy Delphiniums

On calm, sunny days, delphiniums are the stars of late June and early July. I cannot imagine why they have become identified with laborious out-of-date gardening as they are one of the wonders of a gardener's world. They are far more spectacular than ornamental grasses and clumps of knotweed in prairie plantings. They are obliging in return for a few minutes of attention, and the effort makes me fonder and prouder of them.

It has taken a while to accept the truth about this family, that with delphiniums you only get what you pay for. If you buy unnamed seedlings or mixed hybrids with group-names like Galahad or King Arthur you will have respectable second-class results. The flower spikes will be relatively short and the flowers will fade quickly up the length of the stem. If you buy named prize-winning varieties like the cream 'Butterball' or the deep 'Blue Nile' you will pay twice as much but you will be rewarded many times over. The spikes are longer and better-furnished and the lower flowers will not have dropped before the upper flowers have even opened. Their colour and shape put the cheaper varieties to shame. The expensive ones are no more difficult to grow, but they cost more because they have to be raised from cuttings taken off a mature parent of the same name.

Long delphinium borders of these named varieties are still the summit of their experts' aspirations. At Godinton House, near Ashford in Kent, the British Delphinium Society has planted a magnificent example beside the local old brick walls. The garden is open to the public and in early July this border is as good of its kind as you can hope to see. There are a few late flowers as July advances and if the first crop is thoroughly dead-headed, there is a second showing in early autumn. The problem is that these long, exclusive borders look drab in the intervening weeks. I prefer to mix a few individual delphiniums as focal points in a varied border rather than in a border of their own. In relatively small beds they can stand alone as individuals without having to go in the very back row in conventional groups of three or five. When they flower, they draw the eye but as soon as they fade, they are dead-headed and become lost once again in an emerging haze of asters and late summer daisies. Used in this way they do not become a mildewed and messy back row throughout most of July and August. A strong delphinium will tolerate neighbours in a border but it ought to have a circle of about three feet in diameter entirely to itself.

One of the happier sights at recent Chelsea Flower Shows has been the return to form of the traditional specialists in named delphiniums, Blackmore & Langdon of Stanton Nurseries, Pensford, Bristol. The company's season for sending out young plants ends in June but they can be pre-booked for next April, at a cost of about £7 for what will only be a rooted little plant in a three-inch pot. In the first year there might be a flower or two, but at only a fraction of the plant's eventual height. If possible, grow on the new arrivals in a well-manured bed and only transplant them later for their second, more glorious season. As recent cold winters have proved yet again, even the biggest and finest delphiniums are unaffected by frost. When they have died down in winter their enemy is not frost but the tireless slug. These hungry pests are still active below soil level where you cannot see them. Always leave slug bait around a delphinium from November to March.

Most of the named varieties will grow in dry conditions but they are far better in ground which does not harden like a hot brick. Traditionally, they were planted in soil that had been dug with animal manure and then topdressed with yet more rotted manure to keep in the dampness. The nutrients given by this manure can be given more effectively by adding a slow-release fertilizer to the planting-hole or to the soil around an established plant's neck. This fertilizer makes all the difference to named varieties, which have to put so much energy into their main season. Dampness can then be retained by a separate mulch of bark or compost around the plant. Many of the best results come from artificially fed delphiniums in beds with artificial irrigation systems. There is no special magic in growing them by 'organic' methods.

Here are some extra-special varieties, noted at the Chelsea shows and proven in my own borders. 'Celebration' is a lovely cream-white with a dark eye and 'Sandpiper' is a classic white with a black eye as a contrast. 'Blue Nile' has a charming white eye and 'Pandora' is a bright mid blue with a blue-and-black eye. All these fabulous forms are offered by Blackmore & Langdon, as is the softer blue 'Pericles' with its white eye. 'Pericles' appeals to me particularly because of its namesake, the great political leader of classical Athens who dominated the people much as Pericles dominates a border in July. Amateur breeders have developed many other winners which are worth hunting down in the *RHS Plant Finder*. One of the best is 'Clifford Sky', a form with an intensely clear sky-blue flower on a very long spike, but a slug finally slaughtered my plants of it and I am consoling myself with the free-flowering 'Merlin', a clear blue, too, with a white eye.

What about the staking and tying? They were used as reasons for banishing delphiniums from 'labour-saving' gardens, as if we could never enjoy this brief, yearly task. Pressed for time, I leave it late, until the first buds are opening and the ground is usually hardened by a dry spell. Some of the necessary bamboo canes then break when they are poked into the surrounding soil, but even this regular setback has an anticipated rhythm. When a cane finally stands straight for every one or two flower spikes and the green twine is circling each stem, I feel pleased at the sight of orderliness achieved within an hour. If you place highly-priced delphiniums as individual focal points along a border, they will make a strong impact and develop strong stems which have less need to be tied up. When their flower spikes fade, the canes come out too as the second flowering, if any, is slighter, and is better able to support itself. The delphinium never deserved to become a symbol of laborious gardening. Its few needs are pleasant variations in the usual round of weeding and dead-heading. We have banished it for the wrong reasons.

The Etna Broom

My garden's best shrub in early to mid-July is yellow-flowered and minimally leaved. The family of broom bushes does not have many champions nowadays and the related family of gorse has even fewer. Nonetheless my winner looks like a broom and is classed in a family with gorse bushes in it. It has no thorns or prickles and it throws off a great shower of bright flower. It is *Genista aetnensis*, the Mount Etna broom, which is native to the hot, volcanic Sicilian mountain. No wonder it likes excessive sun and drought and is in its element in the days of debilitating heat in European gardens.

I first realized how good this tall shrub is when I saw it in the early 1990s in the once-famous Irish garden at Malahide, a short bus ride from the centre of Dublin. Emerald Ireland was suffering in one of the hot Augusts of the early 1990s, but the Etna broom was untroubled. In its heyday Malahide was celebrated for its collection of rare shrubs from Asia, Australia and New Zealand which had been amassed by its owner, Lord Talbot. They have dwindled over time, but *Genista aetnensis* remains a star in the diminished pack. Shortly afterwards I visited Mount Etna and understood why this plant is such a survivor. The lower slopes of the volcano are covered in fine black grit, the lapilli of previous eruptions. The conditions are dry but the genista's leaves need little water and are designed to retain it. The plants grow up to fifteen feet tall and erupt into a shower of yellow flowers when the Sicilian summers are starting to hit the heights of heat.

Back in Britain this genista was a favourite of Vita Sackville-West at Sissinghurst. She planted it cleverly in the back row of one of the narrow beds below her castle's old brick walls and recommended it to her many readers for its cascades of flower, describing it as an 'arrested fountain of molten gold'. Not many readers followed her enthusiasm, possibly because the flowers were yellow at a time when strong yellows were becoming unfashionable. Worse, some of the genistas are prickly gorse bushes. By gardeners, gorse is thought to belong on down-at-heel hillsides in Ireland or on Britain's Celtic fringe. Such fashions in flowers are very restricting. Actually, gorse's orange-yellow flowers are extremely pretty there in early May. It has also been thought to belong with hunting, not gardening. 'There is never a story about fox-hunting,' remarks a sceptical lady in one of the best short stories by Saki, the master-artist of the genre, 'which does not have gorse bushes in it.' Foxes still shelter from the wind in gorse coverts, but a single bush in a garden is not enough to interest them.

When I first grew prickly forms of genista, I was delighted to read that the Swedish founder of botanical naming, Carl Linnaeus, went down on his hands and knees with delight when he landed on the English coastline and encountered their relations, gorse bushes. 'Swedes are always a bit odd,' said an American gardener to whom I told this story, but in this case the Swede had kept his wits. I learned only recently, in Linnaeus' centenary year, that the story of his thanks to God for prickly British gorse is a legend. The expert historian Brent Elliott of the Lindley Library in London pointed out that Linnaeus would have seen masses of gorse in flower all along his route through Germany before he ever took ship for England.

Some of this 'gorse' in Europe was *Ulex europaeus*, whereas spiny Spanish gorse and prickly English furze are genistas. The genista family does not need any help from a Swede on his knees. It includes the planta genista of the old Plantagenet kings of England. The seedpods of its flowers are wonderfully visible on the robes of the Plantagenet courtiers and angels in the National Gallery's great Wilton Diptych, the double painting of King Richard II and his earthly and heavenly attendants. My favourite genista, the Sicilian *aetnensis*, has no Spanish prickles, no strong orange in the golden yellow of its flowers and no special appeal for foxes, either. It is a great shrub, ideally suited to a warming world and extraordinarily free with its little yellow flowers. In a restricted space it can be pruned by taking out the central stem and letting the sideshoots spray sideways at a height of only five or six feet. If unpruned, it will eventually make a tall, widely branched tree, up to twenty feet tall but never so dense that it blocks out the light. The biggest and best in my experience used to belong to Howard Colvin, a former professor of English architectural history in Oxford. In hot summers we would sit beneath its wiry curtain of leaves and flowers, beside the bank of limestone tufa, his substitute for Sicilian lava, in which he grew alpines. Wind may eventually knock a branch or two off a big tree but the branches are light and thin and do no damage if they snap. An Etna broom would be an excellent choice for a large sunny back garden.

Perhaps this broom has suffered by being muddled with a lesser substitute. Similar pea-shaped flowers, bigger and brighter, are found on a shrubby Spanish plant, *Spartium junceum*, which is known as Spanish broom. This plant is only a shrub, never a tree, and has much more solid, pointed stems. It is good in its own right, especially in hotter summers and Mediterranean holiday gardens, but it is not so fine as the Etna genista. I was surprised to hear from a nurseryman that *Genista aetnensis* had suffered from recent cold winters. Outdoors it is totally hardy and I can only ascribe the losses of Etna broom in the trade to the plant's over-wintering in vulnerable plastic pots. For nearly twenty years I have failed to kill the Etna broom. I can give it no better recommendation.

Sickly Chestnuts

No pest or disease affects the Etna broom, but during its weeks in flower, all too visibly an epidemic is infecting one of our loveliest families of trees. It has a high chance of wiping out yet another mainstay of the British landscape. In the early 1970s, as Dutch Elm disease broke out, the one consolation was that elm trees were not the only trees in Britain's open countryside. The bark beetle was starting to destroy them, but the great stands of horse chestnut still stood foursquare in the face of danger and seemed to be indestructible. In May their huge branches were set with white flowers like candles. As children, we used to shred the green surfaces off the chestnuts' big leaves and leave the supporting ribs to look like fishbones. What could ever destroy such giants which have towered in England for more than 400 years?

This optimism was misplaced. Horse chestnuts have now begun to die at short notice, or to look sick and lose their green leaves by early July. Even their conkers fail to develop, and drop off the tree too soon. Few of the trees in distress are suffering from lack of water. The culprits are insects and bacteria, and although the effects of the bugs and the bacteria are distinct, it is hard to know what to do about either of them. The offending bug is a leaf miner called *Cameraria ohridella* which was first recognized in Britain in 2002. It is known in parts of the Balkans and has a toughness verified in Slovenia and active in parts of ancient Macedonia. It has the stamina of the army of Alexander the Great and is as difficult to destroy. Sometimes I wonder if I brought it in on my walking shoes after a trip looking for the elusive homes of his highland officers. The Balkans, however, may not be its homeland. No predator has yet proliferated by making a meal of it and the reason may be that the bug originated even further afield. Western China has been suggested, explaining why nothing in Europe yet eats it.

These leaf miners cluster in thousands and eat their way through the early summer leaves of juicy chestnuts. They cause pale blotches all over the leaves while their larvae wait to mature. The leaves then roll up like browned cigarettes and look extremely sick. There is also a leaf fungus, which attacks chestnuts and deposits brown-red smudges on the tips and edges of leaves, but it is easily distinguished from the leaf miner's action. At first, the insect's damage looks white and transparent and if the leaf is held up against the light, the larva's excreta will show through. The damage then becomes a dry brown patch, causing many leaves to drop off by early September. The only good point is that an attack is not fatal. It spoils the summer look of the tree and, after several years, it will surely weaken it. A few branches may then fall off, but the tree as a whole will not die. It is wretched if a tree has these insects but the only hope is to sit them out, waiting for a remedy or a predator to emerge.

Will a cold winter kill the insect? Unfortunately not, as the pest can survive 20 °C of frost. The best strategy is to remove all the leaves as they fall and to burn them or bag them up for destruction. An ordinary compost heap will not kill off any insects which are wintering in the leaves, as it does not generate enough heat. Instead, if you cover small piles of leaves with about three inches of earth you will prevent many of the larvae from emerging. However, the pest is not susceptible to a green offensive if you have a large quantity of leaves to collect. Piling up sufficient earth becomes too laborious and an adequate covering is hard to maintain.

This leaf miner is one more refutation of the dotty view that gardeners should simply 'work with nature'. Nature comes up with the most lethal pests. This one is able to produce more than 4,000 moths from one kilo of dead leaves, and in spring each one of these natural menaces then lays another 80,000 eggs. We need a chemical control, and quickly. One possibility is to inject the trunks of important trees with that great human invention, Imidacloprid, which already protects the tomatoes and lemons which we eat. It would be best applied when the tree is in flower, but it is expensive and would have to be repeated every year.

Even then, there could be problems. Injections might encourage two other enemies of chestnut trees, both of which are bacterial. Whereas leaf miners are rarer at altitudes of 500 feet or more, these bacteria are active in the north of Britain too, including Scotland.

Bacteria have had less publicity but they are the supreme menace to the chestnut's future. For years we have known one of them, a basic 'bleeding canker', which attacks the crowns and lower branches of horse chestnuts and causes them to ooze a black drip. This sort of attack is due to two forms of that fungal hold-all, *Phytophthora*, a word which is based on Greek and simply means 'plant destruction'. The symptoms look nasty but these bacteria do not kill bigger trees and the only option is to try to ignore them. The other type of bacteria is far worse. It is a newly active one which is at present traced to the *Pseudomonas syringae* group. Unfortunately, it causes more of a tree's bark to drop off and quickly cuts a circle around the stem of bigger branches. It is a killer and will wipe out a tree in one year. Other members of the pseudomonas family can be controlled but not destroyed, but unfortunately, the one which attacks chestnuts cannot as yet be killed. Here, too, we need a chemical and when we find it we need to be less fussy about rules for its use by farmers and gardeners in a crisis. The one bit of good news is that this particular bacterium seems less active on big old trees. Usually it destroys trees between ten and thirty years of age.

The dangers, then, are multiple. If you have a horse chestnut whose bark is loose and sticky, you should wait and see whether it is the deadly pseudomonas or not. If in doubt, do nothing meanwhile, because it may only be phytophthora. It seems, however, that the red-flowered horse chestnut is much less susceptible to the killer variety. Unfortunately, the lovely white-flowered chestnut is most at risk. As ever, neighbours like to depress us. One of my neighbours has a bleeding avenue and has raised the possibility that there will soon be blood on my avenue too. I have a line of tall limes which are close to intervening houses. They are not horse chestnuts, but my neighbour tells me that the more dangerous of the two bacteria may well travel by wind and attack limes, too. At present he is downwind from me but if he exports his bacteria, I think I will move to a high-rise flat.

Lotuses and Lilies

Unsettled by brown chestnut trees, I try to look outwards in July, at gardens further afield where the disease is less in evidence. From time to time I visit a garden and have a transcendental moment. Sometimes I have two, a twinned excitement which lives in the annals of a gardening lifetime.

One such excitement arose from a horse-ride through south-west France, where the chestnuts are sweet chestnuts and the horses were hired for the occasion. Turning for home, I rescued a brochure before my mount could eat it and found that the two of us were within cantering distance of the garden of Monsieur Latour-Marliac. So what, you might wonder? So almost everything, I would reply, because this particular monsieur was the man behind the water lilies which we all enjoy. Until he began his life's work, we were limited to a vigorous white-flowered variety, the only hardy water lily in Europe. From 1879 onwards, Latour-Marliac crossed this variety with wonderfully coloured forms from tropical climates. Meticulously he selected the results and in 1889 dared to display them for six months in the water gardens at Bagatelle on the edge of the Bois de Boulogne in Paris. They were a sensation, so he repeated the display. Two years later they caught the most distinguished eye in the history of the water lily: Claude Monet. Monet had just become the tenant of the ground at Giverny which he was to make into his famous garden. In 1893 he acquired the right to extend it round its big lake, and the rest is art history. When his paintings of water lilies are shown in museum exhibitions, they are still the biggest magnet for crowds of visitors.

Where did Monet find the water lilies which he painted? He

ordered them directly from Latour-Marliac, and amazingly the breeder's ponds, flowerpots and nurseries are still in commercial existence at Temple-sur-Lot in the Lot-et-Garonne, east of Bordeaux and not far from the town of Agen. Here, Marliac lived, studied and experimented after giving up his work as a lawyer. He built water-basin after water-basin and it is possible to visit the remains of his nursery and see the best of his hybrid lilies in place. Better still, if you penetrate to the nursery's tool shed, you will find copies of Latour-Marliac's replies to the orders of Monet himself. These exchanges of letters are great documentary survivors. Through them the most famous lily pond in the history of art was furnished with flowers. Monet had a fine eye and it was he who introduced a Japanese bridge at Giverny and added an upper storey to it to support wisteria. Nobody knows if Monet came down to see Marliac among his lily-ponds. Marliac certainly went to see Monet because he imitated the Japanese bridge. His compressed version of it still stands in his garden.

In ponds all over the world, the water lily follows the schedule of elderly academic life. The flowers wake up after 10 a.m. to face the daylight and then fall pleasantly asleep around teatime. You would never find one in a place like Goldman Sachs. The Latour-Marliac garden contains more than 200 such varieties, many of which were bred by Marliac himself. They float in long narrow canals or in circular ponds where they have been tended for years by the devoted Sylvie Benedetti. A Corsican by birth, she explained the lilies' needs to me while holding a sharply toothed knife of the sort which I last saw being used to castrate a pig. She was preparing to take cuttings and divisions to sell to the garden's daily visitors.

In Marliac's day, young lily plants were allowed to float in hundreds of shallow circular pots which he placed on the edges of his network of concreted canals. The pots are still there but there is nothing in them. '*Voleurs*,' Sylvie explained to me: the French would steal them if they were set out in Marliac's trusting style. Before you feel smug, the English are even worse. When I last opened my garden, I lost several of my rare alpines in one afternoon, probably to the middle-aged ladies who arrived with handbags.

So many of the great water lilies are still in Marliac's canals: the rose-pink 'Nigel' which he bred in 1892, the famous yellow 'Marlia-cea Chromatella', a stronger yellow called 'Texas Dawn' and some tender blue varieties around the big Victoria lily, *Victoria amazonica*, which lives in a necessary greenhouse. If you time your visit correctly you will be enchanted.

In the 1990s the collection in France had a link with Britain's own Stapeley Water Gardens, near Nantwich in Cheshire, who hold and sell many of the same varieties. Whatever happens to this link, I hope that their historic French nursery will continue to thrive. In 2004 the garden was declared a '*jardin remarquable*' in French national list-ings, but over time, its long raised ponds have inevitably started to leak. The honour should encourage French funding to restore it because the nursery is a doubly remarkable site.

Water lilies are not its only heavenly item. Latour-Marliac also grew semi-hardy forms of lotus which will survive outdoors at tem-peratures down to minus 7 °C. We can see from the surviving bills that Monet ordered lotuses too but soon lost them, refuting Marliac's belief that they would be hardy in the Giverny area. Down at Temple-sur-Lot, however, Marliac went on crossing lotuses and selecting superior forms. They still flower briefly there above their glistening grey-green leaves and when I called, the pink forms were at their exquisite best. Behind the pink lotus stretches the shadow of another genius, Alexan-der the Great. It was he who found the pink lotus flowering in India and who reached a conclusion which I now understand. When he saw it, he was on the river Indus, but he believed that he was at the head of Egypt's Nile. 'Egyptian beans,' he thought, were growing along the banks of the Indian river, proving that it was linked to Egypt. After his conquests a pink-flowered lotus ended up in northern Greece near his native Macedon, where it was a great wonder. I quite see why, but I now understand the muddle of the 'Egyptian beans' too. The Nelumbo lotus has the most exquisite flower, the sacred symbol of Indian reli-gions. Its seed-heads look like green watering cans and if you look closely inside, as you can in Marliac's garden, you will see that the seeds are hard, black and shiny, exactly like a type of bean. Alexander was not such an idiot as some historians like to claim. As I looked at the pink lotus I might well have made his mistake too.

Is there anything lovelier in the natural world than the leaf and flower of a lotus at a moment of perfection? Its loveliness inspired a Chinese essay on 'Love for the Lotus' in the eleventh century AD which praises its subtle scent and the purity of its flowers above the muddy floor of a lake. It is particularly lovely when it is safe from mud in the concrete breeding-pens of the French genius who transformed our awareness of the family. He sold specimens to Monet and added to the parcels some plants of the water lilies which became subjects of the most famous stretches of canvas in the world. Despite Marliac's optimism I cannot believe that a pink-flowered lotus will survive outdoors in Oxford, even in a modern winter. It will have to go indoors in a confined tank. I am starting to think about sinking one in my college's ante-chapel, where it will float as an object of veneration.

Sociable Deutzias

A few years ago I went into deutzias, a family of plants which continues to intrigue visitors to western China but never makes it into the British limelight. June and July are the deutzias' cue. There are dozens of them, all extremely easy to grow. They put up with lime soil, unlike many of the best white-flowering shrubs from south-east Asia, and they do not droop in the drought. The best forms have to be tracked down and are much better than the limited range which is on display in an average garden centre. Deutzias are very sociable and can be pruned and contained in a convenient shape. They are classic companions for shrub roses, with whose flowering most of them coincide. They look pretty in such company but they are even better in quiet isolation or at the backs of a mixed border. My favourites include the brightest and boldest, the excellent white hybrid *Deutzia* × *magnifica*. It is a big plant but its flowers make a strong impact, confounding critics who think that deutzias' flowers are small and for fanciers only. It has a squashed pink relation which is separately listed as *Deutzia* × *hybrida* 'Strawberry Fields'. Nearly twenty nurseries in Britain now offer this excellent hybrid which has an unusual colour. It flowers with exceptional freedom, but I do not rate it so highly as 'Magicien', its brother hybrid, which has a touch of lilac in its mixture of pink.

The deepest pink deutzia is upright and very useful in the middle-to-back row of a big border. *Deutzia* × *elegantissima* 'Rosealind' is a product of the old Slieve Donard nursery in Ireland and has small flowers of a deep pink. It grows up to five feet high and puzzles visitors who have forgotten how useful this old variety still is. These hybrids are all very pretty but I prefer forms which are closer to their wild Chinese origins. They must be a beautiful sight among low bushes in Yunnan, but the first collectors in China chose to idolize rhododendrons instead. I first discovered *Deutzia monbeigii* in the wilder parts of the garden of my first landlady, Nancy Lancaster, who grew it in rough grass, lightly shaded by tall trees. This Yunnan native is in full flower by late June, is hardy and reaches a height of seven feet or so. I am glad I encountered it early in life. It is one of a group of taller deutzias, all of which can be trimmed, or even thinned, after flowering. Thinning is the classic advice in the old handbooks which tell us to cut out shoots of our deutzias once they have flowered and prune them to the ground like raspberry canes. From time to time, I thin but I am never so drastic. The alternative is to reduce the bulk of these taller shrubs enough to slim them down, a reason why they are so convenient in a mixed border. After their flowering, if a late summer clematis is planted beside them, it will scramble prettily up through the deutzia's branches.

Two of my best deutzias resulted from a raid on the excellent nursery at Longstock Park, near Stockbridge in Hampshire. On one golden afternoon, I came back with a large white-flowered *Deutzia longifolia* 'Veitchii', which commemorates a great nurseryman. It is spectacularly pretty, and I also bought the unusual *Deutzia × wilsonii* which commemorates the great plant-hunter Ernest Wilson. It seems to be smaller than 'Veitchii' but is equally good. The stars in the family, however, are two other Chinese forms which are distinctive. Ever since I began to read books on plant-hunting, I have had a dreamy mental image of the Ningpo mountains. On them grows *Deutzia ningpoensis* which is now offered by a dozen or so suppliers in Britain and is unusual in having long and narrow leaves and flowering late in July. It seems to be extremely easy and I expect it to reach about seven feet, surprising me with its late cool show of flowers. Fine though it is, the winner is the good deutzia from Sichuan, *Deutzia setchuenensis*, especially the *corymbiflora* variety. It is not the easiest deutzia to propagate, a reason why it is scarce in standard garden centres, and in a very cold winter it may die out. It is not the right deutzia for a cold, exposed place, but it lasts in flower longer than the others and has a slight bloom on its small leaves which sets off the white flowers delightfully. I expect my plants to stop at about four feet, the height at which I first saw spectacular specimens in the paved pool garden at Kiftsgate Court in Gloucestershire. They start to flower in July and persist on through the month long after the other deutzias are over. Casting around for complaints, critics observe that it has no scent. Instead, it has elegance and its little clusters of unopened white buds are enchanting. We are unfair to deutzias which add such class to thoughtful gardens during July.

We have also forgotten an old trick, practised by thoughtful gardeners until the 1930s. Youngish deutzias can be grown in a reserve bed and potted up in early November for sheltering in a moderately heated greenhouse (up to 14 °C). Plants can be brought under glass in sequence, some in mid-November, some in early January and February, and if they are sprayed quite often with warm water, they will break into leaf and bud, giving a fine, unseasonal show which can be shown off indoors. After flowering, the flowered stems should be cut to their base to promote new growth for next season's display and to keep the plants within bounds. Obviously, the smaller deutzias are best suited to the purpose and in due course, after a couple of indoor winters, they can be planted outdoors and younger plants brought in to replace them.

Blue Flax

What would the world look like if the sky were green and the ground were blue? In early July, a few fortunate parts of England have a chance to see a hint of the result. Whole hillsides in the south of the country are a shimmering sea of sky-blue as their crops of flowering flax glisten in the wind. In full flower, flax looks heavenly. When Moses and the elders saw the God of Israel, we are told that 'there was under his feet as it were a pavement of sapphire, like the very heaven for clearness'. A field of flax is a reflection of it.

Early July is an excellent time to start flaxing. Seeds of the best perennial varieties can be bought easily from the leading seedsmen and sown in trays of light compost where their firm, glossy seeds are easily spaced and persuaded to germinate. They are extremely satisfying as they grow quickly and prepare to flower in the following summer. The seed needs no special heat or protection and before the seedlings become too straggly, they can be moved on into separate trays, about twenty to the normal size of seed-tray. They can then be potted up and transplanted in late April.

The flax family has some singular beauties and a few peculiarities. One of the best is a small variety with brilliant yellow flowers, known as *Linum flavum* 'Gemmell's Hybrid', which cannot be raised true from seed. It has to be increased by cuttings, but they are not easy to root. Nonetheless, I have grown it on and off for years, but even on the poor soil which it prefers, 'Gemmell's Hybrid' is quicker to go off than on. It is not a long-lived plant and cannot take credit for stamina. It remains a lovely thing, but thoughtful gardeners are not much worse off with *Linum arboreum* or the small *Linum flavum*

'Compactum'. These yellow-flowered varieties show up clearly at the edge of the flowerbed and are well worth the effort. The blue ones, however, are what we want under a summer sky. The best known is *Linum perenne*, which is a shimmering sky-blue and comes in several varieties, including 'Blue Sapphire' and *alpinum* 'Alice Blue'. All of them are good, but none is as lovely as the darker blue of *Linum narbonense*, which grows wild in parts of southern France. From a seed packet, this dark blue form is the one to prefer. Potted plants cost about £3 each but are no better than the scores of seedlings which you can raise by sowing seed for the following year. Unlike the flax in the fields of our farmers, these blue forms will go on flowering for many weeks, but they must stand in sunshine so that their flowers open fully and show off the heavenly sheen on their petals. The plants are slender so as to thrive in poor conditions without too much water and the leaves are minimal so that the plants can survive wherever the soil is poor and stony. Flaxes thrive in Mediterranean surroundings, but few British gardeners remember to try them round their summer bolt-holes. I clip them lightly in late summer and instead of hacking them down to ground level in autumn, I allow them to regrow freely in spring. They seem to live longer if they are starved and left alone.

In my mind's eye, I picture a sapphire pavement of flax emerging from plants which spread rapidly across the ground from late July onwards. The airy pink flowers of the low-growing *Gypsophila* 'Rosy Veil' would be one possibility, perhaps with the freer-flowering forms of herbaceous potentilla, especially the unstoppable 'Gibson's Scarlet'. The last of the flax would coincide with the first exhalation of flower on the pink 'Rosy Veil' and then the brilliant red of the potentilla would take over. These plants are all happiest in a dry soil in sunshine.

The Tivoli Garden

Flax flowers most freely in a sunny summer, but in the heat of such summers I soon dream of water extravagantly used. I do not mean gallons of water leaking from the pipes of the local water authority. I mean tumbling waterfalls, foaming fountains and rushing streams with no ambition except to look good. Recently I took the plunge and in a hot spell went to revisit the most famous water garden in Europe, the Villa d'Este at Tivoli near Rome.

When I told a distinguished garden designer that I was going to the villa, he looked pained and told me that I should not bother. It was the sort of place, he thought, which is only popular with tours and coaches. Many of the best things are, and I think he was muddling the villa with those later copies called Tivoli Gardens which make a feeble use of water. The real villa's gardens are magnificent. They are even more magnificent nowadays because they have been given a new life as part of Italy's clean-up for the millennium. In Britain, we suffered the Millennium Dome. In Italy, they cleaned historic buildings and restored garden fountains which work. At the Villa d'Este, more fountains now run at one time than I have seen previously. They power up to a great height and make the fountains at Marble Arch in London look pathetic.

Visitors to the Villa d'Este enter a garden which is more than 400 years old. In the 1550s it was laid out by a patron who defied rules which would now restrict it. He was a frustrated candidate for the papacy whose unfettered attitude to the surrounding landscape demolished anything in his way and took anything worth burgling in the neighbourhood. Nowadays he would be sued on at least five counts and would be regarded as a crowning scandal of the Catholic Church. Instead, his garden is a national heritage monument.

Ippolito d'Este was a grand cardinal who found himself appointed to govern the town of Tivoli. He was the son of the scandalous Lucrezia Borgia, and was so handsome that he had been fancied in his youth by the King of France. His family was immensely grand. The d'Estes had long patronized the arts and all the refinements of court living at Ferrara, their charming seat in northern Italy. Few families could meet them as equals, but the Farnese family was one, already enmeshed in the history of the Roman papacy. The d'Estes wanted a pope too, but the honour continued to elude them. Ippolito made two attempts to be elected and one way of understanding his garden is to see it as his compensation for a failed electoral bid at the Vatican.

It was not an unpleasant compensation. Ippolito's name recalled the ancient Greek hero Hippolytus who was famous for his love of hunting: 'hunting he loved,' as Shakespeare put it, 'but love he laughed to scorn.' Ippolito d'Este followed his namesake's example. The 1550s were a time when every self-respecting cardinal would withdraw from Rome during the season for blood sports, maintaining the Gospel while chasing anything on four legs. Round the Villa d'Este, Ippolito annexed large areas of land in his property's main view and preserved it for duck-shooting and deer-hunting, his cardinal pleasures in life. He also had an informed mind. He kept several historical advisers, of whom the most learned was Pirro Ligorio, the Papal adviser on classical archaeology. His Tivoli villa lay near the vast garden-park of the Roman Emperor Hadrian and like several popes before him, Ippolito would visit the site with his archaeological adviser and remove any pillars and bits of stonework which caught his fancy.

Up on his hill, he then set about improving the dull façade of an old Benedictine monastery. The monks had had no idea of the potential genius of their place. During the next twenty years the cardinal had the hillside excavated by hand and arranged for steep staircases to descend from one level to the next. Each level made a terrace with a cross-view on which he could install extraordinary displays of water. While serving in France, Ippolito had seen great waterworks in European gardens, powered by devices of a new mechanical era. He set out to surpass them. The result was a garden which visitors to the house cannot fully appreciate nowadays. In the cardinal's day, the entry was from the bottom of the hillside so that visitors would be humbled by the ascent to his main terrace. We first see the garden nowadays only from the first-floor windows where the slope is so steep that the intricacy of the descending terraces is hardly visible. The bold entrance-prospect is lost to us.

On his terraced slope the cardinal installed running stairways of water and a long line of 100 fountains beside which floated model boats and items with mythical allusions. Four enormous set-pieces spouted water to tremendous heights and even played musical tunes. Ippolito was helped by the natural landscape of surrounding Tivoli, which had once been the site of ancient Roman aqueducts and stylish villas. Its local rivers had already powered the water supplies for ostentatious ancient Roman owners of nearby country seats. The cardinal diverted part of Tivoli's main water supply in the hills and dug out his own aqueduct-tunnel with an unchristian indifference to the community, an attitude which garden owners, restricted by modern laws, both fear and secretly admire.

The result is one of the most spectacular designs in the world. If you arrive in the garden early or during the last hour of its opening, the crowds are hardly visible and the water seems to be running everywhere. The intricacies of the fountains have never been better displayed in modern times. One of the few losses is the cardinal's sculpted display of Rome's seven hills, but the fountain connected with them is now being restored. The Fountain of the Birds is running merrily again and the rocky seat of Tivoli's mythical sibyl is in gushing form. The gigantic water organ has never been heard to better advantage and nearby, the water rushes again down the main staircases and fills three serene fishponds. There is even a Diana grotto, which eclipses the one on the lower floor of Fayed's Harrods store in London. In the evenings, Cardinal Ippolito and his educated friends would read ancient lives by Plutarch and the matchless Latin poetry of the local villa owner, Horace. I think that there are many undercurrents to his villa which nobody has recently understood. Through a haze of spray I thought of two.

On one of the terraces the famous fountains of Rome stand at one end while the other end is closed off by a vast representation of Tivoli. Surely the cardinal and his visitors thought here of the poet Horace, the first man to immortalize the modern commuter's sentiment: 'When in Rome, I love Tivoli, fickle as I am; when at Tivoli, I love Rome.' This famous line of poetry was surely in the minds of visitors who could walk here between a model Rome and a model Tivoli on one and the same terrace. Further down, the great fountain which powers the water organ was controlled to pour forward in a deluge and obscure the cave of the ancient Sibyl which opens on to the terrace behind. Spectators would have known that the Sibyl was thought to have prophesied great apocalyptic floods, including the one which washed away the world in the Biblical story. In his garden, I think, the cardinal recreated the event. It explains why visitors were then treated to a second, calmer array of fountains along the fishponds. As they sat there, these lesser fountains caught the light and shimmered, we are told, like rainbows. I think this effect was deliberate. First, the ancient sibyl foretold the flood. Then, the water fountains simulated it. Then, these smaller fountains recreated the rainbow by which God was believed to have promised that the world would never be washed away again.

I would not wish the garden to seem too cryptic. It has these thoughtful dimensions but it also has such a sense of fun. Since 2000, brilliant engineers have restored the water and the wind-powered music which issues from the fountains. Once again we can hear the twittering birds and the hooting owl in the cardinal's fountain of birdsong. We can even hear tunes on a version of his original water organ. Great gardens often have a complex underlying meaning, but like the Villa d'Este, they are great if they are also capable of setting solemnity aside.

Coneflowers

As an alternative to waterfalls in hot summers, 'New Wave' planters and writers keep telling me to turn the garden into a prairie. I find this advice ironic, because I have spent years trying to turn an impoverished flat patch like a prairie into a garden. Nor do I want great swathes of their favourite 'prairie' plants: those bilious pink knotweeds with flowers like pipe cleaners or their ornamental grasses which flutter delightfully in the wind and seed themselves where they are least wanted for the next five years. I am happy to plunder the prairie-school, pinch its best idea and leave its enthusiasts to cope with their own sea of dead-heads, scruffy leaves and hours with the strimmer among dripping winter stems.

Their best idea is a family which nurserymen have recently improved. Gardeners want something tall and classy which will last well from August onwards, and here the family of echinaceas has come into its own. For years, I used to believe that echinaceas would only look good on damp soil. White-flowered varieties with names like 'White Lustre' and 'White Swan' were recommended for cool, damp surroundings where they could keep company with the damp-loving blue of *Salvia guaranitica* 'Argentina Skies'. The prairie-planters established the opposite: many echinaceas do not need to be damp at all.

Perhaps you need to be reminded what their daisy flowers look like. They are close relatives of that other self-descriptive coneflower, the rudbeckia. They have a prominent yellow or dark central cone made up of tiny florets, attached to spiny bracts. These tough little spines in the central boss explain their curious name, which derives from the ancient Greek word for a hedgehog. The central cone is surrounded by daisy-like ray petals which come in shades of purple, rose or white. Some of the best forms come from the American Midwest, where they once earned a reputation as a herbal remedy. Chief Sitting Bull was probably given a dose of echinacea whenever he caught a chill. Extracts of the plant were also used against snake bite, giving it the name 'snake root'. The most fascinating use of the plant was as an insulation for feet and mouths. An extract of echinacea was turned into a juice which protected Native American fire-walkers and fire-eaters during their antics. Herbalists are fascinated by the properties of this prairie flower, which are still not fully understood.

Echinaceas are best compared in the National Collections which have sprung up in Britain. The most varied is at the Herb Garden, Chesterfield Road, Hardstoft, Pilsley, Chesterfield, Derbyshire, but even the National Collections are struggling to keep up with the latest varieties, the best of which are coming from Germany. Echinaceas hate a wet winter soil, not a dry summer one. As a result they are not good on clay, but they are excellent in gardens which are dry from mid-July onwards. The older varieties and the natural forms have the habit of holding their petals at a reflex angle, so that they look as if they have started to put their ears back in anxiety. I like this habit, but breeders have struggled to correct it by aiming for varieties which hold their petals horizontally. In most gardens, the usual choices are variations on the purple coneflower, *Echinacea purpurea*, from eastern North America. There are some rich colours available, especially the new 'Augustkönigin' which is more pink than purple and holds its petals horizontally. The older 'Robert Bloom' is about four feet high and flowers in a splendid combination of purple petals and orange cones which I still recommend. Any number of white forms are now on the market, but the simple *purpurea* 'Alba' remains one of the easiest and most charming. The tallest variety is 'The King', with bright crimson flowers on stems as much as five feet high. I value this height, although breeders have done their best to reduce it in other varieties.

Exciting new echinaceas are now waiting to spread over our gardens. One is 'Purple Knight' with dark purple stems and flat purple-pink flowers at a modest height of about two feet. On my soil, a winner is the pale pink coneflower, *Echinacea pallida*, which comes from Midwestern America and is well up to life in the Cotswolds. Its petals are finely divided, about three inches long, and wave elegantly in a slight breeze, best seen in the variety 'Hula Dancer'. Usefully, it puts up with bone-hard soil and refutes the old view that this family only grows well in a swamp. Other recent excitements are *purpurea* 'Rubinglow' and 'Rubinstern', two excellent short-stemmed varieties, one with big, heavily petalled red-purple flowers around dark brown centres, the other with huge ruby-red flowers from August till early October. 'Rubinglow' is about two feet high, 'Rubinstern' a little taller. They are outstandingly good new plants, first choices for thoughtful gardeners.

I cannot yet endorse the latest range of colours, the oranges, yellows and reds with names like 'Art's Pride' and 'Harvest Moon'. For the moment I am content with whites and rubies, less usual in August's range. There is no need to have a vast prairie carpet of these easy, bright flowers. Instead, fit them into your existing borders where they will prolong the season when the campanulas are gone and the phloxes are looking tired. It took a new style of gardening to bring them to prominence, but the style is not essential for their enjoyment. Ten years ago echinaceas seemed likely to be much more fussy, but we now know that they will survive a tough summer. The rose-purples and ruby reds are fresh colours for thoughtful gardeners to add among stylish white dahlias and the first blue flowers on a haze of small-flowered Michaelmas daisies.

Asphodels of the Negroes

Exile induces nostalgia for one's home flora. In the 1940s, during self-imposed exile in South Africa, the great Greek poet George Seferis surveyed the landscape and felt profoundly homesick. There were no olives, no cypress trees, so he transposed his memory of Greece's flowers to those along the African roadsides. In a fine poem, he described the stands of blue and white agapanthus as the 'asphodels of the negroes'. From the Mediterranean to the Cotswolds, early August is the peak of the agapanthus season. I much prefer their flowers to the 'romantic' flowers of asphodel, a wishy-washy thing. However, the agapanthus has enjoyed an uneven fate in our gardens. At first, it was regarded by Edwardian gardeners as a tender and exotic beauty which had to live in glasshouses during the winter and was only a flower for the rich. The first agapanthuses to reach Britain from the Cape were the least hardy, so it took a second wave of introductions to bring in hardier varieties. The breeding of the hardy sorts is famously associated with the Hampshire experiments of Lewis Palmer whose results are still commemorated in the Headbourne hybrids. In the 1950s Palmer did much to publicize the strength of these stunning flowers when he crossed them for hardiness and found them to be admirably suited to life on the warm chalk of his Hampshire garden.

While he worked, many gardeners still associated agapanthuses with the French Riviera gardens of the pre-war rich. In them, varieties with thick leaves flourished on hillsides running down to the sea. The agapanthus is still a star performer for anyone caught in a hot zone of France during summer, but Palmer opened the way to a wider use of agapanthus in Britain. He bred hybrids that could survive the winter. Headbourne hybrids are widely advertised nowadays, although their connection with Palmer's original crosses is tenuous. As the agapanthus is easy to raise from seed, it has developed dozens of natural hybrids in the past fifty years. Named hybrid varieties can only be truly transmitted by controlled propagation of stock plants. We can all buy an agapanthus from a big garden store, but there are few suppliers who understand what they are offering and why. Hence the importance of the endeavours of Dick Fulcher in mid-Devon. He holds the National Collection of agapanthus and lists about forty of them for sale through his nursery, Pine Cottage Plants, Fourways, Eggesford, Chulmleigh, Devon. From September to June he sends out young plants by mail, but stocks of the best older named varieties are still scarce and his customers need to list substitutes with their order. On principle, Fulcher has tracked down parents of known provenance, but his list goes far beyond the hybrids which Palmer introduced. He even has young plants of my particular favourite, the hardy 'Ardernei' which was bred before Headbourne was a name to drop. *Agapanthus* 'Ardernei' has white flowers with a grey line down their middle and holds them for a longer season than many of those which purport to be Palmer's blues. Mr Ardern has been unjustly forgotten in the annals of the agapanthus and we ought to reinstate him. Newer named forms range in colour from the excellent 'Bressingham White', raised in the heyday of Alan Bloom and his nursery, to the unusual 'Lady Grey', whose flowers are violet and white, and the splendid late-flowering 'Lilac Time'.

Meanwhile, extremely important work is continuing to be done to the family in New Zealand. The lovely results could be rebranded as the 'asphodels of the Kiwis'. The colours of these Antipodean agapanthuses are distinctive and many of the best varieties are hardy. They also flower for so long, surpassing the brief fortnight in August when the hardy Headbourne varieties are at their best. Two New Zealanders to look for are 'Jack's Blue' and the vivid 'Timaru'. They will still be sending up flowers in early October and are extremely free-flowering, though at different heights. 'Jack's Blue' is tall, with stems up to four feet, and the flowers appear in quantity in a shade of rich purple-blue. Marginally, I prefer 'Timaru', which is about two feet high and generous with a long succession of strong blue flowers on many separate stems. The most conspicuous variety is the excellent 'Purple Cloud', which takes the family into a new colour-range as its strong heads of flower are a shade of deep purple. These new varieties suffer from no diseases and are well up to everything which the English winter throws at them. In open ground they all survived the snow and frost of early and late 2009. There is even a prolific pure white variety which is about a foot high, an excellent arrival known as 'Snowdrops'. I recommend it for the front of any border which looks tired in mid-August. Two years ago, I also bought a single plant of *Agapanthus* 'Streamline' and I rate this one, too, as a winner. The flowers are a grey-blue with dark lines, a combination which never occurred in Palmer's old Hampshire range. The remarkable virtue of 'Streamline' is that it goes on flowering for about two months. It is now quite widespread in the trade and is better than the low-growing 'Tinkerbell', which tends to be promoted with it.

There is nothing difficult about growing these lovely flowers. I have never known any of them to be attacked by slugs. They like sunshine, a south or west aspect which is not a frost-pocket, and a light soil which is full of lime. Their central clump of roots soon becomes a thick tangle but unlike snowdrops, the plants do not flower more freely if they are regularly divided. They can, however, be split very easily into another dozen plants when new green shoots begin to appear like tabs in April. If they are given a liquid feed with Tomorite when the leaves first show they build up strength more quickly.

Fine though these new arrivals are, the finest agapanthuses in the world are not in gardens. They are in Monet's late paintings where they stand out brilliantly, outclassing his lilac-pink water lilies or his muddy views of the Giverny garden's main walks. The best of them live on canvas in the basement of the Marmottan Museum in Paris. If anyone would like to send me an offshoot, I would treat it with grateful respect.

Dead-Heading

If I go to a godless heaven, I hope to spend an hour every evening on the business of dead-heading. An hour of help each day from fellow faithless gardeners should ensure a perpetual season. Dead-heading is the most enchanting of garden tasks and is timely in early August.

Gardeners who complain that their gardens look wretched after mid-July have usually failed to dead-head them sensibly. This careful cutting helps in several ways. It removes the mess on popular early-flowering plants like the hardy geraniums. Geraniums which flower in late May and June are sometimes attributed a longer season by their hopeful nursery's catalogues, but they have this longer season only if they are dead-headed. A good recent arrival is *Geranium* 'Patricia', a lower-growing variation on the tall magenta *psilostemon* which is the mainstay of many borders in early July. 'Patricia' responds nobly to dead-heading from August onwards and will then flower again in early September. Another good arrival, the starry-flowered deep purple 'Nimbus', is also responsive. It will flower from June to November at a height of about eighteen inches if its span of two feet or so is regularly trimmed. Other varieties like violet-blue 'Spinners' or 'Johnson's Blue' have to be tidied at once. They finish flowering in early July and until you have cut them back to a central clump of leaves about a foot high, you cannot imagine what an improvement the tidying makes.

The most rewarding dead-heading is aimed at encouraging a second flush of flowers. I set about the willing varieties with nothing more than the kitchen scissors, reckoning that I will cut back as often as cutting off. Dead-heading, pinching out and shortening of stems are affiliated skills. Excellent candidates for shortening in early August are the lemon-flowered forms of anthemis, the daisy-flowered family which is potentially such a long flowerer. As you cut off the discs of the first dying flowers, you will often find that a second crop of buds is already breaking from the leaves beneath. My favourite is still the tall lemon-yellow *Anthemis tinctoria* 'Wargrave Variety', a great repeater when carefully dead-headed. The job is seldom the simple one of heading and usually requires a cut further down the anthemis's stem to a point where side-shoots will develop. The natural pair for this treatment is the admirable helenium. This daisy-flowered plant will often break into side-shoots and flower again. One of the winners in its family is the wonderful 'Moerheim Beauty', which quickly sends up a second mass of flower-buds below the first dead-headed crop. It has now been overtaken by an even better performer, 'Sahin's Early Flowerer'. Its main British supplier, Bob Brown of Cotswold Garden Flowers, used to remark in his nursery catalogue that 'like *Come Dancing*, it goes on for ever and ever'. *Come Dancing* has added *Strictly . . .* on television, but 'Sahin's Early Flowerer' is flowering on and on. The flowers are a mixture of orange and red-brown markings and some gentle dead-heading will keep it going happily until autumn.

Phloxes are also responsive to an informed snip. Immediately after flowering they need to be cut back to their upper pair of leaves, and then if the weather is not too dry, a worthwhile second round of flowers emerges. To help this second coming, you are advised to feed the plants with a weekly spray of Phostrogen which helps them to regain their stamina. It also helps delphiniums, which are so conspicuously ugly after flowering that it is essential to cut off the dead spikes at once. If the plants are then fed with a regular spray of Phostrogen on their leaves, they develop shorter side-stems of flower which open in early autumn.

Younger plants are more capable of repeating their season. This sad fact of life is particularly obvious in the penstemons, among which old plants in their third year or more flower earlier but tend not to repeat themselves. Younger ones will have a second or third flowering if you continue to dead-head them and feed them gently. I need hardly say, too, how important dead-heading is for annuals from August onwards. The botany is simple. The annuals are hurrying to set and ripen seed in one season, and if we can stop them, they will continue to flower, hoping to outwit us. It is a pleasant race to prolong the best of the bedding plants' display, from heavenly blue cornflowers to brown-orange rudbeckias, feathery cosmos daisies and all types of scabious. If you maintain a constant war on their seed-heads, you can keep them going until early October.

Dead-heading is the one profoundly rewarding war. It tidies away the signs of death and encourages yet another show of flowers. It was wonderfully understood by Vita Sackville-West, in her garden at Sissinghurst Castle. 'Dead-heading roses on a summer evening,' she wrote, 'is an occupation that carries us back into a calmer age and a different century. Queen Victoria might still be on the throne. There is no sound except the hoot of an owl and the rhythmic snip-snip of our secateurs.'

Gendered Landscape

In mid-July, when dead-heading becomes urgent, the first flowers begin to open on border phloxes. As a gardener in a university, I associate them with the last of the questions which have to be marked in the papers for university exams. The questions are hard enough for the hordes who have to answer them, but a thought should be spared for those who set and mark them. Summer is punctuated by unimaginable attempts at answers and by unthinkable questions which some of my brilliant colleagues set.

One such question haunts me, long after the results of its exam were published. In a General Paper you might think that historians are asked to write generally about class war, economic growth or social identity. You would be wrong, even in Oxford. 'What,' one of my fellow examiners recently wished to ask the under-23s, 'is the relation between gender and landscape?' Until now, gender studies may not have shaped your interpretation of green, rolling countryside. Nonetheless, they are everywhere. Sexual distinctions are biological, but gender ones are cultural. Your body parts, to be blunt, are sexual. The fact that females think of buying high heels, whereas I buy semi-brogue shoes, is gendered. So where does gender show up in the landscape?

After an hour's thought, I could think of little as an answer, except that separate lavatories for men and women have been placed by the National Trust along the acres of English coastline which have been preserved by its Operation Neptune. So I wrote to the examiner who set the question and asked what she had in mind. 'There is a list here,' she said, 'which lays out areas in which questions can be asked: one is landscape, one is gender, and as I could not think of a question on either, I ran them together and asked a question on both.' None of the candidates answered it.

Nonetheless, it has not gone away. Once you start looking for answers, they turn up in casual reading, even in reports of the most recent researches on two great British gardens, one at Stowe, the other at West Wycombe. At Stowe, the theory now is that the inscriptions on some of the garden temples referred to the ageing libido and decreasing prowess of the garden's male owner in the early eighteenth century. They might have been subtitled 'Waiting for Viagra'. In reply, witty and outrageous guests at the nearby West Wycombe Park encouraged its owner to lay out one part of his garden in the shape of a naked woman lying flat on her back. There were mounds in appropriate places and a sort of entrance tunnel, surrounded by a thicket of brambles. Their gendered garden was a vigorous answer to Stowe's gendered Georgian inscriptions. Would these researches count as a first-class answer?

My fellow examiner was not giving up. No, she said, the answers need to be much more general and not just show knowledge of a few odd things about odd places in the middle of England. Snubbed, I started to think again and have been thinking ever since. My conclusion is that the landscape is highly gendered but nobody talks about it. In Britain, the whole of it is overwhelmingly male. Men have owned most of it. Men have farmed it, fertilized it and cultivated it. Men, for the most part, have designed it. Why have we all been so slow to point this out?

Half of you, perhaps, are already protesting and saying that this conclusion is untrue. There have been women gardeners and landscapers, even if we exclude the present era in which the professions are finally open and both sexes can gender gardens as they wish. Women's earlier activity is most easily traced through the upper social classes, where a well-studied line runs through women of the nobility from 1600 onwards and includes several members of the royal family. It begins with Lucy, Countess of Bedford, who married at the age of thirteen in 1594 and then had the fortune to have a husband who was permanently mute after a fall from a horse. She liaised with King

James I's wife, Anne of Denmark, who had a parallel problem: her husband's homosexuality. The two of them took to gardening and befriended artists and poets, including John Donne and Ben Jonson. The most impressive result was Lucy's second garden at Moor Park in Hertfordshire, whose symbolic and architectural design cost a fortune. Lucy never put a spade in the ground herself, but she is one of the first English patronesses who contributed to grand gardening, a socially acceptable outlet for frustrated females.

Several members of Britain's royal families shared this outlet, especially Queen Mary of William and Mary, and Queen Caroline, wife of George II. Queen Mary had a real interest in plants, although I doubt that she ever put them in the ground. Caroline enjoyed the help of the enchanting William Kent and built a famous garden at Richmond Lodge which contained an array of allusions to Great Britons of the past. In a Gothic cottage, she even maintained a poetic hermit, who represented the supposed prophecy of Merlin that the kings of ancient Britain would one day return to rule as the Georgian House of Hanover. The garden was a fascinating comment on the idea of Britishness, another hardy perennial in general exam-papers for historians.

These women and others plainly enjoyed gardens, but were prevented by convention from enjoying gardening. It is not entirely clear when that convention began to change. The mid nineteenth century is the likely turning point, represented in books with titles like *Every Lady Her Own Flower Gardener* (1837) and in the famous output of Jane Loudon who started *The Lady's Magazine of Gardening* in 1840. Even then, it was assumed that 'ladies' would not occupy themselves in vegetable gardens or in growing their own fruit. They might manage a flower garden, no doubt with a male labourer under their direction, but it was not considered wise for them to bend over for any length of time. Up to this point, their main contributions had been patronage and spending their husband's money.

So far as I know, the change to practice comes in the 1890s and in 1902 the first School for Lady Gardeners was founded by Frances Wolseley at Glynde in Sussex. Women had become fit students of the practical art of gardening. From the 1890s onwards, therefore, trained female gardeners began to invade Adam's sphere. By 1896, females were working at Kew Gardens. 'Who wants to see blooms now you've bloomers at Kew?' asked a witty magazine in 1900. Since then, the gender balance has continued to even up. Female landscapers include Sylvia Crowe and Brenda Colvin, both of whom laid out acres of ground. At Sissinghurst, there was Vita Sackville-West. In America, there was Beatrix Farrand. In Surrey, there was Gertrude Jekyll. In Germany, there was Elisabeth von Arnim, famous for her book *In a German Garden*.

Indeed there were, and there still are, others, but were they not gardening in a gendered male slipstream? Vita wrote frankly: 'I could not have done it by myself.' She depended for her great garden's structure and design on her talented husband, Harold Nicolson. Beatrix and Gertrude were extremely good at planting, but were they ever effective in a wider landscape, and did they ever come up with a distinctively feminine style of design? Out in Germany, Elisabeth certainly did not. She was always tip-toeing around her awesome male partner, whom she called the Man of Wrath. If Mr Wrath wanted a big alley on the estate, I am sure he drove one into the landscape in an imperious, masculine way without ever asking her advice.

There is a famous letter, written in 1749, which nearly refutes men's dominance, but turns out to confirm it. The valiant Lady Luxborough wrote to the poet and landscape gardener William Shenstone detailing all the alterations which she had just carried out in her garden. 'The upper garden is now ungravelled and is making into a bowling-green; the pavilion will be set up next ...' However, she begins and ends by thanking Shenstone for his book and sketch-plans, and hopes that he will go on helping her. She has only one idea of her own, and she puts it to him as a 'proposal'. She is evidently wanting assurance from a differently gendered hand.

I have excluded the recent, dysfunctional fountain in memory of the Princess of Wales. Instead, I should mention the May Day style of celebrations at America's all-female university, Bryn Mawr College. Recently, the ladies banned the traditional maypole because it was wrongly gendered and too erect. Instead, they dug a cleft in the ground and welcomed the dawn of May by sitting round their Mayhole. They gendered the festival, but the idea has not caught on. To understand why, I suggest you look out of a train window and ponder while it speeds into the concrete jungles of a town. Those haystacks and hedges, those pleasant little coverts, those magical clumps of beech trees: all of them go back to men in the landscape, imposing their masculine gender for the sake of artistry, profit and their beloved country sports. The landscape has a masculine orientation. It is so masculine that I even risked putting the fact to a free-thinking feminist over lunch and asking her what she thought. How would she feel driving home now that she realized that the landscape is imprinted with the tyranny of the phallus and the patriarch? 'Sexy,' she answered, 'incredibly sexy: it really grabs me.' An alternatively gendered landscape is not what the other gender wants.

Lacecaps Under Trees

In a corner of my male-gendered landscape, near the drainpipe for my washing machine, I have an old pink lacecap hydrangea, which my father and I bought in 1963 after a visit to Hidcote Manor gardens in August, where the lacecap hydrangeas are so good. It is a historic hydrangea because it was acquired on a visit which opened my gardening eyes. For five years I had already been keenly growing alpines and annuals but at Hidcote I first realized that there was so much more to shrubs and climbers than our family gardens contained at home. Ever encouraging, my father agreed. We planted this lacecap hydrangea in the angle of two evergreen thuja hedges, a site of dry shade. Remarkably, it survived. It then moved house once, to my home as an adult, and it has never been better than in the years of its late middle age.

Intrigued by it, I set off on a hunt for a place where hydrangeas look really good. In England their qualities remain the subject of controversy. Some of you may be thinking that I should have gone to a major racecourse where mophead hydrangeas are such a frequent decoration of the stands. Others may be thinking of a bad hotel by the seaside where the hydrangeas in the front garden are neither pink nor blue. In fact, I went to Normandy, where hydrangeas are in their element. On the Normandy coast, almost every garden uses them because they love the dampness in the air and the days of sea mist. In an open field near Varengeville-sur-mer, hydrangeas are tended in the National Conservation Collection of the Shamrock gardens. The gardens can be visited on any day of the week as French growers take hydrangeas seriously. Their nurseries list many more varieties than ours do. In

Angers there is even an association which takes a scientific approach to one major branch of the family.

The Shamrock gardens are remarkable. They have been built up by Robert Mallet, whose family's great garden at Parc des Moutiers was partly designed by England's Edwin Lutyens. In 2001 Robert and his wife Corinne had to think carefully about how to transfer their prized collection to a new site, and came up with an unexpected answer. They planted a thick canopy of paulownia trees, which have big leaves like green handkerchiefs and flowers like purple-blue foxgloves if they are not caught in England by spring frosts. Paulownias grow extremely fast, and I would have imagined that hydrangeas would hate to try to grow around their trunks. In fact, they love it, even more than they loved my father's thuja hedge.

The Mallets had studied paulownias and realized that their roots drive deeply down through the soil and draw up water like pumps. In the classic days of old Japanese gardens, the paulownia was highly prized for other reasons: its flowers and its distinctive wood. Parents would make boxes from paulownia wood and give them to their daughters when they married so that they could keep the last dress of their virgin years in a safe, dry place. Nowadays, such a dress would probably be an ageing party dress from childhood, but even so, the paulownia is a tree with a future. Its big leaves open late in the year and fall early, but its roots can draw up water even in the sandiest soil and spread it around, making a garden possible. This brilliant combination is in action in the Shamrock gardens. Their paulownia trees are only six years old but great mounds of hydrangeas are already hugging their trunks. This pairing will work even on very dry soil and this excellent collection has changed my ideas of the hydrangea family's prospects.

It is odd to think that hydrangeas did not even arrive in Europe before the late nineteenth century: Wordsworth and Milton never saw one. They are at home, above all, in Asia, especially in Japan where there are hundreds in the wild which we have yet to collect and understand. I remember Germaine Greer remarking that the sound of the word 'hydrangea' in Australian-English nearly scared her off gardening for life. Actually, the family is popular down under and there are several named Australian forms. A visit to Shamrock transforms our ideas about what is globally available. All over the world growers are busy breeding new forms and we are seriously behind the game in Britain. The soil at Shamrock is acid, and therefore the blue varieties flower in a proper shade of blue. Forget those old varieties like *macrophylla* 'Blue Wave'. The Swiss have bred a blue mophead called 'Blaumeise' which is in a different class. Over in Germany breeders are developing low-growing forms with big flowers and naming them after leading European cities. 'Eibtal' is a cracking blue and they may be telling us something when the one called 'London' is big-headed in a boozy shade of wine-purple.

It will be hard for the Shamrock collection to keep up with the rate of progress. New varieties are pouring in, more than 100 every year. There is also a historic obligation to track down prize varieties raised by great breeders in past decades. One of them was England's H. I. Jones, whose Hertfordshire hydrangeas have almost disappeared from English lists. There is the further problem of uncollected varieties. Corinne Mallet made a recent trip to the Japanese mountains and found several low-growing unnamed lacecaps which have yet to appear in gardens anywhere.

In cultivation, no branch of the hydrangea family has been spared improvement. Some gardeners grow the paniculata forms, which have long, pointed heads of flower, but most of them are unaware that they vary in season and hardiness between their homes in north and south Japan. Paniculatas from the north flower early and should be pruned immediately after flowering because they set buds on the previous year's wood. Paniculatas from the south of Japan flower late and can be pruned later. There are even some low-growing ones with names like 'Dart's Little Dot'. Many of the best are grown in Alabama and are unknown to English gardeners. So, too, are good forms of the much-loved quercifolia, which is popular for its oak-shaped leaves and white heads of flower in August. There have been many recent improvements, some of which flower earlier and make a better show. As for the rest of the family, if anyone offers you a *serrata* 'Miranda' or a 'Mousseline', accept them with delight.

Two problems face everyone who tries to grow hydrangeas: how do you make the flowers go a true shade of pink or blue? How do you prune them? Most of the pink-flowered forms need an alkaline soil, but should be given extra lime between April and July if they stray towards purple-blue. True blue forms need an acid soil but can be maintained elsewhere with a good colour if you dose them on Sequestrene or any chemical compound which allows azaleas to survive on limey ground. The pruning is easy when you know the trick. It is wrong to leave the dead-heads on hydrangeas for months after flowering as if they will protect the plant against damage from frost. At Shamrock they cut them off as soon as they can. Each stem should be traced back to a pair of leaves by a visible pair of lower buds and cut back to that point. The buds are quite easily found on the stem when you look for them.

I set out on my travels thinking that hydrangeas live for ever and that my father's lacecap will outlive me. I returned realizing mopheads have a bright future too, and much more variety than I imagined. If you think they are fit only for the seaside, you are missing the point of a worldwide story.

Le Jardin Plume

Not so far from this garden of hydrangeas lies the best garden with a modern twist which has come my way in years. It represents a thoughtful vision which combines the traditions of several nationalities into an independent and intelligent style. There is a superb sting in the tail. I hate to say it but it makes an excellent use of ornamental grasses. Almost nothing in the vegetable kingdom has had a worse press from me during the past ten years, but I am forced to moderate my convictions. At last, I have seen them ingeniously employed.

During the past decade, Patrick and Sylvie Quibel have quietly been making a remarkable garden on a patch of Normandy so difficult it would have deterred me from even starting. For more than twenty years they have been nursery people with a critical eye for the changing styles of modern gardening. In 1996 they started to imprint their personal vision on a difficult landscape scarcely ten miles from Rouen. On their chosen site, the wind is severe and the soil is unfavourable clay. They had to garden on eight acres of it, but without much external help. Their site would have struck me as a flat, forsaken pancake, but they saw possibilities in it which would allow a plan to come true. The result is Le Jardin Plume, Le Thil, 76116 Auzouville-sur-Ry in Normandy. The garden is open every afternoon from Wednesday until Saturday with a few morning openings listed on the website at www.lejardinplume.com. In 2003 they won a prize for the best modern garden in France. They must have won by a distance. I have not seen a better modern garden anywhere. In 2009 they won a similar award from London's Garden Museum.

At Le Jardin Plume they have combined geometrical formality

with natural freedom, arranged so that symmetry and solidity lead out into unregulated wildness. What does this planning mean in practice? They began with a flat expanse of ground which stretched away from undistinguished buildings, now modernized to serve as their house, and nursery's barns. They raised the ground immediately around the house by the height of a single step and began to adorn it with a strict formal pattern of clipped green box and a tightly controlled planting whose flowers are mainly strong, pure yellow. From this one step up, you look down into a brilliant innovation, a rectangular pond which sits without edging or paving in the surrounding ground. It acts like a mirror and sounds even better in French: *un bassin miroir*. Beyond it, between fruit trees, stretches a carefully planned sequence of rectangular patches of the ornamental grasses which I most deplore. Here, they look brilliant because they are contained in rectangular borders and interplanted with flowering perennials which cheer up their brown waving plumes and give an impression of a man-made wilderness. These rectangles extend for more than an acre down the view across a flat prairie. They are many times prettier than the wildflower meadows which obsess gardeners in Britain and then look a mess for five months of the year. Here, the 'meadows' are rigidly controlled by a formal French eye and the mown paths between them are given the width of a boulevard. It is a fine experience to look down the central length of this extraordinary garden which is not in the least hostile to flowers. There is no brutal modernism, no silly sculpture and no unsympathetic concrete. There is an orderly sense of tightly controlled nature. I love it.

Round the house the colour is intense in several different sections. When I first visited in July the main terrace was a blaze of strong yellow from excellent types of coreopsis, emerging rudbeckias, carefully chosen dahlias and so forth. The strong colour goes well with the fresh green of the clipped box and makes an excellent contrast with the directed wilderness of grasses and perennials beyond. The wilderness is not like the shaggy banks of a British motorway, even when they are dotted with meadow geraniums.

The Quibels are excellent nursery people. They have worked out exactly which types of veronicastrum, tall thalictrum and desirable sanguisorba will compete and survive in a general setting of waving grasses. Like all patrons of '*les graminées*', known to me as eurograss, they emphasize the way in which this type of planting waves in the wind and fluctuates like waves when breezes penetrate the surrounding hedges. What differentiates the style at Le Jardin Plume is the intelligent interplanting with flowering perennials and the strict controlling vision which has not lost a reassuring formality underneath the seed-heads.

Patrick is most likely to take you round the garden and talk about its plan. It sounds so chic in French and makes me think of the formal mind of Descartes applied to a flat patch of the natural world. As it is a deeply thought garden, it does not stop with beds of grass or a single season. On one side of the house the spring garden faces east towards the rising sun and is cheered in the autumn by plantings of lowly *Aster divaricatus*. On the west side of the house, a segregated autumn garden includes very tall plants with flowers like spires. Clear yellow daisies rise here among clumps of bright pink and purple Michaelmas daisies and a central backbone of silvery grass. I can well imagine that it is spectacular when in season.

As you stand on the terrace's single step and look out, to your half-right is an enchanting potager which has rambling gourds, clumps of flowery coriander, the right kind of woven hurdles and a good display of upturned flowerpots. They are just like the pots from which Laurence Olivier used to extract earwigs while playing John Mortimer's blind father in his *Voyage Round My Father*, reliving those memorable scenes among dahlias which Mortimer's father would never see. The style in the potager is highly cultivated, intimate and immediately lovable. Beyond it you enter a forest of grassy miscanthus, the rampant grass which, for once, is rather exciting. Beyond it again, the white-flowered willowherb, or epilobium, has run wild in magnificent profusion. In spring, the flat rectangles of grasses on the main axis are full of brilliantly coloured bulbs. As an informal Englishman I might have been tempted to vary the rectangles and include one rectangle of flowering perennials to every two of grass. No doubt it would have looked awful but I would like to try. Meanwhile, I urge you to go and see the existing plan.

When you talk to Patrick and Sylvie you realize how considered and how serious is their engagement with nature and gardens. This quality does not always belong to the people who become most famous or who write the most books. The Quibels knew what they wanted to do. They looked carefully at the new styles of wild gardening in the Netherlands and adapted ideas which they found there, giving them a personal turn which transforms them. So often I found that they put into French what I quietly think in English. I am sure they will never exhibit at fancy Chelsea but I give them a gold medal. They also run an excellent nursery whose prices depend on the British pound's rate to the euro. Before the pound fell, they were lower than specialists' prices in England. There are no fewer than fourteen kinds of excellent helenium, eight of which are new to me, and eleven varieties of the sanguisorbas which they use so well but which are not easy to propagate. If you have a car boot, I suggest you fill it, because there is plenty there which you will not easily find back in England. All the plants are properly grown, not in peat-based compost, but proper soil, what is called in French 'terre universelle'.

Dealing With Dry Shade

In August, those of us at home can put the garden under critical review. In sunny weather, the first problems which hit the eye are areas of dry shade. We all have dry shade and not many of us make much of it. When the sun is hot, we retire towards it and then realize the space we are wasting. After many experiments I have a core of reliable colonizers which survive on these awkward sites. I am not thinking of dry shade under a wall so much as the shade cast by tall trees, a difficult constraint, especially on a light soil. The answer is not to aim for anything exotic and not to plant phloxes, which may like light shade but are miserable without water. Go for something quieter which will not look as if it is struggling.

One of the best choices is a first cousin to our Michaelmas daisies, an aster called *schreberi*. Its flowers are star-shaped and white above leaves which are an excellent shade of dark green. *Aster schreberi* is quite without diseases and never catches grey mildew. It flowers for about three months, starting in July, and is even more robust than its striking blue relation, the daisy-flowered *Aster macrophyllus* 'Twilight' which will also put up with difficult conditions. 'Twilight' does not cover the ground but it shows up well from August onwards in a pretty shade of blue. It is excellent to see its fresh flowers among other survivors which have had their season. In front of it I plant groups of the pleasantly sprawling *Aster divaricatus*, another neglected winner with small starry white flowers, dark black stems and exceptional stamina in drought.

The greatest such survivors are the hardy geraniums, many of which throw out long stems of flower and fall forwards untidily after midsummer. They must be cut back promptly with a pair of lawn shears and reduced to a central clump. Some of these sprawlers will grow well in difficult settings, but my standby is a tidier one, *Geranium macrorrhizum* 'Album'. It is a quiet plant but never seems to fail, although the flowers are not actually white, as the third of its Latin names implies, but a pale shade of pink-white from May onwards. The leaves are tidy and it is fun to discover that they are pleasantly scented of the geranium oil which is used for bath essence. One or two plants can soon be divided and multiplied to make a long line. The plant is a godsend in dry conditions.

If you also choose shade-lovers with height, they will break up the lower layers of this cover and stop them looking like an effort to block the ground. An excellent option is to plant the deeper blue form of what is sometimes wrongly known as 'chicory'. *Cicerbita plumieri* is an indestructible plant which gives great pleasure in high summer at a height of about four feet. It is not the sky-blue 'chicory' which is often seen flowering by roadsides in Mediterranean countries. Its flowers have a deeper colouring, almost violet-blue, and its thick, water-retentive roots will grow where the going is tough.

Shrubs also give a layer of height and the best of them flowers in late spring, although it is happy with minimal water. The familiar choisya, or Mexican orange blossom, is a surprisingly good performer under tall deciduous trees, a discovery which has come late in my experience. A choisya's leaves have a shiny green coating and although they are not at their seasonal best when the flowers appear in May, they soon recover and remain a glossy green presence which is cheering from June onwards. The entire plant is tougher than was thought forty years ago, when there were fears that it might not be hardy. Few modern winters are going to trouble it in the shelter of tall trees and it is good to discover that a dried-out summer does not bother it, either. I am also puzzled why an equally tough form of honeysuckle is not more widely available. *Lonicera tatarica*, preferably the form called 'Hacks Red', is a reliable shrub with an exceptional ability to put up with next to no water wherever the developing roots of trees cause problems. Its leaves look dusty in dry weather but it is almost indestructible and the red flowers in the joints of the leaves are pretty. They puzzle people who know honeysuckles only as climbers.

If you prefer to allow a small, narrow strip of a dry bed to be invaded so that it never needs attention, I recommend a wild runner, a relation of comfrey but one which never seeds itself widely. *Symphytum cooperi* is not yet in the *RHS Plant Finder* but is excellent value if given its head in a dark, dry corner. The flowers are tubular, combining a hint of dark purple with blue and white without being overpowering. Alternatively, I would choose evergreen *Phlomis russeliana*, which has quite big leaves and sends up green-yellow flowers to a height of about three feet. The leaves will flag if the weather is persistently dry, but the plant never dies.

In August, it is easy to think only of yet more flowers for August but the best plants in dry shade flower much earlier. Even when they are in competition with sycamore roots, hellebores will make an excellent show in dry ground from February until April. The ones to choose are the many varieties of the Lenten rose, *Helleborus orientalis* and the × *hybridus* garden forms. From August onwards, in dry places, it is worth feeding their clumps once a fortnight with diluted fertilizer to be sure of spectacular shows of flower in the following spring. Some of their experts write as if they must have a deep soil, lightly shaded, but in fact, they will grow in less than a foot of soil over a stony subsoil, only six feet away from the trunks of tall sycamores and chestnuts. I know, because I tried them there, at first with a sinking heart, as I had ordered them before I discovered with a crowbar how bad their chosen position was to be. An autumn feeding has helped them but in these tough conditions they are as beautiful as those in more favoured parts of the garden.

In the past ten years, crossing and selecting have extended the charm of these excellent plants. The good work has accelerated through the positive attitude of Ashwood Nurseries at Kingswinford, near Kidderminster, whose owners took a splendidly contrary view. For years, there had been fears that hellebores would deteriorate when their famous keepers gave up or died. Two of the great experts were Helen Ballard in Worcestershire and Elizabeth Strangman in Kent, and fortunately they had the generosity of true experts and were prepared to make their best plants available to the Ashwood team. While other experts were inclined to moan that all the good forms were dying out, Ashwood rose to the challenge and set out to breed even better ones. You can now go to their splendid nursery and buy the results in selected colours. The Ashwood crosses will ensure that you have high-class winners of your own, although other forms have been bred elsewhere and are often very good. I have had excellent value from an ugly-sounding hybrid, *Helleborus* × *nigercors*, which is a cross between the Christmas rose and the vigorous green-flowered Corsican hellebore. The big white flowers come in bunches and last very well and the Corsican bloodline gives the leaves a point and the plant some extra strength.

Dry shade is not a disaster for gardeners. It is a challenge which limits options and needs thought if it is to be turned to good effect.

19. Wilhelm and Frau Schacht inspect an alpine sink at Waterperry

20. Sir David Scott and his bride Valerie, an hour after their wedding

17. Miss Havergal in uniform leaflets a visitor to Waterperry

18. How to use a trowel: Miss Havergal, her dog and a student at work

21. Herterton in July

22. Rose 'Long John Silver'

23. *Delphinium* × 'Centurion Lilac Blue Bicolour' will flower in its first year from seed sown in January

24. *Deutzia setchuensis corymbiflora* at Kiftsgate

25. My lacecap hydrangea, now 47 years old

26. *Hydrangea macrophylla* 'Blaumeise'

27. Part of the potager in Le Jardin Plume

28. Rosemary Verey under the laburnum arch

29. Autumn in the Picton Garden, Colwall, near Malvern

30. *Aster × frikartii* 'Wunder von Staffa'

31. Arthur and Gay Hellyer in their Jersey garden

32. The thoughtful future: my son and grandson plant their first tomato

Rosemary Revisited

Dry shade was the sort of challenge which Rosemary Verey liked to overcome with a forgotten cure. Ever resourceful, she became the Queen of English gardening until her death in June 2001, and I still reflect on her fame and style. As a writer, lecturer, planter and gardener, she became celebrated throughout the English-speaking world for her densely planted garden at Barnsley House in Gloucestershire. It was promptly sold by her heirs, but was bought and turned into a hotel by neighbours who had admired Rosemary in action. The garden remains open in her memory.

Rosemary was first propelled to fame by the book *The Englishwoman's Garden*, which she wrote with the talented gardener Alvilde Lees-Milne, famous for her fine garden, also in Gloucestershire, at Alderley Grange near Wootton-under-Edge. The title caught a mood of gentle feminism and showy gardening in the early 1980s, although with hindsight, many of the gardens in the book were made by men or jointly with men as partners. On the strength of it, Alvilde became a garden designer for Mick Jagger and Rosemary, too, would soon be advising a male celebrity world. Increasingly known from her writing, she emerged as a garden designer with influence. In imitation of her Gloucestershire garden, ever more people wanted to own a tunnel of trained laburnum, dripping with yellow flowers. She emerged in middle age, an achievement which seems unusual now because subsequent garden-princesses have been launched through television, for which youth and beauty are a help. Whereas Alvilde had gardened for decades, having known (and loved) Vita Sackville-West in the 1950s, Rosemary only began gardening in her early fifties when her children had grown up and her husband was encouraging her to fill the empty spaces in the garden with flowers. One of her shining qualities was that she was always clear and generous about the people who inspired her to try to garden seriously. She recalled how Russell Page, the landscape gardener, had just brought out his classic book *The Education of a Gardener* and it caught her fancy. She often told me of the encouragement she received from Arthur Hellyer, the impulse behind so many well-known gardeners.

Her gardening career took off at an age when many people think of downsizing their garden or giving up. Undaunted, she showed what a female gardener could do through her own talent at an older age. Rosemary was extremely well organized and had a clear, efficient mind. In her youth she had read for a degree in Economics in London and throughout her years of motherhood she was a skilled horsewoman, applying her talents for organization to the horse-shows and local Pony Club meetings around her Gloucestershire home. The death of her beloved husband David, himself an architect and man of style, impelled Rosemary to apply her skills to a new, absorbing occupation. She chose gardening in which she had already progressed but in a different era and place she might well have chosen a public career.

Rosemary Verey began late, but she hit on the right style at the right moment. She coincided with a new wave of English-style gardening, propelled by economics and a subtle change in technology. The technical change was not horticultural. It was a change in book-production which encouraged the rise of the book-packager and book-designer: English publishers realized that good, cheap colour printing could be bought in from Italy or Hong Kong. As a result hers was the first grand garden to be stunningly photographed and marketed through full-page colour spreads in such affordable books as her *Making of a Garden* (1995) and *Garden Plans* (1993), among the most rewarding of her titles. She soon began to think clearly in photographic terms. In the 1960s, most colour picture books had been feebler: Rosemary's set a new standard by the way in which her gardens were presented.

The revolution in presentation went together with various social novelties and a particular character of her own. Until the late 1970s, the main theme in most gardens had been the continuing urge to 'save labour'. Gardeners were still struggling to use 'ground cover' and surmount the shock to their parents or themselves caused by the disappearance of cheap labour since 1945. Rosemary went in the opposite direction, helped by an increasing team of gardeners. She liked themed features, colour, thick layers of planting, and anything which was not drab. As her fame and fortunes grew, the variety of features at Barnsley grew too and the lavishness of the planting and upkeep were able to be sustained by the profits of her advice. In the early 1980s, a new free-market mood in Britain made riches and their display more accessible and more acceptable and gardening regained a scale and extravagance lost since the 1930s. The Prince of Wales, recently married, set high society an example of grandiose gardening round his newly bought home at Highgrove, on whose themed gardens Rosemary gave early advice. In the new social climate well-off garden-owners began to want to compete with the illusory perfection which was caught in the photographs of her plantings. She stood for a new affirmation of a generous 'English style', one which had been in retreat for fifty years.

English gardening had always been popular in America, especially on the East Coast, and the newly lavish style of her flower gardening appealed to American owners too, who were also prospering in a free-market age. Rosemary was quick to develop transatlantic contacts which multiplied through mutual friends, impressed by her garden, her royal contacts and her clear views. She had the special cachet of being a woman, one who was at ease in high society and very well presented as a lecturer. She became a major bridge between keen American gardeners and English gardeners who had previously written off much of America's gardening out of ignorance. Back in Gloucestershire, she found in her friend and neighbour, the dress-designer Hardy Amies, exactly the person to dress her in style for lectures and meetings on her transatlantic circuit. They had a splendid rapport, as Sir Hardy was also a sharp-eyed gardener of taste and independence, with a fine eye for old-fashioned roses, his 'last collection', he would tell me, while showing off his roses with French names as if they were ladies in a couturier's salon. Characteristically, Rosemary loved learning from the many fine American gardens which she was now able to visit: she especially admired the artistic style of Bob Dash on Long Island and the exceptional planting by Ryan Gainey in Atlanta, Georgia. 'The dry brown hills,' she once wrote, 'of the Yakima Reservation in Oregon, with their tawny look, remind me of the brown stems and trunks of my winter shrubs and trees at Barnsley. It has taught me to think about the expansiveness of nature . . .'

As the books and their authoress travelled, Rosemary became in demand as a designer and garden-planter to a degree which no Englishwoman in recent decades had equalled. Throughout, she retained a concern for natural solutions to the artificial art of gardening. She liked to look for such practices in older garden books which dated back to the 1600s and before. Her strength was to suggest ideas, not to design on paper, an art which she never mastered. She could not draw. Instead, she liked novel experiments, so much so that she was one of those who urged me to mulch my garden with cocoa-shells, a fashionable war cry in the battle against peat, and one which I am glad I never followed. Her 'countrywoman's notes' from Gloucestershire are some of her most enjoyable writings, but here too her fancies can seem idiosyncratic in the modern world. 'If your son or daughter is facing an important examination,' she once suggested, 'encourage them with angelica ("inspiration"), red clover ("industry") and pink cherry blossom ("education") . . .' From my practical observations, the young recipients' first thought would be to try to smoke them.

At Barnsley, her knot garden was a brilliant revival of an old fashion, using forgotten green germander as well as box. Her laburnum tunnel was not an original idea, but it was a master-stroke to underplant it with the tall purple onion-heads of *Allium aflatunense*, a choice which she told me she owed to the Dutch nurseryman van Tubergen. It was, however, her own happy idea to plant the long paved path from the main rooms of her house with bright helianthemums, or sun roses, a scheme which ought to be imitated. By the mid 1980s, she had also planted a formal vegetable garden, or potager, which became famous through photographs of its standard gooseberry trees and richly coloured Swiss chard. It was a difficult space to visit, not least with the owner, who would bend among the elegant cloches and accentuate a visitor's sense of fighting for space, like a car-parker in Knightsbridge. Here, especially, she had thought to a photographic scale, rather than to a workable width for a long-term garden.

Monarchs are also adept at looking past people, or putting them down, arts which Rosemary sometimes failed to realize she possessed. To those whom she acknowledged, she was extremely loyal and generous, but at her packed memorial service in Cirencester, one of her many beneficiaries, the fine plant photographer Andrew Lawson, recalled how he once came to photograph the Barnsley garden. He started work very early in the morning, a garden photographer's necessary licence. He went to the yellow laburnum tunnel and found a few flowers fallen on the ground beneath, so he brushed them away to suit his picture. Breakfast followed, and Rosemary surprised him by remarking on his tidying of her tunnel's appearance. There was a pause and while Andrew reached for a reply, Rosemary cut him short. 'I preferred it,' she told him, 'the way it was.'

I am not sure that she always preferred the garden the way that it became. Winters in Gloucestershire can be bleak, and as the years passed, a bottle or two of spirits used to help her through dark, solitary evenings. In due course her own garden became a victim of the very photography which made it wondrous. Photographs fix a perfect instant, but as time passed and plants grew too freely, she was prone to pass off the jungle of her later decades as a 'meadow style'. She was a great magpie and noticer, but how deep and broad was her knowledge? Once, when we returned from a walk to admire her orange-flowered asclepias, I responded to her offer of a shrub from her plant stall. I asked for a plain old ceratostigma, the prince of blue-flowering autumn shrubs, which grows well enough at Barnsley. Rosemary surprised me by saying she did not know it and certainly did not have it.

Television viewers may share a different memory. In front of the camera, Rosemary Verey was magnificently poised and true to her class, but she was seen on one widely watched programme walking down the broad borders of a lovely Cumberland garden with its panama-hatted owner. After passing some fine urns, he turned to her to ask for advice, as he felt the garden needed a bit of a lift at the point where they were standing. There was a brief silence and she replied: 'Urns, more urns . . .'

Rosemary remains justly honoured as a great ambassador for English gardening, here and abroad. One of her clients was the singer Elton John and she once wrote that she loved to hear him singing, and even hoped that 'one day, it will be a song about the orange marigold that has found its way into his white garden'. Was she chiding him for the oversight, or was she celebrating nature's wayward manner? Either intention would be true to her way with gardeners and gardens.

Swinging Baskets

Up and down historic Britain, sweaty August brings the public crop of hanging baskets into overheated bloom. They dangle on the lamp-posts in heritage Oxford (twinned with Leon, Nicaragua), conservation Bath is crawling with them, and they are swinging far and wide in Leamington Spa.

Why ever have councils assumed that their taxpayers want to pay for this public fiesta? The cost is not only the cost of the baskets. Cast-iron poles have to be drilled into the pavements to hold them above head height. While publicizing their low-emission buses and writing on their nuclear-free notepaper, councils send out teams of water-carriers to soak their hanging baskets with precious water which could otherwise help them in their mission to 'save our planet'. The watering is done in the twilight before dawn, away from spectators who might question it. In a vivid image, Germaine Greer has given the display a new meaning. Hanging baskets in our city centres remind her, she has written, of 'severed heads on the way to the Roman Forum'. Were there really heads on show in the central space of ancient Rome? Romans were capable head-hunters, and they first cut the head off a presiding consul and displayed it in the Forum in 87 BC. Forty years later, Julius Caesar had a neat little bout of head-hunting at the expense of his enemy Pompey's remaining men in Spain. In cele-bration, his troops stuck the heads on the fortifications of Spanish towns. In 43 BC, there was the beheading of poor old Cicero, the acknowledged master of oratory. Head-hunters sent his head to his enemy Mark Antony, whose wife is then said to have pierced the tongue with hairpins. Head-hunting has ancient roots in the history of Western civilization.

Severed heads in Rome's forum were always male, but is the most thought-provoking analogy for baskets in a crowded town centre a Cicero with petunia-dreadlocks or a Gaul with a grimace of busy Lizzie? Not according to one of my former gardening suppliers in the Vale of Evesham. He declared himself king of the hanging basket and delighted both sexes by offering them a choice of hanging baskets in cup-sizes ranging upwards from double-D. He changed my perception of a council's underwired basket of blue lobelia, delicately lined with green moss. In return I told him about Queen Pheretima, attested in Herodotus' ancient histories. She took revenge on the women of a Libyan city by cutting off their breasts and fixing them on the outside of the city wall. In her honour he introduced a special basket called Pheretima's Revenge. When you next see the municipal baskets on city walls, think of Pheretima and look again.

Why are these great balls of colour so often an affront? One reason is their context, another, their contents. They have become part of the mission to jolly up town centres and give them a festive mood. Poles topped with streaky petunias are a strange idea of a festival. They derive from the municipal obsession to turn town centres into a vision of Toy Town, spattered with pointless signposts and multi-coloured distractions. Towns with serious architecture are lucky enough not to need them, as they have their own dignity without being told to join in a frolic. Has anyone seen a row of hanging baskets in the centre of Venice or Paris?

Perhaps you wonder why petunias, trailing 'surfinias', lobelias, 'geraniums' and busy Lizzie are the overwhelming types of planting in each severed basket. The reason is commercial. These particular types of plant are raised in vast quantities by wholesalers who then pass them on as young 'plugs' or ready-grown plants, to the 'gardening' departments of local authorities. If you wrote and suggested that the baskets might be filled next year with trailing morning glory, the problem would be that somebody locally would have to germinate it and grow it. This pre-selection is an anathema to thoughtful gardeners. They look on the contents of a typical hanging basket much as keen cooks look on supermarkets' rock-hard apologies for 'fresh nectarines' or Class One pears.

Is there a suitable place for rounded holders of colour, clamped above head-height on posts or on buildings' façades? If you live in a festive building like a pub, you might as well go festive and cover it with anything which flowers. The problem is not the basket itself but the transfer of decoration fit for a pub to settings which have no need of it. Why, too, does the container always have to be a basket? In the south of France or in Italy a cluster of single flowerpots often stands beside steps or windows and shows plantings of a carefully chosen scarlet geranium or a flower of the homeowner's choice. On the walls of a big square in Cordoba the trailing geraniums are spectacular. In bright sunlight, these single flowerpots are so charming because they lack the over-stuffing which comes with a double-D basket in full flow. They also avoid the carmine colours which are chosen by city parks departments without thought for their setting in a sober street. Breeders have proudly developed trailing petunias which will flower for weeks and 'add value'. The trouble is that most of these varieties are available only in veined or streaky colours.

It is time for council taxpayers to answer back. Each year, busy judges go out and assess the annual planting which local authorities, 'working with the environment', have plastered over their town centres. They then give them prizes in the name of Britain in Bloom. Then the taxpayers pay all over again so that a winning of this prize can be inscribed on the road signs which identify the city and its foreign twins. Instead, the judges should request that slips be sent out with each demand for council tax, asking the payers whether they continue to want baskets and artificial watering all over their environment at their own cost. There could be a space for comments and another for suggestions of colour-coding. The extravaganza would then disappear, along with the pretensions which introduced it.

Forcing Nature

'The French build gardens and the English like to think that only they can plant them.' Is this bit of popular garden history true? I have been checking it out at one of those dreamy French country houses which activate the planting instincts of English gardeners as soon as they see avenues of trimmed limes and beech trees.

Near Bayeux and within sight of the 'Gold Beach' of the Normandy landings in 1944, the Château de Brécy is a rare delight. Formal French designs for gardens are usually on such a grand scale that modern gardeners struggle to apply them to their own setting. They 'force nature', we are taught, but at Brécy nature looks as if she has been happily seduced into submission. Neither the château nor the formal garden is impossibly large. Nonetheless the virtues of fine stonework and mathematical planning are in evidence on the three terraces, which ascend in due proportions from the main vista. Their former owner and partial restorer, the man of letters Jacques de Lacretelle, described the garden as the 'finery of an Italian princess thrown over the shoulders of a little Normandy peasant girl'. It was thrown there in the 1660s and has lived on wondrously as the backbone for a medium-sized formal garden, which is once again at its peak. I wish I could inherit it.

Plagued by small black thunder-flies, I stood on the roof of the château with the present genius of the place, Didier Wirth, and asked him to take me through the evolution of the garden beneath us. Its mastermind is still unknown, although some have suggested a genius of formal landscaping, François Mansart, who worked earlier in the vicinity and helped to teach the great Le Nôtre. Its patron is better known, a local man of law, Jacques Le Bas. His supplementary fees while in office would fascinate the modern British press but they were also the income on which his plans for Brécy's house and its ascending garden of steps, parterres and balustrades were based. Their main vista is a triumph of rational French calculation and demonstrates that mathematical proportion applies to all houses and homes, whatever their extent.

Brécy's garden lies on the site of a former monastic seat for Benedictine monks. Even now Didier Wirth and his gardeners hit on the bones of holy brothers when they dig the foundations for new hedges and plantings near the surviving priory church. In the French Revolution this church and its lands were taken over by the villagers. The sculpted entrance gates and formal backbone of the Brécy garden survived in gentle decay, until they were encountered by the renowned French actress Rachel Boyer on holiday in the summer of 1912. Enchanted by them, she bought the place on sight and even acquired the superfluous priory. Everybody's property had sunk to the value of nobody's property. She paid 101 francs for the church, one of history's great post-Revolutionary buys.

In her care Brécy first benefited from the attentions of French professionals, experts who cared for the preservation of '*monuments historiques*'. A lull followed, including a merciful escape from shelling in 1944, when Brécy was taken without a fight in the first flush of the Allied landings. In 1955 the writer de Lacretelle bought the place and set to work on the formal garden near the house. He reintroduced a smart box parterre and a formal pattern of diagonal lines for the main terraces. He based his patterns on drawings by the master designer André Mollet, preserved in the classic handbooks of the period when Brécy was built. Brécy began to smile again, but its smile has been lengthened and greatly improved by Barbara and Didier Wirth, owners since 1992.

As I looked at their excellently chosen old roses round the church, I remembered the cliché about English planting and French building. Modern Brécy challenges it. At home, on the hedges of my English old vicarage, I have sheets of white flower from the apt climbing rose 'Rambling Rector'. Beside the Church of 101 Francs, the Wirths have

'Rambling Rectors' too. I had left for France while two valiant tree-cutters struggled to restore shape to my English avenues of hornbeam and evergreen *Pyrus calleryana* 'Chanticleer', a self-inflicted penance which drains money every two years. At Brécy, Wirth's gardeners keep a long run of hornbeams to the shape of a green cloister, complete with arched windows. They emerge on ladders through this cloister's green ceiling and clip every twig in sight. Neat cones of hornbeam flank a path by the church, clipped so tightly that you could bounce a ball off them. In England my avenues of hornbeam become so fluffy before their clipping that I have sometimes thought of felling them. The difference is that Brécy's hornbeams are cut three times a year from a French platform which makes my platform at home look like a clumsy parody of a guillotine. Brécy is proof that hornbeam hedging, tightly clipped, is the right choice for sites in full sun, whereas beech hedging is best in partial shade.

Brécy is fortunate in its present owners. They have emphasized the garden's strong architectural lines by intelligently extending its green hedging. On the far end of its main axis they have added formal barriers of limes and hornbeams in a style which struck a distant English chord in my mind. A widely spaced line of pleached trees stands as a back row with its trunks neatly clipped. In front of it runs a line of tightly clipped hedging, matching the variety of tree behind it. I remembered the excellent green lines of similarly clipped hedging in the Buckinghamshire garden of the famous decorator and designer David Hicks. It was not a random memory. Barbara Wirth, I then learned, had run the David Hicks shop in Paris and had been a good friend of the designer, whose garden had indeed influenced her style.

Clichés begin to become fuzzy. Here is a formal French garden with lessons in planting and maintenance for English gardeners. Its formal style is a supreme witness to the classic age of French planning, but one of its initiatives owes a debt to an English designer's example. Happily confounded, I turned back to consider the garden's most unusual keynote, globe artichokes modelled in stone on the garden's impressively restored fountains. Wirth explained the underlying idea. They imitate the globe artichokes which survive carved in stone near the top of the property's Benedictine priory church. They puzzled later historians, but the answer lies in medieval Benedictine bibles. The globe artichoke is not a symbol of the hors d'oeuvres which await us in a starred French restaurant in paradise. It represents our human relation to God. God is in the artichoke's heart, below the layers of choking fluff and prickles. We are the artichoke's leaves which surround His presence at the centre. Is that why I often find the artichoke's heart so indigestible? At Brécy, I am happy to accept that the designs on the Wirths' new fountains are telling us that the garden is close to heaven.

Later Clematis

Clematis which flower in late summer are the most reliable members of their family. The best of them never catch the disease of clematis wilt and are able, too, to survive a long dry spell. The best of all is *Clematis* 'Bill MacKenzie'. It is a tangutica hybrid with yellow flowers, but the flowers are larger and more open than in close relations, and it is a name on which you should insist. Tangutica comes from Mongolia and north-west China and should not be confused with the smaller-flowered *Clematis orientalis*. The 'Bill MacKenzie' name commemorates a great gardener who did much for London's admired Chelsea Physic Garden during the 1960s. It was he who selected this exceptionally good variety while visiting Valerie Finnis at the Horticultural College which flourished at Waterperry, Oxford. It was the happiest selection, and you should insist on it when you are shopping.

The reason is that it flowers spectacularly, grows strongly and makes an exceptional show. The flowers have four broad yellow 'petals' which open out and show a contrasting cluster in the centre. It grows more than fifteen feet high with great speed and is not fussy about a dry place below a tall wall. For years, I never realized that it would thrive when facing south on the front of a house. I now wonder why I bother with anything else. 'Bill MacKenzie' goes on and on flowering and is still at its best in early October on my walls. Not only does it have the best flowers in the yellow group, it also has the enchanting grey-silver fluffy seed heads of the main species. An *FT* reader once wrote to describe them to me as resembling 'imitators of the early Beatles' haircuts, now in their late middle age'. Indeed, they look like grey-haired survivors from those carefully styled fans whom

I saw screaming in the Hammersmith Palais in late 1963. Fortunately, Bill MacKenzie's clematis is silent.

One of my other late favourites is a useful sprawler. *Clematis* × *jouiniana* was raised as a cross between two wild parents, one of which is the vigorous Traveller's Joy of hedgerows. It falls around happily at ground level and makes a mound, off which long side-growths spread. The small flowers are shaped like an X and are a pleasing shade of milky blue-white. The advantage of this plant is that it will spread and hide gaps or ugliness at ground level. It is not ever-green, but it makes a good job of hiding an old tree stump or a big drain cover if you plant it some distance away and fix wide-meshed netting over the offending object. If you ever need to open the drain cover, the stems of × *jouiniana* can easily be brushed aside. Alterna-tively, you can build it a frame of pea-sticks and leave it to scramble into a longish thicket about three feet high. It will also grow up a wall, but it is as a late sprawler that I value it most. On poor soil, I have found that its flowers are much smaller, but they are always better in a wet year. There is an earlier form, conventionally called × *jouiniana praecox*, but I think that this name is freely applied in the trade, irre-spective of the start of the plant's flowering season. A true *praecox* should already be in flower in July.

One of the main ambitions of breeders nowadays is to create a late-summer clematis which will stay small and flower well as a pot plant. None of the candidates has yet persuaded me, but there is one established item, a neat little number from Guernsey called 'Petit Fau-con'. The merit of this plant is its exceptional length of flowering, which sometimes stretches across three months. The height is not more than a metre, but the flowers are prolific from the tips of new growth and open to a good shade of deep blue. They twist round as they open, showing pretty orange-yellow stamens, and then the col-our becomes more pure. 'Petit Faucon' is a good choice for the middle row of a flower border, where it can be centrally supported on a cane. Alternatively, it can be placed to fill in the bare space which develops at the base of many climbing roses, especially if they have not been pruned sufficiently hard in their early years. 'Petit Faucon' is an excel-lent plant which fills a gap in gardens and in its family.

Over early-flowering shrubs I grow late-flowering clematis, a cloak which gives these shrubs a second season. The best ones for the purpose are members of the Viticella Group, coloured from white to deep velvety maroon-red. They grow to a convenient routine. In February, they should be cut down to within a foot of ground level, a cutting which keeps their stems off the flowering growth of forsythias, viburnums and early shrub roses. When the shrubs have flowered, the viticellas begin to spread through them, but not so quickly that the shrubs, too, cannot be pruned lightly after flowering. In August my white-flowered *Viburnum* × *carlcephalum* would look dull and dusty without their covering of white-flowered *Clematis* 'Alba Luxurians'. This white variety with green markings shows up best on a shrub, whereas the darker purple and red viticella forms are blurred by the branches over which they run. For this purpose, a clematis should be planted on a cane about three feet away from the shrub's main stems. The cane should be tilted towards the shrub's lower branches, so as to guide the clematis to clamber in the right direction.

On quite a different scale, another winner was bred in the Crimea about forty years ago, also by capitalizing on vigorous Traveller's Joy as a parent. It is called now correctly 'Paul Farges' (formerly, *fargesioides* 'Summer Snow') and is one to watch. The flowers are small, but they are cream-white with a slight scent and a long season. It is a favourite with beekeepers because bees love it and turn it into palatable honey. 'Paul Farges' is a favourite with me because it is so vigorous that it will bolt up a tall tree or hedge. I have even let it loose up a shaggy barrier of Leyland cypress. I am now thinking of aiming it up a big pine tree which a passer-by has kindly killed by lobbing a cigarette over the garden wall from the nearby footpath.

One place not to put this rampageous Russian is in a pot on a terrace, where I saw it, lovingly labelled, in Fulham. Thoughtful gardeners have much scope for placing clematis, old and new, but a pot is no place for varieties with so much energy.

Autumn

I remember a clear morning in the ninth month when it had been raining all night. Despite the bright sun, dew was still dripping from the chrysanthemums in the garden. On the bamboo fences and criss-cross hedges I saw tatters of spider webs; and where the threads were broken the raindrops hung on them like strings of white pearls. I was greatly moved and delighted.

As it became sunnier, the dew gradually vanished from the clover and the other plants where it had lain so heavily: the branches began to stir, then suddenly sprang up of their own accord. Later I described to people how beautiful it all was. What most impressed me was that they were not at all impressed.

Sei Shōnagon, The Pillow Book *(c. AD 1000),*
translated by Ivan Morris

Vita Sackville-West, the most beguiling of garden writers, once compared the seasons of the year to the stages of human life. March and April, she thought, were youth, and May to June ran up to one's thirtieth birthday, 'that disagreeable milestone'. June to July 'is the stage between thirty and forty, or should we say fifty?' In August 'we enter the painful stage when we know we are going on for sixty, and then comes September when we approach seventy'. Her garden at Sissinghurst had some fine features in September and October, including a border of bulbous pink-flowered nerines and blue *Aster × frikartii*, two essential autumn plants for us all. Her pessimism has not survived our new attitudes to our advancing years and our wider range of garden plants.

Autumn's first six weeks are often the loveliest in the garden's entire year and they have regained the limelight as barriers of prejudice have fallen away. I emphasize in this section the exceptional beauty of dahlias, Michaelmas daisies and chrysanthemums, but each of them has been frowned on in my lifetime by gardeners who preferred pale colours and plants without links to the florist's trade. At least we can all agree that the blue flowers on *Ceratostigma willmottianum* are one of the entire year's high points. This shrub is entirely hardy in modern winters and is one of the indispensable plants for a garden. I still leave its top growth uncut in winter in honour of the old advice that it will protect the plant in case of an extreme frost. I am less confident that many hebes will survive hard weather, but as they grow so quickly and flower so young, they are worth the risk and regular replacement. My two favourites are among the hardiest: *Hebe*

'Watson's Pink', which is a magnificent survivor up at Kiftsgate Court, even higher than my garden in the Cotswolds, and 'Nicola's Blush', which goes on producing pale pink flowers until early December on bushes about three feet high. There is usually a 'Watson's Pink' for sale on Kiftsgate's excellent plant stall in summer, from which I acquired my original plant and learned how good this variety is. 'Nicola's Blush' originated at Rushfields Nursery, near Ledbury in Herefordshire, whose owners once told me that they had named it after a young garden assistant who was prone to blush during conversation. Nicola's name and habit are now commemorated nationwide and I rate her namesake as one of the best buys for a later season.

Lemon-yellow tall *Helianthus* 'Lemon Queen' ran back into favour about twenty years ago, an excellent choice for a border's back row and only slightly invasive, though best in soil which is not too dry. It gives valuable height at six feet behind clumps of middle-ranking asters and it goes very well with the blues of the tough aconitums, *carmichaelii* being my mainstay here, though newer ones, named after English rivers, have just appeared on sale and need careful study. September and October are months in which it is very easy nowadays to plant a classic border with graded height through a back row, middle row and front row. As in spring, that old 'colour wheel' is irrelevant, because the autumn light is mostly softer and the effect of a multi-coloured finale does not need to obey artificial rules of visual 'harmony'.

Older gardeners used to look on 15 October as the cut-off point for the half-hardy bedding, the date at which salvias, heliotropes and marguerites must all be brought under cover. Nowadays, they can flower on outdoors until the end of the month, often later, especially in London gardens warmed by their neighbours' hot air. I pick only five of the better salvias here, but they could as easily have been twenty choices, some of which will survive modest winters outdoors. Remember that plants in pots are more sheltered if the pots are pulled back in late autumn against a sunny wall. Terracotta pots are best kept safe in winter propped above hard paving on pairs of bricks, allowing the winter rains to drain through safely. If left on the paving itself, the bottom of the pot may freeze on to the hard surface with water which has drained from it, and when the pot is moved in a thaw, the bottom will break off it. I admire solid terracotta work and have two big urns, made in Impruneta near Florence, which once belonged to Nancy Lancaster. Nonetheless their decoration has been frozen off in various winters and I would not now buy specialized terracotta purely for garden purposes. At prices up to £10, supermarkets offer thin but acceptable clay alternatives which will last for quite a while. If their colour annoys you, the answer is to paint them in your favourite shade of Majorelle blue or dove-grey. Paint will even hide the horror of chunky plastic substitutes, making them welcome too in a garden's green surrounds.

Until mid-October I am still picking flowers off perennial penstemons, the essential family for the front rows of autumn flowerbeds. Young plants flower best, so it pays to take cuttings off a parent and root them in September, ready to be potted on and grown for the following season. I remember the fuss which used to surround the scarlet-red *Penstemon* 'Schoenholtzeri' even before it changed its trade name to 'Firebird'. Was it hardy? How could ghostly gardening cope with its strong red? Some gardeners were even persuaded to plant *Penstemon* 'Garnet' instead, on the grounds that its flowers were a muted shade of purple-red. It is not just that 'Garnet' then changed its name correctly to 'Andenken an Friedrich Hahn', making it unsaleable in Britain. Its colour had a stale drabness which is outside my personal limits. Scarlet-red 'Firebird', meanwhile, turned out to be entirely hardy, willing to flower well for several years, and a welcome shade of red at a time when colour needs to be cheerful. Dozens of less hardy penstemons have now appeared on sale in its wake, of which dark black-purple 'Blackbird' and white 'Snow Storm' are good, but among the least hardy. The way forward is to track down the new 'Pensham' varieties, which have a long season, near-hardiness, varying height and a marked willingness to flower until October. Bred in the Vale of Evesham they are fine additions to the autumn armoury and are very easy to root from early September cuttings.

Not that the first frosts finish a thoughtful garden's interest. Berries are not just a subject for columnists out of season. As I reiterate in this section and exemplify under 'Crabs in Flower', they are a high point of the year. Mine begin on the admirable *Sorbus americana* in August, the most unjustly neglected tree in this book. They end with late coto-neasters, especially the good *lacteus*, big red *frigidus* 'Cornubia' and yellow-berried 'Exburiensis', two strong growers for any soil. In between come the maluses, of which I write with a new, clearer know-ledge. I now regret my choice of *Malus* 'Golden Hornet' among the yellow-fruited varieties, for reasons which I explain. Books on thoughtful gardening are not written by faultlessly thoughtful gardeners.

Fluttering Buddleias

When it is too cold and wet in English gardens and too hot for Mediterranean ones, is there anything seasonal in August which will grow
well in them both? My answer is one of my favourite floral families:
the buddleias. Many gardeners think of buddleias only as tall, easy
shrubs with coarse leaves and plumes of flower in shades of purple or
white which are beloved by butterflies. Their seedlings blow all over
the place and have a troublesome way of lodging themselves in walls
or stonework. They have been great uninvited colonizers on bomb
sites, but there is so much more charm in the family's members. They
have been on a five-year trial in the Royal Horticultural Society gardens at Wisley but until the trial's results settle down I prefer to
consult a grower whose livelihood is linked to the family. The biggest
buddleia collection in England is in the fine nursery at Longstock
Park, near Stockbridge in Hampshire. Longstock Park is owned by
the John Lewis Partnership and the nursery lies in the grounds of its
enlightened founder, the late John Spedan Lewis. Buddleias have yet
to appear at the tills of the Waitrose stores in the John Lewis group
but the nursery sells more than a thousand pot-grown specimens
yearly. Mature specimens can be viewed in beds outside the nursery's
walled garden on any day of the week because Longstock's owners
have had the good fortune to employ a buddleia fanatic and breeder,
Peter Moore. Peter worked for years for the nearby nursery of Hillier's, but has found his true home in Longstock's smaller enterprise.
There, he can attempt to improve on nature by breeding exciting new
hybrids in popular families of shrubs.

In the Longstock collection I thought I had made an instructive study of the parent buddleias until I dared to interrupt Moore while he was active nearby in his Waitrose working overalls. We spent another hour-and-a-half studying the buddleias which I had overlooked. The lessons included many of the most important specimens on the site. There are spring-flowering buddleias, pale pink-flowered buddleias and even a Mexican one, *Buddleja cordata*, which attracts flies rather than butterflies. I am about to become a buddleia bore, not least because I have bought too many varieties and have no idea where I can fit them into my gardens. Mainstream buddleias are very easy to look after. They like a sunny site and are unfussy about soil. Most of them are best cut down to about a foot above ground level every spring. At Longstock they are cut down in late March, a job which needs a leap of faith, because the yearly top-growth of a buddleia looks so luxuriant. It is so dense that veterans even do the cutting with their powered hedge-clippers. The plants survive it well and then regrow to a manageable height, liberally covered in flower by August. The other essential is to continue dead-heading the bushes so as to treble their flowering season. As we walked round the collection I noticed how Peter Moore would cut the dead and half-dead flowers off his buddleia-children, reproaching himself for not having done so for at least two days. Gardeners are obsessed about dead-heading their roses but never think of dead-heading their buddleias so carefully. Many varieties show dead brown plumes of flower among their fresh flowers but if the dead ones are cut off, their stems will usually send up new, short plumes from their lower leaf-joints. When dead-headed, most of the popular varieties will flower on into mid-September.

If your mental image of the best buddleia is still an old *davidii* hybrid like 'Royal Red' or 'Black Knight', you are contending with coarse untidy leaves and a tall habit which is hard to fit into a border. At the entrance to the Longstock collection, I realized how far I had fallen behind the new age. A five-foot-high beauty called *davidii* 'Adonis Blue' was showing dark, slaty blue spikes of neat flower above tidy, slender leaves. It had been bred at Notcutts nursery in Suffolk. In front of it were the striking short white-grey leaves of 'Silver Anniversary', a new silver-leaved buddleia which stands out in a crowd. Its terminal flowers of white even have a honey scent. It has been bred at

Longstock by Moore himself, so I bought one of each variety, thinking how well they will look in the driest part of my garden. 'Adonis
Blue' and 'Silver Anniversary' are both hardy and would flourish in a
hot garden nearer the Mediterranean. Many buddleias are native to
dry parts of China, and in Europe they colonize dry, untended ground
along railway lines. If their flower spikes droop in hot weather, water
the plants in the evening, whereupon they will recover and continue
to attract butterflies. To us, these flowers smell like the hair-oil of an
old-style city slicker but to male butterflies they smell like female
butterfly-flappers.

Over-stocked with buddleias in my garden, I asked Moore to name
his top picks for keen gardeners. I coaxed him into naming two of his
own, the shining white 'Silver Anniversary' and the palish blue *davidii*
'Summer House Blue'. He even recommends the former for big pots
which can be brought indoors in November so that their 'Silver Anni-
versaries' can be persuaded to go on producing scented white flowers
in winter. 'Summer House Blue' is a taller variety but it is not coarse
and is easily contained by annual pruning. It arose at Longstock as a
random seedling by the property's golf course and was never part of a
breeding programme. Such are the wonders of plants in national collections, where marriages are free and easy. We then argued about the
third choice, concentrating on *davidii* varieties. I much like the recent
'Nanho Blue', which has chic leaves and good blue flowers. Moore
picked 'Nanho Purple' instead, insisting that its rose-purple flowers
were far better when lit up by late sunlight. I think he was being very
precise. We agreed that 'Camberwell Beauty' is another pink-purple
possibility, with the agreeable habit of holding little sprays of flowers
above a main plume. Many know the similar habit of 'Dartmoor', but
'Camberwell Beauty' is less rampant. Among the whites, you should
choose 'White Profusion', which is still the best of this class. Among
the yellows with balls of flower, the best is *Buddleja* × *weyeriana*
'Sungold'.

I listened, noted and tested the flowers like a happy butterfly while
many more varieties pressed forwards to be bought. The buddleia is
now so varied and improved that it deserves to be sent fluttering out
across Europe.

Sorrel Soup

When did you last see sorrel in a supermarket? I have kept the same three plants going for fifteen years and if archaeologists were ever to analyse my diet they would be hard put to identify the source of its natural acidity. The answer is sorrel, picked in green leaf and consumed in heavy quantities. I even have a recipe for sorrel soup which was written out for me in ballpoint pen on an old payslip by the great French chef Raymond Blanc. It involves sweating a chopped carrot and an onion in butter and adding torn sorrel leaves late in the process. Reading hungrily, I then hit on a neglected wonder in that unsurpassed classic, *French Provincial Cooking* by Elizabeth David: the recipe for a sorrel omelette. It involves making an omelette in the usual pan and putting some chopped sorrel leaves in the centre just before you roll it up. Sorrel omelette is delicious and puzzles even the most serious food bores. Miss David's firm advice is often neglected: never put too much of a filling in an omelette, especially a sorrel one. A few finely chopped leaves give the distinctive tang of lemon which transforms a simple dish. *Omelette à l'oseille* is not to be found on menus nowadays in France. The only person to recognize it at my table was a Russian visitor. In Russia, sorrel is a staple survival from peasant life.

My third sorrel trick is Greek. It consists of top-dressing a stew of diced lamb with sorrel leaves added to finely beaten egg yolks. The top dressing goes on at the last minute and must not be allowed to set. I ate this excellent dish in an ordinary establishment in Athens in the early 1990s and took the recipe away with me, written in Greek on the back of the bill. I then found it given as Arni Fricassée in Claudia

Roden's *Mediterranean Cookery*, although the sorrel leaves ought to go in nearer to the last minute than she implies, as their strips become too soggy otherwise. Lamb and sorrel have gone down well, except when I forewarned a guest, a brilliant cook, that the recipe was Greek. She promptly assumed that the lamb cubes were goat and left them untouched on the plate.

Between them, these options consume masses of my sorrel between April and September. It is as well that the plants earn their keep because I bought my three original sorrels as pot-grown plants for a silly price. Actually you can raise them easily from seed sown out-doors, one source of which is the interesting 'heirloom' list of vegetable seeds from Pennard Plants at East Pennard, Shepton Mallet, Somerset BA4 6TU. 'Growing the dream' is its slogan and it offers two types of sorrel at £1 each per packet. I do not like the sound of the red-veined one, which is described as a 'staple in French cooking' and is com-pared with a sprightly spinach or chard. The green one is better, although the list calls it 'Cuckoo's Sorrow', claiming that birds are believed to use its sharp lemony leaf to clear their throats. I had just slashed my old sorrels to the ground and dumped the top growth when I heard the call of the cuckoo for the first time in years. I do not believe it had been at the compost heap but I do believe in cutting the tall stems off sorrel plants in mid-May. Otherwise they bolt, set seed and deteriorate. Pennard Plants has several other rare types of forgot-ten vegetable, including strawberry spinach with salad leaves and shiny fruits like mulberries.

Elizabeth David is my source for another classic summer dish: chicken with tarragon. Her real thing, *poulet à l'estragon*, is unafraid of the necessary cream and is unsurpassed. The trick here is the var-iety of tarragon. Supermarkets sometimes offer pots of a useless herb, the Russian tarragon, which is hardy in British winters and quite tasteless. The only cookable variety is the frost-prone French tarra-gon, which smells exactly right when you pinch its leaves. I buy it as a named plant from reliable garden centres which offer both types separately and know their business. The plants grow freely in light soil until mid-November but are then at high risk to most winters' frosts. Dig up some pieces, plant them in pots and protect them until spring.

The other con on the market is chainstore 'spinach', which is labelled 'French spinach' and packaged as pale heart-shaped leaves. This bland browse is fit only for a pet hamster. It is a tame sort of beet, justly called *Beta*, as the labelling admits in small print on the pre-packed plastic bag. The true alpha spinach is dark green and totally different. To find it you must grow your own from seed: true dark green English spinach, the only type which will make the classic salad with chopped, darkly fried bacon and a dressing which is strong on vinegar, added to the leaves after the bacon fat has been poured on from the pan. True spinach prefers a wet summer in rich soil.

Even if you are a minimal gardener, flatter your skills by sowing radish seed, too. The seeds come up so easily and are ideal as a crop for children who need some summer amusement at home. Like everything from basil to tomatoes, radishes now come in shapes and colours which have left the prototype far behind. I link my first years of radish-growing with a short story by H. E. Bates, the supreme describer of hot English summer days. It involved an elderly man with a round bald head, reddened in the sun like a radish, who intruded on a neighbouring lady's garden and was set to work by her, tossing lettuce and helping in the kitchen. Slightly drunk on her cocktails, he fell slightly in love and stayed, I remember, for days. Modern radishes could no longer be compared with his bald head because they are white, long or twisty, or something called 'mooli'. In honour of H. E. Bates's story, I sow 'Rougette', an all-red rounded variety with a root like a sunburnt head. It is not very hot on the palate but I use it in this classic pasta dish which I met near Naples, a radish-growing area. Lightly fry an onion, put in about two dozen sliced radishes and the chopped leaves from their tops. Add garlic and cook until the leaves flop. Add the mixture to a big spoon of the water in which you have just cooked some tagliatelle. Mix in the pasta, add grated cheese (strong Cheddar does the trick) and top it all with fresh parsley. The result is remarkably satisfying, a *pasta del giardino* which is within the competence of us all.

Founded on Love

For readers, the one great garden on Long Island is the garden of a literary mind. 'There was music from my neighbour's house through the summer nights', music which still echoes to readers of F. Scott Fitzgerald and his tale of the rise and fall of Jay Gatsby who 'told me once he was an Oxford man'. On Mondays, there were eight servants in his pay, including an extra gardener, and at weekends there were the parties. 'In his blue gardens men and girls came and went like moths among the whisperings and the champagne and the stars.' Young Englishmen were dotted about, 'all looking a little hungry, and all talking in low, earnest voices to solid and prosperous Americans . . . agonizingly aware of the easy money in the vicinity and convinced it was theirs for a few words in the right key'.

For gardeners, there is a finer garden on Long Island, also founded on love, but not on a desire to impress or on deals done on the wrong side of the law. In 1903, the son of Andrew Carnegie's first partner in business went down on one knee in the heather in Scotland and proposed to his young English bride. If you will marry me, he told her, and come and live in America, I will make you a garden as fine as any abroad. She accepted, so her husband, J. S. Phipps, took her to Long Island, to Old Westbury Gardens where the gates are carved with emblems of the sport of hunting and you can scent the sea between the driveway's avenues of limes. True to his word, Phipps began to make the garden which now draws 80,000 visitors a year. I owe the story of Phipps's promise to the authority of his surviving daughter, then in her nineties, who remained a presiding genius of the place.

Like other great gardens, Westbury has been made from a marriage of English and American talents. Phipps's English bride introduced an English style of planting, and entrusted the design of the house and garden to George Crawley from England, a name no longer honoured as it deserves in the annals of English gardening. Crawley's plan is still impressive in its American setting and is marked out by broad hedges of hemlock, fine trees, bold steps and a stylish use of water. The Phipps family were Crawley's patrons and have continued to influence the garden, the scene of their halcyon days since 1903. Old Westbury Gardens is now run by a board which draws on the family's endowment but it retains its original character as it has never called in an outside group and been forced to diverge from the family's sense of style.

Westbury Gardens runs on a budget of $2.6 million a year, about a fifth of which comes from gate money and as much again from annual fund-raising. Four horticulturists and five working gardeners are assisted by part-timers who are each paid by the hour. There are also interns, up to six in any one year. Money alone never makes a great garden, and when I entered the walled enclosure, some way from the house, I was enchanted by the mixing of plants and colours which went beyond the usual English range. Huge standard bushes of purple-flowered tibouchina stood as backing to the drooping flowers of tall white tobacco plants. Familiar cosmos daisies fluttered beside unusual types of salvia and groups of *Pentas lanceolata*, a plant which never seems to be grown from seed in England. In borders by the wall, a tall *Abelmoschus* had flowers which looked like a clear yellow hibiscus, and its forthright woman supervisor said that it grows with such ease that even an Englishman should try it. Sky-blue plumbago covers another brick wall beside cotoneaster clipped in an espalier shape. Perhaps we English should try that combination too. A cross-vista divides the walled garden and at one end a curving pergola concludes the view across a semicircle of water. It is made as exotic as New York's Lotus Club by the leaves and seed-heads of the vivid lotuses which are growing in its depths.

Long Island's sea-driven climate is not so relentless that the garden is browned by winds in autumn. Great maples, limes and beeches luxuriate, including a gigantic beech tree which was moved to be nearer the side terrace in days when the moving of such a big tree cost only $100. Very large gardens risk losing their atmosphere, but Westbury's is secure in the careful attention given to its bedding and to the green views through parkland and clipped hedges which run away from the house. Order and scale have not been lost in flowery detail, even where unusual ipomoeas romp in the walled garden beside *Clematis terniflora* and big groups of pale *Salvia coccinea* 'Snow Nymph'. The trees, the ground plan and the yearly succession of such well-chosen flowers are a reminder that gardens may indeed grow best on a founding promise of love. It could never be a place like Gatsby's where 'a sudden emptiness seemed to flow from the windows and the great doors, endowing with complete isolation the figure of the host who stood on the porch, his hand up in a formal gesture of farewell'. Westbury was made for happy family life and was duly blessed by it.

Back To The Fuchsia

If you think European winters are permanently warming, the fuchsia should be your first stop. So many varieties have hovered on the borders of hardiness, showing a willingness to survive in all but the hardest frosts. Now that frost is proving less of a problem, the boundaries of the fuchsia family have been noticeably advanced. Following the climate, I am going back to the fuchsia and profiting from the cool summers which they love.

The facts have been clear for years in California. British gardeners are mostly unaware that fuchsia growing has a long history in parts of California where the winter temperatures are far removed from frost, and the summer humidity reaches the high level which fuchsias enjoy. Not for nothing are so many of the best varieties named after sites around the Los Angeles area. In the 1930s, breeders developed vigorous varieties with names like 'Beverly Hills' and 'Hollywood Park' which flower all year round and have to be stopped by a firm pruning in the new year. In Britain one of the best suppliers of fuchsias is Roualeyn Nursery at Trefriw, Conwy, North Wales, who prefer to supply rooted plants by mail in spring, when their prices are extremely reasonable. Their catalogue now lists more than forty varieties which their years of Welsh experience show to be hardy. I have had confidence in their choices and have not lost a single one of their recommended range in the past eight years.

If you buy a young fuchsia, you can train it up quickly into a special shape. In spring, standard fuchsias with tall stems come on sale at prices up to £100 but there is no magic about training a fuchsia into this form, except patience and basic knowledge. Take a normal bush variety and cut off all side shoots except for the main stem and its growing tip. The stem should be supported on a cane and when it has grown up to two or three feet, about a foot less than the height you want, the side shoots should be left to develop freely without being pinched out. Traditionally, four or five pairs of side shoots are left to grow free at this height and then the growing tip is snipped out to limit the plant's height. The entire operation is simple but the result looks exotic and somebody, somewhere will pay extraordinary prices for it. Standards are less hardy than ordinary branched varieties and as they become bulky to protect under glass in winter, it is convenient if only the hardy forms are chosen for the purpose. They have the strength to survive in unheated settings.

One of the best is the excellent red-flowered 'Rufus', which was bred nearly fifty years ago. It flowers madly and has an upright habit which trains well into a standard. If you start a 'Rufus' off now and trim it, you will have an excellent standard specimen within eighteen months. It pairs well with the larger-flowered 'Blue Gown', which is double-flowered and a classic combination of scarlet and blue, changing to purple. 'Blue Gown' flowers heavily, and as it always needs staking, it might as well be staked as a standard. Roualeyn Nursery classes it as hardy nowadays.

Down at ground level, there is a neat combination for gardeners who are more lazy than they care to admit. If they lay out box-edged beds in a formal pattern of evergreen compartments, they can plant the gaps with hardy fuchsias for the summer and underplant the fuchsias with small narcissi for a spring display. The results look dreadful in late May when the narcissi's leaves are dying down and the dead stems on the fuchsia are breaking into growth. If you can live with them for this one drab fortnight, they then give you two seasons of colour for minimal effort without the bother of yearly bedding-out. In autumn, the fuchsias take over and look charming in full flower against the clipped evergreen box. A good group of fuchsias to choose here is the low-growing range with names of the seven dwarfs from Snow White: 'Sleepy', 'Dopey' and so forth. In early spring, low-growing small-flowered narcissi make a patchwork of flower in the bare earth between the dwarfs' bare stems.

I have two other tips about fuchsia growing, one nutritious, the other historical. It pays to feed all fuchsias with regular doses of balanced Phostrogen, directed at them through a watering can from July onwards, because they revel in humidity and an inorganic supplement to their health. Historically, the family is the subject of a famous story for entrepreneurs. It does not involve liquid fertilizer, but it does involve some fertile business practice.

Traditionally, the flowering fuchsia is said to have originated at Wapping in east London in the 1780s, before anyone thought of printing newspapers on the site. A great nurseryman, James Lee of Hammersmith, is said to have heard news of an exotic new plant with hanging flowers which was growing in the window box of a Wapping housewife. She said that it had been brought to her by her husband from the West Indies. Though tempted to retain the fuchsia, she was more tempted by the colour of Mr Lee's money and handed over her stock plant for about £10. The nurseryman then stripped it for cuttings, multiplied the stock and began the next season with 300 plants which were already showing buds. Smart society rushed to buy them, propelled by competitive females. Their 'horses smoked off to the suburb', breaking the speed limit in order to buy the remaining stock, but, justly, Lee gave the housewife one of the first of the new batch so that she could keep it safe for her husband. Lee himself sold so many fuchsias in one year that he turned £10 into more than £300, all from a woman's memento.

Quite probably, this story is exaggerated. It emerged only fifty years later on the authority of a curator at the Botanical Gardens in Liverpool, and in its first published form, the newspaper which told it seems to have misprinted the plant's point of origin as a 'widow' in Wapping, not a 'window'. Authorities therefore argue whether the housewife lost her husband as well as her fuchsia. However, nobody can dispute that James Lee the entrepreneur brought gardeners a flower from which they have derived ceaseless pleasure.

Botanical Palermo

Throughout Europe there is a truth much neglected by travelling gardeners: always head for the botanic garden. Across the ages most of their founders were inspired by the arts of herbal medicine and the results linger on, gardens which are not fully about gardening and centres of botany which are not fully at the centre of genetic science. For decades, I have visited such gardens from Leiden to Vienna, Urbino to Berlin. There are many more in waiting, but there is one where the plants, history and design are an ageing paradise on an unlikely plot of earth.

In Palermo, in north-west Sicily, the Botanic Garden is a witness to the enlightened ideas of the 1790s. The place still gives off a neo-classical atmosphere. By its entrance, three regular, classical buildings express the values of order and reason which their mustard-yellow paint cannot conceal. They still have friezes, pilasters and pediments, with sphinxes in front and statues inside. By the garden's original entrance, two pillars support statues of the great ancient botanists Theophrastus and Dioscorides on honey-coloured stone at a height of thirty feet. The two classical masters survey a formal setting whose flowerbeds have been laid out on the sexual system of the Swedish botanist Linnaeus.

There is a pleasant irony of time and culture in this garden's architectural form. Work on it began in early 1789, just before the events in France which ended in revolution. A French architect laid the plans for the garden buildings and was ably supported by Italian sculptors and collaborators, encouraged by the Bourbon King Ferdinand I and his courtiers. Local Palermitan notables and prominent clergymen also contributed funds, but when the garden opened in 1795, its classical style had acquired new overtones after six French revolutionary years. The garden's backbone is a bold series of straight avenues which are endowed with names of significant figures in its history. These avenues, or *viali*, radiate at a series of angles and each one is flanked by different types of tree. Evergreen oaks edge one, palms and pelargoniums another. The roots of huge old specimens of *Ficus magnoloides* and its relation, the sideways-rooting banyan tree, unsettle the central pathway beside tall oriental planes and rare eastern neighbours. Some of these fine trees are nearly two centuries old, great survivors from thoughtful curators of the past. To walk down these uneven avenues is to recapture a sense of the main avenue in the fine garden at Tresco in the Scilly Isles before a storm in the late 1980s destroyed its canopy of tender trees.

The avenues are a challenge for tree-lovers, but they are not the garden's only distinction. The central *viale* ends at a circular garden of water, donated by Palermo's archbishop in 1796. Ice-blue water lilies, lotus, papyrus and much else float in the neatly divided sections of its pool, and around it a forest of bamboos makes a tall green fluttering curtain. Big banyan trees are in the background and even the skeletal shape of the modern gasworks beyond the boundary makes little impact on the immediate view. Down each of the avenues run hundreds of flowerpots, carefully labelled, and in autumn showing few signs of growth. The empty, labelled flowerpot is a speciality of Italian botanic gardens, but at Palermo the pots are planted with bulbs for all seasons and are very much alive. A few autumn-flowering varieties suggest what the spring will also bring. On the flowerpots, the bust of a sphinx is stamped as a hallmark, matching the sphinx which stands in sculpture outside the garden's main buildings. In the 1790s, sphinxes acquired new meaning through Napoleon's Egyptian conquests, but I doubt if the Palermo garden was moving to this rhythm.

In Palermo, there is hardly any rain between April and mid-September, but some spectacular residents are not deterred. Huge spiky specimens of *Dracaena draco* stand near an artificial mound of rocks. Old plants of *Yucca elephantipes* rise to a height of thirty feet, while hundreds of cacti, cycads and agaves are tended in yet more flowerpots. I treasure the sight of a scarlet bougainvillea, which scrambles over an outbuilding in the company of sky-high yuccas. The nearby garden has orderly greenhouses, one of which was given by Queen Maria Christina in the 1830s and based on French design. Like the flowerpots, the greenhouses are lovingly maintained in a city whose public services are not exactly overfunded. The houses are an excuse for yet more collections of flowerpots, holding anything from aloes to mimosa.

Among the dry fallen leaves and the highs and lows of the surviving trees, one spectacular avenue flowers prolifically in September. In a far side of the garden, Palermo's curators have planted a long run of the flowering false kapok tree, or chorisia, from South America. They have become huge trees, thirty to forty feet high. In nature their trunks swell with age like bulging bottles and are fitted with botanical prickles to deter animals. Their flowers are a five-petalled mixture of pink and yellow, and drop by the hundred on to the garden's paths. Fully mature and swollen, the trees are an astonishing sight.

This botanic garden has also become a home for the mother of all Palermitan plants, one which the garden's earliest foreign admirer, Goethe, never saw when he visited in the 1790s. About fifty years after Goethe's visit, gardeners in Palermo discovered the charms and strengths of the frangipani. In Palermo, this superb flower is everywhere. It has been the subject of a special exhibition at the Botanic Garden, and there are tremendous trees of it in front of Palermo's older houses and dozens of specimens on private balconies. It even has its own folklore. Experts from the Botanic Garden described the frangipani to me as the object of an all-female cult. Women, they tell me, are the 'priestesses responsible for tending it'. When a girl marries, her mother traditionally gives her a piece of the family's frangipani for her new balcony. If it fails, it is a bad omen. Frangipani plants on balconies 'remain a female province from which males of the family are excluded'. Men are allowed to look after them only outdoors, and preferably they are 'retired males and experienced gardeners'.

The plant has the most extraordinary history. Technically, it is plumeria, the name under which it appears in nursery catalogues. Our name, frangipani, commemorates a titled count of that name who invented a similarly scented compound in seventeenth-century France. The people of Palermo call it 'pomelia', a name which reflects the plant's wide diffusion. This marvellously scented flower goes back to the brutal empire of the Aztecs in America, who venerated it, mainly because its bark and juice were so good for healing wounds. The earliest picture of the plant is in the famous *Codex Badianus* which dates from 1552 and shows plants known to the Aztecs. There are four main species, all of which centre on tropical America or the Caribbean, but nowadays the tree is all over India and the Far East and is famous as the source of flowery necklaces in Polynesia, where Paul Gauguin's girls loved to wear them. Spanish travellers carried bits of the plant with them to the Far East, and established them away from its native habitat. On Hawaii, frangipani is believed to originate from plants brought by an American diplomat in 1860.

The mild climate in Palermo was well suited to frangipani, so it multiplied rapidly, spreading outwards from the gardens of the rich nobility in the early nineteenth century. The frangipani is such a brilliant traveller because cuttings from it root easily and are even able to come into flower on a branch which has been cut from a parent-tree. In the Far East, the public were delighted by this rare ability which seemed to symbolize eternal life, so they planted frangipani by burial grounds and temples. In the Palermo Botanic Garden there are no fewer than eighteen types of frangipani, arranged against a wall beside the greenhouses. The flowers range from pink through yellow to white and the garden has been important in spreading this plant to the balconies of well-trained Sicilian women. It is one of the many American imports which make the plants of the Botanic Garden much richer than its architect's original classicizing conception.

In Britain, frangipani is not too difficult if grown in a heated greenhouse until frosts are over. The plants should be kept in pots, with or without sphinxes, and will survive the tender care of an English male. They lose their leaves in late autumn and should be brought back into a heated house before the danger of frost in October. Out in Palermo, the ladies of the balcony sometimes protect the tips of their plant's branches by capping them with empty eggshells, making them into a sort of egg tree. With female cunning, they have found that this ovarian trick protects the growing points against frost. In Britain, the climate is too cold and the eggshell trick is superfluous.

Great modern botanic gardens hum with technology, order and research. Palermo's is now under reconstruction with help from the European Union and is at grave risk of unwary modernizing. Even so, it has a great basic design, teeming contents and an enchanting contrast of age and youth. Delighted by it, I went up to one of the garden's blue-overalled interns and told him that his botanic garden was the best in Italy. No, he corrected me, with winning local patriotism, not just in Italy, but in Europe, perhaps the world. There are so many pots to water and a reconstruction to survive, but work with a hosepipe has not dimmed the staff's affection for their home.

The Haunt of Ancient Peace

In hot weather, flower gardens have the worst of it, but architectural gardens retain their style. They depend on big evergreen building-blocks, strong design and an elegant use of stone and hard surfacing. The best are often the gardens of architects, whose sense of space and proportion stops a flowerless garden from being dull.

Just to the south of Bath, but still in Wiltshire, the garden at Iford Manor is a calm architectural masterpiece. Its design goes back across a hundred years to 1899 when it was bought by a genius of landscape design, the architect Harold Peto. He had matured in the late Victorian era when many still wrongly think that the style of gardens was bizarre. Peto had a superb eye, an architectural training and no family ties to hold him down. By his mid thirties, he had travelled widely and discovered the charm and artistry of Italy. He had also opened his eyes to gardens in North Africa and Japan. Twenty years before the great planter Miss Jekyll began to extol her herbaceous borders, Harold Peto had laid out gardens with an architectural mastery which was quite beyond the famous old lady's skills. One of his early assistants was Edwin Lutyens, the man who would later put the backbone into many of Miss Jekyll's plantings.

At Iford Manor, this master-architect's design survives around the house which he chose for himself. It stands on a steep hillside which he shaped and landscaped with great skill. The result is not just a flower garden. In its central core, Peto found room for superb flights of ascending steps, a noble Italian-style terrace complete with ancient pillars, a small Mediterranean-style house (his '*casita*') and a most remarkable private cloister.

In the 1880s, geometric patterns of bedding plants were popular, even when set among patterns of pebbles and reflecting glass. Peto the architect wanted none of them. He reintroduced English gardening to architectural Italian style while the same style was independently reaching the new mansions of East Coast America through the work of Charles Platt. In garden history, he is a forerunner of the formal style which shaped the theories of Sir George Sitwell in Derbyshire and is so dramatic at Hidcote Manor, where it blossomed in his younger American contemporary, Lawrence Johnston. Iford remained in the Peto family until 1964, and thanks to restoration and the dedication of the present owners, Elisabeth Cartwright and John Hignett, it now attracts 10,000 visitors a year. Until the mid 1980s John had been a farmer on nearby land, but he then turned his energy to restoring Peto's buildings and stonework, which had started to crack after years of neglect, not least because they stood on a hillside whose geology is unstable. Elisabeth Cartwright had arrived in her mid twenties from the classic Georgian mansion at Aynho in Northamptonshire. She, too, had a family background which could warm to the challenge of Iford, and with her came Leon Butler, her mother's garden boy. Appointed as head gardener, he has just retired after nearly forty years of work on Iford's behalf.

Those forty years have been well spent. The place has a natural holiness which Peto's style has helped to enhance. He believed that a garden of nothing but flowers would be boring, so he introduced stonework because stone is as expressive as plants. At Iford, he introduced some very remarkable stones, the spoils of his collecting and travelling in Spain and Italy. Every piece was honestly bought, and nobody has yet made a fuss about repatriating the Peto Marbles, but it is astonishing what this artful magpie was able to bring back to Wiltshire. His terrace has some fine ancient Roman sarcophagi and his stairway has a spare column from one of the greatest churches at Ravenna, constructed in the sixth century. His cloister contains fragments of fine Italian doorways, coats of arms, rare marble pillars and a relief of the Virgin Mary protecting survivors from a great plague. All of them would be treasured antiquities nowadays, but in the early twentieth century, Peto bought them because nobody else wanted them. He even acquired twelfth-century stone lions and some pieces from the Ca' d'Oro in Venice.

Iford Manor is a charming house of many different periods, but it is Peto who intuited a particular quality in its setting and overgrown hillside. On a hot afternoon, there is no more tranquil landscape in England than the view from his antique colonnade to the grass-green meadows beside the River Frome. Peto had a well-formed culture and taste which guided his canny expenditure. He was not extravagant and he had a public dimension to his art: he expressed increasing distress at the breakdown of the uneasy balance of power in Europe. In 1907 he put up an unusual memorial to King Edward VII as a peacemaker and then built his rectangular cloisters, basing them on the cloisters which he had seen and loved at Granada in the Alhambra. He was enchanted by Granada's great gardens because Granada, he rightly saw, was a place which could match up to the artistic standards set by Venice, Rome and Florence. When he returned to London after a Spanish tour, he wrote how he had 'sat next to a Spaniard at dinner who had been in London and said he should really die if he lived there a year: everything is black, the sheep, grass, houses, even birds'. Spaniards can be rather macabre. Peto's landscape gardening is an expression of a brighter vision which was rooted in an undergrowth of contemporary taste in English society. In his early lifetime, polite society had rediscovered Florence; millionaires were bidding competitively for Italian master-paintings and Florence was seen as the wellhead of the arts and crafts. As so often before, Italy had jolted England out of barbarity.

Iford is only one of Peto's gardens but it is the most personal. His public masterpiece is Ilnacullin on the island of Garinish in Ireland's Bantry Bay. He was also taken up by rich Edwardian migrants who used his talents freely, not least on Cap Ferrat in the South of France. Would a new Peto be possible nowadays? Iford is not a big garden, but our age of global tourism has a weakened awareness of the classical underpinning of Western art, and so Peto's Italian taste has a different emphasis to modern eyes. We no longer take his assumptions for granted. Sharing them, I cherish his inscription in the year in which he finished Iford's cloisters. He carved into the stone: 'The Haunt of Ancient Peace'. The year was 1914. In our own late summers, the words have a contemporary resonance.

Space Invaders

Gardeners draw some fine lines, and none is finer than the line between nature and culture. Standing back, I have been thinking that parts of my garden are at last full of plants which look after themselves. They knit together and spread into self-sustaining communities. They are not scrupulously tidy but they survive the winter, and one day they may even survive me.

In Europe this style of planting is fashionable and much photographed. In America, I now find, many of its components are listed as 'menaces'. I have been checking them in a fascinating guide, *Invasive Plants, Weeds of the Global Garden* which was published in 1996 by the Brooklyn Botanic Garden in New York. In 1993 the Congressional Office of Technology Assessment compiled a report entitled 'Harmful Non-Indigenous Species in the United States', which tried to quantify the main dangers and their damage. It concluded that seventy-nine of them have caused losses worth $97 billion and that fifteen 'high impact species' will cause another $134 billion of damage in future. What neither they nor I realized is that I have been lovingly planting some of their most dangerous 'weeds of the global garden' for my own pleasure. A hit squad needs to come over and poison my anti-global garden, using compounds like picloram or imazapyr, which is sold in America under the blunt name of Arsenal. It is not that I am growing the dreadful Japanese knotweed. I have a relation of the lovely giant hogweed, but its habits are restrained. I am looking after some ground elder, but it is the elegantly variegated form and I wage vigilant war on the green-leaved variety. I have banished almost all milky euphorbias, whose juice is so painful if it ever sprays into an eye. My invaders are plants which other British gardeners also choose and admire.

Like many of them, I look forward in May to the flowers on the silver-leaved Russian olive, the suckering *Elaeagnus angustifolia*, which has intensely scented, small yellow flowers. There is even a selected form called 'Quicksilver', which is especially silver in May. It becomes rather dingy by July, a fault which disqualifies it as a shrub for a main vista, and it spreads slightly, but the American assessors are having none of it. Since it arrived in the States, it is 'choking out native vegetation', particularly in the western plains, and should be attacked by 'girdling, stump-burning and depositing rock salt into holes drilled into the stump'. For years, I have been even more fond of the green-leaved *Elaeagnus umbellata*, which is equally well scented when in flower. It is now a declared enemy in the Midwest, where it arrived in 1917, and unfortunately, the register tells me, 'periodic fires' do not control it. What about the good old guelder rose, the *Viburnum opulus* which was so beloved by Britain's revered Miss Jekyll? Advisers to the Pennsylvania Department of Conservation would have gone straight into her Munstead Wood and attacked in hard hats: 'Natural area managers recommend a 20 per cent solution of glyphosate herbicide to the cut stump and chipping the brush to prevent seed dispersal'. Apparently, it has started to interbreed with native highbush cranberry and may soon produce 'a truly innovative child'.

In southern Britain we treasure big paulownia trees and their occasional displays of lavender flowers like foxgloves whenever they survive the late spring frosts. In colder counties, many of us enjoy this big-leaved tree as a showy shrub for a border, where we cut it down every year and cause it to sprout again with emphatic foliage. In my view, we should plant more shrubs around it as its roots are such helpful pumps of water from the subsoil. Over in the Great Smokey Mountains National Park, however, they want us to declare war on this 'princess tree', which is capable of producing twenty million seeds and colonizing banks, roadsides and 'utility rights of way'. 'Treat cut stumps immediately with triclopyr herbicide to prevent sprouting.' Last year, unwarned, I planted three more paulownias to give a bold emphasis to three of my garden's strategic points.

Instead, you might be tempted by thoughts of the shimmering leaves of a white poplar tree in the middle distance, or foolish enough to risk the Far Eastern *Acer ginnala* as an ornamental tree. Forget them both. The poplar suckers horribly and has escaped into American landscapes since the Colonial era. The acer produces thousands of seeds which 'have the potential' to become a major weed, even in Canada. Burn them both, Americans are warned, and spray herbicide over the stumps. As for the old English holly, abandon it. It is now a 'recent invader of the American north-west' and is changing the structure of forests not by adding a foreign hint of Christmas but by bringing in a layer of tall vegetation, which casts shade and competes with native plants. When birds eat the fruits, they drop the seeds far and wide, but at least this invader is vulnerable. 'Fortunately, English holly is easy to remove mechanically.' It is fortunate that these machines have not been prowling round English churchyards.

Much of my planting at home turns out to be on America's most unwanted list of immigrants: Chinese privet (costing £7.50 a plant in garden centres); *Nandina domestica*, an evergreen bamboo which is infiltrating 'pine flatwood communities in the south-east'; and even Scotch broom, which 'currently occupies more than 2 million acres in Washington, Oregon and bits of California' and needs to be removed with a 'brush hog machine'. It has been a hard horticultural slog to grow anything in my garden of Cotswold glacial shingle, and I plead for mercy if most of the shrubs which I have established are classed as anti-American terrorists.

At least, you may think, English herbaceous borders are safe havens. On poor soil, I am glad to grow *Hesperis matronalis*, or sweet rocket, in late May, perennial potentilla in June and baby's breath in July, with a few clumps of ornamental silver-leaved cardoons and some Michaelmas daisy species for autumn. Please do not tell the American Office of Assessment. After next year's poppy-spraying mission in Afghanistan, agents may descend on me and spray them all to death. The cardoons had occurred in 'thirty-one counties' by the 1950s and are classed as an American agricultural pest. Sweet rocket is spreading rapidly from seed and 'should never be included in roadside plantings of wild flowers'. I treasure my pale yellow *Potentilla recta sulphurea* and the vivid yellow *recta* 'Warrenii', two plants which a highly decorated member of the Royal Horticultural Society once described to me as her favourite herbaceous plants. In the northern Rockies, forget her: this potentilla is becoming a 'serious wild land invader' and people are being told to remove it by 'slipping a sturdy digging tool under the crown'. Michaelmas daisies are a pest on the edges of woodland and as for baby's breath, it is a feared problem in Michigan and is likely to try to terrorize the 'open dune habitat' on the surrounds of the Great Lakes.

I have just been cutting back my beloved form of baby's breath, *Gypsophila* 'Rosy Veil', and blessing the day when I discovered this plant whose stems spread so usefully in late summer. The Michigan Department of Natural Resources has a different view. 'Early in the growing season, spot-burn all plants with a hand-held propane torch.' The line between 'gardening' and 'wilderness' is drawn differently in our two allied lands. In the garden, as in other areas, England and voices in America are fighting different wars.

Odessan Odyssey

Gardens do not have to be perfect to be rewarding. They are often evocative in ways which depend on their viewer, not their level of care. No two people see quite the same when they look beyond the surface, and often it is easiest to see more in gardens abroad, partly because they use a different flora, partly because these sites can evoke a world remembered by an outsider's restless eye.

When I looked recently at Ukrainian gardening, I found an interest which went deeper than appearances. In the Black Sea city of Odessa, first impressions are curiously familiar. Horse chestnut trees line many of the central streets, and like their British brothers, they turn brown in August in a premature announcement of autumn. They too are beset with the chestnut-infesting insect which has spread as fast as the internet in the past ten years. Its presence in southern Ukraine supports the theory that its ultimate home lies further east, probably in China, from where its natural predators have yet to pack their bags and fly in pursuit.

Under these browning chestnuts, Odessa's city gardeners surprised me by the plantings of lines of narrow-leaved hostas. English gardeners reserve these plants for richer soil and never plant them round tree trunks, but Odessans ignore our rules. I watched as hundreds of hostas were planted out and saw how their gardeners begin by removing a spade's depth of the surface soil and replacing it with rich compost. In prominent places they add leaking hosepipe below the surface to irrigate the new arrivals. In Odessa, too, preparation is more than half the battle.

In the elegant main city square, gardeners must also be irrigating their splendid cannas. Newspaper readers used to send me postcards from former Soviet countries of hideous beds of cannas, sometimes with an exclamation mark on the back of the card. The sight of them made me glad to be living in the free West. Christopher Lloyd then began to champion the charms of cannas in his garden at Great Dixter, but I pictured a bust of Lenin glowering over them when he took up their cause as if it was new. In Odessa, gardeners have not been reading Lloyd's books. They exclude the forms with purple leaves and rose-purple flowers. In the city's main square only clear scarlet or yellow cannas are used in masses, and then only in forms with clear green leaves.

What happens, I wondered, in the Odessan botanical garden marked 'Botanichesky Sad' on my city map? Up in Kiev the botanical garden is remembered for its fine display of the little-known flora of the Ukraine. In the Crimea, just outside Yalta, the huge Nikitsky Sad includes a yew tree which is more than 500 years old. This vast horticultural enclave became the experimental centre of agriculture in the Soviet era, extending over 600 acres with another 1,500 acres of outstations. It has remained almost wholly unknown to Western lovers of plants. Odessa's botanical garden has a very different air. In Odessa, a port-city, the pride of the botanical garden is the oak tree which once made the English navy great. Superb specimens of our beloved English oak tower over a garden of evocative neglect. Under the oaks are yet more hostas, freshly watered, as if somebody, somewhere is still trying to do their best. I recalled how the garden historian Edward Hyams wrote of this very garden in 1969: 'It consoled us for its neglect by producing hoopoes for our delight.'

Instead of hoopoe birds among the acacias, it consoled me with its personnel. In the heart of the garden, I watched the only gardener, an elderly lady who was hosing the last of the hibiscus and rose-pink gladioli. She was wearing a smock whose style had surely not changed in the last hundred years. An aged magnolia sagged in the background and panes were missing in the nearby greenhouse, whose heating chimney had corroded. Inside the house, cacti and tender plants were jumbled in big clay pots. Outside, pear and plum trees overlooked the Black Sea and, with a sudden shock of recognition, I realized I had been in such a garden before. It evoked for me the garden of the Bolkonsky family outside Moscow, to which Prince Andrei returns before battle in the matchless pages of Tolstoy's *War and Peace*. Andrei, too, found panes gone from the greenhouse and plants lying on their sides in tubs. In his garden, too, there was a magnolia with broken branches and only one worker was visible: not a woman watering the hibiscus, but an old man weaving a shoe from raffia-twine. He, too, was undistracted among adversity, as if life must simply go on. There were fruit trees, too, in the Bolkonsky garden. A group of young girls, Andrei found, had been pillaging them in their noble owners' absence. These girls ran unawares into their former master while carrying stolen fruit in the folds of their dresses.

Andrei had come to say farewell to his home 'from a characteristic desire', so Tolstoy tells us, 'to aggravate his own suffering'. I had come to say hello, out of a gardener's curiosity. Amazingly there were sounds of a scuffle in the bushes and fiction became fact before me. Three young girls appeared by a hovel, two of whom were carrying plums, like the girls in Tolstoy's novel. The old lady went on with her work, watering, not weaving, but as unconcerned as Tolstoy's old man by a spectator's existence. The plane trees which towered above the five of us were old enough to have existed in Odessa's garden in the year when Tolstoy was writing his chapter.

Andrei had turned away, 'unwilling to let his girls see that they had been observed'. He sympathized with them and 'a new sensation of comfort and relief came over him when he realized the existence of other human interests entirely aloof from his own and just as legitim-ate as those that occupied him'. The girls in his garden ran away through the meadow-grass, carrying their stolen fruit and showing their bare, sunburned legs. Instead, my girls pushed the eldest to the front so that she could ask if I needed a guide to the garden. She was riding a Western-made bicycle. Like Andrei, I 'shared their wish for the success of their enterprise', but I needed no guide because I could retrace my path by following the English oak trees.

Desirable Dahlias

By September, dahlias are at their brilliant best. They have had a chequered history because they were not at first a success with gardeners, and even now many people fail to exploit their beauty. Dahlias were discovered by Spanish settlers in Mexico but at first were thought to have a bright future as vegetables. The local Indians used to eat their fat tubers, and when a few plants were sent to Madrid the hope was that they would vary the fashionable diet of potatoes. It took a while for the British to catch on to them and only in the 1810s do we hear of dahlia seeds and species being sent for experiment to a titled lady in London. Her gardener failed to make anything of them, and it was left to Napoleon's wife Josephine to see their potential. French contemporaries slyly called her 'the lubricious Creole', but she showed excellent taste in plants. At her Malmaison garden she paid for superb roses and lilacs, immortalized by her painter Pierre-Joseph Redouté. She also patronized new forms of the dahlia, flowers which shared her connection with the New World. Back in Mexico the Indians had been calling the dahlia *cocoxochitl*. I would like to hear the Empress Josephine pronounce that teaser in a Creole accent. Fortunately, the botanists came up with a pronounceable name. It was given in honour of Andreas Dahl, one of the favoured 'apostles' who travelled the world to bring back new plants for classification by Linnaeus in Sweden.

Even then, many gardeners looked down on the new wonder in their midst. It became entangled with boundaries of social snobbery, as if it was fit only for the bungalow-gardens of the working class. Polite English society banished many of the available colours to kitchen gardens, where they could be grown in hiding and used as cut flowers. Breeders continued their work, but in the south-east of England there was a prejudice against many of the new shapes, as if they were all balls of lilac-mauve. It took years for dahlias to be integrated in full glory into mixed borders, where they prolong the season in a flush of fine colour.

Like many gardeners, I was alerted to the best dahlias' potential by the autumn exhibits which Aylett's of Hertfordshire used to put on at the Royal Horticultural Society halls in London. During September it is still a treat to see these dahlias on their home ground at Aylett's garden centre near London Colney in Hertfordshire. Off the M25 at Junction 22, on the A414, Aylett Nurseries have kept up high standards in the cultivation of the dahlia for more than fifty years. In 2005, I attended the celebration of their fiftieth anniversary. It was held in a temporary tent installed by the main garden centre. The displays of dahlias were backed by a brass jazz band.

Aylett's began trading in 1955 when Roger Aylett and his family took on seven-and-a-half bare acres and set up premises in a former chicken shed. They were quick to pick on dahlias as their speciality and found that exhibiting was in their blood. Their first show was coordinated by Muriel, mother of the family, in the Harpenden Public Hall. They then staged their own dahlia festival, charging an entrance fee of 15p, to include a cup of tea. By 1977 the company had won one of the highest medals in the RHS. It continued to exhibit until the late 1990s when it stopped, having won most of the other major medals too. Exhibiting in London had made little difference to the company's business at home.

Back in Hertfordshire the garden centre grew far beyond the old chicken shed. It now employs 120 people and turns over £5 million a year. It has remained a family business with a firm grip on what it stocks, but it is the dahlias which bring in migrating customers. In spring there are even enthusiasts who come all the way from Norfolk to buy them, because Aylett's sell young pot-grown plants. They are so convenient for those of us who have no frost-proof greenhouse or shed.

I first realized dahlias' tremendous presence in a mixed border when I saw them beautifully grown by the brilliant head gardener, Jimmy Hancock, at the National Trust's property at Powis Castle in Shropshire. Dahlias in beautiful colours filled the middle and back rows of his great borders on the main terraces and made my August gardens look extraordinarily boring by comparison. Since then, dahlias have gained from the warmer climate. Converts to the family find that nowadays they are usually able to leave the tubers lazily in the ground even when a frost has killed the top growth. Until early 2009 the winters were so mild that the plants came through in strong form for a second year. I still shy away from this idle habit, and the early months of 2009 and 2010 were so cold that they exposed it as bad practice. If you still want to take the risk, put straw or chopped compost on top of the dahlias after cutting their shoots down. Do not try to plant them deeply in the belief that they will come through the winter more easily. They do not.

After fifty years, I asked Mr Aylett which dahlias are his favourites. While a tuba and trombone played in the background, he evaded the question by telling me the variety which his wife likes best. Mrs Aylett votes for the shell-pink decorative variety 'Dawn Sky', perhaps because it has a long stem and is excellent for picking. Her husband then came up with three selections. The first is the salmon-pink blend of 'Scaur Swinton', a colour which I would never have chosen but which he knows as a grower and guarantees as a fine performer with level, steady growth. The second is my personal number one, although stocks of it have now dwindled and my plants are rarities: the superb 'Maltby Whisper', which is a small-flowered cactus variety in clear yellow, a star which flowers freely in large pots or in the middle-to-front of a border. At shows in the 1990s I made a note of the alluring 'Vicky Crutchfield', a pink variety which has served me well ever since. However, Mr Aylett thinks that 'Vicky' has had her day and that the silver-pink waterlily dahlia, 'Pearl of Heemstede', is much better. Over the canapés I felt I had extracted fifty years of wisdom. Like me, the Ayletts are not sentimental about many of the old varieties, not least because they have grown them and understand that many of them are mediocre, long before conservationists feared they were being 'lost' and tried to bring them back.

Old or new, dahlias grow well only if given plenty of water. I plant mine with a dusting of Vitax Q4 fertilizer beneath them and I feed them until late July with a growth-promoting fertilizer, Miracle-Gro being my choice. Advised by the experts, I then turn to Tomorite to prepare for good buds and flowers. Before that, I harden my heart and stop the young plants at least once, preferably twice. Stopping means removing the tips of the main growing shoot when about four pairs of leaves are showing. It is something beginners hate to do, but it is crucial. It encourages strong side shoots which will in turn bear flowers. If your dahlias have only two or three buds of flower you are shirking the stopping. Mr Aylett also recommends careful disbudding, the removal of buds which appear on side shoots between mid-July and early August. So long as you then stake the bigger dahlias properly, you will have nothing but pleasure.

How popular are dahlias nowadays? Aylett's raise 120,000 cuttings a year, but dahlias account for only 1 per cent of their garden centre's turnover. They suffer from being gardeners' plants in an era when gardening has become so much less popular than the idea of gardens. They give me exceptional pleasure and each year, the mild sense of satisfaction of having done my best by them. In return, I can take credit for one innovation in the Aylett repertoire. In the late 1980s I reproduced beside my column a picture of Aylett's prize-winning London exhibit of dahlias with young Julie Aylett, the boss's daughter, captioned beside it. The photograph was seen by Adam Wigglesworth, then a commodity trader in vegetable oil, while delayed at an airport in Holland. He had already been wooing Miss Aylett, but when he saw her displayed in the *Financial Times*, his daily bible, he realized that her speciality was even more esteemed than his. Shortly afterwards they married, and he is now a director of the family's garden business. They have been married for twenty years and the dahlias have continued to shine. When my son married too, it was for me to supply the flowers for his church wedding. Naturally, I turned in September to dahlias, and except for the bride, Aylett's pale cream *Dahlia* 'Cameo' and the wondrous yellow 'Glorie van Heemstede' were the beauties of the day. Say it with dahlias, and you too will join the revived fashion of our age.

Appreciating Asters

Whenever I can, I pay a late September visit to the National Collection of Michaelmas daisies, which is beautifully kept by the Picton family at Old Court Nurseries near Malvern in Worcestershire. Paul Picton is the latest member of a distinguished family of gardeners to be involved with the aster family. He has grown them and much else since he was a boy and his family's nursery at Colwall shows England's finest collection of asters, on which Paul is an acknowledged expert and grower. His book *The Gardener's Guide to Growing Asters* was published in Britain and America in 1999 and remains one of my most consulted and most admired recent gardening books.

If you mistrust Michaelmas daisies, you need to look at them more closely. Traditionally, their enemy was mildew. If it spared the old varieties they made a heavy mass of dark leaves and blocked up a border for months before flowering. Most of the mildewed plants were hybrid *novi-belgii* varieties which flowered in brilliant colours and had names which ranged from 'Percy Thrower' to 'Winston S. Churchill'. From August onwards they looked as if they had been showered with grey powder, and steadily went into decline. Thirty years ago, sensitive gardeners never even mentioned them in memories of their gardening progress. They were felt to be plants which the Edwardians had wisely reserved for special Michaelmas borders and which were best reserved nowadays for the sort of bungalow which surrounds itself with purple dahlias.

There is much more to the family than mildew, mites and wilt. For years, I blamed *novi-belgii* asters on Belgium because of their name. They are not Belgian at all. Their name was an early attempt to render

New York in botanical Latin, so they are the New York asters, which were rampant on Park Avenue and in Times Square before the human Astors took over. They still grow wild up America's east coast as far as Maine.

Paul Picton's book gives informed advice about coping with the problems in this lovely section of the family, from the early lilac-blue 'Ada Ballard' to the purple-red 'Winston S. Churchill', which spoils in wet weather. I urge you to read his instructions and to pay attention to his personal list at the end of the book. It gives the varieties which his long experience has found to be less prone to mildew. His personal favourite is the double blue 'Marie Ballard', the best blue of all autumn daisies and an exquisite variety wherever it remains healthy. New York asters were not much developed by New Yorkers or Americans, although their varieties are widespread in the American trade.

It is odd, too, that the other great branch of the family, the *novae-angliae* varieties, are under-represented in American gardens. These asters are also American, deriving their name from New England, and in the wild they grow as far south as Carolina. In Europe, gardeners have been defecting to the New England aster because it is so much stronger and not prone to mildew. The best varieties have lilac to purple-blue flowers, although there are whites and a well-known 'Harrington's Pink'. 'Rosa Sieger' is a valuable tall pink, and the purple-red 'Lou Williams' is six feet high at the back of a border. It was only bred in 1995. I like many of them, but they are not as sensational as the New York forms. The most sensational turned out to be a disappointment. 'Andenken an Alma Pötschke' began by promising to be a brilliant splash of autumn colour in Britain but the flowers did not open well, especially in wet years, and recent autumns have left it looking its worst. Hopes of its cherry-red flowers, fully open in October, have faded in the past decade.

The exciting revivals belong to related species, on which Picton's book is excellent. America's favourite aster is *Aster* × *frikartii*, and many British gardeners too would rate this lavender-flowered single variety in their top half-dozen of all border plants. Confusions about the true variety are neatly cleared up in Picton's text and I would only add that this aster is a brilliant plant for twining and propping among other plants from July onwards while the first summer flush of flowers in the front of a border is fading. Staking is essential for a proper display of almost all asters, and the best method is to use bamboo canes of moderate height, artfully placed and secured.

In America, there is a great following for the long-flowering violet-blue 'Fanny's Aster', which we hardly grow in Britain. It owes its name to a grower's housemaid, whereas names from domestic servants are more usually found among English varieties of the past. In Florida and the south-east, gardeners also grow the remarkable climbing *Aster carolinianus*. It is rather untidy but shows thousands of flowers in a shade of pale purple to a height of more than ten feet. In Britain, not even the Pictons have been able to grow it. British gardeners, however, have at last woken up to the beauty of early-flowering *Aster sedifolius* and the small-flowered variations of *Aster cordifolius*. If I could have only one of them, I would choose the metallic single blue 'Little Carlow', which is wonderfully vigorous. I owe my first knowledge of its excellence to a passing remark by John Sales, former adviser to the National Trust's gardens in England. When he was confronted with miles of flowerbed needing colour until the end of the public season, 'Little Carlow' was his suggestion, a great aster with thousands of smallish flowers in a shade of steely clear blue so intense that I find it almost best against the dark background of a green yew hedge. The time to plant and divide 'Little Carlow' is early spring, because it dislikes a wet winter and, when young, is susceptible to slugs. As my own asters multiply and add an entire month to the high point of my garden, I have to say that this easy variety remains top of my list.

My other star turn is tall, pale blue *cordifolius* 'Chieftain', which holds a handsome place towards the back of the border, growing up to five feet high. It is even taller than the light sprays of flower on *Aster turbinellus* or the little white stars which then begin to open on admirable *Aster tradescantii*. Again, these varieties prefer the opposite conditions to modern mildewed hybrids. They like a light, well-drained soil and will tolerate dry weather, although it turns their leaves brown.

The broader range of asters shows us that the season is far longer than we usually realize. With me, it begins with the pale blue *Aster thomsonii* 'Nanus' in early August, joined a little later by the admirably easy *Aster sedifolius*. Without mildew, the focus then moves to the *novae-angliae* varieties, and it is usually mid-October before we see the best from *Aster amellus* 'King George' and its wonderful flush of violet-blue. October is the season for the low-growing *Aster lateriflorus* 'Prince', which has very small flowers of pink-white and stems and leaves of a remarkably dark purple. These dark-stemmed asters are always worth watching and I am particularly keen on the tall *Aster laevis* 'Calliope'.

From August till late October thoughtful gardeners can have asters without diseases and a prairie of first-class colours. Michaelmas daisies are no longer limited to Michaelmas and the strongest of them give the garden a good two months of colour.

Coloured Crabs

In Britain, our trees' autumn colour may be disappointing, but their berries and fruits are another matter. They are an excellent way of prolonging a garden's impact and are invaluable for those of us who like arranging seasonal displays indoors. In August there are already undamaged bunches of big scarlet fruit on one of my top tips, *Sorbus americana*, an upright tree which is untroubled by dry summers. This tree is always good, but it excels itself now that so many garden birds are in hiding. Maybe the birds are on the run from the aggressive wildlife which we are being encouraged to cherish in our gardens.

It is worth planning carefully for a good blaze of fruits. For a small garden in Britain, Europe or America, I would turn first to the family of *Malus* or flowering crabs. The best of them are extraordinarily tough. They are beautiful in flower, fruit and autumn leaf, with two high seasons of special interest. Most of them will grow in dry or cold climates and are more or less foolproof. My deepening knowledge is based on visits to an outstanding nursery collection of the best maluses, where I realize that my view of them needs revision. I have learnt my lessons from Landford Trees at Landford Lodge, Salisbury, Wiltshire whose catalogue has grown gratifyingly during the twenty years in which I have been using and recommending it.

The stock is grown on thirty acres of exposed Wiltshire farmland and is the backbone of a nursery which hardly ever buys in its trees from other sources. An alphabetical collection of the maluses on offer has been steadily developed in and around an area of its walled garden, and I met the proprietor, Christopher Pilkington, beside his visible catalogue of maluses in green growth. We walked up and down his densely planted lines and tried to rank them in an order which would help gardeners to find their way to the best. To my initial relief, we agreed on the one which holds its fine red fruits for the longest time and continues to catch the eye throughout the winter. *Malus* 'Red Sentinel' is an old favourite and ranks near the top after Landford's careful assessment of many of its rivals. It holds its red fruit from November until February in my college garden in Oxford, at least until one of the fellows discovers that the fruits can be turned into jam. 'Red Sentinel' is healthy, arching in outline, and pretty in pink-white flower. So long as you do not expect a tree of a simple, upright form, it is a superb choice.

We also agreed on a lesser-known species which has the prettiest combination of flower, fresh young leaf and sideways-spreading growth. *Malus transitoria* has my favourite leaf in the entire family. It is extremely tough, drought-resistant and delicate in its young greenery. The yellow fruits are a further pleasure and should earn the tree a wider public.

Some of my other initial choices turn out to be not so well advised. 'Golden Hornet' is as common in the trade as *transitoria* is not. It is a tough variety, but its shape is upright, the leaves look dusty and drab, and the brilliant yellow fruits have a way of vanishing by early November. For years, I have blamed birds for their disappearance, but Pilkington remarks that the culprit is always the first hard frost. He rates *Malus* × *robusta* 'Yellow Siberian' much more highly and considers it the best of the yellow fruiters. I am stuck with two 'Hornets', my penance for life.

Several of the most popular types of malus have dark-purple flushed leaves. I would probably have named 'Profusion' as a top variety in this group, but the expert assures me that it looks increasingly wretched as the summer proceeds and is not especially healthy. We hear much less about the related *Malus* × *moerlandsii*, which is unusual in the trade but happy in the Landford nursery. I saw it growing strongly to a height of about fifteen feet and its red-purple leaves and healthy nature deserve more attention. A combination of dark red flowers and shiny purple leaves is also an attractive possibility, best found in 'Liset', an upright variety which is selected from ×

moerlandsii but more widely available. The red colouring of many maluses' leaves has a way of fading and looking tired as the years go by, but the most persistent red is the one called 'Royalty', which begins by growing straight before spreading pleasantly outwards in later years. The darkest shades of red come from fruits, not leaves, and are best seen on a dark-fruited new arrival, *Malus* 'Indian Magic'. The big fruits are distinctive and when stocks of this fine variety build up, they ought to be widely planted.

My favour for 'Golden Hornet' and 'Profusion' has been misplaced. It is pleasant, then, to agree on the virtues of varieties which others wrongly consider to be ordinary. *Malus × robusta* is the Siberian crab from which 'Red Sentinel' and others are derived. It is a very good tree itself in flower and fruit, retaining red crab-apples well into the winter. It is as robust as its name and an excellent choice for a double season of beauty in flower and fruit. Its close relation is the Japanese crab, *Malus floribunda*, which is spectacular in flower, making a conveniently small tree whose crimson-red buds open to white flowers. It becomes more wide than high and allows itself to be clipped into a pretty, semi-floral shape. It is very strong, and although I thought it was too hackneyed when I was first offered it, I have learned to love it as one of the best of the family when in flower.

Finally, two modern varieties which are on the up and are difficult to kill. Pilkington's first choice is 'Evereste', a transatlantic variety with white flowers and green leaves which age unusually well. Its masses of orange-red fruits are pretty in October. I appreciate the expert's tact in choosing this one as 'idiot-proof'. 'Evereste' is the variety to which I gave a central position in my garden some years ago and which I have prided myself on growing with unusual success. That pride can now be transferred. In Landford's maloretum there is a new variety which suits me particularly well. Known as *Malus × zumi* 'Professor Springer' it bears masses of orange-red fruits on a super-healthy tree. At Landford they know it as the 'zoomy professor'. I have zoomed in, and given it a prime place at home.

Cutting Corners With Chrysanthemums

Thoughtful gardeners can prolong their gardens' late flowering by the clever use of chrysanthemums. These flowers have had all sorts of symbolic associations across the world, from China to France. They represent love or death or scholarly perfection, and in parts of China their leaves would be infused in water to make a liquid which was supposed to give eternal youth. Elsewhere in China admirers used to examine them and mark them on a scale used in the exam for entrance into the Chinese civil service. I like the idea of coaching chrysanthemums for an Oxford degree and deciding which of them deserves a low second ranking. In Britain, there is an obstacle: like dahlias, chrysanthemums are bound up with the British sense of class.

Up the social scale, garden-owners look down on chrysanthemums as if they are common. They scorn mounds of them in simple front gardens and dislike those yellow-flowered varieties in plastic pots from florists. Anything which calls itself a 'Mum' and flowers like a fancy cushion is beyond the bounds of acceptability. As a result, chrysanthemums have receded into vegetable gardens, where they can be visited but never confronted in the main view.

The family should not be damned because a few members of it are used in odd ways. The choice is not between a Mums' outing or a complicated system of training spray-chrysanthemums under glass. Nowadays I enjoy ten weeks of chrysanthemums by the dozen because I cheat. I grow chrysanthemums only from the end of April and have none of the bother of rooting, rotting or prolonged heating which deters beginners. In busy times, thoughtful gardeners can let others do the initial work. I turn to Halls of Heddon-on-the-Wall,

Northumberland NE15 0JS, who specialize in dahlias and chrysanthemums and are committed to helping customers cut corners. If customers send in orders for chrysanthemums before early March, Halls will deliver rooted cuttings of named varieties in late April or early May. Each rooted piece should then be set in a four-inch pot filled with a good garden compost and kept in a sheltered place. Watch for warnings of a late frost, and if forewarned, bring the plants indoors for the night only. I use no heat, no glass and receive my plants at the end of April, potting them and growing them on for planting outdoors on 15 May. It is so easy, and in ten years I have not lost a single one.

The results are extremely pleasing, especially from early-flowering varieties which give such a lift to the garden from the third week in August onwards. My winners are the old and well-loved 'Bronze Max Riley', flame-red 'Membury' and pale yellow 'Dana', which is good for cutting. The range of colours is widened by the stalwart 'Allouise' and the sports from it in many colours. They come in shades of white, peach, red and gold and flower early enough to be at their best long before the weather turns in mid-November. Experts emphasize the importance of stopping the early varieties in order to encourage side shoots and many more flowers by removing the growing tip, or upper few inches, of a young plant. I stop mine at the end of May, whereupon the side shoots multiply and keep the season going. Feeding and spraying are important too. I fork the fertilizer fish, blood and bone into the soil a day before planting out the young cuttings. From mid-July until mid-August, I spray the developing plants with diluted Phostrogen, but I stop the fertilizer when colour begins to show in the bud. Pests are only a problem because the young green leaves look so appetizing between May and July. The RHS Wisley handbook calls greenfly 'virus vectors', but the way to stop them vecting is to spray them early with Tumblebug. If the plants are unsprayed, leaf miners will also cause the leaves to curl up and look as though something is tunnelling through them. Again, Tumblebug keeps them away.

These foes are hazards, but are not inevitable. Can we also be lazy and keep these varieties through the winter? We can, if we remember that in November a parent plant should be cut down to about six inches, lifted and laid in a good peaty compost. It can then live in an unheated glasshouse and be brought back to growth by resuming the watering and increasing the heat in early March. Within three weeks, young shoots will be bursting everywhere and can be rooted easily as the cuttings for next year. Alternatively, you can order again from Halls in early spring and reckon that the time saved is worth the modest cost. If you cannot be bothered with lifting plants, you can cut them down, cover them with sandy soil, straw or peat to a depth of several inches and trust to luck. The early varieties will survive quite a heavy frost under covering and are a worthwhile gamble in light soil outdoors.

Alternatively, choose varieties from the hardy group, which flower from late September into early November and usually survive the winter. Excellent varieties are now being marketed again, after being rescued by keen conservationists. The single dark pink 'Anne, Lady Brockett' is a cracker but she had to be rediscovered by expert nurserymen at Monksilver Nursery, Cottenham, Cambridge. Her ladyship had decamped to France, where healthy plants were duly found and repatriated. Admittedly, she had always had what nursery lists call a 'running habit'. Two of the commonest hardy varieties are good value too, yellow-apricot 'Mary Stoker' and the double red 'Duchess of Edinburgh'. The prettiest is the late-flowering 'Emperor of China', which grows up to four feet high and combines a red flush on its leaves with beautifully shaped flowers of pale double pink. I look on these fine chrysanthemums with eyes formed not by China but by the unsurpassed *Tale of Genji*, the Japanese classic which was written by Lady Murasaki at the start of the eleventh century. Such a sensitive work is unimaginable in dreary old northern Europe at that date, but in Japan it was already traditional to debate the relative merits of gardens in spring and autumn. Fashions were fickle and as Lady Murasaki neatly puts it: 'Women who are seduced by the spring garden (so it is in this world) are now seduced by the autumn.'

In his youth Prince Genji, she tells us, prepared to sing and dance for the court during their autumn excursion. He had been wearing a branch of maple in his cap, but as the leaves fell, 'it seemed at odds with his handsome face'. An unlikely character called the General of the Left replaced Genji's branch with chrysanthemums, which 'stood in his cap, delicately touched by the frost, and gave new beauty to the prince's form and motions'. Everyone was profoundly moved. 'Even the unlettered menials', who were thinking of 'rocks and branches', were stirred to tears at the sight. I picture Genji with 'Anne, Lady Brockett' in his hair and can well understand the menials' reaction.

Genji's cousin was a concubine of the emperor, and in her garden an entire 'chrysanthemum hedge would blossom in the morning frosts of early winter'. In the tale translated as 'The Ivy', a prince who is believed to be Genji's son attempts to seduce a secluded daughter of the Eighth Prince. She casts a quick look at him from behind a silk curtain and starts to cry behind her fan. He pities her, but he knows that her charm will bring other men flocking and, as a result, his 'doubts come back and also his resentment'. He turns away to the nearby chrysanthemums and notices how the better they are cultivated, the slower they are to show their last, prized flush of colour. As he looked, one flower was already turning to its grand finale and the prince was moved to poetry. 'I do not love among flowers the chrysanthemum only,' he began, quoting a famous old Japanese poem. Neither do I, but it was he who then had the luck. He captivated his young target and stayed on with her among the flowers for some days, 'with music and other diversions to break the monotony'.

At Home With Hellyer

Not until 2002 did I break one of the most welcome treaties of my life. It ran for twenty-five years and protected me from exposure to serious expertise. During its lifetime, I shared the role of writing weekly gardening columns for the *Financial Times* with a senior partner, Arthur Hellyer. His career as a gardener and writer had begun more than fifty years before mine. Born in 1902, he was the supreme expert when I began to write in 1970, but the treaty was his suggestion.

The terms were beautifully simple. Neither of us would visit the other's garden during our tenure of the job. Perhaps Hellyer did not wish to be interrupted. Perhaps he was shy of one of my first pieces, which attacked the entire family of flowering heathers. He knew far more about them than I did and grew some fine varieties near his own house. As I moved around in earlier life, I was glad he never came to see my less established efforts. He eventually visited the gardens of my Oxford college, but told me later that he did not know I was in charge of them. He never expressed an opinion.

I finally visited his garden, Orchards, in Rowfant, near Crawley, West Sussex, about ten years after he had died. In Arthur's older age there had had to be economies of scale, but since his death in 1993, his daughter Penelope had done her best to cope with the framework and the inevitable replanting. I found my visit extremely touching. It reflected the history of a particular era, now lost. As a schoolboy in Dulwich, the young Arthur Hellyer had had a sound, practical mind. He then contracted tuberculosis and for his health's sake was advised to work in the open air. During the First World War, emphasis was soon laid on the need to 'dig for victory'. Many people were digging for death in their trenches in France, but behind the lines, civilians were encouraged to grow vegetables to help feed the nation. Hellyer once told me that his early interest in gardening owed much to the need to dig up the family lawn and try to save Britain in 1916.

His garden at Orchards survived as a witness to the sort of self-sufficient vision which returned to fashion in the dark days of the early 1970s and was brilliantly satirized in the TV series *The Good Life*. Arthur's lifelong partner was certainly no Penelope Keith. He married Gay in 1933 when he was thirty-two and she was working at the John Innes Research Institute. Gay had a BSc and the clear mind of a natural teacher. She was an ideal match for Arthur's own practical and scientific outlook and his faith in the possibility of a self-sustaining life. In 1934, they did what many of us once dreamed of achieving: they bought seven acres of bare land, which was to be their home for the rest of their life. On it Arthur the gardener planted excellent magnolias, camellias and acers in a design which he developed on the ground rather than on the drawing board. He also built the house at Orchards. He continued for many years to work to a routine which makes life in a modern office seem a cushy number. In summer, he would begin the day at 5 a.m. He would garden until 6.45 a.m. He would then make cups of tea, one of which would be given to his young daughter, Penelope. He would leave at 7 a.m. for the daily train to London. Whenever possible, he would take with him some home-grown fruit and produce to sell to the greengrocer on his way to the station. In London he would edit the immortal magazine *Amateur Gardening*. He would return home just before 7 p.m. to take an early supper. Then, he would write, breaking only for one programme on the television, the *Nine O'Clock News*.

An old black-and-white photograph from the 1930s captures the resolution of this pair of pioneers, he pushing a plough through virgin soil, she following it to beat the ground into shape. At the time, Arthur and Gay were living in a temporary shed on the lower slopes of Orchards. I found it enchanting that their early settlement survived seventy years later with orange blossom, lily of the valley, raspberries and indestructible shrubs around it. Of course, there had been a goat, a cow and various chickens. Arthur managed the heavy machinery, but Gay would help him with every other garden job. Once in the hot summer of 1976 she too contributed to the *FT*, publishing her excellent recipe for cucumber soup. Behind it lay her own practicality and hard work as a scientifically minded land girl.

Sometimes, I look back at old copies of *Country Life* magazine, published between 1935 and 1955, whose house prices make one sick with envy – 'offers around £5,000 for an enchanting Georgian rectory with two cottages, stables and 10 acres of land' in what is now the M25 corridor. Articles in these magazines reflect the Hellyer ethic, the bravado of 'back to the land' and the virtue of growing one's own vegetables and becoming a self-sufficient unit. Like that era's house prices, these assumptions now seem a distant echo of history. Most of us now 'pick our own' somewhere else or scour the supermarket. The old *Country Life* assumptions, however, were ones which guided Hellyer's life, but in his case, they had a further depth. For a while, his wife Gay had inclined to the sect of Plymouth Brethren, a group which opposed her marrying a non-member. Their settling at Orchards marked a personal escape, but the Brethren's values of personal responsibility, work and dedication stayed with him throughout his life.

There was a shared culture of science between Arthur and his wife which shaped their outlook and their clear way of teaching. He was profoundly uninterested in spin, though quietly appreciative of style. This clear, practical modesty gave him a style of his own. It also made him aware of gardening's many pitfalls, and generous, therefore, about others' efforts. If he had broken our treaty and called on me, I would have learned so much, and somewhere, he would have found something to admire.

Selecting Salvias

Twenty-five years ago my garden was living in an autumnal Dark Age. Since then plant-hunters and breeders have transformed the range of late-flowering plants from which we choose. One of the best transformations has been the discovery of so many new salvias. The best are not really hardy, but they are so free-flowering from mid-July onwards, in such exceptional colours, that it seems a small effort to protect them from extreme frost.

If I could choose only five out of more than 100 on the market, which would I pick? The colour might be startling, but I think the vivid *Salvia involucrata* would make it into the top group. The flowers of this vigorous Mexican are a marvellous shade of lipstick rose-magenta. It will withstand quite a sharp frost and continue to flower into late November. I have learned its special value in border plantings, where the art is to dot individual plants at intervals down a bed and let them develop their full potential so as to draw the eye down the bed's entire length. Each involucrata is best staked on a central cane, but there is no need to tie in the upper stems, as they are prettier if they spread out naturally at a horizontal angle. They grow furiously to a height of four feet and will even put up with light shade.

Also from Mexico, my favourites for small pots are the various forms of a natural hybrid, *Salvia* × *jamensis*. 'La Luna' is an excellent yellow, and there are fine pinks and shades of cream, including 'Moonlight Over Ashwood', which has yellow leaves and very pale yellow flowers. These fine little plants are not hardy in an English winter and need to be kept alive in the dark months as rooted cuttings sheltered indoors. Among the blues, my favourite is *Salvia cacaliifolia*. Its spikes of blue flowers have an exceptional depth and intensity, deserving the description 'royal blue'. It has two cardinal needs. It must have plenty of water and as it is spoilt by the first few degrees of frost, it needs to be sheltered. I simply take it indoors. At a growers' lunch at Chelsea Flower Show, I learnt that the easiest way to propagate it is to heap a mulch of compost round the central root stock and then pull off the root-bearing stems which emerge from the base.

Salvia microphylla also has to feature in the top five, but only in a form with a true red to its flowers. 'Kew Red' is excellent, flowering freely above shiny mid green leaves. For years now, I have also grown 'Newby Hall', which is tall enough to reach five feet and has bright red flowers with yellowish leaves. These plants tolerate a lack of water for up to a fortnight, allowing one to go on holiday with a clear conscience. At a recent RHS Autumn Show in London, I bought plants of the small *Salvia chamaedryoides*, a pretty number from Texas which has small deep blue flowers and grows to a foot in height. On balance, I think I prefer the tender *Salvia darcyi* which has big bright red flowers until late October. The leaves are quite sticky and the plant needs to be staked to show itself well at a height of three feet. The inevitable first frost in a modern November or December will ruin it, but salvation for all these salvias is easy. From late October onwards I bring the likes of *Salvia darcyi* and *cacaliifolia* into the house in pots and enjoy them for another month or two as indoor plants. If they are dead-headed there, they will go on flowering until December. They then go into a greenhouse and produce dozens of rootable cuttings when they start to grow again in spring. If you shelter these vivid new arrivals, you will never be short of stock to carry you cheerfully through a winter.

Goodnight at Gamberaia

The end of each season of flower gardening lives on in thoughtful gardeners' memories. One of my most memorable endings occurred on a hill outside Florence, the setting for the garden of the Villa Gamberaia, which has been widely praised as a supreme example of a garden with features in a Renaissance style. The site is easily reached by the number 10 bus from Florence's main railway station, which takes you up into the hill town of Settignano, once the home of distinguished sculptors and artists. The Villa Gamberaia's garden owes its continuing evolution to a series of dedicated private owners, and nowadays paying visitors are welcome. In its well-defined space, the final scene in my year of flower gardening involved China roses, lemon trees and some boisterous ladies.

First, I should explain the Villa's celebrated garden and its history, which has had admirable attention in recent years. In 1944 the house and garden were heavily damaged when a German officer set fire to the place, before abandoning the site. Three years later, despite the ruin and neglect, the sensitive eye of the great art critic Bernard Berenson described the place as still able to 'inspire longing and dreams, sweet dreams'. I do not think that Berenson had much knowledge about flower gardening but he had an eye for design, and it was Gamberaia's design which had endured. In his lifetime the place had become widely known in English circles through the book by the novelist Edith Wharton, *Italian Villas and their Gardens*, which described it as 'the most perfect example of the art of producing a great effect on a small scale'. Even if the villa had no garden it would still be a fine place to visit for the sake of its views across an enchanted landscape.

It is hard to believe that the great urban sprawl of modern Florence lies so near, concealed beneath it in the valley. From the lawns, the views to the distant hills of Chianti country are unspoilt and, on one side, the landscape is fit to be included in a great Florentine painting from the fifteenth century.

What we see nowadays is only a temporary point in a long history. As so often, an admired garden makes nonsense of simple ideas of historical conservation. The garden which we admire has continued to be altered, and to what point in the past would purists for garden history now want it to be restored? The villa's name, 'Gamberaia', goes back to the old Italian word for a crayfish, and as there has always been good water on the site, the name suggests to some that the villa began life as a simple farmhouse on a property where this fish was farmed. There may have been a link between the fishponds and the nuns of a nearby convent, but others believe the name merely came from a like-named Florentine family. The villa which we see today took its main shape rather later, in 1610.

As experts on Edwardian gardening remarked, the villa garden is confined. On one side, the main distinction is the superb view over Florence. On another, it is a long green vista of grass which was once a bowling green and now ends in an imitation grotto. There is still some dispute about the origins of this pretty walk, which appealed to English visitors' love of lawns. In the Edwardian era, a visiting American student ascribed it to a member of the Lapi family in the later seventeenth century. Others think, as I do, that the credit goes to a later owner, Scipione Capponi, a member of a great Florentine family. He was a man of taste who admired classical antiquities, and his brother helped to fund the Botanic Academy in Florence. Certainly Scipione changed and improved the site and a map from the mid eighteenth century suggests that the best-known part of today's garden already had a formal outline during his ownership. It shows some twisted evergreen embroidery and a circular island for rabbits, confined by water.

What we now see and admire is due to very different hands. In 1896, the villa was bought by a Romanian, Princess Giovanna Ghika, who had studied arts and sculpture in Paris. She took over ground which had been given to vegetable gardening and introduced an attractive plan of formal water ponds which she edged with roses and oleanders in order to make a parterre. She planted a concluding wall of evergreen cypress beyond it and may already have cut tall windows into their green mass. These interludes of open space give brilliant views through the hedge to this day.

During the Princess's lifetime, the Oxford aesthete and historian Harold Acton lived at the fine villa La Pietra on the opposite line of hills. He loved the atmosphere at neighbouring Gamberaia and recalled how he 'began to frequent this paradise, then belonging to a narcissistic Romanian who lived mysteriously in love with herself, perhaps, and certainly with her growing creation, the garden'. At this point Acton's memory has airbrushed out of his text the Romanian's most beloved companion, the elusive Mary Blood with her blue-grey angora cat. I think there was more to these ladies' relations than narcissism. The Gamberaia garden should be recognized as a forerunner of Britain's Sissinghurst in histories of female love and the landscape. It is not that Acton suppressed Miss Blood on purpose. On another occasion he recalls her and describes her as 'a great artist'. He even preserves what are some of her only surviving words. She told him as a boy to 'plant umbrella pines. You can never have enough of them.' It is not bad advice. The Princess and Miss Blood did most to make the parterre garden which visitors still admire, but in the mid 1920s the next owner, Baroness von Kettler, simplified some of their planting and introduced more evergreen yews. None of these ladies, however, were the ladies in the scene which concluded my year.

In the late November sunshine I climbed Gamberaia's stairway to the garden's upper levels where the planting is more formal. In summer, the big terracotta pots here contain handsome lemon trees, but over the garden wall came something else: an operatic chorus of laughter, cheering and occasional swear words. The olive trees were swarming with women in aprons who were shaking the branches and pushing off their crop of fruits with long-handled mops. The olives then fell on to large sheets around the tree trunk, no doubt to be gathered and pressed. The female pickers played up to my male gaze, but they did not know that I was thinking of the unchanging techniques of olive-gathering. On ancient Greek vases, Greeks are shown up olive trees shaking fruits on to similar sheeting. They have sticks, not mops, and significantly, they are all men.

In front of me the big lemon trees in their heavy pots had just gone into the lemon house, the *limonaia*. They stood there in rows, sheltered from the November frost. On the sloping ground towards Florence, a line of China roses was still in pink flower, showing how good this sort of rose is in a dry and difficult season. The November light began to fade and suddenly the bells struck the hour in the town below. I felt part of the evolution which is every great garden's history. The landscape architect Geoffrey Jellicoe once described the Villa Gamberaia as 'more Italian than the Italians'. He ought to have seen my Italian ladies expressing their Italian natures and recanted his patronizing view. They were the right finale for a year of flowers outdoors, and I quietly covet them up the trees. Their singing would be most welcome as I set about pruning my avenues of ornamental pears.

Sophie's World

As Christmas approaches, old readers of my gardening column always resurface with news of their gardens' progress. Young ones join them, propelled by new ambitions, so I end this book with two young hopefuls whose public debut earned them many fans. The first of them represents my claim to have invented Facebook as early as 1997, although I was too unworldly to pursue the most lucrative idea in this book.

The years of the dotcom boom were hectic for all of us, but for none of those with whose gardens I keep in touch were they half as hectic as for the young Sophie Click-Portal. I can hardly believe that it is already fifteen years since that snowy afternoon in December when we rejected her application to read for a degree in Classics at New College, Oxford. My notes at the time said her spelling was appalling and she believed that the Elgin Marbles were carved in the second century BC. In her translation test she twice mistook an active for a passive. She went on to Cambridge, much as we expected, and two years later I heard from a colleague that she was taking their newly designed option called Classix instead.

Sophie's world turned out to be social rather than intellectual. When her graduation loomed, her friends were adamant that her choices lay only between headhunting or helping to write an agony column in the weekend press. They were not reckoning with Derek, Sophie's boyfriend, who had been working during her degree as a partner in a technology start-up in Cambridge's silicon fen. Every Sunday, she would commute to his flat in Biggleswade. It was there that she was introduced to the World Wide Web.

In 1997, Sophie decided to try agony-aunting online and set up a website for social and personal encounters and photos, the area where her strengths lay. On friends' advice, she approached nearby celebrities for venture capital and after she had been in touch with a number of offshore trusts, the funding was sorted out, although part of it arrived as banknotes in an envelope. By autumn her site was up and running and her plans for Intimate.com were born. Or, rather, they would have been born but for Sophie's talent for misspelling. By one of those lucky chances which lie behind most successful entrepreneurs, the name which she actually registered was Intermate.com instead.

The name suggested its own agenda and Sophie has developed it into Britain's most exclusive online encounter and dating service. Intermate is now the City's best-kept secret. If you think your financial adviser has been underperforming, the reason is that he has been obsessed with time on Intermate instead. The service is available only on subscription and only to individuals of high net worth or otherwise impeccable assets. On the site Sophie soon introduced a Call Option which went like wildfire. Her move into spread-betting was also inspired, but it had to be suspended when two European users misunderstood what it meant. Meanwhile, Intermate roared secretly ahead on Wall Street despite severe anxieties about security. When a very exclusive brokerage house discovered that its senior male partners were starting to date each other online, they decided that the only way to hush up the rumour from the private clients' ears was to buy Sophie out, monopolize the service and give her a vice-presidential role.

What do you do aged twenty-six with a pay-out of £60 million and a lifetime stretching in front of you? Sooner or later, you go back to your roots, and the Click-Portal roots go deep into northern Nottinghamshire. There, Sophie remembers a golden haze of childhood set in a dreamy summer garden of old-fashioned roses and scented jasmine. The memories, too, are hazy, because her mother could not face the Nottinghamshire winters and the obligatory shooting lunches, so she decamped to the South of France without Sophie's father when Sophie was only six. Thanks to her new-found riches Sophie can at last begin to integrate her past. She will recreate those golden afternoons and update them on a site of her own choosing.

She could afford to buy a house almost anywhere, but she liked the sound of the special section called Desperate To Impress on Britain's coolest internet start-up, lastminute.com. Among dozens of tempting offers she found a magnificent Georgian villa in Twickenham whose gardens slope down to the Thames near historic Marble Hill House. She bought it with one click of a mouse and became the proud owner of a long-neglected garden site. However, even in our enterprise culture, massive riches incite the envy of workers in the old economy. Her sister, Cathy, is the brains of the Click-Portal family and is slowly writing a doctoral thesis on early Georgian landscape poetry. When Sophie set up in Twickenham, Cathy sent her a moving-in card with a message inside from a malevolent poem written by Jonathan Swift in 1727. Impersonating a Georgian house in Twickenham, Swift had written as follows: 'Some South-Sea broker from the City / Will purchase me the more's the pity, / Lay all my fine plantations waste, / To fit them to his vulgar taste.' Cathy had scratched out the words 'South Sea' and 'his' and written 'online' and 'her' instead. She has not been invited to stay at Christmas.

Her sister's conscious plan, meanwhile, is to ride the new wave in gardening and take it forward beyond the stereotypes of the pre-electronic age. Her guiding design concept is to represent the telecosm in natural materials, and link the garden and the new global village by a subtle use of allusion. Her front door leads out on to some avant-garde wooden decking which she has had painted with red and yellow wavebands to suggest intercontinental communication. Beyond the decking visitors pass through a living 'portal', a block of evergreen hedging made from clipped leylandii conifers to symbolize rapid growth. Beyond the portal, students from Kew have worked at the weekends to lay out a complex web of clipped box. It is web-like to symbolize the internet and golden, not green, to symbolize the bags of money which can be made from it. Beyond her golden web, Sophie has sited an echo of her Classix training and her studies of the 'appropriation' of the ancient world by modern taste. On a pedestal she has put a statue of Hermes, the ancient god of rapid messages, or heavenly e-mail. To move with the times, Hermes' sandals are no longer winged: they are webbed.

Beyond the telecosm the ground slopes down towards the River Thames where Sophie has fertility-stripped the turf and replaced it with hundreds of plants from the category of ornamental grasses. This part of the design is to be known as the Wild West, symbolizing the open frontiers which stretch beyond the telecosm for the next generation of Sophies who are quick enough to see where they lie. In mild, wet winter weather, the top growth of these grasses looks much dirtier and drabber than Sophie expected. She is still hoping for a sharp frost over Christmas to make it look like the glistening photographs in her colour books of garden design.

Sophie sees it all as cool gardening at the cutting edge, but it looks much less effective than the adjacent rectangular garden where Sophie, unwittingly, has gone back to her dislocated roots. Drifts of campanulas from her father's Nottinghamshire garden mix with pale yellow evening primroses, the lovely white peony 'Kelway's Glorious' and a range of purple-blue summer salvias which hark back to the times before Sophie's mother bolted to France. The part of the garden with the most personal warmth is the part which evokes a fractured past.

In Sophie's eyes, the only problems in the landscape are two unanticipated visitors. Her elderly father, Tommy Click-Portal, has invited himself for Christmas and expects to be entertained with something as old fashioned as conversation. He has never got on with Derek, and Sophie was not anticipating that Derek would migrate from Biggleswade and set himself up on the top floor in Twickenham, near his beloved rugby football, with plans to telecommute by long-range terminal to Cambridge without ever leaving the house. Derek's motto is copied from the American head of Intel, who told the world that 'only the paranoid survive'. Sophie has always believed the opposite: 'only the extrovert succeed'. It has occurred to her that as she no longer owns the site, she can advertise herself on Intermate as a seasonal Christmas Call Option, keep quiet about the details and check the back-to-back offers. Deep down she knows that by the end of the holiday season she will have had more than enough Face Time with Derek, especially if he spends most of the day entrenched upstairs with his computer-game called *Heads Down*, which is advertised online as 'better than the best rugger scrum'.

As Intermate is so secure, Derek will never know that Sophie has put herself up for a cyber-relationship, under the general description of 'a multi-millionairess in her twenties with an ever-open portal'. As ever, Sophie is confident of success. She is only a mouse click away, she believes, from someone with whom to take telecosmic gardening into the new age. Deeper still, she is farther from what she needs, a soul-mate to repair the past and join her in scattering bonemeal on the ground which her parents ploughed and buried in her heart.

À La Carte de Tendre

Post-Christmas tension is also the subject of prolonged telephone calls from my column's favourite readers, and over the years none has been more prolonged or enjoyable than my calls from Annabel Swift-Decking. She has always had a sharp financial brain, and nine years ago in March she did something truly last-minute: she took a vast short position in a dotcom company and made so much money that it changed her life. She then cashed in her holding in Asset.missmanagement, the one-stop website for high-flying women, and bought herself a charming Georgian rectory in my nearby Gloucestershire village of Upper Quartile. Friends in fund management had never thought of Annabel as anything so interesting as a 'wild card'. The most interesting thing about her was her string of unsatisfactory transatlantic boyfriends.

In January, everything changed, the way life can, when she met Thierry over dinner in a friend's flat in Onslow Gardens. Seven months later, he left Paris and came to spend a year in the depths of the English countryside. At first sight, anyone would fall for Thierry Taille Chic. His business is selling time-dated options on the pound's precise moment of entry into the euro and as sterling has fallen steeply, he has done a cracking business down in Gloucestershire. It is surprising how many of the local members of Business for Sterling have secretly opened positive positions in Thierry's book. His charm is still stronger than his English, but both are very much stronger than Annabel's French. This gap explains the recent fuss over Christmas presents.

In the summer, Thierry began to complain that Annabel was spending more time on her flowerbeds than she was spending on him. It was not very tactful, but in November he was pleased to find the perfect peace-offering in the Hatchard's Christmas catalogue, a book called *The Constant Gardener*. It will not go down well, because Annabel hates spy-writing. However, she cannot claim the high ground, either. Friends told her that the way to convert Thierry to Britain's national pastime was to buy him a book in French on gardening, so she went to Paris and looked for one. Much the best catalogue of gardening books is issued by the Maison Rustique in the Rue Jacob, and among some very scholarly treatises, Annabel found the perfect thing in the Maison's personal collection at the end of its list. It was called the *Livre des Caresses*. She imagined something sweet about flowers and the language of kisses, and the thought of them awoke pleasant memories. After her first lunch with Thierry, he had touched her heart by faxing to her office a sort of map which was called a 'Carte de Tendre'. Apparently, it was dreamed up in the 1660s by the authoress of an unreadable French novel called *Clélie*, whose heroine had forthright views on the pitfalls of a woman's love-life and the problems of feminine emotion. On the 'Carte de Tendre', the River of Inclination runs northwards between two well-mapped bits of country. The right bank is the Land of Reason, settled with such solemn virtues as Sincerity, and leads away to the Lake of Indifference. The 'rive gauche' is the land of emotion, tenderness and '*petits soins*' in which a woman risks being swept away to the left-hand side of life. Emotionally, Annabel has always felt decidedly Left Bank, and never more so than when Thierry drew a little route for himself entirely on the map's left side.

When Thierry opened his present at Christmas, the *Livre des Caresses* turned out to be something altogether different. Gardening in France is a broader subject, it seems, and this book from Paris's leading catalogue turned out to describe the '*géographie sensuelle*' of the female of the human species. Thierry took it as a hint and an insult but it was only the beginning of a very bad day. There were the usual problems over the morning's church services, because Thierry's Catholic service took place in a tin shed on the outskirts of town, while Annabel sang 'Glory to the new-born King' in the grand church in the centre of Cirencester. When they returned home, Annabel knew better than to suggest watching the Queen's Christmas Message after all the dreadful things which *Paris Match* has said about royalty in the past fifty years. They went straight in to lunch and Annabel thought she was justified in assuming that traditional Christmas pudding is now an acceptable currency Europe-wide. Thierry took one mouthful, spat it out and started talking in fast French about the joys of 6 January, the Feast of the Epiphany, and a pudding called *galette des rois*. After lunch, Annabel searched high and low in her kitchen bible, *Constance Spry's Cookery Book*, but this particular cake was never one which was taught to English debutantes in their dreamy days at Wingfield.

Christmas evening was definitely more right bank and reasoned than full of '*empressement*' on the left. There was more hope for Boxing Day, as Annabel had promised Thierry that they would go to watch a meet of Gloucestershire's famous Beaufort Hunt. She ended by wishing that Parliament had been more decisive and passed an act against Hunting With Dogs which actually worked. Thierry had seen the sport in France and was most put out not to be offered a plate of *fraises des bois* at the meet. He was expecting an array of horn-blowers to play something by Poulenc, but the elderly Beaufort huntsman, an ex-captain of little military distinction, blew three flat notes on his hunting horn and everybody moved off. Seeing his disappointment, a tweed-wrapped woman in mittens assured Thierry that it was not real hunting anyway because the 'unentered hounds' had not been able to go cubbing properly in the autumn and the legislation was beginning to bite. 'Unentered hounds' conjured up an alarming image in Thierry's mind, which was not helped when the woman added that everything had been ruined by fears of foot-and-mouth. When he looked completely blank, she explained in her best county French that it was all the fault of '*pied-bouche*'. Thierry was horrified, thinking it must be something that minor royalty do with their financial advisers on holiday.

To jolly things up Annabel had arranged lunch with her cousins, Julian and Veronica Sloane-Wally, in their nearby Old Rectory. She explained to Thierry that the Sloane-Wally garden was famous, but in winter he could only admire the golden thuja hedge. Lunch went off well enough, with devilled turkey on the menu, but when conversation returned to the topic of hunting, Veronica exclaimed that the government had very odd priorities as it had given so much parliamentary time to a ban on the noble art of fox-hunting but so little time to debate before reversing the admirable ban enshrined formerly in Section 28. Thierry again looked puzzled and when Veronica briskly explained the sexual behaviour which '*Section vingt-huit*' was supposed to discourage, he shrugged his shoulders and said that in Paris, these things were '*plus chic*'. Veronica looked as if she had been given a euro in her small change in W. H. Smith. Matters did not improve when Thierry later remarked that in Paris, he lived in the rue des Francs-Bourgeois in the Marais. Veronica muttered audibly that if so, it was the first time she had ever heard of a pansy living in a swamp. Soon after, they left, but their hosts' wariness about kissing anyone goodbye caused a slight unease in Annabel's mind.

For some weeks, Thierry had been talking fondly about the imminent arrival of his beloved Delors, the dog which lives with a friend in Paris and which Annabel has not yet seen. He has been telling her that it represents one of his two infidelities. During their early exchanges of local vocabulary, Annabel was charmed to discover that the French for a 'fox terrier' is the same as the English but pronounced in the French way. She assumed that they would be collecting '*le fox-terrier*' from Heathrow next week, but on the morning after Boxing Day she opened a parcel from Paris. Inside it she found a thick collar with big metal studs and an inset portrait of something which looks alarmingly like a Rottweiler. Worse, there was a medallion on the collar, engraved with the following words, '*Titi: baisers, Jules*'. Am I the second infidelity, she has begun to wonder, and if so, am I second after the dog or after whom? In matters of her personal 'Carte de Tendre', her cousin Veronica has a maddening way of being right. When Annabel last wrote to me, therefore, she was anticipating a grim time of further researches which would take her way out to the right of the River of Inclination. Down in Upper Quartile, it has been a poor Christmas for European union, but Annabel is determined to get to what she calls the bottom of it, even if it involves plumbing the right bank's Lake of Indifference.

Further Reading

I owe special debts to several older books, now mostly out of print, to which I continue to refer. I especially recommend J. Coutts, *Everyday Gardening* (London, 1945), which first taught me techniques of gardening, and the two masterpieces by A. G. L. Hellyer, *Your Garden Week by Week* (London, 1936) and *Amateur Gardening Pocket Guide* (Feltham, 1971). Christopher Lloyd, *The Well-Tempered Garden* (London, 1970) is also full of practical advice, based on experience, and remains essential. I find these practical books cheaper and more use than subsequent encyclopaedias written by many authors and diluted by too many colour pictures. As wide-ranging guides to particular types of plant, the titles by Martyn Rix with the photography of Roger Phillips are in a class by themselves, uniting expert knowledge of every plant discussed with superb colour pictures, frequently of the plants in their wild habitats. Roger Phillips and Martyn Rix, *Bulbs* (London, 1989), *Perennials* (London, 1994–6), *Roses* (London, 1988), *Shrubs* (London, 1989) and the remarkable *Summer Annuals* (London, 1996) are outstandingly good value. Among more specialized books I turn often to Paul Picton, *The Gardener's Guide to Growing Asters* (Devon, 1998) and only slightly less often to the other titles in this excellent series, all of which are worth reading. In the old, now defunct series of Penguin Handbooks, E. B. Anderson's *Rock Gardening* (London, 1960), Lanning Roper, *Hardy Herbaceous Perennials* (London, 1960) and E. B. Anderson, *Hardy Bulbs, volume I* (London, 1964) are unsurpassed. Peter Beales, *Classic Roses* (London, 1985) is invaluable and has greatly widened my love of this fine family of plants. Helen Dillon, *Helen Dillon on Gardening* (Dublin,

1998) and *Helen Dillon's Gardening Book* (London, 2007) combine great wit and clear, direct sense from one of our greatest flower gardeners. Among books on designing gardens I have written a preface to Russell Page, *The Education of a Gardener* (New York, paperback edn, 2008) and also to Vita Sackville-West, *The Illustrated Garden Book, A New Anthology by Robin Lane Fox* (London, 1986). Tracy DiSabato-Aust, *The Well-Tended Perennial Garden* (London, new edn, 2006) is a valuable encouragement to try new ways of cutting back border plants and changing their seasons. Jane Taylor, *Plants for Dry Gardens* (London, 1993) is very well founded and makes good use of earlier German reference books. Among the many recent accounts of making a garden as a beginner or an ignoramus, I like Roy Strong, *The Laskett: The Story of a Garden* (London, 2003).

My fellow journalists and broadcasters in Britain continue to produce many books which address aspects of gardening in accessible styles, sometimes reprinting their selections of their newspaper columns. Ursula Buchan, *Good in a Bed* (London, 2001) and *Better Against a Wall* (London, 2003), Monty Don, *The Ivington Diaries* (London, 2009) and Hugh Johnson, *Hugh Johnson on Gardening: The Best of Tradescant's Diary* (London, 1993) are recent collections of such articles, compiled from differing starting points. More general works include Stephen Anderton, *Rejuvenating a Garden* (London, 1998), Rachel de Thame, *Gardening with the Experts* (London, 2003), Jane Fearnley-Whittingstall, *Peonies: The Imperial Flower* (London, 1999), Mary Keen, *Creating a Garden* (London, 1996), Stephen Lacey, *Real Gardening* (London, 2002), Anna Pavord, *Anna Pavord's Gardening Companion* (London, 1992) and Alan Titchmarsh, *The Complete How To Be a Gardener* (London, 2005).

Selected References

I have begun from the *RHS Plant Finder 2009–10* when checking the plant names in this book and only departed from it when the names proposed are newly revisionist or manifestly at odds with general nursery lists and gardeners' practice. Most of the plants I discuss are listed in it with UK suppliers to whom readers should turn. There is also the helpful website www.britishplantnurseryguide.co.uk, which gives details of British nurseries of all sizes and lists their current plants and events. More generally, the website www.gardenersclick.com is a network of value for keen gardeners who are 'digitally included'.

Of the gardens I mention, two in France need further detail. Shamrock Garden (pp. 215–8) is at Route du Manoir d'Ango, 76119 Varengeville-sur-mer, and from the UK the telephone number is 0033-02-35-04-02-33. Brécy (pp. 236–9) lies between Caen and Bayeux to the west of the departmental road 82 between Rocqueville and Saint Gabriel-Brécy. Opening times currently include afternoons from 14.30 to 18.30 on Tuesdays, Thursdays, Sundays and (in June) Saturdays, from Easter to All Saints Day. The fax number in France for further details is 02-31-80-11-90.

An excellent way to visit these and other French gardens is to take a tour with French Gardens Today (www.frenchgardenstoday.co.uk), a meeting place for many keen gardeners. I am grateful to the founder and admirable organizer, Clare Whately, for all I have learned from her and her team.

In Britain the gardens which I discuss are open at times listed in the current *RHS Garden Finder*, but Kiftsgate Court in Gloucestershire, just down the road from Hidcote Manor, also has a particularly helpful website at www.kiftsgate.co.uk.

In Ireland the superb garden of Helen Dillon at 45 Sandford Road, Ranelagh, Dublin 6, mainly opens on afternoons in March, July and August but on Sunday afternoons only from April to June and in September. Times can be checked by calling 01-497-1308 within Ireland.

Specific references to other texts in this book include:

Thoughtful Gardening (pp. 1–8): L. Wittgenstein, *Zettel*, ed. G. E. M. Anscombe and G. H. von Wright (Oxford, 1967), sections 100–107 on 'thoughtful activity'. L. Wittgenstein, *The Brown Book*, in *The Blue and Brown Books* (Oxford, 1960), 178, discusses pansies, a reference which I owe to Peter Hacker. Erasmus describes flowers in literary terms in his *Colloquia*, in his *Opera Omnia* 1 (Amsterdam, 1972), 235, which I owe to William Marx, *Vie du Lettré* (Paris, 2009), 78.

Jardin Majorelle (pp. 62–5): for Majorelle, see Alain Leygonie, *Un Jardin à Marrakech: Jacques Majorelle, Peintre-Jardinier, 1886–1962* (Paris, 2007).

'Oh dear, I do love gardens!' (pp. 66–9): the geraniums are described by Katherine Mansfield in J. Middleton Murry, ed., *The Journal of Katherine Mansfield* (London, 1954), 156–7, a reference I owe to Laura Marcus. The letters are superbly edited by Vincent O'Sullivan and Margaret Scott, *The Collected Letters of Katherine Mansfield*, Vols. 1–5 (Oxford, 1984–2008), and for her last days see Vol. 5, 303–48.

Let Them Eat Squirrel (pp. 88–90): Julia Drysdale, *Classic Game Cookery*, is itself a classic in paperback (London, 1983). It first appeared in hardback in 1975 as *The Game Cookery Book* (London, 1975).

Harassed by Perpetual Bother (pp. 102–04): the unsurpassed letters of John Clare are best available in Mark Storey, ed., *The Letters of John Clare* (Oxford, 1985), and I quote from pp. 630 and 643.

When Connie Met Oliver (pp. 117–20): I have used D. H. Lawrence, *Lady Chatterley's Lover*, in the Cambridge edition, ed. Michael Squires (Cambridge, 1993), and then for the earlier versions *The First and Second Lady Chatterley Novels*, ed. Dieter Mehl and Christa Jansohn (Cambridge, 1999).

Corona's Imprint (pp. 125–8): Altamont is signposted off the main N80 road from Carlow to Wexford. The garden is near Tullow, Co. Wicklow, and the weekly opening times can be checked on the Irish telephone and fax number 0503-59444. They include Saturdays throughout the gardening season.

Valerie Finnis (pp. 132–5): I have drawn on Ursula Buchan, *Garden People: Valerie Finnis and the Golden Age of Gardening* (London, 2007), which ends with an invaluable survey of individual 'garden lives' by Brent Elliott.

Separate Beds on the Bay (pp. 147–50): I refer to Statius, *Silvae*, 2.2, 2.7 and 3.1, which are brilliantly interpreted by R. G. M. Nisbet, '*Felicitas* at Surrentum (Statius, *Silvae* II. 2)', *Journal of Roman Studies*, LXVIII (1978), 1–11.

Irises on Drugs (pp. 159–61): Aldous Huxley, *The Doors of Perception* (London, 1954).

The Tivoli Garden (pp. 197–200): David R. Coffin, *The Villa in the Life of Renaissance Rome* (Princeton, 1979), gives the facts of the Villa d'Este's history. I quote Horace, *Epistles*, 1.8.12; and for the Sibyl and floods, see J. L. Lightfoot, *The Sibylline Oracles* (Oxford, 2007), 116–17 and 416–17.

Asphodels of the Negroes (pp. 204–06): I allude to the poem 'Stratis Thalassinos Among the Agapanthi', in George Seferis, *Collected Poems*, trans. Edmund Keeley and Philip Sherrard (Princeton and London, 1995), 144–5. It was written in Transvaal on 14 January 1942.

Gendered Landscape (pp. 210–14): an excellent survey of Englishwomen in the garden is given by Sue Bennett, *Five Centuries of Women and Gardens* (London, 2000), which I draw on with gratitude. It accompanied the fine exhibition at London's National Portrait Gallery in 2000.

Rosemary Revisited (pp. 227–32): Rosemary Verey, *A Countrywoman's Notes* (Gloucestershire, 1989), collected some of her monthly articles for *Country Life* magazine, written between 1979 and 1987. It has been reprinted in miniature editions in London since 1993.

Forcing Nature (pp. 236–9): Eric T. Haskell, *The Gardens at Brécy: A Lasting Landscape* (Paris, 2007), gives a full historical account of the garden.

The Haunt of Ancient Peace (pp. 265–7): Robin Whalley, *The Great Edwardian Gardens of Harold Peto: From the Archives of Country Life* (London, 2007), is a magnificent account of Peto's work.

Space Invaders (pp. 268–71): I refer to John M. Randall and Janet Marinelli, eds., *Invasive Plants: Weeds of the Global Garden* (New York, 1996).

Á La Carte de Tendre (pp. 304–7): George de Scudéry, *Clélie* (Paris, 1661–5), is the source of the Carte de Tendre, my knowledge of which is owed to the kind help of Dr Wes Williams. The author was in fact female, Madeleine de Scudéry. The Carte is discussed in fascinating detail by James S. Munro, *Mademoiselle de Scudéry and the Carte de Tendre* (Durham, 1986).

Picture Acknowledgements

I am particularly grateful for the help of Peter Beales, supplier of so many fine roses through Peter Beales Roses, London Road, Attleborough, Norwich NR17 1AY, and of Thompson and Morgan Ltd, suppliers of so many fine seeds at Poplar Lane, Ipswich, Suffolk. Paul Picton has helped me with excellent pictures of the asters and autumnal plantings which are exemplified in the Picton gardens at Old Court Nurseries, Colwall, near Malvern, Worcestershire WR13 6QE. Anne Chambers has provided the pictures of Britain's finest garden flourishing in long family ownership, Kiftsgate Court in Gloucestershire, whose regular opening times for visitors are given on the website at www.kiftsgate.co.uk. Andrew Lawson, king of English gardenphotographers, has been a patient source of images from his archives. Lucy Waitt and staff at the RHS Lindley Library have made available the pictures taken by Valerie Finnis (Scott), now in the RHS's keeping. Clare Whately has been an invaluable help with the pictures from France, whose gardens I know through her organized tours, available at www.frenchgardenstoday.co.uk. I have made every effort to trace underlying copyrights, but if any has been overlooked, it will, if possible, be acknowledged in future editions.

The following sources apply for illustrations as listed: Michael Walker 1, 25; Didier Wirth 2, 16; Thompson and Morgan 3, 23; Robin Lane Fox 7, 13, 14; Valerie Finnis (Scott) and RHS Lindley Library 4, 11, 17, 19, 20; Melissa Wyndham; Anne Chambers 24; Andrew Lawson 5, 12, 21, 28; Kim Wilkie 6; John Fairey 8; Arabella Lennox-Boyd 9; Marquis of Lansdown 10; David Astor; Patrick and

Sylvie Quibel 15, 27, 29; Melinda Manning of the New York Botanical Garden; Isabelle Brunetière; Peter Beales 22; Robert Mallet 26; Paul Picton 30; Peter Moore; Ayletts; David Hall; Peter Hellyer 31; Tara Lane Fox 32.

Index